Student Quick Tips

Use this Student Quick Tips guide for a quick and easy start with McGraw-Hill Connect. You'll get valuable tips on registering, doing assignments, and accessing resources, as well as information about the support center hours.

Getting Started

TIP: To get started in Connect, you will need the following:

- Your instructor's Connect Web Address

  Sample of Connect Web Address:

  http://www.mcgrawhillconnect.com/class/instructorname_section_name

- Connect Access Code

TIP: If you do not have an access code or have not yet secured your tuition funds, you can click "Free Trial" during registration. This trial will provide temporary Connect access (typically three weeks) and will remind you to purchase online access before the end of your trial.

Registration and Sign In

1. Go to the Connect Web Address provided by your instructor
2. Click on **Register Now**
3. Enter your email address

TIP: If you already have a McGraw-Hill account, you will be asked for your password and will not be required to create a new account.

4. Enter a registration code or choose **Buy Online** to purchase access online

(Continued: **Registration and Sign In**)

  5. Follow the on-screen directions

  TIP: Please choose your Security Question and Answer carefully. We will ask you for this information if you forget your password.

  6. When registration is complete, click on **Go to Connect Now**

  7. You are now ready to use **Connect**

Trouble Logging In?

  • Ensure you are using the same email address you used during registration

  • If you have forgotten your password, click on the "Forgot Password?" link at your Instructor's Connect Course Web Address

  • When logged into Connect, you can update your account information (e.g. email address, password, and security question/answer) by clicking on the *"My Account"* link located at the top-right corner

Home (Assignments)

  TIP: If you are unable to begin an assignment, verify the following:

  • The assignment is available (start and due dates)

  • That you have not exceeded the maximum number of attempts

  • That you have not achieved a score of 100%

  • If your assignment contains questions that require manual grading, you will not be able to begin your next attempt until your instructor has graded those questions

(Continued: **Home Assignments**)

> **TIP:** Based on the assignment policy settings established by your Instructor, you may encounter the following limitations when working on your assignment(s):

- Ability to Print Assignment

- Timed assignments – once you begin a "*timed assignment*," the timer will not stop by design

> **TIP:** "*Save & Exit*" vs. "*Submit*" button

- If you are unable to complete your assignment in one sitting, utilize the "*Save & Exit*" button to save your work and complete it at a later time

- Once you have completed your assignment, utilize the "*Submit*" button in order for your assignment to be graded

Library

> **TIP:** The *Library* section of your Connect account provides shortcuts to various resources.

- If you purchased ConnectPlus, you will see an *eBook* link, which can also be accessed from the section information widget of the *Home* tab

- *Recorded Lectures* can be accessed if your instructor is using *Tegrity Campus* to capture lectures. You may also access recorded lectures when taking an assignment by clicking on the projector icon in the navigation bar

- Many McGraw-Hill textbooks offer additional resources such as narrated slides and additional problems, which are accessible through the *Student Resources* link

Reports

TIP: Once you submit your assignment, you can view your available results in the *Reports* tab.

- If you see a dash (-) as your score, your instructor has either delayed or restricted your ability to see the assignment feedback

- Your instructor has the ability to limit the amount of information (e.g. questions, answers, scores) you can view for each submitted assignment

Need More Help?

CONTACT US ONLINE

Visit us at:

www.mcgrawhillconnect.com/support

Browse our support materials including tutorial videos and our searchable Connect knowledge base. If you cannot find an answer to your question, click on "Contact Us" button to send us an email.

GIVE US A CALL

Call us at:

1-800-331-5094

Our live support is available:

Mon-Thurs: 8 am – 11 pm CT
Friday: 8 am – 6 pm CT
Sunday: 6 pm – 11 pm CT

ENGAGING QUESTIONS
A Guide to Writing

Carolyn E. Channell, *Southern Methodist University*

Timothy W. Crusius, *Southern Methodist University*

ENG-W 131
Reading, Writing, & Inquiry
Indiana University/Purdue University – Ft. Wayne

Mc
Graw
Hill
Education

2 3 4 5 6 7 8 9 0 BKM BKM 17 16 15 14

ISBN-13: 978-1-259-33385-9
ISBN-10: 1-259-33385-X

Learning Solutions Consultant: Bradley Ritter
Project Manager: Tricia Wagner
Cover Photo Credits:
87658218 – JupiterImages
106513624 – Jeff Huting
87465423 – Hemera Technologies

DEDICATION

For James L. Kinneavy

ABOUT THE AUTHORS

Carolyn E. Channell taught high school and community college students before joining the faculty at Southern Methodist University, where she is now a senior lecturer and specialist in first-year writing courses. She has served as a writing program administrator and is currently coordinator of computer-assisted instruction. Her research interests involve literacy in the digital age. She resides in Richardson, Texas, with her husband David.

Timothy W. Crusius is professor of English at Southern Methodist University, where he teaches beginning and advanced composition. He is the author of books on discourse theory, philosophical hermeneutics, argumentation, and Kenneth Burke. His long-standing interest in the relation between dialogue and rhetoric has led in recent years to a fascination with the art of questioning, his current research focus. He resides in Dallas with his wife, Elizabeth, and with two adults who used to be their children, Micah and Rachel.

BRIEF CONTENTS

CONTENTS

PART I
Exploring Writing and Reading 1

PART II
Practicing Writing 63

PART III
Researching Writing 395

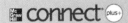

CHAPTER 22
Interpreting Short Stories

What Is Interpretation?

Why Interpret Short Fiction?

How Do Writers Interpret Short Stories?

A Short Story and Example Interpretation

THE ASSIGNMENT

How Do I Write an Interpretation? Questioning the Rhetorical Situation

How Do I Write an Interpretation? Engaging the Writing Process

Editing Your Revised Draft

Three Short Stories for Interpretation

R E A D I N G S

The Man to Send Rain Clouds by Leslie Marmon Silko

On *The Man to Send Rain Clouds* by Helen Jaskoski

Separation and Hope in The Man to Send Rain Clouds by Nina Williams

CHAPTER 23
Claiming Voice

What Is Voice?

Why Care about Voice?

THE ASSIGNMENT

How Do I Recover My Voice? Engaging the Writing Process

How Do I Use Spontaneous Style?

How Do I Use Conscious Style?

How Do I Extend My Voice?

R E A D I N G   *Where My Writing Came From, and Where It Went* by Allison Griffin

CHAPTER 24
Designing Documents and Using Graphics

What Are Document Design and Graphics?

Why Consider Document Design and Graphics?

WHY ENGAGING QUESTIONS?

> **Judge a person by their questions, rather than their answers.** VOLTAIRE

Engaging Questions takes a practical approach to composing, with a view that effective writing occurs in the context of critical thinking. By using a consistent methodology that prompts students to learn and practice "the art of questioning," *Engaging Questions* presents writing as one essential part of the critical thinking whole, ultimately empowering students to become skilled thinkers and confident writers.

In a time when many people look at textbooks as either too expensive or too expansive, it is only appropriate that we extend the practical approach of *Engaging Questions* to the way we present and distribute its content. We know that less is more and access is crucial. We offer students the guidance they need but not more than they need; we do not distract, overburden, or confuse instructors or students with too much detail and too many considerations that belong to advanced writing courses. *Engaging Questions* is available seamlessly within Blackboard® and other learning management systems, so students will not need to travel outside the course syllabus for assignments, readings, or reference. In summary, we tried to create a useful, efficient text that promotes writing based on questioning and thinking, a writing guide that is responsive to contemporary students, instructors, and current writing programs. We welcome your suggestions for making it better.

Carolyn Channell
214-768-3682
cchannel@smu.edu
Timothy Crusius
214-768-4363
tcrusius@smu.edu

ENGAGING QUESTIONS
ENGAGING MINDS

CHAPTER 10

Making a Case

YOU HEAR OR READ ABOUT SOME TOPIC THAT INTERESTS YOU (CALL IT "X"), and soon enough you form an opinion about it. Nothing much happens until someone asks you a key question, "What do you think about x?" This question starts many serious conversations, but it leads to stating opinions, not to **argument,** which means *a reasoned defense of an opinion.* To get to argument, you need a question with a sharper edge, a critical thinking question: "*Why* do you think this about x?" That is, "What reasons do you have to explain and justify what you think? What evidence do you have to back up your opinion?"

When you answer these questions, you are making a **case,** *arguing for a position by advancing reasons and evidence in defense of it.* Arguing a case occurs in many genres, including newspaper editorials, letters to the editor, blog posts, speeches, and personal letters. Following is a brief example of making a case from a doctor responding to a news article about vegan diets, which include no meat or dairy products.

The Art of Questioning

The writing instruction in *Engaging Questions* is structured around questions designed to lead to confident, effective writing that is based on skillful, open-minded reading and thinking. The concept of questioning is introduced in Part I—providing a background for questioning when reading and writing—and then applied consistently throughout the text.

> *The important thing is not to stop questioning. Curiosity has its own reason for existing.* ALBERT EINSTEIN

How Do I Write . . . ?

When students are ready to write, they need to know how to write for a particular purpose and within a selected genre or medium. Practical guidance for writing within a particular genre or medium is provided through nine *How Do I Write . . . ?* guides. These appear within the print text, while four additional guides can be found in the *Engaging Questions* eBook. *Engaging Questions* also can be customized to include an instructor's preferred selection of the *How do I Write . . . ?* guides. Remove any you do not plan to assign and/or add ones from the eBook.

Rhetorical Analysis
Blog
Reflection
Visual Analysis
Review
Editorial
Proposal
Research Proposal
Annotated Bibliography
Prospectus ⊕
Lab Report ⊕
Instructions ⊕
Abstract ⊕

HOW DO I WRITE A BLOG?

BEFORE PERSONAL COMPUTERS, CELL PHONES, AND ELECTRONIC SOCIAL NET-working, people expressed opinions as they always have and still do, in conversation with relatives and friends. However, *publishing* one's opinions beyond the circle of face-to-face talk was much more difficult. You had to find a source, such as a magazine or newspaper, willing to put something you wrote in print. Relatively few people had the time and talent to take advantage of print publication. Blogging changed the situation entirely: Now tens of millions of people the world over publish their opinions via the Internet, and many millions more visit blogging sites and are influenced by what they read.

What Is a Blog?

The word **blog** is short for *weblog, a site on the Internet where people post entries about their ideas, opinions, and experiences.* The entries, called **blog posts,** are *arranged chronologically descending from most recent to oldest.* There are group blogs and blogs by individuals. Blogs often focus on a single area of interest, such as one's work, hobbies, health, or politics. Unlike diaries or journals, blogs are public; blog posts take you into the world of ideas, current events, and

> *Rarely do we find men who willingly engage in hard, solid thinking. There is an almost universal quest for easy answers and half-baked solutions. Nothing pains some people more than having to think.* MARTIN LUTHER KING, JR.

Activities for Practice and to Build Skills

Four types of activities give students a chance to practice the chapter's writing concepts: *Thinking as a Writer, In Your Own Work, Writer's Notebook,* and *Collaborative Activity.* Additional skill-building activities are organized by learning objective on Connect Composition Plus and can be assigned and managed through Blackboard®.

Instructors may choose to start the course with a comprehensive online adaptive diagnostic tool, which assesses student proficiencies in five core areas of grammar and mechanics and generates a continually adaptive personal learning plan. Powered by metacognitive learning theory, the personal learning plan continually adapts with each student interaction, while built-in time management tools help students achieve their overall course goals in every session. This personalized and constantly-adapting online environment is designed to increase student readiness, motivation, and confidence, and allow classroom instruction to focus on thoughtful and critical writing processes.

ACTIVITY 1.1 *Thinking Like a Writer*

Finding a Writer's Moves in a Different Reading

Analyze the reading selection you previewed, read, and annotated (as instructed on pages 20 and 23). Note the major subdivisions and the main point of each subdivision. Make an outline to show (1) how each subdivision functions (the role it performs) and (2) what it says (the point it makes). Use the example outline above as a model. ■

ACTIVITY 1.2 *In Your Own Work*

Checking the Accuracy of Statements

Freewrite for five minutes on an opinion you hold, explaining why you believe that opinion is correct. Then look over what you wrote. Did you make any statements that you are not positive are totally accurate? ■

ACTIVITY 1.2 *Writer's Notebook*

Drawing Inferences from a Political Cartoon

- What other details in the cartoon contribute to your interpretation of Luckovich's commentary? What inference do you draw about Luckovich's opinion of who is to blame for the destruction and pollution caused by the explosion? What evidence from inside and outside the text leads you to this interpretation?
- How does the genre (or type) of selection—the fact that this is a political cartoon rather than, say, an editorial—affect your understanding? ■

ACTIVITY 1.3 *Collaborative Activity*

Thinking through What Walzer Says

In groups of two or three, discuss the limits of toleration. What behavior can we peacefully coexist with and what behavior must we oppose by persuasion, law, or force? For instance, can we tolerate organizations in the United States that promote terrorism and other forms of violent protest? ■

Readings

The market-tested professional and student readings in the print version of *Engaging Questions* were chosen to engage students and provoke thoughtful questioning and writing.

Readings in *Engaging Questions* can be customized—added, removed or replaced—easily through Create. Additional readings can be assigned through Connect Composition Plus.

ENGAGING QUESTIONS
ENGAGING YOU

The Option of a Custom Text

It's Your Course; Make It Your Text with Create.
Craft your teaching resources to match the way you teach! With McGraw-Hill Create, you can easily rearrange chapters and add material from other content sources. Create even allows you to personalize your book's appearance by selecting the cover and adding your name, school, and course information. Order a Create book and you'll receive a complimentary print review copy in 3 to 5 business days or a complimentary electronic review copy (eComp) via e-mail in about one hour. Go to **www.mcgrawhillcreate. com** and register today.

> *If you believe everything you read, you better not read.*
>
> JAPANESE PROVERB

With Create you can

1. Choose which
   - chapters to include—choose from the 21 print chapters and 6 eBook-only chapters
   - readings to include—choose from readings that are part of the text as well as selected alternative readings for each chapter and from more than 700 selections in our readings database, all with supporting pedagogy.
   - How Do I Write...? guides to include—choose from the 9 print guides and the 4 eBook-only guides
   - personal course content to include—upload your course syllabus, teaching notes, or other material
   - other McGraw-Hill material to include
2. Include or exclude the handbook.
3. Determine whether you want a print and/or electronic text.

Include only the chapters you plan to cover, add readings, add your course outcomes—it's your course, so make it your text.

The Connect Composition Plus eBook

The Connect Composition Plus eBook provides *Engaging Questions* content in a digital format that is accessible from within Connect and Blackboard®. In support of the engaged learning experience, students can link directly to activities and assignments within Connect Plus from the eBook.

The CourseSmart eBook

At CourseSmart your students can take advantage of significant savings off the cost of a print textbook, reduce their impact on the environment, and gain access to powerful web tools for learning. CourseSmart eTextbooks can be viewed online or downloaded to a computer. The eTextbooks allow students to do full-text searches, add highlighting and notes, and share notes with classmates. CourseSmart has the largest selection of eTextbooks available anywhere. Visit www.CourseSmart.com to learn more and to try a sample chapter.

Peer Review

Superior peer reviewing capability enables students to collaborate online, benefit from their classmates' comments, and create a revision plan based on that feedback. This collaborative experience, managed through an efficient and fun-to-use online system, will prepare students for the group writing projects they will encounter throughout their college careers and in the workplace.

> *Whenever you find yourself on the side of the majority, it is time to pause and reflect.* MARK TWAIN

Documentation

Online interactive documentation tools will help students acknowledge their sources in MLA and APA styles.

Optional Handbook

The *Engaging Questions* handbook can be added to a custom text through Create. The brief handbook includes a section on Signaling the Reader and one on Common Errors.

> *The most important training, though, is to experience life as a writer, questioning everything, inventing multiple explanations for everything. If you do that, all the other things will come.*
> ORSON SCOTT CARD

ENGAGING QUESTIONS
ENGAGING WRITING PROGRAMS

Blackboard®

All the content of *Engaging Questions*—writing instruction, readings, assignments, documentation flowcharts—is integrated with the Blackboard® course management system to offer single sign-on, seamless use of all Connect Composition Plus assets within Blackboard®, and synchronization for all assignment and grade book utilities.

> *It's better to know some of the questions than all of the answers.*
>
> JAMES THURBER

Tegrity

Tegrity Campus is a service that makes class time available all the time by automatically capturing every lecture in a searchable format for students to review when they study and complete assignments. With a simple one-click start-and-stop process, you capture all computer screens and corresponding audio. Students replay any part of any class with easy-to-use browser-based viewing on a PC or Mac.

> *Curiosity is the very basis of education and if you tell me that curiosity killed the cat, I say only the cat died nobly.*
>
> ARNOLD EDINBOROUGH

Continually Adaptive Personalized Learning Plan

With a simple, self-guided adaptive diagnostic that assesses student proficiencies in five core areas of grammar and mechanics, students can generate a unique learning plan tailored to address their specific needs in the allotted time students determine they want to study. Students receive a personalized program of writing lessons, videos, animations, and interactive exercises to improve their skills and are offered immediate feedback on their work. Powered by metacognitive learning theory, the personal learning plan continually adapts with each student interaction, while built-in time management tools ensure that students achieve their course goals. Results can be sent directly to the instructor's Connect Composition Plus and Blackboard® grade book for easy course management. This personalized, constantly adapting online environment is designed to increase student readiness, motivation, and confidence, and allow classroom instruction to focus on thoughtful and critical writing processes.

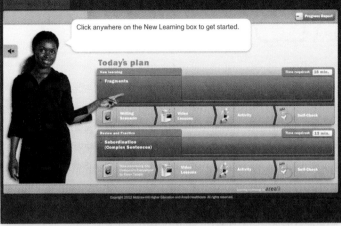

> *Research is formalized curiosity. It is poking and prying with a purpose.*
> ZORA NEALE HURSTON

Outcomes-Based Assessment of Writing

Connect's powerful Outcomes-Based Assessment tool presents writing instructors and coordinators with simple reports—suitable for program evaluation or accrediting bodies—to review student progress toward program goals. Prebuilt, customizable grading rubrics, written specifically for composition, can be adapted to your program's unique assignments and goals to make the set-up, management, and reporting of outcomes-based writing assessment efficient, professional, and useful for informing instruction within your program.

ENGAGING RESOURCES

Instructor's Resource Manual

Written by John Haywood, *Waubonsee Community College*; Ted Rollins, *Johnson County Community College*; Matthew Schmeer, *Johnson County Community College*; Julia Roth, *Waubonsee Community College*; Sarah Stupegia, *Waubonsee Community College*; and Jessica Wedemeyer, *Waubonsee Community College:*

The instructor's resource manual, designed for both the new and experienced instructor, includes suggestions for activities and teaching resources.

Handbook for Engaging Questions: A Guide to Writing

The *Handbook for Engaging Questions: A Guide to Writing,* available packaged with your printed text, as part of your custom text through Create, and through Connect+, includes sections on Signaling the Reader and on Editing for Common Errors.

Connect Composition Plus with self-guided adaptive diagnostic and eBook

Connect Composition Plus for *Engaging Questions* allows instructors to assign quizzes, learning activities, additional readings, videos, and writing assignments. All assets are organized by chapter and learning objectives, and tied to WPA outcomes. Additionally, instructors can assign the self-guided adaptive diagnostic that assesses student proficiencies in five core areas of grammar and mechanics, students can generate a unique learning plan tailored to address their specific needs in the allotted time students determine they want to study. Students receive a personalized program of writing lessons, videos, animations, and interactive exercises to improve their core area skills and are offered immediate feedback on their work. Results from the adaptive diagnostic and other self-graded activities can be sent directly to the instructor's Connect Composition and Blackboard® grade book for easy course management. Finally, the full ebook is housed in Connect for easy access and completion of assignments. Contributors include Andrew Preslar, *Lamar State College, Orange;* DaRelle Rollins, *Hampton University;* Brittany Stephenson, *Salt Lake Community College;* and Matthew Schmeer, *Johnson County Community College.*

The CourseSmart eBook

At CourseSmart your students can take advantage of significant savings off the cost of a print textbook, reduce their impact on the environment, and gain access to powerful web tools for learning. CourseSmart eTextbooks can be viewed online or downloaded to a computer. The eTextbooks allow students to do full text searches, add highlighting and notes, and share notes with classmates. CourseSmart has the largest selection of eTextbooks available anywhere. Visit www.CourseSmart.com to learn more and to try a sample chapter.

Tegrity [McGraw Hill] ✆egrity

Tegrity Campus is a service that makes class time available all the time by automatically capturing every lecture in a searchable format for students to review when they study and complete assignments. With a simple one-click start and stop process, you capture all computer screens and corresponding audio. Students replay any part of any class with easy-to-use browser-based viewing on a PC or Mac.

ACKNOWLEDGMENTS

A book like this could never be brought to completion without the work of a host of people, far too many to be recognized in the space we have. We would like to call special attention to Barbara Heinssen, who took a partial rough draft and did so much to turn it into the first complete draft, a long process during which she freely shared her wisdom and experience. Jane Carter helped us see that questioning was at the heart of this book and guided us through a revision that improved the book in many ways. Finally, Cara Labell took over the project as we were composing final drafts and moving toward production, bringing with her ideas that greatly impacted the book's questioning focus, visual design, reading selections, and overall readiness for actual use in the classroom. We owe more to these three talented developmental editors than we can adequately express.

We also wish to acknowledge the work of an outstanding research librarian at SMU, Rebecca Graff, who went far beyond professional duty in helping us, and of Rebecca Innocent, who wrote the draft of what eventually became the handbook.

Next, the support of the good people at McGraw-Hill Higher Education must be recognized. They kept the faith and backed this project generously when it took considerable courage to stay committed. In this regard, Dawn Groundwater, with her tireless energy, honesty, and vision, deserves special mention.

Finally, our appreciation goes out to our colleagues across the country who provided feedback on our evolving plans for the project, drafts of manuscript, and our digital vision. Thank you.

Angelina College
Diana Throckmorton

Baylor University
Jesse Airaudi

Brigham Young University
Brett McInelly

Cedar Valley College
Andrew Anderson
Elsie Burnett (Board of Advisors)
Suzanne Disheroon
Beth Gulley
Rebekah Rios-Harris
Marilyn Senter

Central New Mexico Community College Main
Jonathan Briggs

Claflin University
Linda Hill (Board of Advisors)
Peggy Ratliff (Board of Advisors)
Mitali Wong

Clayton State University
Mary Lamb

College of Coastal Georgia
Anna Crowe Dewart
Meribeth Huebner Fell

Dutchess Community College
Angela Batchelor

Eastern Washington University
Polly Buckingham
Justin Young

El Centro College
Carrie Sanford

Georgia Southwestern State University
Paul Dahlgren

Hampton University
Shonda Buchanan
Bryan Herek (Board of Advisors)
DaRelle Rollins (Board of Advisors)
Christina Pinkston Streets

Highpoint University
William Carpenter

*Indiana University-Purdue University,
Fort Wayne*
Stevens Amidon (Board of Advisors)
Karol Dehr
Jennifer Stewart (Board of Advisors)

*Indiana University-Purdue University,
Indianapolis*
Scott Weeden
Mel Winniger

Ivy Tech Community College, Indianapolis
Judith LaFourest

Ivy Tech Community College, Terre Haute
Phyllis Cox
Lucinda Ligget
Leslie Stultz

Johnson County Community College
Maureen Fitzpatrick
Sayanti Ganguly-Puckett
Ted Rollins (Board of Advisors)
Matthew Schmeer (Board of Advisors)

JS Reynolds Community College
Beth Bersen-Barber
Marti Leighty

Kansas City Kansas Community College
Jim Krajewski

Kapiolani Community College
Georgeanne Nordstrom

North Central Texas College
William Franklin (Board of Advisors)
Rochelle Gregory (Board of Advisors)

North Dakota State University
Amy Rupiper-Taggart
Joshua Webster

Northwest Arkansas Community College
Audley Hall (Board of Advisors)
Curtis Harrell (Board of Advisors)
Timothy McGinn

Oakland Community College
Subashini Subbarao

Pima Community College
Kristina Beckman-Brito

Pittsburg State University
Lyle Morgan

Purdue University North Central
Jesse Cohn
Bob Mellin
Jane Rose

Queens University of Charlotte
Marion Bruner (Board of Advisors)
Helen Hull (Board of Advisors)

Quinnipiac University
Glenda Pritchett

Rowan-Cabarrus Community College
Donna Johnson Ginn
Shelly Palmer

Sacramento Community College
Jeff Knorr

Salt Lake Community College
Ron Christiansen (Board of Advisors)
Brittany Stephenson (Board of Advisors)

Savannah State University
Emma Conyers
April Gentry (Board of Advisors)
Gwendolyn Hale

Seminole State College
Ruth Reis-Palatiere

Sinclair Community College
Susan Callender
Kate Geiselman

Southeast Missouri State University
Trishina Nieveen Phegley (Board of Advisors)

Southern Illinois University
Ronda Dively

Southern Illinois University, Edwardsville
Anushiya Sivanarayanan

Spokane Community College
Angela Rasmussen

Tidewater Community College, Chesapeake
Joseph Antinarella (Board of Advisors)

Truckee Meadows Community College
Robert Lively

Truman State University
Monica Barron
Christine Harker

University of Idaho
Jodie Nicotra (Board of Advisors)
Karen Thompson (Board of Advisors)

University of Rhode Island
Kim Hensley Owens

University of Utah
Jay Jordan
Susan Miller

University of Wisconsin, Stout
Andrea Deacon

Virginia State University
Michael McClure

Waubonsee Community College
Mary Edith Butler
Gary Clark
Billy Clem
Ellen Lindeen
Jeanne McDonald (Board of Advisors)
Daniel Portincaso
Sarah Quirk

Western Michigan University
Jonathan Bush (Board of Advisors)

Exploring Writing and Reading

CHAPTER 1

Critical Thinking and the Art of Questioning

MOST PEOPLE EQUATE INTELLIGENCE AND EDUCATION WITH KNOWLEDGE— that is, having a large store of information in one's head. Of course, knowledge is important. A college education is partly about acquiring more knowledge by taking a wide range of courses. However, what you can do with what you know matters more. You can look up information you lack. You cannot look up the ability to think critically, interpret information, evaluate it, and put it to new uses.

By **thinking critically** we mean *the ability to examine anything you or someone else has done, said, or written to discover how sound or useful it is.* Critical thinking depends on **the art of questioning**, which means *finding, asking, and pursuing the questions that enable you to examine what you or someone else has done, said, or written.* Thinking critically and questioning go hand in hand. Together, they promote genuine engagement with writing and the other language activities essential to success in college, career, and life.

Why Is Questioning Important?

Questioning helps you become engaged when performing any of the following language activities:

- **Thinking**   Thinking underlies everything we do. Without it, any other activity—including discussion, reading, and writing—is meaningless. Critical thinking first begins with questioning what we think, read, observe, or hear. Through critical thinking, we examine and revise our beliefs and opinions.

- **Discussing**   Talking with other people, which means listening to them and asking them questions, not just holding the floor ourselves, has enormous value. It is central not only to forming friendships but also to learning from and collaborating with classmates, colleagues, and others. Discussion allows us to try out and refine first thoughts in response to the thoughts and reactions of other people. Thought nurtures discussion; discussion nurtures thought.

- **Reading**   Reading is central to both college and career. It fuels our thinking and discussions. Whether the text is a magazine or a book, an e-mail or a report, reading it effectively means not just passing the eyes over the page but going beyond the surface to understand and question what the text says. Like thinking critically, reading critically requires thoughtful engagement.

To learn more about reading critically, see pages 13–37.

FIGURE **1.1**

**The Circle of
Language Activities**

What is the common
thread in the activities
that these people are
engaging in?

- **Writing**   Because writing requires us to express our ideas completely and precisely, it is central to both college and career. Lab reports, essay exams, and research papers are common tools used to measure whether students have absorbed facts, mastered concepts, and become engaged enough to think critically and creatively about what they have learned. Writing does not end with graduation. In our knowledge-based economy, people spend up to 30 percent of their time at work composing e-mails, reports, proposals, letters, and so on.[1] Even in community and personal activities, from writing letters to the editor to updating a Facebook page, writing is how we represent ourselves. Most importantly, writing our thoughts down helps us examine them; writing is a tool for questioning what we think and read and discuss.

Thinking, discussion, reading, and writing are too deeply intertwined to describe fully; Figure 1.1 will help you envision how intertwined they are.

---

1. Brandt, Deborah. "Writing for a Living: Literacy and the Knowledge Economy," *Written Communication* 22.2 (Apr. 2005): 168. Print.

BEST PRACTICES | The Importance of Informal Writing

Throughout *Engaging Questions,* we will invite you to write in various informal ways. Each Writer's Notebook provides valuable informal writing practice, but the activities can take many different forms, such as online journals, files on your computer, or even old-fashioned notebooks.

Informal writing supports all of the language activities described above. While thinking, people make outlines, flowcharts, lists, and notes. During class discussions and meetings, people write notes to hold onto interesting ideas. While reading, people annotate the margins of books or ebooks with informal notes to themselves. And writing itself usually begins with informal writing, sometimes called freewriting, intended to get early thoughts out where they can be examined. The more you write informally, the easier it will be for you to write in more formal ways. ■

Thinking, discussing, reading, and especially writing all start with asking questions. The sections that follow demonstrate how focusing on a few crucial questions, such as What do I really think? What does that word mean? Is that statement accurate? and Is that statement true? can help us become more critical thinkers, readers, writers, and discussion participants. These and other questions will appear throughout this book. We hope you will keep them with you and use them to dig deeper and discover what is important to you and to your readers.

■■■■ ACTIVITY 1.1 *Collaborative Activity*

Exploring the Connection between Writing and Discussing

Spend five minutes freewriting (writing nonstop) about a question that interests you, such as a course to take as an elective or the qualities that make a good friend. Then, discuss these questions in groups of three or four. Add to your freewriting any further thoughts that occurred as a result of discussion. Finally, write a paragraph about this process: Did your freewriting stimulate thought about your topic? Why or why not? To what extent did discussion help refine your ideas? ■

What Do I Really Think?

"What do I really think?" is a serious and challenging question. It is serious because critical thinking must be honest, and it is challenging because being honest is not easy. Sometimes students are taught to keep their opinions out of their writing, yet critical thinking cannot begin without opinions. Frequently, we know what we are supposed to think because other people tell us what the "right" opinions are. To get beyond what "everybody thinks," however, we must consider what we really think, as student Tony Lee does in the following blog post.

Steroids for Your Brain

Sunday, October 26, 2008

Coffee. Red Bull. Adderall.

Set for another study session, I am enhancing my focus and ability to stay awake so that I can do better in my classes. The truth of the matter is that with the drugs and energy supplements I can push myself to study longer and work more than someone not taking the supplements can. Basically, I'm taking steroids for my brain to help me achieve a goal. Unlike steroids, however, there are no long-lasting side effects, and my reward is knowledge.

Is using these drugs a form of cheating? Is using them similar to an athlete taking steroids? The thing with steroids is that they don't themselves build muscle; you have to be willing to put time in to lift weights. In the same way, although Adderall or Ritalin helps you stay awake and focus on what you study, you actually have to open a book and learn the material. So is it any different from physical enhancers?

Lee knows what he thinks and has expressed his opinion clearly. The problem is that too often thinking *stops* with stating an opinion, whereas critical thinking *begins* with an opinion. Now we have something to examine, to explore with questions. What questions can we ask?

What Does That Word Mean?

The meaning of even the most ordinary word needs examination. What prevents us from asking, "What does that word mean?" is the assumption that "everybody knows" what it means, and therefore we do not need to ask. The assumption is usually wrong.

For example, what does *enhancement* mean? It means *anything* people can do to improve their ability to perform a task better. Certainly Adderall, a drug used to treat Attention Deficit Disorder (ADD), can increase concentration and therefore enhance Lee's ability to study. However, if Lee takes Adderall on a doctor's prescription to treat ADD, what he is doing may qualify not as enhancement, but only as restoring the normal ability to concentrate.

What does *cheating* mean? It means *violating the rules that all participants in an activity are supposed to observe.* Steroid use is dangerous and unwise for people who train with weights, but it is cheating in professional baseball because the rules governing the game prohibit it.

So what can we say about Lee's question, "Is the use of a drug like Adderall a form of cheating?" The answer is: It depends. It would be cheating if the honor code at Lee's university prohibited the use of brain-enhancing drugs. Otherwise, it cannot be called cheating.

Just by examining what the words *enhancement* and *cheating* mean, we can answer Lee's question and therefore advance the thinking begun in his blog post.

■■■■ ACTIVITY 1.2 *Writer's Notebook*

To learn more about exploring a concept, see pages 147–72.

Reflecting on Key Terms

Return to the question you freewrote about in Activity 1.1 on page 4. In one or two paragraphs, explore the meaning of a key term, such as *elective* or *friend*. ■

Is That Statement Accurate?

What other questions might help us examine Lee's blog post? Just as we can fail to examine the meaning of words because we think "everybody knows" what they mean, we can fail to examine statements because "everybody knows" that they are accurate.

Consider Lee's statement that drugs like Adderall have "no long-term side effects." Is this accurate? The answer to the question is a matter of fact. To answer it, we must locate authoritative information. Perhaps Lee is right, perhaps he is wrong, or perhaps the long-term effects depend on the individual, how much the person takes, and for how long. Whatever the case may be, the question needs to be asked and answered, or else we may assume that a statement is accurate when it is not. Letting inaccurate statements slide by is another common way critical thinking can go wrong; it is just as common as not thinking about what words mean.

■■■■ ACTIVITY 1.3 *In Your Own Work*

To learn how to conduct an effective Internet search, see pages 420–23.

Checking the Accuracy of Statements

Freewrite for five minutes on an opinion you hold, explaining why you believe that opinion is correct. Then look over what you wrote. Did you make any statements that you are not positive are totally accurate? Did you make any statements that you think are accurate but that someone else might challenge? Do an Internet search to check the accuracy of any factual statements you made. Then revise your statements to eliminate inaccuracies and to incorporate information that improves what you wrote. ■

Is That Statement True?

There are many other questions we could ask about Lee's blog post. A short list of such questions follows on pages 8–9. First, let's consider a general point: If we are truly dedicated to critical thinking, then nobody should get a free pass. We have been considering a student's blog post, but the same process can be applied to the work of others, no matter who they are. Let's consider the passage below, excerpted from a book by a distinguished philosopher:

> *My subject is toleration—or, perhaps better, the peaceful coexistence of groups of people with different histories, cultures, and identities, which is what toleration makes possible. I begin with the proposition that peaceful coexistence (of a certain sort: I am not writing here about the coexistence of masters and slaves) is always a good thing.*
>
> —Michael Walzer, *On Toleration*

We value "toleration" and "peaceful coexistence," so we are likely to agree with Walzer's proposition without thinking it through. Nevertheless, we should resist this temptation and ask, "Is peaceful coexistence *always* a good thing?"

Note that we are asking a question that is different from the one we asked about Adderall's long-term side effects. That one—"Is it accurate to say that Adderall has no long-term side effects?"—is a question of fact. This one—"Is peaceful coexistence always a good thing?"—is a question of value. Data, or facts, can answer the first question, but no amount of data can answer the second, because questions about what is good or desirable are questions of *belief* and not of accuracy. The answers to questions of belief must be based on our knowledge and experience.

How, then, can we think critically about Walzer's statement that peaceful coexistence is always a good thing? The sentence in parentheses—"I am not writing here about the coexistence of masters and slaves"—offers one way to think about what he says. Clearly, Walzer does not believe that *everything* should be tolerated. He excludes masters and slaves because he considers slavery intolerable. What other conditions might also be intolerable?

▨■■ ACTIVITY 1.4 *Collaborative Activity*

Thinking through What Walzer Says

In groups of two or three, discuss the limits of toleration. What behavior can we peacefully coexist with and what behavior must we oppose by persuasion, law, or force? For instance, can we tolerate organizations in the United States that promote terrorism and other forms of violent protest? Can we peacefully coexist with Iran when its government seeks the destruction of Israel? Then write one or two paragraphs in which you explore your beliefs about this topic. ■

What Do You Gain from Thinking Critically?

You gain a number of things by devoting time and effort to thinking through a statement like the one Walzer made about toleration and peaceful coexistence:

1. Instead of letting what he says slide by, your mind is engaged with what you are reading.

When you think critically and respond thoughtfully, you take part in the conversation—a key goal of education.

2. You have something to look for as you read and to talk about. If you go on to read the book that contains the passage quoted above, you will read in part to see if the author deals with the relation between tolerance and peaceful coexistence in a way that answers your questions and resolves your doubts.

3. You become interested in words and the relation of words to reality. You are not only thinking but also *thinking as a writer thinks,* as a person who works with words and their meanings. If you write about tolerance and peaceful coexistence yourself, you are much better prepared to do so because you thought critically about what Walzer said. Indeed, *the very ability to say something of your own depends on asking questions.* Otherwise you can do little more than repeat what someone else has said.

4. You claim power by asking and pursuing questions. Usually people defer to authority figures like Walzer and let him ask the questions. Asking one yourself can help you claim authority. All it takes is finding a good question, being willing to ask it, and then pursuing it wherever it leads.

5. You take part in the conversation—a key goal of education—by thinking and responding thoughtfully. When you ask a question, you show that you are listening carefully enough to think of a question worth asking.

In sum, from practicing the art of questioning you gain the ability to think critically, to determine what you really think, to challenge what "everybody knows," and to decide for yourself what is really true and why. We invite you to turn the world upside down. Instead of being satisfied with obvious answers, learn to value questions. For only when you pose questions, especially those that challenge the obvious answers, can real thinking begin.

THE ART OF QUESTIONING | Common Critical Thinking Questions

In this chapter we have seen the value of asking four critical thinking questions:

1. **What do I really think?**
2. **What does that word mean?**
3. **Is that statement accurate?**
4. **Is that statement true?**

There are many more such questions. Indeed, *any question that helps you explore what you or someone else has said is a good question.* Here are a few more commonly asked critical thinking questions.

5. What does "x" assume?

Almost every statement is based on assumptions. Asking questions can help us determine whether we should accept or challenge assumptions. For example, consider this statement: "Jane is smart; her IQ is 130." It assumes that the tests purporting to measure intelligence are reliable. Because the reliability of these tests is frequently disputed, we can challenge this assumption.

6. What does "x" imply?

Asking questions about what follows from a statement can help us determine whether we should accept it. For example, if someone says, "Internet privacy should be protected no matter what," then you can ask, "Are you willing to give up free Internet access to protect your privacy?" "Are you willing to protect the privacy of terrorists?" You can ask these questions because the statement implies them.

7. Is "x" a good analogy?

Frequently statements are based on analogies or comparisons. The claim that animals have rights, for example, is based on an analogy, a comparison with people's rights, such as the right to vote or the right to a trial by jury. Obviously animals do not have the *same* rights as human beings, so what rights should they have and why?

8. How many kinds of "x" can we distinguish?

Often a single word or concept has many meanings. *Love* can mean the feelings of a parent for a child or a lover for the beloved. The biblical command to "love thy neighbor as thyself" has nothing to do with emotions. Here *love* means treating others with courtesy and respect. Many concepts are like "love"; they are used to refer to numerous situations or behaviors. We often need to distinguish among the meanings of a word.

9. What is a good example of "x"?

Thinking of concrete examples can often help us understand and think critically about abstract ideas. For example, *peaceful coexistence* may initially seem a wonderful thing. However, when we think about a concrete example of peaceful coexistence, such as Britain and France peacefully coexisting with Nazi Germany in the 1930s, we realize that it may come at a high price.

10. What are the likely consequences of "x"?

With any proposal for action, we should consider what is likely to happen. If someone says, "We should withdraw our troops from Afghanistan as soon as we can," we should ask questions like the following: "If we pull out, will Afghanistan again fall under Taliban control?" "Will the Taliban allow al-Qaeda to reestablish a base of operations there?" "What will happen to women and girls there?" ■

Study: Students Need More Paths to Career Success

CHRISTINE ARMARIO (ASSOCIATED PRESS)

The art of questioning can help us critically examine any kind of text, from cartoons to academic books and articles. Use the ten questions on pages 8 and 9 to examine the following news item. Bear in mind that you can question both what the writer said and anything said by others that the writer quotes.

The current U.S. education system is failing to prepare millions of young adults for successful careers by providing a one-size-fits-all approach, and it should take a cue from its European counterparts by offering greater emphasis on occupational instruction, a Harvard University study published Wednesday concludes. 1

The two-year study by the Pathways to Prosperity Project at the Harvard University Graduate School of Education notes that while much emphasis is placed in high school on going on to a four-year college, only 30 percent of young adults in the United States successfully complete a bachelor's degree. 2

While the number of jobs that require no post-secondary education has declined, the researchers note that only one-third of the jobs created in the coming years are expected to need a bachelor's degree or higher. Roughly the same amount will need just an associate's degree or an occupational credential. 3

"What I fear is the continuing problem of too many kids dropping by the wayside and the other problem of kids going into debt, and going into college but not completing with a degree or certificate," said Robert Schwartz, who heads the project and is academic dean of the Harvard Graduate School of Education. "Almost everybody can cite some kid who marched off to college because it was the only socially legitimate thing to do but had no real interest." 4

The report highlights an issue that has been percolating among education circles: That school reform should include more emphasis on career-driven alternatives to a four-year education. 5

The study recommends a "comprehensive pathways network" that would include three elements: embracing multiple approaches to help youth make the transition to adulthood, involving the nation's employers in things like work-based learning, and creating a new social compact with young people. 6

Many of the ideas aren't new, and leaders, including President Barack Obama, have advocated an increased role for community colleges so the country can once again lead the world in the proportion of college graduates. 7

U.S. Education Secretary Arne Duncan delivered opening remarks at the report's release in Washington on Wednesday, saying career and technical education has been "the neglected stepchild of education reform." 8

"That neglect has to stop," Duncan said. 9

But the idea of providing more alternatives, rather than emphasizing a four-year college education for all, hasn't been without controversy. Critics fear students who opt early for a vocational approach might limit their options later on, or that disadvantaged students at failing schools would be pushed into technical careers and away from the highly selective colleges where their numbers are already very slim. 10

"Nobody who spends much time in America's high schools could possibly argue that they are focused on college for all, or ever have been," said Kati Haycock, president of The Education Trust, a nonpartisan Washington, D.C.-based think tank. "Most schools still resist that idea, instead continuing long-standing, unfair practices of sorting and selecting like an educational caste system—directing countless young people, especially low-income students and students of color, away from college-prep courses and from seeing themselves as 'college material.'" 11

Schwartz said efforts should be intensified to get more low-income and minority students into selective institutions, while also strengthening the capacity of two-year colleges. 12

"You've got to work on both fronts at once," Schwartz said. 13

The study recommends that all major occupations be clearly outlined at the start of high school. Students would see directly how their course choices prepare them for careers that interest them—but still be able to change their minds. Students should also be given more opportunities for work-based learning, such as job shadowing and internships. 14

Students, the researchers recommend, should get career counseling and work-related opportunities early on—no later than middle school. In high school, students would have access to educational programs designed with the help of industry leaders, and they'd be able to participate in paid internships. 15

The report notes that many European countries already have such an approach, and that their youth tend to have a smoother transition into adulthood. And not all separate children into different paths at an early age. Finland and Denmark, for example, provide all students with a comprehensive education through grades 9 or 10. Then they are allowed to decide what type of secondary education they'd like to pursue. 16

Barney Bishop, president and CEO of Associated Industries of Florida, said he would advocate an approach that provides more alternatives and greater inclusion of the business community. 17

"The problem for the business community is where you have kids who don't have the rudimentary skills, and you have to take the time and effort to train them, get them some of the rudimentary skills, plus the special skills," he said. 18

Sandy Baum, an independent higher education policy analyst, said she thinks there needs to be more counseling in advising students about how to make the right choices. "I don't think the problem is too many people going to four-year colleges," she said. "The problem is too many people making inappropriate choices. 19

"What we'd like is a system where people of all backgrounds could choose to be plumbers or to be philosophers," Baum added. "Those options are not open. But we certainly need plumbers, so it's wrong to think we should be nervous about directing people in that route." 20

CHAPTER 2

Reading Critically and the Art of Questioning

WHY INCLUDE A CHAPTER ON READING IN A BOOK ABOUT WRITING? READING is complementary to writing. It provides the raw material for having something to say. It also increases vocabulary, making it easier to think and express ideas. And it develops the art of questioning and critical thinking described in Chapter 1. The habit of questioning when you read carries over to the habit of questioning when you write, allowing writers to see where their writing needs rethinking and revising.

There are many ways to read, depending on your purpose. Skimming may be appropriate when you are looking for bits of information. Slower, repeated reading is needed when your goal is to understand and retain the specialized information in textbooks. When the goal deepens from just gathering information to following an author's train of thought in order to respond to his or her ideas and opinions, then critical reading is necessary. Most of the reading you do in college—and in business—requires this kind of critical engagement.

What Is Critical Reading?

Critical reading is *active and involved interaction with a text, not just reading to find out what it says, but reading to respond to it by asking and answering questions.* Reading critically is like engaging in a silent dialogue with the text and its author. When we read, we seldom think about our dialogue with the text, but we are often unconsciously asking and answering questions like the following:

What does this word mean, based on the words around it?

What is likely to come next?

Is the author being ironic?

Why do I find this part of the text confusing?

Is this a convincing argument?

What do I think about this new idea?

Through questions like these, we not only monitor our comprehension but construct our own ideas about the meaning of a text.

The following passage provides an example of a reader's dialogue with a text. In this excerpt from an *Atlantic Monthly* article, the writer is concerned that his use of the Internet is undermining his ability to read deeply.

Is Google Making Us Stupid?

NICHOLAS CARR

The main source?

Prediction: He's going to talk about McLuhan. "The medium is the message."

For me, as for others, the Net is becoming a universal medium, the conduit for most of the information that flows through my eyes and ears and into my mind. The advantages of having immediate access to such an incredibly rich store of information are many, and they've been widely described and duly applauded. "The perfect recall of silicon memory," *Wired*'s Clive Thompson has written, "can be an enormous boon to thinking." But that boon comes at a price. As the media theorist Marshall McLuhan pointed out in the 1960s, media are not just passive channels of information. They supply the stuff of thought, but they also shape the process of thought. And what the Net seems to be doing is chipping away my capacity for concentration and contemplation. My mind now expects to take in information the way the Net distributes it: in a swiftly moving stream of particles. Once I was a scuba diver in the sea of words. Now I zip along the surface like a guy on a Jet Ski.

Digital files. Artificial intelligence an aid to human intelligence.

Here comes his point.

Clever metaphor to illustrate the point.

Questions for Discussion

1. Do you agree with Carr that using the Internet reduces your ability to concentrate when reading? How would you describe the difference between your experience of reading online and reading a printed book? Are there some kinds of texts for which you prefer one medium over the other?

2. Marshall McLuhan is famous for saying "The medium is the message." Discuss what this means. Do you think the medium (printed versus online, for example) of your communication affects the message? For example, consider how e-mail messages differ from text messages or posts on Twitter or Facebook.

How Does Critical Reading Work?

What distinguishes critical reading from reading to get the gist is the ability to find underlying meanings, to "read between the lines." Reading between the lines means following complex lines of thought, understanding what is implied but not stated explicitly, and noting how the parts add up to construct the big picture. An important skill for reading between the lines is the ability to draw inferences from evidence in the text.

CONCEPT CLOSE-UP | **Drawing Inferences**

Inferences are educated guesses about what we do not know, based on facts we do know. In a windowless classroom, for example, we may not know whether it has started to rain, but by observing students entering with wet hair and soaked jackets, we would be able to infer that it is raining.

Readers infer meanings of unfamiliar words by looking for synonyms or, better yet, patterns of synonyms in a text. Consider the sentences below from the reading selection on page 14:

> For me, as for others, the Net is becoming a universal medium, the conduit for most of the information that flows through my eyes and ears and into my mind. . . . As the media theorist Marshall McLuhan pointed out in the 1960s, media are not just passive channels of information.

Unfamiliar word

Context clue

Synonym for

If the word *conduit* is unfamiliar, you can infer its meaning because you know that liquids usually "flow" and that "channels" (like the English Channel) are waterways. Putting these pieces of information together, you realize that *conduit* must mean a pipeline or waterway.

Readers also infer meaning by bringing outside knowledge to a text. When Clive Thompson, quoted in the passage on page 14, talks about the "perfect recall of silicon memory," the reader infers that he is talking about information stored on computers. This inference is based on knowledge that computers store data on silicon chips. ■

■■■ ACTIVITY 2.1 *Writer's Notebook*

Drawing Inferences from a Political Cartoon

Visual texts also require readers to draw inferences. This is especially true of political cartoons, which require knowledge of current events. Readers have to use both prior knowledge of some event in the news and specific observations of the cartoon to draw inferences about meaning.

The following cartoon by Mike Luckovich appeared in May 2010, about a month after the Deepwater Horizon oil rig owned by British Petroleum exploded in the Gulf of Mexico.

To infer the point of the cartoon, you have to connect outside knowledge with observations of the text. In your Writer's Notebook, answer the following questions. Be prepared to discuss your answers in class.

- You observe the man in the beach chair wearing shorts, flip flops, and a top hat decorated with a star and stripes. How do you interpret this figure? What evidence from both inside and outside the text leads you to infer his significance?

- You observe the musical notes and infer that the man is singing. Most readers would recognize the lyrics as a parody of "Margaritaville" by Jimmy Buffett. What differences do you notice between the lyrics of "Margaritaville" and the words in the cartoon's thought bubble?   *(continued)*

◼◼◼ ACTIVITY 2.1 *Writer's Notebook*   (continued)

Readers must draw inferences from visual texts such as political cartoons, which require knowledge of current events. Copyright © Atlanta Journal-Constitution

- What other details in the cartoon contribute to your interpretation of Luckovich's commentary? What inference do you draw about Luckovich's opinion of who is to blame for the destruction and pollution caused by the explosion? What evidence from inside and outside the text leads you to this interpretation?

- How does the genre (or type) of selection—the fact that this is a political cartoon rather than, say, an editorial—affect your understanding? ◼

◼◼◼ ACTIVITY 2.2 *Collaborative Activity*

Interpreting a Visual

Working with a partner, find a cartoon on another issue in the news. Bring copies to class or arrange to project the image. In a brief oral presentation, explain what observations you used to draw inferences about the cartoonist's comment on the news. How would you state the cartoonist's point in your own words? ◼

What Questions Guide Critical Reading?

Because critical reading is interacting with a text, you need to be able to focus your attention on it. Begin by finding a place where your friends are unlikely to seek you out, and turn off your BlackBerry or iPhone. Like any serious task or skill, critical reading is more successful if you work methodically by doing the following:

- *Preview the text.*
- *Read* the text slowly to discover the key ideas and the author's angle on the topic.
- *Reread* the text to deepen your comprehension and to evaluate the author's reasoning.

Previewing the Text

Find out what you are getting into before you plunge into reading a text. Besides gauging how long it will take you to read it, you should also ask the following questions about the text and its rhetorical situation. The **rhetorical situation** means *the variables in any writing situation:* the author and his or her purpose for writing, the audience to whom the text is addressed, and the decisions the author makes in constructing the text to suit purpose and audience. Chapter 3, Writing and the Art of Questioning, explains rhetorical situation in more detail. (See page 39). Questions to ask include:

- **What is this text about?** From the title, what can you infer about the *topic* and the author's *angle,* or point of view, on the topic? Skim the subheadings if the text has them; if not, look at the opening of each paragraph. Skim the introduction and the conclusion. Based on your preview, try to predict what questions this text will answer. Make a list of questions about the topic that you expect to find answered in the reading. Looking for answers to these questions will make your reading more purposeful.

- **What do I already know about the topic? What opinions do I have about it?** Before reading, take a moment to recall what you may already know about the topic of the text. Refreshing your memory about relevant facts and issues readies you for thinking about what the text will offer. Reflect as well on your own bias, if you have one, and what the origins of that bias might be.

- **Who wrote this text? When and where was it published?** What can you find out about the author or authors? Biographical details about an author (such as date of birth and level of education) and the author's political or philosophical positions and other writings offer many clues for comprehending the text. The Internet is a good resource for this step.

- **Who is the audience for this text?** The author had a readership in mind while composing. Your comprehension will be better if you consider who this readership was and why the author wrote to them. How do you match or differ from those readers?

- **What special features does the text contain that might aid comprehension?** Aspects of layout and visual presentation such as photographs and other images, charts or graphs, boxes or sidebars, and subheadings can all aid understanding. Subheadings are especially helpful when sampling a text to predict what it will say.

- **Epigraphs** (from the Greek, meaning "to write on" or inscribe) are another common feature. Epigraphs are usually *brief quotations from some other text, set above and apart, followed by the author's name and sometimes the title of the source.* They set up the theme of a reading. Take a moment to look up the source and author of an epigraph; this information will help you draw inferences about the relevance of the passage.

We will work with a reading titled "Notes of an Alien Son: Immigration Paradoxes" to illustrate the stages of critical reading. Skim the reading on pages 19–20. Then look at our answers below to the questions for previewing a text.

- **What is this text about?** Skimming Codrescu's essay through to the end, we see that he is describing his mother's experience as a Romanian immigrant. It will show the contradictions between her expectations for a better life in America and what she actually found—and why immigrating might have been a "good deal after all."

- **What do I know about the topic? What opinions do I have about it?** From the title, you might infer that the author is an immigrant, the son of immigrants. Skimming it, you notice that he is describing his mother's difficulties in adjusting to life in America. What do you know about some of the problems people have when coming to the United States from other cultures? What opinions do you have about American customs and culture and why adjusting to it is sometimes difficult?

- **Who wrote this text? When and where was it published?** The author is Andrei Codrescu, a well-known writer of essays, novels, and poetry. He is the MacCurdy Distinguished Professor of English at Louisiana State University and a regular columnist on National Public Radio. Codrescu was born in Romania and lived there with his family while the country was under communist rule, which ended in a revolution in 1989. The family left in 1966 when Codrescu was twenty. This essay was published originally in 1994 in *The Nation* magazine.

- **Who is the audience for this text?** Readers of *The Nation* are the well-educated public, people concerned with political and social issues. This essay has been reprinted in numerous anthologies or collections of essays on the immigrant experience.

- **What special features does the text contain that might aid comprehension?** This is a brief text, without a need for subheadings. However, a closer look reveals that Codrescu uses signal words, like *first* and *second,* to clue the reader to the moves he makes in writing the essay. He speaks of "one" paradox, the two stages of his mother's sense of loss, and the two things she learned. He also uses chronological signal words, such as *at this point* to help readers see the evolving process of her understanding.

Notes of an Alien Son: Immigration Paradoxes

ANDREI CODRESCU

M y mother, ever a practical woman, started investing in furniture when she came to America. Not just any furniture. Sears furniture. Furniture that she kept the plastic on for fifteen years before she had to conclude, sadly, that Sears wasn't such a great investment. In Romania, she would have been the richest woman on the block.

Which brings us to at least one paradox of immigration. Most people come here because they are sick of being poor. They want to eat and they want to show something for their industry. But soon enough it becomes evident to them that these things aren't enough. They have eaten and they are full, but they have eaten alone and there was no one with whom to make toasts and sing songs. They have new furniture with plastic on it but the neighbors aren't coming over to ooh and aah. If American neighbors or less recent immigrants do come over, they smile condescendingly at the poor taste and the pathetic greed. And so, the greenhorns find themselves poor once more: This time they are lacking something more elusive than salami and furniture. They are bereft of a social and cultural milieu.

My mother, who was middle class by Romanian standards, found herself immensely impoverished after her first flush of material well-being. It wasn't just the disappearance of her milieu—that was obvious—but the feeling that she had, somehow, been had. The American supermarket tomatoes didn't taste at all like the rare genuine item back in Romania. American chicken was tasteless. Mass-produced furniture was built to fall apart. Her car, the crowning glory of her achievements in the eyes of folks back home, was only three years old and was already beginning to wheeze and groan. It began to dawn on my mother that she had perhaps made a bad deal: She had traded in her friends and relatives for ersatz tomatoes, fake chicken, phony furniture.

Leaving behind your kin, your friends, your language, your smells, your childhood, is traumatic. It is a kind of death. You're dead for the home folk and they are dead to you. When you first arrive on these shores you are in mourning. The only consolations are these products, which had been imbued with religious significance back at home. But when these things turn out not to be the real things, you begin to experience a second death, brought about by betrayal. You begin to suspect that the religious significance you had attached to them was only possible back home, where these things did not exist. Here, where they are plentiful, they have no significance whatsoever. They are inanimate fetishes, somebody else's fetishes, no help to you at all. When this realization dawned on my mother, she began to rage against her new country. She deplored its rudeness, its insensitivity, its outright meanness, its indifference, the chase after the almighty buck, the social isolation of most Americans, their inability to partake in warm, genuine fellowship and, above all, their deplorable lack of awe before what they had made.

This was the second stage of grief for her old self. The first, leaving her country, was sharp and immediate, almost toxic in its violence. The second was more prolonged, more damaging, because no hope was attached to it. Certainly not the hope of return.

5

And here, thinking of return, she began to reflect that perhaps there had been more to this deal than she'd first thought. True, she had left behind a lot that was good, but she had also left behind a vast range of daily humiliations. If she was ordered to move out of town she had to comply. If a party member took a dislike to her she had to go to extraordinary lengths to placate him because she was considered petit-bourgeois and could easily have lost her small photo shop. She lived in fear of being denounced for something she had said. And worst of all, she was a Jew, which meant that she was structurally incapable of obtaining any justice in her native land. She had lived by the grace of an immensely complicated web of human relations, kept in place by a thousand small concessions, betrayals, indignities, bribes, little and big lies.

6

At this point, the ersatz tomatoes and the faux chicken did not appear all that important. An imponderable had made its appearance, a bracing, heady feeling of liberty. If she took that ersatz tomato and flung it at the head of the Agriculture Secretary of the United States, she would be making a statement about the disastrous effects of pesticides and mechanized farming. Flinging that faux chicken at Barbara Mandrell would be equally dramatic and perhaps even media-worthy. And she'd probably serve only a suspended sentence. What's more, she didn't have to eat those things, because she could buy organic tomatoes and free-range chicken. Of course, it would cost more, but that was one of the paradoxes of America: To eat as well as people in a Third World country eat (when they eat) costs more.

7

My mother was beginning to learn two things: one, that she had gotten a good deal after all, because in addition to food and furniture they had thrown in freedom; and two, America is a place of paradoxes; one proceeds from paradox to paradox like a chicken from the pot into the fire.

8

■■■ *Writer's Notebook*

Practicing Previewing

Choose a different reading and preview it on your own. This might be a reading your instructor assigns, or one of the readings in Chapters 3 through 12. Write answers to the questions that appear on pages 17–18. ■

Reading the Text

After you have skimmed a text and answered the previewing questions, you are ready to settle in and read the text slowly, straight through. Try to keep moving forward. You can go back over difficult passages, but do not stop reading just be-

Annotating helps you preserve your thoughts as you read. This is essential to reading critically.

cause you do not fully understand them. Finishing the text will give you insights that will make the difficult passages more accessible when you go back to them. Have a pen or pencil ready to mark up the reading as described below.

As you read, mark the text with **annotations**—that is, *notes in the margins*. Annotating is essential to reading critically. If you do not want to mark up a book, photocopy the reading or use sticky notes. The important thing is to use a pen or pencil, not a highlighter. You want to preserve your thoughts as you read; you cannot do this with a highlighter.

ART OF QUESTIONING | Some Questions for Annotations

How should you annotate? Here are some questions your annotations might answer:

- **What words do I not know?** You can look them up now and write the definition in an annotation or circle them and look them up later. Why is it important not just to skip them? In the short run, the more you skip, the less you comprehend. In the long run, looking up the words will help build your vocabulary and enable you to infer the meaning of words in future readings, allowing you more time to engage with the ideas as you read.

- **What are the main points as opposed to subordinate passages?** Mark the main ideas in the margin so you can easily find them later. Use brackets to show which paragraphs go together to develop each main idea.

- **What words signal turns in the author's train of thought?** Words like "however" and "but" show that the author will contradict something just stated. Expressions like *for example* suggest that the author will elaborate on an idea. Circle or underline these words, and note how the author's train of thought shifts.

- **Where does the author introduce viewpoints other than his or her own?**
  Authors often introduce other people who agree or disagree with their ideas.
  These may be direct quotations but often are paraphrases.

- **How well am I connecting with this reading?** If you find some parts of a text
  difficult to comprehend, put a question mark in the margin to tell yourself what
  you need to return to later. If you can connect any prior knowledge, observation,
  or personal opinion to something in the text, note it in the margin. ■

We have reprinted the first two paragraphs of the reading by Codrescu to demonstrate the kinds of annotations a critical reader could make.

My mother, ever a practical woman, started investing in furniture when she came to America. Not just any furniture. Sears furniture. Furniture that she kept the plastic on for fifteen years before she had to conclude, sadly, that Sears wasn't such a great investment. In Romania, she would have been the richest woman on the block.

> In other words, cheap furniture. Tone is humorous, ironic.

Which brings us to at least one paradox of immigration. Most people come here because they are sick of being poor. They want to eat and they want to show something for their industry. But soon enough it becomes evident to them that these things aren't enough. They have eaten and they are full, but they have eaten alone and there was no one with whom to make toasts and sing songs. They have new furniture with plastic on it but the neighbors aren't coming over to ooh and aah. If American neighbors or less recent immigrants do come over, they smile condescendingly at the poor taste and the pathetic greed. And so, the greenhorns find themselves poor once more: This time they are lacking something more elusive than salami and furniture. They are bereft of a social and cultural milieu.

> Signals the first major point.

> Here is the point, the paradox: They have plenty but they are still poor.

> Shifts to the neighbors' point of view.

> An inexperienced person.

> Hard to find.

Comparing Annotations

Write annotations to the remainder of Codrescu's essay. In small groups, compare
your annotations. Did you agree on the main points? Did you have similar questions about any part of the reading? ■

▨▬■ ACTIVITY 2.4 *Writer's Notebook*

Adding to Your Vocabulary

In your reading journal, make a list of words that you had to look up or for which you had to use context clues to infer the meaning. Write the definition next to each. You might also "flex" your knowledge of this word by writing some other words with the same root:

indignities—indignity—dignity

Then, for each vocabulary word, write an original sentence using the word in an way that demonstrates your understanding of its meaning. Using the word a few times will help you establish it in your working vocabulary. ■

▨▬■ ACTIVITY 2.5 *Writer's Notebook*

Annotating a Different Reading

Do this "notebook" activity in the margins of the reading you selected and previewed, as described for the activity on page 20. Read it through now and write annotations. Annotate in any way that will aid your comprehension and critical reading, but also use the kinds of annotations suggested in the list on pages 21–22. ■

Rereading the Text

When you are preparing to discuss a reading in class or to use it in your own writing, you will want to reread it or at least portions of it. Go back to passages that you marked as difficult. You will understand them better once you have finished the entire reading. Activities 2.6–2.11 help you get the most out of rereading.

Recognizing Shifts in Point of View and Voice

Writers shift point of view more often than you might expect. Attentive readers note where the author is speaking for himself or herself, and where he or she has slipped into someone else's perspective and voice. For example, an author might present an opposing view without signaling the shift with quotation marks or a transitional expression. If you have been paying attention to the point of view established by the author, you can infer where the point of view shifts.

We noted in Codrescu's essay that he briefly shifts in paragraph 2 to the perspective of the American neighbors who might view new immigrants as having "poor taste" and "pathetic greed." You know that this is not Codrescu's own point of view, not his voice, because he sympathizes with his mother and other immigrants who, as he says in paragraph 4, seek out material objects as "consolations."

■■■■ ACTIVITY 2.6 *Collaborative Activity*

Identifying Voice

In pairs or small groups, reread the paragraph below and decide in which sentences Codrescu shifts from his own point of view and voice to the point of view of his mother.

> My mother, who was middle class by Romanian standards, found herself immensely impoverished after her first flush of material well-being. It wasn't just the disappearance of her milieu—that was obvious—but the feeling that she had, somehow, been had. The American supermarket tomatoes didn't taste at all like the rare genuine item back in Romania. American chicken was tasteless. Mass-produced furniture was built to fall apart. Her car, the crowning glory of her achievements in the eyes of folks back home, was only three years old and was already beginning to wheeze and groan. It began to dawn on my mother that she had perhaps made a bad deal: She had traded in her friends and relatives for ersatz tomatoes, fake chicken, phony furniture. ■

Analyzing Figurative Language

Figurative language (or figures of speech) is *language used in a nonliteral way to convey meaning in a vivid and powerful way.* Two common figures of speech are metaphors and similes. **Metaphors** make *an implicit (or not-on-the-surface) comparison between two things that are not apparently very much alike at all:* "The news story went viral" implicitly compares the spread of news with the spread of a virus. A **simile** also *makes a comparison between two unlike things, but it does so explicitly,* using words such as *like* or *as:* "The news spread like a virus." Other common figures of speech include analogy (an extended metaphor or simile), personification (attributing human qualities to animals, ideas, or objects), and hyperbole (exaggeration for emphasis).

We already noted on page 14 that Nicholas Carr used a metaphor to describe his former reading style ("Once I was a scuba diver in the sea of words") and a simile to describe what has happened to his reading ("Now I zip along the surface like a guy on a Jet Ski"). Figurative language adds voice and angle to writing. The metaphor of the scuba diver suggests depth and silence, while the "guy on a Jet Ski" suggests superficiality and noise.

■■■■ ACTIVITY 2.7 *Writer's Notebook*

Interpreting Figurative Language

Reread paragraph 4 in Codrescu's essay on page 19. In your Writer's Notebook, discuss the effect of Codrescu's use of death as a simile for the loss experienced by new immigrants. Codrescu also uses the word *religion* metaphorically in this paragraph, but he is not referring to an actual religion such as Judaism or Christianity.

How would you interpret the meaning of "religion" in the context of this paragraph? Writers often extend an idea through a series of related metaphors, as Codrescu does here. Highlight or underline all of the references to religion in paragraph 4. How do these assembled religious metaphors contribute to the point Codrescu is making about material objects in the lives of immigrants who are experiencing "a kind of death"? Be ready to discuss your answers to these questions in class. ∎

Paraphrasing Difficult Passages

The reading you do in college is sometimes difficult. Paraphrasing can help you make sense of challenging passages. A **paraphrase** is a *restatement in your own words and sentences*. Paraphrasing is like translating the passage into language you can better understand—using shorter, more direct sentences and more familiar vocabulary. It ought to substitute your own language for the author's voice, sentence patterns, and word choices. A paraphrase should be in your own voice, which usually means trading more literal language for any metaphors or similes, unless you put them in quotation marks.

To learn more about paraphrasing, see Chapter 18, pages 441–42.

Below is a passage from Codrescu's reading in which he explains the immigrant's disillusionment with American material goods. Note that the paraphrase, on the right, is approximately as long as the original. A paraphrase is not a summary, and it should contain all of the points in the original passage. As the color coding indicates, all the points in the original appear in the paraphrase.

Original Passage	**Paraphrase**
When you first arrive on these shores, you are in mourning. The only consolations are these products, which had been imbued with religious significance back at home. But when these things turn out not to be the real things, you begin to experience a second death, brought about by betrayal. You begin to suspect that the religious significance you had attached to them was only possible back home, where these things did not exist. Here, where they are plentiful, they have no significance whatsoever. They are	New immigrants to America feel the loss of their friends, family, and culture. Codrescu compares this sense of loss to mourning a death. To console themselves, they turn to material objects such as cars and furniture, things that they could not buy in the old country but could only dream of possessing. They believed in the power of these objects to give meaning to life. But the immigrant discovers, sadly, that the products are cheap and shoddily made. This discovery is a second loss, as the immigrant mourns the loss of

inanimate fetishes, somebody else's fetishes, no help to you at all.

hope. Paradoxically, the products had meaning only in the old country, when they were out of reach. Here, they are nothing but junk, and the buyer finds that they are useless in providing any sort of consolation.

■■■ ACTIVITY 2.8 *Writer's Notebook*

Practicing Paraphrase

Using the advice and the example paraphrase above, write a paraphrase of another passage. More help with writing paraphrase is available in Chapter 18; see pages 441–43. For a passage to paraphrase, you might look at the alternative reading you may have already previewed and annotated, or you may use the passage below, from Codrescu's essay. You will need to go back to see where the passage fits into the text so that you can write a good paraphrase that clarifies what point in time Codrescu refers to here.

> At this point, the ersatz tomatoes and the faux chicken did not appear all that important. An imponderable had made its appearance, a bracing, heady feeling of liberty. ■

Finding the Writer's Moves in a Text

One way of seeing the big picture of any text you are reading is to go behind the scenes and think about how the text was constructed. **What moves did the writer make in creating it?** Groups of paragraphs often work together to perform a function, such as providing an introduction, background information, an opposing view, or an illustration.

Recognizing these universally available moves and distinguishing them from their specific content is a way to analyze any text. A good strategy is to make a descriptive outline showing the major subdivisions. For each subdivision of the reading, a descriptive outline answers two questions:

■ What is the move or function of this section? In other words, what is it doing?

■ What is the main point or content of this section? In other words, what is it saying?

Writing a descriptive outline requires two skills: analyzing the function of each section and paraphrasing the most important point or points in each section. Following is an example showing the subdivisions of this short reading by Codrescu.

Subdivisions of "Notes of an Alien Son: Immigration Paradoxes"

Paragraphs 1–2

> **Does:** Gives an example of one problem, or paradox.
>
> **Says:** When Andrei Codrescu's mother emigrated from Romania, she found a better life materially, but she had to accept the loss of her home, friends, and family—her supportive social and cultural environment.

Paragraphs 3–4

> **Does:** Gives an example of another problem, or paradox.
>
> **Says:** American products turned out to be cheaply made junk that did not last. They had been more powerful as dream than as reality. Realizing their dreams were built on false expectations is an even greater loss for the immigrants than leaving home and family.

Paragraph 5

> **Does:** Sums up the two main points of the essay so far.
>
> **Says:** His mother suffered two losses: first, the loss of her cultural and social environment, and second, the loss of her belief in products as a consolation for the first loss.

Paragraphs 6–7

> **Does:** Puts the problems into a larger context or perspective.
>
> **Says:** She realized that going back to Romania would be worse. In Romania, her life was bound by a bureaucracy run by favors and bribes. In America, she had freedom, an amazing discovery.

Paragraph 8

> **Does:** Sums up the main point of the whole essay.
>
> **Says:** His mother learned that the benefits of emigrating were worth the costs and also that life in America was more complicated than she had envisioned.

▪▪▪ ACTIVITY 2.9 *Thinking as a Writer*

Finding a Writer's Moves in a Different Reading

Analyze the reading selection you previewed, read, and annotated (as instructed on pages 20 and 23). Note the major subdivisions and the main point of each subdivision. Make an outline to show (1) how each subdivision functions (the role it performs) and (2) what it says (the point it makes). Use the example outline above as a model. ▪

Summarizing the Text

Writing a summary of a reading helps you see the text as a whole, not a series of parts. It is often necessary to sum up the entire content of a reading, such as when you want to explain someone else's argument in a paper of your own or

To learn more about summarizing, see Chapter 18, pages 443–45.

when writing an annotated bibliography to let others know the content of your sources.

To write a summary, you must first sort out the main ideas from the supporting details and then put the main ideas into your own words—that is, paraphrase them. Writing a descriptive outline, as explained above, is an excellent strategy for drafting a summary. Once you have found the major subdivisions of a reading and paraphrased their key points, you have material to work with for a summary.

Simply splicing the paraphrases together, however, may not result in a smooth summary. The biggest challenge is to unite these paraphrases into a coherent piece of writing that reflects the train of thought in the original passage. You will need to add transitions and possibly some additional information from the original text. You may use brief quotations. Bear in mind, however, that a summary should be no more than one-third the length of the original.

An example summary of "Notes of an Alien Son: Immigration Paradoxes" appears below. The original complete text is on pages 19–20.

Summary of "Notes of an Alien Son: Immigration Paradoxes"

When Andrei Codrescu's mother emigrated from Romania she had to accept the loss of her home, friends and family, her social and cultural support. In exchange, she dreamed of a better lifestyle materially, with new furniture and a car. However, she was disappointed by the reality: mass-produced food with no flavor and cheaply made cars and furniture that fell apart. She felt that she had "been had." In her anger, she saw only the bad side of America—the greed, the selfish individualism, people's blasé lack of appreciation for what they have. Realizing that her dreams were built on false expectations was an even greater loss than leaving home and family, because now she had no hope for any kind of consolation.

But then she realized that going back would be worse. In Romania, she had had no rights. Even where she lived could be dictated to her. As a Jew, she had no legal standing. Her life was bound by a bureaucracy run by favors and bribes. In contrast, the freedom in America gave her a "heady feeling of liberty." She could protest, she could even throw things and be confident that the penalties would be light.

Codrescu's mother realized that even if America was a "place of paradoxes" where a good tomato costs more than it would in a Third World country, freedom made emigrating "a good deal after all."

Margin annotations:
Covers paragraphs 1 and 2
Covers paragraphs 3 and 4
Covers paragraph 5
Covers paragraphs 6 and 7
Covers paragraph 8

■■■ ACTIVITY 2.10 *Writer's Notebook*

Summarizing a Reading

After having worked through the critical reading stages for an alternative reading, write a summary of it using the advice and model on page 28. You should also consult Chapter 18 for more advice on how to write summaries; see pages 443–46. ■

Responding to a Reading

During and after rereading, you should have more extensive responses to a stimulating text, with more thoughts than can fit in a marginal note. That is why serious readers and researchers keep reading response journals for recording thoughts, reactions, and opinions that are more extensive than brief annotations.

You could simply write your thoughts in a spiral notebook or in a file you keep on your computer, or you could follow the suggestion of many reading experts and use a double-entry journal, a notebook, or online document divided into two columns with quotations or paraphrases of the text in one column and your reactions on the right. Following is an example of a double-entry reading journal:

What the text says:	What I say back to the text:
Par. 2: Codrescu shows how isolated immigrants can be: "there was no one with whom to make toasts and sing songs."	This passage explains why many new immigrants want to live in neighborhoods with others who share their customs and language. I think as they assimilate, they lose this dependency, but that is sad too because their children often forget about their roots.
Par. 3: "She had traded in her friends and relatives for ersatz tomatoes, fake chicken, phony furniture."	His mother expected American products to be a good part, and they weren't. Why not? Possibly because Americans are more interested in saving money on necessities like food and furniture so they can spend it on other more status-symbol things.

What the text says:	What I say back to the text:
Par. 4: "She deplored its rudeness, its insensitivity, its outright meanness, its indifference, the chase after the almighty buck, the social isolation of most Americans, their inability to partake in warm, genuine fellowship and, above all, their deplorable lack of awe before what they had made."	This is a pretty harsh description of Americans. It shows how an outsider notices the downside of our fast-paced, materialistic lifestyle—things that we might acknowledge if pointed out to us, but that we just accept as how it is. It would be interesting to get other opinions about this, such as from exchange students.
Par. 6: "... she had left behind a vast range of daily humiliations."	Romania has changed now that it is a democracy and part of the European Union. She may not even want to leave if she lived there today, but the point of the essay is still relevant because it describes a universal experience for the many who still want to escape to America for freedom and a better life.
Par. 8: "America is a place of paradoxes. ..."	What does he mean here? What other examples can I think of? An example would be American middle-class women who can choose to eat a healthy diet but are forced by fashion images to eat the calorie intake of someone in a developing country. They are free and yet they are controlled by media messages. That's a paradox.

The advantage of the double-entry journal is that it shows the connection between what you read and what you thought about what you read. The double-entry journal is useful for stimulating your own thinking in response to the text. You can also consult it for citing the passages in the text when writing in response to a reading.

■■■■ ACTIVITY 2.11 *Writer's Notebook*

Double-Entry Journal

Use the double-entry template on this book's website, to make your own notes and responses to Codrescu's text. Is there any connection among the comments you made in the right-hand column? Write two or three paragraphs describing these connections. ■

The Assignment

Just as writing a summary of a reading helps you to see the whole text coherently, writing a personal response essay helps you assess your own thinking in response to a reading. Writing your response helps you examine, revise, and possibly gain new insights into the text. On his blog, the best-selling writer Steven Johnson explains how writing a book review helps him appreciate the book more deeply: "... [A]ctually sitting down to write out a response to something makes you see it in a new way, often with greater complexity." For this assignment, write a short essay explaining your response to a text that you choose or that your instructor assigns. Begin by reading the text critically using the process and strategies described in this chapter.

What Could I Write About?

To stimulate your thinking, ask yourself questions like the following:

■ What is the central issue raised in the reading? What are the author's views on this issue? Did you have views on the issue before reading? If so, how would you compare your prior thinking with the author's?

■ Do your observations and experiences confirm, illustrate, or contradict what the text says?

■ Did the reading present any new ideas that had not occurred to you before? Did the reading raise some new questions you had never considered? Did it question some assumption or belief you had been holding?

■ If you could ask the author one question, what would it be? Why would this question matter to the line of thought or argument in the text?

■ What other writers' views have you read on this topic? How do their views compare with the views expressed in this reading?

■ Even if you did not accept all of the views and ideas in this reading, what can you take away from it to add to your knowledge about the topic?

When writing your response, tie your own thoughts to specific passages in the text.

What Is My Rhetorical Situation?

When previewing a reading, readers should ask questions about the rhetorical situation, as explained on pages 38–40. Likewise when preparing to write, writers should consider the rhetorical situation for their own texts. Consider the rhetorical situation for an essay responding to a reading.

Writer: What Is My Purpose?

The purpose of a response essay is to express the writer's ideas about the text. A response can be an evaluation of the reading or it could simply discuss the ideas that the writer found important and worth further thought. See the list of moves in the section below on Text: What Moves Can I Make?

Reader: Who Is My Audience?

The response essay shares the results of your critical reading with other readers of the same text.

Text: What Moves Can I Make?

Response essays can do some or all of the following:

- *Draw connections between the world of the text and your own world,* things you have experienced, prior knowledge you bring to the text.
- *Offer insights into the meaning of the text,* as revealed by relationships between parts of the text, analysis of the language, style, arrangement, and voice of the author.
- *Evaluate the thinking;* tell why the writing is convincing to you or not.
- *Reflect on the significance of the text,* explaining the degree to which reading it contributed to your understanding of the topic.
- *Make specific and accurate references* to passages in the text while making any of the moves listed here.

Following is a passage from a book by Lee Siegel about the Internet, *Against the Machine: Being Human in the Age of the Electronic Mob.* The reading is followed by two student responses. Note that the students disagreed about the validity of Siegel's argument, but each wrote a good response, showing real engagement with the ideas in the reading.

Information Is Powerlessness

LEE SIEGEL

Born in 1957, Lee Siegel is a prominent cultural critic whose writing has appeared in many publications, including Harper's, The New Republic, *and* The Wall Street Journal.

Why does anyone not employed in the news media need a constant flow of news and information? One of the Internet boosters' proudest claims is that the Internet can deliver the news to its users with unprecedented immediacy. If someone gets shot in a supermarket parking lot in Flagstaff, Arizona, an Internet user in New Jersey will know about it in hours, maybe even days before someone who depends on his local evening news. But who really needs to know that? Who needs to assimilate the unrelenting reams of information directed at us twenty-four hours a day? . . .   1

Well, no one can ingest so much information at once. Yet, again, if you push an Internet enthusiast's claims that the Internet delivers news faster than the speed of light, he will answer your question with the tautological reiteration of his claim. Information is good because information is good. Democracy depends on information and on full access to information, he will tell you. An informed citizenry is an empowered citizenry. For too long, the elite media outlets controlled access to information. The Internet has thrown those exclusive and excluding doors wide open. And on and on.   2

The Internet does indeed have achievements in the news business. It has forced the traditional news outlets to seek out more and more trivial news, in order to compete with the Internet. And it has engorged the "old" media with streams of useless information. . . .   3

Now, information is a good thing. In situations of emergency or crisis, it is a vitally good thing. But information is composed of facts with which one has only recently become acquainted, facts that have value because they are communicable entities that many people want to possess. You desire knowledge for its own sake, not for the sake of knowing what someone else knows, or for the sake of being able to pass it on to someone else. Knowledge guarantees your autonomy. Information gets you thinking like everyone else who is absorbing the same information.   4

To put it another way: knowledge means you understand a subject, its causes and consequences, its history and development, its relationship to some fundamental aspect of life. But you can possess a lot of information about something without understanding it. An excess of information can even disable knowledge; it can unmoor the mind from its surroundings by breaking up its surroundings into meaningless data. Distraction has the obvious effect of driving out reflection, but because we are reading or watching the "news" rather than enjoying a diversion, we feel serious and undistracted. Never mind that the news has often been more diverting than the most absorbing diversions, and now more than ever. The more we concentrate on the news, the more distracted we are. . . .   5

Taylor 1

Abigail Taylor

Professor Channell

English 1301

September 30, 2010

Response to Lee Siegel's "Information Is Powerlessness"

Our nation is in serious trouble intellectually. I am disgusted by people's inability, and often refusal, to look beyond the surface. Our current political environment is the clearest example of this kind of intellectual incompetence. Today, politics are polarized because so many citizens are black-and-white thinkers. They are unable to see the gray area or middle ground of political issues because they lack the insight and understanding necessary to evaluate the issues for themselves.

> This opening paragraph does not refer to Siegel's text but it does put the text into a larger context, voters' ignorance of the issues, giving a purpose to Taylor's response.

Lee Siegel expresses a similar repulsion at the intellectual state of society in his book *Against the Machine: Being Human in the Age of the Electronic Mob*. In a section of the book about the Internet as news media, Siegel says "a constant flow of news and information" (par. 1) can disable our minds from understanding or even valuing real knowledge (par. 5). Instead, we worship information for its own sake. This change in values threatens our freedom as a society.

> This paragraph grounds the response in the text. It summarizes the main points and refers to specific passages, citing the paragraph numbers in parentheses.

Siegel agrees that information is a good thing, but he says that you have to be able to do something with it, namely: Think about it! Instead, people want to possess the latest "communicable entities" (par. 4) to show each other up. A perfect example is a friend of mine from back home in Virginia. Whenever I talk to her, she gets on the topic of the latest news. If I have not heard about the flooding yesterday in North Carolina or the deportation of Roma gypsies from France, she puts me down. It makes her feel good to know all this stuff, but she doesn't do anything or act in a way that would allow her to use her knowledge constructively.

> Presents a supporting point from Siegel that Taylor could connect with from personal experience.

> Taylor uses a personal experience to confirm Siegel's point.

Adding to our national ignorance, the Internet "has forced the traditional news outlets to seek out more and more trivial news, in order to compete . . . ." (par. 3). How

> Presents another supporting point that Taylor connects with from personal observation. She again cites the text to keep her response connected to Siegel's specific points.

34

Taylor uses her own voice and observations to confirm Siegel's point.

true this is! Trivial stories litter every broadcast. NBC's "The Today Show" is only about 30 percent straightforward news and 70 percent petty human-interest stories. "Today" recently aired a report about starlet Lindsay Lohan's trouble with the law. The show presented the vapid, inconsequential gossip story the same way they would present a serious story about election results. The anchor cut to a reporter "in the field" who then showed a video segment of Lohan entering a courtroom for her probation hearing. Siegel is right when he says that the news has become just another distraction.

I realize that Siegel is an idealist. There is no way to turn off the flow of news on all the online news sources, and no way to stop the conventional news media from catering to the public demand for constant stimulation. However, if people realize how little voters know about the issues or care about candidates' knowledge and character, they will see that Siegel has a point: Sheer information in quantity does not guarantee a free society. The result is that everyone thinks alike. On the other hand, Siegel says, "Knowledge guarantees your autonomy" (par. 4). A free society depends on autonomous citizens who can think for themselves, not an "electronic mob."

5

Returns to her opening theme and shows how Siegel's reading provides insight into the problem of an ignorant voting public.

Taylor brings her opening idea about uniformed voters together with Siegel's point about the need for independent critical thinkers in a democracy. She ties her conclusion to Siegel's text.

■ ■ ■ ACTIVITY 2.12 *Collaborative Activity*

Noting a Writer's Moves and Responding to a Reading

Notice that the annotations to Taylor's response essay above point out how Taylor moved back and forth between Siegel's text and her own responses as she developed her response. Following is a second student example responding to Lee Siegel and offering a different point of view on the reading. Working in pairs or groups of three, annotate Will Bost's essay as we have done above to point out the various moves made by the student writer. ■

Will Bost

Professor Channell

English 1301

September 30, 2010

A Response to Lee Siegel

Behold, the Internet's unstoppable surge of information and its dooming consequences.   1

These are the words I hear Lee Siegel whimpering after reading an excerpt from his book,

Against the Machine: Being Human in the Age of the Electronic Mob. Perhaps we should pay

more attention to our growing technological reliance, but does a technological reliance

actually mean we are giving up free thought and the ability to discern knowledge from

information? Siegel thinks so. I don't buy his claim that we as a society are incapable of

distinguishing news from knowledge.

Siegel mocks the advocates of free information by condescendingly labeling their   2

defense as a "tautological reiteration" (par. 2). Yes, Siegel does use big words to convey

his point, but he does this at the risk of losing what seems to be his target audience, the

"electronic mob"—people who appreciate the ability to stay informed thanks to the Internet.

If asked whether we would be better off with less access to information, most people would

not hesitate to answer "no."

There are a few points in Siegel's essay that are accurate. For example, the quantity of   3

information has grown substantially and comes at us with "unprecedented immediacy" (par.

1). And some of the news is frivolous or at least irrelevant. But that does not mean that the

quality of all the information will diminish. Instead, users learn to seek the better sources

of information, which can be found through intelligent parsing. Wikipedia, for example, is

disreputable because any user can contribute to its database. However, Wikipedia users sift

through sources, throwing out the bad ones and linking to the sound, dependable ones.

Siegel actually preferred the way things were in the past when "elite media outlets   4

controlled access to information" (par. 2). He prefers traditional journalism over the "wide open" doors of the Internet. Here, he reveals his own elitist stereotyping of the American public. He assumes that the public is incapable of critically judging the news or thinking independently about it. But if you look at the comments on the news stories and columns online, you see healthy discussion, not a mob mentality.

The bottom line is that everyone's use of technology is unique; we make it what we want. Instead of concentrating on the negative effects of technology and how much we rely on it, we should put forth our efforts to increasing the benefits of our technological advances. Technology's greatest contribution to our modern society is not a superficial reliance on electronics, but increased accessibility to information for people of all cultures, classes, professions, and stages of life.

5

CHAPTER 3

Writing and the Art of Questioning

THE KEY POINT IN CHAPTER 1 IS THAT THINKING BEGINS WHEN YOU ASK QUES-tions. In this chapter we consider the kinds of questions that writing requires. A good place to begin is to think about the act of writing. What are you doing when you write?

What Is Good Writing?

Writing well is not simply writing correctly. It is **communicating effectively.** Good writing, whether a letter, a memo, a report, or a paper in school, sends a message from a writer to a reader. All communication starts with *someone who has something to say to someone else and a reason or purpose for saying it:*

- We send a text or write an e-mail to a professor to set up a meeting.
- We write letters to customers to explain a new service.
- We write a letter to the editor to tell the community our views on a proposed law or policy.
- We write a paper in a class on popular culture to share our research on how popular music shapes group identity.

Short or long, formal or informal, in school, at work, or in another setting, writing is always communication, and good communication responds appropriately to its *rhetorical situation.*

What Is the Rhetorical Situation?

Rhetoric, *the study of effective communication,* helps us think critically about the texts we write. The relationship among the **writer,** the **reader,** and the **text** forms the **rhetorical situation;** *these are the variables always present when we think about a writing task.* (See Figure 3.1.)

The effectiveness of any piece of writing depends on how well the author has thought about these three basic elements of communication and how they relate to each other. Here are some questions to consider:

Writer

Reader

Text

FIGURE **3.1**

The Rhetorical Situation

About the Writer

- Why am I writing this text? What is my **purpose** (to inform, to persuade, to entertain, to express my feelings, and so on)?

- What is my **angle,** or **point of view,** on the topic?

- What does my angle imply about my **voice,** how I want to sound to my readers?

About the Reader

- For whom am I writing this text? That is, who are my **readers,** people I most want to reach?

- Will my readers find my topic and my angle useful, interesting, something they can relate to?

- What **prior knowledge** of my topic do my readers have or what background do they need?

- In what **context** (academic, business, public, personal) will my audience read and talk about this text?

About the Text

- What kind, or **genre,** of text is this, and what **conventions** govern it?

- What **expectations** do readers have for texts of this genre?

- In what **medium** (print or digital, spoken or read) is this genre typically available?

- What **design** features are associated with this genre?

Notice that the categories overlap and interrelate: The context for a piece of writing determines what is appropriate to include in the message. Facebook, for example, is a more public context than a personal e-mail or text message. Audience also influences the text, as writers choose what to put in or leave out depending on how much the audience already knows about a topic.

Why Ask about the Rhetorical Situation?

Without a sense of audience and purpose, no one can write well. Inattention to the rhetorical situation results in disorganized memos that employees ignore or misunderstand, in public speeches that last too long and make an audience drowsy or restless, and in lectures that leave students confused.

When we ask about angle, we are looking for something of our own to say, a key point we will say more about shortly. If we find something we want to say, we are more likely to care about saying it well. If we have something to say, we also think about readers we want to reach. Connecting with them suddenly matters to us, so we care about how we sound. That is, we care about *voice*.

What Is Voice?

Voice refers to the writer's presence in a text, *how the writer "sounds."* When we read carefully, we can "hear" a person—a personality—in the words. Once again, the rhetorical situation determines how you want to sound. In informal social writing such as comments on a Facebook page, there is almost no such thing as too much personality. In other rhetorical situations, such as when writing a letter to a customer, the voice will sound more formal and reserved: Impatience, anger, and even humor in excess can be offensive in workplace communications. In some science writing an objective tone is appropriate. Voice varies according to the situation, but in all cases we should hear a person saying something that matters in a way that holds the reader's attention and is appropriate to the context and the genre of the text.

Read to hear the voice in each of the following two passages on the same topic, paleontology. The first is from a museum website at the University of California. The author is not identified. The second is from an essay published originally in the literary magazine *Harper's*. The author, David Quammen, writes with a concern for the environment.

The writer's voice reflects his or her stake in the topic.

What Is Paleontology?

UNIVERSITY OF CALIFORNIA MUSEUM
OF PALEONTOLOGY

... [P]aleontology is the study of what fossils tell us about the ecologies of the past, about evolution, and about our place, as humans, in the world. Paleontology incorporates knowledge from biology, geology, ecology, anthropology, archaeology, and even computer science to understand the processes that have led to the origination and eventual destruction of the different types of organisms since life arose.

Planet of Weeds

DAVID QUAMMEN

Hope is a duty from which paleontologists are exempt. Their job is to take the long view, the cold and stony view, of triumphs and catastrophes in the history of life. They study the fossil record, that erratic selection of petrified shells, carapaces, bones, teeth, tree trunks, leaves, pollen, and other biological relics, and from it they attempt to discern the lost secrets of time, the big patterns of stasis and change, the trends of innovation and adaptation and refinement and decline that have blown like sea winds among ancient creatures in ancient ecosystems.

▓■ *Writer's Notebook*

Analyzing the Rhetorical Situation

Write one or two paragraphs answering the following questions about the pair of reading selections above on paleontology.

1. How do the contexts for each piece of writing determine the author's choices of what material to include? What information is similar in the two? What is different?
2. How would you describe the difference in purpose for each passage?
3. How would you describe the writer's angle on paleontology in each passage?
4. How would you describe the writer's voice in each passage? How do the elements of purpose, context, audience, and angle affect the writer's decisions about voice? ■

Why Does Voice Matter?

Learning to control the voice in your writing can increase your satisfaction with a writing project and improve your grade. A former student at the University of Hawaii, Monique Fournier, describes her discovery of the difference voice can make:

> *Six years ago, I dropped out of college after completing my sophomore year. I assumed that it was because college wasn't for me, that I just wasn't meant for the classroom. It turns out that I wasn't ready for college writing. I now believe that once a writer finds her voice, she can easily apply it to any college-level writing assignment. Writing those first two years was difficult for me because I was simply plugging chains of words into every paper without any "me" glue to hold them together. Realizing I had a voice, and taking steps to uncover it, has helped me (and my grade point average) immensely.*

> —MONIQUE FOURNIER, "BEES AND FEARS, WHY I WRITE"[1]

Fournier realized that she had a voice and took "steps to uncover it." That sounds easy, but what steps did she take? Where does voice comes from?

To write with voice, we need the following:

- An angle, a point of view toward whatever we are writing about
- The courage to assert it

Writers adjust their voice to suit their purpose, topic, audience, and genre, but the essential question at the heart of writing with voice is, **What stake do I have in my topic?**

What Is an Angle?

What is this "me" that Fournier calls the glue that holds her words together? It comes from personal engagement, having a stake, in your topic. Writers often refer to this as "having an angle." For example, consider the two passages on page 41 on paleontology. On the museum website, the writer's angle is the broad range of knowledge included in the modern study of paleontology. This angle promotes paleontology; it suggests that the reader might want to visit the museum or even take a course.

The other passage shows a darker angle on paleontology as the study of nature's indifference toward the plants and animals that have become extinct. Listing the specific objects that paleontologists study, the author shows his view of paleontology as a study of ancient mysteries. Not everyone would see it that way, but Quammen's angle shows his personal interest in the topic. In each case, the author has a point of view that gives voice to the writing.

A good way to think about angle is to compare writing with taking a photograph. Through your camera lens, you decide how to frame a scene or a person.

---

1. Dobrin, Sidney I., and Anis S. Bawarski, eds. *A Closer Look: The Writer's Reader*. New York: McGraw-Hill, 2003. 763. Print.

FIGURE **3.2**

A Writer's Angle Shows Point of View

A writer's angle is similar to a photographer's angle on a subject. The angle reflects the creator's point of view.

You may try out different angles, with different amounts of background, foreground, and contrast between light and dark. All of these decisions affect how you want to present your subject. Pictures show the photographer's angle on the subject (see Figure 3.2).

Engaging with Topics: How Can I Find an Angle?

Whether you are writing about a social problem like bullying or a scientific topic like climate change, reflecting on your experiences and prior knowledge will help you find an angle. On any topic (represented here by "x"), questions that help to find an angle include the following:

- How does "x" affect me? Why does "x" matter?
- What is my opinion of "x"? What does it mean to me?
- What is the most interesting thing about "x"?
- How is "x" relevant to anything else I have observed or experienced?
- How is "x" relevant to anything else I have read about or studied?
- If I had to put "x" into a larger picture or category, what would that be?

Angle and Rhetorical Situation

A writer's angle on a topic is also influenced by the rhetorical situation, such as the audience, the purpose, and the genre or kind of text that he or she needs to write. Following is a promotional description of a suburb of Dallas:

about richardson

Discover Richardson!

Richardson is located within minutes of all the amenities of Dallas Fort Worth and enjoys a temperate climate with mild winters and warm summers. Spanning 28 square miles and nestled just to the north of downtown Dallas, Richardson is a City like no other.

Known nationally as the Telecom Corridor® which, is home to over 500 high tech and telecommunications companies, today, Richardson has found its place as a sophisticated, modern suburb featuring award winning family festivals, nationally ranked championship golf courses, 30 beautiful parks, more than 40 miles of hike and bike trails and our cultural gem, the Charles W. Eisemann Center for the Performing Arts.

Because the audience for this description is people interested in finding locations for meetings, this description of the city plays up its proximity to Dallas as well as its many cultural and recreational amenities.

■■■ ACTIVITY 3.1 *Writer's Notebook*

Changing the Angle

Revise the description of "About Richardson" based on one of the following angles:

- The viewpoint of a zoologist *celebrating the survival of wild animals in suburban areas.*

- The viewpoint of a resident *interested in honoring and preserving the city's history.*

- The viewpoint of a bicyclist *informing other fitness enthusiasts about the city's bike trails.*

- The viewpoint of an environmentalist *opposed to suburban sprawl.*

Be sure to consider how the voice, message, and purpose of this writing would change with the angle. ■

■■■ ACTIVITY 3.2 *In Your Own Work*

Describing Your Hometown

Write a one- or two-paragraph description of your hometown from an angle that interests you. Who would be an appropriate audience for a paragraph written from this angle? To share your description with classmates, post it on an online discussion board or on a blog. ■

The Assignment

The start of a college writing class is a good time to take stock as a writer. What strengths or abilities do you have, and in what areas do you hope to improve? Looking at the learning goals for your course or writing program will help you assess your skills.

For this assignment, you will focus on some aspect of your writing that matters to you. Maybe there is something about writing that you particularly enjoy, or something that challenges you, such as a problem you would like to overcome. Maybe it is an experience you had with writing—in your childhood, in high school, or maybe outside of school—that influenced your development. This will be a brief essay, so focus on a specific topic connected with your writing. What might you benefit from thinking more about? How might readers benefit from knowing about your experiences with writing?

What Could I Write About?

Some ideas for topics include:

■ A teacher, relative, or other role model of a writer

■ Some advice or instruction that helped or did not help

■ A book, reading, or author that inspired you or influenced you

■ A particular assignment or some writing that you did outside of the classroom

What Is My Rhetorical Situation?

As we discussed earlier, the rhetorical situation is a combination of a writer with something to say, a reader the writer wishes to reach, and a kind (or genre) of text appropriate to the writing task.

Writer: What Are My Purpose and Angle, and How Will They Be Reflected in My Voice?

Your purpose is to reflect on some aspect or experience that has influenced you as a writer.

We have been talking about angle because it is what makes your writing matter to you and matter to your readers. If you do not have something you want to say, your writing will be empty. What do you really think about your development as a writer? What point would be worth sharing with your teacher and your classmates? Why would your point matter to them?

All of the elements discussed influence how you sound in your essay. Envision your audience as the real people they are, and speak to them in the same voice you would use in a conversation or class discussion about writing. Your voice and angle grow out of your life, so do not discount the specific details of your experience, such as teachers' comments, books you read, papers you wrote.

Reader: Who Is My Audience?

Your instructor and your classmates are a natural audience for your essay. In your class, you are part of a community focused on developing as writers. Your instructor is your guide, so sharing some experience or reflecting on some aspect of your writing will help him or her get to know you. You and your classmates will share work and helpful critiques. Getting to know each other as writers will make everyone more comfortable exchanging writing and advice.

Text: What Moves Can I Make?

The genre (kind of writing) for this writing project is the **essay**. An essay is *a short composition in which the author expresses his or her personal views on a topic.* The word itself comes from the French *essai,* meaning "to attempt" or "to try or test out." The writing shows the thought processes of the writer. Essays are more polished than journal entries. A main point or central idea gives the essay coherence, and transitions signal the writer's train of thought.

The following short essay was written by a student in response to the activity outlined above. Read through it once just to see what she has to say, and then go back to note her attention to elements of the rhetorical situation discussed in this chapter.

Griffin 1

Allison Griffin

Professor Channell

English 1301

September 10, 2010

Where My Writing Came from, and Where It Went

As a child, I loved to write. I wanted to be a writer. I wrote about anything and   1

everything. I created fictional stories to release my imagination and poems to express my emotions. I wrote down prayers and kept journals that preserved my deepest worries, fears, and moments of happiness, and kept track of my changing aspirations. I remember getting lost in my writing time. I would jot down my thoughts and watch them develop into something interesting, to me at least.

I had special places I put pen to paper. My most inspirational times were when I was surrounded by nature; the solitude I found crouched under a tree liberated my thoughts. I also remember turning my closet into a writing sanctuary equipped with pens, paper, and pillows. My mom sometimes worried when I disappeared into my closet for hours, but she also looked forward to my reappearance with a new creation for her to read. I had this pure gratification from writing, the desire to write for its own sake, but also competed successfully in writing contests, which fed my dream to be a writer. I could transform my voice for creative writing prompts, poetry and stories that other people liked.

2

Notice I've been writing in the past tense. I wish it weren't true, but long ago I betrayed my longing to create with words. When did my attitude change, and why? I am studious, and in middle school devoted all my writing time to school assignments. I didn't realize it then, but the formulas and guidelines caused me to lose my appetite for simply expressing myself. Sentences with huge SAT words dominated my writing. I got caught up in writing the ideal essay to please my teachers. Each year a new teacher would offer a "better" formula for the "perfect" paper.

3

Of course, there were occasional essays in high school that I felt good about—and I couldn't wait to share them. Somehow they were different from the rest, but my teachers always seemed to find the parts that broke the rules, diminishing my pride and satisfaction. Gradually I learned to strangle my voice because the more "me" I put in a paper the more I was criticized.

4

My mom has wondered about what happened to that part of me that loved to write. Maybe it was all the formulas and rules that caused me to lose my voice, or maybe during adolescence I became too afraid to reveal myself. After not using my voice for so long, I found this paper hard to write and harder to share with others. But maybe I did find my voice again, or perhaps it was always there, hidden beneath all the rules and formulas for a while. Whatever happened, I realize what I have lost and want to recover my passion for writing.

5

Questions for Discussion

In small groups or as a class, discuss the following questions:

1. What is Griffin's **purpose** for writing?
2. For whom is she writing—that is, what **readers** does she have in mind and how does she make it interesting for them?
3. What is her **angle** or point of view on her past writing experience?
4. How would you describe her **voice,** the way she sounds to you? Point out specific places in the text where you can "hear" Griffin's voice. Is it appropriate for her **purpose,** her **audience,** and her **angle** on the topic?

GENRES FOR FURTHER PRACTICE

HOW DO I WRITE A RHETORICAL ANALYSIS?

IN A TYPICAL ANALYSIS OF A TEXT—A LITERARY PIECE, A SPEECH, A CONVERSA-tion, a commercial, an image—you carefully examine the text, often to figure out what it means. In a rhetorical analysis, you study the text not only to determine what it means but how it creates and communicates this meaning.

What Is a Rhetorical Analysis?

Rhetorical analysis involves *taking apart or breaking down a text; separation of the parts from the whole enables understanding and evaluating how the strategies being used work together to achieve the text's purpose.* First, you read the text to understand its purpose: to explain an idea, to share information, to convey a feeling or emotion, to argue a position—whatever you think the text was created to do. Second, you read the text to see how it works: for example, its tone, choice of words and kinds of sentences, the emotion created, the context implied, or the relationship to the audience.

ART OF QUESTIONING | Anatomy of a Rhetorical Analysis

Ask and answer the following questions:

- Description: **Who wrote or created the text? When? Where?**
- Reader identification: **Who is the target audience? How does the author try to reach the audience?**
- Stated or implied goal: **What is the text's purpose?**
- Strategies: **How does the text appeal to logic, emotion, or credibility?**
- Structure: **How are the ideas or images put together?**
- Key words: **What language choices do you find?** ■

Why Write a Rhetorical Analysis?

People do rhetorical analysis whenever they want to understand the way an idea is presented to them. At halftime during the Super Bowl, you might think about the similar ways that commercials try to convince you to buy a product and wonder about the assumptions those businesses have made about who their audience is. While walking across campus, you might notice a flyer that catches your attention, post its image on your Facebook page, and offer your rhetorical analysis in the caption.

In college and in your work life, you will be expected to analyze the rhetorical situation whenever you read critically, whether it is a piece of literature or a letter from the CEO to the company's stockholders. When you write a rhetorical analysis, your task is not simply to state all of the elements of the situation (author, purpose, and audience) or to itemize all of the ways that the writer or creator uses language, images, or emotions. *Your task is to make a point or come to a conclusion about how the text communicates meaning to its audience.*

An Example of Rhetorical Analysis

Rhetorical Analysis of the Section on the Church in "Letter from Birmingham Jail"

GINNY NORTON

The text of "Letter from Birmingham Jail" is available online. Search by the title to read the entire text. The analysis deals with paragraphs 33–44.

Introduction: explains context and background of text analyzed.

On April 12, 1963, eight Alabama clergymen published a letter in the local newspaper as a response to the protests being enacted to affect the desegregation of Birmingham, Alabama, in which they asked the African Americans to wait for a more opportune time to begin their protests. Meanwhile, Martin Luther King had been arrested and imprisoned in the Birmingham jail for his participation in one of his non-violent action campaigns. While in jail, he read the letter from the clergymen and was inspired to write a rebuttal, which asserted why African Americans have waited long enough to receive equality and freedom, and also why it is the moral responsibility of the Church, which has remained uncharacteristically silent "behind the anesthetizing security of stained glass windows" to endorse racial equality. This rebuttal became known as his "Letter from Birmingham Jail." In this letter, Martin Luther King masterfully uses rhetorical appeals . . . to convince the American public that African Americans need the support of the Church as they act immediately to eradicate racial inequality.

1

Transitional sentence: alerts reader analysis about to begin.

Focuses on the appeal of character (*ethos*), moving an audience by generating respect for the writer. Provides specific citations from the text as evidence.

King uses ethos early in his section on the complacency of the Church on racial issues, which serves to build his credibility as a minister and civil rights leader. Dr. King demonstrates his long-standing relationship with the Church by telling us he is a third generation preacher. He then adds to his credibility by praising a few notable examples of Churches that have taken a stand for racial equality, such as Reverend Stallings, who held a non-segregated Sunday worship service the previous Sunday. King also

2

demonstrates his worthiness as a civil rights leader by nonchalantly mentioning that he "was suddenly catapulted into the leadership of the bus protest in Montgomery [Alabama]." He once again emphasizes how experienced he is in matters involving the Southern Church, by exclaiming that he has heard "numerous religious leaders of the South" implore their congregations to conform to desegregation merely because it is a law. However, Dr. King laments that those Southern religious leaders do not encourage desegregation because it is the morally right thing to do, which lays the foundation for King's logical argument. King's use of *ethos* is a very effective tool at establishing him as a knowledgeable, veteran preacher and civil rights leader.

Transitional word moves reader from paragraph 2 to 3.

3   Additionally, King's impassioned, potent word choice creates several instances of *pathos*. At the beginning of his argument about the Church, he first explains that he is critiquing the Church as someone who deeply loves and respects it and will continue to do so "as long as the cord of life shall lengthen." This beautiful explanation of King's relationship with the Church has the effect of making readers sympathize with a man whose dearest institution has let him down. Midway through his critique, King uses deliberately short, adamant sentences to point out that the early Christians were once so fired up for the Lord that they were not intimidated by the masses. During this period, the Church used its influence to bring an end to infant sacrifice, as well as brutal conquests. Next, King shifts his focus to the modern Church, and acerbically asserts that the Church of today "is so often a weak, ineffectual voice with an uncertain sound." This accusation leads into King's main argument as it emotively demonstrates that the Church has fallen from its powerful position of setting the moral agenda on issues to an outdated, fruitless institution.

Focuses on the appeal to feeling or emotion (*pathos*). Note: last example of emotional appeal linked to discussion of the appeal to reason in next paragraph.

4   Dr. King concisely uses logos throughout his argument about the ineffectual nature of the contemporary Church on the topic of immediate racial equality. King succinctly reminds his audience that the early Church frequently occupied towns and rearranged their entire power structure with the conviction that "they were a 'colony of heaven' and had to obey God rather than men." King shows that the contemporary Church is conversely an "arch supporter of the status quo." In fact, King illuminates how the power structures of today's cities are reliant upon the Church's placating, "silent . . . sanction of things as they are." Lastly, King ardently explains that the civil rights movement will succeed, because, as he so eloquently proclaims, "the sacred heritage of our nation and the eternal will of God are embodied in our echoing demands." As a minister, King hoped that the Christian values of morality and universal brotherhood in Christ would be incentive enough for the Church to realize the dire need for immediate action in favor of racial equality. Dr. King expresses disappointment in the Church's uncharacteristic silence on the issue of racial injustice, when it is so clearly morally wrong. King goes on to express fears that if the Church fails to regain the sacrificial spirit of the bygone era, it will soon be "dismissed as an irrelevant social club with no meaning for the twentieth century."

Lead sentence is topic sentence signaling to the reader what the entire paragraph is about.

Focuses on the appeal to reason or logic (*logos*). Note: backed by citation from the text and commentary by the author.

Asking Questions: What Can I Write About?

You could write a rhetorical analysis of virtually anything—a political speech, a newspaper editorial, a blog, a literary passage, a scene in a film or play, an overheard conversation. When choosing a text to analyze for an assignment, look for something that intrigues you, that you want to comment on or explain the workings of. Here are some possibilities:

■ An advertisement. Print ads in magazines are often good choices. Because magazines have definite, well-defined readerships, you can assess the ad's effectiveness especially well.

■ A commercial or institutional website, especially the home page. Because online access matters so much to businesses, universities, government agencies, museums, and so on, special effort goes into creating the right impression.

■ A song lyric, if the words are interesting enough to make analysis worthwhile.

How Do I Prepare to Write a Rhetorical Analysis?

When preparing to write a rhetorical analysis, consider what the task requires, voice and style, and development and organization.

Thinking as a Writer: Task Requirements

First read the text carefully and critically. Before drafting your analysis, examine all of the elements of the text by asking yourself the following questions:

■ **What is the writer's or speaker's overall point (thesis) and purpose** (to persuade, to shock, to criticize)?

■ **Who is the intended audience?**

- **What kind of emotion or tone does the text create** and how do you respond to it on an emotional level?
- **What kind of language is used** (slang, technical jargon, formal, conversational) and how are sentences structured (short and choppy, questions or exclamations)?
- **Are there any significant shifts in pattern and structure or in tone and language?**

As you answer these questions, think about the details in the text that helped you answer them and why the author chose them. This will help you make a strong argument in your analysis.

Thinking as a Writer: Voice and Style

The voice and style of your analysis need to match the context. For example, an overly formal tone when analyzing a singer's connection to the audience in a hip hop song might diminish your credibility, creating questions in your audience's mind about your ability to understand the song. Similarly, an angry tone in an analysis of a political speech might lead your readers to question whether you are unbiased enough to assess the speech fairly.

Thinking as a Writer: Development and Organization

A key feature of a good rhetorical analysis is demonstrating where the text itself supports your claims. This means you cannot simply state that a pop song is targeted at an audience of teenage girls; you need to include quotations from the song to show how you have arrived at this conclusion. Good ideas need details to back them up.

What Are the Steps in Writing a Rhetorical Analysis?

Because a good rhetorical analysis requires very close examination of the text it discusses, you will need to move back and forth between writing your analysis and rereading the text. Keep an open mind throughout this process, and you might discover new angles and points to develop in your analysis.

1. **Draft your analysis.** As you write your first draft, you will begin building the argument for the thesis of your analysis, which is the point that you want to make about the rhetorical situation in your text. Work your way through the text, gathering evidence to support your thesis and all points you make in developing your thesis. Careful reexamination of the text can result in discovering a different or better point you want to make. Allow yourself time, then, to draft and revise so that you can change the direction when a new idea comes to you.

2. **Revise your analysis.** Read your analysis critically by asking these questions:
   - **Does the opening introduce the text and make my main point clear?**

- **Am I moving from point to point based on the needs of my argument?** Does the logic of my essay too closely follow the sequence of the text? Structure your analysis to meet the needs of your argument.
- **Does my analysis offer more than a summary of the text?** A brief summary at the beginning of the analysis is fine, but after that you should be making points about how the text works and providing evidence and commentary about the evidence.
- **Have I offered enough detail to support my claims?** Are there any comments that I have made but not supported? Have I used the best evidence in the text to support each point?

3. **Edit your analysis.** A rhetorical analysis needs to integrate its own ideas with the ideas from the text it is examining. Be sure to link what you are saying to whatever you are citing from the text to back up your point. That is, your reader must understand clearly which point your evidence supports and how it supports each point.

4. **Proofread your analysis.** Any paper should be proofread carefully for errors. In a rhetorical analysis, you need to pay extra attention to quotations to ensure that you have cited them accurately.

BEST PRACTICES | Writing a Rhetorical Analysis

When you are writing a close analysis of a text, you must refer to details from the text, quote it, and describe it. A fine line exists between enough detail and too much. You must draft, revise, and edit with this in mind to ensure that you are not flooding your audience with too much information not relevant to the point you are making.

A good rhetorical analysis is itself rhetorical, an effort to convince others that your analysis has merit. Assume the audience has read the text you are analyzing but lacks information that will help them understand the text better and needs your interpretation to grasp how the text works. ■

HOW DO I WRITE A BLOG?

BEFORE PERSONAL COMPUTERS, CELL PHONES, AND ELECTRONIC SOCIAL NET-working, people expressed opinions as they always have and still do, in conversation with relatives and friends. However, *publishing* one's opinions beyond the circle of face-to-face talk was much more difficult. You had to find a source, such as a magazine or newspaper, willing to put something you wrote in print. Relatively few people had the time and talent to take advantage of print publication. Blogging changed the situation entirely: Now tens of millions of people the world over publish their opinions via the Internet, and many millions more visit blogging sites and are influenced by what they read.

What Is a Blog?

The word **blog** is short for *weblog, a site on the Internet where people post entries about their ideas, opinions, and experiences.* The entries, called **blog posts,** are *arranged chronologically descending from most recent to oldest.* There are group blogs and blogs by individuals. Blogs often focus on a single area of interest, such as one's work, hobbies, health, or politics. Unlike diaries or journals, blogs are public; blog posts take you into the world of ideas, current events, and community issues that provoke other people's thinking. Blogs have a **comment feature** that allows readers to post their responses.

Why Write a Blog?

People blog because they want to make their interests and opinions public or to share their experiences in deeper ways than are possible on social networking sites. Politics are the focus of many blogs, but so are hobbies, family topics, and professional interests. People read and write blogs in order to join communities for exchanging ideas and offering support.

Blogs are often part of college class activities across the curriculum. Writing and maintaining a blog develop skills essential for academic, personal, and professional writing:

- Reading closely and critically
- Forming opinions on a wide range of topics
- Expressing your ideas in clear, concise, and interesting ways
- Responding to reader feedback on your writing

CONCEPT CLOSE-UP | Anatomy of a Blog

The following blog post by novelist Tayari Jones, who teaches creative writing at Rutgers-Newark, shows all the elements of a blog.

- ■ Blog Title: The entire weblog that you create that contains all of the entries you post. Like a book of essays, your blog will have a title of your choice.
- ■ Blog Platform: The software you use to create your blog, such as Blogger.
- ■ Blog URL: Your blog will have a unique URL, or address on the Internet. The blogging platform you use to create your blog will help you make a unique URL.
- ■ Display Name, also called "signing name": Bloggers may use their own names or blog under pseudonyms.
- ■ Post: Posts are the messages you place on your blog; they appear in reverse chronological order with the most recent at the top. Each post will have:
  - Post Date: The date and the time of the message.
  - Title: You will give each post a title, indicating content. Titles are important in attracting readers to your posts; we will have more to say about titles later.
  - Body: The body of your post can range from one paragraph to several. Some posts are as long as a short essay.
  - Links: Your blogging tool, whether through Blackboard, Connect Composition from McGraw-Hill, or a commercial platform like Blogger, will allow you to put links to other webpages into your posts. Jones's post contains a link to the Twitter site for readers who want more information about the topic.

- Comments: When others read your post, they can reply using the comment function.

- Design and Graphics: Blogging platforms make Web publishing easy because they give you a choice of templates for your blog's colors and styles. ■

Asking Questions: What Can I Write About?

Topics for blogging are everywhere—current events; popular culture; campus life; college classes; other people's blogs; books; magazines; the Internet; music; personal experiences; and observations of people, places, and events.

However, an interesting topic alone will not engage readers; you need an angle or point of view on the topic. Your angle shows your personal engagement with your topic, and it gives a point to your post that readers might want to respond to. Here are four questions to help you come up with ideas for topics and angles on them.

- **What interesting experiences have I had recently?** Good blog posts arise out of personal experiences that make you stop and think. For example, one student blogged about a conversation she and her friends had one night in the dorm about choosing a major and the problems that students face when parents' ideas of a good choice conflict with the student's ideas. The post drew sixteen comments because so many readers were dealing with similar issues.

- **What ideas am I learning about?** In college you learn new ideas and concepts, some of which may be unsettling. Your blog is a good place to explore them. If the concept is confusing, you might grow to understand it by explaining it to other bloggers.

   Another student explored her understanding of a concept she learned in sociology: the "looking-glass self." In her blog, she explained the concept to students who had no prior knowledge of it. Doing so helped her to grasp it herself. Then she explained why she resisted the concept as an explanation of her own identity. Her blog post was short—just two paragraphs—but it could have been the beginning for a paper.

- **What decisions or problems am I wrestling with?** Everyone has problems, decisions, and dilemmas. People use their blog posts to explore their thinking and ask for others' input. Common topics in this category have to do with time management, problematic roommates, raising children, and relationship issues.

- **What opinions do I have?** Reading the news, seeing films, observing campus life—all of these can expose important issues and strong opinions. Students write about campus issues; cultural events such as plays and movies; and topics in the news, whether local, national, or world.

- **What have I been reading lately?** Any leisure reading can inspire ideas for blogging. Read online newspapers and magazines so you can link to them in your posts. You can also get ideas for topics from reading other students' blogs. If you get an idea from someone else, be sure that you have your own point to make about the topic; before you write about it on your own blog, it would be courteous of you to write a comment on theirs to keep the discussion going on that blog.

The best blog posts are not necessarily on the most sensational topics or stories in the news. The best posts are often about what is close to your own and your readers' life experiences, concerns, and attitudes. Topics associated with campus culture and social interaction usually lead to good posts if the blogger takes a critical or analytical stance.

How Do I Prepare to Write a Blog Post?

Blogging is a special medium requiring an approach somewhat different from diaries, journals, or paper assignments for classes. You need to select a blogging platform, consider voice and style, organization, development, and visual appeal.

Thinking as a Writer: Task Requirements

If you are blogging for a class, the instructor may stipulate a blogging platform for you to use, such as the blogging tool on Blackboard or Connect Composition. You may have the option of using a free Web tool. Setting up your blog can be done in less than fifteen minutes on free platforms like Blogger.

Thinking as a Writer: Voice and Style

Consider the differences between writing papers and a blog post. First, blog posts are personal, expressive: They are your own thoughts, ideas, opinions and experiences. Blog posts are informal. Papers are like you in your dress clothes; blog posts are like you in your jeans and a t-shirt. Finally, blog posts should be short enough to encourage readers to read.

One of the best things about blogging is its ability to allow you to experiment with voice and style. Different topics will bring out different sides of your personality: You can be serious, satirical, comic, and so on. No matter what tone you take, write posts that sound like you talking. When you read them, you should be able to hear your voice.

Thinking as a Writer: Development and Organization

Coming up with a good idea for a post and developing it takes time. So does reading your classmates' blogs, finding posts that you want to respond to, and writing well-developed and thoughtful comments. Blog posts and comments can be as short as a long paragraph or as long as a short essay. Having *a concise post with a clear point* is especially important when your readers are surfing and not required to read what you have written.

See Chapter 24, Designing Documents and Using Graphics, for more on design features.

Thinking as a Writer: Visual Appeal

Most commercial blogging platforms like Blogger give you a wide array of templates to choose from when creating your blog. Within the templates, you can choose colors for background and type, font style and size, and other design features.

When writing your posts, consider readers' eyes as well. Reading on screen is different from reading on paper. Readers are less patient with long blocks of text on screen, so it is good to break up your blog posts into short paragraphs and even put some space between the paragraphs.

What Are the Steps in Writing a Blog Post?

Posts should be more than offhand, top-of-your-head writing, sent without a second look. Sketch them out in Word and look them over before pasting them into your blog for publication.

1. **Draft your post.** You should rough out a draft post in a word processing program, not on the site itself. If you write on the site and accidentally close the window, you could lose everything. Another reason to draft before posting is that you may not be sure about your point until you start writing. Drafting is for thinking. Revising is for writing. Drafts can be long and messy; they are ways of discovering what you have to say.

2. **Revise your post.** Look over your post with these questions in mind:
   - **Does my opening generate reader interest?** How might I improve it?
   - **What and where is my main point?** Am I making too many points?
   - **Is the post as long as a paper?** If it is more than 500–750 words, you probably need to narrow the focus. Ask yourself: What is the heart of my post, and what could I delete without hurting the point and the support for it?

See Chapter 16, Finding Sources, pages 421–22, for help with searching for information on the Internet.

   - **Is the post as short as a paragraph?** That may be fine, given your point and purpose, but most good posts develop an idea. Ask yourself: Am I saying anything my readers would not already know? Do I need to get some facts, examples, specifics to flesh this out?
   - **Does the post have a shape?** Where does the beginning end? Where does the end begin? Have I broken the middle into blocks of text?

See Chapter 14, Editing Fundamentals, pages 435–36, for help with editing for wordiness.

3. **Edit your post.** Blog posts should be concise; your blog is a good place to practice the art of editing. Look for wordy repetitions, long, indirect sentences that do not sound like your speaking voice. Look for passive voice and other vague uses of the verb "to be."

4. **Proofread your post.** Readers find carelessly written posts with many errors annoying and thus easily discount them. Proofread your posts to eliminate spelling, grammar, and punctuation errors.

BEST PRACTICES | Developing Good Blogging Habits

- Think of yourself as a writer who has to produce a column once or twice a week. As you go about your daily activities, pay attention to things that you could write about: something that happened in class, a conversation you overheard, a person whose appearance caught your attention. Keep a notebook or a computer file for jotting down ideas for future blog posts.

- Do not feel that you have to read, write, and post all in the same sitting. Try designating half-hour slots for reading classmates' blogs and for roughing out ideas for your own posts.

- Think of blogging as mental exercise, a place for regular practice with written expression. The more you do it, the easier it becomes. ■

What Are Some Special Considerations for Writing a Blog?

Bloggers need to be aware of some customs that characterize good and ethical writing on blogs.

1. **Using Sources in Your Posts**
   Some form of research usually goes into writing a good post for your blog. On a campus issue, for instance, you may need to go to the school paper to get details. Even popular culture topics such as music or movies may require fact checks. In blogging, research serves real purposes and meets genuine reader needs.

   Bloggers need to be just as careful not to plagiarize when they blog as they are when writing a paper. Blog posts do not have formal citations, but it is important to give credit when you use someone else's words and ideas. Not to do so is unethical and can even be illegal if you violate copyrights. Give credit by naming the source as you lead into the quoted or paraphrased part. Ideally, you "cite" your source if it is on the Internet by putting in a hyperlink that takes readers directly to the webpage. Your blogging platform has a tool for making hyperlinks; this is just a matter of copying the URL of your source, selecting the words in your post that refer to the source, opening the tool, and pasting in the URL.

   For more on the ethics of writing, see Chapter 19, Using Sources Responsibly, pages 456-57.

2. **Writing Comments on Someone Else's Blog**
   A goal of blogging is interaction between readers and writers. Communities form, with the members giving each other support, information, and helpful criticism of ideas. Bloggers want comments and often check the comment indicator at the bottom of their posts to see if someone has commented on their blog. Even a brief comment lets the writer know he or she

reached a reader. However, when you want to contribute to the discussion on a blog, you have to put more thought and effort into your comments. A good comment adds value to a post by:

- Adding new information on the topic
- Correcting any misinformation in the original post
- Providing a new perspective on the topic after clearly showing that you understand the perspective of the post
- Disagreeing and making an argument for your position

A good comment shows that the commenter has read and paid close attention to the original post. Even when expressing disagreement, a good comment is polite.

3. **Projecting Good Character**
   The Internet is a public space that encourages freedom of expression, in some cases, with the option of anonymity. As in any public space—a classroom, a park, a neighborhood—the quality of the community depends on the level of civility the members show towards one another. While satire and humor can engage readers and liven up a discussion, rudeness and insensitivity are never appropriate when blogging.

PART II

Practicing Writing

CHAPTER 4

Interpreting Experiences

WE LEARNED TO LOVE STORIES AS CHILDREN, AND WE CONTINUE TO LOVE them as we grow. This chapter is about one kind of story, the **personal narrative,** *an account of something that has happened to us*. It answers two key questions: What happened? Why does it matter? Answering the first question draws readers into your story simply because people are interested in what happens to other people. Answering the second makes what happened into an experience, something meaningful, worth remembering.

Experiences are not always major events. *The New York Times* has a weekly feature in which readers share their experiences of city life. These "Metropolitan Diary" entries are effective because they have **angles,** *distinctive points of view or interpretations that make you think.* Here is an example.

MICRO-EXAMPLE **Interpreting Experience**

Metropolitan Diary

Erik Torkells

Dear Diary:

I was looking at my phone as I moved into the crosswalk at Fifth Avenue and 53rd Street, and a man bumped into me, dropping his eyeglasses. He said something, but I vaguely remembered hearing about a scam like this, so I walked on.   1

"Hey, man," he said, following me across Fifth Avenue. "You broke my glasses!"   2

I gave him my most stone-faced look. I was annoyed at having to deal with an uncomfortable scene, but I was even more annoyed because he evidently thought he looked like a rube.[1]   3

I'm sorry," I said, "but I'm familiar with this scam."   4

As he turned away, he gave me a big smile and said cheerily, "Have a nice day!"   5

_____
[1] A naïve or inexperienced person.

Gives setting for story.

Use of dialogue provides lifelike interest.

Implies the significance of the story: the sharing of a sophisticated urban awareness.

Leaves the reader with an implied contrast between how this potential conflict is handled and hostile interaction that might have resulted.

What Is Interpreting Experience?

An **experience** is something that stands out in memory, *a departure from the routine*. When we have a memorable experience, we share it with others and talk about how we might understand it. As writers we create **narratives,** *stories based on memorable experiences*. We offer these stories to readers for enjoyment and contemplation, and we interpret them to explore what they mean.

CONCEPT CLOSE-UP | Angle in Personal Narrative

All good writing depends on the writer having an angle on his or her topic. In personal narratives, the angle shows that the writer has thought about the experience and developed a point of view on it. The angle does the following:

- Helps the writer decide what details are relevant to include in the story
- Helps the reader see how the story is relevant to people other than the writer

Consider how the details of the story of the scam artist would change if the writer had taken a different angle, such as one of the following: the city as a place where people of different economic classes rub shoulders; city life as stressful; unemployment as a social problem that touches everyone. ■

ACTIVITY 4.1 *Writer's Notebook*

Interpreting Experience

Has a "little" experience struck you as surprising, funny, or thought provoking? It could be a conversational exchange or some other interaction between people; an observation about animal behavior; something you noticed on the freeway, at the mall, in a restaurant. Describe the experience for your readers, making it as vivid as you can. How would you describe your angle on the experience? ■

Why Write to Interpret Experience?

Narratives are among the most common kinds of writing we encounter. People write and read them because human beings enjoy sharing experiences and exploring what they mean. Personal narratives also develop thinking and writing skills applicable to all kinds of writing, among them the following:

■ Sharing the meaning of an experience enables you to gain and hold reader attention. The key question is, **"How can you connect your experience with the lives, interests, and concerns of other people?"**

■ In narrative genres such as memoirs, travel writing, and blogs, sharing experience provides the opportunity to assert your attitudes, ideas, and opin-

The world is full of amusing, interesting things to write about if you take a look around you. What funny or interesting experiences have you had that might make for a great personal narrative?

ions. In other genres, such as political speeches or newspaper editorials, narratives can provide evidence and make emotional appeals.

■ Interpreting experiences allows you to develop your **voice,** *how you sound to your readers.* Depending upon the purpose of your story, you may sound, for example, serious and sincere or warm and funny.

■ Sharing stories about specific events helps you move beyond **stock responses—***the standard things people say about something that happens.* We all know the typical reaction to a friend's betrayal of trust, but we can get beyond this stock response by posing questions such as the following: Was this person really a friend in whom I should have placed my trust? What role did I play in setting myself up to be betrayed? Critical thinking, which involves asking such questions, matters in all significant writing.

How Do Writers Interpret Experiences?

Narratives share five characteristics with fiction. That is, they work as all stories work by pulling together voice, plot, conflict, concrete and relevant details, and shared insight (see Figure 4.1).

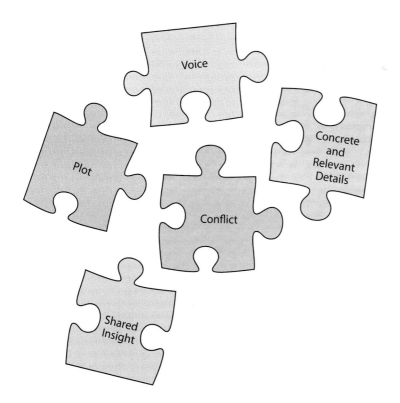

FIGURE **4.1**

The Five Features of Storytelling

There are five important elements to successful storytelling: voice, plot, conflict, concrete and relevant details, and shared insight.

Voice

Stories are told by a **narrator,** *the person telling the story.* You are the "I" who is writing about something that happened to you, and therefore your presence contributes to the story's meaning, mainly as point of view. For example, if you are writing about an event that occurred when you were younger and more limited in your understanding, you might tell the story from your more mature viewpoint but include scenes that show the viewpoint of your younger self.

Plot and Conflict

Every story has a **plot,** another word for plan or *storyline.* Most plots begin by setting the scene and providing background information. Then, as the action of the story builds, the plot develops. The story's action depends on **conflict,** a *problem or source of tension,* which comes from lack of harmony in desires, ideas, or behavior. It can exist within a person, between people, or between a person and the circumstances. In most plots, there is a high point where the action or tension reaches a climax. In an autobiographical narrative, the plot usually ends by showing the narrator's personal growth or increased understanding.

Concrete and Relevant Details

Stories contain sensory details: sights, sounds (including dialogue and people's voices), scents, and the way things feel to the touch or on the skin. Details make experiences vivid. In choosing what to include or leave out, favor details that contribute to bringing out the point of the story.

Shared Insight

Whether stated or implied by the action, personal narratives reveal the significance of an experience. This significance amounts to *shared insight* because readers come to see how your story relates to their lives and how it might help them interpret similar experiences.

A Dark, Skinny Stranger in Cleveland Park

STEPHEN L. CARTER

The following reading is an excerpt from Stephen L. Carter's Civility: Manners, Morals, and the Etiquette of Democracy, *which deals with an African American family moving into a white, upper-class neighborhood in Washington, DC, in 1966. Well-known as a writer of both fiction and nonfiction, Carter is the William Nelson Cromwell Professor of Law at Yale Law School. In the following reading, note especially how well he depicts the limited understanding he had as a boy of the society around him and what a great difference one kind, open-hearted person can make in overcoming fear and alienation.*

> Gives background of family's move to Washington, DC.

In the summer of 1966, my parents moved with their five children to a large house near the corner of 35th and Macomb Streets in Cleveland Park, a neighborhood of Northwest Washington, D.C., and, in those days, a lily-white enclave. My father, trained as a lawyer, was working for the federal government, and this was an area of the city where many lawyers and government officials lived. There were senators, there were lobbyists, there were 1

> Depicts first impression of unwelcoming neighborhood and the children's desire for their old, familiar environment.

undersecretaries of this and that. My first impression was of block upon block of grim, forbidding old homes, each of which seemed to feature a massive dog and spoiled children in the uniforms of various private schools. My brother and two sisters and I sat on the front steps, missing our playmates, as the movers carried in our furniture. Cars passed what was now our house, slowing for a look as did people on foot. We waited for somebody to say hello, to welcome us. Nobody did.

> Explains how African Americans living in the North were conditioned to view the Southern world across the river, within the limits of a child's understanding.

We children had no previous experience of white neighborhoods. But we had heard unpleasant rumors. The gang of boys I used to hang out with in Southwest Washington traded tall tales of places where white people did evil things to us, mostly in the South, where none of us had ever lived, nor wanted to. Now and then, perhaps on a Saturday afternoon, we would take a walk to see the evil empire. We would walk up Fourth Street, beneath the highway and the railroad tracks that separated our neighborhood from the federal areas of the city, past the red-brick police station, a half-mile or so up to the Mall. Then, nudging each other with nervous excitement, we would turn west and continue our march. We wanted to see. We would pass with barely a glance the museums that on any other day would keep us occupied for hours. We would circle around the Washington Monument, whose pointed top with twin windows on each side, some of the older boys said, reminded them of a Ku Klux Klan hood, an image that scared me a little, although at eleven years old, raised in the North by protective parents, I was not too sure what the Ku Klux Klan was. We would walk along the Reflecting Pool and continue past the Lincoln Memorial, which, then as now, seemed under constant repair. At last we would reach the shores of the Potomac River which, in those days, exuded the fetid odors of sewage and industrial waste. And we would stand on the bank; a tiny band of dark, skinny children, still growing into full awareness of our race; we would stand there and gaze across the river at the shores of the forbidden land. Mostly what we saw was trees. Sometimes we could pick out a house, perhaps a mansion, including one named for Robert E. Lee. We knew nothing of General Lee 2

> Refers to familiar landmarks in our nation's capitol, singling out both that of Washington, a Virginia slaveholder, and of Lincoln, the Great Emancipator. Note that the Lincoln Memorial "seemed under constant repair," as if the task of overcoming our history of racial trouble is never complete.

Note combination of truth, myth, bravado, and nervous laughter among the boys as they contemplate Virginia.

except that he had something to do with slavery. On the wrong side. That was enough. We looked, but from our safe distance. There were bridges, but we never crossed them. We had somehow picked up the idea that to go there for more than a short time meant death. Or maybe worse. Emboldened by the river running before us like a moat, we stood our ground and kept looking. A few of the boys claimed to have visited the evil empire, but the rest of us laughed uneasily to show our doubts. We stood, we gazed, we told bad jokes. We poked each other and pointed.

"That's Virginia," we would say, shuddering.   3

Transitional paragraph that acknowledges changes since 1966; sets up conclusion featuring the words and actions of Sara Kestenbaum.

Times have changed. Virginia has changed. I have changed. Today I love the state, its   4
beauty, its people, even its complicated sense of history. But in 1966, sitting on the front step of our grand new house in our grand new lonely white neighborhood of Washington, I felt as if we had moved to the fearsome Virginia of the sixties, which, in my child's mind, captured all the horror of what I knew of how white people treated black people. I watched the strange new people passing us and wordlessly watching back, and I knew we were not welcome here. I knew we would not be liked here. I knew we would have no friends here. I knew we should not have moved here. I knew . . .

And all at once, a white woman arriving home from work at the house across the street   5
from ours turned and smiled with obvious delight and waved and called out, "Welcome!" in a booming, confident voice I would come to love. She bustled into her house, only to emerge, minutes later, with a huge tray of cream cheese and jelly sandwiches, which she carried to our porch and offered around with her ready smile, simultaneously feeding and greeting the children of a family she had never met—and a black family at that—with nothing to gain for herself except perhaps the knowledge that she had done the right thing. We were strangers, black strangers, and she went out of her way to make us feel welcome. This woman's name was Sara Kestenbaum, and she died much too soon, but she remains, in my experience, one of the great exemplars of all that is best about civility.

Clarifies the point of the story: One person's civil behavior does not cancel out how other people behaved, but it did then and does now make a significant difference.

Questions for Discussion

1. Where in the story does the author introduce conflict for the first time? What details in the description of the new neighborhood best reveal the pervasive racial tensions of 1966? Why does Carter devote a lengthy paragraph to his youthful experiences on the banks of the Potomac? Why does the story end with the actions of Sara Kestenbaum?

2. Find examples of *concrete sensory details,* appeals to sight, sound, smell, and so on. How is each example relevant to the interpretation of the experience?

3. Concentrate on the narrator's *voice.* What attitude toward his younger self does Carter imply? How does he show the anxieties he felt as a boy without making the story sentimental?

What Is the Rhetorical Situation?

1. What is Carter's *purpose* in writing this essay? What is his *angle* on the topic? How would you describe his *voice*?
2. Who is Carter's intended *audience*? Many of his readers have no experience with racial prejudice as it existed when he was growing up or now. How did the writer help such people understand and connect with his story?
3. Personal narratives offer shared insight into life. What did you learn about the past and present from Carter's narrative? ■

READING **4.2**

Driving Away

KATHERINE KRUEGER-LAND

The following narrative, written by a student in a first-year composition course at Southern Methodist University, tells a common story—the struggle with substance abuse—in a compelling way. Note especially how well the author handles dialogue.

The first car I ever owned was a fifteen-year-old, lipstick-red, '91 Ford Thunderbird. 1991: The car was too recent to be cool, but too old to be reliable. Still, I loved it. My parents bought it for me when I got out of rehab and moved down to La Grange, Texas, to live with my Aunt Priscilla and Uncle Kelley.

I was lucky that they would take me; I had nowhere else to go. I was considered a serious gamble: no one wanted a relapsed Katherine on their hands. Yet they took me in, helped me get a job waiting tables, and treated me like an adult. I consider them my second family.

Apart from having had relatively few options, there was one other enticing reason to choose Texas: Nick Nolan. Although I intended to stay sober and made him swear never to tempt me, it still seemed a good idea to have an old friend around just in case I changed my mind.

1

2

3

Nick and I had been running buddies since high school. During our freshman year in college, I spent fall and spring breaks down at A&M partying with him. We had a platonic relationship built entirely around getting as stupidly high as possible and sustaining it until we dropped. 4

Nick Nolan was fun: quick to laugh, quick to anger, cruel and uproarious, dishonest, manipulative and narcissistic, and at times disarmingly self-effacing. He was a violent drunk, an adventurous stoner, and a suicidal, self-harming depressive with the impulsivity of a toddler. In short: perfect. 5

Perfect, that is, if you want to grab an 8-ball and a shotgun and trespass on an airfield to shoot off rounds at your own pants hanging in a tree, drive to the coast but miss the sunrise just to pass out stoned watching cartoons in a motel room, and wake up in time to crash your Houston dealer's family dinner—"watch out for the dogs and don't wake the baby"— where your nose bleeds all over the new couch. 6

But that was before I got sober. 7

I had been in La Grange for two months when I finally heard from Nick. I was working at the Marburger Antique Fair helping out a family friend, Becky Barnsdall, at her stall in Tent D. During my lunch hour I would wander around the nearby fairgrounds and comb through the junk. I was admiring a display of decapitated dolls' heads when he called me. 8

"Hey Nick what's up?" 9

"Dude, I had a freakin' heart attack yesterday!" *A heart attack?* 10

"Wait, what?" 11

"I know, right?" 12

"Are you ok?" 13

"Tommy just picked me up from the hospital with a fifth." 14

"Should you be drinking?" I whispered, self-conscious in front of the dolls. 15

"Probably not," he said. 16

With my cell phone still pinned to my ear, I started tracking across the hay-strewn grounds toward my car, past armless mannequins, old Coca-Cola bottles, wooden toy-wagons, and buckets full of colorful glass beads. On the other end of the line Nick told me his story: the chest pains, the gasping, the ambulance, the hospital stay. 17

"So now that I'm better you have to come celebrate." 18

"I'm working." 19

"Quit." 20

"I need the money. Besides, you're drinking; it won't be any fun for me." 21

"Then you'll just have to drink with us." 22

"You know I can't do that, Nick." 23

He sighed, "I know, I know," and paused. "Krueger, man, I'm not going to make you do anything you don't want to do." 24

"I know," I answered. And I believed it. 25

* * *

I was at his house on the Tuesday afternoon three months later when Nick was again rushed to the hospital. We were sitting on the couch inside watching South Park with the 26 dog, JD. Named for James Dean, he was half Dalmatian, half pit bull, and the sweetest dog you ever met. He liked to sit on top of the sofa back like a giant cat and lean his sweet warm face on your shoulder.

Nick had gone into the other room to get his guitar; he generally could not watch TV without doing something else at the same time. Several minutes elapsed before I heard the knocking. I called but he did not answer. All I heard were two more muffled knocks. 27

I got up from the sofa and peered around the doorframe into the bedroom and there he was, lying on his back, his face turning red, his right hand clutching his left side. As he struggled to breathe he looked up at me, his eyes wide and pleading. The sight momentarily shocked me: I'd never known him to be afraid of anything. I bent over him to see if he was hurt, but I already knew what was happening. I reached for my phone. 28

"911, what is your emergency?" 29

"I think my friend is having a heart attack." 30

"Is he breathing?" 31

"Yes." 32

"Is he awake?" 33

"Yes." 34

"Is he able to tell you what's wrong?" 35

"No, he's gasping, he can't talk." 36

"What is your location, ma'am?" I didn't know the address. 37

"I'm on McCommas, past Winding, uhh, hold on—" 38

"Are you in a house?" 39

"Yes. Hold on—" I rifled through the papers on his desk, but couldn't find any letters addressed to him. 40

"And what is the address of the house, ma'am?" 41

"It's his house, I don't know the address, just hold on—" I gave Nick an exasperated look and dashed out of the room, climbing over the dog to keep him from getting out the front door, and ran to the mailbox. "2389 Alhambra. That's 2-3-8-9 A-l-h-a-m-b-r-a." 42

In a rush of nylon jackets and plastic gloves, the paramedics came and with cool efficiency swept him off the floor, onto a gurney, into the ambulance, and off to the hospital. I followed them, and found Nick in a bed divided by curtains from three other patients in a small holding area. He sat up when he saw me. 43

"The doctor said I need to quit doing drugs," he smiled weakly. 44

"How do you feel?" He looked small to me. He's tall and strong, but lying down and wearing a hospital gown, he looked frail. 45

"Bad." 46

"You look like it," I said. He chuckled, and then coughed. 47

"They told me I'd die if I don't quit," Nick said. 48

"So will you?" 49

"Yeah, maybe." 50

I left Nick in the hospital hooked up to an IV watching television and drove home. Being in the hospital had made me claustrophobic. After all, I'd only just checked myself out of a 51 hospital a few months before. Perversely, I felt a little nostalgic for the insanity of living life in self-destruct mode. But I didn't want to go back. I didn't want to wear shoes without laces and have my blood pressure taken at 5:00 am everyday and sit in a group talking about feeling worthless. *Still,* I thought, *it wasn't all bad.*

* * *

The last time I saw Nick, I was just stopping by on my way up from La Grange to Dallas, where I was soon to move. I was sitting out on his back porch on the sofa we had once lit on fire (quite by accident) listening to him tell stories, which he's good at, and make plans, which he's even better at, although he never follows through on anything. After a few minutes he paused, dug around in the dirty seat cushions for a lighter, and lit a cigarette for himself, and one for me. He smoked Camel Turkish Golds, the ones with the pretty blue borders. I smoked Pall Malls, in a soft-pack, back then.   52

"I need to quit smoking," he said. He meant pot, I was sure.   53

"Yeah, maybe."   54

"I need to quit with the coke, too."   55

"You look thin," I told him.   56

"I'm down to 130 now. I was 175 a couple months ago."   57

Jeez, I thought. *At 6'3", 130 pounds isn't much.*   58

"You look really thin," I repeated. And he looked tired, too. And not in a didn't-sleep-last-night way, but in a haven't-really-slept-in-weeks way.   59

"I don't eat much."   60

"That's the coke."   61

"And the pot."   62

"You look tired."   63

"I know. I haven't been sleeping."   64

"Maybe you should quit."   65

"Yeah, maybe."   66

I was surprised to see him so reflective. Maybe he really would quit, maybe he was finally ready. I got up to leave, sliding open the glass back door—JD bouncing cheerfully into the house behind me. I grabbed my purse, slipped on my shoes, and was just trying to open the front door without letting the dog out when I looked up and saw Nick standing by the back door.   67

"Hey, wait, if I'm going to quit, then you need to smoke with me one last time."   68

"I can't, Nick, you know that."   69

"Sure you can. I'll even let you roll it, old school."   70

"No, Nick." *But I could.*   71

"Come on."   72

"No, Nick." *But I want to.*   73

"Just one more time, and then we'll both quit together."   74

"I already quit. I quit a year ago."   75

"Exactly, it'll be no big deal."   76

"It *is* a big deal," I said, angrily. He had promised not to pressure me.   77

"No, it's not." *You pathetic fool,* I thought. *You have no idea what I went through. You have no idea how hard it was to leave everything behind.*   78

"You just don't get it, Nick. You can't stick with anything, and you don't understand how anyone else can either. That's why you'll never get sober. That's why the stuff is going to kill you."   79

And with that, I climbed over the dog and squeezed out the front door. I was shaking with anger and fear as I paced down the driveway, and started to climb into my old red T-Bird. I was tempted to turn back, to apologize and have one more good time with my old running buddy, but I was already in motion, the decision already made. *No, I won't do it. I want to, but I won't.* I had passed the test.   80

I glanced back and saw him standing there, one hand holding open the front door, the other firmly grasping JD's collar as he wriggled wildly, desperate to run after the passing cars.   81

We looked at each other, and it seemed to me he was a lot farther away. He was miles away, years away. Already he was part of another time, another life, one I could not go back to. There was a gulf between us and a long narrow bridge: I had driven across, and he had not, and that's all there was to it.   82

"Have a good drive," he called.   83

"Thanks."   84

"Come back soon."   85

"I will," I lied, and drove away.   86

Questions for Discussion

1. Note especially in paragraphs 8, 17, and 26 the use of effective descriptive detail. How do the details contribute to the themes of the story?
2. Conflict is essential to a good narrative. What are the sources of conflict in "Driving Away"? How does the author develop them?
3. Review two instances of conversation in the story. What are the exchanges like? How and why is the writer's use of dialogue effective?

■■ *Thinking as a Writer*

What Is the Rhetorical Situation?

1. What is Krueger-Land's *purpose* in writing this essay? What is her *angle* on the topic? How would you describe her voice?
2. Who is the writer's intended *audience*? If you have never struggled with addiction yourself, how did the writer help you to understand and sympathize with people who do struggle with it ?
3. The story gives us insight into friends, people we love and need but whose impact on us can be negative as well as positive. How would you describe this insight? How does the insight apply to your friendships? ■

The Assignment

Write a narrative sharing a personal experience and offering insight into its meaning. The goal is to tell an interesting story that leaves your readers with insight they can relate to their own lives.

How Do I Interpret Experience?
Questioning the Rhetorical Situation

Begin by picturing a **rhetorical situation** for your writing project, a real-world context for communicating. You should consider the *key variables in any act of communication:*

- A writer with something to say
- A reader the writer wishes to reach
- A kind of text appropriate to the writing task

These three variables will affect many decisions in the composing process.

Writer: What Is My Purpose, and What Impression Should Readers Have of Me?

Autobiographical narratives share an interesting and meaningful experience with an appropriate readership. Because the experience comes from your life, your purpose is self-expression. You are revealing a part of yourself. Because you are sharing a part of yourself with others, you want them to enjoy reading the story and gain from it insight that they will remember.

Your purpose implies your role as a writer for this assignment. Both Carter and Krueger-Land assume the role of the experienced person, someone who is "in the know" from having experienced being a minority in a white neighborhood or being a recovered addict. Your role in writing your story will be much like theirs: No one else knows your life better than you do; no one else is in a better position to say what it means.

Being experienced does not mean that you know everything or have all the answers. You can freely admit to gaps in your knowledge, even to being puzzled about your own motives or the motives of someone else in your story. Just be honest about what happened to you and how well you understand it.

Audience: Who Is My Reader?

Because almost anyone can read and enjoy an interesting story, it is tempting to think of your readers as everyone. However, stories are always told *to someone*, and actual readerships are never everyone. The key question is: Who might gain most from reading about your experience? They should be your readership.

Why is it important to have a definite readership in mind? First, you have to assume a certain level of existing knowledge. Carter, for example, does not explain what a "lily-white enclave" is or what Virginia's "complicated sense of history" means. He has to assume a certain amount of knowledge about Washington, DC, its nearness to the North/South divide, and the prominent role Virginia played in the Civil War, because otherwise he would have to explain too much; likewise, you will not want to clutter your narrative with too much explanation. Second, the readership you choose helps you to decide what to include and what to emphasize in your story. Krueger-Land was writing primarily for people who may not fully understand how hard it is to escape addiction, which is why she emphasized her entanglement with a person from her earlier, drug-dominated life.

Text: What Would Be an Appropriate Topic?

Stories that hold the reader's interest involve conflict or tension. Consider experiences that did one or more of the following:

- Resulted in intellectual or moral growth, an increase in maturity.
- Challenged your beliefs, attitudes, or values.
- Allowed you to see your behavior from someone else's perspective.
- Disappointed or surprised you about your own character or the character of someone you thought you knew.
- Led you to see some past event in a new context or category that transformed its meaning.
- Called conventional wisdom about right and wrong into question.
- Created a dilemma, a choice between two paths of action, neither of which is entirely satisfactory.

Remember that the significance of an event is *not in the event itself but in what you make of it,* the angle or point of view you bring to it or discover in thinking or writing about it. Nevertheless, finding the right topic for you does matter. If you are having trouble locating yours, consider the following possibilities.

- **Distinctive People, Places, and Objects**   Carter focused on just one episode in his experience of moving into a new neighborhood; Krueger-Land focused on one part of her experience with drugs, the temptation to go back to them. Stories about places include journeys to wilderness or foreign places and revisiting places from our past.

- **A Troubling Memory**   Perhaps you liked a person that others did not like, perhaps even someone you should not have liked. Or you did something unethical, but you would do it again. Or you visited a place meant to stimulate a certain reaction, but you actually responded "inappropriately."

- **Class Readings**   The readings in this chapter may remind you of an experience you should write about. Perhaps a concept you encountered in one of your courses gives you a new angle for understanding a past event.

- **Your Own or Other People's Blogs** Look over your blog for promising topics, such as reunions with friends from high school, something that happened at work or at home with your family, and decisions you have made since starting college.

- **Work or Community Experience** Consider times of conflict or tension where you work or the insights you have gained from internships, volunteer work, church activities, attending social events, and the like.

How Do I Interpret Experience?
Engaging the Writing Process

Readings 4.1 and 4.2 in this chapter and the student example at the end of this chapter make all or some of the following basic moves:

- Establish the time and place of your experience.

- Provide vivid details in descriptions, selecting from everything you could describe only those details that connect with what your story means.

- Share what you said and thought, using some dialogue or conversational exchange when appropriate.

- Zoom in for "close-ups" of important moments in your experience.

- Supply transitional paragraphs to help your reader move from one part of your experience to another.

- Structure your story around a central conflict.

- Imply or state directly what your story means.

Exploring Your Topic

No two people compose in exactly the same way, and even the same person may go through the writing process in different ways with different assignments. Nevertheless, because no one can attend to everything at once, there are phases in handling any significant writing task. You begin by preparing to write, generating content and finding your angle.

The next phase is planning and drafting your paper, getting a version, however rough it may be, on paper or screen so that you have something to work with during the next two stages. The first stage is revision, where your attention should be on content, arrangement, and style. The second is editing to take care of problems at the paragraph and sentence level, such as loss of focus and coherence, awkward or unclear sentences, and errors of grammar, spelling, and punctuation.

Preparing to Write

When you have decided what story to tell, explore it by writing informally to generate ideas and material for drafting.

No one else knows your life better than you do. When writing your story, be honest and tell it from your point of view.

■■■■ ACTIVITY 4.2 *Writer's Notebook*

Asking Questions about the Elements of Your Narrative

Using lists, diagrams, and/or a series of notes to yourself, jot down your responses to the following questions:

- Characters: Besides you, what other people played a role in this experience? Of these, who were the most important? Why?

- Setting: Picture a scene from the experience. What sensory details have stuck in your memory? What do you recall seeing, tasting, hearing, smelling, or touching? Ask *why* you recall those details: Perhaps you can discover a pattern in what you remember that will lead to an insight or imply what the story means.

- Plot: What conflict or tension makes this experience interesting for you and for your readers? What was the moment of greatest tension? How was the tension resolved? If it was not fully resolved, what problems or issues remain?

- Angle: Explore possible meanings or interpretations of the experience. What was your point of view when you were living it? As you look back on it, has your interpretation of it changed? What central insight or insights can you offer? ■

▓▓▓■ ACTIVITY 4.3 *Writer's Notebook*

Discussing Your Topic Idea

Post your best ideas for your narrative on your class's discussion board. When everyone has posted, read through the posts and send replies to at least three classmates. In your reply, ask questions to stimulate thought about the event's significance, the conflict or tension that could drive a good plot, and the relevance of the experience to others. ■

Asking Questions: Framing the Plot

Choosing where to begin your story is one of the more important choices you will make. For instance, how much background do you need to provide so your readers will understand the story?

Some narratives open with background material, some with the action itself. Either way, draw your readers in with something specific, such as Krueger-Land's new living situation after rehab or Carter's description of his new neighborhood.

Once you have decided how to open the story, plot out the key scenes. Think of your essay as if it were a video with action, setting, characters, and dialogue. Often one of these elements dominates a particular scene. For example, Krueger-Land's memory of the fun she once had with Nick dominates the early scenes in her narrative.

▓▓▓■ ACTIVITY 4.4 *Writer's Notebook*

Listing Key Scenes

Depict your experience in a series of scenes. If you were making a film, which moments would you show in action, and which would a narrator summarize? In Carter's story, there are two key scenes:

- ■ The new neighborhood
- ■ The view of Virginia from the north bank of the Potomac

List two or three key scenes in your experience. How can each contribute to building the tension, and which one will you use to resolve it? ■

Borrowing a Film Technique: The Storyboard

Some writers of fiction and nonfiction borrow the storyboard technique used in filmmaking (see Figure 4.2 on page 82). Carolyn Coman—author of many acclaimed novels for young people, including *What Jamie Saw*—got the idea of storyboarding from reading comic books with her young daughter. Coman draws a blank square for each main scene in a story and, using stick figures, draws the central action of the scene. Sketching the scene is a kind of visual drafting. As with a rough draft, when you reread it, you discover surprises, clues to meaning.

As Coman says, "The size of the stick figures, the amount of white space around them, the kinds of marks you make . . . all of these have things to tell you about tone, distance, point of view."[2]

It also helps you organize around a main idea. If you write a sentence or two beneath each drawing, the storyboard will help you find connections between scenes and identify the angle or main idea of your narrative. Even a single sentence about the emotion or tension each scene conveys will help you organize and sort the material.

A storyboard made of individual diagram cards offers several advantages. You can do the following:

- Add, delete, or rearrange scenes
- Sketch visually or verbally a scene's setting and characters
- Create dialogue
- Indicate what you will be telling the reader

An alternative is to make a series of boxes on sheets of plain paper, in the style of a comic book, and draw your scenes in sequence.

Student Example: Molly Tilton's Storyboard for a Personal Narrative

Figure 4.2 on the next page shows an example of how one student used the storyboard technique to get her story started and focused. Molly Tilton wrote about an experience she had while working as a waitress in a diner. A regular customer, Frank, was waiting for his daughter to join him for breakfast; as the event unfolded, Tilton gained some insight about her own life. Sketching scenes for her story helped Tilton order the events, including the use of a flashback, and decide which moments to focus on in her narrative.

■■■■ ACTIVITY 4.5 *In Your Own Work*

Visualizing Your Story

Using storyboard sketches on index cards, work out a plan for your story. Think about how you might open the essay, how you might work in background information, and how the essay should end. ■

Drafting Your Paper

What should be most on your mind as you are writing your first draft of the narrative? Focus on your voice and on development and organization.

---

2. Coman, Carolyn. "Seeing the Whole Story: Storyboarding," *Highlights Foundation.* Highlights Foundation, n.d. Wed. 4 Aug. 2011. <http://www.highlightsfoundation.org>.

FIGURE **4.2**

An Example of a Simple Storyboard

Storyboards don't need to be elaborate to be helpful in piecing your story together. Grab a pencil and some paper and try sketching out simple "scenes" that capture critical moments of your personal story.

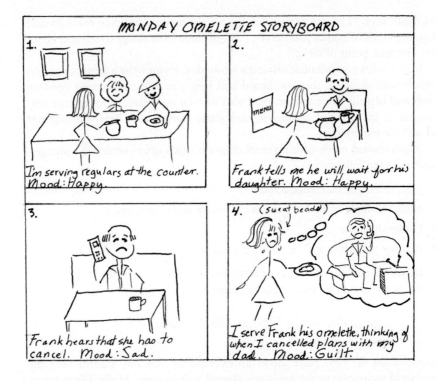

MONDAY OMELETTE STORYBOARD

1. I'm serving regulars at the counter. Mood: Happy.

2. Frank tells me he will, wait for his daughter. Mood: Happy.

3. Frank hears that she has to cancel. Mood: Sad.

4. (sweat beads) I serve Frank his omelette, thinking of when I cancelled plans with my dad. Mood: Guilt.

Thinking as a Writer: What Voice Is Appropriate in Personal Narratives?

When we say that writing has voice, we mean that readers can sense the human presence in the words. The author's personal interest and angle on the topic are evident in the writing. *Well-chosen details convey your lived experience best* and connect with readers more effectively than general statements.

Consider the scene in "A Dark, Skinny Stranger in Cleveland Park" in which Carter describes his small group of young friends looking across the Potomac at "the evil empire."

> *And we would stand on the bank; a tiny band of dark, skinny children, still grow-ing into full awareness of our race; we would stand there and gaze across the river at the shores of the forbidden land. Mostly what we saw was trees. Sometimes we could pick out a house, perhaps a mansion, including one named for Robert E. Lee. We knew nothing of General Lee except that he had something to do with slavery. On the wrong side. That was enough. We looked, but from our safe distance. There were bridges, but we never crossed them.*

Carter expresses well the combination of fear and fascination he and his friends had for a place none of them knew firsthand, only by "unpleasant rumors" and a few half-understood facts, like who Robert E. Lee was and the existence of the Ku Klux Klan.

He doesn't say "we were scared and intrigued"; rather he allows his descrip-tive details to imply what he was feeling.

▨▧▨ ACTIVITY 4.6 *Thinking as a Writer*

Developing and Organizing Your Personal Narrative

You have many options in writing your story. It can start at the beginning, at the end, or in the middle. You can omit events that do not contribute to your point and zoom in on details that do. You can use flashbacks and flash-forwards.

Begin by writing a central episode or scene. Structure the other scenes around it. Then concentrate on background, transitions, and opening and concluding strategies. ■

▨▧▨ ACTIVITY 4.7 *Writer's Notebook*

Composing Your Scenes

Concentrate on details of setting, character, and action. Consider posting your scenes on a blog or discussion board or sharing them with other students in some other way to receive feedback. ■

Revising Your Draft

In revising, concentrate especially on the following:

- **Interpretation** Consider what writing about the experience has revealed to you. Perhaps the meaning of it has changed and therefore needs reformulating.

- **Focus** Look for opportunities to add relevant details that come to mind as you revise.

- **Shape** Craft your story into a well-paced narrative. Get to the action as quickly as possible. Keep the story moving. Make statements of your thoughts and emotions short and simple.

Write a brief assessment of your draft. Exchange draft and assessment with at least one other student and use the revision questions in the Art of Questioning box to help each other decide what needs to improve.

ART OF QUESTIONING │ Revision Checklist for Interpreting Experiences

1. Make a list of the best images in the draft. Do these words and phrases present concrete, sensory details of the place?

2. What do these images have in common? Do they imply a theme or central idea? If you cannot find a theme or idea emerging *through the details,* review the draft again to locate its best scene. What theme for the whole story might be developed from it?

3. What conflict does the narrator face? Do you encounter the conflict early in the story? How does it build and come to a crisis or point of maximum tension? How is it resolved?

4. What parts of the essay do not contribute to the theme or the conflict? Consider cutting them.

5. Can you make any suggestions for improving the organization? Should events be presented in a different order? Should the story open or end more quickly?

6. Are there any places in the story where the author spends too much time talking about emotions, how he or she feels? Replace with details that convey emotion without having to say what it is.

7. Either to clear up confusion or to satisfy curiosity, what might your reader like to know more about? Consider developing parts of the essay to answer questions your reader might have. ■

Student Example: Excerpts from Molly's Draft

The most common revision problem when interpreting experience is underdevelopment, not supplying enough detail for the reader to understand the story. Here is a paragraph from Molly Tilton's first draft of "The Monday Omelette," a story about fathers and daughters, the revised version of which appears on pages 86–87:

> He would ask a lot of questions per usual and tell me how much he missed me that day. I would apologize and say that I would see him tomorrow morning and that we could go to lunch, knowing that the plan would most likely fall through. Then he would drag himself upstairs to bed, without the smile on his face.

Here is the revised version:

> He would ask a lot of questions per usual and tell me how much he missed me that day. He would always assure me it was OK. I would apologize and tell him that I would try to see him the next day. That promise always sounded empty. After the divorce, I couldn't guarantee when I would see him. Alternating between my mother's and father's houses was sometimes too complicated. And then I had my friends. I was busy. I was sorry. After I hung up the phone, I would imagine him turning off the TV and dragging himself upstairs to bed. I pictured the let-down expression on his face. He had been ditched, stood up by his own daughter.

The revised paragraph is not just longer, but better. Note the improvements:

■ "After the divorce" adds important information: It explains why father and daughter have to make plans to see each other.

■ The details about her own life make standing up her father understandable, even if she is using them as an excuse.

■ Because she cannot know for sure how her father reacted when she did not show up, it is better to say "I would imagine" what his response was.

- Taken together, the details she adds give greater support to her feelings of guilt, which readers will then understand and relate to more easily.

Examine your own essay for opportunities to add detail. The key question is: **What do my readers need?** Tilton saw that they needed to know more about the father-daughter situation and why she feels guilty. She added only what she needed to include and the result was a stronger story.

Editing Your Revised Draft

An important concern in editing is cohesion, whether sentences connect smoothly. People sometimes use the word *flow* to describe cohesion. When writing has cohesion, each sentence picks up on something in the one before it, and readers' expectations about what comes next are rewarded. When writing lacks cohesion, it sounds choppy. Below are some examples to show how editing can improve cohesion. In this passage, student Molly Tilton describes the man in the diner waiting for his daughter:

Before Editing

Frank waited for another forty minutes. With a smile, he told me, "My daughter will be here soon, but I am just going to order anyway."

Then his cell phone rang. He was sitting in the beat-up gray booth, and I felt the room go dark. Something had come up. She would not be able to meet him.

I was a daughter. I had done this. I had broken similar news to my own father before.

> This point interrupts the point about the phone call.

> This sentence too abruptly shifts the topic from Frank's daughter to the narrator.

After Editing

Forty minutes later, he was still sitting alone in the beat-up gray booth, waiting. With a smile he told me, "My daughter will be here soon, but I'm just going to order anyway."

Then his cell phone rang . . . I felt the room go dark. Something had come up. She would not be able to meet him.

Suddenly, the scene felt familiar to me. I was a daughter. I had done this. I had broken similar news to my own father.

> This point now helps to set up the scene for the call.

> Adding a transitional sentence helps the reader see the connection that the writer had in mind but left unstated.

The following two passages follow a flashback scene in which the narrator recalls having "stood up" her father when she had told him she would visit him.

Before Editing

I went into the kitchen to bring out Frank's meal. I was sweating from guilt of being a daughter. When I delivered Frank his omelette, his lifted his face, fake smiled, and said "Ahh Miss Molly. Thank you so much!"

> This sentence offers a great image, but it would work better as a transition from the flashback to the present time.

After Editing

Sweating from the guilt of being a daughter, I went back into the kitchen to bring out Frank's meal. When I delivered his omelette, he lifted his face, fake-smiled, and said "Ahh, Miss Molly. Thank you so much!"

> The image now works as a transition from Tilton's thoughts about her own father to her experience with the other father in the diner. By turning the sentence into a modifier, Tilton's edit also gave the passage more sentence variety.

◼◼◼ ACTIVITY 4.8 *In Your Own Work*

Editing at the Sentence Level

Using our suggestions for editing, work through your revised draft to make sentence-level improvements. The best way to find repetitions and wordy passages is to read the paper aloud. They are easier to hear than to see. ◼

◼◼◼ ACTIVITY 4.9 *In Your Own Work*

Editing Your Revised Draft

Every writer has editing problems. Keep a checklist of your editing problems. For instance, list words that you misspelled. If you did not punctuate a sentence correctly, write down the sentence and circle or underline the correct punctuation mark. If you need examples to remember other types of problems—such as editing for flow—take one from your paper. Check your revised draft for your most common problems.

Study your instructor's marks and comments on every paper. Add new editing problems to your list as needed. *Always check your next paper for the problems you have listed.* In this way you can reduce your characteristic editing problems. ◼

REVISED STUDENT EXAMPLE

Tilton 1

Molly Tilton
Professor Channell
English 1301
May 6, 2011

The Monday Omelette

"Hi! My name is Molly and I will be taking care of you today. Coffee, anyone?" These were
the words I spoke daily when working as a waitress at Bacarri's Diner on Cape Cod this past
summer.

> Establishes the setting for the story, both time and place.

1

The weekend people were sometimes tough customers: the grumpy old man whose
orange juice was not cold enough, the woman whose bacon was too burnt, and the
screaming three-year-old girl who threw her pancakes on the ground. A mother complained
about the coffee spills from my hands shaking from nervousness. I apologized, grabbed five
napkins, and blamed it on the wobbly tables.

2

Serving breakfast on Monday morning always seemed so simple. After a weekend of impatient customers, I was delighted to wait on regulars, who were kind and respectful.

Good contrast between hectic weekends and weekday customers.

The diner was an old-fashioned, low-key place. The light blue walls were hung with Marilyn Monroe photos, and Elvis was almost always playing on the jukebox. The paint was chipped and the white tile floor, although clean, looked dingy. These details only augmented the retro feeling. The older folks said they felt like they were back in the sixties.

Details chosen to imply the generation of people who like the diner—her parents' generation.

All the regulars sat at the off-white countertop. Frank came in everyday, usually twice. He smiled like a child, but his white hair gave away his age. He would wear a collared shirt and khaki pants every morning. In the afternoons, he was more relaxed, usually wearing his beat-up jean shorts. His lunch order never varied: a hot dog and a cup of beans. I never really got to know Frank that well. He did not talk much, but called me "Miss Molly" and said I reminded him of his daughter.

Introduces key character and establishes relation in her mind between Frank and her own father.

The weekends were special for Frank. His daughter met him for breakfast, and they would sit in one of the booths, chatting about Hailey's busy life. She was in her third year of law school. Hailey had Frank's smile and his delicate face. Her long brown hair perfectly draped over her sundress. She usually ordered French toast or a grilled muffin. When Hailey was there, Frank upgraded his breakfast order to the egg-white, sausage-and-peppers omelette.

Details indicate the ties between father and daughter in appearance and shows how special seeing his daughter is to Frank.

On this Monday morning, Frank arrived around 8:30 and took a seat in one of the booths instead of his weekday perch at the counter. I poured him a cup of coffee, and he told me he was not going to order at the moment because he was waiting for his daughter to meet him for breakfast. His face was glowing when he told me. I could feel his excitement. He sat there for ten minutes and, still smiling, asked for more coffee.

Forty minutes later he was still sitting alone in the beat-up gray booth, waiting. With a smile he told me, "My daughter will be here soon but I'm just going to order anyway."

Depicts stages in Hailey's standing up of Frank: She is late and then finally calls, well after she should have called him.

Then his cell phone rang. He answered. "Hi, where are you? Oh, that's OK. I know about Mondays. No, it's OK. We'll do it another day." I felt the room go dark. Something had come up. She would not be able to meet him.

Suddenly, the scene felt familiar to me. I was a daughter. I had done this. I had broken similar news to my own father.

I pictured my dad, sitting on the brown leather couch on a Friday night watching the news—anticipating my arrival. He was drifting off to sleep. Then his phone rang.

Develops parallel between Hailey and Frank and the way she has treated her own father.

"Hi, Dad. It's me. I'm sorry, but I'm going to stay at Courtney's tonight. I'll call you in the morning, OK?"

He would ask a lot of questions per usual and tell me how much he missed me that day. He would always assure me it was OK. I would apologize and tell him that I would try to see him the next day. That promise always sounded empty. After the divorce, I couldn't guarantee when I would see him. Alternating between my mother's and father's houses was sometimes too complicated. And then I had my friends. I was busy. I was sorry. After I hung up the phone, I would imagine him turning off the TV and dragging himself upstairs to bed. I pictured the let-down expression on his face. He had been ditched, stood up by his own daughter.

Effective understated ending, with feelings covered up with forced cheerfulness.

Sweating from the guilt of being a daughter, I went back into the kitchen to bring out Frank's meal. When I delivered his omelette, he lifted his face, fake-smiled, and said "Ahh, Miss Molly. Thank you so much!"

3

4

5

6

7

8

9

10

11

12

13

14

CHAPTER 5

Creating Profiles

MOST PEOPLE FIND NOTHING MORE INTERESTING THAN OTHER PEOPLE. THAT is why we gossip, tell stories about ourselves and others at parties, watch television shows about famous people, enjoy Facebook, and read biographies. The important questions are: Who is this person? What is she doing now? Why does this person and his activities matter? The **profile** answers these questions by *depicting people that matter to us so that our readers will know about them too.*

Following is a brief example of a profile from a writer's website.

MICRO-EXAMPLE PROFILE

About Me
Tracy López[1]

I am an Anglo-American, (aka as Caucasian, gringa or white as Wonder bread), but my name is Señora López. No! De verdad! For real, it really is. Here's my story, for those who are now todos confundidos, or just curiosos. (Or maybe you're a metiche. That's okay, too.)

I was born and raised outside of Washington DC. My childhood was fairly typical, if not ideal. Maybe that was the problem.

Have you ever put on a sweater and known it's just not "you"? Maybe there's nothing *wrong* with the sweater, in fact, it could be bien chula, but for whatever reason, it just doesn't *feel* right.

Okay, that's how I feel about being Anglo. It isn't some kind of "White guilt," because I've felt this way since elementary school. And it isn't that I hate myself, because I don't. I love who I am.

It's an unexplained attraction to Latino culture (and really all cultures fascinate me.) If you believe in reincarnation, maybe I was Latina in a former life. ¿Quién sabe?

The Spanish language is what allowed me to meet Señor López, el amor de mi vida. He didn't speak English back then and my Spanish wasn't as good as it is now. Pero who needs words? There's no talking when you're busy besando anyway ¿verdad?

todos confundidos: completely confused
curiosos: curious
metiche: nosy
bien chula: very cute
quién sabe?: who knows?
el amor de mi vida: love of my life
pero: but
besando: kissing
¿verdad?: right?

---
1. López, Tracy. "About Me." *Latinaish.com* N.p., n.d. Web 27 Aug. 2011. <http://latinaish.com/about/>.

What Is a Profile?

A **profile** *describes a subject of interest to the writer, such as a person or place.* While some profiles can be purely informative—facts about a corporation or a prominent figure in business—the profile essay, which is the assignment in this chapter, is more subjective. A **profile essay** expresses the *writer's interpretation of the subject; the writer chooses what to include and omit based on the impression of the subject he or she wants readers to have.* This impression comes from the writer's *angle* or point of view, which gives the paper focus and purpose. Profiles usually do not have a thesis, but the details about the subject should add up to a memorable impression. A profile should show why the subject matters to the writer and should matter to readers as well.

CONCEPT CLOSE-UP | More about Profiles

Profiles depict a person, place, organization, event, or situation. They do the following:

- Provide *snapshots,* not a complete or even necessarily balanced view.
- Seek to create a *memorable impression.*
- *Convey information but not in a detached or objective way*: The interpretation is yours, the writer's, and therefore implies what matters to you.
- Are often *ethical and moral,* concerned with right and wrong, good and bad, the desirable and the undesirable.
- Strive for *lifelike immediacy.* ◼

Why Write Profiles?

We encounter profiles in many places: in human interest pieces written for magazines, newspapers, and television shows; online in blog posts and on websites; in speeches that pay tribute to important people. Profiles are also often part of

Mark Zuckerberg, creator of the social networking site Facebook, has been profiled countless times in recent years. Though celebrity profiles can be very satisfying for us to read, might a profile of the ordinary be more enriching and meaningful to our lives?

larger pieces of writing; for example, a profile of Abraham Lincoln may be included in a book about the Civil War.

In a world of more than 6.5 billion people who inhabit nearly all places on our planet and who come together in an almost infinite number of organizations, events, situations, and online social networks, why single out this person, or that place, organization, and so on, for attention?

In our media-saturated world, one answer is obvious: because someone or something is famous, and people therefore want to know more. It explains profiles of a person like Bill Gates, a place like the White House, an organization like Habitat for Humanity, an event like a basketball team losing a game 100 to 0, and a situation like the unending conflict between Israel and Palestine.

However, some of the best profiles are about the little known, even the seemingly insignificant. How do we explain these? Such profiles reveal a motive more profound than satisfying media-generated curiosity. They are protests against obscurity, a struggle for attention and memory. "This person," they say or imply, "no matter how unknown otherwise, matters." "This place, organization, event, or situation you have never heard of is more important than you think." Such profiles enlarge reader awareness and reveal the value of someone or something that may never make the evening news or even turn up on a Google search.

ART OF QUESTIONING │ **What Matters?**

Profiles involve ethics; that is, they always imply questions such as the following:

- What counts most in life?
- How should I treat other people?
- What's the right thing to do?

■ How can I maintain integrity amid all the pressures to do what others want me to do or what the immediate situation seems to require?

Writers select subjects for profiles based on their values; how they depict their subjects implies what matters to them. Consequently, the most important question when you read or write a profile is this: **Why does this matter?** Put another way: **Why do you care?** ■

The questions, "Why does this matter? Why do I care?" are important in writing profiles. Hold them in mind as you read the profiles by Carl T. Rowan, Luis Alberto Urrea, and Molly Tilton in this chapter. **What do they value? Do you value the same things? Why or why not?** Keep them in mind also as you move into the assignment. The questions have everything to do with the subject you select and how you treat it. **Why do you care about your subject? How can you get your readers to care about it too?**

How Do Writers Compose Profiles?

Profiles strive for lifelike immediacy, ways to connect readers intimately to the subject. Some of the strategies writers use to compose successful profiles include:

■ Vivid description.

■ Interesting details from available background information.

■ Quoting what people say and what others say about them.

■ Use of dialogue to report conversational exchanges.

■ Use of photographs and other visual means of transmitting information, such as maps and drawings.

In the readings that follow you will see how all of these tools work in detail.

Unforgettable Miss Bessie

CARL T. ROWAN

Carl T. Rowan (1925–2000) was a syndicated columnist and deputy secretary of state during President John F. Kennedy's administration (1961–1963). Among his books are Just Between Us Blacks (1974) and Breaking Barriers: A Memoir (1991).

As you read the profile of Miss Bessie, one of his teachers in high school, bear in mind the time period when Rowan was in high school, the late 1930s and early 1940s, well before the civil rights movement and the beginning of integration in the 1960s. What has changed since then? The present is better in many ways, but how much of what happened eighty years ago made the present possible, and what have we lost from the past that we could use now?

> *Establishes central theme: small in stature, big in impact.*

She was only about five feet tall and probably never weighed more than 110 pounds, but Miss Bessie was a towering presence in the classroom. She was the only woman tough enough to make me read *Beowulf*[1] and think for a few foolish days that I liked it. From 1938 to 1942, when I attended Bernard High school in McMinnville, Tennessee, she taught me English, history, civics—and a lot more than I realized. 1

I shall never forget the day she scolded me into reading *Beowulf*. 2

> *Good use of dialogue—creates lifelike sense of the person profiled.*

"But Miss Bessie," I complained, "I ain't much interested in it." 3

Her large brown eyes became daggerish slits. "Boy," she said, "how dare you say 'ain't' to me! I've taught you better than that." 4

"Miss Bessie," I pleaded, "I'm trying to make first-string end on the football team, and if I go around saying 'it isn't' and 'they aren't,' the guys are gonna laugh me off the squad." 5

"Boy," she responded, "you'll play football because you have guts. But do you know what *really* takes guts? Refusing to lower your standards to those of the crowd. It takes guts to say you've got to live and be somebody fifty years after all the football games are over." 6

I started saying "it isn't" and "they aren't," and I still made first-string end—and class valedictorian—without losing my buddies' respect. 7

During her remarkable 44-year-career, Mrs. Bessie Taylor Gwynn taught hundreds of economically deprived black youngsters—including my mother, my brother, my sisters, and me. I remember her now with gratitude and affection—especially in this era when Americans are so wrought-up[2] and after a "rising tide of mediocrity"[3] in public education and the problems of finding competent, caring teachers. Miss Bessie was an example of an informed, dedicated teacher, a blessing to children, and an asset to the nation. 8

> *Background information section; note that it comes after interest-generating opening.*

Born in 1895, in poverty, she grew up in Athens, Alabama, where there was no public school for blacks. She attended Trinity School, a private institution for blacks run by the American Missionary Association, and in 1911 graduated from the Normal School (a "super" 9

---

1. ***Beowulf:*** A long story in poetic form, written in the eighth century in Old English.
2. **wrought-up:** Worked up; upset.
3. **"rising tide of mediocrity":** A reference, from a 1983 report from the National Commission on Excellence in Education, to sinking standards said to be threatening the U.S. educational system.

high school) at Fisk University in Nashville. Mrs. Gwynn, the essence of pride and privacy, never talked about her years in Athens; only in the months before her death did she reveal that she had never attended Fisk University itself because she could not afford the four-year course.

Establishes context of Miss Bessie's teaching—note use of quoted statements, rather than just a summary of what she said.

At Normal School she learned a lot about Shakespeare, but most of all about the profound importance of education—especially for a people trying to move up from slavery. "What you put in your head, boy," she once said, "can never be pulled out by the Ku Klux Klan,[4] the Congress, or anybody." 10

Miss Bessie's bearing of dignity told anyone who met her that she was "educated" in the best sense of the word. There was never a discipline problem in her classes. We didn't dare mess with a woman who knew about the Battle of Hastings, the Magna Carta, and the Bill of Rights—and who could also play the piano. 11

Good use of specific detail about what and how Miss Bessie taught; makes this part of the essay more memorable.

This frail-looking woman could make sense of Shakespeare, Milton, Voltaire, and bring to life Booker T. Washington and W. E. B. DuBois. Believing that it was important to know who the officials were that spent taxpayers' money and made public policy, she made us memorize the names of everyone on the Supreme Court and in the President's Cabinet. It could be embarrassing to be unprepared when Miss Bessie said, "Get up and tell the class who Frances Perkins[5] is and what you think about her." 12

Miss Bessie knew that my family, like so many others during the Depression,[6] couldn't afford to subscribe to a newspaper. She knew we didn't even own a radio. Still, she prodded me to "look out for your future and find some way to keep up with what's going on in the world." So I became a delivery boy for the *Chattanooga Times*. I rarely made a dollar a week, but I got to read a newspaper every day. 13

Miss Bessie noticed things that had nothing to do with schoolwork but were vital to a youngster's development. Once a few classmates made fun of my frayed, hand-me-down overcoat, calling me "Strings." As I was leaving school, Miss Bessie patted me on the back of that old overcoat and said, "Carl, never fret about what you *don't* have. Just make the most of what you *do* have—a brain." 14

Good use of specific detail about what and how Miss Bessie taught; makes this part of the essay more memorable.

Among the things that I did not have was electricity in the little frame house that my father had built for $400 with his World War I bonus. But because of her inspiration, I spent many hours squinting beside a kerosene lamp reading Shakespeare and Thoreau, Samuel Pepys and William Cullen Bryant. 15

No one in my family had ever graduated from high school, so there was no tradition of commitment to learning for me to lean on. Like millions of youngsters in today's ghettos and barrios, I needed the push and stimulation of a teacher who truly cared. Miss Bessie gave plenty of both, as she immersed me in a wonderful world of similes, metaphors, and even 16

---

4. **Ku Klux Klan:** The collective name of several organizations that have persecuted African Americans and other groups since the 1860s.
5. **Frances Perkins:** Secretary of labor under U.S. President Franklin D. Roosevelt and the first woman to hold a cabinet post.
6. **Depression:** Severe economic downturn lasting from the stock market crash of 1929 until the start of World War II.

onomatopoeia. She led me to believe that I could write sonnets as well as Shakespeare, or iambic-pentameter verse to put Alexander Pope to shame.

In those days the McMinnville school system was rigidly "Jim Crow,"[7] and poor black children had to struggle to put anything in their heads. Our high school was only slightly larger than the once-typical little red schoolhouse, and its library was outrageously inadequate—so small, I like to say, that if two students were in it and one wanted to turn a page, the other one had to step outside. 17

Effective and appropriate use of humor.

Negroes, as we were called then, were not allowed in the town library, except to mop floors or dust tables. But through one of those secret Old South arrangements between whites of conscience and blacks of stature, Miss Bessie kept getting books smuggled out of the white library. That is how she introduced me to the Brontës, Byron, Coleridge, Keats, and Tennyson. "If you don't read, you can't write, and if you can't write, you might as well stop dreaming," Miss Bessie once told me. 18

So I read whatever Miss Bessie told me to, and tried to remember the things she insisted that I store away. Forty-five years later, I can still recite her "truths to live by," such as Henry Wadsworth Longfellow's lines from "The Ladder of St. Augustine": 19

The heights by great men reached and kept
Were not attained by sudden flight.
But they, while their companions slept,
Were toiling upward in the night.

Shows that Miss Bessie cared about her students long after graduation.

Years later, her inspiration, prodding, anger, cajoling, and almost osmotic[8] infusion of learning finally led to that lovely day when Miss Bessie dropped me a note saying, "I'm so proud to read your column in the Nashville *Tennessean.*" 20

Miss Bessie was a spry 80 when I went back to McMinnville and visited her in a senior citizens' apartment building. Pointing out proudly that her building was racially integrated, she reached for two glasses and a pint of bourbon. I was momentarily shocked, because it would have been scandalous in the 1930s and '40s for word to get out that a teacher drank, and nobody had ever raised a rumor that Miss Bessie did. 21

Shares experience with Miss Bessie as an adult, creating an effective contrast with the days when he was her student.

I felt a new sense of equality as she lifted her glass to mine. Then she revealed a softness and compassion that I had never known as a student. 22

"I've never forgotten that examination day," she said, "when Buster Martin held up seven fingers, obviously asking you for help with question number seven, 'Name a common carrier.'[9] I can still picture you looking at your exam paper and humming a few bars of 'Chattanooga Choo Choo.' I was so tickled, I couldn't punish either of you." 23

Miss Bessie was telling me, with bourbon-laced grace, that I never fooled her for a moment. 24

When Miss Bessie died in 1980, at age 85, hundreds of her former students mourned. They knew the measure of a great teacher: love and motivation. Her wisdom and influence had rippled out across generations. 25

---

7. **"Jim Crow":** Segregation of African Americans under discriminatory laws and customs.
8. **osmotic:** Like the transfer of substances through a cell membrane (osmosis).
9. **common carrier:** A public transportation system, such as a railway or airline.

Some of her students who might normally have been doomed to poverty went on to become doctors, dentists, and college professors. Many, guided by Miss Bessie's example, became public-school teachers.

26

Good quote from another person who knew Miss Bessie.

"The memory of Miss Bessie and how she conducted her classroom did more for me than anything I learned in college," recalls Gladys Wood of Knoxville, Tennessee, a highly respected English teacher who spent 43 years in the state's school system. "So many times, when I faced a difficult classroom problem, I asked myself, *How would Miss Bessie deal with this?* And I'd remember that she would handle it with laughter and love."

27

Short, to-the-point conclusion.

No child can get all the necessary support at home, and millions of poor children get *no* support at all. This is what makes a wise, educated, warm-hearted teacher like Miss Bessie so vital to the minds, hearts, and souls of this country's children.

28

Questions for Discussion

1. The profile reveals that education and teachers used to be more formal and authoritarian. How did you react to Miss Bessie's manner, the "bearing of dignity" Rowan refers to in paragraph 11?
2. As depicted in paragraph 4, why does Miss Bessie react so strongly to Carl's "ain't"? Is it just "bad grammar" she's objecting to?
3. What does Rowan report that he read under Miss Bessie's direction? Do you see a pattern in the choices? Compare the works of literature Rowan read in high school to what you read. How are they alike? How are they different? How do you explain the differences?

■■ *Thinking as a Writer*

What Is the Rhetorical Situation?

1. What is Rowan's *purpose* in writing this essay? What is his *angle* on the topic? How would you describe his *voice*?
2. Who is Rowan's intended *audience*? Is he writing for other African American professionals, for education reformers, or for some other readership? Is there anything in the article you can cite that implies his target readership?
3. Using Concept Close-Up: More about Profiles (page 89) as a guide, answer the following question: How does Rowan use the *conventions* for creating a subjective profile? Specifically, how does he use background information about Miss Bessie? How does he include her voice, the sort of things she said, and the manner she used in saying them? How does he use detail to give his subject fuller humanity, a view of Miss Bessie from more than one side? ■

The Border Patrol at Wellton Station, Arizona

LUIS ALBERTO URREA

Luis Alberto Urrea is a distinguished novelist and a member of the Latino Literary Hall of Fame. An example of a profile of a place and the people who work there, the following selection comes from a nonfiction book, The Devil's Highway *(2004), a national bestseller and a finalist for the Pulitzer Prize in 2005. The book tells the story of fourteen people who died in the deserts of Arizona seeking work in our country, an instance of the appalling human suffering resulting from poverty in Mexico and U.S. border policy.*

We include a map provided in The Devil's Highway *to help you follow references to places in this profile.*

The town of Wellton is in a wide plain on I-8. It is tucked between Yuma's mountain ranges and the Mohawk Valley, with its strange volcanic upthrusts. The American Canal cuts through the area, and a bombing range is to the south. Running just below I-8 is the railway line that carries freight from Texas to California. Most train crews have learned to carry stores of bottled water to drop out of their locomotives at the feet of staggering illegals. 1

Wellton Station sits atop a small hill north of the freeway. It is isolated enough that some car radios can't pick up a signal on either AM or FM bands. Cell phones often show "Out of Service Area" messages and go mute. 2

Many agents, borderwide, commute a fair distance to their stations. Drives of twenty, forty, even seventy miles are common. But the trips to and from work afford them a period of quiet, of wind-down or wind-up time. It is not always easy to leap from bed and go hunt people. Besides, the old-timers have learned to really love the desert, the colors in the cliffs, the swoop of a red-tailed hawk, the saffron dust devils lurching into the hills. 3

For most agents, it works this way: you get up at dawn and put on your forest green uniform. As you get to work, you pull in behind the station to the fenced lot. You punch in your code on the keypad, and you park beside the other machines safe from your enemies behind the chain-link. Your station is a small Fort Apache. On one side, the agents line up their trucks and sports cars, and on the other side sits the fleet of impeccably maintained Ford Explorers. Border Patrol agents are often military men, and they are spit-and-polish. Their trucks are clean and new; their uniforms are sharp; and their offices are busy but generally squared away. The holding cells in the main buildings—black steel mesh to the far left of the main door—sparkle. Part of this is, no doubt, due to the relentless public focus on the agency. In Calexico, the Mexican consulate has upped the ante by placing a consulate office inside the actual station: prisoners are greeted by the astounding sight of a service window with Mexican flags and Mexican government signs. 4

Inside, Wellton Station is a strange mix of rundown police precinct and high-tech command center. Old wood paneling, weathered tables. Computers and expensive radios at each workstation. In the back building, supervisory officer and mainstay of the station Kenny Smith has a couple of radios going, which he listens to, and a couple of phones ringing every 5

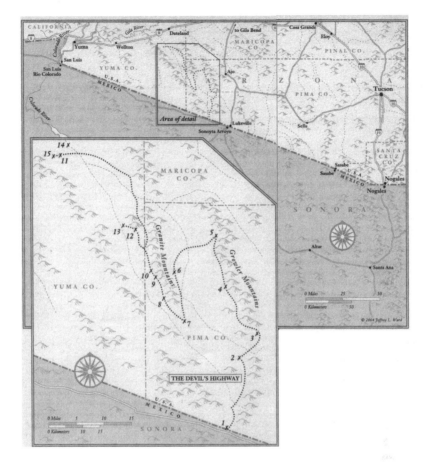

few minutes, which he generally ignores. A framed picture of a human skull lying in the desert hangs on the wall. It has a neat hole in the forehead, above one eye socket. "Don't get any cute ideas," one of the boys says. "We didn't shoot that guy."

A computer is on all the time, and GPS satellite hardware bleeps beside it. Above Kenny's desk is a huge topo map showing the region. He sits in a swivel chair and reigns over his domain. He has an arrow with its notched end stuffed into a gas station antenna ball. He holds the ball in his fist and uses the arrow to point out various things of interest on the map. 6

On the wall is the big call-chart. Names and desert vectors are inked onto a white board in a neat grid. Agents' last names are linked to their patrol areas. In the morning, you check the board, banter with Kenny, say good morning to the station chief, stop by to say hello to Miss Anne, who runs the whole shebang from her neat desk in the big main room out front. 7

The town of Wellton is farms and dirt, dirt and farms. New agents, fresh from the East or West coasts, amuse the old boys by asking where they can find an espresso or a latte. Kenny 8

Smith tells them, "Well, you can go down to Circle K and get a sixteen-ounce coffee. Then put some flavored creamer in it." That one never fails to get a laugh out of the old boys. An agent, sipping his stout coffee, is mid-story: ". . . And here comes Ole José," he says, "all armed-up on some girlie!" Old José seems to be the archetypal tonk [undocumented immigrant] who shows up in stories. The listener, a steroidal-looking Aryan monster with a military haircut and a bass voice, notes: "Brutal." He turns to his computer keyboard and plugs away with giant fingers.

Everybody speaks Spanish. Several of the agents are Mexican Americans. Quite a few in each sector who aren't "Hispanic" are married to Mexican women. 9

Wellton Station is considered a good place to work. The old boys there are plain-spoken and politically incorrect. INS and Border Patrol ranks are overrun with smooth-talking college boys mouthing carefully worded sound bites. Not so in Wellton. Agents will tell you that the only way to get a clear picture of the real border world is to find someone who has been in service over four years. A ten-year veteran is even better. Wellton has its share of such veterans, but any agent who has been in service for ten years knows better than to talk to you about his business. 10

A great compliment in the Border Patrol is: "He's a good guy." Wellton's agents are universally acknowledged by other agents as good guys. Jerome Wofford, they say, will give you the shirt off his back; the station chief will lend you his cherry SUV if you have special business. 11

Like the other old boys of Wellton Station, you love your country, you love your job, and though you would never admit it, you love your fellow officers. Civilians? They'll just call you jack-booted thugs, say you're doing a bad job, confuse you with INS border guards. You're not a border guard, you're a beat cop. Your station chief urges you not to hang out in small-town restaurants, not to frequent bars. Don't go out in uniform. Don't cross the border. Don't flash your badge. Don't speed, and if you do and get tagged for a ticket, don't use your badge to try to get out of it. Don't talk to strangers. In hamlets like Naco, San Luis, Nogales, civilians often won't make eye contact. Chicanos don't like you. Liberals don't like you. Conservatives mock and insult you. And politicians . . . politicians are the enemy. 12

There's always someone working in the office, early or late, every day and every night of every year. They're guarding the cells, monitoring the radios, writing reports. Sometimes, you can't sleep. You can always come in to the clubhouse and find someone to talk to. Somebody who votes like you, talks like you. Believes in Christ or the Raiders like you. You can make coffee for the illegals in the cage, flirt with the señoritas—though with all the sexual assault and rape charges that dog the entire border, you probably don't. Human rights groups are constantly lodging complaints, so you watch yourself. The tonks supposedly have phones in their holding pens so they can call their lawyers to come slaughter you if you do anything wicked. You pull up one of the rolling office chairs, turn your back to them, and sit at a radio and listen to the ghostly voices of your partners out in the desert night, another American evening passing by. 13

Questions for Discussion

1. Elsewhere in his book Urrea states that "Mexican American Border Patrol agents are feared even more by the illegals than the gringos [non-Hispanic whites], for the Mexicans can only ascribe to them a kind of rabid self-hatred." Does Urrea's profile suggest that the Mexicans should fear Border Patrol agents, regardless of ethnicity?
2. "He's a good guy." Urrea tells us that this statement about an agent is "a great compliment" and that the agents at Wellton Station are "universally acknowledged by other agents as good guys" (paragraph 11). What does "good guy" seem to mean in this context? Do you see them as good guys?
3. Visuals can be indispensable in effective profiles. Look again at the map Urrea provided. How did it help you understand the profile?

■■ *Thinking as a Writer*

What Is the Rhetorical Situation?

1. What is Urrea's *purpose* in writing this essay? What is his *angle* on the topic? How would you describe his *voice*?
2. Who is Urrea's intended *audience*? Is he writing for both sides of the political conflict over immigration, for neither side, or for some other group? Is there anything in the article you can cite that implies his target readership?
3. Using Concept Close-Up: More about Profiles (page 89) as a guide, answer this question: How does Urrea use the *conventions* for creating a subjective profile? Specifically, how does he use background information, the voice and behavior of the border patrol agents, and detailed description to create a vivid impression of Wellton Station and its surroundings? ■

The Assignment

Write a profile about a person, organization, place, event, or situation. We recommend writing a single-person profile because it is easier to research and control. We also recommend that you at least be acquainted with the person you choose to profile. Extending and deepening a relationship you already have usually works better than establishing a new one from scratch.

How Do I Write a Profile?
Questioning the Rhetorical Situation

Begin by picturing a **rhetorical situation** for your writing project, a real-world context for communicating. You should consider the key variables in any act of communication: a writer with something to say, a reader the writer wishes to reach, and a kind of text appropriate to the writing task. These three variables will affect many decisions in the composing process.

Writer: What Is My Purpose, and What Impression Should Readers Have of Me?

The purpose of a profile is to depict a person, place, organization, or some other suitable subject that you care about, that matters to you. You are informing, telling readers what they need to know to understand your subject. Using your own point of view, your angle, you are also communicating an interpretation of your subject, what it means, the value it has—in short, why it should matter to your readers. Your readers should perceive you as knowledgeable about your subject, consistent in your point of view, and interested in depicting your subject in a memorable way.

Audience: Who Is My Reader?

Profiles often communicate with a broad audience because human beings are so-cial animals and enjoy reading about other people. However, skillful profiles have *particular readerships* in mind. Given the subject you have chosen and the angle you have on it, ask yourself this question: **What group of people will gain the most from reading it?** What do they need to know to understand your subject? What could you tell them that they will find interesting, intriguing, or challenging? How can you get them involved in the ethical issues your subject raises—that is, questions of right and wrong, good and bad?

Text: What Would Be an Appropriate Topic?

The most important criterion for making your selection is that the subject matters to you. Genuine interest in and involvement with your subject cannot be faked. Here are some possible topics:

- An older family member, a family friend, a mentor (such as a coach or teacher), someone in the community you interact with often, someone you work for or with, or a close, personal friend.

- Profiles in newspapers and magazines are about at least locally well-known people, such as artists, musicians, entertainers, sports figures, politicians, business leaders, and so on. If you happen to know a "high-profile" subject, as journalists call them, they can be good choices.

People working to accomplish something, such as installing a community garden in your neighborhood, make good profile subjects.

- Situations you, your family, or your local community face, such as entering the military, taking your first job, raising children, taking care of older relatives, or coping with illness or injury.
- Places you have lived or visited often, such as a foreign country; places you go to visit family, conduct business, or take vacations; the neighborhood where you grew up or live now.
- Significant happenings or gatherings of people, such as a concert or sporting event; something you witnessed that made the news and/or was a topic of conversation on your campus or in your local community.

How Do I Write a Profile?
Engaging the Writing Process

No two people compose in exactly the same way, and even the same person may go through the writing process in different ways with different assignments. Nevertheless, because no one can attend to everything at once, there are phases in handling any significant writing task. You prepare to write by generating content and finding your angle.

The next phase is planning and drafting your paper, getting a version, however rough it may be, on paper or screen so that you have something to work with during the following two stages: revising your draft by making changes to the content, arrangement, and style of your writing; and editing your draft to take care of problems at the paragraph and sentence level, such as lack of focus and coherence, awkward or unclear sentences, and errors of grammar, spelling, and punctuation.

Exploring Your Topic

Most profiles draw on both what the writer knows already about the person profiled—that is, experience with that person—and additional information gathered from research. Start by investigating your experience.

Asking Questions: Mining for Details about a Person

It is remarkable what we know about relatives, friends, acquaintances, and colleagues yet do not fully realize that we know. The following questions should help you recover some of what you know about the person you have chosen to profile.

In your writer's notebook or in an electronic file, write down everything that occurs to you in response to each of the following questions:

1. What does the person look like?
2. How does the person dress?
3. What is it like to talk to this person? Are there characteristic facial expressions, qualities of voice, mannerisms, gestures, accent, and so on that you recall?
4. How would you describe the person's character? For instance, how does she or he handle problems and setbacks?
5. What achievements and activities is the person proudest of?
6. How self-aware is the person? Does the person's self-conception match your view of him or her?
7. What does the person most like to talk about? What topics does she or he avoid or say nothing about when others raise them?
8. Where have you talked with the person? What did you notice about the home, office, or other place where the two of you talked?
9. What sort of people does your person have as friends or associates? If you have met some of them, what were your impressions? What did they say about your person?
10. If you were talking with someone else who does not know the person as well as you do, what story or stories would you tell? What stories about your person do you recall others telling you?

▨▨■ ACTIVITY 5.1 *Writer's Notebook*

Assessing Your Materials

After you finish brainstorming your topic using the ten questions on page 102, step back and begin looking for *patterns and convergences* in the material. Do you see a dominant theme in your person's life, something that she or he is always concerned with or pursuing? Do you detect fundamental loyalties or commitments, a basic philosophy, outlook, or set of controlling attitudes or values?

Profiles create memorable impressions, and therefore you need to be seeking the impression you want to create for yours. You may not know yet what it will be, but probably somewhere in your first exploration there are clues or intuitions. Write them down, even if you have doubts, even if some of the details do not fit. You are not committing yourself to anything yet, but you need some first ideas for further thought and to help guide the research you will probably need to do. ■

Preparing to Write

You can see from the example profiles at the beginning of this chapter that the amount of research required varies considerably. Rowan's profile drew almost entirely on his own memories; Urrea devoted weeks to visiting Border Patrol stations and talking with the officers. How much you need depends on how long you have known and how well you know the person you have chosen and on your instructor's assignment requirements.

Interviewing is the most common form of research in doing profiles, and we will devote special attention to it shortly. What other ways of acquiring information might be available to you?

BEST PRACTICES | Sources of Information for Profiles

1. Besides interviewing the person you are profiling, talk to people who know your subject as well or better than you do, such as friends, associates, family members, and other relatives.
2. Find out if your person has written anything that you might gain access to: articles, books, texts for speeches, diaries, journals, blogs, even e-mail exchanges she or he might be willing to share.
3. Ask if you may look at scrapbooks or photo albums your subject might have.
4. Look for information via Google, news stories you can find via your local paper's index or your library's databases (see pages 419–20), Who's Who publications, résumés, bios written by your subject or by someone else, and so on. Ask your subject for help in accessing such information.
5. Arrange to attend meetings or other gatherings of people in which your subject plays a prominent role. ■

See Chapter 16, Finding Sources, and Chapter 17, Evaluating Sources, for more on using print and online materials.

Conducting Interviews

Interviews are *guided conversations,* and they are guided largely by the questions you ask. On the one hand, you want as natural and free-flowing a conversation as possible, something close to what would happen if you were sitting next to someone on an airplane and just happened to strike up a conversation. On the other hand, there is information you need and questions you have thought of in advance to elicit it, and you do not want the interview to end with too few of those questions asked and answered. Interviews are, therefore, a challenge, a push-pull between *let it flow* and *steer it toward what you need to know.* Following are important considerations when conducting interviews (also see Figure 5.1):

1. **The medium matters.** We recommend face-to-face interviews over telephone interviews, and telephone interviews over online chats or e-mail exchanges. Of course, you conduct them any way you can, but as you move down the line in methods of communication, you lose more and more information. Face-to-face interviews give you the full experience of good talk, including gestures, facial expressions, changes in posture, and information from the surroundings. Over the telephone, you have only the interviewee's voice in addition to what is said; with online communication you have only the written text to work with.

2. **Bring a camera with you.** Photographs of your subject and places associated with him or her can help supplement descriptions and confirm the impression you want to create. Many profiles include photographs.

3. **Plan to bring an audio recorder.** Ask your interviewee before the conversation begins whether or not you can use the recorder. Have a notebook with you as well for making quick notes between questions, during a response, and immediately after the interview when your memory is freshest. However, do not allow note-taking to intrude into the conversation—fast jottings are all you will have time for during the interview itself.

4. **Bring with you a set of questions** that are printed out or written on your notepad and rank ordered from the most to the least important. The questions should address holes in your knowledge detected after recalling what you know already about your person and after pursuing some of the suggestions in the Best Practices (page 103) for gaining additional information. They should also fill out what you have learned that you and your readers are likely to find most interesting.

   Often your questions will either not lead to anything interesting or will turn up much more than you anticipated. In the first case, be ready to pose another question as soon as you can; in the second case, let the person talk until you sense the well is going dry, even if it means you do not get to ask a few of your less important questions.

5. Finally, as your interview draws to a close, ask if you may arrange another meeting later and/or pose follow-up questions over the telephone or via

1

2

3

4

FIGURE **5.1**

Things to Remember for an Interview

When conducting an interview, there are a few important things to remember to help you get the most of out it: (1) speak to your subject face-to-face, (2) take the person's picture, (3) record the interview, and (4) have good questions prepared.

e-mail. Also ask about additional sources of information listed on page 103 that you can only obtain if the interviewee is able and willing to supply them—texts of speeches, for instance.

Face-to-face interviewing is an art well worth learning how to do. Start practicing it now, on this assignment, because you will need it for information-gathering on the job or for community-based leadership positions.

Selecting Details Based on Your Angle

Profiles are always based on far more information than the writer can actually use in the profile itself. If you feel somewhat overwhelmed by all the information you have gathered, that is normal. Here is how to gain a measure of control over it sufficient to write a first draft.

First, remember that profiles are always *partial depictions of your person, and the source of the partiality is your angle or point of view.* Put another way, you need to create a memorable impression, and it can only come from your point of view. It is time to decide on your point of view and commit yourself to it—at least until you see how well it works in a first draft.

Remember also that your point of view is what it is, and so it cannot be wrong. Have confidence in it and suspend judgment until you get the first draft completed. Only then can you assess your point of view according to the only criterion that matters: Did it work? Were you able to write an engaging profile? If not, adjusting your point of view may be one of the keys to revising it.

What matters now is choosing a point of view that has the greatest potential for connecting with readers. You can see how it works by revisiting the example profiles at the beginning of this chapter (Readings 5.1 and 5.2). For Carl T. Rowan, Miss Bessie is *the* role model for public school teachers, especially those whose students come from disadvantaged backgrounds. His point of view connects with readers because the educational problem he addresses was a major concern in 1985 and remains so today. Luis Alberto Urrea wants to expose the common view of the Border Patrol as corrupt and sadistic for the serious distortion of reality that it is. The problems along our border with Mexico are not caused by the Border Patrol nor are they problems the officers can solve. Readers connect because they want to know what is really going on and what is required to cope better with the situation.

In formulating your point of view, then, ask two questions:

- Why does my subject matter to me?
- How can I connect what matters to me with my readers' concerns and interests?

Answer these questions and you have what you need to select information from all the data you have gathered. If an item relates *directly* to depicting what matters to you and your readers, include it in your plan for the first draft; if not, leave it out.

Drafting Your Paper

As you write your draft, focus on the following concerns.

Thinking as a Writer: What Voice Is Appropriate for a Profile?

Profiles are informative, not primarily expressive, thus the focus is on the subject profiled, not on the writer. Nevertheless, your voice matters, as it always does in writing. Sound like a well-informed insider with an intimate knowledge of your subject. That is how you project authority. Beyond that, voice depends largely on point of view, how you understand your subject.

For example, listen to this paragraph from Urrea's profile of a Border Patrol station:

> Inside, Wellton Station is a strange mix of rundown police precinct and high-tech command center. Old wood paneling, weathered tables. Computers and expensive radios at each workstation. In the back building, supervisory officer and mainstay of

the station Kenny Smith has a couple of radios going, which he listens to, and a couple of phones ringing every few minutes, which he generally ignores. A framed picture of a human skull lying in the desert hangs on the wall. It has a neat hole in the forehead, above one eye socket. "Don't get any cute ideas," one of the boys says. "We didn't shoot that guy."

The description is "objective" in the sense that it tells us only what the author saw and heard, with enough detail to convince us that he knows what he is talking about. The attitudes and judgments are implied: What sort of people would display such a photograph? Why does one of the agents feel the need to say that "we didn't shoot that guy"?

Urrea's point of view is both positive and ironic; he refuses to either demonize the Border Patrol or depict them as Boy Scouts. They are ordinary men doing a difficult job. His reporter's voice—facts implying assessments—is exactly right for the message he wants to get across.

Thinking as a Writer: Developing and Organizing Your Profile

The following organizational principles apply to arranging your materials:

- Start with something memorable, an attention-getting opener that indicates what your profile is about and why it matters to you and your reader.

- Provide most of your background information next, after you have your reader's attention and interest.

- Structure the remaining material by looking for a sequence that makes sense. For instance, you may need to describe a situation before you cite what your subject said or did. Or perhaps one story or memory may provide a good lead-in to or context for another.

- Save something especially memorable for the conclusion. You want to end as strongly as you began.

Commonly writers set out to follow a plan and then depart from it as they draft. The plan they thought would work has to be modified or even abandoned as they write. If that is what happens to you, do not be concerned. As long as the final version of your profile has a structure that readers can understand and follow, you have solved whatever organizational problems you may encounter.

Revising Your Draft

Writing is revising. A first draft is a start, but most need significant rewriting—for instance, parts taken out, new parts added, and parts rearranged. The strongest revisions begin with your own assessment. It is a good idea to put your draft aside for a while, preferably a day or two. Then, when you have some distance from it, go back and read what you wrote.

Try to see it as your readers will see it. The questions in the Art of Questioning will help you find ways to improve the draft.

ART OF QUESTIONING | Revision Checklist for Writing a Profile

1. **Does the draft create a memorable impression?** What word or words best state your angle, or interpretation, of your subject?
2. **Is there anything in the profile that does not contribute to the impression?** If so, it should be background information. Cut anything else.
3. **Does your draft capture your subject's full humanity?** If yours seems "flat," one-dimensional, revise by adding anecdotes, descriptions, comments from other people, and so on to reveal more sides or aspects of your subject. Here is a major opportunity for improving your paper by developing it better.
4. **Does your profile have immediacy and intimacy?** Isolate the places in your paper where you have described your subject, so that the reader can see and hear what you experienced. Go back to the notes you took during exploration and research. **What details might be added?** Sight and sound usually dominate descriptions, but touch, smell, and taste can sometimes contribute as well. Developing your descriptions is another way to make your profile more effective.
5. **Have you quoted your person and/or cited snippets of revealing conversation?** *Your reader needs to hear your subject talking.* What was said and in what way, with what gestures, facial expressions, tone of voice, and so on?
6. **Have you made your relationship with your subject clear?** Read through your paper again, concentrating entirely on voice and self-presentation. **What is your attitude toward your subject?** Where does it emerge most clearly and forcefully? **How do you sound to your reader?** Do you think how you sound is appropriate given your relationship to the person?
7. Does your profile at least imply questions like: **What matters in life? How should we live? How ought we to deal with other people?** Find the places in your essay where ethical questions like these are relevant. Can you develop them better without turning your profile into a sermon or moralistic lesson? ■

■■■ ACTIVITY 5.2 *Collaborative Activity*

Getting a Second Opinion

Either before you attempt a revision or at some point during the revising process, it always helps to have someone else, such as a classmate, a tutor, your instructor, a willing friend, look at your draft. Be sure that the person understands the assignment and what you are trying to do to create the memorable impression profiles make.

Share the questions listed in the previous section with the person reviewing your draft. Show them what you have done or plan to do to improve the draft. Then ask for the person's honest and full assessment and any suggestions for improvement. ■

■■■■ ACTIVITY 5.3 *In Your Own Work*

Revising Your Draft

After assessing the draft yourself and getting a second opinion, formulate a revision strategy—that is, an approach to carrying out the revision. Here are some suggestions:

- First, decide what you think the useful criticism and suggestions are. Not all the feedback will be equally helpful, and some of it will not help at all. Reassess your own self-criticisms—do you still see the same problems?

- Second, being as specific as you can, make a list of items you intend to work on. "The first anecdote on page 3 needs more descriptive detail" is an example of what we mean by specific.

- Third, divide your list into two categories: revisions that will change all or much of the paper—called global revisions—versus spot revisions that require only altering a paragraph or two in one place.

- Fourth, do the global revising first. Ponder the best order for doing them. For instance, if you decide to rearrange sections in your profile, do that first before working on transitions or other flow problems.

- Fifth, after completing the global revisions, deal with the spot revisions by beginning with those most likely to improve your draft the most.

Remember that revisions cannot be done all at once, in one step. Focus your attention on solving one problem at a time. *Remember also that carrying out your plan will often result in unplanned insights.* You might discover, for instance, that in developing one anecdote you now see connections with another. Adjust your plans to take full advantage of revision surprises. ■

Student Example: Excerpts from Molly Tilton's Draft

Molly Tilton's profile, "Mr. Santa Claus," appears on pages 113–15. Let's look at some excerpts from her first draft so you can see some of the significant improvements revision can make.

Excerpt 1: Opening Paragraph

In the back corner of an office in United Liquors' headquarters in Braintree Massachusetts, the phone rang. Terri, the director of The Ray Tye Medical Aid Foundation, answered; she yelled, "Mr. Tye, Senator Ted Kennedy is on the phone, and has a prospective patient for the foundation." Mr. Tye took the call and then came into Terri's office to explain to her a young child's life-threatening situation.

In her revised opening, Tilton gets to the point faster:

In a back corner of United Liquors' headquarters in Braintree, Massachusetts, lives are being saved. Mr. A. Raymond Tye, a prominent businessman and philanthropist, strides into his place of work one morning with his cane and a mission. "Terri," he cries, "Come into my office to discuss some prospective patients for the foundation, twin boys conjoined at the head. They need our help." From that point the real work begins.

Excerpt 2: Paragraph 6 about Terri

Terri, the director of the foundation, is faced with tough decisions every day. She, along with Mr. Tye, decides on the patients the foundation will support. Doctors and politicians call The Ray Tye Medical Aid Foundation asking for financial help for someone they know. Patients and their family members fill out online applications asking for medical assistance. It is Terri's responsibility to contact hospitals to find out more about the patient's condition, as well as keeping in touch with ill patients. The majority of applications come from Haiti, Iraq, China, and Massachusetts; the foundation does not pay for travel costs but usually sets up patients with another foundation who can assist them. The foundation reviews all patient applications but only helps those who are facing life-threatening ailments and do not have health insurance.

In her revision of this paragraph, Tilton uses **specific details** to bring more life-like immediacy to Terri, allowing readers to see her as a real person:

Terri Carlson, the director of the foundation, has worked for the foundation for two years. Prior to this, she worked for United Liquors as credit manager. In recent years, Terri, a devoted wife and mother of two, has worked long hours while juggling her responsibilities at home. She wears business attire every day to work, showing her serious attitude, but her bright red hair exemplifies her bubbly spirit. Even though Terri is in her 40s, she has the high-pitched voice of a child and gets excited over the littlest accomplishments. Her lovable personality makes it easier for people all over the world to connect with her, even over the phone. As the director, Terri has the responsibility to read through the applications, contact hospitals about patients' conditions and medical histories, find the hospitals with the most expert specialists, keep in touch with current patients, and establish lasting relationships with recovered ones. She is able to accomplish all of this with only the aid of a computer, a telephone, and a calculator.

■■■■ ACTIVITY 5.4 *In Your Own Work*

Revising for Focus and Development

Exchange your draft with another student and help each other find ways to improve focus and development. Look especially for lack of sufficient detail in description. Also remember other options for development in profiles, such as quotations and reported conversations. ■

■■■■ ACTIVITY 5.5 *In Your Own Work*

Using Visual Supplementation

A picture may not be worth a thousand words, but having some can help your reader visualize your subject and places associated with the information gathered through interviews and conversations. They can also confirm what you say about your subject. Consider using photos if you have not included them; if you have included them, consider how to acquire better ones if you are not entirely happy with them. Also consider order and placement. If there is more than one, which should come first, second, and so on? Where in the paper should you place a photograph? Usually placing it close to the paragraph it is most relevant to works best. ■

Editing Your Revised Draft

Excessive repetition is a common editing problem. When the same word is used too frequently, readers notice. Writers seldom detect unintentional repetitions by silent reading; read your draft aloud so you hear them.

Because Molly Tilton's angle on the founder and the foundation itself was so respectful, and because Mr. Tye was so much her elder, Molly chose to refer to him throughout the essay as Mr. Tye rather than by his full name on first mention and from then on by his last name only, as is customary. This decision created some passages where editing for repetition would have streamlined the writing, such as the excerpt below from paragraph 5.

Original Version

Mr. Tye has provided hope to thousands of people all over the world with his selfless acts and has constantly encouraged others to share what they can for those in dire need. The impact Mr. Tye has had on others shows tangibly in the hundreds of thank you notes and hugs he has received since 2002, the year of the foundation's establishment. Mr. Tye's office is decorated with wooden sculptures from Africa and steel plaques from organizations that have honored Mr. Tye for his remarkable work. In May 2009, Catholic Charities honored Mr. Tye for his philanthropic efforts throughout the city of Boston; making him the first Jewish man to receive a Catholic Charities award.

There are several options for ways to refer to people:

1. Use a pronoun
2. Use a synonym or substitute word
3. Use a different version of the person's name

Using these options, Molly created the edited version below:

Revised Version

A. Raymond Tye has provided hope to thousands of people all over the world with his selfless acts and has constantly encouraged others to share what they can for those in dire need. The impact his generosity has had on others shows tangibly in the hundreds of thank you notes and hugs he has received since 2002, the year of the foundation's establishment. Mr. Tye's office is decorated with wooden sculptures from Africa and steel plaques from organizations that have honored him for his remarkable work. In May 2009, Catholic Charities honored him for his philanthropic efforts throughout the city of Boston; making Mr. Tye the first Jewish man to receive a Catholic Charities award.

■■■■ ACTIVITY 5.6 *In Your Own Work*

Editing for Other Repeated Words

When you notice the same word appearing in sentences in sequence, there are two ways to reduce the repetition:

1. Think of a different word but one that still sounds natural—not as if you found it in the thesaurus.
2. Combine two of the sentences into one.

In the sixth paragraph of Molly's essay, the word *work* appears several times, as a verb and as a noun. Practice reducing repetitions by editing the passage below. Compare your edited version with those of others in your class.

> Terri Carlson, the director of the foundation, has worked for the foundation for two years. Prior to this, she worked for United Liquors as credit manager. In recent years, Terri, a devoted wife and mother of two, has worked long hours while juggling her responsibilities at home. She wears business attire every day to work, showing her serious attitude, but her bright red hair exemplifies her bubbly spirit. . . . ■

■■■■ ACTIVITY 5.7 *In Your Own Work*

Detecting and Editing Repetitions

Read through your revised draft with special attention to the problem of repeated words. You might ask someone else to read the paper and circle or underline repetitions if you have trouble detecting them. Use the suggestions in the student examples above to add more variety or conciseness as you reduce the repetitions. ■

R E V I S E D   S T U D E N T   E X A M P L E

Tilton 1

Molly Tilton
Professor Channell
Writing 205
April 4, 2011

Mr. Santa Claus

Short introductory paragraph gets to the point and the action quickly. Gains reader interest and attention.

In a back corner of United Liquors' headquarters in Braintree, Massachusetts, lives are being saved. Mr. A. Raymond Tye, a prominent businessman and philanthropist, strides into his place of work one morning with his cane and a mission. "Terri," he cries, "Come into my office to discuss some prospective patients for the foundation, twin boys conjoined at the head. They need our help." From that point the real work begins.

At the end of Campanelli Drive sits a gray warehouse. The mirrored glass walls on the sides of this building contribute a faintly contemporary architectural style, but the building is of little significance to the town of Braintree otherwise. The only cars that travel down the road are large supply trucks and employee vehicles. When you walk into the building's lobby, Sheila, the Braintree division's secretary, greets you with a smile and asks how she might assist you. On the first floor, over sixty United Liquors employees work diligently in cubicles. Up the stairs, in a recently renovated part of the building, you reach a common meeting room and a door to the right with a sign reading, "The Ray Tye Medical Aid Foundation." Inside are three cubicles, and in the back left corner is Mr. Tye's personal office. Terri Carlson is the only employee of the foundation. Her cubicle has one large desk, one computer, a chair, two file cabinets, a printer, and three cabinets full of office supplies, all she needs to operate this foundation.

This and following paragraphs supply needed background knowledge.

The Ray Tye Medical Aid Foundation was started to offer financial assistance to people around the world who suffer life-threatening illness and need in-hospital medical care to save their lives. In honor of Tye's 80th birthday, his wife, friends and family collected two million dollars in order to establish The Ray Tye Medical Aid Foundation. This small foundation has helped to save or prolong 183 lives. Patients have been helped no matter what their location, race, sex, or religious affiliation. The patients that the foundation has helped are from all over the world, including the U.S. This past year, I had the privilege of being the first volunteer to work at this foundation; it was in this capacity that I became closely acquainted with Terri and Mr. Tye.

Establishes writer's connection with her subject and, therefore, her authority.

Mr. Tye is a first-generation entrepreneur who started his own company, United Liquors, which went on to become one of the largest liquor distributors in Massachusetts. Living a

1

2

3

4

colorful life, he attended Tufts University, fought in World War II, and fathered five children. Now in his 80's, he has dedicated his life to helping others, and received countless accolades for his philanthropic efforts. He always dresses in professional attire, making him a serious business man, which most find intimidating, until he lets out his vibrant smile. His appearance speaks to his kind spirit, from his white bushy eyebrows to his portly belly. In fact, Terri often tells the story of one patient, a cancer survivor, who referred to Tye as "Mr. Santa Claus."

Needed background material, but includes personal details about Tye that make him human, engaging.

Mr. Tye has provided hope to thousands of people all over the world with his selfless   5
acts and has constantly encouraged others to share what they can for those in dire need. The impact Mr. Tye has had on others shows tangibly in the hundreds of thank you notes and hugs he has received since 2002, the year of the foundation's establishment. Mr. Tye's office is decorated with wooden sculptures from Africa and steel plaques from organizations that have honored Mr. Tye for his remarkable work. In May 2009, Catholic Charities honored Mr. Tye for his philanthropic efforts throughout the city of Boston, making him the first Jewish man to receive a Catholic Charities award. Mr. Tye states on the foundation's website:

Use of memorable detail to confirm Tye's achievements.

> It is a strong belief of my own that giving should really be called receiving because the elemental act of giving returns many pleasant rewards to the giver. In fact, it might be said that there is not a more self-serving act than a liberal manifestation of generosity. . . . Seeing the happiness generosity creates in the recipients is another positive reinforcement—a big return for a small investment.

Good use of material gathered from her subject's own writing.

Accordingly, the motto of The Ray Tye Medical Aid Foundation is simply "We will never stop caring."

Terri Carlson, the director of the foundation, has worked for the foundation for two   6
years. Prior to this, she worked for United Liquors as credit manager. In recent years, Terri, a devoted wife and mother of two, has worked long hours while juggling her responsibilities at home. She wears business attire every day to work, showing her serious attitude, but her bright red hair exemplifies her bubbly spirit. Even though Terri is in her 40s, she has the high-pitched voice of a child and gets excited over the littlest accomplishments. Her lovable personality makes it easier for people all over the world to connect with her, even over the phone. As the director, Terri has the responsibility to read through the applications, contact hospitals about patients' conditions and medical histories, find the hospitals with the most expert specialists, keep in touch with current patients, and establish lasting relationships with recovered ones. She is able to accomplish all of this with only the aid of a computer, a telephone, and a calculator.

Each week, the foundation receives four or more lengthy applications from people   7
around the world seeking help. All prospective patients must fill out an online application. Terri and Mr. Tye review all patients' applications but help only those who face life-threatening conditions and do not have health insurance.

Recently, media in the United States told the story of twin Egyptian boys whose heads   8
were conjoined. These boys, Mohamed and Ahmed Ibrahim, are patients that Tye discovered himself. On a Sunday morning in August 2002, he read an article about them in *The Boston*

Use of specific, extended example to illustrate the help Tye's foundation provides.

Globe and decided to help them. Their operation was estimated to cost two million dollars; the Ray Tye Medical Aid Foundation donated $100,000, making it one of the leading donors. The thirty-four hour operation was successful in October 2003, and the boys have been making steady progress since then. After their extensive surgery and therapy, the boys learned how to walk on their own and learned how to speak English.

Mohamed and Ahmed live happy and healthy lives with their family, thanks to Mr. Tye and Terri's tireless efforts to make a difference in their lives. They were able to see for themselves the progress the twin boys had made when they visited Braintree, Massachusetts, in September 2009. At the time of the twins' visit, Mr. Tye stated to a Boston news reporter: "If you can do something to save a life there is an inner feeling of satisfaction that you can derive from nothing else."

Short, to-the-point concluding paragraph wraps up the profile in a memorable way.

9

CHAPTER 6

Presenting Information

WITH MORE THAN 161 BILLION GIGABYTES OF DIGITAL CONTENT CREATED IN 2007 alone, no one can doubt that we live in the information age. That much information would fill twelve stacks of books stretching all the way from the Earth to the Sun.[1] With all this information at hand, and browsers like Google to help us find it, we can answer one key question about information rather easily: What is known about "x"? with "x" representing almost any topic. However, two other questions matter more when we write to communicate information:

- **What do my readers need or want to know?**

- **How can I help them understand what the information means?**

These questions are so important that no other purpose for writing has so many genres devoted to answering them: maps, brochures, newspaper and magazine articles, dictionaries, encyclopedias, journals for people in specialized areas of study, documentary films, websites, and owner's manuals, among many others. The list is so long and includes every communication medium because modern, open societies depend on access to information. Every context for writing—college, business, community, government, even personal communication—generates enormous amounts of informative writing. Presenting information well, then, is an important skill. As the following example shows, visuals are a key element in presenting information in all media.

---

1. Palfrey, John, and Urs Gasser. *Born Digital: Understanding the First Generation of Digital Natives.* New York: Basic Books, 2008. 185. Print.

Home Page

National Endowment for the Arts[2]

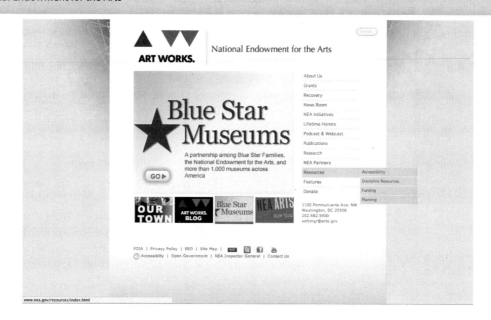

Questions for Discussion

Visit the home page of the National Endowment for the Arts (NEA at www.nea.org.). Examine the links offered on the "About Us" page and consider how they are categorized. How do these categories address reader needs and desires for certain kinds of information? Select a link to find more information. If you were writing on an arts topic, how could you use the NEA's site to help discover both topics and ideas for research?

---

2. Home Page. National Endowment for the Arts. National Endowment for the Arts, n.d. Web. 20 Feb. 2009. <http://www.nea.gov/>.

As the NEA site shows, information has value only in *relation to a reader's needs and desires.* **Presenting information,** then, amounts to *selecting, organizing, and displaying data to make it accessible and useful for readers.*

Sixteenth-century philosopher Sir Francis Bacon said, "Knowledge is power." But knowledge only has power when it is communicated well.

What Is Presenting Information?

Information is **data**, *what we commonly call "the facts," interpreted and organized to make it useful to others.* By interpreting and presenting the information we are exposed to, we construct **knowledge**, *our understanding of any subject.* "Knowledge is power," as the philosopher Francis Bacon said: It enables us to do things we otherwise could not do. For most of history we had no idea that microscopic organisms existed, much less that some cause disease. The science we call microbiology put all the information together and interpreted it, so that now we know this virus or that bacterium causes a particular disease. Because of such knowledge we have gained the power to both prevent and cure many diseases.

The Concept Close-Up shows the relation of data to information and to knowledge.

CONCEPT CLOSE-UP | Assessing Data

Data (the facts) are *statements about a topic that are not in dispute.* From all the facts gathered about a topic, writers select **information,** *data a particular readership needs or wants to know.* **Knowledge** results from *the interpretation the writer gives the information*—what the writer takes it to mean. The following triangle depicts the relation between data, information, and knowledge:

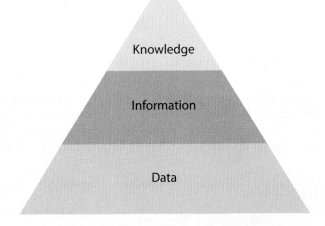

Because data are the base of the triangle, what we assume to be true beyond question, it is especially important to be critical of "the facts." Data must be all of the following:

Accurate	We can be misled by sources who thought they were telling the truth (misinformation); we can be misled by people who knew they were telling lies (disinformation).
Current	Data can be out of date: once true, but false now.

| Sufficient for the need at hand | Data can be too little or too much: If too little, we do not have enough to go on; if too much, we are confused or overwhelmed. |
| Communicated in a way the intended readership can understand | Much technical data is accurate, current, and sufficient but useless to us because we do not understand the words and numbers that express it. ■ |

Why Present Information?

Knowledge is always power—the power to help others, to correct misinformation, to increase our understanding of ourselves and the world.

Communicating information is so important that it dominates writing in all areas of our society. In the academic world, textbooks, handouts, lectures, and course websites are all primarily informative. In the business world, e-mails, memos, reports, performance assessments, and quarterly earnings are primarily informative. In community life, local magazines, community newsletters, signs posted along streets announcing meetings, and most presentations done in schools and other civic gathering places are primarily informative. Indeed, our society moves by and through a sea of information that keeps everything afloat and at the same time threatens to drown us in too much of a good thing. For this reason we all have a high stake in managing information so that it does not overwhelm us. The next question, therefore, is especially important.

How Do Writers Present Information?

The key idea in informative writing is the *reader's need or desire to know something.* We lose sight of this sometimes when we go to a standard reference work, like a dictionary. What we find seems "just there," off by itself in a book without relation to anything else. Yet we would not be checking up on a word if we felt no need to know what it means or how to use it correctly. All information is motivated by need or desire, and therefore, for a writer, *sizing up a reader's need or desire and satisfying it* define the challenge of presenting information.

Consequently, the most common features of informative writing are meant to catch readers' attention and keep them reading. These include:

- **Anecdotes,** *short narratives* that help readers connect with the topic and relate it to their lives.
- **"Up-front" statements that indicate why the information matters** or how readers can profit from knowing it.
- **Headings that indicate where the writer will answer the reader's key questions,** such as why something happens, how the reader can avoid bad consequences or act to make good ones more likely, and so on.
- **Statements that create a realistic context for readers,** such as how to buy or sell something wisely, solve practical problems, or understand a widely discussed issue better.

The simple truth is that we have abundant information and a shortage of reader attention. Informative writers, therefore, compete with each other to gain and hold readers. Remember this and you will understand how to compose effective informative writing.

Beyond reaching readers, what matters most is **genre,** *the specific kind of informative writing you are doing.* We are about to examine two of many informative genres: a magazine article and a newspaper story. As all genres do, each of these conforms to certain **conventional expectations**—that is, *what people expect to find in a specific genre.* As you read the following selections, consider how each meets your expectations for the kind of writing usually found in a magazine article and a news story.

READING 6.1

Procrastinating Again?
How to Kick the Habit

TRISHA GURA

The following magazine article comes from Scientific American Mind, *a good source for interesting topics in the cognitive and social sciences. It deals with a problem almost all people have to some degree: putting off what we know should be done immediately or soon. As you read, consider your own habits and motivations. Are you a procrastinator? If so, what kind?*

Raymond, a high-powered attorney, habitually put off returning important business calls and penning legal briefs, behaviors that seriously threatened his career. Raymond (not his real name) sought help from clinical psychologist William Knaus, who practices in Longmeadow, Mass. As a first step, Knaus gave Raymond a two-page synopsis of procrastination and asked him to read it "and see if the description applied." Raymond agreed to do so on a flight to Europe. Instead he watched a movie. He next vowed to read it the first night at his hotel, but he fell asleep early. After that, each day brought something more compelling to do. In the end, Knaus calculated that the lawyer had spent 40 hours delaying a task that would have taken about two minutes to complete.

> Introduction: Note case example followed by definition in paragraph 2 of the key concept, "procrastination."

Almost everyone occasionally procrastinates, which University of Calgary economist Piers Steel defines as voluntarily delaying an intended course of action despite expecting to be worse off for the delay. But like Raymond, a worrisome 15 to 20 percent of adults, the "mañana procrastinators," routinely put off activities that would be better accomplished ASAP. And according to a 2007 meta-analysis by Steel, procrastination plagues a whopping 80 to 95 percent of college students, whose packed academic schedules and frat-party-style distractions put them at particular risk. . . .

> Calls attention to group especially vulnerable to the problem.

1

2

Built-in Bias

First of four subheadings. Subheads help writers to organize information, readers to follow content.

Procrastination is as old as humans are. For people living in agrarian societies, a late-planted crop could mean starvation. Thus, our ancestors, including Greek poet Hesiod in 800 BCE, equated procrastination with sin or sloth. The industrial revolution may have facilitated the practice of putting off important jobs. Technical advance brings some protection from the forces of storms and famine as well as an increase in leisure time, in consumer goods and in the number of possible *choices* of activities. Contemporary society offers a surfeit of distractions, including computer games, television and electronic messaging—not to mention cars and planes to take us to more stuff to see and do—all enticing us to move off task.

3

Explains source of stigma against procrastinators in evolutionary, survival terms.

Calls attention to the serious consequences of procrastination. Indicates why the information matters.

Succumbing to such enticements can be costly. Experts estimate that 40 percent of people have experienced a financial loss because of procrastination, in some cases severe. In 2002 Americans overpaid $473 million in taxes as a result of rushing and consequent errors. And Americans' dearth of retirement savings can be attributed, in part, to people putting off putting away cash.

4

Divides negative consequences into financial loss (paragraph 4) and impact on health (paragraph 5). Allots one paragraph to each.

Procrastination can also endanger health: after screening more than 19,800 people for high cholesterol, epidemiologist Cynthia Morris and her colleagues at the Oregon Health and Science University reported in 1990 that 35 percent of those who learned they had elevated cholesterol put off consulting a physician for at least five months. In 2006 psychologist Fuschia Sirois of the University of Windsor in Ontario reported in a study of 254 adults that procrastinators had higher stress levels and more acute health problems than did individuals who completed jobs in a timely manner. The procrastinators also received less frequent medical and dental checkups and had more household accidents, a result of putting off dull jobs such as changing smoke detector batteries.

5

Note data cited confirming that procrastination endangers health.

Discusses two causes of procrastination, devoting paragraph 6 to "task aversiveness" and paragraph 7 to "temporal delay."

Task aversiveness is one of the main external triggers for procrastination. Who puts off doing what she loves? According to Steel's meta-analysis, half of the college students surveyed cited the nature of the task itself as the reason they put it off. Undoubtedly, few leap at the chance to write a dissertation about nematode reproduction or clean out the garage. "Procrastination is about not having projects in your life that really reflect your goals," Pychyl says.

6

The amount of time before a project's due date also influences the tendency to procrastinate. In particular, people are more likely to dawdle when the deadline is far away. The reason for this lies in a phenomenon known as temporal delay, which means the closer a person gets to a reward (or a feeling of accomplishment), the more valuable the reward seems and hence the less likely he is to put off performing the work needed to earn it. In other words, immediate gratification is more motivating than are prizes or accolades to be accrued in the distant future.

7

Definition and explanation of "temporal delay," a key concept.

Such a preference may have a strong evolutionary basis. The future, for those in the Stone Age, was unpredictable at best. "Thus, there was truth to the saying 'a bird in the hand is worth two in the bush,'" Pychyl says. "For survival, humans have brains with a procrastination bias built in." . . .

8

Getting Personal

Develops three explanations for why people procrastinate: lack of conscientiousness, impulsiveness, and fear of failure.

At the end of the 20th century, psychologists began studying the so-called big five personality traits that blend to describe any human being: conscientiousness, agreeableness, neuroticism, openness and extroversion. According to Steel, the extent to which a person displays each of these traits helps to determine that individual's proclivity to procrastinate.

The characteristic most strongly linked to procrastination is conscientiousness—or lack thereof. A highly conscientious person is dutiful, organized and industrious. Therefore, someone who is not conscientious has a high probability of procrastinating. A person who is impulsive also is a procrastinator at risk. "People who are impulsive can't shield one intention from another," Pychyl says. So they are easily diverted by temptations—say, the offer of a beer—that crop up in the middle of a project such as writing a term paper.

Procrastination can also stem from anxiety, an offshoot of neuroticism. Procrastinators postpone getting started because of a fear of failure (*I am so worried that I will bungle this assignment*), the fear of ultimately making a mistake (*I need to make sure the outcome will be perfect*), and the fear of success (*If I do well, people will expect more of me all the time. Therefore, I'll put the assignment off until the last minute, do it poorly, and people won't expect so much of me*). . . .

The Psychology of Delay

Develops major motivations for procrastination.

Two key elements in the urge to let projects slide are an uneasy feeling about an activity and a desire to avoid that discomfort. "A procrastinator says, 'I feel lousy about a task,'" Pychyl explains, "and thus walks away to feel better." Psychologist Joseph Ferrari of DePaul University has coined "avoidance procrastinator" to describe a person for whom avoidance is the prime motivator.

Another psychological driver is indecision. An "indecisive procrastinator" cannot make up her mind about executing a task. Say a woman intends to visit her mother in the hospital. Rather than simply grabbing the keys and heading out, the indecisive procrastinator starts debating whether to drive or to take the train. *The train is a hassle, but parking is expensive and I'll have to drive back at rush hour. But then again, the train will be packed, too.* The internal debate continues until enough time passes that visiting hours are over.

A third oft-cited explanation for unreasonable delay is arousal. The "arousal procrastinator" swears that he works best under pressure, loving—perhaps needing—the rush of a last-minute deadline to get started. Such a person believes procrastinating affords a "peak" or "flow" experience, defined by psychologist Mihály Csikszentmihályi of the Drucker School of Management at Claremont Graduate University as being completely involved in an activity for its own sake. Time disappears. The ego dissolves. But procrastination does not facilitate flow, according to social scientist Eunju Lee of Halla University in South Korea. In 2005 Lee reported surveying 262 students and finding that procrastinators tended to have *fewer*, not more, flow experiences. After all, a person must be able to let go of herself to "get lost" in an experience, and procrastinators are generally self-conscious individuals who have trouble doing that.

9

10

11

12

13

14

Nor is the thrill of a looming deadline an actual reason people put off uninviting jobs. Pychyl and his graduate student Kyle Simpson measured traits associated with arousal, including thrill seeking and extroversion, in students who often procrastinated. In Simpson's unpublished doctoral thesis, Pychyl and Simpson show that neither of these qualities accounted for the dawdling the students reported. Thus, procrastinators are probably not really in need of arousal, Pychyl says, but use the belief *I need the pressure of a last-minute deadline* to justify dragging their feet, which they do for other reasons, such as circumventing unpleasantness.

15

Other procrastinators strategically delay projects to excuse poor performance, should it occur. They tell themselves or others, "I could have done better if I had started earlier." Such a strategy might, in some cases, serve as a shield for a fragile ego. . . .

16

Preventing Procrastination

Develops ways to deal with procrastination, a fitting way to end the article.

Steel's meta-analysis suggests that 95 percent of procrastinators would like to break the habit but cannot, because it has become automatic and ingrained. "Habits become nonconscious brain processes," Pychyl says. "When procrastination becomes chronic, a person is, essentially, running on autopilot."

17

Some experts suggest replacing the reflex to postpone with time-stamped prescriptions for action. Psychologist Peter Gollwitzer of New York University and the University of Konstanz in Germany advises creating "implementation intentions," which specify where and when you will perform a specific behavior. So rather than setting a vague goal such as "I will get healthy," set one with its implementation, including timing, built in—say, "I will go to the health club at 7:30 a.m. tomorrow."

18

Setting such specific prescriptions does appear to inhibit the tendency to procrastinate. In 2008 psychologist Shane Owens and his colleagues at Hofstra University demonstrated that procrastinators who formed implementation intentions were nearly eight times as likely to follow through on a commitment than were those who did not create them. "You have to make a specific commitment to a time and place at which to act beforehand," Owens says. "That will make you more likely to follow through."

19

Smart scheduling can also thwart procrastination. In an experiment published in 2002 Duke University behavioral economist Dan Ariely, then at the Massachusetts Institute of Technology, and marketing professor Klaus Wertenbroch of INSEAD, a business school with campuses in France and Singapore, asked students in an executive-education class to set their own deadlines for the three papers due that semester. Ariely and Wertenbroch set penalties for papers turned in after the self-imposed deadlines. Despite the penalties, 70 percent of the students chose deadlines spaced out over the semester, rather than clustering them all at the end. What is more, those who set the early deadlines scored better, on average, than did students in a comparable class in which Ariely set one due date for all three papers at the end of the semester. Such planning can buck any inclination to put off the work. "The deadlines made them better performers," Ariely says.

20

More simply, Pychyl advises procrastinators to "just get started." The anticipation of the task often is far worse than the task turns out to be. To demonstrate this fact, his group, in

21

work that appeared in 2000, gave 45 students pagers and checked in with the volunteers 40 times over five days to query them about their moods and how often they were putting off a task that had a deadline. "We found that when students actually do the task they are avoiding, their perceptions of the task change significantly. Many times, they actually enjoyed it."

In Raymond's case, getting to the task was, indeed, the hard part. Knaus helped him to do that by first determining the reason for his instinct to delay: Raymond feared being tested on the synopsis and looking foolish. So Knaus asked him to pick the lesser of two evils, doing his work—and risking imperfection—or avoiding difficult tasks and losing his job. When Knaus put it that way, the lawyer was able to "just grind it out." Instead of being fired, Raymond became a "superstar" at his firm.

22

Return to Raymond's case ties ending to beginning, concludes with a successful example of overcoming procrastination.

Questions for Discussion

1. Gura blames "technological advances" for some of our problems with procrastination. How big a role does social networking or other time spent online (watching videos, looking up information, playing games) play in your tendency to put off tasks? How big a role does it play in accomplishing such tasks?
2. The reading says that some motives for procrastination are "deep," that is, unconscious, such as fear of failure. It also says that procrastination is often "automatic and ingrained," that is, merely a bad habit. Which view seems more plausible to you?
3. How did Gura attempt to gain your attention at the beginning of her article? If you wanted to keep on reading, what did she say that piqued your interest?

■■ *Thinking as a Writer*

What Is the Rhetorical Situation?

1. What is Gura's *purpose* in writing this essay? What is her *angle* on the topic? How would you describe her *voice*?
2. Who is Gura's intended *audience*? Is she writing for instructors, for college students who procrastinate, for all college students, for lawyers, or for some other more general readership? Is there anything in the article you can cite that implies her target readership?
3. Using the Concept Close-Up: Assessing Data (page 118) as a guide, answer the following questions: What data does Gura draw on? How did the article inform you—that is, what does it say that is news to you? What do you know about procrastination as a result of the information she presented and how she led you to understand it? ■

■■ *Collaborative Activity*

Organizing Headings

As a class or in small groups, analyze the structure of the four subheadings in Gura's article. How does she divide each heading into parts, points, or kinds of information? Does her organization of the headings seem logical to you and easy to follow? Why or why not? ■

■■ *Collaborative Activity*

Integrating Sources

Gura handles source material well by integrating it into her prose; identifying the names and qualifications of her sources; and mixing summary, paraphrasing, and quoting. As a class, work through all or part of her article, studying what she does with each use of source material and listing the various techniques employed. ■

For more on using and documenting sources, see Chapters 19, 20, and 21.

READING 6.2

Major Survey Challenges Western Perceptions of Islam

AGENCE FRANCE-PRESS (AFP)

The following news story comes from AFP, the French equivalent of our AP (Associated Press) or UPI (United Press International), whose purpose is to inform the public about what is happening in the world. As you read, consider how you might use the article if you were preparing to write a paper about Muslim popular opinion.

Feb 26, 2008

WASHINGTON (AFP)—A huge survey of the world's Muslims released Tuesday challenges Western notions that equate Islam with radicalism and violence. 1

The survey, conducted by the Gallup polling agency over six years and three continents, seeks to dispel the belief held by some in the West that Islam itself is the driving force of radicalism. 2

It shows that the overwhelming majority of Muslims condemned the attacks against the United States on September 11, 2001 and other subsequent terrorist attacks, the authors of the study said in Washington.

3

"Samuel Harris said in the *Washington Times* (in 2004): 'It is time we admitted that we are not at war with terrorism. We are at war with Islam,'" Dalia Mogahed, co-author of the book *Who Speaks for Islam,* which grew out of the study, told a news conference here.

4

"The argument Mr. Harris makes is that religion is the primary driver" of radicalism and violence, she said.

5

"Religion is an important part of life for the overwhelming majority of Muslims, and if it were indeed the driver for radicalisation, this would be a serious issue."

6

But the study, which Gallup says surveyed a sample equivalent to 90 percent of the world's Muslims, showed that widespread religiosity "does not translate into widespread support for terrorism," said Mogahed, director of the Gallup Center for Muslim Studies.

7

About 93 percent of the world's 1.3 billion Muslims are moderates and only seven percent are politically radical, according to the poll, based on more than 50,000 interviews.

8

In majority Muslim countries, overwhelming majorities said religion was a very important part of their lives—99 percent in Indonesia, 98 percent in Egypt, 95 percent in Pakistan.

9

But only seven percent of the billion Muslims surveyed—the radicals—condoned the attacks on the United States in 2001, the poll showed.

10

Moderate Muslims interviewed for the poll condemned the 9/11 attacks on New York and Washington because innocent lives were lost and civilians killed.

11

"Some actually cited religious justifications for why they were against 9/11, going as far as to quote from the Koran—for example, the verse that says taking one innocent life is like killing all humanity," she said.

12

Meanwhile, radical Muslims gave political, not religious, reasons for condoning the attacks, the poll showed.

13

The survey shows radicals to be neither more religious than their moderate counterparts, nor products of abject poverty or refugee camps.

14

"The radicals are better educated, have better jobs, and are more hopeful with regard to the future than mainstream Muslims," John Esposito, who co-authored *Who Speaks for Islam,* said.

15

"Ironically, they believe in democracy even more than many of the mainstream moderates do, but they're more cynical about whether they'll ever get it," said Esposito, a professor of Islamic studies at Georgetown University in Washington.

16

Gallup launched the study following 9/11, after which U.S. President George W. Bush asked in a speech, which is quoted in the book: "Why do they hate us?"

17

"They hate . . . a democratically elected government," Bush offered as a reason.

18

"They hate our freedoms—our freedom of religion, our freedom of speech, our freedom to vote and assemble and disagree with each other."

19

But the poll, which gives ordinary Muslims a voice in the global debate that they have been drawn into by 9/11, showed that most Muslims—including radicals—admire the West for its democracy, freedoms and technological prowess.

20

What they do not want is to have Western ways forced on them, it said.

"Muslims want self-determination, but not an American-imposed and -defined democracy. They don't want secularism or theocracy. What the majority wants is democracy with religious values," said Esposito.

The poll has given voice to Islam's silent majority, said Mogahed.

"A billion Muslims should be the ones that we look to, to understand what they believe, rather than a vocal minority," she told AFP.

Muslims in 40 countries in Africa, Asia, Europe and the Middle East were interviewed for the survey, which is part of Gallup's World Poll that aims to interview 95 percent of the world's population.

21
22
23
24
25

Questions for Discussion

1. All informing is motivated by some need or desire to know something. What need or desire does this article satisfy? How does it attempt to catch and hold reader attention?

2. Information often corrects misinformation or disinformation, which in turn leads to misunderstanding. How might this article correct some misunderstanding?

3. Information varies in the degree of importance it has for individual people. How important is the information in this article for you? How could you use it for a paper in a college course?

■■ *Thinking as a Writer*

What Is the Rhetorical Situation?

1. What is the writer's *purpose* in this article? What is the AFP's *angle* on the topic? How would you describe the piece's *voice*?

2. Who is this article's intended *audience*? Is it written for people who are experts about Muslim culture and beliefs, for people who are curious to learn more about Muslims, for people with some degree of bias against them, for Muslims themselves, for politicians, for the French or American reading public, or for some combination of these groups? Is there anything in the article you can cite that implies its target readership?

3. Using the Concept Close-Up: Assessing Data (page 118) as a guide, answer the following question: How does this AFP article turn information into knowledge? Specifically, how does it interpret the data from the survey so that readers understand what it means? ■

The Assignment

Compose an informative article that satisfies a readership's need or desire to know something. Depending on your instructor's requirements, your article can draw from personal experience (for example, a hobby, sport, or internship) and incorporate information gained from all forms of research (for example, print and online materials, interviews, and questionnaires).

How Do I Present Information? Questioning the Rhetorical Situation

Begin by picturing a **rhetorical situation** for your writing project, a real-world context for communicating. You should consider the *key variables in any act of communication*: a writer with something to say, a reader the writer wishes to reach, and a kind of text appropriate to the writing task. These three variables will affect many decisions in the composing process.

Writer: What Is My Purpose, and What Impression Should Readers Have of Me?

Your purpose is to provide accurate, current, and sufficient information to meet the needs and interests of your readers. "Accurate" and "current" simply mean that you should avoid, to the best of your ability, **misinformation,** *data that misrepresents reality or was once accurate but is not so now.* Because misinformation is common, both in print and Internet sources, check the information you find against other sources, especially if the content seems biased, inconsistent with common sense, with what you know already, or otherwise suspect. "Sufficient" is entirely relative to your reader: If you are an experienced stamp collector, for instance, you could easily overwhelm readers just taking up the hobby with too much information or assume that they know things beginners would not know.

See Chapter 17, pages 426–30, for guidance on how to evaluate sources.

Informative writing has a wide range of voices and styles, depending mainly on the topic and the readership. A light touch joined with humor might work well for informing amateur cooks about the amazing array of olive oils currently sold, but a piece for parents about the relative safety of car seats for young children must sound serious and concerned throughout.

An informative writer should be a helpful guide and therefore use **plain style:** *simple, direct sentence structure and ordinary, everyday vocabulary and illustrations.* Include technical information only as required, and be sure to explain what you include at the level your audience can comprehend.

Audience: Who Is My Reader?

The key question in selecting your readership is: **Who would profit most from knowing what I know?**

All good writing is reader aware, but informative writing is especially so because *what qualifies as information depends on who is reading it.* For example,

Understanding your reader is critical to writing an informative article. If, for example, you are writing about the latest video game, an experienced gamer such as these students would probably not also need instructions on how to use an Xbox.

an article describing ways to protect your computer from viruses might be informative for a new computer user but not informative to a technical expert or to someone who does not own a computer.

Select your readership with care, paying special attention to the background knowledge you assume they have. If you assume too little, you will have to provide too much background; if you assume too much, you can have a readership you cannot reasonably expect to inform. An article about the latest computer game, for example, might be written for readers at an intermediate or advanced level of experience but not written for someone without experience or for people who create them and thus know as much or more than you do.

Text: What Would Be an Appropriate Topic?

Promising informative topics can come from readings in any college class, from national and local news, from personal experience, or from online sources. Consider the following possibilities.

- **Personal experience.** Hobbies, sports, physical fitness, diets, gardening, cooking, and the like can be promising topics.
- **Work experience.** Businesses rely on the flow of information, so topics where you work are good possibilities. You may be an expert on something interesting to other people, such as how to get the best deal in purchasing a car.
- **Your community.** Community affairs are also a rich source of informative topics, such as the rules that govern home renovation in certain historical districts or the policies for coping with homeless people.

Consider writing in one of the common informative genres:

- **Book or movie review.** Provides guidance for what to read or see.
- **Technical description.** Explains how something works—for example, hydroponics, growing plants in liquid mediums rather than soil.

- **Cause-and-effect essay.** Explains why things happen, such as the increase in allergies when most other human health problems have declined in the United States.
- **Report.** Summarizes the findings of surveys, tests, field observations, for example, how effective red-light cameras are or how well new software for class registration works.

How Do I Present Information? Engaging the Writing Process

No two people compose in exactly the same way, and even the same person may go through the writing process in different ways with different assignments. Nevertheless, because no one can attend to everything at once, there are phases in handling any significant writing task. You begin by preparing to write, generating content and finding your angle.

The next phase is planning and drafting your paper, getting a version, however rough it may be, on paper or screen so that you have something to work with during the next two stages: (1) revising your draft, making changes to the content, arrangement, and style of your writing, and (2) editing your draft to correct problems at the paragraph and sentence level, such as lack of focus and coherence, awkward or unclear sentences, and errors of grammar, spelling, and punctuation.

If you are assigned to write about a topic you know little about, organizing a "plan of attack" by answering some preparatory questions—such as, "What do I already know?" and "What do I still need to know?"—will help get the process rolling.

BEST PRACTICES | Informative Writing

The basic moves of informative writing are:

- Identify your topic.
- Define and illustrate key terms.
- Supply background information as needed, depending on the level of knowledge you assume your readers have.
- Provide a context for your topic, such as how common procrastination is, misinformation about Muslims, or the costs of some problem in the workplace.
- Indicate why your topic matters—for example, it will help people cope better with procrastination; it will show that the opinions of a minority of Muslims should not be confused with the opinions of most Muslims; it will help people vote as well-informed citizens.
- Limit your topic as necessary to meet space requirements (for instance, discuss the amount of time wasted as a result of some workplace problem).
- Divide your topic into parts, and divide those parts into parts, so that your reader can concentrate on one large point or issue at a time and so that each large point or issue has a set of paragraphs that deal *only* with that issue or point.
- Depending on the nature of your topic, describe *how* it works, *what* motivates it, *how* to use it appropriately or safely, and so on, *going into detail in those places where your reader most needs the information.*

For examples of these strategies at work, consult Readings 6.1 and 6.2 or the revised student example at the end of this chapter. ■

Exploring Your Topic

In this phase you are *finding something to say*, generating ideas and content, which includes discovering your angle or point of view.

Let's assume the most challenging informative writing situation: a "cold" topic, one selected by someone else—a professor, a boss, the head of a committee you are on—and one that requires research because you know little or nothing about it. How do you begin? Organizing your efforts by answering the following questions will help.

Asking Questions: What Does the Task Require?

Some informing situations call for only minimal interpretation. If your assignment is to trace sales patterns over the past ten years for a particular item your company makes, you can do that with charts and graphs combined with short commentary. In contrast, if your assignment is to write about potential power struggles among the various ethnic groups in Afghanistan, you will need to do more than tell your readers about the ethnic groups. You will need to analyze the potential for conflict, cooperation, and alliances, not only as they exist now but also as they are likely to exist in the future. Clearly, in this case, far more interpretation is necessary and appropriate.

However, make *a firm distinction between informing and arguing*. Informative writing typically avoids **open advocacy**—that is, *defending a position on a controversial issue with the intent to convince or persuade your readers*. Because many informative topics are controversial, you may need to describe the range of existing opinion. In interpreting existing opinion, you can say which point of view seems most acceptable to you and explain why. However, defending your opinion or someone else's at length would be inappropriate.

Asking Questions: What Research Will I Need to Do?

We recommend brainstorming your topic first, writing down what you know and think about it in two or three fifteen-minute sessions separated by short breaks. Write whatever comes to mind without being concerned about how good it is. Step back and examine what you have; then ask, **"What do I need to know?"** Make a list in answer to this question, and you are prepared to get the most from research.

ASKING QUESTIONS | Assessing News Stories

When you encounter a news story in doing research, use these questions to help you assess it.

1. **What is the writer's point of view?** Every news story is written by someone who has a point of view, a purpose for writing, and the potential for bias.
2. **Who would find this story worth reading?** Information is told to someone, some audience or readership.

3. **What makes this information newsworthy?** Information is published because it is newsworthy: that is, it is surprising, interesting.
4. All news stories include answers to the prime journalistic questions: **Who? What? When? Where? Why? How?** Answer these questions for the article you are assessing, being careful to distinguish what the writer says from sources cited.
5. **Who and what are mentioned and why?** News stories often mention people, books, organizations, conferences, and the like connected with the story. Use the references to pursue further research. ■

Information comes either from print and online sources or from **field research,** which involves *collecting your own information, such as conducting polls, interviewing experts, making firsthand observations, or carrying out simple experiments.* See Chapter 15, Planning a Research Project, and Chapter 16, Finding Sources, for guidance. Be sure to keep careful notes as you work your way through the source material (see pages 412–424) so you know which information came from what source and so you do not confuse your own comments about the source material with the material itself.

Asking Questions: How Can I Evaluate the Research?

Answering the following questions will be especially useful when evaluating research.

1. **Is the data current?** Remember that a book or article published this year is likely to contain information that is at least two to three years old. Check it against more up-to-date sources of information, such as online data banks.

2. **How was the data generated?** In general we rely on a source's reputation for reliability, credentials, and qualifications. However, some information requires more. The newspaper article about Muslim popular opinion we examined earlier (pages 125–27) does not tell us what questions the 50,000 respondents were asked, what choices they were given in answering the questions, how they were selected, or the time period during which the poll was taken. All of these factors can strongly influence the results, so we cannot rely simply on the good reputation of the Gallup organization. We need to find out more to assure that the results are reliable.

3. **What sources did your source use?** Most published articles cite multiple sources of information. For information you are relying on most, go to the primary source: for example, the reporter who was an eyewitness to the event, the scientist who conducted the experiment, or the expert who recorded the observations. In short, *consult the sources your source cites.*

4. **What interpretations are consistent with the data?** The first three questions focus attention on assessing your information; this question asks you to assess your own response to it. No one can do research without forming conclusions about what the information means. Forming conclusions helps you interpret the information that matters most in informing your reader. However, *let the best information you have drive your interpreta-*

tion rather than imposing an interpretation you had before researching the information. Put another way, adjust your thinking to the information rather than the information to your thinking.

▨▦■ ACTIVITY 6.1 *Writer's Notebook*

Evaluating Sources

First, use the guidelines for evaluating sources (Chapter 17, pages 426–30) to assess your sources. Some might be too old, not directly relevant, or suspect because the writer may be biased by affiliation with a special interest group.

Second, sort the sources that are left into two groups by relevance and quality:

- The two or three you will rely on the most.
- The two or three you will probably use less, such as for only one section or paragraph in your paper.

As you assess your sources, be sure to preserve your thinking in notes to yourself. You may need to refresh your memory as you write and revise. ■

Preparing to Write

In evaluating your sources, you are already sorting out information you might use from all the information you have.

Asking Questions: How Can I Decide Which Information to Include?

Consider the following questions:

1. **What do my readers know already?** You can either not mention such information or briefly refer to it to remind your readers.

2. **What do my readers need to know?** This is the key question. For most topics you can find much more general information than you can possibly include. However, what counts is only (1) what will be news to your readers, information they do not have, and (2) selecting from that news what is most relevant to how your readers will use the information. In a student essay about illegal immigration (available online), for example, the writer selected information she considered most relevant to voters in the general election of 2008. That is, she asked herself, "Of everything I know about illegal immigration, what do well-informed voters need to know?" Ask yourself a similar question in deciding what information to include on any topic.

Asking Questions: How Can I Find My Angle?

1. **What impact do you want your information to have?** In informative writing, what even qualifies as information depends on your readers. It makes sense, then, that your angle will also be reader centered. The student example

(pages 140–46) provides a good illustration of angle. The student wanted to impress upon her readers that not treating people kindly at work is not just a social or personnel problem, but a big financial problem.

2. **In what framework is my information best understood?** In the case of illegal immigration, economics provided the best angle because supply-and-demand drives the entire process. There are usually jobs on our side of the border, well-paid jobs from a migrant worker's point of view, and grinding poverty and lack of opportunity on Mexico's side. Readers must understand the economics of illegal immigration to understand the topic at all. Hence, the student's choice of economics as her framework was ideal for her topic.

Drafting Your Paper

Begin by recalling what informative writing does: *It makes information relevant or interesting for readers; turns facts into something that matters, has meaning, a point.* What this means in practice is that selection depends on giving your readers "news"—things they do not know—and getting them to understand why the new information matters.

Select from all your information *what counts or is significant*: the results of the latest research, data your readers will not know, information that is surprising and/or that runs counter to what most people believe or imagine. Also select information *based on the story you can tell about it*—that is, in how it comes together to make a point, illuminate a problem, clarify a cause or effect.

Thinking as a Writer: What Stance and Voice Are Appropriate for Presenting Information?

It is important to inform your readers, to provide facts or data they do not know or may have forgotten. Even more important, however, is interpreting the information you provide. *What you have to say about the information should be center stage.*

Consequently, reconsider your **stance** and angle, your point of view on your topic. For example, which of the following are you doing?

- Challenging beliefs and attitudes based on misinformation or disinformation?
- Enabling your readers to do something they otherwise could not do or not do as well?
- Explaining a cause-and-effect relationship?
- Describing a problem and ways to solve it?
- Giving advice based on experience with your topic?

There are many other possibilities—*what matters is that you know what you are doing and why.* Perhaps you will change your angle as you write; perhaps in assessing your draft you will find another angle you like better and write the second draft around it. Nevertheless, being as clear as you can about what motivates the information you are providing helps to focus and sustain your first draft.

Also consider what **voice** is appropriate for this aim and genre. Information requires your take on what the information means and why it matters, and therefore your voice will emerge mainly in your commentary. Trisha Gura's voice (see pages 120–24) emerges best in *commenting on her information*, as, for example, in the following sentences:

> But like Raymond, a <u>worrisome</u> 15 to 20 percent of adults, the "mañana procrastinators," routinely put off activities that would be better accomplished <u>ASAP</u>. And according to a 2007 meta-analysis by Steel, procrastination <u>plagues</u> a <u>whopping</u> 80 to 95 percent of college students, whose <u>packed</u> academic schedules and <u>frat-party-style distractions</u> put them at particular risk. . . .

The underlined words convey her attitude toward procrastination, the seriousness of the problem, the urgent need to understand and attend to it.

Thinking as a Writer: How Might I Use Images and Graphics to Present Information?

When appropriate, plan to use photographs, drawings, maps, tables, and graphics for presenting readers with new information. Use graphics when you can because they:

- Take less space than giving information in prose.
- Are easier for readers to understand, remember, and refer to.
- Separate data from your commentary on what the data means.

Here's the basic principle in deciding whether to use graphics: *Use graphics to present information; use writing to tell your story about the information.*

Thinking as a Writer: Developing and Organizing Your Information

Develop an informative article effectively by doing the following:

Images and graphics are an effective way to present information because they are easy for readers to understand and they add visual interest.

See online Chapter 24 for detailed guidance on the design and use of visuals.

- Pull together closely related material from several sources.
- Offer your own comments—explanations, illustrations, and ways of understanding the source material.

Consider this example from Gura's article:

> A third oft-cited explanation for unreasonable delay is arousal. The "arousal procrastinator" swears that he works best under pressure, loving—perhaps needing—the rush of a last-minute deadline to get started. Such a person believes

Passage pulls together information from two sources; also defines "arousal procrastinator" and adds comments to explain "flow experience"—"Time disappears. The ego dissolves."

procrastinating affords a "peak" or "flow" experience, defined by psychologist Mihály Csíkszentmihályi of the Drucker School of Management at Claremont Graduate University as being completely involved in an activity for its own sake. Time disappears. The ego dissolves. But procrastination does not facilitate flow, according to social scientist Eunju Lee of Halla University in South Korea. In 2005 Lee reported surveying 262 students and finding that procrastinators tended to have *fewer*, not more, flow experiences. After all, a person must be able to let go of herself to "get lost" in an experience, and procrastinators are generally self-conscious individuals who have trouble doing that.

Organizing information boils down to *answering reader questions in a sequence that makes sense.* The answer to one question implies another question, the answer to which implies yet another question, until you run out of questions that need answering to adequately inform your audience. In "Procrastinating Again? How to Kick the Habit" (pages 120–24), Gura answers the following questions:

- What is procrastination? (paragraphs 1–2)
- What harm does it do? (paragraphs 3–5)
- Why do people procrastinate? (paragraphs 6–7)
- What personality traits contribute to it? (paragraphs 9–11)

Start to finish, she is answering questions. Furthermore, she is answering them *in a logical sequence.* She tells us that, distinct from other kinds of delay, procrastination is: "delaying an intended course of action despite . . . [being] worse off. . . ." If procrastination causes harm, her next question follows: What harm does it do? If it causes such significant harm, we want to know, why, then, do people do it?

This simple notion—*answers to implied questions linked together to form a sequence*—is the key to organization in informing and can keep you on track as you are writing the first draft.

■■■■ ACTIVITY 6.2 *In Your Own Work*

Planning Your Draft

You have the information selected from the research you did for your topic. You know the readers you want to reach. Now imagine a conversation with your readers. Given your topic, what questions would they ask? List those questions as they occur to you. Look also at the information you have selected. What questions do they answer? List those as well.

Looking at your list of questions, ask, **"What question comes first?"** Often it will be the definitional question, **"What is it?"** Sometimes the first question is, **"Why does my topic matter?"** Or, **"What background knowledge does my reader need to understand or appreciate the importance of my topic?"**

Whatever you decide the first question must be, it will imply the next, which in turn will imply still another. Order your questions accordingly, and you have a plan for your draft. ■

Revising Your Draft

When you complete your draft, do a self-assessment. The revision questions listed in Asking Questions will help.

ASKING QUESTIONS | Revision Checklist for Presenting Information

1. Early in the paper **have you indicated why your information is important**? How does it relate to your reader's life, crucial decisions, or topics she or he would find interesting?
2. Facts or data amount to misinformation if they are not reported accurately. **Are there any instances where the facts or data you report seem unlikely or contradictory?** Check what you say the facts are against your source.
3. Currency matters because information becomes misinformation if the data is seriously out of date. **Are there any instances where data cited might be too old?**
4. Information must be sufficient for the need at hand, which means there must be enough to satisfy your readers. **Are there places where you need more than you provide? Are there places where you offer too much,** which might confuse or bore your readers?
5. Information does no good if your readers cannot understand it. **Have you explained what the information means *at the level appropriate to your readership?***
6. Informative writers need to be consistent in their assumptions about what their readers know and think about the topic. **Have you assumed too much or too little about what your readers know before reading your paper?** Have you addressed misconceptions and unwarranted positive or negative attitudes they are likely to have?
7. **Have you adopted an angle, a single point of view, to help your readers follow your presentation?** Have you limited your discussion only to matters relevant to your angle?
8. **Have you organized your information into sections—major divisions of your topic—and structured each section to develop content relevant to that section only?** Would using headings, as Trisha Gura does (pages 120–24), help both you and your reader understand your paper's organization better?
9. **In reporting your data, have you mixed quotation, paraphrase, and summary? Have you identified the qualifications of your source?**

10. **Are there places where the information could be handled more efficiently by using visuals, such as photographs, drawings, and/or graphics?** If you have used graphics or plan to add them in revision, be sure to refer to each graphic and discuss what it means in your paper. ■

Excerpt from Amie Hazama's Draft

When writers use subheadings to identify the purpose of different sections of their papers, they still need to attend to the need for transitions as well, to show how each subdivision connects with the one before. Here is an example from the draft of the student paper printed in final form on pages 140–46.

Introduction

A typical day at the office begins for Amanda. Walking to her cubicle, she passes Joe, who seems in a hurry and returns her "Good morning" with just a nod. Later, in a meeting, a phone goes off, distracting everyone. The owner shuts it off but does not offer an apology. On her lunch break, Amanda fills the empty coffee pot in the kitchen and throws out the empty sugar packages lying crumpled on the counter. After lunch, her boss asks her to make some copies, but first she has to spend extra time fixing the jammed photocopier. Back at her desk, she tries to concentrate on a project while two co-workers talk loudly in the next cubicle about a basketball game the night before. Finally, after a long day at work, Amanda is fatigued and stressed.

What Is Workplace Incivility?

Workplace incivility is the subject of much research. Christine Pearson and Christine Porath (2005) define the problem as "low intensity deviant behavior that violates workplace norms for mutual respect and may or may not be intended to harm the target" (p. 8). It is called "low intensity" because it is subtle, often unconscious, and frequently not even recognized by managers and workers. Examples of uncivil behavior range from sending a nasty, demeaning note and publicly undermining an employee's credibility to not returning phone calls and failing to acknowledge others in the hall. More extreme examples include bullying by bosses (Hauser, 2011).

The problem is the writing's **flow,** its *movement from paragraph to paragraph.* In her revised version, she opened the second section with a short transitional paragraph.

What Is Workplace Incivility?

Little acts of insensitivity like those described above are just part of the job for many employees. However, they are also part of a problem that is costing businesses in lost productivity and workers in lost job satisfaction.

Editing Your Revised Draft

A rule of thumb is that no more than 10% of the total words in your paper should be direct quotations. (See Chapter 18 pages 440–43 for more about when and when not to use direct quotations.) The solution is to use paraphrase, but when the source contains simple data, rewording it adequately takes some effort. In the original passage below, Hazama's wording is too close to that of the source.

Original Version of the Draft

In her book *Rude Awakenings,* Gonthier (2002), researchers found that as a result of workplace incivility 22% <u>decreased work efforts</u>, 10% <u>decreased the amount of time spent at work</u>, 37% <u>reduced their commitment to the organization</u>, and 12% quit companies to avoid rude instigators (p. 26).

The actual source wording was: "The researchers found that as a result of uncivil behavior at work:

- 22 percent of respondents intentionally decreased work efforts,
- 10 percent decreased the amount of time they spent at work (absenteeism),
- 28 percent lost time avoiding instigators, . . .
- 37 percent reduced their commitment to the organization, . . . and
- 12 percent actually quit companies to avoid rude instigators."

In the edited version Hazama made the wording more her own.

Edited Version

In her book *Rude Awakenings,* Gonthier (2002) reports that 22% of the victims of incivility decreased their work efforts, 10% increased their absenteeism, 37% felt less commitment to their employer, and 12% went so far as to quit their jobs to get away from the offenders (p. 26).

■■■ ACTIVITY 6.3 *In Your Own Work*

Editing for Adequate Paraphrasing

When editing, pay special attention to the passages of information you have taken from sources. You may need to do more rewording to avoid accidental plagiarism, which is just as serious as intentional plagiarism. You may want to recast some of the material into charts or other visuals, not only to avoid a poor paraphrase but also to present the information more vividly. ■

Being Nice Is GOOD Business

Amie Hazama

ENGL 1302, Section 002

Professor Channell

March 23, 2011

Being Nice Is Good Business

Hazama decided to use an anecdotal introduction just as Trisha Gura did in her article on procrastination. After reading through this paper, consider what other options would have made an equally effective opening to draw in readers.

A typical day at the office begins for Amanda. Walking to her cubicle, she passes Joe, who seems in a hurry and returns her "Good morning" with just a nod. Later, in a meeting, a phone goes off, distracting everyone. The owner shuts it off but does not offer an apology. On her lunch break, Amanda fills the empty coffee pot in the kitchen and throws out the empty sugar packages lying crumpled on the counter. After lunch, her boss asks her to make some copies, but first she has to spend extra time fixing the jammed photocopier. Back at her desk, she tries to concentrate on a project while two co-workers talk loudly in the next cubicle about a basketball game the night before. Finally, after a long day at work, Amanda is fatigued and stressed.

1

Hazama's angle is to show the wearing effects of incremental exposure to small acts of incivility. She wants to make readers care about the victims.

What Is Workplace Incivility?

Hazama uses questions as subheadings to let the reader know what they will learn in each section of the paper.

Little acts of insensitivity like those described above are just part of the job for many employees. However, they are also part of a problem that is costing businesses in lost productivity and workers in lost job satisfaction.

2

Workplace incivility is the subject of much research. Christine Pearson and Christine Porath (2005) define the problem as "low-intensity deviant behavior that violates workplace norms for mutual respect and may or may not be intended to harm the target" (p. 8). It is called "low-intensity" because it is subtle, often unconscious, and frequently not even recognized by managers and workers. Examples of uncivil behavior range from sending a nasty, demeaning note and publicly undermining an employee's credibility to not returning phone calls and failing to acknowledge others in the hall. More extreme examples include bullying by bosses (Hauser, 2011).

3

This paper is documented according to APA (American Psychological Association) style, which is commonly used in the social sciences. See pages 508-15 for a full treatment of APA style.

Hazama uses the comparison mode of development to define the concept of incivility.

Incivility is the opposite of civility, which is being aware of and respecting others. P.M. Forni is a civility expert and Professor of Italian Literature at Johns Hopkins University. In his book *Choosing Civility,* Forni states, "Courtesy, politeness, manners, and civility are all, in essence, forms of awareness. Being civil means being constantly aware of others and weaving restraint and consideration into the very fabric of this awareness" (Forni, 2002,

4

p. 9). Forni's "Three R's" of civility are "respect, restraint, and responsibility" (as cited in Hauser, 2011). Saying a simple "please" and "thank you," putting trash in the proper receptacles, and signaling before making a right hand turn are examples of civility (Forni, 2002, p. 9). Civility is everywhere in daily life. Unfortunately, so is incivility.

What Are the Causes of Workplace Incivility?

Incivility has become common in the workplace. Pearson and Porath (2005, p. 7) surveyed close to 800 U.S. employees to find out about their personal observations of incivility while at work. Ten percent said they witnessed it on a daily basis, and twice that number, twenty percent, said they themselves were victims of it "at least once per week." Experts give several reasons for the increase. Oddly, one cause suggested by Giovinella Gonthier (2002), a civility consultant in Chicago, is the rise of equality in the workplace, caused by the feminist and civil rights movements of the 1960s. In the past, people who were superiors showed their high positions through manners and other "rituals of behavior" (p. 8), but in a more democratic society, we have dropped the manners that used to "prop up" unequal relationships (p. 9). In that same period, young people disillusioned by government and the Vietnam War "lost respect for tradition," and this generation went on to raise their children permissively. Everything just became more casual (Gonthier, 2002, pp. 4–5).

Pearson and Porath (2005) bring in a more recent cause: In our high-tech, fast-paced workplaces, people believe being nice takes too much time and "impersonal modes of contact do not require courtesies of interaction . . ." (p. 7). Also, there is the "me first" attitude common in the competitive workplace (p. 7) and the Gordon Gekko types, with the "impetuous, rude, 'everyone else be damned' personality" that many people associate with success ever since the movie *Wall Street* (Gonthier, 2002, p. 3).

What Are the Ramifications of Incivility at Work?

All of this incivility is costly to businesses. Porath estimates that "stress and lost productivity" as a result of incivility costs the United States' total economy multi-billion

5

6

7

As a transition into the causes of incivility, Hazama sets up a context for learning more about incivility— its prevalence in the workplace today.

Hazama now turns from the causes of the problem in business to the effects on business.

dollars each year (as cited in Hauser, 2011). Pearson and Porath (2005) have found that "incivility corrodes organizational culture and that employees who are on the receiving end will respond in ways that are costly to their organizations" (p. 8). For example, two thirds of the victims of incivility reported that they put less effort into their work, four out of five said they lost time worrying about bad experiences, and 63% said they went out of their way to avoid being around the person who offended them (Hauser, 2011). In her book *Rude Awakenings,* Gonthier (2002) reports that 22% of the victims of incivility decreased their work efforts, 10% increased their absenteeism, 37% felt less commitment to their employer, and 12% went so far as to quit their jobs to get away from the offenders (p. 26). Incivility and disengagement go hand in hand, and they result in a very high level of people who are not actively engaged with their jobs. A Gallup study (2006) found that only 27% of workers reported feeling "engaged" while at work, while 59% described themselves as "not engaged." Still another 14% were "actively disengaged," which means they purposefully undermined the efforts of their co-workers.

There are additional costs to management. Resolving worker conflicts can take up 13% of executives' time, almost seven weeks of the year for any one boss (Pearson & Porath, 2005, p. 8). Replacing workers who leave can cost as much as 2.5 times the annual salary of the job if it is a high-profile job and interviewees have to be flown in and paid to move (Gonthier, 2002, p. 27). Replacing lost customers is another concern because sales will decline if disgruntled workers are in customer service positions and take out their frustrations on the customers, a common occurrence. Forni (2002) states, "A stressed, fatigued, or distressed person is less inclined to be patient and tolerant, to think before acting, and to be aware of the needs of others" (p. 139). Gonthier (2002) reports that 58 to 62% of customers will change to a different company if employees treat them rudely (pp. 30–31).

What Can Be Done to Reduce Workplace Incivility?

In order to accomplish civility in the work place, leaders must lead the way. Robert D. Ramsey (2008), who works in personnel administration and writes for management

8

Note that Hazama has done a good job of synthesizing sources. This paragraph blends information from her three major sources.

A logical question to end this discussion is, "What can be done to solve the problem?"

9

publications, says supervisors have the ability to do the most to turn around a bad working atmosphere (p. 4) and "create a culture of civility at work"(p. 5). Ramsey has devised a six-step action plan. First, managers must act as role models; they must represent civility in all their actions. Forni agrees, saying, "The attitude of the leader . . . has an enormous impact on the overall climate" of the workplace (as cited in Hauser, 2011). Programs like CREW (Civility, Respect, and Engagement in the Workplace) have shown that when leaders set the example, civility has a way of going viral, "infecting" other workers to act in equally courteous ways (Hauser, 2011).

Secondly, Ramsey (2008) says business relationships should become more personal,   10
encouraging considerate and respectful behavior. A worker is more likely to act in a rude fashion through an impersonal encounter through the telephone or e-mail. Some businesses will not allow e-mails between workers who have offices on the same floor (p. 5). Next, issues between workers must be addressed. A leader needs to actively mediate disputes and remind workers of expectations and boundaries for behavior. Pearson and Porath (2005) echo this advice. They tell leaders, "When incivility occurs, hammer it" (p. 14). Ramsey's fourth step is about consequences. An authority figure must make policies and rules that delineate the proper conduct on the job, and carry through with the consequences when workers violate them. Ramsey says it is amazing how quickly people become more civil when their raise or promotion depends on it (p. 5). Fifth, business leaders can offer training programs, civility courses, and workshops on ethics, respect, responsibility, awareness, and etiquette. An example is the CREW program mentioned earlier and created for the Veterans Health Administration. Workers from all over the country fly to Cincinnati for three-day training sessions (Hauser, 2011). Ramsey's last step addresses how to develop trust among workers. Leaders should devise exercises that involve teamwork, even if they seem "childish," like "having an employee fall backwards into the arms of co-worker, counting on the other party to catch him safely" (p. 6).

Through their individual actions, employees can also maintain civility in their   11
workplace. As Forni states, "Corporate responsibility does not erase individual responsibility" (Forni, 2002, p. 140). The little things add up to make either a bad day, like Amanda's, or a

good one. Gonthier (2002) says, "Always say hello or good morning or good afternoon as you encounter co-workers on your rounds. And, of course, respond in kind if they initiate the exchange" (p. 110). A simple greeting shows a concern for their well-being. Also, compliments for a job well done will influence others to continue to work hard.

Listening properly will result in better teamwork and acceptance of each other's ideas. 12 Being a cooperative listener includes responding in the right manner with questions and body language. A listener must show that he or she is listening by making eye contact, saying remarks to show engagement and repeating the speaker's thoughts to show comprehension (Forni, 2002, p. 52).

Other people's space must also be respected in a working environment. In order to 13 maintain privacy, workers should keep noise levels down and distractions to a minimum (Forni, 2002, p. 102). Many tensions in the workplace arise from common facilities and resources. Resources at work are shared with all of the workers; therefore, if a worker creates a mess, he or she must clean it immediately so others do not have to clean up after them. Anyone who uses an appliance must make sure that he or she has left it in working condition (Gonthier, 2002, 125). If each worker takes responsibility for his or her actions, everything runs more smoothly and people are not tired and irritated by the end of the day.

Conclusion

Everyone benefits from a civil workplace. Joan Wrangler, an executive coach working 14 at NASA's Goddard Space Flight Center, created a personal relations program there. She has discovered the huge difference that civility makes in productivity and creativity: "Civility is part of the foundation for bringing out people's brilliance. If you want to touch people's smartness and bring out their brilliance, then you need to be able to create a space where people feel safe enough to speak, to listen to one another, to be heard, to offer support, to coach one another" (as cited in Hauser, 2011). That sounds like the kind of place everyone would like to work.

This quotation sums up the civil workplace and points to its outstanding quality from the standpoint of both the employer and the employee: Every boss wants brilliant workers and every worker wants a chance to shine.

References

Forni, P. M. (2002). *Choosing civility: The twenty-five rules of considerate conduct.* New York, NY:
St. Martin's Press.

Gallup study: Feeling good matters in the workplace. (2006, January 12). *Gallup Management Journal.* Retrieved from http://gmj.gallup.com/content/20770 /Gallup-Study-Feeling-Good-Matters-in-the.aspx

Gonthier, G. (2002). *Rude awakenings: Overcoming the civility crisis in the workplace.* Chicago, IL: Dearborn Trade Publishing.

Hauser, S. (2011). The degeneration of decorum: Stress caused by rude behavior in the workplace might be costing the U. S. economy billions of dollars a year. *Workforce Management, 90.1,* 16. Retrieved from http://find.galegroup.com.proxy .libraries.smu.edu/gtx/start.do?prodId=AONE&userGroupName=txshracd2548

Pearson, C., & Porath, C. (2005). On the nature, consequences and remedies of workplace incivility: No time for "nice"? Think again. *Academy of Management Executive, 19.1,* 7–18. Retrieved from http://www.realmarcom.com/documents/conflict/pearson _incivility.pdf

Ramsey, R. (2008). The case for civility in the workplace. *Supervision, 69.12,* 3–6. Retrieved from http://find.galegroup.com.proxy.libraries.smu.edu/gtx/start.do?prodId =AONE&userGroupName=txshracd2548

CHAPTER 7
Exploring a Concept

IN THE FIRST CHAPTER, WE INTRODUCED A KEY QUESTION FOR CRITICAL THINKing: What does that word mean? It is an especially valuable question because the meaning of many words is open to question. For example, when someone claims that the Internet is the most *democratic* communication technology ever developed, what does the person mean by "democratic"? Is the Internet any more democratic than, say, television? If so, in what ways? Question what the word *democratic* means and you begin thinking critically about a statement that usually passes as uncontroversial.

This chapter is about how to explore the meaning of words. We are most interested in exploring words that name concepts like "democracy"—words that we use in talking about ideas that are important to us. We use these words so often and in so many different contexts that we might wonder if they mean anything at all. Consequently, writers who use words responsibly often elaborate on their meaning, or they may write simply to explore the meaning of a concept.

Following is a brief example of concept exploration at work in a newspaper opinion piece. In this excerpt, the author explores what the word "empathy" means.

MICRO-EXAMPLE   **Concept Exploration**

The Disconnect of the Connected
Keith O'Brien

The background or history of a concept is often used in exploring the meaning of a concept.

Note the different meanings "empathy" has for people who study it. Explains *why* the author is exploring the concept, which is important to establish in any concept exploration.

Empathy is such a basic ingredient of the human experience that even babies exhibit it, crying when other children cry or reacting to the facial expressions of adults and parents. Yet the word is relatively new: It didn't enter the English lexicon until the early 1900s, derived from the German word *einfühlung,* according to Daniel Batson, a researcher of empathy and professor emeritus at the University of Kansas. 1

Psychologists studying empathy disagree on some basic questions about how it should be defined: Is it feeling for others? Feeling as others feel? Understanding how others feel? Or some combination of the above? 2

States the problem that motivates exploration: An important concept with many possible meanings.

Effort at a "core" or basic meaning for "empathy" developed by citing an authority, Aaron Pincus. Establishing "core" meanings is an important move in exploring concepts—otherwise we are left with only all the different meanings.

"It's all over the place," Batson said. "There's no agreed-upon definition." 3

But at the most basic level, most concur that empathy is some sort of emotional 4 response to another person's plight, pain, state or suffering. "It's not just putting oneself in another's shoes," said Aaron L. Pincus, a professor of psychology at Penn State University. "It's truly grasping what they're experiencing. . . . Your emotional state will move in a direction more similar to the person you're empathizing with."

In small ways, psychologists say, empathy is constantly driving our daily lives, as we 5 take into consideration how other people might feel before we act. Some suggest that empathy is the foundation for social norms, even basic etiquette. We typically don't insult people to their faces, Davis explained, in part because we know they're not going to like how that feels.

Establishes the significance of the concept of empathy, why we should care about what the concept means and use it more precisely—also a key move in concept exploration.

Question for Discussion

Sometimes "empathy" is contrasted with "sympathy." What does "sympathy" mean to you? Does the concept exploration above preserve the distinction between empathy and sympathy? If so, how? If not, do you think the distinction is worth holding on to?

■■■■ ACTIVITY 7.1 *Collaborative Activity*

Thinking about the Core Meaning of Concepts

The **core meaning** of a concept refers to *what most people think of when the concept is mentioned*. It is therefore important in exploring concepts. The following graph depicts the results of a survey of Americans, who were asked this question: "As I read you a list of different arrangements, please tell me whether you consider each to be a family or not."[1]

In small group or class discussion, consider the following questions:

1.   What do these results tell us about the core meaning of "family" among Americans? How would you describe the core meaning as implied by these survey results?

---

1. Pew Research Center. "The Decline of Marriage and Rise of New Families." *PewResearchCenter.* Pew Research Center, 18 Nov. 2010. Web. 1 Sep. 2011. <http://pewresearch.org/pubs/1802/decline -marriage-rise-new-families>.

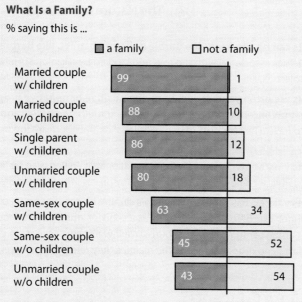

What Is a Family?

% saying this is ...

■ a family   □ not a family

	a family	not a family
Married couple w/ children	99	1
Married couple w/o children	88	10
Single parent w/ children	86	12
Unmarried couple w/ children	80	18
Same-sex couple w/ children	63	34
Same-sex couple w/o children	45	52
Unmarried couple w/o children	43	54

Note: "Don't know/Refused" responses are not shown.

Source: Pew Research Center

2. How would you answer the question for each arrangement? Explain why you think each arrangement is or is not a family. What do your choices reveal about the core meaning of "family" for you?

3. The extended family, where two or more generations of people live together in the same residence, was once common in the United States and still is among some groups. Where would you locate the concept "extended family" in your notion of the core meaning of "family"?

4. Increasingly Americans are living in what might be called "improvised families," close associations of friends and relations who may not all live together but form close-knit groups. Do you consider such an arrangement part of the concept "family"? Why or why not? ■

What Is Concept Exploration?

A **concept** is *a category, a way of grouping objects, attitudes, beliefs, and behavior that we consider related.* Cars, trucks, SUVs, and golf carts are all grouped as "vehicles." **Concept exploration** *examines concepts in an effort to understand what they mean and how they are used,* often with some practical question in mind. Should flag-burning count as "free speech"? The Supreme Court has ruled that it does, but many Americans believe that burning a flag is not speech and amounts to an unpatriotic act that should not enjoy constitutional protection.

CONCEPT CLOSE-UP | The Nature of Concepts

- **Concepts can be concrete, like Barbie dolls, or abstract, like Barbie culture,** a set of values associated with the toys and studied by sociologists interested in gender roles.

- **Concepts are often value laden, implying positive or negative judgments.** For instance, the concept of "empathy" designates something positive and good for people to have. The concepts of being "callous" or "uncaring" are the opposite of empathy and therefore negative.

- **Concepts vary across cultures.** What is "fashionable" in Paris can be "immoral" in certain Islamic societies and just "odd" in many places in the United States.

- **Concepts vary across time.** As a society's circumstances change, its concepts also change. "Exurb," for example, arose as a concept when people moved farther out from urban centers, beyond suburbs. We invent new concepts to characterize new realities and drop old ones as the realities they refer to cease to exist. ■

Why Explore Concepts?

Concepts can vary across cultures. What may be considered "fashionable" in one country may be considered odd or immoral in others.

We *define* concepts like "quark" to explain what they mean for readers unfamiliar with the terms, but we seldom explore scientific or technical concepts because of their precise, limited meaning. We *explore* abstract concepts like "democracy" and "empathy" because their meanings are not so precise and limited. Understanding them better matters because such words belong to our value systems and influence our behavior. For example, Mike Rose, now a distinguished professor of English, explains in his book *Lives on the Boundary* that he almost flunked out of college his freshman year. Influenced by the concept "individualism," he refused to seek help when he could not understand the assigned books. Similarly, Jamie Cummins, who explores "gender" at the end of the chapter, does so to determine whether we might be "trapped . . . by our ideas of appropriate behavior for men and women."

Concept exploration appears in newspaper stories and editorials, in scientific and philosophical books and articles, online in blogs, and in many other **genres,** or *kinds of writing.* It also appears in every context for writing. In a workplace setting we might need to assess how "democratic" the Internet is; in personal writing, we might explore what being a "friend" to someone ought to mean; and in academic writing, defining the word "novel" might be crucial to an essay exam.

How Do Writers Explore a Concept?

What should we ask when we want to think seriously about the meanings of a concept and its applications to life? Following are some basic questions that stimulate thinking about exploring concepts.

1. **What are the dictionary definitions of the concept?** Have definitions changed over time? Have the word's emotional associations changed, especially in a negative or positive direction? Four centuries ago, for example, "innovation" was a negative word, implying the work of a troublemaker, whereas now the word glows with all that is good and desirable.

2. **What are the root meanings of the word?** "Democracy," for example, comes from two Greek words meaning "people rule." It is not surprising, then, that "democratic" now means for many Americans much the same thing as "popular."

3. **In what contexts do people use the concept?** In one situation, "fairness" means that everyone gets an equal share of something—as even young children know when a treat is being distributed. In another situation, "fairness" means *unequal distribution,* as when one person or one group has contributed more than another to a successful enterprise and therefore deserves a greater share of the reward.

4. **Is conflict or disagreement at hand when the concept is used?** "Freedom" often runs headlong into "social responsibility." Smoking in enclosed public spaces was once common in the United States; now it is rarely permitted.

5. **What is the practical impact of the concept?** "Subprime mortgages" and financial contracts called "derivatives" so damaged the American and global economy that the investor Warren Buffett called them "weapons of mass destruction." Many people do not understand that file-sharing of copyrighted materials is "theft" in the same sense, as, for example, stealing someone's car.

6. **What company does this concept keep, and what distinctions are there among related ideas?** "Marriage," for example, connects with many other concepts, such as "soul mate," "monogamy," the "union of a man and a woman," "reproduction," and so on. Increasingly the connected concepts are being separated from the institution as the institution itself changes.

7. **What have other writers said about the concept?** About "justice," for example, a Supreme Court justice famously said, "Justice too long delayed is justice denied." What is the relation of "justice" to "timeliness"?

8. **What confusions or uncertainties surround the use of the concept?** For example, the concept of "preemptive war" is used to justify a surprise attack on an enemy who is about to attack you. Can we distinguish between "preemptive war" as self-defense and the use of the concept to disguise a motive like expanding a country's territory by attacking a weak neighbor?

Operation Seduction[2]

ELAINE SCIOLINO

HAND GESTURE — As Jacques Chirac demonstrated to Laura Bush in 2003, a kiss is never just a kiss. *Philippe Wojazer/Reuters*

Foreign languages provide a rich source for concept explorations. The following reading by Elaine Sciolino, a prominent writer for The New York Times, *investigates the concept of "seduction" in France, a concept far more complex and interesting in French culture than in English culture. As you read, note how Sciolino draws on her experience with French culture to provide a context for exploring the various meanings of seduction.*

It is not enough to conquer; one must also know how to seduce.
                              —Voltaire, "Mérope"

The first time my hand was kissed *à la française* was in the Napoléon III salon of the Élysée Palace. The one doing the kissing was the president of France.   1

In the fall of 2002, Jacques Chirac was seven years into his 12-year presidency. The Bush administration was moving toward war with Iraq, and the relationship between France and the United States was worse than it had been in decades. I had just become the Paris bureau chief for *The New York Times*. Chirac was receiving me and Roger Cohen, then *The Times's* foreign editor, to make what he hoped would be a headline-grabbing announcement of a French-led strategy to avoid war. When we arrived that Sunday morning, Chirac shook hands with Roger and welcomed me with a *baisemain,* a kiss of the hand.   2

The ritual—considered old-fashioned nowadays by just about everyone under the age of 60—was traditionally a ceremonial, sacred gesture; its history can be traced to ancient Greece and Rome. In the Middle Ages, a vassal paid homage to his lord by kissing his hand. By the 19th century, hand kissing had been reinvented to convey a man's gallantry and *politesse* toward a woman. Those men who still practice it today know the rules: never kiss a gloved hand or the hand of a young girl; kiss the hand only of a married woman, and do so only indoors.   3

Politesse: formality, politeness

Opening secures reader attention immediately.

Provides necessary background information.

Interesting historical details about the *baisemain.*

---

2. Print. *New York Times Magazine* 22 May 2011: 63–64.

Chirac reached for my right hand and cradled it as if it were a piece of porcelain from his private art collection. He raised it to the level of his chest, bent over to meet it halfway and inhaled, as if to savor its scent. Lips made contact with skin.

4

The kiss was not an act of passion. This was not at all like the smoldering scene in Proust's "Swann's Way"[3] in which the narrator "blindly, hotly, madly" seizes and kisses the hand offered to him by a lady in pink. Still, the kiss was unsettling. Part of me found it charming and flattering. But in an era when women work so hard to be taken seriously, I also was vaguely uncomfortable that Chirac was adding a personal dimension to a professional encounter and assuming I would like it. This would not have happened in the United States. It was, like so much else in France, a subtle but certain exercise in seduction.

The power-kiss of the president was one of my first lessons in understanding the importance of seduction in France. Over time, I became aware of its force and pervasiveness. I saw it in the disconcertingly intimate eye contact of a diplomat discussing dense policy initiatives; the exaggerated, courtly politeness of an elderly neighbor during our serendipitous morning encounters; the flirtatiousness of a female friend that oozed like honey at dinner parties; the banter of a journalist colleague that never ended and never failed to amuse. Eventually I learned to expect it, without quite knowing why.

Séduction and *séduire* (to seduce) are among the most overused words in the French language. In English, "seduce" has a negative and exclusively sexual feel; in French, the meaning is broader. The French use "seduce" where the British and Americans might use "charm" or "attract" or "engage" or "entertain."

The word's omnipresence in the French consciousness can be unsettling. During a trip to Israel in May 2009, the pope was said to have "seduced the Palestinians" with his call for the creation of a Palestinian state.

The milk producers of northern France were not simply on strike; they were on a "seduction mission" to explain to consumers why they were blocking trucks and collection points.

When the sales of Dell laptops declined, it was because the company had "a hard time seducing." The left-leaning newspaper *Libération* once ran a two-page article illustrated with a photo of a French soldier in full battle gear and pointing a large automatic weapon under the headline "Afghanistan: The French in Seduction Mode."

Clearly, seduction in France does not always involve sex. A *grand séducteur* is not necessarily a man who easily seduces others into making love. The term might refer to someone who never fails to persuade others to his point of view. He might be gifted at caressing with words, at drawing people close with a look, at forging alliances with flawless logic. The target of a seduction—male or female—may experience the process as a shower of charm or a magnetic pull or even a form of entertainment that ends as soon as the dinner party is over.

What is constant is the intent: to attract or influence, to win over, even if just in fun.

Seduction can surface any time—a tactic of the ice cream seller, the ambulance driver, the lavender grower. Foreigners may find themselves swept away without realizing how it happened. Not so the French. For them, the daily campaign to win and woo is a familiar game, instinctively played and understood.

---

3. Marcel Proust (1871–1922), famous author of *In Search of Lost Time*.

A key component of seduction—and of French life—is process. The rude waiter, the dismissive sales clerk, the low-ranking bureaucrat who demands still another obscure document are all playing a perverted version of a seduction game that glorifies lingering. It may be a waste of time and end without the desired result. But played well, the game can be stimulating. And when victory comes, the joy is sweet.

14

That's because seduction is bound tightly with what the French call *plaisir*—the art of creating and relishing pleasure of all kinds. The French are proud masters of it, for their own gratification and as a useful tool to seduce others. They have created and perfected pleasurable ways to pass the time: perfumes to sniff, gardens to wander in, wines to drink, objects of beauty to observe, conversations to carry on. They give themselves permission to fulfill a need for pleasure and leisure that America's hard-working, super-capitalist, abstinent culture often does not allow. Sexuality always lies at the bottom of the toolbox, in everyday life, in business, even in politics. For the French, this is part of the frisson[4] of life.

15

Offers interesting contrast with American cultural values.

---

4. Frisson: From French, "A brief moment of emotional excitement." Merriam-Webster Online <http://www.merriam-webster.com/dictionary/frisson>.

Questions for Discussion

1. Note the author's mixed response to Chirac's *baisemain* (paragraph 5). Why does she react as she does? If you are a woman, how would you feel? If you are a man, how would you feel about such an act of "seduction" as the French conceive the concept aimed at your wife or girlfriend?

2. Explain what "process," "*plaisir,*" and "frisson" have to do with the core meaning of seduction in French. How do these related concepts help you understand the French concept of seduction better?

3. In the next to last sentence, the author says that "sexuality always lies at the bottom of the tool box." What do you think she means? At bottom, how different is our American notion of seduction from the French notion?

■■■ *Thinking as a Writer*

What is the Rhetorical Situation?

1. What is the author's *purpose* in writing this article? What is her *angle* on the topic? How would you describe her *voice*?

2. Who is the intended *audience*? The article appeared in a section of *The New York Times Magazine* called "culture." Who would read this section? Is there anything you can point to in the article that implies her target readership?

3. Using the eight questions for how to explore a concept (page 151) and the marginal annotations to the article, evaluate how the author develops her view of seduction. That is, how does she define, illustrate, and explore the notion of "seduction" in French culture? ■

What Is Civility?

P. M. FORNI

Maybe I was coming down with change-of-season influenza. If so, I should really consider buying a little white half mask for my subway ride home.

—Sujata Massey

This reading comes from a best-selling book, Choosing Civility: The Twenty-five Rules of Considerate Conduct. *The author is a professor of Italian literature and civility at Johns Hopkins University, where he directs The Civility Initiative at Johns Hopkins. Before offering readers his "rules" for showing consideration toward others, Forni lays the groundwork by exploring the concept of* civility.

For many years literature was my life. I spent most of my time reading, teaching, and writing on Italian fiction and poetry. One day, while lecturing on the *Divine Comedy,* I looked at my students and realized that I wanted them to be kind human beings more than I wanted them to know about Dante. I told them that if they knew everything about Dante and then they went out and treated an elderly lady on the bus unkindly, I'd feel that I had failed as a teacher. I have given dozens of lectures and workshops on civility in the last few years, and I have derived much satisfaction from addressing audiences I could not have reached speaking on literature. I know, however, that reading literature can develop the kind of imagination without which civility is impossible. To be fully human we must be able to imagine others' hurt and to relate it to the hurt we would experience if we were in their place. Consideration is imagination on a moral track.   1

Sometimes the participants in my workshops write on a sheet of paper what civility means to them. In no particular order, here are a number of key civility-related notions I have collected over the years from those sheets: 2

Respect for others	Decency	Trustworthiness
Care	Self-Control	Going out of one's way
Consideration	Concern	Friendship
Courtesy	Justice	Friendliness
Golden Rule	Tolerance	Table manners
Respect of others' feelings	Selflessness	Lending a hand
Niceness	Etiquette	Manners
Politeness	Community service	Morality
Respect of others' opinions	Tact	Moderation
Maturity	Equality	Propriety
Kindness	Sincerity	Listening
Being accommodating	Honesty	Abiding by the rules
Fairness	Awareness	Compassion
Good citizenship	Being agreeable	Peace

This list tells us that

- Civility is complex.
- Civility is good.

- Whatever civility might be, it has to do with courtesy, politeness, and good manners.
- Civility belongs in the realm of ethics.

These four points have guided me in writing this book. Like my workshop participants, I am inclusive rather than exclusive in defining civility. Courtesy, politeness, manners, and civility are all, in essence, forms of awareness. Being civil means being constantly aware of others and weaving restraint, respect, and consideration into the very fabric of this awareness. Civility is a form of goodness; it is gracious goodness. But it is not just an attitude of benevolent and thoughtful relating to other individuals; it also entails an active interest in the well-being of our communities and even a concern for the health of the planet on which we live.   3

Saying "please" and "thank you"; lowering our voice whenever it may threaten or interfere with others' tranquility; raising funds for a neighborhood renovation program; acknowledging a newcomer to the conversation; welcoming a new neighbor; listening to understand and help; respecting those different from us; responding with restraint to a challenge; properly disposing of a piece of trash left by someone else; properly disposing of dangerous industrial pollutants; acknowledging our mistakes; refusing to participate in malicious gossip; making a new pot of coffee for the office machine after drinking the last cup; signaling our turns when driving; yielding our seat on a bus whenever it seems appropriate; alerting the person sitting behind us on a plane when we are about to lower the back of our seat; standing close to the right-side handrail on an escalator; stopping to give directions to someone who is lost; stopping at red lights; disagreeing with poise; yielding with grace when losing an argument, these diverse behaviors are all imbued with the spirit of civility.   4

Civility, courtesy, politeness, and *manners* are not perfect synonyms, as etymology clearly shows. . . . *Courtesy* is connected to *court* and evoked in the past the superior qualities of character and bearing expected in those close to royalty. Etymologically, when we are courteous we are courtierlike. Although today we seldom make this connection, courtesy still suggests excellence and elegance in bestowing respect and attention. It can also suggest deference and formality.   5

To understand *politeness,* we must think of *polish.* The polite are those who have polished their behavior. They have put some effort into bettering themselves, but they are sometimes looked upon with suspicion. Expressions such as "polite reply," "polite lie," and "polite applause" connect politeness to hypocrisy. It is true that the polite are inclined to veil their own feelings to spare someone else's. Self-serving lying, however, is always beyond the pale of politeness. If politeness is a quality of character (alongside courtesy, good manners, and civility), it cannot become a flaw. A suave manipulator may appear to be polite but is not.   6

When we think of good *manners* we often think of children being taught to say "please" and "thank you" and chew with their mouths closed. This may prevent us from looking at manners with the attention they deserve. *Manner* comes from *manus,* the Latin word for "hand." *Manner* and *manners* have to do with the use of our hands. A manner is the way something is done, a mode of handling. Thus *manners* came to refer to behavior in social interaction—the way we handle the encounter between Self and Other. We have good manners when we use our hands well—when we handle others with care. When we   7 rediscover the connection of *manner* with *hand,* the hand that, depending on our will and sensitivity, can strike or lift, hurt or soothe, destroy or heal, we understand the importance— for children and adults alike—of having good manners.

Civility's defining characteristic is its ties to *city* and *society.* The word derives from the Latin *civitas,* which means "city," especially in the sense of civic community. *Civitas* is the same word from which *civilization* comes. The age-old assumption behind civility is that life in the city has a civilizing effect. The city is where we enlighten our intellect and refine our social skills. And as we are shaped by the city, we learn to give of ourselves for the sake of the city. Although we can describe the civil as courteous, polite, and well mannered, etymology reminds us that they are also supposed to be good citizens and good neighbors.

8

Questions for Discussion

1. Forni begins by arguing that learning to be kind to others is as important to a college education as learning about literature—or presumably any other area of academic study. Do you agree? If so, can kindness be taught? How?
2. A common way to explore concepts is to write about other closely related concepts. Forni offers a long list of other concepts associated with civility (paragraph 2). Does the list help you to understand civility better? Why or why not?
3. Much has been written in recent years about the loss of civility in American life. Writers point to people engrossed with their laptops and cell phones rather than talking with the people around them. They also point to lack of cooperation in our politics, saying that Democrats and Republicans view one another as enemies rather than people who have different views on policy issues. Do you see a loss of civility? If so, do you see the alleged decline in civility as a problem?

■■ *Thinking as a Writer*

What is the Rhetorical Situation?

1. What is the author's *purpose* in writing this passage? What is his *angle* on the topic? How would you describe his *voice*?
2. Who is the intended *audience* for this passage (and for the larger book)? Is Forni writing for students in an academic setting or for a more general public? Is he writing for people who are already well informed about notions of civility or for people who might not have thought much about the concept? Is there anything in this excerpt you can cite that implies the author's target readership?
3. A common way to explore concepts is to consider their etymologies, their root meanings or origins. Forni does this in his discussions of *courtesy, politeness,* and *manners.* Do the root meanings of these words, including *civility* itself, help you to grasp these concepts better? Why or why not? ■

The Assignment

See Chapter 16, Finding Sources, pages 412–25, and Chapter 17, Evaluating Sources, pages 426–36, for kinds of sources you could consult.

Write an essay exploring a concept. Depending on your teacher's instructions, you may draw from personal experiences, interviews, and observations as well as from reference works, books, and articles. Be sure to use the key questions for exploring a concept (page 151). Some or all of them will help you see how to think critically about your concept and discover options for writing about it.

How Do I Explore Concepts? Questioning the Rhetorical Situation

Begin by picturing a **rhetorical situation** for your writing project, a real-world context for communicating. You should consider the key variables in any act of communication: a writer with something to say, a reader the writer wishes to reach, and a kind of text appropriate to the writing task. These three variables will affect many decisions in the composing process.

Writer: What Is My Purpose and What Impression Should Readers Have of Me?

Exploratory writing is "thinking aloud," for this assignment, putting on screen or paper how you have gone about trying to understand a concept. You may explain the concept and concepts related to it, but your primary purpose is to explore, not to inform or explain. You may also argue *for* your understanding of the concept—usually near the end of your essay, after your exploration is over—but your primary purpose is to explore, not to argue for your interpretation. The key to exploration is to **postpone closure**, which means *letting your mind play with the concept* rather than informing or arguing.

Consequently, your readers should see you as a *thoughtful guide* to the concept, someone asking and pursuing interesting questions. They should see you as someone with an open mind, not as someone who has all the answers.

Reader: Who Is My Audience?

As with all writing projects, you should imagine a group of people who might read your paper. Your instructor will evaluate your work, and part of that evaluation is how well you communicate with your reader. Beyond that, you need to write for a reader because it will help you decide what to say and how to order what you say. Therefore, one of the key questions you need to ask yourself often as you write and revise a draft is, **"What does my reader need?"**

Remembering this will help you imagine your reader: *Your purpose for writing determines your role as a writer, which in turn implies a role for your reader.* In this case, your purpose is exploration and your role is an explorer, someone engaged with the meaning of a challenging concept. You are displaying your thought process as you ponder the concept's dictionary definition, its root meanings, what other writers have said about it, how the concept is used, and so on. Without having to say it, you are inviting your readers to "Come and think about this concept with me." You are saying, "Here's what I am thinking," which implies that you want what you say to stimulate their thinking.

Note how different this role for the reader is from informing or arguing. When you inform, your readers become somebody who needs or wants to know what you know. When you argue, your reader becomes someone you are trying to convince or persuade. Exploration is different: You want your readers to think through a concept with you.

Text: What Would Be an Appropriate Topic?

Your instructor may assign a concept to explore. When asked to choose your own, consider the following:

- **Personal experience.** Draw on your personal experience to select a concept for exploration. For example, seeing mothers interacting with their children in line at the bank or grocery store may prompt you to consider the concept *child rearing*. An experience from childhood or adolescence that made you consider concepts such as *innocence* or *naïveté* could also be explored.

- **Blog posts.** A student from Sweden described how the concept of friendship in his country differs from the concepts in the United States. The post received many comments from other bloggers, opening up further exploration of a challenging concept.

- **Book reviews.** Nonfiction books especially can offer either new concepts or interesting analyses of familiar ones. You can respond to the author's exploration with comments of your own.

See Chapter 4, Interpreting Experiences, for guidance, and pages 77–78 for more ideas.

Here are some other sources for concepts to explore.

- **Class readings.** Concepts from the readings in this chapter—seduction, *plaisir*, courtesy, gender roles—or in other texts you are reading for class could provide concepts for exploration.

- **Personal reading.** An article in your campus newspaper or in a magazine like *Time* or *Sports Illustrated* could provide a concept ("fairness in the media," "cheating in sports").

- **Campus issues.** For example, "plagiarism" or "going green" are good concepts for exploration. Speakers at your college or university may also discuss intriguing concepts.

- **Concepts in your community.** For example, "third place" is used to designate where people spend time besides home and work.

- **Concepts in your workplace.** For example, in a summer or regular job you may have encountered a concept such as "malware," a name for computer viruses, Trojans, and worms.

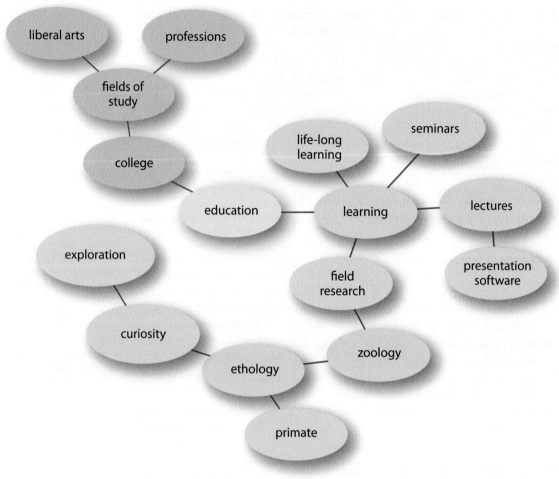

FIGURE **7.1**

What Should I Write About?

Think of one interesting broad concept and then come up with as many concept "offshoots" as you can. Sometimes brainstorming with a visual diagram can help you come up with the perfect topic to write about.

- **Concepts from foreign languages or cultures.** If you have studied a foreign language, you have probably encountered concepts unique to that language, which have no precise English equivalents. Such concepts can make interesting explorations, especially if you have lived or visited countries that speak the language and can offer insight into how the concept is actually used.

- **Concepts from cultures in the United States.** Our country is in large part a collection of cultures, people of different races, ethnicities, nationalities, religions, languages, and so on. Perhaps you were raised in or have extensive experience with one of these cultures and can discuss a concept its people often use.

How Do I Explore Concepts?
Engaging the Writing Process

No two people compose in exactly the same way, and even the same person may go through the writing process in different ways with different assignments. Nevertheless, because no one can attend to everything at once, there are phases in handling any significant writing task. You begin by preparing to write, which includes generating content and finding your angle.

The next phase is planning and drafting your paper, getting a version, however rough it may be on screen or paper so that you have something to work with during the next two stages: revising your draft by making changes to the content, arrangement, and style of your writing; and editing your draft to take care of problems at the paragraph and sentence level, such as lack of focus and coherence, awkward or unclear sentences, and errors of grammar, spelling, and punctuation.

Exploring Your Topic

BEST PRACTICES | How Do I Explore Concepts?

The genre represented in Readings 7.1 and 7.2 and in the student example at the end of this chapter (pages 169–72) is the exploratory essay. The basic moves are clear from the micro-example (page 147):

- ■ Introduce the concept you intend to explore.
- ■ Indicate why the concept needs to be explored.
- ■ Cite the views of experts on the concept and comment on what they say, and/or . . .
- ■ Cite dictionary meanings, root meanings, examples of how the concept is used and so on (see the key questions on page 151 for other possibilities) and comment on them, and/or . . .
- ■ Cite your own experiences or observations that contribute to your thinking about the concept.
- ■ Propose a core or basic meaning for the concept.
- ■ Offer your view of what the concept means, including, when relevant, your evaluation of how the concept is used or misused. ■

In this phase you are *finding something to say,* generating ideas and content, which includes discovering your angle or point of view.

■ ■ ■ ACTIVITY 7.2 *Writer's Notebook*

Will It Work? Testing Your Concept

If you are in doubt about a concept you have chosen, try writing about it as fast as you can for about 15 minutes. If you find the ideas are flowing, you probably have a concept suitable for you to write about. As an alternative, write an e-mail to a friend or classmate explaining why you have chosen the concept and what you foresee saying about it. Ask for feedback. Either or both methods should help you test the concept before you commit yourself to a draft. ■

Asking Questions: Generating Ideas and Gathering Materials

See Chapter 15, pages 408–10, for guidance on keeping a working bibliography.

The following six questions will help you come up with ideas and more than enough content for your essay. Make handwritten notes as you work your way through these questions or preserve your notes and comments on a computer file reserved for this assignment. Be sure to indicate the sources from which all your information comes.

1. **What is the definition and history of the concept?** Start with the meanings of the concept as listed in a college-level dictionary. Distinguish the *concept's meanings* (called **denotation**) from the *implications of the concept* (called **connotation**). For example, "empathy" means the ability to feel what someone else is feeling (denotation); its connotations are always positive, implying a sensitive, caring person. Many dictionaries also show the word's **etymology** (*its derivation or root meanings*). The *Oxford English Dictionary (OED)* is particularly good for illustrating etymology because it gives example sentences showing how the concept has been used in the past.

2. **What other concepts are related to the concept you are exploring, and how are they related?** Concepts can only be discussed by using other concepts. What words were used to define your concept? What **synonyms** *(words that mean approximately the same thing)* did your dictionary supply? What synonyms can you think of? What synonyms are listed in a thesaurus?

   Consider also concepts closely related to your concept that are not synonyms. Forni offered a list of forty-two concepts related to civility (page 155). You can find things to say about your concept by simply listing all the related concepts you can think of. Add to your list by writing down related concepts other writers have used to discuss your concept (see question 4).

3. **What metaphors are used to discuss your concept?** A metaphor is an implied comparison. People talk about "argument," for instance, using the concept of "war." Arguments are won and lost; we shoot down or demolish opposing views; evidence is ammunition. Consider how this metaphor influences how people think about argument and behave when they argue.

It certainly works against listening thoughtfully to people we disagree with or empathizing with opponents in a dispute.

Concepts are metaphorical more often than we realize. Expose and examine the metaphors in your concept. Remember also that language is full of **dead metaphors,** *comparisons used so habitually that people no longer recognize them as metaphors.* The language of war used to discuss argument is a good example. When you encounter dead metaphors, invent fresh ones that might restore life to your concept. For example, why not present argument as dialogue or negotiation?

4. **What has been written about my concept?** Using your library's online catalog and an all-purpose periodicals database, such as Academic Search Complete, InfoTrac, JSTOR, and ProQuest, find sources in which your concept is discussed. Then conduct a Google search on your sources' authors to learn about their background, their areas of expertise, and their perspectives on your concept. Keep copies of your sources, make notes about what the authors say, and add your own reactions and comments.

   See Chapter 16 for advice on finding suitable print and online sources.

   See Chapter 18 for advice on taking notes and making comments on source material.

5. **Do different groups of people use the concept differently?** The most common sources of difference are race and ethnicity, gender, class, age, religion, and sexuality. "Equal opportunity," for example, may mean one thing to those born into privilege, something else to those born into poverty. "Community" may mean one thing to your grandparents and another thing to you. Consider how your concept may be understood by members of different groups. What conflicts or misunderstandings might result? How might your view of the concept help reduce conflict or misunderstanding?

6. **How do people actually use the concept?** Field research, such as surveys and interviews, can help you gain insight into your concept. One student exploring gender surveyed her fellow musicians' choices of instruments and found that instruments were "masculine" and "feminine"—that is, women tended to choose certain instruments (the flute, for example), while men tended to choose others (such as the drums). She was intrigued by how these gender concepts influenced musicians' choices. Consider conducting your own survey or interviewing a campus expert to learn more about your concept.

   See Chapter 15 for guidance in conducting field research.

■■■■ ACTIVITY 7.3 *Collaborative Activity*

Discussing Your Concept

If you keep a blog or if your class has an online discussion board, write a post about the concept you are exploring. Include any interesting results from answering the six questions above for generating ideas. Ask participants to post comments, contribute questions for exploration, and share their own experiences. ■

Drafting Your Paper

As you move toward writing your first draft, focus attention on angle, organization, and voice.

Thinking as a Writer: How Can I Find My Angle?

Angles are typically **contextual**, *derived from your life situation*. For example, the context for "Operation Seduction" was the author's experience as a journalist working in France. She wanted Americans to understand a pervasive concept in French culture. The context for a college student wrestling with the concept *indie music*, might be her own role as a DJ at the college radio station and the kinds of music her definition of "indie" would allow her to play. Concept exploration is usually motivated by practical needs, problems, or questions that arise at work, at home, in the community, or in one of many other contexts provided by life.

To determine your angle, consider the following questions:

1. **What context do I bring to the concept?** A student who surveyed fellow musicians about gender and instrument choice brought the context of playing in an orchestra. Any way that your concept can be connected with school, work, sports, family, or social life can help you find an angle.

2. **What outcome do I want for my exploration?** Forni wanted his readers to appreciate how complex "civility" is and to understand why he considers civility so important. Cummins explored "gender" to call attention to how limiting rigid notions of "masculine" and "feminine" can be.

3. **How can I challenge existing notions of the concept?** Everything you read about a concept can be questioned in some way, and often your angle can come from finding a particularly fertile question. When we read Sciolino's

Finding an angle often means writing about what you know. For example, if you work at an indie radio station and have an opinion about what indie is, write about it.

article, for example, we wondered whether the behavior of older French-men in kissing the hands only of married women implied anything sexist. Why do the rules prohibit the kissing of a gloved hand or of the hand of a young girl, and why only indoors? Because "seduction" is never innocent, what exactly is going on underneath the effort to charm?

4. **What distinctions might I make?** By their nature, concepts lump things together. Perhaps your angle can come from making one or several distinctions. The Swedish student who explored "friendship" thought Americans confused friend with acquaintance. That was his angle, and it worked well.

Thinking as a Writer: Organizing Your Exploratory Essay

Consider arranging your material as described below.

Introduction   A good technique for opening exploration papers is to say what most people think about a concept and why it needs rethinking. Other options include:

- A quotation showing a particularly good or particularly bad understanding of the concept.
- A personal narrative about how your exploration got started.

Body   One way to organize the draft is chronologically, beginning with your initial view of the concept and explaining the stages in which your understanding grew. See the student essay at the end of this chapter for an example. A chrono-logically organized draft would emphasize breakthrough moments, when your major insights occurred.

You can also organize around sources. Arrange your sources around a se-quence of points they make or a set of question they help to answer, and be sure to comment on them as they relate to your angle.

Conclusion   Depending on your angle, conclude with the results of your explo-ration, whatever they are:

- How does your understanding of the concept work or fail to work in the context you brought to it? For example, the idea that band or orchestral instruments have a gender might end by considering boys who choose the flute and girls who choose the tuba. How do you explain choices that do not fit gender stereotypes?

- What outcome did you want from exploring the concept? Emphasize the re-sults of your exploration, such as a clearer notion of friendship, a healthier view of romantic love, or an understanding of how much human society depends on civility.

- What challenge to the typical notion of your concept can you offer? For example, instead of the sharp contrasts that usually go with masculine and feminine gender categories, you could say that most people are a mix of the two genders, and therefore "masculine" and "feminine" tend only to distort reality.

- What distinctions seem important to you? For example, besides the usual distinction between friend and acquaintance, it might be interesting to discuss something relatively new—"friending," which can occur with people who are neither friends nor acquaintances.

Leave your readers with the feeling that your exploration made headway, but you need not resolve all issues or questions. Some explorations end by calling attention to problems, issues, and questions requiring further thought.

Thinking as a Writer: What Voice Is Appropriate for Exploring a Concept?

Saying what you mean involves voice, how you sound to your readers, so we need to consider voice in exploratory writing. Voice depends on function, on what a writer is doing. When we explore concepts, three functions are in play: informing, questioning, and asserting. All three functions and voices are present in "Operation Seduction" (pages 152–54), but listen especially to the author's voice in the following passage:

> Clearly, seduction in France does not always involve sex. A grand séducteur is not necessarily a man who easily seduces others into making love. The term might refer to someone who never fails to persuade others to his point of view. He might be gifted at caressing with words, at drawing people close with a look, at forging alliances with flawless logic. The target of a seduction—male or female—may experience the process as a shower of charm or a magnetic pull or even a form of entertainment that ends as soon as the dinner party is over.

Her voice sounds like the knowledgeable insider, who is sharing with us the subtle range and never-fully-explicit meanings of seduction in France. Note especially the word choices in phrases like "caressing with words" and "forging alliances with flawless logic."

Revising Your Draft

Because exploration depicts the thought process itself, laying it out for readers to follow, revision should not conceal or obscure the twists and turns of your thinking. Instead, *revise to highlight discoveries,* to expose how your thought unfolded. The Asking Questions: Revision Checklist provides questions to guide assessment of your or another student's draft.

ASKING QUESTIONS | Revision Checklist for Explaining a Concept

1. Does the paper explore the concept, opening it up to questioning rather than only informing or presenting an argument? Isolate passages that clearly explore. How can they be improved?

2. Is the author's angle on the concept clear, and does the writer provide a reason for exploring the concept in the introduction? What is the angle? Where is the reason discussed?

3. Does the author explain the context within which she or he will be exploring the concept? Recall that "context" for this paper means the concept's place in the writer's life. Where specifically are the connections with context made? What possible questions might a reader have that go unanswered?

4. Is the paper organized around the stages marking the writer's unfolding insights into the concept, around sources and the insights into the concept they provide, or in some other way that makes sense? If not, what changes in organization would help the reader follow the exploration better?

5. Has the author made the exploration specific enough to show how the concept is used, by providing examples and illustrations that demonstrate how people use the concept? Where in the paper does this happen? Where might the author provide additional supporting evidence?

6. If the author has used sources, how well are the authors of these sources introduced as people whose opinions on the concept should matter? To see how to incorporate sources, look at the micro-example (page 147), one of the readings (pages 147–48, 152–54, and 155–57), or the student example (pages 169–72).

For more help on incorporating sources into your text, see Chapter 18, pages 438–40.

7. Is there too much quotation, paraphrase, and summary of sources and not enough commentary on the sources? Find places where the author has said something about sources cited. To what extent do the comments express his or her own point of view and voice?

See Chapter 18, pages 440–44, for guidance on using quotations, paraphrase, and summary.

8. Has the author brought the exploration to some degree of closure by drawing a conclusion about what he or she learned? Should more be concluded? Why? Remember that closure in exploratory writing can include mentioning problems, issues, and questions that need further thought. ■

Student Example: Excerpts from Jamie Cummins's Draft

Student Jamie Cummins explored the concept of gender. He encountered specific challenges with his opening and using sources.

Problems with the Opening   A paper's opening is important because it is the first thing your audience will read. In the rough draft of this chapter's featured student essay (see pages 169–72 for the revised draft), Cummins opened with a dictionary definition and then moved into a quotation from one of his sources, an expert on the topic of gender roles:

> Gender is defined in the dictionary as "kind, sort, class; also genus as opposed to species." And that's just it. Gender is a word meaning what *kind* of human are you. Most would say, "I am a male" or "I am a female." But the words "male" and "female" refer to their sex. Gender has nothing to do with one's biological make-up, but more of an element of one's identity—"'gender' is masculinity and femininity" (Kimmel 3).

Compare this opening with the opening of his second draft (page 169). Which do you like better? Why?

Problems with Using Sources   Because your readers have not read the sources you cite, you need to comment on what they say and set up quotations and paraphrases with enough context so they can understand them. Here is Cummins's first effort to integrate a source:

> The idea that our gender is influenced and developed in elementary, middle and high school is explored by C. J. Pascoe, a sociologist at the University of California at Berkeley. Among many things, Pascoe explores the idea that school is "an organizer of sexual practices, identities, and meanings" (26) in her book, *Dude, You're a Fag: Masculinity and Sexuality in High School.* She also notes that "the heterosexualizing process organized by educational institutions cannot be separated from, and in fact is central to, the development of masculine identities" (27). Specifically, C. J. Pascoe refers to the "Mr. Cougar" competition in the high school she did her field work in. Candidates for the "Mr. Cougar" title performed short skits, usually mocking boys who are less masculine than the stereotypical "manly man". These skits reinforce the idea that the stereotypical "manly man" is strong, big and powerful. The "manly man" must also have a girlfriend and must frequently have sex. The skits made being a "manly man" seem essential, and "male femininity [. . .] is coded as humorous" (4). Referring to one of the "Mr. Cougar" skits, Pascoe writes that "the skit fostered and encouraged masculinity as heterosexual" (45). The "Mr. Cougar" skits make it seem like one has to prove his own masculinity to be considered heterosexual. She reinforces the concept that because of "heterosexualizing" schools, gender is shaped and developed in elementary, middle and high school.

Compare this version to paragraphs 6 and 7 in the revised version. Note how much better he handles context for and commentary on his source.

Editing Your Revised Draft

In working with sources, you often need to summarize what they say. A wordy summary can obscure the ideas rather than present them clearly. Compare the following two versions of a summary Jamie Cummins used for one of his sources. The original version reads like a list of disconnected points stated by author Michael Kimmel:

Original Version

These sentences describe the original source by listing points Kimmel makes, but they do not show how the points relate to each other.

> Kimmel explains that "virtually every society known to us is founded upon assumptions of gender difference and the politics of gender inequality" (2). He believes that "gender difference is the product of gender inequality" (4) rather than the other way around. Kimmel focuses more on gender inequality and the "differences *among* men and *among* women" (9) rather than just explaining how they are different. He also mentions that "gender difference is the product of gender inequality" (4). Because of the inequality between men and women, their resulting gender is affected. Kimmel notices that "the organizations of our society have evolved in ways that reproduce both the differences between women and men and the domination of men over women" (15). His words reinforce that it is society that determines and develops our gender.

Passive voice obscures the point: Inequality causes gender differences.

The original passage is 132 words; in the revised version, Cummins cuts the word count down to 95. In the following passage, note how Cummins makes this summary both shorter and easier for readers to follow.

Edited Version

Kimmel explains that "virtually every society known to us is founded upon assumptions of gender difference and the politics of gender inequality" (2). While most people assume that inequality is caused by gender difference, Kimmel sees inequality as the cause, not the result, of gender difference. Gender inequality exists because "the organizations of our society have evolved in ways that reproduce both the differences between women and men and the domination of men over women" (15). In other words, societies dictate that the sexes have distinctly different roles in order to keep the sexes unequal.

> The color coding in this revision shows the improved coherence in the revised summary, as each sentence picks up a point from the one before and carries it forward.

> Sums up argument's main point.

REVISED STUDENT EXAMPLE

Cummins 1

Jamie Cummins
Professor Channell
Writing 205
August 24, 2011

Exploring the Concept of Gender

In her book *Mindfulness,* Ellen J. Langer says that people can be "trapped by categories" or concepts from the past. One example she gives is "masculine/feminine" (11). I began to wonder how trapped we might be by our ideas of appropriate behavior for men and women. Many will say that because of men and women's biological makeup, our gender is simply something one is born with—an instinct, of sorts. But is this true? I decided to explore the concept of gender and gender roles to see how different the sexes really are.

> Explains motivation for his exploration of "gender."

First, I looked into definitions of the word *gender.* I found that it can be interchanged with the word *sex* in common use, but social scientists use gender to refer to social roles and sex to refer to biological differences. According to the *Oxford English Dictionary*, gender is a "euphemism for the sex of a human being, often intended to emphasize the social and cultural, as opposed to the biological, distinctions between the sexes." If it's just a euphemism for sex, do we need it at all? Why should social distinctions need to be emphasized?

> Results of dictionary information, including root meanings. Note his comments on the information.

1

2

I read the introduction to a book by a leading writer on gender, Michael Kimmel, titled *The Gendered Society*. He says, "'Sex' refers to the biological apparatus, the male and the female—our chromosomal, chemical, anatomical organization. 'Gender' refers to the meanings that are attached to those differences within a culture" (3). Kimmel believes that these meanings are socially constructed (9) in order to keep the sexes unequal.

3

Use of another writer's view of gender.

Kimmel explains that "virtually every society known to us is founded upon assumptions of gender difference and the politics of gender inequality" (2). While most people assume that inequality is caused by gender difference, Kimmel sees inequality as the cause, not the result, of gender difference. Gender inequality exists because "the organizations of our society have evolved in ways that reproduce both the differences between women and men and the domination of men over women" (15). In other words, societies dictate that the sexes have distinctly different roles in order to keep the sexes unequal.

4

This is an interesting theory, but I wonder how different are men and women, really? Kimmel acknowledges the biological differences but his social constructionist approach explores "the differences *among* men and *among* women" and has determined that "these are often more decisive than the differences between women and men" (9). The diagram below, taken from his book, shows that there is greater variation within the bell curve representing each sex than there is between the sexes. The shaded area in the middle is the overlap showing how similar men and women really are. Kimmel says the "interplanetary" view of men as from Mars and women from Venus just reinforces the myth of gender difference, but really, we are all from planet Earth (11).

5

So if men and women are not so different, where do they get the idea that they are? Kimmel says it is the social institutions of family, workplace, politics, and schools "where the dominant definitions are reinforced and reproduced and where 'deviants' are disciplined" (15). I saw gender roles at my high school, but I never thought school itself played a role, but a recent book shows how this happens.

6

C. J. Pascoe, a sociologist, observed a typical public high school for an entire year and found that the school reinforced ideas of masculinity as white, athletic, and heterosexual. In her book, *Dude, You're a Fag: Masculinity and Sexuality in High School*, she describes a popularity contest called the "Mr. Cougar" competition. Candidates for the "Mr. Cougar" title performed short skits, in which they mocked boys who did not fit the stereotype of the "manly man."

7

Use of another writer as a concrete example of gender role conditioning.

In one skit, titled "The Revenge of the Nerds," the candidates for Mr. Cougar appeared at first as weak and effeminate, dressed in nerdy clothes. Pascoe says the audience thought this was hysterically funny because "male femininity . . . is coded as humorous" (4). The nerds' girlfriends were then kidnapped by other boys dressed as "gangsta's." To get "their women" back, the nerdy boys had to bulk up by lifting weights. The girls were depicted as trophies awarded to the nerds once they had transformed themselves into manly men and proved their masculinity by rescuing the girls from the gangsta's (45). When our class discussed this reading, many students reported that their high schools had similar contests, but they

8

thought Pascoe was overanalyzing, and it was all just in fun. But I have seen all of this first hand.

Many different organizations promote male masculinity. At all levels of education, there is pressure to conform to the "normal" gender image. If one does not act "girly" or "manly," they are shunned. Most will eventually find out that one does not have to have sex, lift weights, or have a girlfriend to prove their masculinity. Actually, no one should ever have to *prove* their gender, especially since exaggerated gender roles reinforce inequality of the sexes.

9

Draws on his experience in this paragraph to illustrate gender role conditioning.

But women have made gains in equality, so it's logical to ask, since concepts of gender change with time, could our society's concept of masculinity be changing? Sharon Jayson, the author of the article "Guys Try to Read Society's Road Map for Behavior," says yes and no. Boys are getting mixed signals about sexuality and how to develop their masculine identity. An American Psychological Association study found 19% of the male high school students in the study received conflicting messages; some told them they had to be tough and others that they had to be nice. Andrew Smiler, an assistant professor of psychology at the State University of New York-Oswego, says boys learn that women are equals, but "we haven't changed masculinity" (qtd. in Jayson). Jayson quotes a professor of counseling who says "a large proportion of young males [still] view drinking and having sexual conquests as the appropriate way to begin to prove they are an adult male." Girls send boys the message they should be sensitive and show their feelings, but boys are still sending each other the old "macho" message.

10

Poses a significant question explored in the paragraph.

I was ready to accept that gender differences are totally social, but I still had to ask, "Is it possible that male and female brains are different in a way that would affect their behavior?" Some researchers believe that the sexes have innately different ways of thinking. Simon Baron-Cohen, a psychologist at Cambridge University, believes that "there are interesting differences between the *average* male and female mind. Recognizing these could lead to a mutual respect of difference" (77). He says studies show that females have more empathizing brains, while men have more systemizing brains (78). Women are more likely to share, take turns, show sensitivity to facial expressions, talk about emotions, and make eye contact. In contrast, a male brain is more likely to pay attention to relevant details, pursue math, science and physics, read maps, and show interest in mechanical systems. Even one-day old baby boys will "look longer at a mechanical mobile, which is a system with predictable laws of motion, than at a person's face, an object that is next to impossible to systemize" (86). This may be evidence that difference is innate, not learned.

11

Poses another key question he explores in this paragraph.

What disturbed me was that Baron-Cohen's article supports the idea that men are the dominant sex. Baron-Cohen tries to avoid discussing the politics of power and inequality in his article. He insists that the differences are "on average." Researchers found individual men with empathizing brains and individual women with systemizing brains; thus, "there is no scientific justification for stereotyping . . ." (92). However, by claiming that men have more systemizing brains, he shows why they are the dominant sex. We all know that those who are

12

Calls attention to a disturbing implication of the innate difference view.

talented mathematicians, scientists and physicists get paid more than people in caretaking roles. And in today's society, money *is* power. If men are biologically stronger in these fields, they will be the ones who are more apt to make the money.

I have begun to think that gender is not a helpful concept for the human race, since as Kimmel argues, it is based in inequality. He says that if we could eliminate gender inequality, "we will remove the foundation upon which the entire edifice of gender difference is built" (4). Eliminating the concept of gender would be impossible, but we need to be aware of how it creates inequality and causes both men and women to be trapped in stereotypes.

13

> Concludes with his tentative view of "gender" as the source of stereotypes.

Page break

Works Cited

Baron-Cohen, Simon. "Does Biology Play Any Role in Sex Differences in the Mind?" *The Future of Gender*. Ed. Jude Browne. New York: Cambridge UP, 2007. 77–97. Print.

Jayson, Sharon. "Guys Try to Read Society's Road Map for Behavior." *USA Today* (26 August 2008): 09D. *InfoTrac*. Web. 20 November 2008.

Kimmel, Michael S. *The Gendered Society*. 3rd ed. New York: Oxford UP, 2008. Print.

Langer, Ellen J. *Mindfulness*. Cambridge, MA: Da Capo Press, Perseus Books, 1989. Print.

Pascoe, C.J. *Dude, You're a Fag: Masculinity and Sexuality in High School*. U of California P, 2007. Print.

CHAPTER 8

Comparing Perspectives

IN CHAPTER 1 WE DISCUSSED THE DIFFERENCE BETWEEN A QUESTION OF FACT and a question of opinion. "Does playing video games improve visual response time?" is a question of fact. It can be answered by finding reliable current data. Questions of opinion, however, are open to debate. "Should sales of violent video games be restricted to people age 18 or older?" is a question of opinion. On questions like this, we find a range of perspectives, all of which could be well informed.

Who is right? What should we think? When people encounter conflicting perspectives, two responses are common:

1. "It's just a matter of opinion." It *is* a matter of opinion, and to that extent the response is justified. However, this response usually implies that all opinions are equally sound.

2. "Since everyone is entitled to his or her opinion, I'll take whatever position appeals to me."

The problem with these responses is that they shut down further critical thought on the question.

A third response—one that opens up further thought—is to compare conflicting perspectives carefully, identifying the most intelligent perspective by asking questions like the following:

- Which opinion is backed by the best current information?
- Who offers the most convincing reasoning?
- How can I reconcile the best points in one opinion with the best points in another?

As we explore viewpoints, we accept some ideas and reject others. Eventually we draw our own informed conclusion about where the truth lies.

In the example that follows, several experts on higher education bring different perspectives to the question: "Does it matter where you go to college?"

MICRO-EXAMPLE   **Comparing Perspectives**

Does It Matter Where You Go to College? From Room for Debate: A Running Commentary on the News

The New York Times

Does It Matter Where You Go to College?

Debaters

What You Do vs.
Where You Go
Martha O'Connell

Access to Money
and Power
Anthony P.
Carnevale

Merit and Race
Luis Fuentes-Rohwer

Graduate School
Matters More
David W. Breneman

Numbers Favor
Top Schools
Richard D.
Kahlenberg

Skip the
Admissions Game
Kevin Carey

The Specialization
Trade-Off
James Shulman

Introduction

Will you have a better life if you graduate from an elite school? Students and their parents think the answer is yes, and competition for slots at top-ranked (and costly) schools seems higher than ever. Having a big name college on your resume can impress employers, friends and the opposite sex.

The Times columnist Gail Collins says this national fixation makes little sense. "We can do a great service to the youth and parents of America by telling them to stop obsessing about choosing a college," she <u>wrote</u> recently in The Conversation blog. "Kids, you do not need to go to a school with a name that impresses your friends. Go to a school you can afford."

If enough people took her advice, the spell might be broken. In the meantime, what should sensible and ambitious students keep in mind about where they go to school?

Daren McCollester/Getty Images
Tourists in front of the John Harvard statue in Harvard Yard.

Within this large topic, three of these authors address a more specific question: Does it matter if you attend a top-ranked school? Here, we compare their answers.

Martha (Marty) O'Connell is the executive director of Colleges That Change Lives, *a* nonprofit organization that assists students in choosing a school that is the right fit for them.

She says no. The elite brand is less important than the educational experience: "The key to success in college and beyond has more to do with what students do with their time during college than where they choose to attend." What does matter? The "opportunity for engagement and critical, creative and collaborative learning with faculty, peers and community."

Richard D. Kahlenberg is a senior fellow at The Century Foundation, a progressive research institute concerned with public policy.

He says yes. Kahlenberg says that "attending a selective college with a large endowment offers numerous advantages, which can put students on a more favorable trajectory in life." Compared to graduates of the least selective schools, graduates of elite schools have greater likelihood of graduating, greater chance of going to graduate school, 45% higher entry level earnings, and "unparalleled access to the leadership class in this country."

Kevin Carey is the policy director of Education Sector, a think tank on education problems and policies dedicated to improving students' opportunities for success.

He says yes, but other options can be just as good. Carey admits, "For those who can afford it and can get admitted, any elite school would be a good choice." Students looking for a great, affordable education should look into rankings of community colleges because "the best community colleges do a better job than the average elite research university at teaching freshmen and sophomores."

Comparison Paragraph

A comparison of perspectives brings key points together and notes where they agree and disagree.

O'Connell says attending an elite school should not matter; her purpose is to help students find the best educational experience. Kahlenberg says it does matter because his purpose is to point out the disparities in U.S. higher education. Carey's perspective aligns more with O'Connell's because he shows how the quality of the educational experience, at least for a freshman or sophomore, could be better at a community college than a prestige research institution. For both Carey and O'Connell the student's experience is more important than the prestige of the degree.

Question for Discussion

Is the student's experience more important than the prestige of the degree? If you say yes, why do you think so? If you say no, what are your reasons?

What Is Comparing Perspectives?

Comparing perspectives is the examination of the differences among *perspectives* (*opinions or points of view*). People have different perspectives because of different backgrounds and prior knowledge. For example, parents of young children are more likely to favor restricting the sale of violent video games, while people who work in the video game industry are more likely to favor open access.

Central to writing a comparison of perspectives is **synthesis**, a *Greek word* that means "*putting together.*" An effective mash-up, for example, is a synthesis of different songs to create a new whole. In the academic world, most writing relies on synthesis, blending information and ideas from multiple sources to develop and support a single point of view. The comparison paragraph in the example above—"Does It Matter Where You Go to College?"—illustrates synthesis by bringing three views together into one.

Why Write to Compare Perspectives?

Your answer to any question depends on your perspective. For example, if someone asked you whether Facebook has been a positive social influence on young people, your answer would depend on your experience with Facebook. To get a broader perspective, you must move beyond your own knowledge and experience, deepening your understanding by comparing and evaluating the views of other people. On the Facebook question, for example, you might evaluate what psychologists and educators have had to say and compare their perspectives with those of your friends and classmates. The key questions for comparing perspectives, then, are the following:

- **How do different people answer the question?**
- **Which perspectives seem most valid after careful examination?**
- **What can I use from these perspectives to answer the question more fully and thoughtfully for myself?**

Finding what others think can complicate our thinking. But getting a mix of viewpoints stimulates thought. A good panel discussion can be more invigorating to an audience than a single person lecturing. Similarly, reading multiple perspectives opens your mind.

Why *write* to compare perspectives? Writing helps us do the following:

- Identify the specific points being discussed
- Analyze where opinions intersect and diverge
- Determine, point by point, the differences and similarities
- Reflect on the points under debate
- Formulate our own view

Writing a comparison of perspectives results in more precise and informed thinking about a question.

Comparisons of perspectives are common in business and community contexts, such as deciding which candidate to vote for, choosing a course of action after hearing a range of proposals, or soliciting the views of multiple consultants on some complicated issue or problem. In personal and academic contexts, people compare perspectives whenever they read reviews of colleges, books, and movies, and all researched writing involves exploring what experts have said.

Genres that compare perspectives include the introductions to books and scholarly articles in which the writer surveys previous scholarship on the topic, book reviews that compare how two or three books treat the same subject, and exploratory essays using multiple sources.

How Do Writers Compare Perspectives?

Like any kind of serious thinking, comparing perspectives works best if you have a method for your investigation:

1. Start by posing a question, not of fact but of opinion, a question on which reasonable people might disagree. It could be a question you wish to research, such as, "Do sports build character?" or "Do same-sex schools educate girls (or boys) better than coeducational ones?"

2. Next, ask how people have answered the question. This involves some kind of research.

3. Compare how people have answered the question. Asking Questions (below) lists questions to ask when comparing.

ASKING QUESTIONS | **Some Ways Writers Compare Perspectives**

1. **What is the central question addressed in all the readings?** What is the key question implied in each viewpoint you have read?

2. **What are the key terms or concepts used in discussing this question, and how do the writers define these terms?** Is there disagreement about the meaning of key terms?

For more on concepts, see Chapter 7, Exploring a Concept, pages 147–72.

3. **How do the authors answer the question, and where do their answers agree or disagree?** Which authors provide the best evidence in support of their views?

4. **What conclusions or insights into the central question have you been able to reach as a result of comparing perspectives on it?** Which perspectives do you want to incorporate into your own answer to the question? ■

The following reading is an example of comparing perspectives. Note that the author answers all four of the questions listed above.

Which Character Should Sports Develop?

ANDY RUDD

The reading below is excerpted from an academic article in the social sciences by a psychologist at Florida State University. It is the introduction to a long article on the relationship between sports and character. In the social sciences, such as psychology, writers typically preface their articles with an abstract and a comparison of viewpoints uncovered through their research, a genre known as the "literature review."

An *abstract* is an article summary common in scientific journals and databases. Helps researchers decide whether an article is relevant to their research without having to read it.

Abstract

For years, strong claims have been made that sport builds character. Despite such claims, a "winning at all cost" mentality can frequently be seen within all of sport. The reason for this paradox may relate to confusion around what it means to demonstrate character. The purpose of this article is to show that there are indeed two distinct types of character that are espoused in the sport milieu. One type is related to social values (social character) the other related to moral values (moral character). Following an explication and comparison of these types of character, a recommendation is made for a needed emphasis towards the development of moral character.

Explains and compares the views before making his recommendation.

Passive voice is customary in articles in the social sciences and natural sciences.

Introduction

Typically when an athlete or team at any level of sport is considered to have displayed character, the word "character" is associated with a host of values such as teamwork, loyalty, self-sacrifice, perseverance, work ethic, and mental toughness. As a specific example, a high school athletic director defined an athlete's character as "a willingness to try no matter what the situation. An attempt to continually improve; a willingness to give all up for the cause; and sacrificing without expectations." In another example, a high school coach asserted: "Character is the belief in self-worth and your own work ethic. . . ." (Rudd, 1999).

1

Article uses APA (American Psychological Association) documentation style, common in the social sciences.

In professional sport, character has been defined similarly. For instance, consider a newspaper article that headlined, "The Arizona Diamondbacks Attribute Their Success to Character." Specifically, the article highlighted the Diamondbacks as players who work hard and don't complain about salaries (Heyman, 2000). Consider also an issue of *Sports Illustrated* in which New England Patriots' Troy Brown commented on former teammate Drew Bledsoe's ability to play with a broken finger and lead his team to victory. Brown stated, "It showed a lot of character" (Zimmerman, 2001, p. 162).

2

Presents more examples of *character* as a social value to demonstrate that this understanding of character is widespread.

However, in contrast to the notion that an athlete of character is one who displays values such as teamwork, loyalty, self-sacrifice, perseverance, work ethic, and mental toughness, sport scholars in the area of character development have defined character with a different set of values. Sport scholars, including sport philosophers and sport psychologists, more commonly define an athlete of character as one who is honest, fair, responsible, respectful, and compassionate (Arnold, 1999; Beller & Stoll, 1995; Gough, 1998; Shields & Bredemeier, 1995). For example, Arnold (1999) states, "In terms of moral goodness, or what I refer to as

3

Offers the other perspective of *character* as a moral value and cites several writers who hold it.

moral character, it involves a life that complies with such virtues as justice, honesty, and compassion" (p. 42).

It does indeed seem, therefore, that there are two distinct definitions of character maintained by two camps. The first camp consists of coaches, administrators, and players who may typically define character with social values such as teamwork, loyalty, self-sacrifice, and perseverance. This could be designated as "social character." The second camp consists of sport scholars, and people of earlier generations still alive, who typically define character with moral values such as honesty, fairness, responsibility, compassion, and respect. This is commonly referred to by many of them as "moral character." The existence of these two camps, each with their respective definitions of character, suggests that there is confusion and disagreement concerning the definition of character in sport. (Of course, there may be some "in the middle" who accept an overlapping, possibly conflicting set of values to describe the term "character.")

As a result of the above, the differences in the way character is defined may provide strong evidence why many feel there is a lack of sportsmanship in competitive sport today. Similarly, these same people decry the "winning-at-all-cost" mentality that seems to prevail in athletics (see, for example, "A Purpose," 1999; Hawes, 1998; Spencer, 1996). Many coaches, athletic administrators, and parents may indeed place such a premium on social values such as teamwork, loyalty, self-sacrifice, and work ethic that they forget, or at least downplay, any emphasis on time-honored moral values such as honesty, fairness, responsibility, and respect.

4 — Identifies patterns in the viewpoints and sums up the differences between the two.

5

Offers an insight into what the comparison has revealed and why it matters. Concludes with view he favors.

References

Arnold, P. (1999). The virtues, moral education, and the practice of sport. *Quest, 51*(1), 39–54.

Beller, J. M., & Stoll, S. K. (1995). Moral reasoning of high school student athletes and general students: An empirical study versus personal testimony. *Pediatric Exercise Science, 7*(4), 352–363.

Gough, R. (1998). A practical strategy for emphasizing character development in sport and physical education. *Journal of Physical Education, Recreation, & Dance, 69*(2), 18–23.

Hawes, K. (1998). Sportsmanship: Why should anybody care? *NCAA News*, 1, 18.

Heyman, J. (2000, May 22). They're 'good guys, good players.' *Statesman Journal*, 3B. A purpose pitch. (1999, May 17). *Sports Illustrated, 90*, 24.

Rudd, A. (1999). [High school coaches' definitions of character]. Unpublished raw data.

Shields, D., & Bredemeier, B. (1995). *Character development and physical activity.* Champaign, IL: Human Kinetics.

Spencer, A.F. (1996). Ethics in physical and sport education. *Journal of Physical Education, Recreation & Dance, 67*(7), 37–39.

Zimmerman, P. (2001, September 3). New England Patriots. *Sports Illustrated, 95*(9), 162–163.

1. In the first and second paragraphs, what similar ideas connect the examples Rudd provides?
2. One of the keys to responding to anything we read is to evaluate it according to our own experience. What have you learned about character from participating in sports or from observing sports events?
3. Which of the two groups does your perspective on character in sports conform to, or does it include some of both views? If so, do you see conflict in your definition?

■■■ *Thinking as a Writer*

What Is the Rhetorical Situation?

1. What is Rudd's *purpose* in writing this literature review? What is his *angle* on the topic? How would you describe his *stance* and *voice*?
2. Who is this essay's intended *audience*? Is Rudd writing for his psychologist peers, for students with an interest in the topic, for athletes, for a more general public, or for another specific group? Is there anything in this essay you can cite that implies his target readership?
3. Using Asking Questions on page 177 and marginal annotations to the article, explore how the author develops his comparison of perspectives. What are the key moves he makes and in what order does he make them? ■

Portfolio of Readings on Narcissism

The following three readings offer different answers to the question, "Is narcissism increasing among young people in the United States?" These essays are arguments intended to provide an opportunity for you to explore and compare their perspectives. Rather than pose questions about them here, we will use these readings to demonstrate how to compare perspectives in the assignment section.

Changes in Narcissism

JEAN M. TWENGE

The first narcissism reading argues that narcissism has increased in recent decades, causing emotional problems for people under 35. The author, Jean M. Twenge, born in 1971, describes herself as at the "leading age" of the generation she writes about. Twenge is an associate professor of psychology at San Diego State University. The selection is from her book Generation Me: Why Today's Young Americans Are More Confident, Assertive, Entitled—and More Miserable Than Ever Before *(Free Press, 2006).*

N arcissism is one of the few personality traits that psychologists agree is almost completely negative. Narcissists are overly focused on themselves and lack empathy for others, which means they cannot see another person's perspective. (Sound like the last clerk who served you?)[1] They also feel entitled to special privileges and believe that they are superior to other people. As a result, narcissists are bad relationship partners and can be difficult to work with. Narcissists are also more likely to be hostile, feel anxious, compromise their health, and fight with friends and family.[2] Unlike those merely high in self-esteem, narcissists admit that they don't feel close to other people.

1

All evidence suggests that narcissism is much more common in recent generations. In the early 1950s, only 12% of teens aged 14 to 16 agreed with the statement "I am an important person."[3] By the late 1980s, an incredible 80%—almost seven times as many—claimed they were important. Psychologist Harrison Gough found consistent increases on narcissism items among college students quizzed between the 1960s and the 1990s.[4] GenMe students were more likely to agree that "I would be willing to describe myself as a pretty 'strong' personality" and "I have often met people who were supposed to be experts who were no better than I." In other words, those other people don't know what they're talking about, so everyone should listen to me.

2

In a 2002 survey of 3,445 people conducted by Joshua Foster, Keith Campbell, and me, younger people scored considerably higher on the Narcissistic Personality Inventory, agreeing with items such as "If I ruled the world it would be a better place," "I am a special person," and "I can live my life anyway I want to."[5] (These statements evoke the image of a young man speeding down the highway in the world's biggest SUV, honking his horn, and screaming, "Get out of my way! I'm important!") This study was cross-sectional, though,

3

1. Campbell, W. Keith. 2005. *When You Love a Man Who Loves Himself.* Chicago: Source Books.

2. Helgeson, V. S., and Fritz, H. L. 1999. Unmitigated Agency and Unmitigated Communion: Distinctions from Agency and Communion. *Journal of Research in Personality,* 33: 131–158.

3. Newsome, C. R., et al. 2003. Changes in Adolescent Response Patterns on the MMPI/MMPI-A across Four Decades. *Journal of Personality Assessment,* 81: 74–84.

4. Gough, H. 1991. "Scales and Combinations of Scales: What Do They Tell Us, What Do They Mean?" Paper presented at the 99th Annual Convention of the American Psychological Association, San Francisco, August 1991. Data obtained from Harrison Gough in 2001.

5. Foster, J. D., Campbell, W. K., and Twenge, J. M. 2003. Individual Differences in Narcissism: Inflated Self-Views across the Lifespan and around the World. *Journal of Research in Personality,* 37: 469–486.

meaning that it was a one-time sample of people of different ages. For that reason, we cannot be sure if any differences are due to age or to generation; however, the other studies of narcissism mentioned previously suggest that generation plays a role. It is also interesting that narcissism scores were fairly high until around age 35, after which they decreased markedly. This is right around the cutoff between GenMe and previous generations.

Narcissism is the darker side of the focus on the self, and is often confused with self-esteem. Self-esteem is often based on solid relationships with others, whereas narcissism comes from believing that you are special and more important than other people. Many of the school programs designed to raise self-esteem probably raise narcissism instead. Lillian Katz, a professor of early childhood education at the University of Illinois, wrote an article titled "All about Me: Are We Developing Our Children's Self-Esteem or Their Narcissism?"[6] She writes, "Many of the practices advocated in pursuit of [high self-esteem] may instead inadvertently develop narcissism in the form of excessive preoccupation with oneself." Because the school programs emphasize being "special" rather than encouraging friendships, we may be training an army of little narcissists instead of raising kids' self esteem.

4

---

6. Stout, Maureen. 2000. *The Feel-Good Curriculum*. Cambridge, MA: Perseus Books, 178.

READING 8.3

Generation Y and the New Myth of Narcissus

DUNCAN GREENBERG

This next narcissism reading is skeptical of Twenge's research. The author was a senior at Yale when he wrote this opinion column defending his generation against the charge of narcissism.

In our 10 or 20 years of existence as an age group, we've been called a lot of things, but "narcissistic" is the slur *du jour*. A controversial study at San Diego State University, which trickled down to papers this week, found that "30 percent more college students showed 'elevated narcissism' in 2006 compared with 1982." The study was authored by Jean Twenge, the cynic behind the book *Generation Me: Why Today's Young Americans Are More Confident, Assertive, Entitled—and More Miserable Than Ever Before.*

1

Twenge consolidated data from 25 years of surveys and found—or claimed to find—that the Millennials had reached unhealthy heights of self-esteem.

To you and me, narcissism remains an elusive term. But words have different meanings in common parlance than in academic jargon, and there is a general consensus in the psychology community as to the symptoms of "narcissism." Some of the more familiar characteristics, as defined by the Mayo Clinic, include a "need for constant praise," a "grandiose sense of one's own abilities or achievements," a "lack of empathy for other people," and an "expectation of special treatment." 2

Twenge's study hasn't been published yet,[1] but newspaper articles give us glimpses of her methodology: In an annual poll conducted for 25 years, students were asked if they agreed with statements like, "If I ruled the world, it would be a better place," "I think I am a special person," and "I can live my life any way I want to." Each student's answers were ranked on a scale from egocentric to empathetic. 3

Having circumscribed the malady, though, we are left with the problem of diagnosis. You can't just flat-out ask people if they're narcissistic (a true narcissist will never admit it); your only hope is to trick your subject into signing off on statements that indirectly expose his inflated ego. That's why psychologists use oblique and ambiguous statements like, "I think I am a special person." The downside of obliquity, however, is questionable results. 4

Take the second question for example: if someone thinks he's special, does that make him a narcissist? Isn't everyone "special," in the etymologically related sense of "species," implying a unique combination of color, shape, and size? And where exactly is the line between narcissism and self-confidence? Given our high achievement and low rates of violence, maybe we Millennials are entitled to some self-esteem. Remember, surveys are like a house of mirrors: You can appear fat or thin, tall or short, depending on which study you happen to be to looking at. UCLA's annual report, "The American Freshman National Norms for 2006," for example, paints a radically different picture. Its finding? "A record number [of college freshmen]—83 percent—say they volunteered at least occasionally during their senior year of high school." 5

Either we're narcissistic, or we're compassionate—we can't be both. But rather than reconcile the two studies, Twenge dismisses the redeeming evidence, arguing that more and more high schools require students to meet a not-for-profit quota—the drive to do community service, she suggests, is coming from without, not from within. Admittedly, as university acceptance rates have fallen, students have turned increasingly to volunteer work to gild their applications. But if you eliminate competitive pressure from the equation, two-thirds of college freshman still believe it is "essential or very important to help others who are in difficulty, the highest percentage in a quarter century." I'm not calling Twenge a quack, but for every study that supports her point, there's another that contradicts it. And the fact of the matter is that when it comes to giving back, we've more than done our part. 6

"Okay," the critics say, "maybe you're not selfish, but you're self-absorbed." True, Millennials have been known to flaunt their lives on YouTube and MySpace. But it's not as if 7

---

1. Twenge's book was published in 2006. [Editor's note]

our predecessors didn't get attention other ways—you're telling me the hippie and grunge movements weren't attempts to attract eyeballs by raising eyebrows? Besides, while there's no denying that YouTube and MySpace are perfect outlets for the world's narcissists, vanity is not the only trait those websites cater to. Would YouTube be worth $1.65 billion to Google if users only posted videos of themselves without so much as a glance at others' postings? Critics get hung up on the egotism of the prefixes "my" and "you," but these sites are only successful because they're about other people—about meeting other people, about seeing what hidden talents other people have. Social networking, whether virtual or in person, is always going to entail a little window-dressing; the quasi-narcissistic practice of putting one's best foot forward in social settings is hardly confined to cyberspace.

In a recent *Los Angeles Times* editorial, William Strauss and Neil Howe ["Will the Real Gen Y Please Stand Up?" 2 March 2007] hit upon a baffling phenomenon: "Whenever youth behavior seems clearly positive, critics cynically find a way to dismiss it." Maybe these critics begrudge us our youth, maybe they mistake young-looking bodies for immature minds—your guess is as good as mine. For not only do we care about what other people think, seeking the approval of our peers through YouTube ratings and FaceBook friend requests, but we care about how other people feel, volunteering for heroic causes on an unprecedented scale. Yes, we feel entitled—to a world without terrorism and global warming and to politicians who will take these scourges seriously. And, no, we don't need constant praise—but a little positive feedback, when we deserve it, would be nice. 8

Will the Real Gen Y Please Stand Up?

WILLIAM STRAUSS AND NEIL HOWE

Is the narcissism of young people a fearsome national problem? Absolutely, according to a new study by San Diego State psychology professor Jean Twenge. In a book published last year, *Generation Me,* and a new report issued this week, Twenge 1

The final perspective on narcissism comes from two writers who specialize in the study of generations throughout American history. This article, based on different surveys, draws a completely different conclusion from Twenge's about today's young people. It appeared in 2007 in the Los Angeles Times.

draws a portrait of under-socialized young people fated to depression, self-destruction, violence and civic decay as they grow older.

Her study, "Egos Inflating over Time," draws on 25 years of personality surveys that test youth for narcissism. Today's teenagers stand condemned for being more likely to agree with statements such as "I think I am a special person." The study's conclusions fuel endless negative media commentary on today's kids that will always find an audience—stories about crime, cheating, sexual license and celebrity worship. 2

But Twenge and others are wildly mistaken about the Millennial generation—those born since the early 1980s, which some persist in calling Generation Y. No matter what teens say on surveys, there is scant evidence that they act more selfishly. In fact, the trends in youth behavior support the opposite conclusion—namely, that Millennials have much greater regard for each other, their parents and the community than Gen X'ers or baby boomers had at the same phase of life. 3

Consider crime as an obvious index of self-centered behavior. Since 1994, the rate at which people under age 25 commit serious violent crimes has fallen by more than 60%. Even as states build new prisons, the incarcerated population under age 25 is shrinking. 4

Or look at the rate of pregnancy and abortion for girls under age 18, both of which are down by roughly one-third since the mid-'90s. Apparently (experts say) teenagers are having sex less and protecting themselves more, backtracking against the sexual revolution ignited by the boomers. 5

Drug abuse too is a classic barometer of self-involved behavior. According to the highly regarded annual Monitoring the Future survey, cigarette and alcohol consumption in grades 8, 10 and 12 are now at their lowest levels since the survey began in 1975. The rate of illicit drug use is much lower for today's kids than it was for their parents when they were in high school. Selfish kids would seem unlikely to get along with their parents. Yet several surveys indicate that today's teenagers are very close to their moms and dads. Record numbers claim they "share their parents' values" or "have no problem with any family member." Increasingly they say they want to live near their parents later in life—a reassuring prospect if Social Security collapses under the demographic weight of the boomers. 6

A healthy civic indicator is the boom in youth volunteering, a finding the "Egos" study discounts because so many high schools require community service. But other indicators point to the same positive trend. Voting rates for Americans 25 and younger have surged since the late 1990s. According to the UCLA College Freshman survey, 76% of new college arrivals, a record high, now say that "raising a family" is a very important goal—and a record low, only 27%, agree that "realistically, there is little an individual can do to change society." 7

But the scolders of the young argue on. Many are themselves boomers, a generation that pushed up most indicators of self-seeking behavior during their own youth: violence, risk, rage and rebellion. The original Me Generation has spent a lifetime obsessed with the journey within. Thanks to boomers, a vocabulary of self-esteem and self-love so permeates today's schools and media that professors like Twenge can now blame kids for obligingly repeating it back to them on personality tests. 8

Whenever youth behavior seems clearly positive, critics cynically find a way to dismiss it. If teenagers are doing more homework, passing more AP tests and making longer-term life plans, that just shows how selfishly they want to get ahead. If they flock to social network sites for mutual support, that's a sign of me-first showboating. If youth suicide rates have fallen, that's only because of new drug therapies. In order to claim that kids are "more miserable than ever before," Twenge needs to deny that they're emotionally healthier. 9

No message from 40- and 50-year-olds to today's 20-year-olds could be so perverse and contrary to fact as the accusation of selfishness. Boomers and X'ers would do a lot better by finding within themselves the sort of authentic moral leadership that will inspire Millennials to build a better society as they mature. 10

The older generations also should go easy on themselves. They should be proud that maybe they've raised their children pretty well after all—even if those children are not turning out to be as endearingly egocentric as themselves. 11

The Assignment

To get a broad perspective on a topic, compare and evaluate the views of other thinkers. Does everyone, for example, think that Facebook improves friendships? Which perspectives seem most valid after careful examination?

Read at least two perspectives addressing a topic of current interest. In an essay, explore the perspectives by noting where authors address the same or similar questions, and compare their answers. Decide which views seem most valid. Conclude by discussing how your exploration contributed to your understanding of the topic.

How Do I Compare Perspectives? Questioning the Rhetorical Situation

Begin by picturing a **rhetorical situation** for your writing project. Remember that rhetoric means *effective communication*. You are not just writing a paper, you are also communicating. You should consider the key variables in any act of communication: a writer with something to say, a reader the writer wishes to reach, and a kind of text appropriate to the writing task. These variables will affect many decisions you make during the composing process.

Writer: What Is My Purpose and What Impression Should Readers Have of Me?

The assignment in this chapter specifies a purpose for comparing perspectives: to explore the range of opinions on a single question and to draw an original conclusion informed by your reading and critical thinking. In college writing, this is a common purpose, since most research papers begin with an exploration of the research.

This project, then, will help you develop a crucial college skill you will also use regularly in daily life as you analyze competing bids, for example, or assess the arguments of political candidates vying for your vote.

Audience: Who Is My Reader?

As with all writing projects, imagining your audience will help you decide how best to represent the viewpoints you are comparing. You will need to place perspectives in context for your readers by identifying each writer and providing information about their background. Readers expect writers to represent the competing viewpoints fairly by providing accurate summaries of the various positions. Because the assignment requires comparing and evaluating viewpoints, your readers will need you to go beyond summary to identify the strengths and weaknesses of each position.

Text: What Would Be an Appropriate Topic?

If your instructor does not provide you with a set of readings that provide different views on a single question, you have several options for finding them:

- **Reviews of artistic works and performances.** You could compare reviews of a film, play, or musical performance.

- **Opinion columns assessing political candidates or proposed legislation.** If you are writing in an election year, you could compare candidates' positions on a single issue. Newspapers often run opinion columns where you can find at least two views on a current political issue.

- **Viewpoints on issues in current events or popular culture.** News articles often cite a few expert viewpoints on the topic, which you could use as a starting point. Use a library database to search for articles by these authors. You can also search using keywords for opinions and articles on an issue. Newspapers often run "debates," in which they publish several columnists' responses to a single question. For example, see the online feature "Room for Debate" in *The New York Times*. The reference librarians at your school can also help you locate a variety of views on a topic.

See Chapter 16, pages 419–20, for guidance in using library databases.

See Chapter 16, pages 420–21, for guidance in using search engines and for information about newspapers.

How Do I Compare Perspectives? Engaging the Writing Process

No two people compose in exactly the same way, and even the same person may go through the writing process in different ways with different assignments. Nevertheless, because no one can attend to everything at once, there are phases in handling any significant writing task. You begin by preparing to write, generating content and planning your draft. The next phase is drafting your paper, getting a version, however rough it may be, on screen or paper so that you have something to work with during the next two stages: revising your draft by changes to the content, arrangement, and style of your writing; and editing your draft to take care of problems at the paragraph and sentence level, such as lack of focus and coherence, awkward or unclear sentences, and errors of grammar, spelling, and punctuation.

We will illustrate this process for comparing perspectives using this chapter's portfolio of three readings (pages 181–86) on narcissism. We will guide you through strategies for finding points for comparison and organizing an exploratory essay around them.

Exploring Your Topic

Plan to spend at least half of the time allotted for this project on the preparation stage: careful reading and considerable informal writing, both in the margins and in notes either online or in a notebook.

Asking Questions: Choosing and Narrowing Your Topic

As you choose readings on your topic, be sure that the authors are addressing not just the same topic but *the same question or questions* about the topic. For example, *The New York Times* "Room for Debate" on choosing a college was titled "Does It Matter Where You Go to College?" This is a broad question that could take into account many variables. The perspectives actually addressed a question: "Does it matter if you attend a top-ranked school?"

Read your selections critically, as described in Chapter 2, pages 13–37. These strategies for preparing to read will help:

1. Find out about the author and his or her likely bias.
2. Skim the reading to see the main ideas as evident in the introduction, paragraph openings, and the conclusion. Look for key words that appear in other readings you are considering for your comparison.

Asking Questions: What Does That Word Mean?

On any topic, certain words are central to the discussion, as in our reading about the concept of character in sports. In the example question for our illustration of the writing process, the key term is *narcissism*. An in-depth dictionary is a good place to start your exploration. According to the *Oxford English Dictionary (OED)* **narcissism** is:

> Excessive self-love or vanity; self-admiration, self-centeredness.

The *OED* also tells us that the term *narcissism* alludes to a character in Greek mythology. It describes Narcissus as "a beautiful youth who fell in love with his own reflection in water and pined to death."

Narcissus contemplating his own image. Painting by John William Waterhouse, 1903.

■ ■ ■ ■ ACTIVITY 8.1 *Writer's Notebook*

Exploring Terms

List the key term (or terms) that are used in your question. Then look up the term(s) in a comprehensive dictionary like the *OED*. Write a paragraph or two explaining what you discovered about the origins and definitions of your key term (or terms). ■

Preparing to Write

Beyond gathering your readings and assessing them critically, the key step in preparing to write is to look for ways to synthesize what the perspectives say.

Asking Questions: Finding Ways to Synthesize

Writing a good comparison depends on synthesis, bringing together what different people have to say on similar points. A useful strategy for finding connections among sources is to identify the main points in any one source and turn them into questions. For example, in Jean Twenge's perspective on narcissism (pages 181–82), she says:

> Narcissists are overly focused on themselves and lack empathy for others, which means they cannot see another person's perspective. . . . They also feel entitled to special privileges and believe that they are superior to other people." They are "more likely to be hostile, feel anxious, compromise their health, and fight with friends and family" and to "admit that they don't feel close to other people."

The implied question is, "What are the traits of a narcissist?"

BEST PRACTICES | Advantages of Turning Key Points into Questions

1. Different sources will give different answers to the same question, but *stating the question* will help you bring the readings together.
2. Questions can help you *organize your essay point by point,* showing how each question is addressed by different sources; this approach is preferable to presenting entire perspectives, one after another. The latter organization results in summaries, whereas the former compares and comments on specific differences among the perspectives. ■

▨▨■■ ACTIVITY 8.2 *Collaborative Activity*

Turning Main Points into Questions

In groups of two or three, review the three readings on narcissism, identifying the main points in each. State the question that each main point answers. Then find passages in two or all three of the readings that answer the same question. What similarities and differences do you find among the answers? ■

Mapping Ideas on a Comparative Grid

Another way to identify points of similarity and difference in multiple sources is to map the ideas on a grid, such as the one that follows. Begin by identifying the questions answered by the main points in each selection. Then indicate where the answers are in the readings.

Question	Twenge (pages 181–82)	Greenberg (pages 182–84)	Strauss and Howe (pages 184–86)
What are the traits of a narcissist?	par. 1	par. 2	
Is there evidence that narcissism has increased?	Yes: par. 2, 3	No: par. 4, 5	No: par. 3
Is there evidence that narcissism has not increased?		Yes: par. 3, 4, 5, 6	Yes: par. 5, 6
What has caused the increase or the appearance of an increase?	par. 4: schools, media	par. 7: YouTube and MySpace	par. 8: schools

Additional Ways to Track Connections across Perspectives

As you read into a second or third person's perspective, try one or more of these suggestions to help keep control over your sources:

■ Annotate each reading with references to page numbers in other sources that address the same questions.

■ Use color-coded highlighters to mark passages addressing the same questions in different readings.

- Write informally to discuss where the authors agree or disagree and re-spond with your own opinion about who has the best viewpoint. See Chapter 2, pages 29–30 for a model. In the next section, we show an example of a student's informal writing in response to one question in common across the readings on narcissism.

Using Informal Writing to Join the Discussion

One of the best ways to generate content is to write informally about how different people answer the same questions and to say what you think about their answers. You can do this as freewriting, a notebook entry, or a post on a discussion board to share with classmates who might be reading and comparing the same sources.

The advantage of this kind of informal writing is that you can later use it as part of the draft of your paper. It will need cleaning up, but it will have two essential qualities:

- A comparison with specific references to the sources you have read
- Commentary showing your own thinking in your own voice

You need to be part of the synthesis, too, so it is never too soon to begin to evaluate the viewpoints. Following is an example of a freewriting from student Ian Fagerstrom, whose comparison of perspectives on narcissism concludes this chapter (see pages 198–201).

Student Example

Ian Fagerstrom's Freewriting to Compare and Comment

So—is narcissism more common in my age group? Twenge says yes. To prove it, she has done a lot of research, looking at surveys about what people say when asked to agree or disagree with certain statements. Over a 40-year period, the number of people who agreed with the statement "I am an important person" went up from 12% to 80%. She says this is an "incredible" increase, but I personally don't find it surprising. The numbers look impressive, but what is the reality? Does it mean a huge jump in narcissists or a change in thinking about the word "important"? Most self-confident people today aren't likely to say "I am an unimportant person." If I heard somebody say that, I'd think they were depressed. The problem has to do with the statements on the survey, as the savvy Yale student, Greenberg, says. They "trick" people into saying things that sound egotistical, like "I think I am a special person." Greenberg looks more closely at the word "special." This is smart because it shows how Twenge's research could be way off base. "Special" can just mean unique, not superior. If you interpret "special" in a bad way, you hear a narcissist talking, but if you see the word as more positive, it's just a self-confident person talking. And self-confidence is good. Without self-confidence, I wouldn't be pushing myself to take on new challenges in college.

Raising a central question like this is a good way to open freewriting and also a section of your comparative paper.

Twenge's perspective.

Includes specifics about what the source says.

Responds to Twenge's perspective and evidence.

Brings in another perspective on the question of whether narcissism has increased and whether the evidence supports Twenge's claim.

Shows why Faegerstrom agrees with Greenberg.

▖▖▖▪ ACTIVITY 8.3 *In Your Own Work*

Respond to Ideas in Your Readings

As you read and reread each of the perspectives, record key points in a reading and respond to them with your own evaluations. Be sure to *refer to specific passages in the readings,* as highlighted in blue and gray in Fagerstrom's freewriting example. ▪

Drafting Your Paper

Begin by considering the guidance in the following:

BEST PRACTICES | **Writing an Exploratory Essay Comparing Viewpoints**

The basic moves are illustrated in Andy Rudd's comparison of views on character in sports (pages 178–79). The student example (pages 191–92) also illustrates the moves. In sum they are as follows:

1. Introduce a question upon which people take different positions.
2. Define any key terms central to the question.
3. Present the main point of each perspective in brief summary statements.
4. Look for patterns of agreement and disagreement, and compare what different people have to say on the same point.
5. Use quotation and paraphrase to show what different people say in defense of their viewpoint.
6. As you present your sources' viewpoints, respond with your own comments evaluating them.
7. Conclude with an evaluation of the viewpoints and what you learned from comparing them. ▪

Thinking as a Writer: What Is My Angle?

Getting a draft started will be easier if you find an angle on the material you have generated. An angle is a slant, an approach, a way to engage your topic.

Each of the three reading selections on narcissism has an angle:

▪ Jean Twenge's angle comes from her own experience as a member of the generation she studies. She and her peers were told "Put yourself first" and "You are special." In college, she studied psychology. She noticed a correlation between her generation and self-centered attitudes, loneliness, and other personality problems. When she discovered the narcissistic personality surveys, she had an angle for her research on this data.

▪ Duncan Greenberg's angle derives from the fact that his experience of Generation Y did not jibe with Twenge's research. Writing for his college newspaper, he knew that debunking Twenge's theory would strike a chord with his readers. Greenberg had his angle for a column.

■ Strauss and Howe had been studying generational differences for many years. They had the experience of knowing that older generations often criticize younger generations, asking, "What is wrong with kids these days?" Seeing Twenge's research as another example of the same old criticism gave them their angle for writing.

These three readings, however, are arguments, not explorations. How does a writer find an angle while keeping an open mind? The answer is to think about why exploring the question matters to you personally. What perspectives are you inclined to hold? As you read to discover and compare other perspectives, put your own attitudes to the same test. Consider the following questions:

> To insert your voice into perspectives you have gathered from other people, try freewriting about what you think about what they say. You can use it as part of your draft.

1. **What context do I bring to the question?** A person exploring perspectives on the relationship between wealth and happiness began by considering how her own upbringing in a military family fostered frugality and self-discipline.

2. **What outcome do I want for my exploration?** Having an angle means believing that your exploration matters. What do you hope to learn from reading multiple viewpoints? Someone planning to become a teacher chose to read about different perspectives on how young children learn. Her interest in education gave her an angle.

3. **Which perspectives are commonly held, and should they be challenged?** On any given question, we can usually name some popular perspectives. An angle can derive from challenging popular perspectives. For example, many Americans believe that everyone should go to college. We can look for selections supporting this perspective, as well as perspectives that challenge it.

Thinking as a Writer: What Voice Is Appropriate for Exploratory Writing?

You do not want your essay to read like a list of points: "Source A says _____. On this question, Source B says _____." Such a paper would be monotonous. *You need to be present in the paper, speaking as someone thinking through the questions and evaluating the various viewpoints.*

Use the informal writing you did as you read, evaluated, and responded to the readings to get your own voice into your project. Ask yourself what you would say to the author if he or she were present and you were doing an interview. Challenging perspectives is a good way to put voice into your paper, but make sure that your challenges are well reasoned, not attacks. You should sound fair, thoughtful, and receptive, willing to consider points of view that you do not find persuasive but that may contain valuable points or insights.

Developing and Organizing Your Synthesis

Drafting the essay for this project should not be difficult if you have highlighted your sources to identify passages that answer the same questions, annotated your sources to note points in common, and written informally to compare and respond to the perspectives you have gathered. Review your notes and then consider the following advice.

1. **Introduction:** How might I begin the paper? For your introduction, you could do the following:

   - Open with your own view before reading. In the body and conclusion, indicate how your thinking changed.

   - Open with the question that is the focus of your exploration. State it clearly and explain its importance.

   - Open with one of the main questions that cut across the readings, such as, "Some people think narcissism is a growing problem. Is it?" You could move directly into your paper this way.

2. **Body:** How can I introduce and compare the perspectives?
   You could devote one or two paragraphs to setting up all of the perspectives, summarizing the main position of each and introducing the key figures who hold that position, including full names and some background about their research. Or you could begin with the first question that cuts across at least two of the perspectives, introduce the perspectives, and present what each says in response to that question. Then move on to another question.

   The essential point is that a paper that synthesizes ideas from multiple authors *needs to be organized around the questions that cut across the readings,* not around the readings themselves. If you devote the first part of your paper to just one author's views, the second to the second author's views, and so on, your paper will read like a summary rather than an exploration.

3. **Conclusion:** Your conclusion should review your evaluations of the different perspectives. Whose reasons were the most persuasive? What evidence the most compelling? Construct a perspective of your own using what you have found convincing and compelling from all the sources. Use your conclusion to explain how you developed deeper insight based on comparing your sources.

BEST PRACTICES | Tips for Organizing Your Paper around Questions

- Check the lists of questions you have made for each perspective. Put these lists together now and identify questions that appear in multiple readings.

- Consider whether narrowing the focus of your exploration might help. An exploration of narcissism, for instance, might deal only with the difference between healthy self-esteem and genuine narcissism.

- Based on length requirements for the paper and how much you have to say about the questions, select the ones you intend to address.

- Order the questions logically. For example, a definition question makes more sense at the beginning of the paper. Discuss causes, then effects.

- Plan on multiple paragraphs for each question. You could, for instance, devote one paragraph to one source's answer and another to what the others say on the same question.

- Create transitions so that your reader will know when discussion of one question is over and another is beginning. ■

Revising Your Draft

Revising this kind of paper usually involves improving the organization, looking more closely at the perspectives to make your exploration more specific, and including more of your own reactions to the authors' views. Asking Questions lists specific activities for helping you revise.

ASKING QUESTIONS | Revision Checklist for Comparing Perspectives

This checklist moves in descending order, from major challenges of this project to concerns to consider in every piece of formal writing.

1. **Did you explore?** Exploring means entertaining a question. To entertain a question means to hold it open and consider it thoughtfully. If you disputed a point before considering its merits, revise to show more open-mindedness before you declare that someone is wrong.

2. **How well did you represent the ideas of all the authors?** Did you draw on the sources to represent their views accurately and fully? Did you introduce the authors with full name on first mention and provide information about their credentials?

3. **How well did you organize the paper?** Check to see that you focus on one question at a time, not one source at a time. Did you bring in comparisons throughout your draft?

4. **How well did you work quotations into your paper?** Did you introduce quotations and follow up with explanation and commentary as needed?

5. **How well did you respond to the sources?** Did you provide enough commentary to show exactly what you agreed or disagreed with and why?

6. **How smoothly did the sentences flow?** Each sentence should prepare the reader for the one coming next. Read your draft aloud, listening for places where transitions are needed. ■

When you have limited time to revise a paper, you have to prioritize. Take care of the bigger problems first, the ones that alter your essay substantially. If smaller problems remain, solve as many as you can in the time you have. One common problem of drafts is inadequately developed paragraphs.

Student Example: Excerpt from Ian Fagerstrom's Draft

The following excerpt from Ian Fagerstrom's draft omits important information.

Draft Version

Jean M. Twenge, an Associate Professor of Psychology at San Diego State University and author of *Generation Me,* also tends to put the young generation in a negative light, accusing us of being obsessed with ourselves and putting the blame for it on the schools, media and parents. She believes narcissism is on the rise, almost an epidemic. However, offering the perspective of someone in the Millenial generation, Duncan Greenberg, an undergraduate student at Yale, wrote an editorial in his campus newspaper titled "Generation Y and the New Myth of Narcissus." Greenberg says that narcissism is actually not a problem at all, but a misinterpretation of data. He takes the opposition and points out that our generation is actually more empathetic than most.

> Fails to mention Twenge's use of the NPI (Narcissistic Personality Inventory).

> Without data from Twenge, reference to data confuses the reader, who would ask: What data?

Revised Version

Jean M. Twenge, an Associate Professor of Psychology at San Diego State University and author of a book called Generation Me, says yes. She accuses young people of being obsessed with themselves. In her book and in a National Public Radio interview, she places the blame for this problem on media messages, indulgent parents, and the self-esteem movement in the schools. She believes narcissism is on the rise, almost an epidemic, as indicated by college students' responses over the years to a psychological survey known as the NPI, for Narcissistic Personality Inventory.

However, representing the perspective of someone in the Millennial generation, Duncan Greenberg, an undergraduate student at Yale, wrote an editorial in his campus newspaper titled "Generation Y and the New Myth of Narcissus." Greenberg says that narcissism is actually not a problem at all, but a misinterpretation of the NPI data. He points out that our generation is actually more empathetic than most. Greenberg refers to a Los Angeles Times article by William Strauss and Neil Howe, who have written several books about the role of generations in America. I read their article, which contains evidence pointing in the opposite direction, showing no indication of narcissism. So—who has it right?

> Sets up the second perspective.

> Sets up the third perspective.

Editing Your Final Draft

Nearly every draft can be improved by editing to reduce wordiness, vary sentence structure, and make word choices more specific. This is especially true in introductions. Once your writing project is complete, revisit the opening to see if it contains repetitions and other wordy sentence constructions, such as overuse of the verb "to be."

The first draft of Ian Fagerstrom's introduction included too many uses of "it is" and other forms of the verb "to be."

Original Version

Living in a bustling city like Dallas, <u>it is</u> not hard to see self-absorbed people everywhere I turn. <u>It is</u> all too easy to get caught up in the idea that "you <u>are a special person.</u>" Honestly, <u>it is</u> an appealing idea; who does not want to feel important and special. <u>It is</u> a good feeling <u>to be</u> at the top of the class, or <u>be</u> the first person to have the newest iPod. <u>Isn't</u> this focus on ourselves natural for people when they <u>are</u> young? Does it make us narcissists? Some authors recently claim that American culture and young Americans especially are suffering from an epidemic of narcissism. I wonder. <u>Is</u> this "problem" really not a problem at all, or just some new ideas that critics are blowing out of proportion?

Edited Version

Some authors recently claim that young Americans are suffering from an epidemic of narcissism. Could they be right? Living in a bustling city like Dallas, I see self-absorbed people everywhere I turn. We live under a barrage of messages suggesting ways to announce that we are "special." Honestly, it is an appealing idea; who does not want to feel important? Who does not want to be the one at the top of the class or the one with the newest iPhone? But isn't this focus on the self a natural thing for people when they are young? Does it make us narcissists?

REVISED STUDENT EXAMPLE

Fagerstrom 1

Ian Fagerstrom

English 1301: Rhetoric

Professor Channell

November 2, 2011

Comparison of Perspectives on Narcissism

Introduces the question.

Some authors recently claim that young Americans are suffering from an epidemic of narcissism. Could they be right? Living in a bustling city like Dallas, I see self-absorbed people everywhere I turn. We live under a barrage of messages suggesting ways to announce that we are "special." Honestly, it is an appealing idea; who does not want to feel important? Who does not want to be the one at the top of the class or the one with the newest iPhone? But isn't this focus on the self a natural thing for people when they are young? Does it make us narcissists?

1

Sets up the first perspective.

Jean M. Twenge, an Associate Professor of Psychology at San Diego State University and author of a book called *Generation Me,* says yes. She accuses young people of being obsessed with themselves. In her book and in a National Public Radio interview, she places the blame for this problem on media messages, indulgent parents, and the self-esteem movement in the schools. She believes narcissism is on the rise, almost an epidemic, as indicated by college students' responses over the years to a psychological survey known as the NPI, for Narcissistic Personality Inventory.

2

Sets up the second perspective.

However, representing the perspective of someone in the Millennial generation, Duncan Greenberg, an undergraduate student at Yale, wrote an editorial in his campus newspaper titled "Generation Y and the New Myth of Narcissus." Greenberg says that narcissism is actually not a problem at all, but a misinterpretation of the NPI data. He points out that our generation is actually more empathetic than most. Greenberg refers to a

3

Sets up the third perspective.

Los Angeles Times article by William Strauss and Neil Howe, who have written several books about the role of generations in America. I read their article, which contains evidence pointing in the opposite direction, showing no indication of narcissism. So—who has it right?

Introduces first point in comparison.

Two sources by same author requires title in the citation.

We might begin by checking to see if the authors agree on the meaning of the key term "narcissist." Twenge describes narcissists as "overly focused on themselves"; they are people who "feel entitled to special privileges and believe that they are superior . . ." (*Generation,* 68). She makes the distinction between high self-esteem and narcissism. People with high self-esteem feel close to others; narcissists on the other hand do not (69). Greenberg uses the Mayo Clinic's symptoms of narcissism: traits such as "a need for constant praise" in addition to an "expectation of special treatment" (qtd. in Greenberg). So there is no disagreement about what narcissism is between these writers, but they reach different conclusions about whether it is a growing problem.

4

Shows two perspectives in agreement about what narcissism is.

Introduces the question: Is there evidence that narcissism is increasing?

Twenge's perspective.

Twenge says yes. To prove it, she has done much research, looking at surveys about what people say when asked to agree or disagree with certain statements. In her National Public Radio interview, she says 30% more college students score above average on the Narcissistic Personality Inventory than in 1982 ("Study"). In her book, she reports that over a 40-year period the number of people who agreed with the statement "I am an important person" went up from 12% to 80%. (*Generation,* 69). She says this is an "incredible" increase, but I personally don't find it surprising. The numbers look impressive, but what is the reality? Does it mean a huge jump in narcissists or simply change in thinking about the word "important"? Most self-confident people today aren't likely to say "I am an unimportant person." If I heard somebody say that, I would think they were depressed.

5

Includes specifics about what the source says. What evidence supports this perspective?

Responds to Twenge's perspective and evidence.

The problem has to do with the statements on the survey, as the savvy Yale student, Greenberg, says. They "trick" people into saying things that sound egotistical, like "I think I am a special person." Greenberg looks more closely at the word "special." This is smart because it shows how Twenge's research could be based on too much faith in the results of survey responses. "Special" just means unique, not superior. "Isn't everyone 'special,'" he asks, "in the etymologically related sense of 'species,' implying a unique combination of color, shape, and size?" If you interpret "special" in a bad way, you hear a narcissist talking, but if you see the word as more positive, it's just a self-confident person talking. And self-

6

Uses Greenberg to call Twenge's evidence into question.

Responds to the second perspective and its reasoning.

confidence is good. Without self-confidence, I wouldn't be pushing myself to take on new challenges in college. Greenberg's interpretation makes more sense to me.

States his evaluation of whose argument seems better.

Strauss and Howe provided a missing piece to the puzzle that helped me think through what might be causing the rise in concern about narcissism. They point out that the older "Boomer" generation, through schools and TV programs, encouraged children to develop self-esteem. So today young people who say they are special are just "obligingly repeating" what parents and teachers have told them all their lives. On a survey, they may talk like narcissists, but that doesn't mean they are narcissists. On the other hand, Twenge says that the schools went so far in teaching self-esteem (*Generation,* 69–70), that they wound up producing narcissists.

7

Asks the question, "Aside from the surveys, where is there evidence for narcissism increasing?"

But what real day-to-day evidence is there of an increase in narcissism? Twenge says you see it in people who are hostile, who have relationship issues, and who "compromise their health" (Generation, 68). But has there really been an explosion of people like this? Strauss and Howe offer statistics about a decline in crime by people under 25, a decline in risky sex and drug use, and an increase in close relationships with family. Greenberg defends our use of social networking sites as evidence of our interest in other people, not self-obsession. Greenberg, Howe, and Strauss say the rise in volunteerism shows empathy for others.

8

Compares Twenge, Greenberg, and Howe and Strauss on the evidence.

Last two paragraphs state author's view after careful consideration of all three perspectives.

At first, I was inclined to accept Twenge's argument that schools, media, and parents are going too far in telling children they are the best, most special kids ever ("Study"). But now I am not so pessimistic about the future, based on my generation's values. After considering the evidence offered by Strauss and Howe, I agree with them that Generation Y is not any more self-obsessed than generations before us. I think Greenberg is right to say that my generation may be "entitled to some self-esteem."

9

Strauss and Howe make a valid point about older generations' tendency to dismiss positive youth behavior. When a younger generation is praised for something, older generations tend to put us down, call us spoiled and scoff at us. I have met my fair share of narcissists, but it is hard to prove that it is such a big problem that we need to name my generation "Generation Me."

10

Works Cited

Greenberg, Duncan. "Generation Y and the New Myth of Narcissus." Editorial. *The Yale Herald,*
8 Mar. 2007. Web. 20 Feb. 2007.

Howe, Neil and William Strauss. "Will the Real Gen Y Please Stand Up." *Los Angeles Times.* 2
March 2007. Web. 24 Nov. 2010.

Twenge, Jean M. *Generation Me: Why Today's Young Americans Are More Confident, Assertive,
Entitled—and More Miserable Than Ever Before.* New York: Free Press, 2006. Print.

——— "Study Sees Rise of Narcissism Among College Students." Interview by Alex Chadwick
and Luke Burbank. *Day to Day.* Natl. Public Radio. WNYC, New York, 27 Feb. 2007. *NPR.
org.* Web. 19 Feb. 2008.

CHAPTER 9
Critiquing an Argument

WHEN YOU HEAR OR READ AN ARGUMENT ABOUT A TOPIC YOU FIND INTEREST-ing, the first question you ask is, "What exactly did it say?" That is, you recall or reread the content. Then, depending on your reaction to the argument, you likely ask the following questions that respond to it: What do I agree with? What do I disagree with? Why?

When you answer these questions, you are engaging in **critique,** *offering a reasoned assessment of an argument.* We encounter critiques in letters to the editor in newspapers, in magazines that include reader responses to articles published in the previous issue, and in blogs devoted to some controversial issue or cause. The basic situation is always the same: First, someone writes an argument urging readers to believe or do something; next, a reader responds by agreeing or disagreeing (or doing some of both) and explaining why.

What Is a Critique?

A critique is a written assessment or review of the merits of someone's work. Reviews of concerts, for instance, are critiques; so are book reviews. When an instructor grades your work, he or she usually offers a brief critique of its strengths and weaknesses. In each case, the person evaluates the work according to a set of standards appropriate for the type of performance it is.

An argument offers reasons for believing or doing something. Therefore, a critique of an argument is a rational assessment of it, organized around one or more points of evaluation. It is not an attack or even necessarily negative. Critiques do not have to find fault; you can write to defend arguments, especially when you think others have wrongly criticized them.

Rational assessment includes understanding why people disagree. In large part, people disagree because they think about controversial issues or questions in different **contexts**—that is, *different frames of reference based on how they were raised; the life experiences they have had; what they know, believe, and value.*

CONCEPT CLOSE-UP | Context and Critique

Arguments in newspaper opinion columns or magazines or websites are not actually the isolated pieces of writing they seem to be. They arise out of contexts, real-world situations as experienced and interpreted by their authors. People argue in response to things that happen in the news or in their lives. Real-world circumstances like economic class, political beliefs, or religious values influence people's arguments.

Context always matters for the following reasons:

■ **Context is the key to understanding an argument as rhetorical communication.** Arguments are designed to move readers. We can only understand an argument by asking, "Who is the writer trying to convince or persuade?"

■ **Context is the key to understanding why people disagree.** People look at issues from their own perspectives. An argument for making tuition loans easily available to college students might appeal to young people who cannot afford the cost of college. However, a student whose older sibling graduated from college and is now trying to repay a $20,000 debt might argue that easy loans are not the best solution to the problem.

■ **Context is the key to understanding your response.** Arguments are also read within contexts, the background, knowledge, and experiences of the reader. Your initial reaction to an argument will depend on the point of view you bring to it. To judge an argument fairly, you will have to take this context into account. ■

Why Write to Critique an Argument?

Every day you hear or read the arguments of other people, in conversation, in books and magazines, on television, radio, and the Internet, in business meetings and community gatherings. There is no way to avoid arguments designed to influence what you think and do. Nor should we want to avoid them: Arguments and counter-arguments are democracy in action, one of the ways an open society works. However, good arguments must be distinguished from bad ones. This is the stake that you and all thoughtful people have in critique.

It is important to distinguish between a reaction and a critique. A reaction is just a "thumbs up" or "thumbs down" judgment, like responses to films we have seen. In responding to arguments, a reaction is simply agreement or disagreement without explaining why or offering any justification. In contrast, a critique offers reasons for agreeing or disagreeing. It attempts to defend an evaluation of an argument. Consequently, a critique can help us distinguish good arguments from bad ones.

ABC's long-running talk show *The View* is a great place to see arguments in action. The hosts and their guests discuss a variety of topics and engage in interesting, and often heated, discussions. An episode of *The View* may be a great place to start for practice with evaluating good, well-supported arguments versus bad ones.

How Do Writers Critique Arguments?

An argument advances a thesis or **claim,** *what the writer wants us to believe or do.* The claim is defended with reasons that explain and justify the claim, and the

For more on the structure of argument, see Chapter 10, pages 231–57.

reasons are backed with evidence for accepting each reason. Critiques challenge the claim, the reasons, the evidence, or all three.

As you read the following arguments, focus on what the critiques challenge and why.

READING 9.1

Point Person: Our Q and A with David H. Freedman

JIM MITCHELL

*S*cience and business writer David H. Freedman has pondered why smart people get it wrong so often, and he says the answer is that we're too eager to accept—and promote—the most deeply flawed but attention-getting conclusions. He describes his new book, "Wrong: Why Experts Keep Failing Us—and How to Know When Not to Trust Them," explores "what pushes experts—be they top scientists, high-powered consultants, pop gurus, financial whizzes or journalistic pundits—into offering misleading advice and ways to tell good expert advice from the dubious stuff."

1

David H. Freedman published a book arguing that our media-dominated society is too dependent on the cult of the expert. He was interviewed by Jim Mitchell, an editorial writer for the Dallas Morning News. *An excerpt from that interview appears below, which summarizes the argument of the book. A reader of the newspaper, William Brown, then wrote a response to the interview in Reading 9.2. He objects to one of Freedman's key ideas— the notion that there is no such thing as "absolute truth." As you read the interview and Brown's critique, consider your own view of truth. Do you see truth as Freedman does, as Brown does, or in some other way?*

Why is there so much bad research out there?

2

People are encouraged to do bad research. We like really simple answers, but we live in a very complex world. We're essentially asking for the wrong sort of answers and then rewarding people for giving them to us. We reward them with our attention. We read their books and articles. In this way, researchers get pushed toward giving simple, "breakthrough," exciting answers.

But doesn't expertise naturally evolve as we learn more?

3

A friendly way of putting it is to say that experts start off wrong, but get more and more right over time. But there also are steps backward where things get more wrong for while and then get right again.

What's become more wrong over time? 4

Diet advice. It's getting worse and worse and has been for some time. We used to have a better idea of the problem, which is essentially overeating and lack of exercise. Now we're bombarded with all sorts of exotic explanations.

Are we too consumed by metrics, especially in business? 5

Absolutely. The ability to measure more and record it better also hurts us. Sometimes we measure the wrong things or measure the right things poorly. We have to take a step back and take a more holistic view and use our common sense. Yet, we often check our brains at the door and allow computer analysis tools to take over, and the results are often tremendous errors, big mistakes.

Are the Internet and social media contributing to the "expertise" problem? 6

The Internet is miraculous in its ability to give more of us better access to better information. It also gives us much better access to much worse information. Right now, bad information tends to overwhelm good information, and the net effect has been negative. I've not seen a lot of good things come out of social networks, either. The problem is generations are growing up on this stuff and are never going to question it.

Does absolute truth exist? 7

> The key statement that Brown will object to.

No, and we should not have an idea of absolute truth. One person's truth is another person's falsehood. We see it in politics, science and other things. It is so easy to find people and supposedly good evidence that back up your point of view. Everyone becomes more and more convinced that they are right and less and less willing to look at the other point of view. Everyone gets the sense that they have the absolute truth when, in truth, they're getting further away from it.

Does this mean we're trained in school to consume, not analyze, information? 8

From a very early age we are taught that there are people out there whose opinion is much more valid than our own and that we should treat those people as absolute authorities. We are not taught early on to question what we see in textbooks. Look at any textbook that is 10 or 20 years old. You'll find so much wrong information. We are overly trained to be much too accepting of what passes for expertise.

Is this a uniquely American issue? 9

It's almost universal. I haven't been able to find any culture anywhere in the world at any time in history that hasn't had a significant problem with expertise. We all can't be super-smart about everything.

Who are the most clueless: economists, scientists, financial experts, educators, journalists? 10

What a wonderful concept. We all have a pretty impressive horse in that race, and it is neck and neck. They all have terrible problems of different types.

How do we know when someone has it all wrong?

Recognize that there is no solution, that because of the general nature of our complex world, the simple answers aren't out there. We need to pay attention to the kinds of expertise that build up to a consensus over many, many years.

11

So do you consider yourself an expert on expertise?

I have to admit I've become a little bit of one. I hate to say it, but I've spent a lot of time studying this stuff, and I think it would probably cause more problems than it would solve for me to claim that I'm not. And, yes, it probably means that I succumb to all the problems that all experts succumb to. I urge people to not take my word for anything. What I'm really trying to do is to provoke thinking and raise awareness.

12

R E A D I N G **9.2**

A Question of Absolutes

WILLIAM BROWN

First paragraph reminds audience of the topic.

Freedman was debunking the bad advice of researchers and others who claim to be in the know in his recent book, *Wrong: Why Experts Keep Failing Us—and How to Know When Not to Trust Them*.

1

Singles out what Freedman said, the statement the writer considers wrong.

When asked, "Does absolute truth exist?" Freedman answered: "No, and we should not have an idea of absolute truth. One person's truth is another person's falsehood. We see it in politics, science and other things." This is absurd on its face if you accept the dictionary definition of "truth," which is that which is in accordance with fact or reality.

2

Argues that Freeman's notion of truth is not consistent with it usual meaning.

Writer contends that "truth" becomes meaningless if there is no standard for truth.

To say that there is no absolute truth is another way of saying everything is relative. This is a fanciful indulgence in never-never land that, for some strange reason, seems to be a popular view today. However, not to accept the dictionary definition of truth is to engage in nonsensical, meaningless talk.

3

Concludes by challenging the notion that truth is only someone's point of view.

If Freedman had intended to say that truth is that which conforms to reality, but one person's way of looking at truth may be different than another person's, I would agree. But alas, that is not what he said.

4

Questions for Discussion

1. Note that Brown does not call Freedman's argument about our general reliance on experts into question, but concentrates instead on one idea, "absolute truth." Is this one idea important to Freedman's argument? Why or why not?
2. Letters to the editor in newspapers have to be short. Consequently, Brown could not explain what he meant by relativism or why he considers relativism a "fanciful indulgence." What does relativism mean? Why is it "a popular view today," as Brown says? What is your view of relativism?
3. Imagine yourself as Freedman responding to Brown's critique. What would you say?

■■ *Thinking as a Writer*

What Is the Rhetorical Situation?

1. What is Brown's *purpose* in writing his critique? What is his *angle*, his way of challenging what Freedman said? How would you describe his *voice*, the attitude his letter conveys?
2. Who is Brown's intended *audience*? Is he writing to convince Freedman that he is wrong about truth? Is he writing to convince readers who read the interview that they should not accept Freedman's view of truth? Is there anything in the letter you can cite that implies the target readership?
3. Using the marginal annotation to the letter, describe how to critique by raising a single objection to someone's argument. What are the moves that Brown makes? ■

See Chapter 3, pages 40-45, for definitions of purpose, angle, and voice.

Responses to Arguments against the Minimum Legal Drinking Age

DAVID J. HANSON

David J. Hanson, professor emeritus of sociology at SUNY, Potsdam, has researched and written on the topic of alcohol for more than thirty years. This piece came from his website at SUNY, Potsdam, for which Hanson received some unrestricted funding from the Distilled Spirits Council of the United States.

Hanson responds to arguments advanced by a government agency, the National Institute on Alcohol Abuse and Alcoholism (NIAAA), against lowering the drinking age to 18. He uses a pattern in critiquing these arguments. First, he gives the standard argument for lowering the drinking age. Second, he gives the NIAAA's counter-argument. Third, he gives his critique of the counter-argument. Keep these three levels in mind as you read.

Context: The first two sentences identify the source of the argument critiqued and what it is about.

The federal government is spending taxpayer money in a questionable political campaign to defend the minimum drinking age against attempts in some states to lower it. In "Responses to Arguments against the Minimum Drinking Age," the National Institute on Alcohol Abuse and Alcoholism (NIAAA) identifies arguments against the minimum legal drinking age and then suggests counter arguments. But in doing so, it plays fast and loose with the facts, a common tactic in politics. 1

States the main point of the critique.

Critique organized around the common arguments for lowering the drinking age, showing weaknesses in the NIAAA's rebuttals of these arguments.

Argument: "If I'm old enough to go to war, I should be old enough to drink." 2

Actually the argument is much stronger than the NIAAA acknowledges. The fact is that citizens are legally adults at the age of 18. They can marry, vote, adopt children, own and drive automobiles, have abortions, enter into legally binding contracts, operate businesses, purchase or even perform in pornography, give legal consent for sexual intercourse, fly airplanes, hold public office, serve on juries that convict others of murder, hunt wildlife with deadly weapons, be imprisoned, be executed, be an employer, sue and be sued in court, and otherwise conduct themselves as the adults they are. And, of course, they can serve in the United States armed services and give their lives defending their country. One of the very few things they can't legally do is consume an alcohol beverage. They can't even have a celebratory sip of champagne at their own weddings. 3

Supports first reason in favor of lowering the drinking age by adding more evidence—one way to increase the strength of an argument you support.

Counter-Argument: Federal agents suggest pointing out that people can obtain a hunting license at age 12 and a driver's license at age 16. Ironically, this actually strengthens the argument against treating legal adults as children with regard to alcohol beverages. People can hunt wildlife with a deadly weapon at age 12 but can't be trusted with a beer at age 20? 4

The government also suggests pointing out that people must be 25 to serve in the U.S. House of Representatives, 30 to serve in the Senate, and 35 to serve as President. But these unusual restrictions were imposed well over two hundred years ago in a new country that was still largely reluctant to grant rights and in which neither women nor African Americans were trusted to vote. We're now in the 21st century enjoying widespread rights and also a time when young people are infinitely more sophisticated. 5

Clearly, the agency's arguments are extremely weak and unconvincing. 6

Argument: "Europeans let their teens drink from an early age, yet they don't have the alcohol-related problems we do." 7

Counter-Argument: The NIAAA responds that "the idea that Europeans do not have alcohol-related problems is a myth." But no one suggests that Europeans have no drinking-related problems. Here the agency is guilty of using the straw person tactic—create a very weak argument and then shoot it down. 8

Exposes the NIAAA's use of a logical fallacy, which he defines.

In reality, research for decades has demonstrated that those countries and groups in Europe and elsewhere in which most people regularly drink but have few drinking-related problems all share three common characteristics: 9

1. Alcohol is seen as a rather neutral substance in and of itself. It's neither a poison nor a magic elixir. It's how it's used that's important.

2. People have two equally acceptable choices:
   - Abstain or
   - Drink in moderation.
   What's never acceptable is the abuse of alcohol by anyone of any age. Period.

3. People learn about drinking alcohol in moderation from an early age in the safe and supportive environment of the home, and they do so by good parental example. All of these groups would agree that it's better to learn about drinking in the parents' house than in the fraternity house.

Shows how outside information can be used in critique.

For help with gathering information from sources, see Chapter 16, pages 412–24.

Presents a different point of view on the legal drinking age by putting it into a larger context worldwide.

Age 21 is actually the highest minimum legal drinking age in the entire world and is a radical social experiment both internationally and in terms of our own national history. Those who call for all adults to be able to drink are traditionalists; whereas those who insist on age 21 are radicals. 10

Argument: "Lower rates of alcohol-related crashes among 19- to 20-year-olds aren't related to the age 21 policy, but rather they're related to increased drinking-driver educational efforts, tougher enforcement, and tougher drunk-driving penalties." 11

Counter-Argument: The agency wants us to argue that "careful research has shown the decline was not due to DUI enforcement and tougher penalties, but is a direct result of the legal drinking age" and that "achieving long-term reductions in youth drinking problems requires an environmental change so that alcohol is less accessible to teens." 12

However, there are a number of weaknesses in what the bureaucrats want us to say. It's true that lower rates of alcohol-related traffic accidents now occur among drivers under the age of 21. But they've also been declining among those age 21 and older, with one notable exception. 13

Arguments often cite only those facts that support their position. Critiques should ask, "What do the data really show?"

Raising the minimum legal drinking age has resulted in an apparent displacement of large numbers of alcohol-related traffic fatalities from those under the age of 21 to those age 21 to 24. In short, raising the drinking age simply changed the ages of those killed. 14

The argument that we need to make alcohol less accessible to adults under the age of 21 fails to recognize the fact, well established by governmental surveys, that it's easier for young people to obtain marijuana than alcohol. 15

It's also foolish to think that effective prohibition can be imposed on young adults. The 16 U.S. already tried that with the entire population during National Prohibition (1920–1933). The result was less frequent drinking but more heavy, episodic drinking. The effort to impose prohibition on young adults has driven drinking underground and promoted so-called binge drinking. This is a natural and totally predictable consequence of prohibition.

Argument: "We drank when we were young and we grew out of it. It's just a phase that 17 all students go through."

Counter-Argument: Interestingly, NIAAA wants us to argue that "Unfortunately, many 18 teens will not 'grow out of it'." Implicit is the belief that adults should not consume alcohol even when legally able to do so. The agency apparently envisions a society in which abstention from alcohol is the norm, a vision that it shares with temperance and prohibition advocates.

While not all students will try alcohol, virtually all normal young people will do so 19 and they will do so without ill effects. But NIAAA wants us to promote the discredited and simplistic "stepping stone" hypothesis that suggests that drinking leads to smoking which leads to marijuana, which leads to crack, which leads to cocaine, which leads to degradation and illness, which leads to death.

Argument: "Making it illegal to drink until 21 increases the desire for the 'forbidden fruit.' 20 Then, when students turn 21, they'll drink even more."

Counter-Argument: NIAAA wants us to assert incorrectly that "Actually the opposite is 21 true. Early legal access to alcohol is associated with higher rates of drinking as an adult."

In reality, research has clearly demonstrated the "forbidden fruit" phenomenon among 22 adults under the age of 21. On the other hand, there is no evidence that the increased desire to drink continues after students turn 21. In fact, upon turning age 21, many adults find that it's no longer so much fun to get into bars and drink precisely because it is legal for them to do so.

Showing that a past policy has failed, one similar to the one advocated or defended in an argument, provides a strong point for critique.

Exposing a hidden agenda is another powerful strategy for critique; the NIAAA's general antidrinking position is also at odds with the twenty-one law it advocates.

Critique ends with the author's strongest point: that the twenty-one drinking age has an effect opposite to its intention.

Questions for Discussion

1. Which of Hanson's points pose the best challenges to the NIAAA arguments? Explain why you think so. Did you find any weaknesses in Hanson's critique?
2. Visit the website of the NIAAA. What is the stated purpose of this organization? In what context does it view alcohol consumption? Is it opposed to all consumption of alcohol?
3. Based on your experience, would you say there is any merit to the "forbidden fruit" argument?

What Is the Rhetorical Situation?

1. What is Hanson's *purpose* in writing this essay? What is his *angle* on the topic? How would you describe his *voice*?

2. Who is Hanson's intended *audience*? Is he writing only for those people who already support lowering the drinking age, or does he also try to reach people who support the legal age of twenty-one or have no definite position on the issue? Is there anything in the article you can cite that implies his target readership?

3. Using the Concept Close-Up box on page 202 and the marginal annotations to the article, show how Hanson uses *context* and the *conventions* of critique to raise doubts about the current legal drinking age. Did his critique help you to see more ways to support lowering the legal age? If you were not convinced by his critique, what exactly did you resist in his arguments and why do you resist them? ■

The Assignment

If your instructor does not assign one, locate any short (750–1,000 words) argument on a controversial topic and write a critique of it. Your instructor may specify a length for your paper. If not, write a critique of about 500 to 1000 words. Later in this chapter, we offer some arguments for critique, including David Fryman on responding to opinionated professors (pages 214–15), Thomas Sowell on patriotism (pages 228–29), and Linda Chavez on the right to bear arms (pages 229–30).

How Do I Write a Critique?
Questioning the Rhetorical Situation

Begin by considering the **rhetorical situation,** *the key variables associated with you as writer; with your audience; and with the genre, conventions, and expectations of your text.* Understanding the rhetorical situation will give you a stable sense of the whole, something definite to hold in mind as you work your way through the process.

Writer: What Is My Purpose, and What Impression Should Readers Have of Me?

Your purpose in writing a critique depends entirely on the argument you are responding to and how you feel about it. Sometimes you agree with the argument and wish to offer additional reasons and evidence for it; sometimes you partly agree and wish to indicate why you cannot accept the argument entirely; and sometimes you disagree completely and wish to refute the argument. Regardless of your exact purpose, your readers should see you as someone who has listened carefully to the argument, understood it, and taken the time to write a well-considered response. Above all, you should be concerned that your readers understand what you agree and disagree with and why.

Audience: Who Is My Reader?

Most critiques address the same readership that the argument hoped to reach. Therefore, one of the more important questions you can ask is, **"Who is the reader for the argument I am responding to?"** The answer to that question tells you who your reader is. However, some critiques deliberately respond to an argument from the point of view of another possible audience, usually one the argument overlooked or chose not to address. For instance, a representative of MADD (Mothers Against Drunk Driving) might critique Hanson's argument (see pages 208–10) from the standpoint of parents who have lost children to drunk driving, clearly not the readership Hanson had in mind. When most of what you have to say would appeal to a different readership or when you want to call attention to reader concerns the argument fails to consider, shifting audience can be an effective strategy.

Text: What Would Be an Appropriate Topic?

This assignment could be written in many genres, the most common of which is a letter to the editor of a newspaper or magazine. But it could also be an op-ed piece; a response to a post on a blog; a short article for a newspaper, magazine, or newsletter; an assessment of a classroom discussion, debate, chat room exchange, public speech, or some other oral argument.

We suggest that you pick an argument you disagree with or an argument you partly agree with and partly disagree with in almost equal measure. It is harder to write a critique of an argument you find wholly convincing.

You can locate suitable arguments by recalling something you read in a newspaper, magazine, or on a website; by doing subject searches in online library indexes like LexisNexis or Academic OneFile (see pages 420–23 for how to use these resources); and by using Google to search for information on a topic in the news. Consider also the following possibilities:

- **Class Readings** Class readings can provide arguments for critique, especially if the readings themselves are arguments.

- **Local News or Observation**   Read your local and campus newspapers for arguments relating to your community. Sometimes these can be more interesting than overworked topics such as abortion or gun control.
- **Internet Discussions**   Blogs are often good sources for arguments. Visit blogs on issues of public concern, such as National Public Radio's blog.

How Do I Write a Critique? Engaging the Writing Process

No two people compose in exactly the same way, and even the same person may go through the writing process in different ways with different assignments. Nevertheless, because no one can attend to everything at once, there are phases in handling any significant writing task. You explore the topic to get a sense of whether it will work for you and what you might be able to do with it; if the topic is working out for you, then you move into preparing to write, generating more content and planning your draft.

The next phase is drafting your paper, getting a version, however rough it may be, on screen or paper so that you can work toward the final draft. Getting there involves two further phases: (1) revising your draft, making major improvements in it, followed by (2) editing your draft, taking care of errors, sentences that do not read well, paragraphs lacking focus and flow, and so on.

Exploring Your Topic

To see how to explore the argument you are about to critique, we need an example argument to illustrate the process. Here is one on an issue of some concern on most college campuses. Read it once or twice, just to understand what it says and to form a first reaction to it.

Open Your Ears to Biased Professors

DAVID FRYMAN

David Fryman was a senior at Brandeis University when he wrote this opinion column for the school's newspaper, the Justice. *He is offering advice to younger college students who often encounter professors with political opinions different from those endorsed at home or in their local communities. Fryman's question is, How should they respond?*

One of the most important lessons I've learned in three years of higher education is the value of creativity and critical thinking, particularly when confronted with a professor whose ideology, political leanings or religious viewpoint fly in the face of what I believe. In fact, with a good professor, this should happen often. It is part of a professor's job to challenge you, force you to reconsider, encourage you to entertain new ideas and the like. My first year here, it bothered me. Some professors subtly endorsed certain ways of thinking over others without always justifying their biases. They offered opinions on issues beyond their academic expertise. Many showed partiality to the political left or right.   1

How should we react when a professor with a captive audience advances a perspective we find offensive, insulting or just ridiculous? Perhaps we would benefit from treating our professors, who often double as mentors and advisers, the same way that we're taught to approach great works of literature: with critical respect.   2

The truth is many faculty members are at the top of their fields. They read, write and teach for a living. We're generally talking about the most well-educated and well-read members of society. So when a professor has something to say about politics, religion, war or which movie should win the Academy Award, I think it's a good idea to take him seriously.   3

It certainly doesn't follow, though, that there's a direct relationship between what a professor says and what's true. In fact, there may be no relationship at all. While our professors generally are leading scholars, some are also biased and fallible. I don't mean this as an insult. Professors are human beings and, as such, carry with them a wide array of hang-ups and prejudices.   4

Interestingly enough—if not ironically—our professors often teach us how to deal with biased and opinionated scholars like themselves. When we read novels, journal articles, essays and textbooks for class, we're taught—or at least this has been my experience—to be critical. We're expected to sift through material and distinguish between what holds water and what doesn't, what is based on reasoned analysis and what is mere speculation.   5

If we treat our professors similarly it should no longer bother us when they use the classroom as their soapbox. They have important things to say and we're here to learn from them. I've come to appreciate professors' opinions on a variety of issues not directly related to the subject at hand, and I think it helps us build relationships with them. While it's unfair for a professor to assign high grades only to students who echo their view or to make others feel uncomfortable to disagree, I prefer that professors be honest about what they think.   6

While it's a disservice to our own education to be intimidated or too easily persuaded by academic clout, it's just as problematic, and frankly silly, to categorically reject what a professor has to say because we take issue with his ideology, political leanings, religious views or cultural biases.

It's become popular, particularly among conservatives responding to what they perceive as a liberal bias in academia, to criticize professors for espousing personal views in the classroom. The ideal, they argue, is to leave students ignorant about their instructors' beliefs.

First of all, I think there's a practical problem with this strategy. It's more difficult to be critical if we're unsure where our professors stand. For the same reason that it's often helpful to have background information about an author before analyzing his work, it's useful to see our professors' ideological cards on the table. For instance, if I know my professor loves hunting and believes everybody should have firearms in his basement then when I hear his interpretation of the Second Amendment, I'm better equipped to evaluate his thoughts.

Secondly, if we proscribe what views may or may not be expressed in the classroom, we limit our own access to potentially useful information. Even if most of the extraneous digressions aren't worthy, every once in a while we might hear something that goes to the heart of an important issue. To limit this because we don't trust our own critical abilities is cowardly.

To return to the question I posed above: How should we respond to politically-charged, opinionated, biased professors? I think we should listen.

Forming a First Impression

It is impossible to read an argument without having some kind of response to it. Start by asking yourself, **"What is my first impression?"**

▪▪▪ ACTIVITY 9.1 *Writer's Notebook*

State Your First Impression

State your reaction simply and directly. Write it down in your notebook or a computer file reserved for this assignment. Read the selection again. Is your reaction changing? How? Why? ▪

Most of our students' first response to Fryman was favorable. He offered practical advice, and more appealing yet, *safe* advice. You may have had an entirely different reaction. First reactions cannot be right or wrong, good or bad. They just are what they are. The important thing is that *you* know what your reaction is.

Asking Questions: Achieving Critical Distance through Analysis

Critiques require **critical distance** from first responses. "Critical distance" does not mean "forget your first response." On the contrary, first impressions often turn out to be sound. Critical distance does mean *setting your first response aside for a while so that you can think the argument through carefully.*

Use the questions for critiquing an argument in Best Practices to guide your analysis.

BEST PRACTICES | Questions for Critiquing an Argument

1. **What is the context for this argument?** As we said earlier (pages 202–3), arguments take place in contexts—situations that prompt people to write. Ask, therefore, "Who wrote this? What prompted him or her to write? What might explain his or her perspective?"

2. **What is the author claiming?** Find the main point or thesis that the writer wants you to believe and/or be persuaded to do. Sometimes the claim will be stated, sometimes implied. Then ask: Is the claim clear and consistent? Is it absolute, no exceptions allowed? Is it reasonable, desirable, practical?

3. **What reasons does the author provide for accepting the claim?** Reasons answer the question: Why? Given the claim, what explains or justifies it? Like the claim, reasons will be stated or implied. Then ask: Does each reason actually explain or justify the thesis? How convincing is the reason? If the author reasons by means of an **analogy** (*comparison, reasoning that what is true in one case should be true in a similar case*), does the comparison really stand up to inspection?

4. **What evidence has the author given to support the reasons?** Reasons need support using examples, data, or expert opinion. Look at the evidence offered for each reason and ask: Does the evidence actually support the reason? How convincing is each piece of evidence, and how convincing is the evidence for each reason taken together?

5. **What are the key terms, and what do they mean?** Writers use words, often without defining them, that should be carefully examined. When a claim is justified, for instance, as the right or moral thing to do, we need to ask what "right" or "moral" means in this case.

6. **What is the author assuming?** It is impossible to argue without assuming many things, and "assumed" means "not stated." Ask: What must I believe to accept that claim, or reason, or piece of evidence? Is the assumption "safe," something that any reasonable person would also assume?

7. **What are the implications of this argument?** The implications are what the argument suggests or implies. Like assumptions, implications are usually not stated. To uncover them, ask: If I accept this position, what logically follows from it? Are its implications acceptable or not?

8. **What values motivate the argument?** What priorities does the author have? What other priorities or values conflict with those of the author?

9. **What voice and character are projected in the argument?** We talk about voice and presence in writing, and these are important to an argument's effectiveness. How would you describe the speaker and on what evidence from the text?

10. **Who is the audience for the argument?** Who is likely to agree with this argument? Who might want to refute it? What might an opponent object to and why? ■

Example: Critiquing an Argument

Here is a model of how some of these questions could be applied to Fryman's argument (pages 214–15):

1. **Thesis: What is the author's main claim?**
   Fryman: College students should listen with critical respect to biased and opinionated professors.
   Comment: Be clear about the argument's main point. Note that with this argument you have to piece together the thesis from several statements Fryman makes.

2. **Context: What prompted the author to write the argument?**
   Fryman: In paragraph 8, Fryman explains the situation that prompted him to write this argument. Conservative students had been protesting what they saw as an abuse of academic freedom by liberal professors.
   Comment: Fryman is not arguing directly to conservative activists. Whom do you think he sees as his audience? How would his argument be different if he were to address the more politically active protestors?

3. **Reasons: What are some reasons, and how well do they hold up to examination?**
   Fryman: One reason given is: "Many faculty members are at the top of their fields."
   Comment: Clearly, this statement is a reason—it explains why the author thinks students should accord professors respect. We can respond by saying, "Yes, some professors are quite accomplished *in their fields*. But when they venture outside them, do their opinions count for more than any other relatively well-informed person's?"

4. **Key terms: What words are important to the argument, and would there be any confusion about what they mean?**
   Fryman: "How should we react when a professor with a captive audience advances a perspective we find offensive, insulting or just ridiculous? . . . with critical respect."
   Comment: It is important to note that Fryman is not saying that students have to agree or even be neutral but rather that they should think critically as they listen.

5. **Assumptions: Does the author make any assumptions you might question?**
   Fryman: He is assuming that professors airing their views in class will not take away from class time devoted to material that must be covered or will not distract from the course material.

Comment: We might respond by suggesting that Fryman should have qualified his argument by putting a limit on how much class time might be devoted to professors airing their biases.

6. **Implications: What happens in reality if we accept the argument?**
Fryman: He implies that students should tolerate whatever the professor dishes out.
Comment: We can respond by saying, "How much student toleration is too much toleration? Suppose that a professor is openly sexist, for instance? Shouldn't we not only reject the opinions but also report the behavior to university authorities?"

7. **Analogies: How well do comparisons hold up?**
Fryman: He compares the approach students should take to opinionated professors with the critical respect accorded great works of literature (paragraph 2).
Comment: We can respond by saying, "Great works of literature have typically survived for years. We call them classics. Does it make sense to meet the casual opinions of professors the same way that we approach Shakespeare?"

■■■■ ACTIVITY 9.2 *In Your Own Work*

Exploring Your Argument

If you are working alone on an argument, use the ten questions in Best Practices: Questions for Critiquing an Argument (pages 216–17) to find possible content for your critique. Record the results in your notebook, your computer file for this assignment, or online—for example, as a blog that presents the argument and your analysis of it.

If all members of your class are critiquing the same argument, divide into small groups of about three or four people and do an analysis. Share what your group found with the class as a whole in discussion. Summarize what each group came up with in your notebook, computer file, or online as a blog entry or e-mail addressed to the entire class. Indicate which analytical comments you consider strongest. ■

Personal Engagement in Critiques

Critique focuses on *what an argument says*. The challenge of critique is to discover what you can say back.

Part of a good critique is to test the argument against what you know about reality. Test what the argument says against your experience with life and the world, and against what you know about the topic. Add to your knowledge of reality by gathering information through research.

Asking Questions: What Information Is Relevant to My Critique?

The following questions should help you add insights about an argument:

1. **What is my own experience with the topic or issue or problem the argument takes up?** In the case of Fryman's argument, when have the com-

ments of "biased teachers" been illuminating or helpful to you? When have they been boring, irritating, or useless? What's the difference between the two?

2. **What relevant information do I have from reading or from some other source?** Perhaps you have heard other students complain about professors pushing their political convictions on their students. What did the students say? Did their complaints seem justified? Why or why not?

3. **What could I find out from research that might be relevant to assessing the argument?** Most arguments suggest opportunities for at least checking up on information relevant to the argument. For instance, you might investigate the idea of academic freedom. How does it apply to professors? How does it apply to students?

See Chapter 16, pages 412–24, for detailed guidance on ways to research any topic.

4. **If the argument reasons from data, in what other ways might the data be interpreted? What other data might contradict the information given?** Research will often lead you to other arguments that interpret the same or similar data differently or that supply additional data the argument you are critiquing did not know or ignored. For example, arguments for stronger border patrol enforcement sometimes fail to mention that about 40 percent of undocumented immigrants came here legally and simply stayed. Enhanced border control obviously will have no effect on that group.

■■■■ ACTIVITY 9.3 *In Your Own Work*

Assessing the Fit of Argument and Reality

In your notebook or computer file, sum up the results of applying the above questions. Freewrite about what you might add from your own experiences and observations, or from research. Highlight the best insight you gained. It could be a major point in your critique, perhaps even the central point around which you structure it. ■

Preparing to Write

Thoughtful exploration of an argument—responding to what it says and pondering its fit with reality—results in much you could say. However, a critique is not a collection of comments or a list of criticisms. Rather it's *a coherent evaluation from a particular point of view*—your view. Consequently, formulating your position, your main point about the argument's validity, matters most.

Formulating Your Position

Your critique will need to focus on one main point: your position about the merits of the argument. You can reject an argument in general but see value in a part of it. You can accept an argument in general but with major reservations.

In response to Fryman's argument, a wide range of stances are possible. Someone in agreement could say:

> Fryman acknowledges that biased professors can be annoying, but he makes an effective argument that opinions have a role in the education process.

Someone disagreeing could say:

> Fryman would have a stronger argument if he did not imply that students should open their ears but not their mouths.

Or, among many other possible positions, someone could say:

> It is easy to agree with this argument in the abstract because Fryman avoids actually quoting any of the biased views he has heard.

■■■■ ACTIVITY 9.4 *In Your Own Work*

Formulating Your Position

Using the suggestions above, write a position statement. If you are having difficulty, consider the following possibilities:

- Return to your first impression. Perhaps a revised version can be your stance.

- Review the statements in the argument that you found open to question. Is there a pattern in your criticisms? Or perhaps one statement stands out from the rest and seems central? Your position may be implied in your most important criticism.

- Do you detect one place where the reasoning breaks down? You could focus your critique on the major weakness in the argument's case, that is, its claim, reasons, and evidence.

- Look for places where the author's view of reality and/or what is needed or desirable part company with yours. Your position might be that the argument sounds logical but is not realistic or practical.

- Talk through possible positions with another student or your instructor. Just talking helps, and sometimes a comment from someone else can help your stance emerge.

Sometimes you will discover the best statement of your position only through writing a first draft. For now, try out the stance that appeals to you most. You can always revise and rewrite. ■

Drafting Your Paper

In your first draft, focus on organizing and voicing your main points fully and clearly.

Thinking as a Writer: What Voice Is Appropriate for a Critique?

Voice   The voice of critique or analysis shares much in common with the voice of case-making: State your position clearly, directly, and forcefully, using a style more formal than conversation but less formal than a public speech. Remember that critique is not name-calling, insults, outrageous claims, or partisan bickering, but rather the calm voice of reason, opinions stated precisely and defended well.

See Chapter 10, page 249, for a discussion of voice in case-making.

Here is a good example of the voice for critique from Hanson's introductory paragraph:

> In "Responses to Arguments against the Minimum Drinking Age," the National Institute on Alcohol Abuse and Alcoholism (NIAAA) identifies arguments against the minimum legal drinking age and then suggests counter arguments. But in doing so, it plays fast and loose with the facts, a common tactic in politics.

It is acceptable to say that an argument "plays fast and loose with the facts" or that it is illogical or inconsistent, providing that you can back it up and make your accusations stick, as Hanson does in the rest of his article.

Your voice in critique, therefore, depends largely on *how you assess the quality of the argument you are critiquing.* Hanson boldly accuses the NIAAA's argument of being politically motivated, not supported by available data, and poorly reasoned. But his voice is intelligent, informed, and logical because he develops his counter-arguments thoroughly.

▪▪▪ ACTIVITY 9.5 *Writer's Notebook*

Reader, Purpose, and Voice

Add notes about the key variables to your position statement. Answer these questions: **Do you intend to address the same readers that the argument does? Why or why not? How *exactly* does your version of the truth differ from the author's, and how great is the difference? How friendly to the author do you want to sound?** ▪

Thinking as a Writer: Developing and Organizing Your Critique

Organization   Whether you write first drafts in chunks and then fit them together or write from a plan more or less in sequence, have the following organizational principles in mind:

Introduction

- Begin by identifying the argument you are critiquing: who wrote it and for what group of readers, when and where it appeared, what it is about, and the position the author takes.

- Make your own stance clear and give it an emphatic position, near the end of your introduction.

Body

- From everything you found questionable in the argument, select *only* what is relevant to your stance. No one expects a critique to deal with everything an argument says or everything that can be said about it.
- *Don't let the order of the argument determine the order of your critique.* Organize around points that develop *your* position, and think about what order would have maximum impact on your readers.
- If you can say positive things, deal with these points first. Readers listen to the negative more willingly after hearing the positive.

Conclusion

Short critiques of short arguments do not need summarizing conclusions. Strive instead for a clincher, the memorable "parting shot" expressing the gist or main thrust of your response.

Development For each part of your critique, you have many options for development. Here are some of them.

Introduction

Besides identifying the argument and taking your stance, you can also include material about context, background information, and a preview of your critique. A critique of Fryman's argument, for instance, might place it in the context of efforts to restrict academic freedom; research about the author might reveal relevant background information, such as what was happening at Brandeis University when he wrote the article. Previews summarize the points you are going to make in the order in which you are going to discuss them.

Body

Take up one point at a time. Each point will challenge either the reasoning of the argument or its fit with reality. If the former, be sure to explain inconsistencies or contradictions fully so that your reader understands exactly where and why the reasoning went wrong. See Hanson's critique (pages 208–10) for examples. If you want to show that it is unrealistic, provide counter-evidence from personal experience, general knowledge, or research.

Conclusion

To clinch your critique, consider the following possibilities: a memorable quotation with a comment on it from you; a return to a key statement or piece of information in your introduction that you can now develop more fully; a reminder to the reader of your strongest point with additional support or commentary.

Revising Your Draft

Write a brief assessment of your first draft. Exchange draft and assessment with at least one other student, and use the critique revision questions in Asking Questions on page 223 to help each other decide what you each need to improve.

ASKING QUESTIONS | Revision Checklist for Critiquing an Argument

1. Look at all places where you have summarized or paraphrased the argument. Compare them against the text. Are they accurate? Do they capture the author's apparent intent as well as what she or he says?
2. Locate the argument's context—the existing view or views the argument's author addressed. If the critique does not mention context, would it improve if it did? If so, where might a discussion of context work best?
3. Critiques seek the truth about some controversial issue or question. What is the issue or question the argument addresses? Is it stated in the critique? Does the difference between the argument's view of the truth and the view in the critique emerge clearly? If not, what could be done to make the difference sharper?
4. Underline the critique's main point or stance. Is it stated explicitly and early in the essay? Examine each critical point. How does it develop, explain, or defend the stance? Consider cutting anything not related to the stance.
5. Check the flow of the critical points. Does each connect to the one before it and the one after? If not, consider rearranging the sequence. How might one point set up or lead to another better?
6. What voice do you hear in the critique? The tone should be thoughtfully engaged, fair, balanced, and respectful, but also confident and forceful. Look for places where the tone might make the wrong impression. Consider ways to improve it. ■

Exchanging your draft with at least one other student and going over the Critique Revision Checklist together can help you decide what you each need to improve.

Formulating a Plan to Guide Your Revision

The plan can be a single sentence or two: "I'll cut this, rearrange that, and add a section here." Or if you work better from an outline, develop one now. The important thing is to have a definite, clear idea of what you want to do and what moves you will make to get the results you want.

Student Example: Excerpts from J. R. Solomon's Draft

The following passages are excerpted from student J. R. Solomon's draft critique of David Fryman's argument, "Open Your Ears to Biased Professors." These examples all illustrate common problems in first drafts of critiques.

Excerpt 1: Position statement not forceful enough

> Fryman believes that students should treat professors' personal opinions with critical respect. I agree, but think that his view is one-sided and therefore not fully persuasive.

All arguments present one position on an issue, so to say an argument is "one-sided" does not offer a valid critique. In fact, Solomon meant that the argument was unbalanced, tipping too far in favor of professors' powers. Here is the revised version:

> "Open Your Ears to Biased Professors," by David Fryman, a student writing for the Brandeis University paper, *The Justice,* deals with a common complaint among students: teachers who express their political or religious views in class. Fryman believes that students should listen to the personal opinions of professors with "critical respect." I agree, but the argument is not persuasive because Fryman describes an unbalanced situation where the professors have all the rights and the students have all the responsibilities.

Excerpt 2: Paraphrase or summary not accurate

> In my ethics class last year, my teacher . . . believed strongly in the right of homosexuals to marry. Some of the students, including myself, did not agree with her. Yet, when we tried to discuss our side of the issue, she cut us off. **Fryman neglects to discuss such instances when a teacher's opinions infringe on the students' right to open debate. I believe that if teachers can express their opinions openly in class, the students should be able to express theirs.**

The bolded sentences do not accurately represent Fryman's argument. Fryman also believes that students should feel comfortable expressing disagreement with the professor and says so in his paragraph 6. Here is the revised version:

> Unfortunately, some professors do not want students to form their own opinions but rather convert to the professor's ideology. In my ethics class last year, the teacher

told us she was a lesbian. In one of our discussions we spoke about gay rights, and whether or not marriage should be legal for homosexuals. She believed strongly in the right of homosexuals to marry. Some of the students, including myself, did not agree with her. Yet, when we tried to discuss our side of the issue, she cut us off. Although Fryman says "it is unfair for a professor to assign high grades only to students who echo their view or to make others feel uncomfortable to disagree," he does not go far enough to emphasize professors' responsibility in ensuring students have a voice.

Excerpt 3: Unfocused and underdeveloped paragraphs

Because he is writing only to students, Fryman has very little to say about how professors should conduct themselves. He deals with the problem of bias as if only what students should do matters. Actually, professors have more responsibility. They're older, more knowledgeable, and more experienced. I think if professors are going to express their political and religious views in class, they should do so in certain ways or not do it at all.

These sentences move from professors to students and back to professors, ending with a vague point about what professors should do. In the revised essay, Solomon used the two main points to organize his entire critique. You can see parts of this draft paragraph in paragraphs 2 and 5 of the revised draft.

Editing Your Revised Draft

There is almost no revised draft that could not improve with proofreading for habitual errors and editing to tighten up the writing and make some points more clear. The highlighted words below indicate where the passage could be tightened up.

Original Version

In my ethics class last year, the teacher told us she was a lesbian. In one of our discussions we spoke about gay rights, and whether or not marriage should be legal for homosexuals. She believed strongly in the right of homosexuals to marry. Some of the students, including myself, did not agree with her.

The edited version that follows reduces the repetition and tightens up the style by using the pronoun *it*.

Edited Version

In my ethics class last year, the teacher told us she was a lesbian. When the class discussed gay rights and homosexual marriage, she expressed her view that it should be made legal. Some of the students, including myself, did not agree with her.

One grammatical problem remains in the edited passage. The word *myself* is a reflexive pronoun; it should not be used unless the word *I* has already been

See "Common Errors" in the Handbook, Section W-1, for more explanation of reflexive pronouns.

used in a sentence ("I hurt myself"). However, the ethics class anecdote does not use the word *I*; the pronoun is treated as an object and should reflect this. This mistake—using *myself* instead of *me*—is common in casual talk; we tend to make it when we write too. Be alert to reflexives in your drafts.

Edited Version

Some of the students, including me, did not agree with her.

■■■■ ACTIVITY 9.6 *In Your Own Work*

Editing Your Paper

Edit your own draft to eliminate errors, such as confusing plurals with possessives, using singular pronouns to refer to plural nouns, and misusing the reflexive pronoun "myself." Exchange your edited paper with another student. Help each other find and correct any remaining errors. ■

REVISED STUDENT EXAMPLE

Solomon 1

J. R. Solomon
English 1301
Professor Crusius
October 12, 2011

Indoctrination Is Not Education

The introduction sets up the argument to be critiqued with information about its author and publication.

"Open Your Ears to Biased Professors," by David Fryman, a student writing to the Brandeis University paper, the *Justice,* deals with a common complaint among students: teachers who express their political or religious views in class. Fryman believes that students should listen to the personal opinions of professors with "critical respect." I agree, but the argument is not persuasive because Fryman describes an unbalanced situation where the professors have all the rights and the students have all the responsibilities.

The introduction ends with a strong stance, or position, on the validity or merits of the argument.

The first point in support of the stance that the argument is unbalanced.

Because he is writing only to students, he has very little to say about how professors should conduct themselves. Fryman deals with the problem of bias as if only what students should do matters. They should listen and evaluate the professor's views just as they would

1

2

a book or journal article assigned in the class. This is what he means by "critical respect." It sounds good; however, class readings are likely to be on-topic and written by experts, while the professor's personal opinions may be off topic and not as well thought out as something published. The professor's views may not deserve so much critical attention.

Furthermore, the students might not be ready to take on the responsibility for evaluating the professor's opinions. Because professors know so much, they can appear very appealing to students who have not encountered an issue before. By leaving out other interpretations, the professor assures that students hear only the teacher's side, which does not allow students to form their own conclusions. I saw this happen in a government class which discussed the 2008 Presidential election. Most of the class did not know much about politics, and therefore accepted the professor's view completely. They didn't have the critical capacity Fryman assumes all college students have. Certainly professors should challenge students, but what my government professor did was convert.

Unfortunately, some professors do not want students to form their own opinions but rather convert to the professor's ideology. In my ethics class last year, the teacher told us she was a lesbian. In one of our discussions we spoke about gay rights, and whether or not marriage should be legal for homosexuals. She believed strongly in the right of homosexuals to marry. Some of the students, including me, did not agree with her. Yet, when we tried to discuss our side of the issue, she cut us off. Although Fryman says "it is unfair for a professor to assign high grades only to students who echo their view or to make others feel uncomfortable to disagree," he does not go far enough to emphasize professors' responsibility in ensuring students have a voice.

Professors are responsible for educating, not indoctrinating. They are older, more knowledgeable, and more experienced. I think if professors are going to express their political and religious views in class, they should do so in a way that invites critical discussion, not just "critical respect." Students should hear about other viewpoints so they can think about all sides of the issue. The professor's views are one opinion, but not the only right one. Professors should encourage students to form their own opinions.

Finally, Fryman fails to deal with the negative impact when teachers stray from the subject matter of the course. In my ethics class, the teacher was always returning to the issue of gay rights, even when the topic of discussion didn't relate to it. Because she lacked restraint, the class spent too much class time on one issue. It is the professor's responsibility to see that course material gets covered.

I agree that professors should share their opinions with the class and students should listen and learn from them. But the opinions should relate to the course content. Professors should not allow themselves to talk about just whatever happens to be on their minds. Most of all, education should not be indoctrination. Opinions should be discussed, not preached. A professor is a teacher, not a politician.

Margin annotations:

Questions the validity of the comparison between professors' opinions and the views in readings.

The student connects the critique with his own experience of the issue.

Challenges an assumption about professors.

Explains an alternative to "critical respect" and shows why that alternative is more educational.

Shows that Fryman's argument neglects another important responsibility of the professor.

3 Questions an assumption about students at the heart of Fryman's argument.

4 Personal experience showing the frustration when a professor does not allow disagreement.

5

6

7 Persuasive and memorable ending.

Sample Readings for Critique

READING **9.5**

Does Patriotism Matter?

THOMAS SOWELL

A high school dropout who returned to school and completed a doctorate in economics at the University of Chicago, Thomas Sowell is a senior fellow at the Hoover Institution, author of a dozen books, and an award-winning newspaper columnist. The following article came from the Jewish World Review website.

The Fourth of July is a patriotic holiday but patriotism has   1
long been viewed with suspicion or disdain by many of the
intelligentsia. As far back as 1793, prominent British writer
William Godwin called patriotism "high-sounding nonsense."

Internationalism has long been a competitor with patriotism,   2
especially among the intelligentsia. H.G. Wells advocated
replacing the idea of duty to one's country with "the idea of cosmopolitan duty."

Perhaps nowhere was patriotism so downplayed or deplored than among intellectuals   3
in the Western democracies in the two decades after the horrors of the First World War,
fought under various nations' banners of patriotism.

In France, after the First World War, the teachers' unions launched a systematic purge of   4
textbooks, in order to promote internationalism and pacifism.

Books that depicted the courage and self-sacrifice of soldiers who had defended France   5
against the German invaders were called "bellicose" books to be banished from the schools.

Textbook publishers caved in to the power of the teachers' unions, rather than   6
lose a large market for their books. History books were sharply revised to conform to
internationalism and pacifism.

The once epic story of the French soldiers' heroic defense against the German invaders   7
at Verdun, despite the massive casualties suffered by the French, was now transformed into a
story of horrible suffering by all soldiers at Verdun—French and German alike.

In short, soldiers once depicted as national heroes were now depicted as victims—and   8
just like victims in other nations' armies.

Children were bombarded with stories on the horrors of war. In some schools, children   9
whose fathers had been killed during the war were asked to speak to the class and many of
these children—as well as some of their classmates and teachers—broke down in tears.

In Britain, Winston Churchill warned that a country "cannot avoid war by dilating upon   10
its horrors." In France, Marshal Philippe Petain, the victor at Verdun, warned in 1934 that
teachers were trying to "raise our sons in ignorance of or in contempt of the fatherland."

But they were voices drowned out by the pacifist and internationalist rhetoric of the   11
1920s and 1930s.

Did it matter? Does patriotism matter?　12

France, where pacifism and internationalism were strongest, became a classic example　13
of how much it can matter.

During the First World War, France fought on against the German invaders for four long　14
years, despite having more of its soldiers killed than all the American soldiers killed in all the
wars in the history of the United States, put together.

But during the Second World War, France collapsed after just six weeks of fighting　15
and surrendered to Nazi Germany. At the bitter moment of defeat the head of the French
teachers' union was told, "You are partially responsible for the defeat."

Charles de Gaulle, François Mauriac, and other Frenchmen blamed a lack of national will　16
or general moral decay, for the sudden and humiliating collapse of France in 1940.

At the outset of the invasion, both German and French generals assessed French military　17
forces as more likely to gain victory, and virtually no one expected France to collapse like
a house of cards—except Adolf Hitler, who had studied French society instead of French
military forces.

Did patriotism matter? It mattered more than superior French tanks and planes.　18

Most Americans today are unaware of how much our schools have followed in the　19
footsteps of the French schools of the 1920s and 1930s, or how much our intellectuals have
become citizens of the world instead of American patriots.

Our media are busy verbally transforming American combat troops from heroes into　20
victims, just as the French intelligentsia did—with the added twist of calling this "supporting
the troops."

Will that matter? Time will tell.　21

READING **9.6**

Right to Bear Arms

LINDA CHAVEZ

Once the highest-ranking woman in the White House when Ronald Reagan was president, Linda Chavez is an author (best known for Out of the Barrio)*, columnist, and radio talk show host.*

Washington, D.C., will become a safer place to live and　1
work thanks to the U.S. Supreme Court ruling Thursday
against the city's absolute ban on handguns. The Court

ruled that the Second Amendment's guarantee of the right to bear arms is an individual right, not just one that permits states to maintain militias, striking down one of the nation's toughest anti-gun laws. As someone who lived in the District at the time the city imposed its ban 32 years ago, I say it's about time.

I bought my first gun in 1974 after my husband was mugged in broad daylight just blocks from the White House. My husband was picking up our six-year-old son from school when a man approached him and demanded money. When my husband refused, the man picked up a two-by-four and hit him on the back of the head, knocking him to the ground. 2

The event traumatized all of us and sent me to a local gun shop to purchase a handgun. I properly registered the .357 Magnum, according to the District law in effect at the time, learned how to shoot it, and kept it safely in my home for the next two years. 3

But in 1976, the city changed its law, grandfathering in people like me who already owned guns, provided they bring their guns to a government building downtown to re-register them. By that time, I was pregnant with my second child. As the deadline approached, I tried a couple of times to stand in line to re-register the gun but gave up as the wait stretched into hours. On the final day, I went downtown again, gun in tow, only to see a line extending for blocks. As pregnant as I was, there was no way I could stand in line for several hours. So, I returned home, knowing my gun would be illegal if I kept it in my home. 4

For the next several years, I stored my gun in Virginia, where we owned a small cabin, to comply with the law. Ironically, there was no crime in the area where my cabin was located, so I had no need of the gun there. But I had several brushes with crime in D.C. 5

Soon after the gun ban went into effect, an intruder hid in my house one day in what was one of the most terrifying incidents in my life. I happened to see the man lurking near my staircase as I headed into the kitchen. I managed not to scream but continued walking away and quietly phoned the police. I confronted the intruder once I knew the cops were on the way. He acted as if I had somehow wronged him by calling the police but didn't stick around to explain to the authorities what he was doing in my house. 6

Around the same time, a serial rapist started attacking women in our neighborhood, including two women who lived within a block of my house. And even though I still owned a gun, I couldn't legally keep it nearby to protect myself. Police eventually caught the rapist, a teenager armed with a knife, but all of us in the neighborhood lived in fear for the weeks he was preying on victims. 7

Then, two years ago, I was again living in D.C. on Capitol Hill when I heard an awful racket through the walls of my townhouse. It sounded as if someone was being thrown down the stairs, with men shouting and doors slamming. When my husband rushed outside to see what was happening, he found our young neighbor visibly shaken. He had come home to find a man in his upstairs hallway, obviously burglarizing the house. Again, I wished I had my gun in D.C., but bringing it into the city would have made me a criminal. 8

These incidents were all near misses. Many other D.C. residents haven't been as lucky. They fall victim to violent crimes in their homes yet can't do anything to defend themselves. 9

The D.C. gun ban never made a dent in the city's gun crime; it still ranks among the most dangerous places in America. At least now, the Supreme Court has acknowledged the constitutional right of law-abiding citizens to protect their own lives when the police can't. 10

CHAPTER 10

Making a Case

YOU HEAR OR READ ABOUT SOME TOPIC THAT INTERESTS YOU (CALL IT "X"), and soon enough you form an opinion about it. Nothing much happens until someone asks you a key question, "What do you think about x?" This question starts many serious conversations, but it leads to stating opinions, not to **argument,** which means *a reasoned defense of an opinion.* To get to argument, you need a question with a sharper edge, a critical thinking question: "*Why* do you think this about x?" That is, "What reasons do you have to explain and justify what you think? What evidence do you have to back up your opinion?"

When you answer these questions, you are making a **case,** *arguing for a position by advancing reasons and evidence in defense of it.* Arguing a case occurs in many genres, including newspaper editorials, letters to the editor, blog posts, speeches, and personal letters. Following is a brief example of making a case from a doctor responding to a news article about vegan diets, which include no meat or dairy products.

MICRO-EXAMPLE   **Case Making**

Letter to the Editor, *Dallas Morning News*

John J. Pippin

States position.

Offers three reasons to justify a vegan diet.

1 As a cardiologist, I'm thrilled that so many people are adopting vegan diets. Plant-based diets have rightfully gained recognition as a healthier alternative to the typical American meat and dairy diet.

2 Fruits, vegetables and other plant foods are rich in antioxidants and other important nutrients. They are a great source of dietary fiber, woefully lacking in the "meat and dairy" diet. They are also free of harmful elements such as animal fats, hormones and antibiotics.

Cites evidence from authoritative sources.

3 The many benefits of plant-based diets are acknowledged by mainstream medical, scientific and nutrition organizations, including the American Medical Association, the American Heart Association and the American Cancer Society.

More evidence, this time to affirm that veganism is good for all, regardless of circumstances.

4 The American Dietetic Association's official position paper on plant-based diets states that vegan diets are healthful for all stages of life, including infancy, adolescence and pregnancy.

More reasons to become a vegan.

5 It also explains that vegetarians have lower cholesterol levels, lower blood pressure, lower body mass index and lower rates of hypertension, Type 2 diabetes, and cancer.

Question for Discussion

Dr. Pippin's letter to the editor has authority in part because he is a heart doctor. Apart from his authority, is his case for veganism convincing? Why or why not?

What Is a Case?

A **case** develops an opinion about a controversial issue or question. It has three parts:

1. A **claim,** or thesis
   Example: College costs are unjustifiably high.
2. One or more **reasons** that explain or justify the claim
   Example: They have increased much more than inflation over the last thirty years.
3. Appropriate **evidence** to back up each reason
   Example: Data comparing the cost of living in general with increases in tuition and fees over the last thirty years.

CONCEPT CLOSE-UP | Visualizing the Structure of a Case

A case has the following structure:

The claim answers the question, **What are you asserting?**
Reasons answer the question, **Why do you make this claim?**
Evidence answers the question, **What information confirms your reasoning?** ■

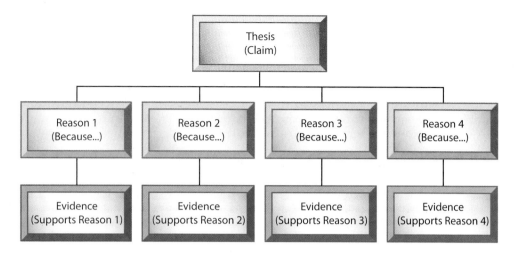

An issue is controversial when reasonable people take different positions on it. One reason to make a case is to convince readers to accept one of those positions. For example, perhaps you feel that texting and talking on a handheld cell phone while driving should be banned. In an editorial or a blog you could make the case by pointing out how dangerous it is.

Why Make a Case?

Proposing a ban on texting and driving is one great example of an issue you could make a case for.

Convincing other people, however, is not the only motivation for making a case. We all have casual opinions we have never thought through. How valid is one of the unexamined opinions you have? The best way to answer that question is to attempt to make a case for it. If you cannot make a good one that other people find convincing, it may be time to change or modify your opinion. Making a case, then, is not only a challenge to convince others but also a testing of how sound your own opinions and reasoning are.

How Do Writers Make a Case?

Cases combine structure (claim, reasons, and evidence) with a strategy for engaging with the readers you most want to convince. For example, many people are in favor of lowering the drinking age from twenty-one to eighteen because they believe the higher drinking age is at least partly to blame for binge drinking. On the other hand, organizations such as MADD, Mothers Against Drunk Driving, support the legal age of twenty-one. They point to thousands of people who die each year in traffic accidents caused by drunk drivers and say that lowering the drinking age will only make a serious problem worse.

Suppose that you wanted to convince supporters of the current drinking age (twenty-one in most states) to alter their opinion. *You have to think as they think.* Everyone agrees that abusing alcohol is a big problem. You could argue that the issue is not age but rather moderation and responsibility whenever people drink. Moderation and responsibility are exactly what the current law cannot promote; prohibition cannot encourage moderation and responsibility. You could allay concerns about drunk driving by advocating stronger enforcement of the law. Without such a strategy, any case you make is likely only to strengthen the views of people who already share your position but not to convince those whose view you want to change.

Building a Better Life through Greenways and Trails

TRAILS AND GREENWAYS CLEARINGHOUSE

An issue that matters to many people is the preservation of trails and greenways in cities and suburbs. Of course, economic incentives sometimes work against using space for these purposes because homes and businesses cannot be built where green spaces exist already or others are being created. Are the green spaces worth the land devoted to them? This article makes the case that they are.

To make a greenway is to make a community.
—Charles E. Little, *Greenways for America*

Necessary background information.

Greenways are corridors of protected open space managed for conservation and recreation purposes. Greenways often follow natural land or water features, and link nature reserves, parks, cultural features and historic sites with each other and with populated areas. Greenways can be publicly or privately owned, and some are the result of public/private partnerships. Trails are paths used for walking, bicycling, horseback riding, or other forms of recreation or transportation. 1

Stresses diversity and nationwide extent of green spaces.

Some greenways include trails, while others do not. Some appeal to people, while others attract wildlife. From the hills of inland America to the beaches and barrier islands of the coast, greenways provide a vast network linking America's special places. 2

Why Establish Trails and Greenways?

Summarizes reasons taken up in order in subsequent headings.

There are many reasons for preserving and improving the trails and greenways we have and for creating new ones. They improve the economy, promote good health, protect the environment, and preserve our rich and diverse American heritage. 3

Economic Benefits

First reason

Trails and greenways provide countless opportunities for economic renewal and growth. Increased property values and tourism and recreation-related spending on items such as bicycles, in-line skates and lodging are just a few of the ways trails and greenways positively impact community economies. 4

Evidence defending first reason. Note evidence includes data from two different sources and the testimony of a local official.

In a 1992 study, the National Park Service estimated the average economic activity associated with three multi-purpose trails in Florida, California and Iowa was $1.5 million annually.[1] 5

According to a study conducted by the U.S. Fish and Wildlife Service, bird watchers spend over $5.2 billion annually.[2] 6

---

[1] "The Impacts of Rail-Trails, A Study of Users and Nearby Property Owners from Three Trails," National Park Service, Rivers, Trails and Conservation Assistance Program, 1992.

[2] "Economic Impacts of Protecting Rivers, Trails, and Greenway Corridors," National Park Service, Rivers, Trails and Conservation Assistance Program, 4th edition, 1995.

The impact on local economies can be significant. As Chris Wagner, Executive Director of   7
the Greater Connellsville Chamber of Commerce, Pennsylvania, remarked,

> Three new gift shops have recently opened, another bike shop, a jewelry store, an
> antique and used furniture store, a thrift shop, a Wendy's Restaurant and a pizza and
> sandwich shop. All this is happening, and only with the *prospect* of the trail opening
> in July. There is an air of excitement and anticipation now within this community,
> something Connellsville has not felt for many years.

Promoting Healthy Living

Second reason   Many people realize exercise is important for maintaining good health in all stages of   8
life; however, many do not regularly exercise. The U.S. Surgeon General estimates that
60% of American adults are not regularly active and another 25% are not active at all.[3]
In communities across the country, people do not have access to trails, parks, or other
recreation areas close to their homes. Trails and greenways provide a safe, inexpensive
avenue for regular exercise for people living in rural, urban and suburban areas.

Environmental Benefits

Third reason   Greenways protect important habitat and provide corridors for people and wildlife.   9
The preserved Pinhook Swamp between Florida's Osceola National Forest and Georgia's
Okefenokee National Wildlife Refuge protects a vital wildlife corridor. This important   Specific example
swampland ecosystem sustains numerous species, including the Florida black bear, timber   used as evidence.
rattlesnake, and the Florida sandhill crane.

Trails and greenways help improve air and water quality. For example, communities   10
with trails provide enjoyable and safe options for walking and bicycling, which reduces air
pollution. By protecting land along rivers and streams, greenways prevent soil erosion and
filter pollution caused by agricultural and road runoff.

Evidence connects
with news stories
of almost annual
floods, something
readers know
about and can
easily appreciate.

Greenways also serve as natural floodplains. According to the Federal Emergency   11
Management Agency, flooding causes over $1 billion in property damages every year. By
restoring developed floodplains to their natural state, many riverside communities are
preventing potential flood damage.

Appeals to
feelings of
alienation
from nature in
metropolitan
America.

Finally, trails and greenways are hands-on environmental classrooms. People of all ages   12
can see for themselves the precious and intriguing natural world from which they often feel
so far removed.

Preserving Our History and Culture

Fourth reason   Trails and greenways have the power to connect us to our heritage by preserving historic   13
places and by providing access to them. They can give people a sense of place and an

---

[3]"Physical Activity and Health: A Report of the Surgeon General," U.S. Department of Health and Human
Services, 1996.

understanding of the enormity of past events, such as Native American trails and vast battlefields. Trails and greenways draw the public to historic sites. For example, the six-mile Bethabara Trail and Greenway in Winston-Salem, North Carolina draws people to the birthplace of the city, the original Moravian Christian village founded in the late 1700s.

Other trails preserve transportation corridors. Rail-trails along historic rail corridors provide a glance at the importance of this mode of transportation. Many canal paths, preserved for their historic importance as a transportation route before the advent of railroads, are now used by thousands of people each year for bicycling, running, hiking and strolling. Many historic structures along canal towpaths, such as taverns and locks, have been preserved.

14

Building a Better Life

As new development and suburbs are built farther and farther from cities, open spaces have disappeared at an alarming rate. People spend far too much time in traffic, detracting from time that could be better spent with their families and friends.

15

Through their votes, thousands of Americans have said 'yes' to preserving open spaces, greenways, farmlands and other important habitat. During the 1998 election, voters in 44 states approved over 150 conservation-related ballot initiatives. Trails and greenways provide what many Americans seek: close-to-home recreational areas, community meeting places, historic preservation, educational experiences, natural landscapes and beautification. Both trails and greenways help communities build pride by ensuring that their neighborhoods are good places to live, so that children can safely walk or bike to a park, school, or to a neighbor's home. Trails and greenways help make communities more attractive and friendly places to live.

16

> Strong conclusion appeals to quality of life issues and sentiments.

Questions for Discussion

1. This case appeared on a website where arguments are usually kept short to encourage online readers not to skip over them. Besides its brevity, what other features of this case should appeal to online readers?
2. Why does the case begin with the economic benefits of trails and greenways?
3. How does the case appeal to the values and feelings of readers? Were you moved by these appeals? Why or why not?

■■ *Thinking as a Writer*

What Is the Rhetorical Situation?

1. What is the *purpose* of the case? What is its *angle* on the topic? How would you describe its *voice*?

See Chapter 3, pages 38–44, for definitions of purpose, angle, and voice.

2. Who is the intended *audience*? Is there anything you can cite that implies the target readership? How do the four reasons appeal to various interest groups and points of view in the United States?
3. Using the chart on page 233 and the marginal annotations, discuss the organization of the case as a claim supported by reasons and backed by evidence. How is the case framed in the opening paragraphs? How does it close or conclude the argument in the last two paragraphs without just summarizing it? ■

READING **10.2**

Why Prisons Don't Work

WILBERT RIDEAU

Wilbert Rideau was convicted of murder at age nineteen and spent more than forty years of his life in Louisiana State Penitentiary at Angola. He edited the prison newspaper and became an award-winning journalist. As you read "Why Prisons Don't Work," pay special attention to Rideau's depiction of how we deal with criminals in the United States and to the solution he proposes. Note also his use of cause-and-effect reasoning, which is common in case-making.

I was among thirty-one murderers sent to the Louisiana State Penitentiary in 1962 to be executed or imprisoned for life. We weren't much different from those we found here, or those who had preceded us. We were unskilled, impulsive, and uneducated misfits, mostly black, who had done dumb, impulsive things—failures, rejects from the larger society. Now a generation has come of age and gone since I've been here, and everything is much the same as I found it. The faces of the prisoners are different, but behind them are the same impulsive, uneducated, unskilled minds that made dumb, impulsive choices that got them into more trouble than they ever thought existed. The vast majority of us are consigned to suffer and die here so politicians can sell the illusion that permanently exiling people to prison will make society safe.

Getting tough has always been a "silver bullet," a quick fix for crime and violence that society fears. Each year in Louisiana—where excess is a way of life—lawmakers have tried to outdo each other in legislating harsher mandatory penalties and in reducing avenues of release. The only thing to do with criminals, they say, is get tougher. They have. In the

1

2

process, the purpose of prison began to change. The state boasts one of the highest lockup rates in the country, imposes the most severe penalties in the nation, and vies to execute more criminals per capita than anywhere else. This state is so tough that last year, when prison authorities here wanted to punish an inmate in solitary confinement for an infraction, the most they could inflict on him was to deprive him of his underwear. It was all he had left.

If getting tough resulted in public safety, Louisiana citizens would be the safest in the nation. They're not. Louisiana has the highest murder rate among states. Prison, like the police and the courts, has a minimal impact on crime because it is a response after the fact, a mop-up operation. It doesn't work. The idea of punishing the few to deter the many is counterfeit because potential criminals either think they're not going to get caught or they're so emotionally desperate or psychologically distressed that they don't care about the consequences of their actions. The threatened punishment, regardless of its severity, is never a factor in the equation. But society, like the "incorrigible" criminal it abhors, is unable to learn from its mistakes. 3

Prison has a role in public safety, but it is not a cure-all. Its value is limited, and its use should also be limited to what it does best: isolating young criminals long enough to give them a chance to grow up and get a grip on their impulses. It is a traumatic experience, certainly, but it should be only a temporary one, not a way of life. Prisoners kept too long tend to embrace the criminal culture, its distorted values and beliefs; they have little choice—prison is their life. There are some prisoners who cannot be returned to society— serial killers, serial rapists, professional hit men, and the like—but the monsters who need to die in prison are rare exceptions in the criminal landscape. 4

Crime is a young man's game. Most of the nation's random violence is committed by young urban terrorists. But because of long, mandatory sentences, most prisoners here are much older, having spent fifteen, twenty, thirty, or more years behind bars, long past necessity. Rather than pay for new prisons, society would be well served by releasing some of its older prisoners who pose no threat and using the money to catch young street thugs. Warden John Whitley agrees that many older prisoners here could be freed tomorrow with little or no danger to society. Release, however, is governed by law or by politicians, not by penal professionals. Even murderers, those most feared by society, pose little risk. Historically, for example, the domestic staff at Louisiana's Governor's mansion has been made up of murderers, hand-picked to work among the chief-of-state and his family. Penologists have long known that murder is almost always a once-in-a-lifetime act. The most dangerous criminal is the one who has not yet killed but has a history of escalating offenses. He's the one to watch. 5

Rehabilitation can work. Everyone changes in time. The trick is to influence the direction that change takes. The problem with prisons is that they don't do more to rehabilitate those confined in them. The convict who enters prison illiterate will probably leave the same way. Most convicts want to be better than they are, but education is not a priority. This prison houses 4,600 men and offers academic training to 240, vocational training to a like number. Perhaps it doesn't matter. About 90 percent of the men here may never leave this prison alive. 6

The only effective way to curb crime is for society to work to prevent the criminal act in the first place, to come between the perpetrator and the crime. Our youngsters must 7 be taught to respect the humanity of others and to handle disputes without violence. It is essential to educate and equip them with the skills to pursue their life ambitions in a meaningful way. As a community, we must address the adverse life circumstances that spawn criminality. These things are not quick, and they're not easy, but they're effective. Politicians think that's too hard a sell. They want to be on record for doing something now, something they can point to at reelection time. So the drumbeat goes on for more police, more prisons, more of the same failed policies.

Ever see a dog chase its tail? 8

Questions for Discussion

1. According to Rideau, why doesn't the possibility of prison deter criminal acts? Based on what you know from how criminals are depicted on the news, TV, in the movies, and in novels, what is your opinion of prison as a deterrent?
2. What does he say prisons do best? What roles should they play in our society's effort to cope with criminals? Do his proposals make sense, given his analysis of cause and effect? Why or why not?
3. What does Rideau contend would truly be effective in reducing crime, especially the violent crime we fear most? What would have to change to pursue the course of action he favors?

■■ *Thinking as a Writer*

What Is the Rhetorical Situation?

1. What is Rideau's *purpose* in writing this essay? What is his *angle* on the topic? How would you describe his *voice*?
2. What is Rideau's intended *audience*? What strategies does he use to counter and disarm objections some in his audience might have to his claim?
3. The Rideau article illustrates cause-and-effect reasoning in case-making, a common strategy in arguments that examine a problem and propose a solution. How does Rideau understand the prison problem? What does he say causes the problem? How does he link his solution to the cause? ■

■■ *Collaborative Activity*

Examining Cause-and-Effect Reasoning

Working in groups of two or three, use the chart on page 233 to create a diagram that shows how Rideau uses the *conventions* for organizing an argument to structure his claim, reasons, and supporting evidence. How does Rideau frame his case? In what situation did Rideau present his case? How might it affect his ability to reach his audience? ■

The Assignment

Make a case for or against a position on a controversial topic, problem, issue, or question. You may propose a solution or criticize someone else's proposed solution. Be sure to analyze your audience, to build common ground, and to offer reasons and evidence that not only support your claim but also respond to readers' concerns.

How Do I Make a Case? Questioning the Rhetorical Situation

Begin by considering the **rhetorical situation,** *the key variables associated with you as writer, with your audience, and with the genre, conventions, and expectations of your text.* Understanding the rhetorical situation will give you a stable sense of the whole, something definite to hold in mind as you work your way through the process of writing your essay.

Writer: What Is My Purpose, and What Impression Should Readers Have of Me?

The *purpose* of a case is to seek assent through logic in the form of a carefully worded claim supported by compelling reasons and accurate, convincing evidence. Your readers need to feel that you have thought your opinion though and that you are knowledgeable about your topic. You may feel passionate about your position, but your stance should be dispassionate, calm, and fair. Treat other opinions and arguments with respect, even as you show that your evidence and reasons are stronger.

Audience: Who Is My Reader?

Cases aim to convince two groups: people weakly inclined to agree with your thesis and those inclined toward another position but willing to consider alternatives. Your case should strengthen the adherence of those favorably disposed to your thesis by giving them good reasons and strong evidence they may have lacked before. Your reasons and evidence should also appeal to readers entertaining other positions, but reaching them requires strategy. (See pages 249–50.)

You cannot expect to convince readers unalterably opposed to your opinion. For example, there is nothing you could say in favor of people living together before marriage that would convince readers who believe it is a sin prohibited by their faith.

Text: What Would Be an Appropriate Topic?

Your topic must be controversial, something about which reasonable people could disagree. Matters of fact are not controversial. For instance, it is a tragic

Topics for case-making must be controversial, such as how to reduce suicide among veterans of the wars in Afghanistan and Iraq.

fact that many veterans of the wars in Iraq and Afghanistan have committed suicide. People do not disagree about this fact but rather about whether enough is being done to help prevent more suicides.

Besides selecting a controversial issue, pick one you know something about from personal experience. Civic activities, internships, and jobs can be rich sources of topics. Here are some other places to find topics:

- **Class readings.** Class readings may suggest possibilities. For instance, reading Rideau's article may lead you to other issues and questions involved with prison reform.

- **Local news.** Read your local and campus newspapers (especially the editorial page) or examine online news sources for controversial topics.

- **Internet discussions.** Visit blogs on topics that interest you. Many newspapers, magazines, and radio shows sponsor blogs that address controversial issues.

As you settle on a topic and begin to organize your thoughts, keep in mind the conventions of the argument described earlier in this chapter.

How Do I Make a Case? Engaging the Writing Process

No two people compose in exactly the same way, and even the same person may go through the writing process in different ways with different assignments. Nevertheless, because no one can attend to everything at once, there are phases in handling any significant writing task. You **explore the topic** to get a sense of whether it will work for you and what you might be able to do with it; if the topic is working out for you, then you move into **preparing to write,** generating more content and planning your draft.

The next phase is **drafting your paper,** getting a version on screen, however rough it may be, so that you can work toward the final draft. Getting there involves two further phases: **revising your draft,** where you make major improvements in it, followed by **editing your draft,** taking care of errors, sentences that do not read well, paragraphs lacking focus and flow, and so on.

Exploring Your Topic

For case-making, exploring your topic means examining the issues involved in it. If your assignment calls for research, do some general reading about your topic to discover what the issues are. See pages 406–11 for how to find and take notes on source material. If your assignment does not call for research, rely on your general knowledge about the topic to formulate the issues.

Asking Questions: Find the Issues

An **issue** is *a point of controversy always or frequently raised in connection with a particular topic.* For your topic, begin by asking, **"What are the questions that people disagree about when discussing this topic?"** For instance, the primary purpose of prisons is always an issue when prison reform is discussed. Some see prisons as primarily punishment for crime; others see them as primarily institutions that should rehabilitate criminals. "What should prisons do?" is the question. Other questions include the following: What should be done about prison overcrowding? How can we reduce assaults on inmates by other, violent inmates? Is prison a breeding ground for more criminal behavior after inmates are released? If so, what can be done to prevent this from happening?

■■■■ ACTIVITY 10.1 *Collaborative Activity*

Isolating the Issues

List the issues connected with your topic. The key question is, **"What do people argue about whenever this topic is discussed?"**

If your class is working with a common topic or you share your topic with at least one other student, you could collaborate to answer the following exploratory questions:

- What issues were you unaware of before you formulated them?
- What positions do people take on these issues?
- What is your view of these issues?

Consider your view of the topic now. If you had no opinion before examining the issues, are you beginning to form one now? If you had an opinion, is it changing significantly? Which issue interests you most? Consider focusing your essay on that issue. ■

Order the Issues (Stasis)

Discussing the issues is an important step in exploring a controversial topic. Ordering them can help as well. Here is an example, one way of ordering the issues involved in committing American troops to combat in a foreign country:

- Are vital American interests at stake?
- If you say no, make a case against committing the troops.
- If you say yes, move on to the next question.
- Have nonmilitary alternatives been exploited fully?
- If you say no, make a case for increased diplomatic effort or some other measure not requiring American troops on the ground.

- If you say yes, move on to the next question.
- Do the announced objectives make sense?
- If you say no, make a case for changing the objectives.
- If you say yes, move on to the next question.
- Can we realize our objectives in a reasonable amount of time with minimal loss of lives?
- If you say yes, make a case for military intervention.
- If you say no, make a case against it based on impracticality.

Ordering the issues in this way is sometimes called **stasis,** *a Latin word that means "stop" or "stay."* That is: If you think a proposed military intervention would not secure vital national interests, you stop with the first question and make a case against it. If you think nonmilitary options have not been pursued enough, you argue for more diplomacy, economic sanctions, or some other alternative. You "stay" with the second question—and so on, through the whole list.

You can order the issues connected with any controversial topic this way. Doing so can clarify your own thinking as you work toward an opinion or assess the one you have.

■■■■ ACTIVITY 10.2 *Writer's Notebook*

Committing to an Opinion

Cases require a considered opinion—that is, an opinion thought through carefully. Consequently, after finding and ordering the issues, you need to decide what your opinion is on the issue or issues you choose to address. Your opinion may change as you write and assess your first draft, but you cannot write a draft at all without one.

In a blog post or notebook entry, state your opinion about the issue you have settled on and the reasons you have for holding that opinion. ■

BEST PRACTICES | Working with Sources in Making a Case

If your assignment involves research, consult pages 433-52 for how to assess and incorporate source material in your paper. Keep the following points in mind as you work with your sources:

- Distinguish evidence from interpretation, or "spin." For example, in 2008 about 6,200 people died in Mexico as a result of the traffic in narcotics. Citing this figure, your source might argue that American tourists should avoid Mexico. There is no reason to doubt the 6,200 figure, but the interpretation is disputable: Drug-related violence seldom involves American tourists, and many destinations in Mexico are no more risky than some cities in the United States.

■ Distinguish information from speculation. **Facts** are *uncontested, established data.* How the stock market performed over the last month is a matter of fact, as measured, for example, by the Dow Jones Industrial Average. Speculations are at most probabilities. How the stock market will perform over the next year is anyone's guess. You cannot ignore the facts, but you can use or not use speculation, depending on whether it helps you to make your case.

■ Strive to maintain intellectual independence from the view your source has of the subject. Avoid distorting or misrepresenting the information in a source to fit what you want to believe, but feel free to interpret the information your own way, as you see the subject. For instance, you may support the screening of passengers before boarding commercial airliners as a necessary counterterrorism measure. If so, you cannot ignore considerable evidence that screening often fails to detect prohibited items that could be used for a terrorist act. Instead of ignoring or denying the evidence, you might argue that screening technology must improve. ■

Preparing to Write

Some writers prefer to go straight to drafting, working out their cases in several drafts. We recommend going through the following steps first, which most writers find helpful:

1. State your opinion as a claim or thesis.
2. Analyze the thesis to determine what you must argue to defend it adequately.
3. State the reasons you will use to explain or justify your thesis.
4. Select and order the evidence you will use to back up each reason.

These steps, described in more detail below, yield a **brief,** *an outline of your case.* Add ideas for an introduction and a conclusion, and you have all you need to guide your first draft.

State Your Opinion as a Claim or Thesis

You are still testing your opinion when you write a first draft of your case, because the value of any opinion depends on how strong a case you can make for it. Writers often change or modify their opinion as they compose or when they evaluate their first draft.

However, your first draft will be stronger if you attempt to state your opinion as a claim in a thesis statement before you begin drafting. An opinion is a general stance or point of view. For instance, in the second reading in this chapter (pages 238–40), Wilbert Rideau tells us that he believes that our prison system is not working because politics rather than reason and an adequate understanding of crime and criminals controls it. That is his opinion. In contrast, his thesis is much more specific: "Society would be well served by releasing some of its older prisoners who pose no threat and using the money to catch young street thugs . . ."

In preparing to write a case, the advantage of a thesis over an opinion is a *sharper focus, with carefully selected key terms.* It is therefore worth your time and effort to work toward a thesis before you draft.

To write a defensible claim or thesis, keep the following in mind:

■ Your claim is a statement you will defend, not just a description of something that is factual.

Not a claim: Student debt for government loans has grown to more than $20,000 for the average graduate, a heavy burden for young people just entering the workplace.

Claim: The economy as a whole would benefit if the federal government would forgive student debts for higher education, which now average more than $20,000 per graduate.

The first in this pair describes a problem. The second makes an assertion for doing something about the problem.

■ The claim should be focused, specific, and directed at a particular audience, or readership.

Too general: Many professors do not know how to make effective use of technology in teaching.

Better: Professors who use presentation technology such as PowerPoint too often stifle creativity and student involvement in the class.

The second example in this pair is more refined, indicating specific directions that the argument will take. It is also clearly directed at educators. The more specific your claim, the easier it will be to decide what your paper will include.

■ Some claims may need to be qualified.

Too absolute: Professors should openly state their opinions on political issues in classes where such opinions are relevant to course content.

Qualified: Provided that they encourage students to discuss their own opinions freely, professors should be able to state openly their opinions on political issues so long as the issue is relevant to course content.

■ Think of objections your readers might have to your claim and modify it to eliminate the possible objection.

Asking Questions: Analyzing Your Thesis

To analyze a thesis means to detect the key terms that make the assertion. For example, consider this thesis: "*Huckleberry Finn* should be required reading in all American high schools." To defend the thesis adequately requires addressing all the key terms: why this *particular book* should be a *required* title on American literature lists and why *high school* is the best place to teach it.

Asking Questions: Thinking about Reasons

The reasoning that led you to your claim will supply the reasons you will offer to explain and justify it to your readers. In listing your reasons, however, you can avoid potential problems by thinking carefully about the following questions:

- Does the statement of each reason say *exactly* what I mean to say? The wording of your reason or reasons matters as much as the wording of your thesis.

- Do I need all the reasons I am thinking of using? As a general rule, two or three reasons are better than four or five because they are easier for the reader to remember. *Concentrate on developing your best reasons well rather than offering all the reasons you can think of.*

- Does each reason clearly connect to the thesis by either explaining or justifying it? Imagine your reader asking, "Why do you believe your thesis?" Each reason should answer this question.

- Are there advantages in taking up my reasons in a particular order? In general, begin and end your argument with your strongest reasons. But also consider the possibility that one reason will lead naturally to another and therefore should come before it.

- If you have more than one reason, are they consistent with each other? Make sure, for instance, that your first reason does not contradict your third reason.

Asking Questions: Thinking about Evidence

Just as the reasoning that led you to your thesis supply the reasons you will develop to convince your readers, so any information that led you to or confirmed your reasons will supply the evidence. Arrange the evidence you have under each reason.

Select and order your evidence in response to the following questions:

- What kind of evidence does each reason require? For example, if you are arguing for making cell phone use by drivers illegal, one of your main reasons will be the link of cell phone use with accidents. You'll need data—facts and figures—to back up your reason. If you also argue that such a law would not restrict personal freedom unduly, you will need other kinds of evidence—for example, laws banning the use of cell phones while driving are no more restrictive than laws against driving while intoxicated.

- How much evidence do I need? The answer is: *enough to overcome the degree of resistance your reader is likely to have.* Many Americans, for instance, assume that the federal government is already too big, too intrusive, and too expensive. Defending any proposal that would increase its role requires significant evidence for both need and positive results.

- Have I mixed evidence types? For example, when a reason requires hard data, you must supply it. But if you also have a statement from a respected expert confirming your reason, consider using it as well. Some readers are convinced more by authoritative statements than by hard data. You could also offer anecdotes, stories from people involved in an event, to confirm a reason. Stories from wounded soldiers who have served in Afghanistan or Iraq, for example, offer strong evidence for improvements in Veterans Health Administration hospitals. Many people find testimony more convincing than any other kind of evidence.

■ Have I selected the best pieces of evidence from all that I could use? Just as it is better to develop two or three reasons well than four or five poorly, so it is better to offer two or three strong pieces of evidence than four or five that vary in quality. More is not necessarily better, and too much evidence can confuse and overburden your reader.

Student Example: Noelle Alberto's Brief

A brief, like the argument it summarizes, has a three-level structure: a statement of the thesis you intend to defend; a statement of each reason that explains why you hold your thesis; and a statement of the evidence that supports each reason.

Here is an example from a student developing a case that urges her fellow students to stop multitasking when they study.

Claim: **Multitasking between recreational technology and studying impairs students' learning and does not prepare them for the real world of work.**

Reason: *Multitasking increases the amount of time spent studying.*

Evidence: Homework takes twice as long to complete with multitasking. (Source: Tugend)

Evidence: Switching tasks makes you have to relearn information to get back on track. (Source: Hamilton)

Reason: *Switching tasks requires relearning.*

Evidence: It prevents students from being able to store information learned through studying. (Sources: Rosen, Jarmon)

Reason: *Multitasking is poor preparation for the workplace.*

Evidence: Businesses don't want people who multitask, they want people who prioritize. (Source: LPA)

Evidence: Multitasking decreases production ability of workers. (Source: Rosen)

Reason: *Multitasking decreases worker productivity.*

Evidence: Ability to pay attention to one thing at a time is a mark of mature thinking. (Source: Rosen)

Drafting Your Paper

Using your brief as a guide, write your first draft. Focus on the following concerns as you write.

Thinking as a Writer: What Stance and Voice Are Appropriate for a Case?

The conventional stance and voice for arguing a case has been the **middle style,** in contrast to the plain style common in informative texts and the passionate style of some public speaking. What does middle style sound like? Here it is in a passage from the Rideau reading (pages 238–40):

> Prison has a role in public safety, but it is not a cure-all. Its value is limited, and its use should be limited to what it does best: isolating young criminals long enough to give them a chance to grow up and get a grip on their impulses.

Read these sentences aloud and you can hear the voice of middle style: *it states its position clearly, directly, and forcefully.* It is more formal than chatting but not as formal as most public speaking.

Avoid the phony, overheated sensationalism of much talk radio and TV. Case-making has nothing to do with name-calling, insults, outrageous claims, and partisan bickering. Rather, argument is the calm voice of reason, one of the voices most admired and respected wherever productive interaction among people occurs: at universities, in business meetings, in community gatherings.

Thinking as a Writer: Finding Common Ground

To convince people who do not already agree with you requires not only that you supply good reasons and strong evidence—your case—but also that you find common ground with them and acknowledge their reasonable concerns and counterarguments. In short, strategy always matters in convincing, and strategy always means engaging with your reader. What can you do as you compose your draft to connect with your reader?

- **Make a concession.** For example, if you are writing against multitasking as a study habit, you can concede that multitasking may be fine—or even an advantage—with other, less demanding tasks than studying.

- **Offer a refutation or a counterargument.** For example, if you are writing in favor of lowering the legal drinking age to eighteen, you can provide evidence that doing so would not increase the number of drunk driving accidents—a central belief of those who support the legal age of twenty-one.

- **Show understanding of and sympathy for other positions.** For example, if you advocate maintaining a U.S. military presence in Afghanistan for an extended period, you can acknowledge the consequent cost in lives and treasure. If you can show that the results justify the costs, your argument is strengthened by confronting the facts directly.

See the Asking Questions box for other strategies for reducing resistance and creating the common ground that case-making requires.

ASKING QUESTIONS | Finding Common Ground

To convince your readers, first ask these two questions:

1. **What are the opinions of people who differ from me?**
2. **Why do they hold these opinions?**

Then, based on your answers to these questions, ask three more:

1. **Do we share any goals, values, attitudes, or beliefs?**
2. **Can I agree with at least some of what they say?**
3. **What reasons and evidence can I present to change their viewpoint?**

Your answers to these questions can reduce the "us versus them" mentality that can make reasoning with those who hold alternative viewpoints frustrating and pointless. Furthermore, connecting with your readers does not mean weakening the case you are making; on the contrary, connecting strengthens your case by taking away objections and reducing resistance to the thesis you are defending. ■

Thinking as a Writer: Developing and Organizing Your Case

Start off by orienting your reader, providing what she or he needs to know to understand your topic and why it is significant. Establish the point of view toward the topic you want your readers to share with you. Make your own position clear. Divide the body of your paper into subheadings. The Best Practices box offers more suggestions to help you as you write.

BEST PRACTICES | Drafting Your Case

1. Openers are important. Start your essay by putting your case in context. For example, the trails and greenways case (pages 235–37) opens by telling us what green spaces are and how they function, important because we can easily take their existence for granted.
2. Your reader may need background information to understand your case. Part of this will come from establishing the context in the opening, but sometimes additional information your reader lacks or may not remember will be necessary or desirable. Rideau (page 238) reminds us of the politics that often prevents prison reform.
3. Avoid summarizing, "in conclusion" conclusions. Strive instead for a memorable "parting shot," something with impact. Rideau's "Ever see a dog chase its tail?" (page 240) is a good example, but you can use, for instance, a well-worded quotation followed by your own commentary.

4. Strive to maintain the dispassionate, calm, and fair voice of the middle style throughout your essay. Simple, forceful statements allow the thesis and its supporting reasons and evidence to stand out for your reader. ■

Revising Your Draft

Write a brief assessment of your first draft. Exchange draft and assessment with at least one other student, and use the revision questions in the Asking Questions box to help each other decide what you each need to improve.

ASKING QUESTIONS | Revision Checklist for Arguing a Case

1. **Who is the target audience?** How is the case framed—introduced—to reach that audience? **Does the writer keep this audience in mind throughout the essay?**
2. Locate the claim as stated or implied. **Is the claim held consistently throughout the essay?**
3. Locate the line or lines of argument and the reasons that explain and justify the claim. Does the writer focus on one reason at a time, staying with it until it is completely developed? How effectively does each reason appeal to the audience? **Is each reason clearly connected to the line of argument it defends?**
4. **Do you detect a logical progression in the ordering of the reasons, so that the first reason leads to the second, the second to the third, and so on?** Is there a better way to order the reasons? Can you find weak reasons that should be cut? Can you suggest reasons not included that would make the case stronger?
5. **How much will the audience resist each reason?** Is there sufficient evidence to overcome the resistance? Is the evidence for each reason clear and relevant to the reason it supports?
6. **Do you see a better way to order the evidence for any of the reasons?**
7. Look at the conclusion. **How does the conclusion clinch the case, leaving the reader with something memorable?** Can you see a way to make the conclusion more forceful? ■

Formulate a Plan to Guide Your Revision

The plan can be a single sentence or two: "I will cut this, rearrange that, and add a section here." Or if you work better from an outline, develop one now. The important thing is to have a definite, clear idea of what you want to do and what moves you will make to get the results you want.

Student Example: Excerpts from Alberto's Draft

The introduction from Noelle Alberto's first draft illustrates a common problem with arguments. It opens with generalizations that do not grab the reader's attention and show how the topic of the paper will matter to them.

> Long before the computer, people have always needed to multitask. Mothers dressed their children while getting ready for work and making breakfast. Men drank their morning coffee and ate breakfast on their drive to work. Multitasking has long been a part of our society, and now, technology has granted us new means of multitasking. This multitasking is now crucial to the younger generation's way of life, but it may be hurting them academically.

Alberto did a good job of creating a context for her case against multitasking, and her thesis is clearly stated in the last sentence. However, she could have used a specific example to connect with her intended audience: college and high school students. By using a source, she was able to revise her introduction to more effectively engage her readers' attention.

> A recent National Public Radio program described the study habits of a modern teenager, Zach Weinberg of Chevy Chase, Maryland. On a typical evening, he worked on French homework while visiting his e-mail and Facebook, listening to iTunes, messaging a friend, and playing an online word puzzle (Hamilton). According to the story, Zach is a successful student, but many studies of multitasking suggest that he could be better if he focused on one thing at a time. While human beings are capable of doing two things at once if one of those things does not require much attention, like driving and drinking your morning coffee, there are some things that require a single focus, like school work. Multitasking between studies and recreational technology is not an effective way to study.

Another common problem in arguments is using sources to support and develop points but not using enough from the source to make the evidence clear and convincing. Here is an example:

> David Meyer, a professor at University of Michigan, found that when you switch to a new task, the parts of the brain that are no longer being used "start shutting things down—like neural connections to important information" (Hamilton). The work you were focusing on isn't as understandable, and when you finally get back to it you "will have to repeat much of the process that created [the information] in the first place" (Hamilton).

The source actually provides additional detail that could help her more clearly explain the issue she is addressing. (Alberto's revised version of this passage appears in paragraph 3 of her final paper on page 255).

To catch this kind of revision problem, ask a friend to read your draft and to be completely honest about evidence from sources that you have not explained clearly.

Editing Your Revised Draft

Alberto's revised draft was well written. Most of her paragraphs were effective; each had an appropriate length and made a single point. In one case, however, a paragraph needed editing for wordiness and unnecessary repetition.

Original Version

Another misconception is that multitasking prepares you for the business world. "Able to multitask" used to be considered a positive on employee résumés. Now, according to the U.S. Departments of Labor and Education, businesses want an employee who "selects goal-relevant activities, ranks them, allocates time, and prepares and follows schedules" ("Skills and Competencies"). Businesses are no longer looking for people who can multitask. They want people who can separate their tasks for the most efficient use of time. School is about preparation for the real world, and if multitasking is not functional there, it is also not functional in school. Furthermore, multitasking in the business world has been found to be completely inefficient. Christine Rosen of *The New Atlantis* writes how multitasking is "a serious threat to workplace productivity" and actually "costs the U.S. economy $650 billion a year in lost productivity" (Rosen 106). A study conducted at the University of London found that "workers distracted by e-mail and phone calls suffer a fall in IQ more than twice that found in marijuana smokers" (qtd. in Rosen 106). Multitasking has no business being in the workplace, and if multitasking is difficult and harmful in the business world, it has no place in a university either.

Margin notes:

This sentence repeats the idea in the first two sentences.

This sentence repeats the point of the third sentence.

The connection between sentences 5 and 6 is not tight.

Before concluding that multitasking is not functional in the business world, the writer should present the evidence for saying so.

The concluding sentence also repeats a point made earlier.

The edited version is more tightly organized and concise.

Edited Version

Another misconception is that multitasking prepares you for the business world. "Able to multitask" used to be considered a positive on employee résumés. However, multitasking has been found to be completely inefficient. Researchers found that "extreme multitasking—information overload—costs the U.S. economy $650 billion a year in lost productivity" (Rosen 106). A study conducted at the University of London found that "workers distracted by e-mail and phone calls suffer a fall in IQ more than twice that found in marijuana smokers" (qtd. in Rosen 106). Future employers do not value multitasking. Now, according to the U.S. Departments of Labor and Education, businesses want an employee who "selects goal-relevant activities, ranks them, allocates time, and prepares and follows schedules" ("Skills and Competencies"). If multitasking is difficult and harmful in the business world, it has no place in a university either.

■■■■ ACTIVITY 10.3 *In Your Own Work*

Editing Your Revised Draft

We called attention to one problem in Alberto's draft: paragraph structure and flow. Look for long paragraphs in your own draft and edit in ways similar to those demonstrated here. Go on to look for other problems, especially ones you know about from previous papers. ■

Every writer has editing problems. Keep a checklist of yours. For instance, list words that you misspelled. If you did not punctuate a sentence correctly, write down the sentence and circle or underline the correct punctuation mark. If you need examples to remember other types of problems—like editing for flow—take one from your paper. Check your revised draft for your most common problems.

Study your instructor's marks and comments on every paper. Add new editing problems to your list as needed. *Always check your next paper for the problems you have listed.* In this way you can reduce your characteristic editing problems.

REVISED STUDENT EXAMPLE

Alberto 1

Noelle Alberto

Professor Channell

English 120

April 29, 2011

Multitasking: A Poor Study Habit

A recent National Public Radio program described the study habits of a modern teenager, Zach Weinberg of Chevy Chase, Maryland. On a typical evening, he worked on French homework while visiting his e-mail and Facebook, listening to iTunes, messaging a friend, and playing an online word puzzle (Hamilton). According to the story, Zach is a successful student, but many studies of multitasking suggest that he could be better if he focused on one thing at a time. While human beings are capable of doing two things at once if one of those things does not require much attention, like driving and drinking your morning coffee, there are some things that require a single focus, like school work. Multitasking between studies and recreational technology is not an effective way to study.

Claim

One misconception that students may have about their multitasking is that they are saving time. Some say that they feel they get more done in a shorter amount of time, but they are actually not doing two things at once. They are switching from one task to another,

1

2

and constant task switching takes more time. Gloria Mark of the University of California Irvine conducted a study in which business workers were interrupted approximately every 11 minutes while working on a project. Each time, it took them about 25 minutes to return their attentions to the original project (Turgend). In study terms, if you interrupt yourself to check e-mail every ten minutes, a chapter that would take thirty minutes straight through takes over an hour to complete.

3

What happens when people shift from one demanding task to another? David Meyer, a professor at University of Michigan, found that when you switch to a new task, the parts of the brain that are no longer being used "start shutting things down—like neural connections to important information." If a student is studying French and interrupts to click open a message, the neural connections to the French homework start to shut down. To restore his level of understanding, Meyer says the student, "will have to repeat much of the process that created [the connections] in the first place" (qtd. in Hamilton).

4

This frequent reconnecting to prior levels of focus and understanding is a waste of time. It is time lost that could be used more efficiently. If students eliminated technological distractions during study time, they would be able to complete more work in a shorter amount of time with greater understanding. There is always time to socialize after homework and studying have been completed.

5

Another misconception is that multitasking prepares you for the business world. "Able to multitask" used to be considered a positive on employee résumés. However, multitasking has been found to be completely inefficient. Researchers found that "extreme multitasking—information overload—costs the U.S. economy $650 billion a year in lost productivity" (Rosen 106). A study conducted at the University of London found that "workers distracted by e-mail and phone calls suffer a fall in IQ more than twice that found in marijuana smokers" (qtd. in Rosen 106). Future employers do not value multitasking. Now, according to the U.S. Departments of Labor and Education, businesses want an employee who "selects goal-relevant activities, ranks them, allocates time, and prepares and follows schedules" ("Skills and Competencies"). If multitasking is difficult and harmful in the business world, it has no place in a university either.

First reason

Paragraph 3 gives more evidence for the first reason.

Paragraph 4 is a transitional paragraph that wraps up the first reason.

Second reason

Third reason

Besides wasted time and money, another unfortunate effect of multitasking is the 6
serious damage to students' ability to learn. Studies by psychology professor Russell
Poldrack show if you multitask while learning, "that learning is less flexible and more
specialized, so you cannot retrieve the information as easily" (qtd. in Rosen 107). Studies of
blood flow in the brain show why. When people are task-switching, they use the "striatum,
a region of the brain involved in learning new skills" (Rosen 107). In contrast people who
are not multitasking "show activity in the hippocampus, a region involved in storing and
recalling information" (Rosen 108). Amy Jarmon, dean at Texas Tech's School of Law, recalls
a study comparing two groups of students in a large lecture class. One group of students
was allowed to use laptops in class; they performed much more poorly on a memory quiz
of lecture content than students not permitted to use laptops. The students who were able
to check their e-mail and update their web pages during class were less capable of recalling
because they were not using the hippocampus section of their brains.

This is the last reason because it has weight in showing how multitasking undermines intellectual potential.

Finally, if students get into the habit of multitasking, they could miss out on 7
developing a personality trait prized by the most highly successful people. As Christine
Rosen writes in *The New Atlantis,* that trait is "a finely honed skill for paying attention" (109).
The great British scientist Sir Isaac Newton said his discoveries owed "more to patient
attention than to any other talent" (qtd. in Rosen 109). The American psychologist William
James wrote that the ability to pay attention marked the difference between a mature and
an immature person: "The faculty of voluntarily bringing back a wandering attention, over
and over again . . . is the very root of judgment, character, and will" (qtd. in Rosen). Maturity
means recognizing that there is a time and place for everything. In meeting the challenges
of college, I have realized the truth of this saying. When I go to the library to study, I leave
my computer behind so that I will not be tempted to multitask. After an hour of focused
school work, I have accomplished a great deal. It is also a good feeling to know that I have
practiced self-discipline by not allowing my mind to wander.

Brings author's personal experience into the paper to confirm a reason.

Multitasking is now part of every student's life. The facts indicate that we need to resist 8
it more. Multitasking is not as helpful as many people think, and its very appeal is part of the
problem. It is inefficient, reduces intelligence, and impairs recall. Zach Weinberg's mother

Brings the paper back around to the student introduced in the opening, as a way to frame the argument.

worries that Zach's multitasking study habits will cause him to "[lose] out on other skills" like the ability to concentrate (Hamilton). To think deeply rather than shallowly, we need to be able to concentrate. Therefore, the best approach is to divide study time from social time. Focusing on one thing at a time will produce better outcomes now and in the future.

Works Cited

Hamilton, Jon. "Multitasking Teens May Be Muddling Their Brains." *NPR*. National Public Radio, 9 Oct. 2008. Web. 7 Apr. 2009.

Jarmon, Amy L. "Multitasking: Helpful or Harmful? Multitasking Has Been Shown to Slow Learning and Reduce Efficiency." *Student Lawyer* 36.8 (Apr. 2008): 30(5). *Academic OneFile*. Web. 23 Mar. 2009.

Rosen, Christine."The Myth of Multitasking," *New Atlantis* 20 (Spring 2008): 105–110. Print.

"Skills and Competencies Needed to Succeed in Today's Workplace." North Central Regional Education Laboratory, Learning Point Associates. n.d. Web. 7 Apr. 2009.

Tugend, Alina. "Multitasking Can Make You Lose...Um...Focus." *New York Times*. New York Times, 25 Oct. 2008. Web. 23 Mar. 2009.

CHAPTER 11

Appealing for Action

APPEALING FOR ACTION, ALSO CALLED PERSUASION, BELONGS TO THE AN-cient discipline of rhetoric established by the Greek philosopher Aristotle about 2,500 years ago. The purpose of rhetoric, he said, was "to discover the available means of persuasion in any given case." Its driving question is, "How can I move this person (or those people) to do what I believe is good, right, or desirable?"

We began to practice rhetoric as children, when we persuaded our friends to play one game rather than another, or when we worked on our parents to persuade them to buy something we wanted. Persuasion has worked on us all our lives, through advertisements; sermons; speeches, books, articles, and videos about controversial topics; editorials; and many other persuasive genres. Entire careers, such as those in communications or marketing, are devoted to persuasion. Persuasion plays a major role in personal and family life, in business, and in the community. It is important to examine more closely what persuasion is and how it works.

What Is Persuasion?

Advertising is one of the most common examples of moving people to action. We can learn a great deal about persuasion by studying advertisers' creative use of persuasive appeals, both verbal and visual, to appeal to targeted audiences.

MICRO-EXAMPLE **Persuasion**

Subaru Advertisement

Impossible is possible with the new 2011 Impreza WRX STI. A 305-hp SUBARU BOXER® engine and Symmetrical All-Wheel Drive scream performance. An aggressive new body and a re-tuned suspension give you the confidence that will make you a believer. Amazing? Yep. Impossible? Not at all. Love. It's what makes a Subaru, a Subaru.

WRX STI: Well-equipped at $33,995¹

As the Subaru ad shows, *persuasion asks us to do something:* spend money, give money, join a demonstration, recycle, vote, enlist, convict or acquit. Like convincing people to change their perspective on an issue (see Chapter 10, pages 231–257, for an explanation of convincing), persuading them to take action for a cause also involves making a case, providing reasons and evidence for doing something, but it also appeals in other ways, especially by gaining our trust and confidence and by arousing emotions favorable to the action advocated.

CONCEPT CLOSE-UP | When Should You Persuade?

Pay close attention to what your course assignments call for, because the full range of persuasive appeal is not always appropriate. The more purely intellectual your topic and the more academic your audience, the more you should emphasize logical appeal, or making a good case. A clear thesis, supported by good reasons and backed by solid evidence, is usually what professors want.

When the issue is public, matters of policy or right and wrong, persuasion's fuller range of appeal is typically appropriate. Making an argument for the creation of a homeless shelter in your community requires establishing your good character and personal involvement with the project as well as appealing to the emotions of your readers. *Persuasion appeals to the whole person:* mind, emotion, the capacity for trust and cooperation, even the virtue of saying things well.

College assignments calling for persuasion will often ask you to take knowledge gained from a course and use it to persuade others who lack it. For example, using what you learned from a course in environmental science, you might write an article urging Americans to buy smaller, fuel-efficient automobiles to reduce carbon dioxide emissions and consumption of oil. ∎

Why Write to Persuade?

Persuasion brings about change in the world, whether in national or local politics, in neighborhoods, on campus, in the workplace, or in personal relationships. For example, persuasion

- Sways elected officials to favor one policy over another.
- Induces people and nations to resolve conflicts peacefully rather than by violent means.
- Affects business decisions of all kinds, including how to promote a product or service.
- Influences college officials who set tuition rates and housing costs on campus.

No other kind of writing has more practical impact. If you want to make a difference in the larger world or your own community and feel it needs to change in specific ways, learning how to persuade other people is the key.

How Do Writers Persuade?

Getting people to take action requires more than a good case. Aristotle identified three kinds of appeal (Figure 11.1):

- To reason (*logos*)
- To the character of the speaker (*ethos*)
- To the emotions of the listeners (*pathos*)

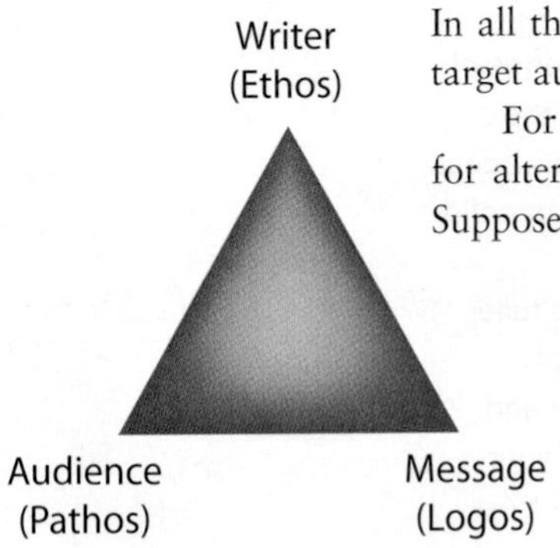

In all three, you adapt your argument to the interests, beliefs, and values of a target audience.

For example, to save money and for other reasons, Americans are looking for alternatives to cars. One of these alternatives is the motorcycle or scooter. Suppose you were writing an essay entitled, "Getting around on Two Wheels."

First, what might you say to appeal to your readers' sense of reason, or logos? You could argue that

- Motorcycles cost far less than cars to buy and maintain.
- They use on average about one-third as much gas.
- They take up only about half as much parking space.
- With proper training and equipment, they are not as dangerous to operate as many people think.

Motorcycles could help solve many problems, including reduction in traffic, greenhouse gas emissions, and American dependence on foreign crude oil.

Next, how could you use pathos, or emotional appeals? The main value here is the fun of motorcycling. Motorcycles are the mechanical horse—you do not

Writer
(Ethos)

Audience
(Pathos)

Message
(Logos)

FIGURE **11.1**

The Rhetorical Triangle

Aristotle identified three types of appeals used to persuade.

drive them, you ride them—and it should be fairly easy to appeal to the American love for freedom and adventure.

Finally, *how could you appeal to ethos, or character?* If you are a motorcyclist yourself, you could draw on your own experience. If not, interview friends who ride and cite what they say: You can borrow *ethos* from others, particularly if they are subject experts.

ASKING QUESTIONS | What Really Persuades Us?

Many people say they are persuaded only by reasons and evidence. That is, *logos* matters most. Aristotle thought that *ethos* might be more powerful: If we think that a writer is intelligent, well informed, trustworthy, and has genuine concern for our needs, we will tend to believe most of what that person says. Look at advertising and you will probably conclude that *pathos* is the prime persuader. Nearly all ads appeal to emotions and attitudes most of all.

What do you think? Consider the last important decision you made. How did you persuade yourself to do one thing rather than another? If someone tried to persuade you, what kinds of appeal did the person use? Which of these appeals had the most impact on the decision you made? ■

READING 11.1

Where Sweatshops Are a Dream

NICHOLAS D. KRISTOF

Nicholas D. Kristof is a two-time Pulitzer Prize–winning columnist for The New York Times. A graduate of Harvard and Oxford, Kristof has lived all over the world and visited 140 countries. As you read the following editorial, ponder the complex issues it raises about opportunities in the developing world.

Before Barack Obama and his team act on their talk about "labor standards," I'd like to offer them a tour of the vast garbage dump here in Phnom Penh.   1

This is a Dante-like vision of hell. It's a mountain of festering refuse, a half-hour hike across, emitting clouds of smoke from subterranean fires.   2

The miasma of toxic stink leaves you gasping, breezes batter you with filth, and even the rats look forlorn. Then the smoke parts and you come across a child ambling barefoot, searching for old plastic cups that recyclers will buy for five cents a pound. Many families actually live in shacks on this smoking garbage.

Phnom Penh, Cambodia

Mr. Obama and the Democrats who favor labor standards in trade agreements mean well, for they intend to fight back at oppressive sweatshops abroad. But while it shocks Americans to hear it, the central challenge in the poorest countries is not that sweatshops exploit too many people, but that they don't exploit enough.

Talk to these families in the dump, and a job in a sweatshop is a cherished dream, an escalator out of poverty, the kind of gauzy if probably unrealistic ambition that parents everywhere often have for their children.

"I'd love to get a job in a factory," said Pim Srey Rath, a 19-year-old woman scavenging for plastic. "At least that work is in the shade. Here is where it's hot."

Another woman, Vath Sam Oeun, hopes her 10-year-old boy, scavenging beside her, grows up to get a factory job, partly because she has seen other children run over by garbage trucks. Her boy has never been to a doctor or a dentist, and last bathed when he was 2, so a sweatshop job by comparison would be far more pleasant and less dangerous.

I'm glad that many Americans are repulsed by the idea of importing products made by barely paid, barely legal workers in dangerous factories. Yet sweatshops are only a symptom of poverty, not a cause, and banning them closes off one route out of poverty. At a time of tremendous economic distress and protectionist pressures, there's a special danger that tighter labor standards will be used as an excuse to curb trade.

When I defend sweatshops, people always ask me: But would you want to work in a sweatshop? No, of course not. But I would want even less to pull a rickshaw. In the hierarchy of jobs in poor countries, sweltering at a sewing machine isn't the bottom.

My views on sweatshops are shaped by years living in East Asia, watching as living standards soared—including those in my wife's ancestral village in southern China—because of sweatshop jobs.

Manufacturing is one sector that can provide millions of jobs. Yet sweatshops usually go not to the poorest nations but to better-off countries with more reliable electricity and ports.

I often hear the argument: Labor standards can improve wages and working conditions, without greatly affecting the eventual retail cost of goods. That's true. But labor standards and "living wages" have a larger impact on production costs that companies are always

---

Margin annotations (left):

Establishes character by depicting what the writer knows firsthand. Also appeals to emotion, sympathy for the plight of the poor in places like Cambodia.

Author opposes Obama's policy. Gains additional character appeal by depicting his opponents as "meaning well."

Testimonials in support of the writer's thesis: factory jobs a step up for many desperately poor Cambodians.

Author shows appreciation for opponent's position, which he sees as moral but not realistic or well-informed.

More appeal to *ethos* or character: believe me, he says, because I know from deep experience what is going on in East Asia.

Shows awareness of argument counter to his and responds to it reasonably.

Margin annotations (right):

3

4 The claim or thesis. In this case it is disturbing to many readers who see sweatshops in wholly negative ways.

5

6

7

8

9 Appeal to reason. You cannot judge Cambodia and similar countries by American norms

10

11

12

trying to pare. The result is to push companies to operate more capital-intensive factories in better-off nations like Malaysia, rather than labor-intensive factories in poorer countries like Ghana or Cambodia.

The practical problems of labor reform in a globalized economy: more appeal to reason.

Cambodia has, in fact, pursued an interesting experiment by working with factories to establish decent labor standards and wages. It's a worthwhile idea, but one result of paying above-market wages is that those in charge of hiring often demand bribes—sometimes a month's salary—in exchange for a job. In addition, these standards add to production costs, so some factories have closed because of the global economic crisis and the difficulty of competing internationally.   13

Author's proposed action: promote manufacturing in poor countries.

The best way to help people in the poorest countries isn't to campaign against sweatshops but to promote manufacturing there. One of the best things America could do for Africa would be to strengthen our program to encourage African imports, called AGOA, and nudge Europe to match it.   14

Among people who work in development, many strongly believe (but few dare say very loudly) that one of the best hopes for the poorest countries would be to build their manufacturing industries. But global campaigns against sweatshops make that less likely.   15

Concludes with powerful emotional appeal to actual people and concrete conditions.

Look, I know that Americans have a hard time accepting that sweatshops can help people. But take it from 13-year-old Neuo Chanthou, who earns a bit less than $1 a day scavenging in the dump. She's wearing a "Playboy" shirt and hat that she found amid the filth, and she worries about her sister, who lost part of her hand when a garbage truck ran over her.   16

"It's dirty, hot and smelly here," she said wistfully. "A factory is better."   17

Questions for Discussion

1. As you can easily imagine, this editorial has been very controversial, resulting in passionate responses, for and against the role of sweatshops. If you are persuaded by Kristof, what does he say that most moved you to agree? If you resist his argument, why did you not find it persuasive?

2. Photographs can be powerfully persuasive. How does the image that accompanies this editorial reinforce what the writer says? Is its appeal logical, ethical, emotional, or some combination of these?

3. Kristof's position is often criticized as a justification for exploiting foreign workers, who are typically paid far less than American workers and endure difficult and sometimes dangerous working conditions. Did he handle this criticism well? Where and how does he confront it? Are you persuaded? Why or why not?

What Is the Rhetorical Situation?

See Chapter 3, pages 40–42, for definitions of purpose, angle, and voice.

1. What is Kristof's *purpose* in his editorial? What is his *angle* on the topic? How would you describe his *voice*?
2. Who is the intended *audience*? Is there anything you can cite that implies the target readership? How do the rational, emotional, and ethical appeals work separately and together to persuade his readers?
3. Using the marginal annotations to the reading, discuss the organization of the editorial. How is it framed in the opening paragraphs? How does it close or conclude the argument in the last two paragraphs without just summarizing it? ■

READING **11.2**

The Factories of Lost Children

KATHARINE WEBER

Katharine Weber's subject matter in the following article (originally published in The New York Times*) is similar to Kristof's, but she bases her argument on tragic incidents involving child labor. How does Weber's use of persuasion differ from Kristof's? As you read, consider which argument is more appealing to you and why.*

Ninety-five years ago, March 25 also fell on a Saturday. At 4:40 p.m. on that sunny afternoon in 1911, only minutes before the end of the workday, a fire broke out on the eighth floor of the Asch Building, a block east of Washington Square in Manhattan. 1

The Triangle Waist Company occupied the top three floors of the 10-story building. There, some 600 workers were employed in the manufacture of ladies' shirtwaists, most of them teenage girls who spoke little English and were fresh off the boat from Russia, the Austro-Hungarian Empire and Italy. The fire, probably caused by a carelessly tossed match or cigarette butt (there were perhaps 100 men working at the Triangle), engulfed the premises in minutes. 2

The factory owners and the office staff on the 10th floor, all but one, escaped onto the roof and climbed to an adjacent building on Waverly Place. But on the eighth and ninth floors, the workers were trapped by a deadly combination of highly combustible materials, workrooms crowded by dense rows of table-mounted sewing machines, doors that were locked or opened inward, inadequate fire escapes, and the lack of any plan or instruction. 3

Before the first horse-drawn fire engines arrived at the scene, girls—some holding hands, in twos and threes—had already begun to jump from the windows. The hundred-foot drop to the cobbled street was not survivable. The firemen deployed their nets, but the force of gravity drove the bodies of the girls straight through to the pavement, and they died on impact. 4

The ladders on the fire trucks were raised quickly, but the New York City Fire Department of 1911 was not equipped to combat fires above six stories—the limit of those ladders. The top floors of the Asch Building, a neo-Renaissance "fireproof" warehouse completed in 1901 in full compliance with building codes, burned relentlessly. 5

The workers trapped near the windows on the eighth and ninth floors made the fast and probably instinctive choice to jump instead of burning or suffocating in the smoke. The corpses of the jumpers, by some estimates as many as 70, could at least be identified. But the bodies of most of those who died inside the Triangle Waist Company—trapped by the machinery, piled up on the wrong side of doors, heaped in the stairwells and elevator shafts—were hideously charred, many beyond recognition. 6

Before 15 minutes had elapsed, some 140 workers had burned, fallen from the collapsing fire escapes, or jumped to their deaths. Several more, critically injured, died in the days that followed, putting the official death toll at 146. 7

But what happened to the children who were working at the Triangle Waist Company that afternoon? 8

By most contemporary accounts, it was common knowledge that children were usually on the premises. They were hidden from the occasional inspectors, but underage girls, as young as 9 or 10, worked in most New York garment factories, sewing buttons and trimming threads. Where were they on this particular Saturday afternoon? 9

There are no descriptions of children surviving the fire. Various lists of those who died 95 years ago today—140 named victims plus six who were never identified (were some of those charred remains children?)—include one 11-year-old, two 14-year-olds, three 15-year-olds, 16 16-year-olds, and 14 17-year-olds. Were the ages of workers, living and dead, modified to finesse the habitual violation of child labor laws in 1911? How many children actually died that day? We will never know. And now 1911 is almost beyond living memory. 10

But we will also never know how many children were among the dead on May 10, 1993, in Thailand when the factory of the Kader Industrial Toy Company (a supplier to Hasbro and Fisher-Price) went up in flames. Most of the 188 workers who died were described as teenage girls. 11

We will never know with any certainty how many children died on Nov. 25, 2000, in a fire at the Chowdhury Knitwear and Garment factory near Dhaka, Bangladesh (most of the garments made in Bangladesh are contracted by American retailers, including Wal-Mart and 12 the Gap), where at least 10 of the 52 trapped in the flames by locked doors and windows were 10 to 14 years old.

And we will never know how many children died just last month, on Feb. 23, in the KTS Composite Textile factory fire in Chittagong, Bangladesh. The official death toll has climbed into the 50's, but other sources report that at least 84 workers lost their lives. It's a familiar story: crowded and unsafe conditions, locked exits, hundreds of undocumented female workers as young as 12, a deadly fire. There may never be another tragic factory fire in America that takes the lives of children. We don't lock them into sweatshops any more. There are child labor laws, fire codes.

13

But as long as we don't question the source of the inexpensive clothing we wear, as long as we don't wonder about the children in those third world factories who make the inexpensive toys we buy for our own children, those fires will occur and young girls and boys will continue to die. They won't die because of natural catastrophes like monsoons and earthquakes; they will die because it has become our national habit to outsource, and these days we outsource our tragedies, too.

14

Questions for Discussion

1. Stories—in this case, an account of a tragic fire—can be as persuasive as an argument. How does the story establish Weber's **ethos,** *the appeal of character*? How does it appeal to her readers' sense of ethics, of right and wrong? How do the details of the story create a powerful appeal to **pathos,** or *emotion*?
2. Weber does argue—in the last paragraph. State her argument in your own words. Does it follow from her story? When we arrive at her argument, what does the story become for us? Is it a source of reasons or evidence or both?
3. As all persuasion does, Weber's article wants us to do something. What exactly does she want us to do? Read Kristof's editorial (pages 261–63). If we did what Weber wants, what impact would it have on Kristof's desired action?

■■ *Thinking as a Writer*

What Is the Rhetorical Situation?

1. What is Weber's *purpose*? What is her *angle* on the topic? How would you describe her *voice*?
2. Who is the intended *audience*? What can you cite that implies the target readership? How does her story and argument appeal to her readers?
3. Discuss the organization of the editorial. How is the story about the Triangle Waist Company told? That is, in what order does the author tell us what we need to know? What does she emphasize and why? How does the argument close without just summarizing what she has said? ■

Using Implied Judgments

Persuasion often depends on *implied judgments,* on *statements of fact that imply the writer's judgments without stating them.* For instance, many of the workers "were fresh off the boat from Russia, the Austro-Hungarian Empire and Italy." This language implies the factory bosses' attitude: The workers were expendable. There was a ready supply of labor on the next boat.

In class discussion or small group work, locate other instances of implied judgments in Weber's narrative. Spell out in each case what the statements of fact imply. Weber makes a clear argument against sweatshops. How would the argument change if Weber spelled out some of her judgments instead of leaving the reader to infer them? When should we say in so many words what the facts imply? When should we let our readers draw inferences themselves? ■

The Assignment

Write an essay on any disputed topic that asks your readers to take action. Your topic must be something about which reasonable people could disagree. In some cases, you might advocate doing nothing when other people want to take action or stop doing something that causes more harm than benefit.

How Do I Appeal for Action? Questioning the Rhetorical Situation

Begin by picturing a rhetorical situation for your writing project, a real-world context for communicating. You should consider the key variables in any act of communication: a writer with something to say, a reader the writer wishes to reach, and a kind of text appropriate to the writing task. These three variables will affect many decisions in the composing process.

Writer: What Is My Purpose, and What Impression Should Readers Have of Me?

The general purpose of persuasion is to move your readers to take action. Given your topic, consider exactly what action your readers can reasonably take. Weber's readers, for instance, cannot do much directly to stop unsafe working conditions, especially in foreign countries, but they can find out about how companies that make their clothes and other consumer products treat their labor force. Her readers can "vote with their pocketbook" by not buying goods produced by careless or grossly exploitive labor practices. Just as Weber does, ask your readers to do something realistic and concrete, something within their power.

Audience: Who Is My Reader?

In many cases, what you want done implies your audience so strongly that virtually no choice exists. For instance, Kristof's article (pages 261–63) addresses the Obama administration because only the president and his officials can influence policy toward sweatshops in foreign countries. In some cases, however, you could reasonably choose between two groups of readers or among or across several. For instance, if your topic is charter schools (privately owned and operated alternatives to public schools), your readers could be students, their parents, local political leaders, state legislators, officials directly involved with educational policy in your state, or some combination of these. In such a case, *choose the readership you know best* because it is difficult to appeal to an audience you know only as an abstract entity, such as state legislators. Once you make your choice, be sure to advocate action your readers can actually take. Parents cannot pass laws, but they can influence educational policy by voting for a candidate in your local district who favors the action you favor toward charter schools.

Text: What Would Be an Appropriate Topic?

Remember that your topic must be controversial: Various courses of action are possible, and genuine choice exists. Matters of fact are not controversial. For instance, it is a tragic fact that many veterans of the wars in Iraq and Afghanistan have committed suicide. People disagree not about this fact but rather about whether enough is being done to help prevent more suicides.

Besides selecting a controversial issue, pick one you know something about from personal experience. Civic activities, internships, and jobs can be rich sources of topics. Here are some other places to find topics:

- **Class Readings** Class readings can suggest topics for persuasion, especially if the readings themselves are persuasive, like the examples in this chapter. For instance, if the sweatshop problem interests you, begin by finding out about the labor practices of the companies that make the clothing you and your friends wear.

  - **Reading in Other Classes** In a political science class, for example, you might study how presidential candidates are selected by the Democratic and Republican parties. The process is highly controversial, and many proposals for reform have been advanced. Perhaps one of the reforms struck you as especially desirable. Do some more reading about it; perhaps you have found your topic.

  - **Local News or Observation** Read your local and campus newspapers for issues and problems of concern to your community. Take a walk around your neighborhood or campus, looking for problems that need solutions, such as wasted energy in offices, dorms, and classrooms.

■ **Internet Discussions** If you keep a blog, you probably have a store of observations about issues that concern you, things you would like to see changed. Or visit blogs on issues of public concern, such as "Opinionator" at *The New York Times,* which gathers opinions from a variety of contributors.

How Do I Write Persuasively? Engaging the Writing Process

No two people compose an appeal for action in exactly the same way, and even the same person may go through the writing process in different ways for different projects. Nevertheless, because no one can attend to everything at once, there are phases in handling any significant writing task. You **explore the topic** to get a sense of whether it will work for you and what you might be able to do with it; if the topic is working out for you, then you move into **preparing to write,** generating more content and planning your draft.

The next phase is **drafting your paper,** getting a version, however rough it may be, on screen or paper so that you can work toward the final draft. Getting there involves two further phases: **revising your draft,** where you make major improvements in it, followed by **editing your draft,** taking care of errors, sentences that do not read well, paragraphs lacking focus and flow, and so on.

Exploring Your Topic

The following questions will help you delve into your topic and begin writing about it.

1. What do you want your readers to do?

2. Who are your readers? Describe them as specifically as you can. What about them will be relevant to your argument? Consider age, religion, income bracket, occupation, political orientation, education, and gender.

3. Reader awareness is important: How much will they know about the problem, question, or issue you intend to address? What is their likely attitude?

4. Why do you care about this topic? What makes you a credible writer on behalf of your position?

5. What is the best reason you can give your readers for doing what you want them to do? State it as a sentence. Do you have a second reason in mind?

6. What additional ideas do you have for appealing to your readers? What values and beliefs can you appeal to?

7. If your topic requires more than general knowledge and personal experience, what sources have you found to support your argument? What additional material might you need?

See Chapter 10, pages 231–57 for more information on case structure and strategy.

■■■ ACTIVITY 11.1 *Thinking as a Writer*

Responding to the Exploration Questions

Write answers to the seven questions above. Consider whether your topic may be too large for the space you have; limiting your topic can save time later, when you have to rewrite a draft that takes on too much. If you have the beginnings of a case in mind—your claim, reasons, and evidence—write them down as well. If you have ideas for appealing to reader emotions, values, and beliefs, write these down too. Include whatever insights you have gained from personal experience. Exchange them with a partner via e-mail and/or in small group sessions in or out of class to help each other refine and develop ideas for and approaches to the first draft. ■

Preparing to Write

Some writers prefer to go straight to drafting, working out their appeals in several drafts. We recommend going through the following steps first, which most writers find helpful.

Asking Questions: Strategies for Appeals

As the readings above (Readings 11.1 and 11.2) and the student example at the end of the chapter (pages 281–85) show, you have many options in persuasive writing. Ask yourself the following questions as you begin to develop your essay:

■ Is there an opportunity to tell a personal or a historical story? Weber provides a good model for storytelling as persuasion.

■ How can I make a **case**, *an argument with reasons and evidence,* to support the action I advocate?

■ How can I join the case to ethical and emotional appeals, persuading my audience through self-presentation and appropriate feelings?

■ When I encounter good reasons for another course of action, how can I refute or use those reasons to favor my own? Kristof is a good model for how to make this move.

■ How can I defend my course of action as the best alternative in an imperfect world? Kristof does not defend sweatshops as ideally desirable but only as a step in the right direction for desperately poor people around the world. Student Natsumi Hazama (see pages 281–85) does not offer a perfect solution to the problem of too much pressure from Asian parents, only an approach that reduces the harm it does.

■ How might I use photos and other visual means of persuasion effectively? For examples, see the Subaru ad and the photo that opens Kristof's editorial.

Doing Research

If the assignment calls for research, use the techniques for finding and evaluating sources (pages 412–34) to find articles, books, and online materials about or related to your topic.

Thinking More about Persuasive Appeals

Thinking through the appeals to reason, character, and emotion helps many writers build up confidence, energy for drafting, and a more detailed plan to guide the first draft.

The Appeal through Logic: Articulating a Claim

You know what you want your readers to do; try formulating it as a claim. These suggestions will help. Your claim is a statement you will defend, not just a description of something factual.

Original Version (not a claim)

Students are choosing majors based on future income instead of interests and abilities.

Revised Version (claim)

Students should find a major that excites their desire to learn rather than one that promises only financial rewards.

The claim should be focused and specific, and directed at a readership.

Original Version (too general)

Parents need to be stricter.

Revised Version

Parents need to teach children to be sensitive to other people in restaurants, stores, and other public places.

The claim uses concrete nouns and verbs, rather than vague and indirect wording, to make its point.

Original Version (vague)

One's natural abilities cannot grow into an established intelligence unless a person learns how to control their attention and concentration.

Revised Version

Even highly talented people need to learn to control attention and concentration to develop their full potential.

Some claims may need to be qualified.

Original Version (too absolute)

High schools need a vocational track.

Revised Version (qualified)

Unless they send all their students to college, high schools should offer a high quality vocational track.

■ ■ ■ ■ ACTIVITY 11.2 *In Your Own Work*

Refining Your Claim

Share several versions of your claim by an e-mail exchange with one or several other students. Ask for feedback based on which version best states your thesis and creates least resistance in your audience. ■

Developing Reasons for Your Claim

Once you have a working version of the claim, begin to formulate reasons for it—why your readers should take the action you are arguing for. Focus on the fit between reasons and the values and beliefs of your readers.

Here are some places to look for reader-oriented reasons.

BEST PRACTICES | Places to Find Audience-Based Reasons

- ■ In the audience's *beliefs and values*. Think about their politics and the values of their culture or subculture.

- ■ In *traditions and traditional texts*. What books, ceremonies, ideas, places, and people do they revere?

- ■ In *expert opinion and/or data*. Draw on the reasoning of qualified experts your audience will respect—mention them by name and cite their credentials. Construct reasons from information and statistics taken from sources your readers will know and trust.

- ■ In *comparisons or analogies* your audience would accept. Analogies work because they liken the less familiar and known to the more familiar and known. Those who oppose genetic engineering, for example, often reason that altering human genes is like altering nature—it has bad side effects.

- ■ In establishing *cause and effect*. If you can show the action you would like the audience to take will lead to positive consequences, you have a good reason. Of course, you will need evidence to show that the cause-and-effect relationship exists. ■

Making a Brief of Your Case

The brief is a concise version of a logical argument. It has three levels:

1. The claim, what you want your readers to do
2. A reason or reasons explaining why
3. Evidence to support each reason

Briefs can help in preparing to write, but keep in mind that new ideas will come to you as you draft. Also bear in mind that a brief is not a plan for the whole paper, only its logical appeal.

Student Example

Student Natsumi Hazama wrote a persuasive paper urging Asian parents not to push their children so hard in school. Here is the brief she developed for her argument:

Natsumi Hazama's Brief

Claim: Asian-American parents need to moderate their demands for high career goals and obedience to parents, allowing their children to find goals and challenges that are right for them.

> *Reason:* Too much pressure can lead to depression and even suicide.
>
> > <u>Evidence</u>: CNN.com article on college student suicides; *Chronicle of Higher Education* online article about depression and suicide at Cornell
>
> *Reason:* Overprotective parenting does not prepare children for the independence of college life.
>
> > <u>Evidence</u>: Asian Outlook website quotes
>
> *Reason:* Students will be more successful at careers they prefer, not the limited choices of engineering and medicine preferred by their parents.
>
> > <u>Evidence</u>: My personal experience
>
> *Reason:* Constant pressure to do better rather than praise for what has been accomplished leads to low self-esteem.
>
> > <u>Evidence</u>: Class reading by Csikszentmihalyi

▪▪▪ ACTIVITY 11.3 *In Your Own Work*

Formulate Your Brief

Outline the logical case you will make—if possible, include supporting evidence for each reason. ▪

The Appeal through Ethos: Presenting Good Character

Ethos is self-presentation. In general, you should

- Sound informed and engaged with your topic.
- Show awareness of your readers' views.
- Treat competing courses of action with respect but show that yours is better.
- Refer to your values and beliefs, your own ethical choices.
- When appropriate, reinforce your ethos by citing information and expert testimony from sources your readers respect and trust.

See Asking Questions below for a more specific list of ideas for establishing good ethos.

ASKING QUESTIONS | Establishing Ethos with Your Readers

1. Do you have a shared local identity—as members of the same organization, the same institution, the same town or community, the same set of beliefs?
2. Can you get your audience to see that you and they have a common cause or perspective?
3. Are there experiences you might share? These might include dealing with siblings, helping friends in distress, caring for ailing family members, struggling to pay debts, working hard for something.
4. Can you connect through a well-known event or cultural happening, perhaps a movie, a book, a political rally, something in the news? ■

■■■■ ACTIVITY 11.4 *Writer's Notebook*

Establishing a Persuasive Ethos

Write about what attitudes you could convey in your paper that will show your good character and values. What can you talk about that will get these appeals across to your readers? ■

The Appeal through Pathos: Using Emotional Appeals

Sharing your own emotions is the most honest way to appeal to your audience's feelings. However, simply saying what your feelings are will not arouse emotion in others. How can you arouse emotions?

Show the audience the *concrete images and facts* that aroused the feelings in you. Kristof used a photo and **testimonials, comments from people supporting his viewpoint,** to appeal to his readers' sympathies. Weber described the bodies of the burned workers in the Triangle fire, "trapped by the machinery, piled up on the wrong side of doors, heaped in the stairwells and elevator shafts . . . hideously charred, many beyond recognition."

In short, *give your readers a picture*, in words or otherwise.

▨▨■■ ACTIVITY 11.5 *Writer's Notebook*

Resources for Emotional Appeal

Freewrite to identify specific details and images related to your topic that move you. If you can, make lists of what you recall. Visit or revisit places relevant to your topic and take notes or pictures. ■

Drafting Your Paper

By now you have generated many ideas for appealing to your readers. As you move toward drafting, first focus attention on two main concerns:

- **Your angle and your voice,** how you want to sound to your reader
- Your draft's **development and organization**

Thinking as a Writer: What Stance and Voice Are Appropriate for Persuasion?

Appealing for action is in part the calm voice of reason described in Chapter 10 (page 249): your opinion stated clearly, directly, forcefully, with confidence. To this persuasion adds the *controlled passion* of emotional appeal, designed to arouse appropriate feelings in your readers.

Look at paragraphs 10–14 in Katharine Weber's "The Factories of Lost Children" (pages 265–266). Here is the voice of controlled passion:

> We will never know with any certainty how many children died on Nov. 25, 2000, in a fire at the Chowdhury Knitwear and Garment factory near Dhaka, Bangladesh (most of the garments made in Bangladesh are contracted by American retailers, including Wal-Mart and the Gap), where at least 10 of the 52 trapped in the flames by locked doors and windows were 10 to 14 years old.

She gives the reader the facts, including the role of American companies in allowing the conditions that result in tragic loss of children's lives. She does not have to say, "This is outrageous, intolerable"; the facts say it for her. Along the same lines, when she cites several tragic instances in paragraphs 10–14, she links them together with the repeated statement, "We will never know how many children died." This is an excellent example of the voice of controlled passion.

Thinking as a Writer: Developing and Organizing Your Appeal

Here are some answers to common questions that will help with both development and organization.

1. *How might I open the paper?* Here are some possibilities:
   An anecdote (short narrative) based on your own experience or something you found in a source.
   A surprising fact or opinion relevant to your topic.
   A question that will stimulate reader interest.

A description of a person or place relevant to your claim.
A memorable quotation, with commentary from you.

Introductions are often more than one paragraph, and your claim can appear anywhere in the paper.

2. *What background material should I provide?* Here are two principles:
Offer *only* what your readers need.
Place it just before the section or sections of your essay where the background is relevant.

3. *Where will I show my connection to the topic?* The introduction is often a good place. Note, however, that Kristof waits until paragraph 10 to mention his Chinese wife, which increases his personal investment in his topic, established throughout the essay by details only firsthand experience with Cambodia could supply.

4. *Will I present opposing views and, if so, where?* How you handle opposing views depends on your reader's relationship to them. If you think your readers will have an opposing view, the best strategy is to engage it first in several paragraphs. Otherwise handle them after your case and with less space devoted to them.

5. *How will I order my reasons?* If your case has three or more reasons, starting and ending with your stronger ones is good strategy. In developing your reasons, *remember that multiple paragraphs are often necessary to develop a reason.*

6. What *visuals might I use and where should they go?* For example, a student who wrote against wearing fur added much to the *pathos* of her argument by including photographs of animals injured by trappers.

See online Chapter 24 for more on using visuals.

7. *How will I conclude my paper?* Try one of these ending strategies:
Look back at your introduction. Perhaps some idea you used there to attract your reader's attention could come into play again—a question you posed has an answer, a problem you raised has a solution.
End with a well-worded quotation, and follow it up with comments of your own.
Repeat an idea you used earlier in the essay, but with a twist. Weber took the word *outsource* and used it in a new way: People "will die because it has become our national habit to outsource, and these days we outsource our tragedies, too."

Revising Your Draft

The strongest revisions begin with assessing the draft yourself. Put it aside for a day or two. *Take the point of view of someone reading your paper.* Ask the questions in Asking Questions to assess it.

ASKING QUESTIONS | Revision Checklist for Appealing for Action

1. Is it clear what the author wants the readers to do? Where is it stated most clearly? Is this the best place to state it?
2. Does the paper have a shape and sense of direction? Does it have parts that clearly play their individual roles in making the argument? Could you make any suggestions for rearranging the parts to make it easier to follow?
3. Do the reasons for taking this action stand out as such? Are they good reasons for the intended audience? Is there a better way to order the reasons?
4. Has the author given enough evidence to support each reason?
5. Has the author shown awareness of and sympathy for the audience's perspective?
6. Are the individual paragraphs unified, and is their contribution to the section in which they appear clear?
7. Can you hear the author's voice in this paper? Do you think readers would find this voice appealing? Does the author exhibit a personal connection with the topic?
8. Where do you see the author using emotional appeals? Are they appropriate? Do they move you?
9. Do you have suggestions to improve the introduction and the conclusion?
10. Has the author smoothly integrated the sources used or just dropped them in? ■

■■■■ ACTIVITY 11.6 *In Your Own Work*

Revising Your Draft

After getting a second opinion, formulate a revision strategy:

1. Decide what you think the useful criticisms and comments are. Reassess your self-criticisms—do you still see the same problems? Make a list of specific items you intend to work on. "The first point on page 3 needs more development" is an example of what we mean by specific.
2. Divide your list into two categories: big revisions that will change all or much of the paper and smaller revisions requiring only adding, deleting, or rewriting a paragraph or two.
3. Ponder the best order for doing big revisions. For example, suppose that you need to rearrange the order of your reasons and improve your tone throughout. Rearrange first because attending to tone will require changing many sentences, and each sentence revision can have an impact on the flow of ideas from sentence to sentence.
4 Finalize your plan with a step-by-step list. Usually the spot revisions can be done in any order, but tackle the ones requiring most work first, leaving the easier ones for last. ■

Student Example: Excerpts from Natsumi Hazama's Draft

Common revision problems include improving opening paragraphs and making points more persuasive.

Revising Opening Paragraphs

A revised draft of Natsumi Hazama's paper appears on pages 281–85. To see how revision improved it, read the following excerpts from her first draft.

Original Version

> One night in 1990, Eliza Noh got off the phone with her sister in college. Eliza knew her sister was depressed and something bad might happen. She sat down to write a letter to support and encourage her. But it was too late. By the time the letter arrived, her sister was dead. She had taken her own life. Eliza believed that too much pressure to succeed contributed to her sister's death. This tragedy led Noh to pursue a career in studying the effects of pressure on Asian-American students.

Revised Version

> Growing up in an Asian-American family I was raised to stay close to my family and always to strive to be number one in my classroom. My parents were both born in Japan and came to America for my father's work. My father was a very intelligent man who wanted me to go into either medicine or engineering. My parents also made me go to Japanese School every Saturday to learn to read and write my native tongue. Going to school six days a week left no time for a social life. The girls at my English school would always have sleep over parties on Friday nights, but I was studying for my next Japanese test. I excelled in school, but that wasn't good enough. Even if I scored a 98 on my math test, my parents would say, "Why didn't you get a 100?"

Do you agree that opening with Natsumi's own story is more effective? The original opening moved to paragraph 15; do you think this arrangement is better?

■■■■ ACTIVITY 11.7 *In Your Own Work*

Revising the Introduction

Look at the opening of your own draft. Why did you choose to open the paper as you did? If you are not happy with the opening, do you see material elsewhere in the draft that might work better? If not, review opening strategies discussed above (pages 275–76) and try one of those instead. ■

Revising to Bring Out the Structure of the Argument

Here is a body paragraph from Natsumi's first draft, offering a reason and evidence in support of her claim.

Original Version

Dr. Henry Chung, assistant vice president for student health at New York University and executive director of the NYU student Health Center, says "Asian-American/Asian students, especially males, are under unique pressures to meet high expectations of parents by succeeding in such traditional predetermined careers as medicine and engineering"(qtd. in Ramanujan). Asian students feel that even though they aren't interested in these fields they must major in them and they end up stressing themselves out. Because students major in fields that they aren't interested in they end up not doing as well in school as they could. If you don't have a passion for your job you feel like you are working twice as hard with loads of work on your shoulders.

Revised Version

Along with bringing home straight "A's," parents also urge their children to major in a subject that they see as respectable. Dr. Henry Chung, assistant vice president for student health at New York University and executive director of the Health Center, points out that "Asian-American/Asian students, especially males, are under unique pressures to meet high expectations of parents by succeeding in such traditional predetermined careers as medicine and engineering"(qtd. In Ramanujan). Even if these fields are not areas of strength or interest, Asian-American students feel that they must major in them. Their grades may start to slip, but as Nguyen at Berkeley says, "Some stay in these majors because they think that they need to. They're reluctant to leave because their parents don't understand: 'If you're not a doctor or engineer, then what are you?'" (qtd. in "Mental").

In the revised version, how has the argument emerged better in the opening sentence? How has it been supported better?

▪▪▪■ ACTIVITY 11.8 *In Your Own Work*

Evaluating the Structure of Your Case

Look over the body paragraphs of your draft. Open with a point of your own; use your sources to support and develop it. Look over your entire draft. How could revising make your reasons stand out more? ■

Editing Your Revised Draft

A common editing problem is integrating source material into your own writing.

Integrating Sources

Using sources responsibly means not only citing the source but also identifying the source by name. Natsumi noticed that she was not always clear about whose words were in quotation marks. Here is an example of the problem:

See Chapter 18, pages 440–41, for more on this important research skill.

Original Version

When kids come to college they receive conflicting messages. "The message at home is that their priority should be to look after their parents and take care of their families" ("Mental"). But the message you get at college and from your friends is that you need to learn to think for yourself and be who you are and do what is best for you. This is a different value than the Asian culture so Asian students feel guilty for not doing what they are supposed to be doing ("Mental").

As the underlined phrases in the edited version show, identifying your sources by name and qualifications not only helps your reader understand who is saying what, but also increases the authority of the quoted statements.

Edited Version

According to Diem Nguyen, a UC Davis student affairs officer, when Asian American students come to college, they sometimes end up partying too much because they are not used to this freedom (qtd. in "Mental"). Also, when kids come to college they receive conflicting messages. Nadine Tang, a psychotherapist who has counseled students at UC Berkeley, says they get the message at home that family is their top priority, but the message at college is "to be who you are, learn to be yourself and do what is best for you. . . . You feel guilty for not doing what you're supposed to and not fulfilling your obligations" (qtd. in "Mental").

■■■■ ACTIVITY 11.9 *In Your Own Work*

Citing Sources

If you are using the words of someone quoted in your source, are you *identifying the actual speaker of the words* as well citing the source? If not, identify this person as Natsumi did in the revised version above. ■

R E V I S E D   S T U D E N T   E X A M P L E

Hazama 1

Natsumi Hazama

English 1301

Professor Channell

August 25, 2011

Is Too Much Pressure Healthy?

Growing up in an Asian-American family I was raised to stay close to my family   1
and always to strive to be number one in my classroom. My parents were both born in
Japan and came to America for my father's work. My father was a very intelligent man
who wanted me to go into either medicine or engineering. My parents also made me
go to Japanese School every Saturday to learn to read and write my native tongue.
Going to school six days a week left no time for a social life. The girls at my English
school would always have sleep over parties on Friday nights, but I was studying for
my next Japanese test. I excelled in school, but that wasn't good enough. Even if I
scored a 98 on my math test, my parents would say, "Why didn't you get a 100?"

When I was in 8th grade my father was diagnosed with colon cancer. He grew   2
very ill, and my parents actually knew that he was dying but didn't tell my sister and
me. One week, all my relatives from Japan flew in; at the end of that week he passed
away. It was a horrible experience, but my mother, sister, and I helped each other, and
with the support of all of our family and friends we got through it.

Starting high school was completely different. Because my mother knew growing   3
up without a father was hard enough, she just wanted me to be happy. Coming home
with a few B's on my report card was okay now. My mother didn't pressure me to get
good grades; she basically let me do whatever I wanted. I wasn't in the top 10% of my

> Opens paper with personal story, allowing non-Asian readers to understand the issue more concretely and the author to build her authority (*ethos*).

> Creates sympathy (*pathos*) for children treated this way—nothing is good enough.

class, didn't get straight A's or take all AP courses. However, I was completely satisfied with my high school experience. I was part of the nationally ranked cheerleading team. I had higher self-esteem. I would give anything to have my father still alive, but I have learned to think for myself and to set my own goals.

My situation before the death of my father is common among Asian-American families. I understand it is part of my culture, which I value. However, Asian-American parents need to moderate their demands and allow their children to find goals and challenges that are right for them.

Wenju Shen and Weimin Mo, experts on educating Asian-Americans, describe our ways as rooted in Confucianism: "The Confucian ethical code . . . holds that the first loyalty is to the family, even above their allegiance to their country and religion."

This closeness to family can bring pressures. In an Asian family the most important thing is to always keep your "face." "Face" means family pride. "Family" means not only immediate relatives, extended relatives, dead ancestors, but also anyone with my last name. To fail in any obligation to the family is to "lose face" and bring shame to myself, my parents, my relatives, and all my ancestors.

While family should be important, this cultural pressure to succeed helps to create harmful stereotypes. As Shen and Mo point out, the "whiz kid" stereotype of Asian-American students encourage their parents to maintain practices "not compatible with the values and beliefs of American society." Asian-American parents need to learn how to balance obligations to the family with the more individual values of Americans.

A more balanced approach to parenting will lead children to more fulfilling lives. Mihaly Csikszentmihalyi, a psychologist at University of Chicago, is noted for his work on happiness, creativity, and subjective well-being. His book, *Finding Flow,* describes the kind of family that leads children to develop their full potential: "they combine discipline with spontaneity, rules with freedom, high expectations with unstinting love. An optimal family system is complex in that it encourages the unique individual development of its members while uniting them in a web of affective ties" (88). Asian-American parents should raise their children more like this. Too much parental

4

5

6

7

8

Strong emotional appeal to American belief in the value of a balanced approach to school and extracurricular activities.

Shows good reader awareness: author not rejecting her culture even as she tries to understand it—especially important for her Asian-American parent audience.

Thesis: Note that it comes in a good place and asks for a course of action Asian-American parents can take.

Important section for explaining cultural norms to non-Asian audience—shows reader awareness again.

First reason to reduce excessive pressure: escape stereotypes.

Second reason to reduce excessive pressure: greater personal fulfillment.

pressure hinders what Csikszentmihalyi calls "flow," a state of mind where the person is fully engaged in what he or she is doing for its own sake (29–32).

For most Asian students, college is the first time they have spent a significant amount of time away from home. Because they aren't used to this responsibility and freedom that they have at college, these students don't know what to do with themselves. They are exposed to new experiences and as a result, they sometimes end up partying too much because they are not used to this freedom that they have.

Third reason to reduce excessive pressure: not good preparation for independence of college.

9

They also receive conflicting messages. Nadine Tang, a psychotherapist who has counseled students at UC Berkeley, says the message at home is that family matters most, but the message at college is "be who you are, learn to be yourself and do what is best for you . . . . You feel guilty for not doing what you're supposed to and not fulfilling your obligations" (qtd. in "Mental").

10

Fourth reason for reducing excessive pressure: puts young people in a bind.

That is what life is all about, fulfilling your own potential, as Csikszentmihalyi says. Unfortunately, even if Asian American students receive excellent grades in school, they tend to have a lower self-esteem than other students (Csikszentmihalyi 24). I think this is because their parents never praise them. Asian-American parents see success as a duty, so children should not receive praise; instead they are told to do even better and aim still higher (Shen).

11

Fifth reason to reduce excessive pressure: improves self-esteem.

Sixth reason to reduce excessive pressure: broadens notion of acceptable fields of study, a better chance to match major with genuine interests.

Along with bringing home straight "A's," parents also urge their children to major in a subject that they see as respectable. Dr. Henry Chung, assistant vice president for student health at New York University and executive director of the Health Center, points out that "Asian-American/Asian students, especially males, are under unique pressures to meet high expectations of parents by succeeding in such traditional predetermined careers as medicine and engineering" (qtd. in Ramanujan). Even if these fields are not areas of strength or interest, Asian-American students feel that they must major in them. Their grades may start to slip, but as Nguyen at Berkeley says, "Some stay in these majors because they think that they need to. They're reluctant to leave because their parents don't understand: 'If you're not a doctor or engineer, then what are you?'" (qtd. in "Mental").

12

Evidence for sixth reason: Asian-American expert opinion.

The result can be destructive to a student's mental health, often leading to   13
anxiety and depression. These problems are more common in Asian-American
students than in the general population ("Mental"). When Asian-American students are
unhappy, they usually don't seek help, even though the best way to recover is to get
counseling. Chung at NYU explains that in Asian culture "suffering and working hard
are accepted as part of life, a cultural paradigm" (Ramanujan). Asian-American students
don't get counseling because discussing emotional problems is a sign of weakness
("Mental"). They also do not tell their parents about their problems. As a psychologist
at Baylor University, Dr. Dung Ngo, says, "The line of communication in an Asian culture
goes one way. It's communicated from the parents downward" (qtd. in Cohen). If
students can't express their anger and frustration, it turns into helplessness; they feel
like there is no way out.

Suicide is therefore common among Asian-American students. According to   14
CNN, Asian-American women age 15–24 have the highest suicide of any ethnic group.
Suicide is the second-leading cause of death (Cohen). At Cornell University, between
1996 and 2006 there were 21 suicides; 13 of these were Asian or Asian-American
students (Ramanujan.)

CNN tells the story of how Eliza Noh, a professor of Asian-American studies at   15
California State University at Fullerton, decided to devote her studies to depression
and suicide among Asian-American women. One night in 1990, she had been talking
to her sister, a college student, on the telephone. She knew her sister was depressed.
She sat down to write a letter to encourage her. It was too late. By the time the letter
arrived, she had taken her life. Noh believes that the pressure to succeed contributed
to her sister's death (Cohen).

I have lived both sides, living with pressure and without. Living without pressure   16
has enabled me to think for myself and be happier. Parents need to give their children
support and encouragement, allow them to make their own decisions about goals,
and most of all, stop pressuring them so much.

Seventh reason to reduce excessive pressure: better mental health.

Use of Asian-American authorities to back up seventh reason, sources her audience must respect.

Strong evidence for the harm of excessive pressure, both data and an actual instance of suicide.

Works Cited

Cohen, Elizabeth. "Push to Achieve Tied to Suicide in Asian-American Women."

    CNN.com/Health. CNN, 16 May 2007. Web. 1 April 2008.

Csikszentimihalyi, Mihaly. *Finding Flow: The Psychology of Engagement with Everyday*

    Life. New York: Basic Books, 1997. Print.

"Mental Health of Asian Youth a Growing Concern." *Asian Outlook— Challenges for*

    Today's Asian American Students. Asian Pacific Fund, Fall/Winter 2007. Web. 15 April

    2008.

Ramanujan, Krishna. "Health Expert Explains Asian and Asian-American Students'

    Unique Pressures to Succeed." *Chronicle Online.* Chronicle of Higher Education, 19

    March 2006. Web. 22 Feb. 2008.

Shen, Wenju, and Weimin Mo. "Reaching Out to Their Cultures: Building

    Communication with Asian American Families." N. p. (1990). ERIC. Web. 15 April

    2008.

CHAPTER 12

Writing an Evaluation

TO SURVIVE, HUMAN BEINGS HAVE ALWAYS ASSESSED THE WORLD AROUND them, asking, "How good is x?" and posing answers to that question, such as, "this plant was good to eat, this place good for hunting." In today's consumer-driven culture, anything can be evaluated and almost everything is; "x" could be a movie, a car, a company, a health care plan.

Evaluation is so common that every genre of writing evaluates in some way or another: Editorials evaluate politicians and policies; consumer reports (including online reviews on sites like Yelp and Hotels.com) evaluate virtually every good and service; reviews and journal articles evaluate literary works, scientific research, engineering designs, public opinion, how well people behaved in the past—in short, anything people can study. In business, we assess how well a corporation did in the last quarter; in public life, we debate the value of a speech; in personal writing, we exchange e-mails or texts that judge yesterday's social event; and in academic writing, we compare solutions to a particular problem, such as how best to feed an overpopulated world projected to exceed nine billion people by 2050.

MICRO-EXAMPLE   **Evaluation**

Fortune's 100 Best Companies to Work For: SAS

CEO Dr. Jim Goodnight, shown here with SAS software company employees in Cary, North Carolina. SAS has been named one of *Fortune* magazine's 100 Best Companies to Work For every year for the last thirteen years due to its outstanding employee benefits.

Evaluation often includes ranking—attaching a number by comparison to other things in a category.

Rank: 1 (Previous rank: 20)

What Makes It so Great?   1

One of the Best Companies for all 13 years, SAS boasts a laundry list of benefits—   2
high-quality child care at $410 a month, 90% coverage of the health insurance
premium, unlimited sick days, a medical center staffed by four physicians and 10 nurse
practitioners (at no cost to employees), a free 66,000-square-foot fitness center and
natatorium, a lending library, and a summer camp for children.

Facts about benefits support the number one ranking and also imply criteria for "best to work for."

The architect of this culture—based on "trust between our employees and the   3
company"—is Jim Goodnight, its co-founder, and the only CEO that SAS has had in its
34-year history.

Facts anticipate and answer key reader questions: How well is this generous company doing? Why such generosity?

Some might think that with all those perks, Goodnight was giving away the   4
store. Not so. SAS is highly profitable and ranks as the world's largest privately owned
software company. Turnover is the industry's lowest at 2%.

Questions for Discussion

Any CEO can claim that his or her company is built on "trust." How does this *Fortune* article appeal to data or the facts to justify the number one ranking for SAS? What additional **criteria**—*standards for judging something*—are stated or implied in the evaluation of SAS?

What Is an Evaluation?

An evaluation is always *someone's* judgment about the quality, utility, value, or beauty of something, so personal or subjective experience comes into play. We can acknowledge the subjective aspect of our judgments in many ways. For example, when warning a friend that a restaurant we recommend serves highly spiced food, we say something like, "You know me—I like hot food," which implies, "Don't go there if you don't."

Open societies like ours—in which people are free to offer opinions about anything—provide and encourage methods for making evaluations less subjective. For example, we are careful to compare "apples and apples" rather than "apples and oranges." We can usefully compare Miami Beach with other beach vacation destinations but not with the mountains of Colorado, where people go to ski, hike, or breathe mountain air.

Magazines like *Consumer Reports* offer evaluations of everything from small electronics to cars, providing reliable information for us to make the best choices possible.

Why Write to Evaluate?

Evaluations are *guides to conduct, ways to make informed choices about something.* Sometimes nothing less is at stake than survival, as when evaluations we consult lead us to drive a safe car, seek medical treatment from a highly rated hospital, or buy nutritious food that promotes health. More often evaluations enhance the quality of life, making it more pleasurable, more efficient, as when we consult *Consumer Reports* or online user reviews before purchasing a refrigerator or laptop. Because some manufactured items are made better than others of the same type, reliable information matters in our selection.

Indeed, when we stop to consider all the evaluations we encounter every day and in every dimension of our lives, little else we can write or read is likely to have more practical impact. Our choices largely determine our present and shape our possibilities for the future, so making good choices matters deeply.

How Do Writers Evaluate?

People are inclined to ignore or dismiss evaluations that seem merely subjective. "It's just his or her opinion," we say. Some judgments, however, just *are* subjective by nature, such as questions of fashion or aesthetic taste. The fashion blogger Scott Schuman of "The Sartorialist" photographs people on the street that he deems fashionable, including this woman in London.

Subjective judgments can have value. Someone's verdict about a style may be a reliable indicator of what is fashionable to people who care about fashion. Most of the blog's readers agreed that this woman has style.

In any case, we cannot exclude subjective judgments from evaluation, nor should we wish to, because they express an individual's **sensibility,** a *mostly nonconscious "feel" for what matters most or has high or low interest or value in his or her experience.* We all have sensibilities, and they matter to us. Tact and civility require us to respect them.

At the same time, we need evaluations that go beyond subjective impressions. The writer needs them for judgments to carry weight so that readers will listen and take an evaluation seriously. Readers need them to guide their conduct—to decide, for instance, if a book is worth reading. How can we offer an evaluation that is more than subjective?

Some evaluations are subjective but still valuable to those who care about the subject, such as opinions on fashion or taste. The fashion blog "The Sartorialist" features photographs of people on the street whom the blogger deems fashionable, such as this woman.

CONCEPT CLOSE-UP | Using Criteria for Evaluating

Criteria, a concept that originated in the Greek word for "judge," refers to *standards for evaluating something.* The singular form of the word is *criterion,* but the plural is more common because people usually have more than one standard in mind when making an evaluation.

Often we do not think consciously of the criteria we use when passing judgment. But when we rank some products or performances, such as Olympic diving, criteria assume great importance. Setting up criteria when writing an evaluation shows your engagement with whatever you are evaluating, implying that your judgment is not casual, hasty, or superficial. It shows that you have asked this important question: **What qualities define excellence in this and similar items?**

An evaluation is a form of argument because the writer makes a claim about the quality of something and supports the claim by showing how it meets or fails to meet the criteria. Evaluators may disagree about which criteria should be used when judging some things, such as a film or a travel destination. Considering the audience for a written evaluation will help the writer choose criteria that readers would find acceptable. ■

READING 12.1

Chevrolet Volt, Car of the Year

ANGUS MACKENZIE

Starts with summary evaluation.

"I expected a science fair   1
experiment. But this is a
moonshot."

    Chris Theodore is a   2
wily veteran of the auto
business, a seasoned
development engineer
whose impressive resume
includes vehicles as
thoughtfully executed as the Chrysler minivan and as
tightly focused as the Ford GT.

Motor Trend, *one of the more influential car magazines, has a group of automotive experts select its "Car of the Year." Eagerly awaited and widely publicized and discussed, the annual evaluation receives careful scrutiny and much commentary. The award went to the Chevrolet Volt in 2011, and the task of justifying the choice fell on Angus MacKenzie, a staff writer for the magazine. As you read, consider how MacKenzie explains and defends the choice.*

As one of the consultant judges on this year's COTY [Car of the Year] panel, Chris brought the deep insight and professional skepticism you'd expect of someone who's spent his entire working life making cars. But our 2011 Car of the Year, Chevrolet's ground-breaking Volt, has blown him away.

"This is a fully developed vehicle with seamlessly integrated systems and software, a real car that provides a unique driving experience. And commuters may never need to buy gas!"

Like all of us on the staff at Motor Trend, Chris is an enthusiast, a man who'll keep a thundering high-performance V-8 in his garage no matter how high gas prices go. But he nailed the Volt's place in automotive history: "If this is the brave new world, then it's an acceptable definition."

In the 61-year history of the Car of the Year award, there have been few contenders as hyped—or as controversial—as the Chevrolet Volt. The Volt started life an Old GM [General Motors] project, then arrived fully formed as a symbol of New GM, carrying all the emotional and political baggage of that profound and painful transition. As a result, a lot of the sound and fury that has surrounded the Volt's launch has tended to obscure a simple truth: This automobile is a game-changer.

Engineering Excellence

The Volt boasts some of the most advanced engineering ever seen in a mainstream American automobile. The powertrain allows the car to run as an EV [electric vehicle], a series hybrid [electric or gas], or a parallel hybrid [electric plus gas], depending on how far you drive and how you drive. The secret sauce is how GM controls the powerflow between the 149-horse electric motor, the generator, and the 84-horse, 1.4-liter naturally aspirated internal-combustion engine. It's fundamentally different from the way Toyota handles things in the Prius.

Attention to detail is impressive. The Volt's wheels, for example, are forged aluminum to reduce weight, shod with specially developed low-rolling-resistance tires. While some consumers may never need to regularly put gas in the car, the internal combustion engine will fire automatically from time to time to ensure the integrity of the fueling system, and to prevent the vehicle being stuck with a tank full of stale gas. And finally, the Volt is built on GM's highly flexible Global Compact Vehicle Architecture (other GCVA vehicles include the Chevy Cruze, the Opel Astra, and the forthcoming Opel Zafira minivan), which means its advanced powertrain can be easily adapted to other vehicle formats.

Advancement in Design

As Toyota discovered with the Camry Hybrid, people who want to buy a vehicle with a highly efficient powertrain want everyone else to know they're driving a car with a highly efficient powertrain. Chevy clearly has watched and learned. The Volt's exterior design brings a unique look to the Chevy lineup. It's a compact that's clearly different from other small Chevys, yet clearly still one of the family. The front end graphic [appearance] is outstanding—strong, confident, and tastefully upscale.

Much of the exterior design obviously has been driven by the pursuit of aerodynamic efficiency. The sharp rear corners and high decklid with integrated spoiler are all about managing the airflow at the rear of the car. But the black graphic under the side windows and the heat-soaking black roof—both artifacts designed to link the car with the fundamentally different Volt Concept—seem somewhat gratuitous.   10

Minor criticism indicates objectivity, making the praise more believable.

Stresses car's high tech appeal.

The interior is relatively conventional, save for the impressive high-resolution—and highly interactive—instrument and center stack LCD [liquid crystal display] screens, and the center stack [instrument panel] itself, whose shiny, white surfacing and slightly hard-to-see, touch-sensitive switch gear seems like an obvious homage to Apple's iPod. (If you can't stand Steve Jobs, the center stack can also be finished in dark gray.) Plastic panels in the front doors allow an effective, low-cost means of changing the Volt's interior colorway [color scheme].   11

Efficiency

The Volt's unique powertrain not only defies established labels; it also defies established methods of determining fuel economy. After all, this is a vehicle that will complete the standard EPA fuel economy test in full EV mode, making conventional mileage calculations impossible.   12

While it is entirely possible that a consumer able to use the Volt in pure EV mode most of the time could use no more than a tank of gas—9.3 gallons—a year (because as noted earlier the car will automatically start the internal-combustion engine at regular intervals to keep the fuel system functional and the gas fresh), it is not a perpetual-motion machine. It requires energy to move. Our testing showed that, in EV mode, the Volt uses energy at the rate 32.0 kW-hr/100 miles or a notional 105 mpg (based on the EPA calculation that a gallon of gas contains 33.7 kW-hr of energy). The internal-combustion engine sips gas at the rate of about 40 mpg.   13

Detailed technical evaluation-analysis of energy use to arrive at an overall equivalent of 72.9 mpg.

In a multiday, 299-mile test that involved a mixture of normal freeway and stop/start city driving (no hypermiling [special ways to drive that increase mileage])—and recharging the car overnight, as most consumers would—we used a total of 58.6 kW-hr of electrical energy, and 2.36 gallons of gas. Just counting the gas, the Volt returned 126.7 mpg. Converting the gas used to energy used (79.5 kW-hr) and adding that figure to the electrical energy used gave us a notional 72.9 mpg. That's impressive.   14

Safety

Treatment of safety divides into two paragraphs: passive (seat belts, air bags) and active (handling, acceleration) to avoid accidents.

The Volt's standard passive safety equipment starts with a complement of eight airbags, including dual-stage front bags, kneebags, and side-impact bags for the driver and front passenger and roof-rail mounted head curtain bags that protect all four passengers. Active safety features include anti-lock brakes, traction control, and stability control.   15

The Volt chassis is nimble and responsive, and the low-rolling-resistance tires deliver better than average grip for this type of rubber. The Volt is not a sports car, but the acceleration (0–60 mph in 8.8 seconds in pure EV mode, and 8.7 in combined gas/electric mode) is competitive with conventional compacts, and more than adequate for safely merging onto a fast-moving freeway.

16

Value

All of that technology is expensive, which accounts for the Volt's $41,000 price tag. Engineering the Volt required considerable investment by GM in vehicle systems integration that would normally be handed off to outside suppliers and contractors. But the cost of the Volt's powertrain and associated systems will come down as GM perfects lower cost components and is able to amortize [distribute cost of] the development across a larger number of vehicles. Meanwhile, consumers can apply for a $7500 federal tax grant, plus state grants, where available, to offset the Volt's relatively high purchase price. And our testing suggests that even if drivers regularly went 80 miles between charges, the Volt is significantly cheaper to run than regular hybrids.

17

> Indicates that GM put unusual amounts of money into developing the Volt.

> Emphasizes cost but sees this criterion in a larger picture where the price tag is not a special concern.

Using EPA average figures of 12¢ per kW-hr for electricity, and $2.80 for a gallon of gas, the Volt costs just 3.8¢ a mile to run in EV mode, and 7¢ a mile with the gas engine running.

18

Performance of Intended Function

The Volt absolutely delivers on the promise of the vehicle concept as originally outlined by GM, combining the smooth, silent, efficient, low-emissions capability of an electric motor with the range and flexibility of an internal combustion engine.

19

It is a fully functional, no-compromise compact automobile that offers consumers real benefits in terms of lower running costs.

20

> Summary evaluation: Delivers for the type of car it is: "an intelligent hybrid."

The more we think about the Volt, the more convinced we are this vehicle represents a real breakthrough. The genius of the Volt's powertrain is that it is actually capable of operating as a pure Ev, a series hybrid, or as a parallel hybrid to deliver the best possible efficiency, depending on your duty cycle. For want of a better technical descriptor, this is the world's first intelligent hybrid. And the investment in the technology that drives this car is also an investment in the long-term future of automaking in America.

21

Moonshot. Game-changer. A car of the future that you can drive today, and every day. So what should we call Chevrolet's astonishing Volt? How about, simply, Motor Trend's "2011 Car of the Year."

22

Questions for Discussion

1. The author admits that the Volt has been hyped and that the car itself is controversial. How does the article attempt to keep the reader from seeing the evaluation as just more hype? How does it imply that the car is solid and therefore should not be controversial?

2. Some Americans resented the federal bailout of GM, but many are also pleased that GM has apparently recovered from bankruptcy. How does *Motor Trend* appeal to patriotic pride in evaluating the Volt?

3. Note the use of **subheadings,** *the division of an article or essay into titled sections.* How did this technique help the author organize what he had to say? How does it help readers follow what he has to say?

▬▬ *Thinking as a Writer*

What Is the Rhetorical Situation?

1. What is MacKenzie's *purpose* in writing this essay? Look at GM's website for the Volt. How is his purpose different from GM's? What is his *angle* or point of view? How would you describe his voice—that is, how he sounds to you?

2. Who is MacKenzie's intended *audience*? That is, who would read *Motor Trend*? What in the article's content best reveals the interests and values of the magazine's readers?

3. MacKenzie makes a strong claim: the Volt is a "game-changer." Such a strong claim requires strong support. How does he attempt to justify his claim? What different kinds of evidence does he use? ▪

'Precious' Mettle

ANN HORNADAY

The 2009 film Precious, *based on the 1996 novel* Push *by Sapphire, won numerous awards: at the Sundance Film Festival, the Audience Award and the Grand Jury Prize for best drama; at the Toronto International Film Festival, the People's Choice Award. Yet the film did not at first have financial backing for distribution and seemed unlikely to be a box office success when it was finally shown in theaters. Its popular success was a surprise—it earned almost five times what it cost to make. The following review by Ann Hornaday* (The Washington Post) *helps to explain the appeal of the film and shows us how to evaluate any work of art that does not fit neatly into existing categories.*

In this drama, based on the novel *Push* by Sapphire, a pregnant Harlem teen (Gabourey 'Gabby' Sidibe) attempts to escape from her abusive mother and build a new life. Movies come, movies go. But a rare few arrive like gifts, sent by some cosmic messenger to stir the senses, awaken compassion and send viewers into a world made radically new by invigorated alertness and empathy. Such is the movie *Precious: Based on the Novel Push by Sapphire*, which surely qualifies as the most painful, poetic and improbably beautiful film of the year.

It's hard to believe that a movie that traffics so operatically in images of brutality and squalor can be so fleet, assured and lyrical. But such breathtaking contradictions abound in *Precious,* which in the course of introducing the viewers to unspeakable despair, manages to imbue them with an exhilarating sense of hope—if not in a bright and cheery future for the film's beleaguered protagonist, then at least in the possibilities of cinema as a bold, fluent and adamantly expressive art form.

That beleaguered protagonist is Claireece "Precious" Jones (played in an astonishing debut by Gabourey Sidibe), a 16-year-old girl who, as the movie opens, is still attending junior high school in 1980s Harlem. Morbidly obese, functionally illiterate, pregnant with her second child after being raped by her father, Precious lives with her mother, Mary (Mo'Nique), in a squalid apartment where she endures the latter's near-constant verbal, physical and sexual abuse. Precious's only escape from this lurid tableau is rich, glittery

1

2

3

fantasy life, in which she has a "light-skinned boyfriend" and "good hair," dresses in ball gowns and carries a little terrier.

Precious is numb, shut down, locked behind protective layers of fat and clothing, her hooded eyes nearly sightless slits. She's invisible, even to herself: When she looks in the mirror, a blond, blue-eyed teenager gazes back. But when an attentive principal enrolls her in an alternative education program, Precious's mountainlike passivity and self-abnegation [self-denial] begin to give way to tiny, seismic temblors of transformation.

Adapted from a 1996 novel by the poet Sapphire, *Precious* has been a hit on the film festival circuit, earning a clutch of audience awards—and, at Sundance earlier this year, the support of Oprah Winfrey and Tyler Perry, who signed on as executive producers.

Director Lee Daniels (*Shadowboxer*), working from a script by Geoffrey Fletcher, doesn't flinch from confronting viewers with the most squalid, violent depredations Precious suffers at her mother's hands. But he instinctively knows when to offer viewers and his heroine much-needed relief, by way of brightly lit, sumptuously staged magical realist sequences portraying Precious's glitzy daydreams. He pulls off this audacious balancing act throughout *Precious,* which toes a vertiginous [dizzying] line between the grim and highly stylized.

But as adroitly as Daniels handles the multilayered details, textures and tones of *Precious's* rich visual design, his most crucial task is giving his cast the space needed to deliver revelatory, searingly honest performances. Sidibe's nuanced, deeply sympathetic portrayal of a character who is almost completely inert for most of the movie recalls Billy Bob Thornton's highly praised breakout turn in *Sling Blade.*

Technically, hers is a far more difficult role than the toxic, rage-fueled monster brought to life by Mo'Nique, who delivers a performance that constantly teeters on the edge of going over the top, but somehow manages to stay on the side of credibility. Mo'Nique, best known and loved for her persona as a stand-up comedienne and comic actress, is rightly being praised for a brave performance untouched by vanity.

Together, she and Sidibe form a formidable dyad that gives *Precious* its dysfunctional centrifugal force. But the entire enterprise is best appreciated as a bracing ensemble piece, in which even the smallest roles harmonize flawlessly within the whole. The gorgeous Paula Patton breathes radiant but bone-weary life into what could have been a stock character of the tireless English teacher. Rather than the reassuring reversals of a miracle worker or "I can *reach* these kids!" speeches, her character, Ms. Rain, wrings incremental victories from a world proscribed by Rolodex contacts and bureaucratic red tape. And not one but two pop stars prove their dramatic bona fides in *Precious*: Lenny Kravitz as a cute, compassionate hospital nurse, and Mariah Carey, in a mousy wig and devoid of makeup, delivering a frank, utterly winning performance as a seen-it-all social worker.

"What does it mean when the author describes the protagonist's circumstances as unrelenting?" Ms. Rain asks at one point. That's precisely the question posed by *Precious,* in which the title character withstands such a constant plague of social ills that she's in danger of becoming little more than a simplistically drawn, even grotesque, poster child. (The same can be said for Mo'Nique's Mary, who in many ways embodies all-too-familiar stereotypes of welfare queens and the pathology of poverty.)

That *Precious* dodges these toxic assumptions, even while coming perilously close   11
to perpetuating them, is a testament not only to the sensitivity and artistry of Daniels's
filmmaking, but also to the fierce performances of actors who, rather than skimming the
surface of their characters, invariably dive ever deeper inside, taking viewers with them.

That journey winds up being excruciating, exhausting, and, against all odds, deeply   12
rewarding. Just how rewarding probably will become clear to viewers when they emerge
from *Precious* to find that life outside the theater has come into a different kind of focus.
Precious performs the same miracle as every great work of art: It gives its viewers new eyes,
and the sense that they'll never see the world—or the people in it—in quite the same way.

Questions for Discussion

1. Whether from popular or high culture, evaluating artistic efforts is challenging. We must get beyond "I love it" or "I hate it." How does Ann Hornaday justify her high rating of *Precious*? What specifics does she offer to back up the positive evaluation?
2. One of the keys to evaluating anything made by human hands is to understand the intent of its maker. What does Hornaday think the director was doing to get the film's material to work? How did understanding the director's contribution contribute to her evaluation?
3. Evaluation often uses comparison as a mode of development. What comparisons does Hornaday make? Did they help you understand points she made better?

■■ *Thinking as a Writer*

What Is the Rhetorical Situation?

1. What is Hornaday's *purpose* in writing this review? In recommending this film, what does she focus on most to establish its artistic merit and appeal?
2. Who is Hornaday's intended *audience*? What does she assume her readers are familiar with? What does she assume they might need to know more about?
3. What relationship does she have with her readers? How would you describe the voice in this review? ■

The Assignment

Write a review evaluating a product, service, cultural event, institution, or anything else your instructor considers appropriate. You should be familiar with the subject of your evaluation and with other, similar products, services, events, and so on, so that you can knowledgeably set up criteria for assessment. If your instructor wants you to support your judgment of the subject with sources such as surveys and expert opinion, you should consider whether such sources are easily available.

How Do I Write an Evaluation? Questioning the Rhetorical Situation

Begin by picturing a rhetorical situation for your writing project, a real-world context for communicating. You should consider the key variables in any act of communication: a writer with something to say, a reader the writer wishes to reach, and a kind of text appropriate to the writing task. These three variables will affect many decisions in the composing process.

Writer: What Is My Purpose, and What Impression Should My Readers Have of Me?

Your purpose is to make a convincing case for your judgment of something. Beyond that, your judgment may serve a variety of purposes, such as helping readers appreciate a movie or a new album, or recommending—or warning against—a restaurant or hotel. You want to sound knowledgeable and be able to justify your opinion since readers may encounter other opinions the opposite of yours. Your readers should see you as someone who has arrived at an assessment thoughtfully. They will need to have confidence in the good reasons you offer for evaluating your topic as you have.

Audience: Who Is My Reader?

As with all writing projects, you should imagine a group of people who might read your paper. Having a readership in mind for your evaluation will help you decide what to say and how to order it. **"What does my reader need to know?"** is therefore one of the key questions you need to ask yourself often as you write and revise a draft.

Readers come to evaluations wanting to know about whatever you are assessing. You can assume interest; what readers want is information, including your assessment and what led you to it, which they will use to help them decide whether to buy the product, use the service, visit the local attraction, and so on. Clearly, readers of *Motor Trend* want and expect technical details such as how miles-per-gallon equivalents work for an electric car. Select the information you think will be most relevant to your readers.

Text: What Would Be an Appropriate Topic?

Your instructor may assign your topic. If you are asked to choose your own topic for this assignment, select something you know well from personal experience. Consider the following categories and examples:

- A manufactured item: a car, electronic device, item of clothing, office machine, sports equipment, home, apartment, or condo.
- A service: a restaurant, travel agency, tax preparation service, online dating service, university or college dining hall or exercise center.
- A cultural item or place: a television show, film, stage play, museum, musical performance, or sports event.
- A print or online publication: a novel, business report, textbook, advertisement, magazine, newspaper, website, blog, or social networking site.
- Software: a video game or computer program.
- Travel destination or other place of interest: a foreign city, attraction in your home town or near your campus, historical memorial, national park, or model community.
- Proposed legislation or policy changes: Proposals to remedy on-campus problems such as parking, off-campus problems such as inadequate public transportation, ecological problems such as clean diesel engines in cars to reduce pollution, or national problems such as the dropout rate in education.

To explore additional topic ideas and see additional models for evaluation, read articles from *Consumer Reports,* book and movie reviews in magazines and newspapers, and online evaluations in blogs and on consumer sites.

When selecting your evaluation topic, choose something familiar and interesting to you, such as a dining experience at a favorite restaurant.

How Do I Write an Evaluation?
Engaging the Writing Process

No two people compose in exactly the same way, and even the same person may go through the writing process in different ways with different assignments. Nevertheless, because no one can attend to everything at once, there are phases in handling any significant writing task. You **explore the topic** to get a sense of whether it will work for you and what you might be able to do with it; if the topic is working out for you, then you move into **preparing to write,** generating more content and planning your draft.

The next phase is **drafting your paper,** getting a version, however rough it may be, on screen or paper so that you can work toward the final draft. Getting there involves two further phases: **revising your draft,** where you make major improvements in your draft, followed by **editing your draft,** taking care of errors, sentences that do not read well, paragraphs lacking focus and flow, and so on.

Exploring Your Topic

Readers read evaluations to know more about a topic, not just how you rate it. Consequently, your task is partly informative, providing facts about your topic. Where will you find this information?

Many evaluations are based entirely on the author's experience with the product, service, vacation destination, and so on—with whatever you are evaluating. Begin, then, by brainstorming what you know from personal experience and observation. Write a list or a notebook entry with facts about your topic. How much do you actually know that is factual? If you cannot generate much by listing or freewriting, you may need to choose a different topic or dig further into the one you plan to write about.

Go back to your topic. If it is a film, watch it again. If it is a product, examine it more thoroughly. You may need to gather some information from sources, such as product information, film credits, and other basic facts appropriate to your topic. You may want to read what other experts have said, but bear in mind that you should make your own judgment aimed at your own audience, based on your experiences and opinions. However, another reviewer might remind you of points or criteria for evaluation.

Asking Questions: Finding Criteria for Evaluating

Which comes first: making a subjective judgment about the quality of something or making a list of criteria and then deciding how well something meets the criteria? Human nature being what it is, most likely we form our opinions and then think of ways to justify them.

Whether you start with a set of criteria or a gut opinion, your evaluation should show that you have thought about reasonable standards of excellence for items similar to your topic, or your readers will not find your opinion credible. Asking questions will help you generate a list of criteria for judging your topic.

When your evaluation of something is solicited, such as when your college asks you to evaluate a course, you usually receive a list of questions: How well was the class organized? Was the professor prepared? How available was the professor for help? For this project, you will have to generate a list of questions appropriate to evaluating your topic.

■■■ ACTIVITY 12.1 *Collaborative Activity*

What Makes Something Good?

Begin by listing the questions that people usually ask when evaluating items similar to your topic. If members of your class are writing about similar topics, get together to compare your lists of questions. Even if you are not writing on shared topics, a classmate or two can help you think of good points upon which to rate your topic. ■

■■■ ACTIVITY 12.2 *Writer's Notebook*

Evaluating Your Criteria and Main Points

After you have generated a list of criteria for evaluating your topic, write informally in your writer's notebook to rehearse the main points you want to make in an evaluation of your topic. If you want to be able to see other classmates' ideas, everyone might post their ideas on an online discussion board. On your list of criteria, are there points upon which you would give your topic the highest rating? Are there other points where your topic falls short? How would you sum up your rating of your topic? ■

Preparing to Write

Some writers prefer to go straight to drafting after having explored a topic thoroughly. Others prefer to lay out a plan for the organization of the paper. Either way, it is good to take stock of the notes you have made and write a tentative thesis for your evaluation.

Stating Your Evaluation as a Thesis

The thesis of an evaluation is simply the main point about the quality of the topic. It does not have to go into all of the criteria used in the evaluation itself, but it should sum up the writer's opinion. For example, consider these sentences from our examples earlier in the chapter.

■ From the evaluation of SAS: "One of [*Fortune* magazine's] Best Companies for all 13 years, SAS boasts a laundry list of benefits . . . ." The evaluation lists the benefits but also speaks of the CEO and his culture of trust as another criterion for choosing it as the best.

- From the evaluation of the Chevrolet Volt: "This automobile is a game-changer." The review's angle is to show how truly revolutionary the car is.

- From the evaluation of *Precious*: "A rare few [movies] arrive like gifts, sent by some cosmic messenger to stir the senses, awaken compassion and send viewers into a world made radically new by invigorated alertness and empathy." The review focuses on the acting and directing that contributed to the movie's power.

▨▨■ ACTIVITY 12.3 *Collaborative Activity*

Trying Out Thesis Sentences

Look over your prewriting notes and lists. What criteria do you think most contributed to your overall estimate of the quality of your topic? Try out some thesis sentences that express your opinion and point to a specific direction that your evaluation might emphasize. In groups of two or three, go over each other's ideas for the thesis and discuss what specific reasons each writer could use to defend that opinion. ■

Drafting Your Paper

Focus on angle, voice, and organization in drafting your paper.

Thinking as a Writer: What Angle and Voice Are Appropriate for an Evaluation?

As you begin drafting your evaluation, you should be conscious of your angle on the topic. A writer's angle is his or her point of view; it is the context in which the writer places the topic. Angle makes writing original and interesting, and gives the writing personality, or what we have called voice. Two writers could give the same item equally excellent reviews based on the same criteria, but their written evaluations will likely have different angles and voice, depending on each writer's attitude toward his or her topic and relationship with his or her readers.

Ann Hornaday, the author of the review of *Precious*, pages 294–96, has a voice appropriate to her evaluation of the movie as art. For example,

> Director Lee Daniels (*Shadowboxer*), working from a script by Geoffrey Fletcher, doesn't flinch from confronting viewers with the most squalid, violent depredations Precious suffers at her mother's hands. But he instinctively knows when to offer viewers and his heroine much-needed relief, by way of brightly lit, sumptuously staged magical realist sequences portraying Precious's glitzy daydreams.

Hornaday's angle is the movie as an integration of opposites, balanced between realism and fantasy. As readers, we feel we are being introduced to a work of art as understood by an insider.

Knowing your topic well enough to have an angle on it and picturing readers that would find your angle interesting—these are the keys to writing with voice.

Thinking as a Writer: Developing and Organizing Your Evaluation

Write a first draft of your evaluation. In planning your draft, consider the suggestions in the Best Practices box that will help you generate material to develop your thesis and organize the evaluation.

BEST PRACTICES | What Moves Can I Make?

The genre represented in the readings above (pages 289–96) and in the student example at the end of this chapter (pages 306–9) is the review or consumer report. Basic moves include the following:

- Indicate what you are evaluating immediately. Catch the readers' attention with an interesting move in the introduction. For example, the Volt evaluation opened with a catchy quotation. The movie review opened with a memorable claim: "the most painful, poetic and improbably beautiful film of the year."

- Provide background information the reader needs to put your topic in an appropriate context—the reviewer of *Precious,* for instance, tells us about the origin of the film in a novel and about the awards it has received.

- Explicitly lay out the criteria for your judgment and explain any criterion whose relevance may not be obvious.

- Use the criteria to structure your essay, as the writer of the Volt review did in a set of headings.

- State your overall assessment, usually early in your review, remembering that it can be positive, negative, or some mix of the two.

- Offer supporting details or specifics to justify and support your assessment, which may be observations from experience, research data, expert opinion—indeed, anything appropriate to your topic that meets your reader's need to know why you have assessed your topic as you have.

- Especially if you offer a negative review of something most people like or a positive review of something most people dislike, offer a defense of your evaluation—acknowledge that you are going against the popular judgment and explain why. ■

Revising Your Draft

Think of the first draft as raw material that could be rearranged for a better flow of ideas or improved emphasis. Have you put your points in the best order to make your evaluation forceful and easy for readers to follow? First drafts often need more development—specific details that readers cannot be assumed to know.

Sometimes you will need to take out material that readers would find either too general or common knowledge or too specific and not relevant to their interest and level of knowledge on the topic. Consider who your readers are and what you might need to explain more or say less about, given their interest in your topic.

ASKING QUESTIONS | Revision Checklist for Evaluation

Use the following questions to review your own draft or to help classmates find ways to improve theirs.

1. Does the evaluation have an interesting opening that would engage readers' interest? What is the opening move, and what other options are possible?

2. Does the writer have an angle on the topic? What is the angle? Does the opening show enough personal engagement with the topic? How could the writer show more connection with the topic?

3. Is the main point about the topic clearly stated as an opinion about the quality of the topic? Does the thesis suggest the author's angle on the topic?

4. Who is the audience for this evaluation? Where might this essay appear if it were to be published online or in print? How much would this audience already know about the topic? Can you think of anything not covered in the draft that these readers might want to know?

5. How well-developed is this evaluation? Does it contain enough specific evidence to support the judgments made about the topic? Where might the draft need more specific development?

6. What other options are there for arranging the main points? Would any other arrangements offer an advantage such as a more logical progression from minor to major criteria for evaluation?

7. How smoothly do the sentences flow? One common problem in first drafts is organization, including organization within paragraphs. It is especially hard for writers to find gaps in the train of thought because the writer knows how the ideas connect in his or her mind, even if the connections are not tight or clearly signaled on the page. Read through the draft again, paying attention to connections between sentences and the flow of ideas. (Read Student Example: Excerpts from Collin Dobmeyer's Draft for more help with checking for coherence.) ■

Student Example: Excerpts from Collin Dobmeyer's Draft

One of the most common problems in first drafts is poor *organization of ideas*, or **coherence.** The writer thinks of several ideas, all worth developing, and wants to get them down in writing. Realizing that there is more to say on some point, the writer comes back to it later in the paragraph—or even in a later paragraph. The reader feels a gap in the train of thought when this happens.

Many drafts can be improved by simple rearrangement of ideas, with clear transitions to signal the reader about turns in the train of thought. The following example of revising for coherence comes from student Collin Dobmeyer's review of the video game *Halo: Reach*. The full revised paper appears on pages 306–09.

Excerpt from First Draft

Dobmeyer assumes his readers know who produced the game.

Bungie really went out on a limb with *Halo: Reach*. They abandoned their previous faceless, emotionless, super soldier hero Master Chief in favor of a squad of Spartan super soldiers with faces and personalities. However, Bungie had better make us care about these characters if they want the player to care about their deaths. Among your teammates there is the able commander Carter, the emotional George, the introverted Emile, the snide engineer Kat, and the talkative sniper Jun. The extent to which they can make these characters relatable is a major deciding factor in the success of the game, which makes it a letdown that it doesn't quite work out. The problem stems from the gameplay. *Halo: Reach* is a game that centers on "run and gun" fighting. It is downright difficult to create sympathetic characters when all we see them doing is murdering every alien life form within 500 yards. It is also a problem because these characters lack depth. Every one of them is an unstoppable, immortal superman that doesn't even flinch when it comes time for their own deaths. The only character with human vulnerability is George, who ironically dies first.

In the draft, Dobmeyer repeats the point about needing to care about the characters.

In the draft, Dobmeyer turns to the problem of the game play style before completing the point about the lack of human characteristics.

Note how much better the flow of thought is after Dobmeyer revised for coherence.

Excerpt from Revised Draft

Sets up the team.

Bungie really went out on a limb with *Halo: Reach*. They abandoned their previous faceless, emotionless, super soldier hero Master Chief in favor of a squad of Spartan super soldiers with faces and personalities. Among your teammates there is the able commander Carter, the emotional George, the introverted Emile, the snide engineer Kat, and the talkative sniper Jun. However, Bungie had better make us care about these characters if they want the player to care about their deaths. The game fails to do so because nearly all the characters lack depth. Every one of them is an unstoppable, immortal superman that doesn't even flinch when it comes time for their own deaths. The only character with human vulnerability is George, who ironically dies first. From then on it becomes difficult to generate any strong emotional attachment to the characters.

After setting up the team, Dobmeyer moves to the need for deeper character development.

This isn't to say that the characters are complete mindless robots; in fact many of them have developing personalities, but the game just doesn't spend enough time developing them beyond the super soldier demeanor. For this, I blame the game play. *Halo: Reach* is a shooter that centers on "run and gun" fighting. It is downright difficult to create sympathetic characters when all we see them doing is murdering every alien life form within 500 yards.

Dobmeyer's revision adds a transition into the role of the game style in failing to allow for the characters' development.

Editing Your Revised Draft

Editing for style can help you emphasize main points and bring out your voice and attitude. The coordinating conjunction "and" often causes a main point to almost disappear or seem like an afterthought. In his earlier drafts, Dobmeyer found a few places where he overused "and," as in the following passage:

Original Version

Will the game successfully build the story to a satisfying climax through a coherent series of events, or will it fall prey to a mindless open season on aliens? These are the factors that will determine *Halo: Reach's* quality, and sadly Bungie missed the mark.

In the edited version, separating the verdict from the setup makes it a more forceful statement.

Edited Version

Will the game successfully build the story to a satisfying climax through a coherent series of events, or will it fall prey to a mindless open season on aliens? These are the factors that will determine Halo: Reach's quality. Sadly Bungie missed the mark.

Consider the value of short sentences when you want to stress a point.

Another stylistic mistake is to put a main point into a dependent cause, especially one beginning with a pronoun like *that* or *which*.

Original Version

Instead of a coherent story, it's more like a series of isolated cut scenes strung together with violence. This problem ties in with a more general issue with *Reach,* which is the general lack of polish.

In the edited version, an appositive set off with a strong punctuation mark gives the second sentence a more forceful ending.

Edited Version

Instead of a coherent story, it's more like a series of isolated cut scenes strung together with violence. This problem ties in with a more general issue with *Reach*: the general lack of polish.

In the final example below, the point about Alex is first made with a dependent "that" clause.

Original Version

It's because she seems like a human with real emotions that Alex becomes an integral, and welcome, part of the story.

In this revision, the point about Alex is promoted to the main clause—and main point—of the sentence.

Edited Version

Because she seems like a human with real emotions, Alex becomes an integral, and welcome, part of the story.

REVISED STUDENT EXAMPLE

Dobmeyer 1

Collin Dobmeyer

Professor Channell

English 1301-010

October 27, 2010

Is Classic Status Out of *Reach*?

Halo: Reach represents the culmination of the Bungie *Halo* franchise, which has run for nine years. Sales of *Reach* hit $200 million on the first day of its release in September 2010. Its popularity suggests it will be a classic, but will it? The series consists of four games: *Halo: Combat Evolved,* which was released back in 2001; *Halo 2; Halo 3*; and *Halo: Reach. Reach* brings the Bungie series to a close with a prequel whose events tie closely with the beginning of the first game. The player joins a group of elite soldiers known as Noble Team as they fight a losing battle to save the planet Reach from aliens. Normally this is where a reviewer should have written "SPOILER ALERT," but the outcome of the battle is quite clear from the outset with your character's helmet sitting in a smoldering crater with a bullet hole through the visor. Because the ending is known, the only chance this game has to make a huge impression on the player is how well Bungie can deliver the story line and personify the human characters.

The question is: did Bungie manage to pull this game off well enough that *Halo: Reach* deserves the title of "classic"? If the characters are not able to engage the

1

2

Margin annotations:

The evaluation opens with the topic clearly stated and an interesting specific fact about it.

This question suggests the writer's angle on the topic: Will it be a classic?

Gives an overview of the game's plot.

Shows the two main criteria that the writer will use as the basis of the evaluation.

players' emotions, then Reach will fail to reach classic status because the story is built around their deaths. The other indicator is how well the story unfolds. Will the game successfully build the story to a satisfying climax through a coherent series of events, or will it fall prey to a mindless open season on aliens? These are the factors that will determine *Halo: Reach*'s quality. Sadly Bungie missed the mark. *Halo: Reach* fails to deliver both characters and plot; as a result it will never be remembered for anything but its sales figures.

The thesis or main point that the evaluation will prove. Memorable summary judgment.

Bungie really went out on a limb with *Halo: Reach*. They abandoned their previous faceless, emotionless, super soldier hero Master Chief in favor of a squad of Spartan super soldiers with faces and personalities. Among your teammates there is the able commander Carter, the emotional George, the introverted Emile, the snide engineer Kat, and the talkative sniper Jun. However, Bungie had better make us care about these characters if they want the player to care about their deaths. The game fails to do so because nearly all the characters lack depth. Every one of them is an unstoppable, an immortal superman that doesn't even flinch when it comes time for their own deaths. The only character with human vulnerability is George, who ironically dies first. From then on it becomes difficult to generate any strong emotional attachment to the characters.

3

This isn't to say that the characters are completely mindless robots; in fact many
of them have developing personalities, but the game just doesn't spend enough time
developing them beyond the super soldier demeanor. For this, I blame the game play.
Halo: Reach is a shooter that centers on "run and gun" fighting. It is downright difficult
to create sympathetic characters when all we see them doing is murdering every alien
life form within 500 yards.

Looking at other classics like *Half-Life* brings the necessity of good
characterization into sharp relief. For those of you who have played the game, think
for a moment about how tedious the experience would have been in *Half-Life 2* if your
supporting character Alex was just one step up from a help screen. Because she seems
like a human with real emotions, Alex becomes an integral, and welcome, part of the
story. The supporting characters in *Reach* just don't work in this position because the
player does not see them as anything more than ordinance support. *Halo: Reach* will
be remembered for trying to develop good characters, but they fall short of really
making those characters human.

Finally we come to the most important part of *Reach*: the story. Too bad that
there really isn't much to it. *Reach* is built around the simple premise of super soldiers
fighting an alien invasion, a story that in the game world is only slightly less common
than trees. *Halo: Reach* pretty much boils down to killing whoever is in front of you and
progressing by finding more to kill. Nothing else actually happens during the game
itself; all of the important dialogue and characterization occur during animated cut
scenes, which gives the game a detached feeling. Instead of a coherent story, it's more
like a series of isolated cut scenes strung together with violence.

This problem ties in with a more general issue with *Reach*: the general lack of
polish. Polish in game creation is like editing and revising for a book, and just as
essential. Having a polished game means that levels flow smoothly from one set to
another, the Artificial Intelligence works without feeling artificial, and the scenes
impart a feeling of wonder.

I do have to give credit to Bungie for delivering the set. The scenery in *Reach* is 8
unlike any other shooter to date. With vast backdrops of war raging in the distance,
they almost manage to give the player the feeling of being part of something greater. I
also give credit to Bungie for the A.I. Enemies in *Reach* react almost like real people and
the Elites are downright cunning in their strategies. Too bad that after you have killed a
few thousand of them as part of the campaign that they cease to be scary or menacing
in any way, shape or form.

What it amounts to is that Bungie liked the run and gun tactics a little too much. 9
They allowed the game to become nothing more than a straight road between the
same boring fight. The gameplay requires the player to keep his eyes glued to the
action. As a result there is very little time to dwell on that wondrous feeling of being
an integral part of a global mission. Polish could have taken care of that. If Bungie had
taken the time to balance, or better yet, incorporate the scenery into the flow of the
game *Halo: Reach* could possibly reach that elusive classic status. As it stands, it feels
like Bungie made a set for *Lord of the Rings* just to perform a puppet show. The general
lack of polish damages Reach's case for classic status to the point where slamming out
patches isn't going to fix the problem. Bungie really dropped the ball on this one.

Despite my despairing tone, *Halo: Reach* is not the worst game on the market 10
today, but it isn't deserving of such massive hype either. The game is mediocre. It is
another generic shooter with some pretty backgrounds and won't be remembered
in a different light in a decade. Games like *Half-life* and *Deus Ex* with their wonderfully
complex stories and in-depth character development will always trump *Halo: Reach*
when it comes to classic status. For all of the people who are considering buying *Halo:
Reach,* I advise putting it on the rent list for now and saving your money for *Half-life:
Episode 3* if Valve ever gets around to making it.

CHAPTER 13

Choosing Strategies of Development

SUPPOSE YOU ARE WRITING AN INFORMATIVE PAPER ABOUT EARTHSHIPS, THE sustainable houses that people build in remote areas off the power grid. You have to get your essay off the ground somehow; you need an idea for an introduction. What are your options?

- You could describe an earthship, giving specific details about the natural and recycled building materials and the ground-hugging architecture.

- You could define the term earthship and explain the ways in which these houses are self-enclosed environments like spaceships.

- You could narrate, or tell the story, of a typical day in an earthship, comparing the experience to a day in a non-sustainable house.

These three options (among other possibilities) are **strategies of development,** sometimes called modes. The strategies are *moves that writers make when constructing a piece of writing.*

What Are the Strategies?

In this chapter, we will examine eight strategies of development.

1. *Exemplifying:* Giving instances or examples
2. *Narrating:* Telling a story or recounting a process
3. *Describing:* Showing the parts or features of something
4. *Evaluating:* Assessing how good something is
5. *Defining:* Telling what something means
6. *Classifying:* Putting something in a group with similar things
7. *Comparing-Contrasting:* Saying what something is like and not like
8. *Showing Cause and Effect:* Explaining why something exists or happens

We list the strategies one by one, but in practice they work in combination, two or three at a time. For example, you might define and exemplify to explain "communism": citing a dictionary definition and providing examples of communist nations, such as Cuba and North Korea. You might also compare and contrast communism with capitalism. The following text shows how strategies work in combination.

Dropping Weight . . .
and Keeping It Off

PAUL RAEBURN

This article appeared in the September 2007 special issue of Scientific American *devoted to "Diet, Health, and the Food Supply." Paul Raeburn is a science journalist and a frequent commentator on science-related issues for National Public Radio.*

This past March, Stanford University researchers published the results of one of the longest and most persuasive comparisons of weight-loss programs ever conducted. Three of the four diets in the study are heavily promoted regimens that have made their originators famous: the Atkins diet and the Zone diet, which both emphasize high-protein foods, and the Ornish diet, a plan that prohibits most fatty foods. The fourth was the no-frills, low-fat diet that most nutrition experts recommend.

The results, published in the *Journal of the American Medical Association,* were a surprise because they seemed to overturn the conventional wisdom. The experts' low-fat diet was beaten by Atkins's steak dinners and bacon-and-egg breakfasts. A year after starting their diets, people on the Atkins plan—which unapologetically endorses high-fat protein such as meats and dairy products to keep dieters sated—had dropped an average of 10 pounds. Subjects on the other diets had lost between three and six pounds. And members of the Atkins test group showed no jump in blood cholesterol levels, despite the high levels of cholesterol in their diet.

Reporters jumped on the obvious headlines: "Atkins Fares Best . . ." stated *The Washington Post.* "Atkins Beats Zone, Ornish and U.S. Diet Advice," the Associated Press declared. It was the same everywhere else: Atkins had bested the competition.

The newspaper accounts were not wrong. But the lead author of the Stanford study suggests a different interpretation of the findings. "What happened in our study was very modest weight loss in all four groups," says Christopher D. Gardner, a nutrition scientist at the Stanford Prevention Research Center. All groups also showed improvement in individuals' levels of cholesterol, blood pressure and insulin, even though none of them followed their diet plans exactly. And far from overturning established ideas about low-fat diets, the Stanford investigation provided resounding confirmation of another generally held belief: most people who try to lose weight, on any kind of diet, will succeed, even if many of them regain the weight later.

Contrast those conclusions with the results of another study published in the April issue of *American Psychologist* by researchers at the University of California, Los Angeles. They analyzed 31 long-term diet studies and found, as Gardner said, that most participants did see results—losing about 5 to 10 percent of their total body mass. And they did it while on all kinds of diets. But most also regained all that weight over the longer term, and some put on even more than they had lost. Only a small minority of

1

2

3

4

5

Strategy: Narrating. In paragraphs 1 through 3, Raeburn tells the story of the release of the study and the reaction it got in the press and medical community.

Strategy: Evaluating. Raeburn shows the researcher's analysis of the results.

Strategy: Describing. Raeburn describes a second study.

Strategy: Describing. Raeburn describes the results of the study.

Strategy: Exemplifying. Raeburn gives examples of headlines about the study.

Strategy: Comparing-Contrasting. Raeburn contrasts results of two studies.

subjects in the 31 studies kept the extra pounds off. The researchers' conclusion? Eat in moderation and exercise regularly.

Strategy: Cause and Effect. Explains why cutting fat has not helped.

Gardner thinks the traditional exhortation to cut dietary fat has turned out to be a bad message. The public health experts got it wrong, he says: "It totally backfired on us." People who consumed less fat often turned to soda and similar corn-syrup-sweetened products, along with other refined, low-fiber, carbohydrate-rich foods. As a result, "the obesity epidemic has continued to grow. Calories have continued to creep up, and it's been predominantly in the refined carbohydrates." 6

Strategy: Evaluating. In paragraphs 6 and 7, Raeburn reviews another analysis by the author of the first study.

The Atkins plan, which advises dieters to be less concerned about fat, steers people toward vegetables and protein and away from sugars and refined carbohydrates. "Maybe low carb is a better simple message to the public than low fat," Gardner says. "We tell them low carb, and they get it. They cut out a couple of sodas or a couple of cookies, and that adds up." 7

Strategy: Evaluating. Raeburn brings in another expert commenting on the diets.

James Hill, a psychologist and authority on weight loss, agrees that the Atkins approach has virtues. "The Atkins diet is a great way to lose weight," he says. But it "is not a way to keep weight off," he asserts. "There's no way you can do it forever." 8

Strategies: Describing and Classifying. Raeburn shows how the study grouped people according to whether they just dieted or dieted and exercised.

Hill is not terribly interested in comparing diets or devising new ones. "I think the weight-loss part is something we do pretty well," he says. One of his areas of research concerns individuals who have reduced their weight and sustained it. Hill and Rena Wing of Brown University have established what they call the National Weight Control Registry to collect data on people who have cut at least 30 pounds and kept them off for a year. Many have lost much more—the average is a 70-pound weight loss maintained for six years. "If you look at how they lost weight, there's no commonality at all," Hill says. But "if you look at how they kept it off, there's a lot of commonality." 9

Strategy: Comparing-Contrasting. Raeburn shows the difference between achieving weight loss and maintaining it.

Strategy: Describing.

The key, he continues, is exercise. "Activity becomes the driver; food restriction doesn't do it. The idea that for the rest of your life you're going to be hungry all the time—that's just silly." People in the registry get an average of an hour of physical activity every day, with some exercising for as much as 90 minutes a day. They also keep the fat in their diet relatively low, at about 25 percent of their calorie intake. Nearly all of them eat breakfast every day, and they weigh themselves regularly. "They tell us two things," Hill says. "The quality of life is higher—life is better than it was before." And "they get to the point with physical activity where they don't say they love it, but they say 'it's part of my life.'" 10

Strategy: Cause and effect. Raeburn shows what caused the weight to stay off.

Strategy: Cause and Effect. Raeburn shows what causes much of the obesity in the first place.

Hill admits that fitting an hour or more of exercise into the day is difficult, which is why he also focuses on prevention. Many of these people might never have become obese initially if they had exercised a mere 15 to 20 minutes a day. "I think you pay a price for having been obese," he states, "and you have to do a lot of activity to make up for that." 11

1. In paragraph 3, why does Raeburn give examples of newspaper headlines reporting the results of the Stanford study? What does this establish in the reader's mind?
2. He uses evaluation, description, and cause and effect in paragraphs 4, 5, and 6. What is the relation of these paragraphs to paragraph 3? What reader question or questions do the paragraphs answer? How do the strategies help get across what he has to say?

How Do Writers Choose Strategies?

Strategies are means of development, ways of saying something. They only make sense, therefore, in relation to the aims a writer is trying to achieve. What does Raeburn's article try to do? Clearly, it informs. But Raeburn also has an angle: He wants to show readers that diet choice matters less than lifestyle changes.

Raeburn chose his strategies based on the aims of his article. In paragraph 5, for example, Raeburn describes the results of another diet study that did not get as much press as the one his article emphasizes. Then, in paragraph 6, he draws on an expert's opinion to evaluate the traditional dietary advice and to explain by cause and effect why reducing fat in diets did not work. He uses these three strategies to give us important information the popular press neglected.

In paragraphs 9 and 10, Raeburn uses two of the same strategies again, description and cause and effect. This time, however, he draws on expert opinion ignored by the popular press to persuade us that exercise matters more than diet choice.

Select strategies to achieve your aim or aims.

BEST PRACTICES | When Should You Apply the Strategies?

The eight strategies are always at work. As you draft, you are using them without thinking about them. However, there are times when thinking about them can help.

1. *After planning your current writing project*
   Ask these questions:
   What aim or aims do I want my essay to achieve?
   Who are my readers? What will they need and expect from me?
   Based on your answers to these questions, look again at your plan and sketch out the strategies you will need for each section. What might you need to define? What must you describe?—and so on, considering all eight options. This will help

to keep you from getting stuck or bogged down with no ideas about where to go next.

2. *When revising a paper*

When you have a paper in first draft, examine it for underdeveloped points. Ask the same questions as in item 1, and sketch out additional or different moves to solve whatever developmental problems you detect.

3. *When assessing graded papers*

Look at the instructor comments. Did they single out places where development could improve? Do you see ways to develop more fully what you said, either by adding strategies or using different ones? ■

What Do the Strategies Look Like in Detail?

In the following section, we look more closely at examples of the strategies in action.

Exemplifying

When you exemplify, you give the reader instances or examples to answer the questions **Who? What?** and **Which?**

Types of examples include

- Brief examples
- Extended examples

Brief Examples

Use brief examples to provide instances of an abstract category or idea. Our first illustration comes from Al Gore's influential book, *An Inconvenient Truth* (see Figure 13.1). It consists of seven photographs showing examples from the category of green technology.

Imagine that Gore had omitted Figure 13.1. Readers would not *see* the technologies and would therefore have a less concrete idea of what is meant by green technology.

How do you choose examples when many are available? Look at the ones Gore chose. He chose examples *to persuade* readers to buy environmentally responsible products and to become advocates of green technologies. *When you write, choose examples that will help you achieve your aims.*

Even a brief example should be specific. Details make examples memorable and effective. Consider this paragraph that describes the consumer tastes of a well-off class of people, known in the 1980s as yuppies. Consider how the details add up to convey the author's angle or point of view:

> Here are just a few of the yuppie badges: yellow ties and red suspenders, Merlot, marinated salmon steaks, green-bottle beer, Club Med vacations, stuff with ducks on it, Gaggenau stoves, Sub-Zero refrigerators, latte, clothing from Ann Taylor or Ralph Lauren, designer water . . . .
>
> —JAMES B. TWITCHELL, "HOW I BOUGHT MY RED MIATA"

FIGURE **13.1**

Kinds of Green Technologies

In his influential book *An Inconvenient Truth,* Al Gore chose examples like these to persuade you to buy environmentally responsible products and to become an advocate of green technologies.

Twitchell might have said: "Yuppies like fancy clothes, wine, broiled fish, special beer, and expensive vacations." Instead, he got very specific. Not fancy clothes, but "yellow ties and red suspenders," not wine, but "Merlot." He is poking fun at the yuppies by showing us how predictable and brand-specific their consumption habits were.

When your instructor asks you to "be specific" when giving examples, think about how you can move down from general words like "car" to words that bring to mind a picture of a particular car: "a fifteen-year-old, lipstick-red, '91 Ford Thunderbird," as Katherine Kreuger-Land described her car in "Driving Away." (See her essay on pages 71–75.)

The more specific your description of something (or someone) is, such as Twitchell's very detailed description of yuppies, the better idea your readers will have of what you are talking about.

Extended Examples

The strategy of exemplification can be used to develop a paragraph or several paragraphs of your writing. These extended examples usually incorporate other strategies such as description or narration. Here is an example from a student paper on gender roles in which the author uses a source to provide an extended example of one way in which high school traditions promote gender stereotypes.

The example is specific in describing the details and smoothly integrates quotations and paraphrases. You might compare this version with the draft on page 168.

Pascoe (2007) observed a typical public high school for an entire year and found that the school reinforced ideas of masculinity as white, athletic, and heterosexual. A popularity contest called the "Mr. Cougar" competition is an example of how the process works.

Candidates for the "Mr. Cougar" title performed short skits in which they mocked boys who did not fit the stereotype of the "manly man." In one skit, titled "The Revenge of the Nerds," the candidates came on stage looking weak and effeminate, dressed in nerdy clothes. The audience thought this was hysterically funny because, as Pascoe explains, in our culture, "male femininity . . . is coded as humorous" (p. 4). The nerds' girlfriends were then kidnapped by other boys dressed as "gangsta's." To get "their women" back, the nerdy boys had to bulk up by lifting weights. The girls were depicted as trophies awarded to the nerds once they had transformed themselves into manly men and proved their masculinity by rescuing the girls from the gangsta's (p. 45).

—Jamie Cummins, "Exploring the Concept of Gender"

Narrating

When you narrate, you tell a story or recount a process. Narratives answer the question **"What happened?"** A narrative usually sticks to chronological order, and it can be combined with other strategies. The extended example of the high school skit, above, combines exemplification and narration to show what happened that reinforced gender stereotypes. Narrative is the primary strategy used in telling stories, whether fiction or nonfiction. When used to develop parts of a larger piece of writing, narrative can play a variety of roles.

Types of narratives include

- Anecdotes
- Dialogue
- Summaries
- Process narratives

Anecdotes

The most common narrative is the **anecdote,** *a short personal account of something that happened,* commonly used to open essays, conclude them, and illustrate important points in between. Below is the first paragraph from an essay about one of the most remarkable accomplishments in baseball, Joe DiMaggio's 1941 56-game hitting streak. The author was a distinguished scholar in the field of evolutionary biology.

> My father was a court stenographer. At his less than princely salary, we watched Yankee games from the bleachers or high in the third deck. But one of the judges had season tickets, so we occasionally sat in the lower boxes when hizzoner couldn't attend. One afternoon, while DiMaggio was going 0 for 4 against, of all people, the lowly St. Louis Browns, the great man fouled one in our direction. "Catch it, Dad," I screamed. "You never get them," he replied, but stuck up his hand like the Statue of Liberty—and the ball fell right in. I mailed it to DiMaggio, and, bless him, he actually sent the ball back, signed and in a box marked "insured." Insured, that is, to make me the envy of the neighborhood, and DiMaggio the model and hero of my life.
>
> —STEPHEN JAY GOULD, "THE STREAK OF STREAKS"

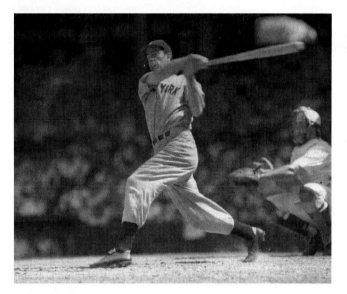

This anecdote connects the writer's childhood experience to his fascination with a baseball record and the man who set it. The result is an effective opener. Anecdotes, like most stories, benefit from the use of dialogue. Dialogue helps to catch the drama of the moment, as in the brief exchange between the son and his father in the example above. Although in this example, both speakers' words are in the same paragraph, it is preferable to make a new paragraph with each change of speaker. Use common identifying tags such as "I said" and "she asked" unless the speaker's identity is so obvious from the context that tags are not needed.

Personal anecdotes, like this story of a boy's father catching Joe DiMaggio's foul ball, are a great way to open or close an essay and make important connections.

Dialogue

Dialogue is a narrative strategy that helps in many genres, such as informative articles, where you might interview an expert and use his or her *exact words* to supply some of the information. Or an entire piece of writing could take the form of an interview or discussion. Ideas can be explored through dialogue. Plato wrote his great works of philosophy as dialogues between his teacher, Socrates, and other characters. Consider using dialogue in your writing when appropriate to add realism and voice, as in the example below from a National Public Radio profile on the Texas town of Marfa, where *Giant* and other more recent movies have been filmed.

Why is Hollywood so attracted to Texas? The drive-in movie critic, Joe Bob Briggs, says it's "because evil thrives in Texas." People seem especially drawn to West Texas, a land of limitless desolation—and possibilities—onto which they can project greed, lust and violence. Which makes it perfect to visit as part of our series On Location, which looks at the places where great American movies were filmed.

Chip Love sits in a conference room of the Marfa National Bank, where he's president. Love is affable, direct and self-deprecating, just like a West Texan. Love had a small role in *No Country for Old Men* as a salesman driving along a lonesome highway who gets pulled over by a police car driven by a psychopathic hitman played by Javier Bardem.

"Frankly, at this point, I've decided I carried that film because of all the lines that I had, which is, 'What's this about?' It's challenging, it's a lot to remember and I was able to remember it," Love says. He repeats the line with a laugh: "'What's this about?'"

Bardem smiles and puts a cattle bolt gun to the banker's forehead. Definitely evil. But why Marfa?

"Yeah, it's a good question," Love says. "The artists will tell you that Marfa has great light. I don't know how to quantify the light other than I know we have some beautiful sunsets. There are still plenty of places you can get and not see anything man-made. Maybe the camera likes that."

—John Burnett, "On Location: 50 Years of Movie Magic In Marfa, Texas"

Summaries

Narratives also work well in creating a **summary** of a complex history or situation, as in the following example:

Humankind has been steadily transforming Earth's surface for some 8,000 years, initially in Eurasia and later on all continents. Initially, we caused these transformations by clearing land for farming; later, other aspects of civilized life joined farming as important causes of this transformation. Well before the industrial era, the cumulative result over many millennia was an enormous loss of what had been "natural" on this planet.

During the 1800's and 1900's, human population increased from 1 billion to 6 billion, an explosion unprecedented in human history. This rise came about because new sanitary standards and medicines reduced the incidence of disease and because human ingenuity led to innovations in agriculture that fed ever-larger numbers of people. As a result, our already sizable impact on Earth's surface increased at a much faster rate.

By most estimates, the explosive population increase still under way will end near AD 2050 as global population levels out at some 9–10 billion people, or roughly 50 percent more people than now. A major reason for the predicted stabilization will be the increase in affluence that has historically resulted in fewer children per family.

—William F. Ruddiman, "Consuming Earth's Gifts"

Writers often use narrative summaries to recap key points made earlier. In this case, Ruddiman sums up key points he made in the preceding chapters of his book, *Plows, Plagues, and Petroleum.*

Note these features:

- Summaries often take more than one paragraph.

- These narratives often help writers make a case. Ruddiman argues that human impact on the environment is nothing new. You can see why, then, he starts his story with the beginnings of agriculture 8,000 years ago. Narratives often emphasize cause and effect. That is, they are efforts to explain why something happens or happened.

See Chapter 10, pages 231–257, for guidance.

Process Narratives

Use **process narratives** to *describe how something is done, how something works, or how something changes over time.* Examine Figure 13.2, an example of a **flowchart,** *a common visual tool that depicts the steps in a process.*

Even simple processes are easier for readers to follow and remember with a flowchart. For complicated processes, such as computer troubleshooting, flowcharts can be indispensable.

A flowchart is a visual example of a process narrative, but many process narratives rely solely on words. This paragraph explains how muscles in the eye respond to light and darkness:

Our pupils naturally expand in darkness and shrink in bright light through the actions of the two opposing iris muscles, the iris dilator and the iris sphincter. The dilator muscle, which extends radially through the iris, contracts to pull the iris outward, bunching it up like an open curtain. The iris sphincter is arranged in a circular pattern, similar to a purse string. Its constriction pulls the iris inward and flattens it, like a curtain drawn closed.

—Donald Mutti, "How Our Pupils Dilate"

Writers use process narratives to explain how something works, how to assemble and operate machines,

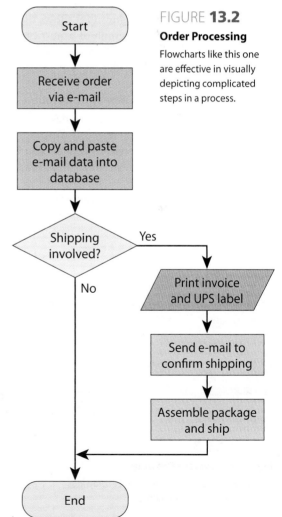

FIGURE **13.2**
Order Processing
Flowcharts like this one are effective in visually depicting complicated steps in a process.

how legislation makes its way through the U. S. Congress, and for a host of other purposes.

Describing

When you describe, you discuss the parts or features of something to answer questions such as **"How does something look, feel, sound, taste, and smell?"** Descriptions can also show readers how the parts of something are related, and description is often used in evaluations to tell readers why something is good or bad.

Types of description include

- Sensory
- Conceptual
- Scientific

Figure 13.3 shows the two primary ways description works. First, as in the photograph of a hurricane, it helps readers see your subject matter or recall what they have seen before. Second, as in the drawing of a hurricane, it reveals what readers cannot see, such as the internal structure of something.

Sensory Description

Use **sensory description** to communicate the concrete details of something you experienced. *Details of sight, sound, touch, smell, and taste* help the reader experience your subject as you did, and thus share your feelings about it. Here is a description that both depicts a scene and shares a feeling:

> It is Easter Sunday, 1950. I am dressed in a green, flocked scalloped-hem dress (handmade by my adoring sister, Ruth) that has its own smooth satin petticoat and tiny hot-pink roses tucked into each scallop. My shoes, new T-strap patent leather,

 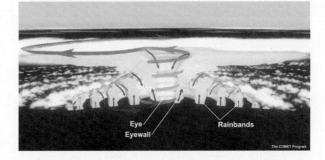

FIGURE **13.3**

Photograph versus Drawing

Photographs capture what we can see; drawings depict structures we cannot see.

again highly biscuit-polished. I am six years old and have learned one of the longest Easter speeches to be heard that day, totally unlike the speech I said when I was two: "Easter lilies / pure and white / blossom in / the morning light." When I rise to give my speech I do so on a great wave of love and pride and expectation. People in the church stop rustling their new crinolines. They seem to hold their breath. I can tell they admire my dress, but it is my spirit, bordering on sassiness (womanishness), they secretly applaud.

—Alice Walker, "Beauty: When the Other Dancer Is the Self"

Appealing both to the eye and ear, this paragraph is effective sensory description, letting us imagine a scene from long ago and the sense of community that went with it. Note how detailed the description is: "tiny hot-pink roses tucked into each scallop." Such detailed descriptions are known as *images* because they paint a picture with words.

Most description leans heavily on sight because human beings rely so much on vision. In your descriptions, do not neglect the other senses: hearing, taste, smell, and touch. They can also contribute to sensory detail in description.

Conceptual Description

Use **conceptual description** to *communicate ideas and categories*. The writer of the following description, an American citizen who was born and raised in India, wants her Americans readers to imagine what growing up in her culture was like.

When I was growing up in Calcutta in the fifties, I heard no talk of "identity crisis"— communal or individual. The concept itself—of a person not knowing who she or he was—was unimaginable in a hierarchical, classification-obsessed society. One's identity was absolutely fixed, derived from religion, caste, patrimony, and mother tongue. A Hindu Indian's last name was designed to announce his or her forefather's caste and place of origin. A Mukherjee could *only* be a Brahmin from Bengal. Indian tradition forbade inter-caste, inter-language, inter-ethnic marriages. Bengali tradition discouraged even emigration; to remove oneself from Bengal was to "pollute" true culture.

—Bharati Mukherjee, "Beyond Multiculturalism: A Two-Way Transformation"

The description in this passage is conceptual, depicting categories rather than things that we see, hear, smell, touch, or taste. Mukherjee does not describe her village or her father's face. Instead, she wants us to "see" something hidden, the Indian mindset. She also wants us to understand that a concept meaningful to us—"identity crisis"—has no equivalent in traditional Indian culture.

As with sensory description, the words and details in conceptual description convey the author's angle or attitude toward what is being described. In the passage above, Mukherjee sounds coolly critical of her native culture's strict rules preserving class and ethnic purity. However, descriptions can be more loaded if the author's purpose is to raise readers' emotions and persuade readers to see a topic from the author's point of view. In the passage below, the writer, Leslie

Marmon Silko, describes young men who have slipped across the border between Mexico and the United States.

> One evening at sundown, we were stopped in traffic at a railroad crossing in downtown Tucson while a freight train passed us, slowly gaining speed as it headed north to Phoenix. In the twilight I saw the most amazing sight: dozens of human beings, mostly young men, were riding the train; everywhere, on flatcars, inside open boxcars, perched on top of boxcars, hanging off ladders on tank cars and between boxcars. I couldn't count fast enough, but I saw fifty or sixty people headed north. They were dark young men, Indian and mestizo; they were smiling and a few of them waved at us in our cars. I was reminded of the ancient story of Aztlán, told by the Aztecs but known in other Uto-Aztecan communities as well. Aztlán is the beautiful land to the north, the origin place of the Aztec people. I don't remember how or why the people left Aztlán to journey farther south, but the old story says that one day, they will return.
>
> —LESLIE MARMON SILKO, "THE BORDER PATROL STATE"

By situating the scene in the historical context of the migration of population groups, Silko shows that she considers the border irrelevant and insignificant.

Writers are sometimes taught to keep their attitudes and judgments out of writing, especially for school papers. For some assignments, like lab reports, that is good advice. For others, however, loaded description is not only appropriate but necessary. For example, an assignment that asks you to take a stance (argue or persuade), will call for a certain amount of loaded description. How strong should your language be? That depends on the topic, how you see it, and how you want your audience to see it.

Scientific Description

Use scientific description to report the methods and findings of research. For example, the following passage describes what naturalists observed when studying the social behaviors of great white sharks. This passage illustrates both description and exemplification.

> At Seal Island, white sharks arrive and depart year after year in stable "clans" of two to six individuals. Whether clan members are related is unknown, but they get along peacefully enough. In fact, the social structure of a clan is probably most aptly compared to that of a wolf pack: each member has a clearly established rank, and each clan has an alpha leader. When members of different clans meet, they establish social rank nonviolently through any of a fascinating variety of interactions.
>
> For example, two white sharks often swim side by side, possibly to compare their relative sizes; they may also parade past each other in opposite directions or follow each other in a circle. One shark may direct splashes at another by thrashing its tail, or it may leap out of the water in the other's presence and crash to the surface. Once rank is established, the subordinate shark acts submissively toward the dominant shark— giving way if they meet, or avoiding a meeting altogether. And rank has its perks, which can include rights to a lower-ranking shark's kill.
>
> —R. AIDAN MARTIN AND ANNE MARTIN, "SOCIABLE KILLERS"

Much scientific description is far more technical, including research methods and statistics, but we can note some common features of description that reports on research:

- Maintains an objective tone
- Avoids first person
- Refers to other researchers and gives credentials
- Draws conclusions about the meaning of the observations or results described

Evaluating

When you evaluate, you assess how good something is. Use the evaluation strategy to answer questions such as these: **How well does this work? How bad would it be if that happened? How should we measure this? Why does this thing work so well?**

Types of evaluation include

- Personal evaluation
- Formal evaluation

Personal Evaluation

Use personal evaluation to offer your judgment or opinion. Most political and social commentary cartoons offer briefly stated evaluations, such as the example in Figure 13.4. Computers have brought us the "information superhighway," but at the price of making wisdom as scarce as water in a desert. That is the cartoonist's view of the Internet, shown in a simple drawing.

FIGURE **13.4**

Where Is Wisdom in the Information Age?

Most political and social commentary cartoons like this one offer clear evaluations. Do not be afraid to make such judgments in your writing.

Copyright Mike Keefe, dePIXion Studios. Reprinted with permission.

When warranted, don't shy away from personal evaluations. Below is an example in which a student expresses his disapproval of the dating culture of his peers.

> The hook-up culture is very deceptive. Hooking-up promises to be liberating and strengthening. Yet people find themselves needing more and more "liquid courage" to even make the first move. Hooking-up promises fun and fulfillment and no regrets, but when morning comes it delivers the "walk of shame." The hook-up culture has tricked us. It has led us to believe that our emotions are disconnected from our bodies, that love is divorced from sex.
>
> —Jack Grimes, "Hook-up Culture"

When you think that something is either good or bad, say so and then explain why, as Grimes does here. The evaluation need not be a moral judgment; it can be any assessment of anything, such as the quality of a movie, the impact of a policy, and so on.

Formal Evaluation

Use **formal evaluations** when you have done some research and serious study of a topic. Like personal opinions, these kinds of evaluations are also *your judgment on a topic, but they are more thought through, and are supported with evidence.* They are often mixed judgments that balance the pluses against the minuses, as in the following example.

> Chat rooms, role-playing games, and other technological venues offer us many different contexts for presenting ourselves online. These possibilities are particularly important for adolescents because they offer what Erik Erikson described as a moratorium, a time out or safe space for the personal experimentation that is so crucial for adolescent development. Our dangerous world—with crime, terrorism, drugs, and AIDS—offers little in the way of safe spaces. Online worlds can provide valuable spaces for identity play.
>
> But some people who gain fluency in expressing multiple aspects of self may find it harder to develop authentic selves. Some children who write narratives for their screen avatars [visual depictions of self in virtual space] may grow up with too little experience of how to share their real feelings with other people. For those who are lonely yet afraid of intimacy, information technology has made it possible to have the illusion of companionship without the demands of friendship.
>
> —Sherry Turkle, "How Computers Change the Way We Think"

The author here is a professor at MIT, a person who has done much research in the social effects of technology. Her stance is critical of information technology, but she knows enough to concede that there are social benefits. Her strategy is to devote a paragraph or so to the positive side, then, with a transition like "but" or "however," devote a paragraph or so to the negative side. When you opt for the positives versus negatives structure, be sure to leave no doubt what your stance is. Turkle clearly thinks genuine intimacy and friendship matter more than experimenting with identity.

Defining

When you define, you tell what something means. Definitions primarily answer who and what questions: **Who is this person? What is that? What does this mean?** A good definition educates the reader by specifying exactly what the writer means. There are many uses for the defining strategy in writing.

Types of definitions include

- Simple definition
- Complex definition
- Negative definition
- Stipulative definition

Simple Definition

Use simple definitions to provide the meaning of words readers might not know. For example:

> Solar cells, also known as photovoltaics, use semi-conductor materials to convert sunlight into electric current.
>
> —Daniel M. Kammen, "The Rise of Renewable Energy"

Kammen defines solar cells because he is writing for a readership that includes people that may not know much about solar energy.

Use simple definitions also to specify the meaning of terms that readers might understand differently or less precisely than you need them to be understood. For example:

> I'm talking about teardowns—the practice of purchasing and demolishing an existing house to make way for a new, much bigger house on the same site.
>
> —Richard Moe, "Battling Teardowns, Saving Neighborhoods"

Moe wants to distinguish the most general meaning of "teardowns," which includes old, condemned houses, from the meaning he intends: the destruction of sound but smaller houses in older neighborhoods to make way for McMansions.

Complex Definition

Some words defy simple definitions. Love, friendship, and wisdom are good examples of concepts that require complex definitions. Use complex definition to show your understanding of a word that has many meanings. Here is an example of one of the most complex concepts in the English language, a word uttered millions of times every day:

> What is love really? What does it mean to love someone?
>
> . . . In *Altruism and Altruistic Love,* Post, Underwood, Schloss and Hurlbutt (2002) raised an important question: "What is at the very core of human altruistic love?" Their answer was that love might be conceptualized as "affirmative affection."

> We all know what it feels like to be valued in this way, and we remember loving persons who conveyed this affective affirmation through tone of voice, facial expression, a hand on the shoulder in time of grief, and a desire to be with us . . . Love implies benevolence, care, compassion, and *action*. (p. 4, italics added)
>
> In our view, actions that fit the description of a loving relationship are expressions of affection, both physical and emotional; a wish to offer pleasure and satisfaction to one's mate; tenderness, compassion, and sensitivity to the needs of the other . . .
>
> —ROBERT W. FIRESTONE, LISA A. FIRESTONE, AND JOYCE CATLETT, "WHAT IS LOVE?"

This kind of definition is also called **operational,** *which means that something is defined by telling how it works.* Regardless of the name, the purpose is clear: to make vague abstractions, with many meanings, into something more precise, with something closer to a single meaning.

Negative Definition

Use negative definitions, saying what a word does not mean, to argue that the common understanding of a word is not correct. Negative definition is especially useful with abstract concepts like love. This use of negative definition comes from the same article as the example cited in the previous section.

> To better understand what genuine love is, perhaps we should also describe what it is not. Love is not what we mean when one is told by a family member that "mommy or daddy really loves you but he/she just doesn't know how to show it." Love is not selfish, possessive, or demanding, or a proprietary right over the other. Love is never submission or dominance, emotional coercion, or manipulation. Love is not the desperate attempt to deny aloneness or the search for security that many couples manifest in their desire for a fused identity.
>
> —ROBERT W. FIRESTONE, LISA A. FIRESTONE, AND JOYCE CATLETT, "WHAT IS LOVE?"

The authors say what love is not because people routinely think that "real love" includes some or all of the situations and motives described. The authors want us to see that much "real love" is not genuine love at all.

Stipulative Definition

In a stipulative definition, a writer gives a specific and often original meaning to a term, usually as part of an argument that challenges conventional thinking about the word.

When you stipulate a definition, you redefine words to suit your purpose. In this example, the author is talking about the use of style in the design of everyday objects.

> In this context, "aesthetics" obviously does not refer to the philosophy of art. Aesthetics is the way we communicate through the senses. It is the art of creating reactions without words, through the look and feel of people, places and things. . . .
>
> Aesthetics shows rather than tells, depicts rather than instructs. The effects are immediate, perceptual and emotional.
>
> —VIRGINIA POSTREL, "THE AESTHETIC IMPERATIVE"

Postrel is arguing for the value of beauty in ordinary, everyday experience, like the design of a bathroom. Because aesthetics is most commonly used in the fine arts, she has to spell out how she is using the word for her topic.

The second type of stipulative definition calls into question the connotations of a word, the emotional overtones it has. Barry M. Goldwater (1909–1998), a U.S. senator from Arizona, was the Republican candidate for president in 1964. Accused of being a dangerous extremist, he made the following remark near the end of his acceptance speech for the nomination that has since often been quoted by conservatives and libertarians:

> I would remind you that extremism in the defense of liberty is no vice. And let me remind you also that moderation in the pursuit of justice is no virtue.
> —Delivered July 16, 1964, San Francisco

Take a word, such as "extremism," used to criticize and condemn, and recast it as something acceptable at least, even worthy of praise.

Classifying

When you classify, you put something in a group with similar things. Classifications can answer several questions: **What kind of thing is this? How is this related to that? Where does that fit in a larger scheme?**

Types of classification include

- Simple classification
- Mixed classification
- Questioning classifications

Among the strategies of development, classifying has special importance because how we divide things into groups has much to do with how we think. Examine Figure 13.5, the two pie graphs that appeared in an article about sources of renewable energy.

Both graphs are examples of classification. We have one big category, Competing Energy Sources: all the ways to generate electricity. This category is divided into six types, one of which is nonhydropower renewables (wind, solar, and so on).

The top pie chart shows us how much of each type the world uses; the bottom pie chart examines one category from the top pie chart by dividing it into four subcategories. Taken together, the graphs show that, despite the vast energy-generating potential of renewables, they do not as yet supply much of our energy.

Organizing information this way is straightforward: Divide something into chunks, then divide the chunks into smaller chunks, and so on, dividing and subdividing as much you need to.

Simple Classification

Use **simple classifications** to *make distinctions between items in one category and items in another,* as in the following example.

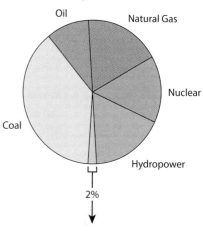

Fraction of Global Electricity Generation

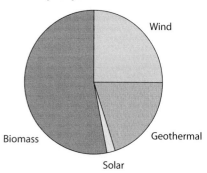

Breakdown of Nonhydropower Renewables

FIGURE **13.5**

Dividing and Subdividing

Organizing information into chunks and dividing and subdividing as needed is a very effective and straightforward way to convey information.

The author is pointing out that grades in courses in the liberal arts category are higher than grades in the sciences and engineering category.

> English departments have basically worked on the A/B binary system for some time: A's and A-minuses for the best students, B's for everyone else and C's, D's and F's for students who miss half the classes or threaten their teachers with bodily harm. At Penn State, A's accounted for 47 percent of the grades in English in 2002. The numbers are similar for sociology, comparative literature and psychology—and indeed for the College of Liberal Arts as a whole. The sciences and engineering, notoriously, are stingier.
>
> —MICHAEL BERUBE, "HOW TO END GRADE INFLATION"

Two large categories, A students and B students, almost cover the possibilities; with a little amusing exaggeration, Berube allows for a small third group that falls outside the A/B distinction altogether, and then finishes the paragraph with another distinction, liberal arts versus science and engineering.

The human mind works largely by "this versus that" distinctions, and therefore simple classification is a common strategy of development.

Mixed Classification

Use **mixed classifications** to depict complex situations in *which objects, or in this case people, can be grouped in different ways according to different classification schemes.*

> One in nine Americans is an immigrant. And half the laborers entering the American workforce in the 1990s were foreign-born. Add in their families and extended families and the picture grows more dramatic still. Together, immigrants and their children now account for one in five Americans. Hispanics, at nearly 14 percent of the population, are already the largest minority, outnumbering blacks. Asian-Americans are still a relatively small share of the nation—at only 4 percent. But despite their numbers, they, too, are going to play a major part in the country's future: already, they make up between 15 and 20 percent of the students at most Ivy League colleges.
>
> Where do these new arrivals come from? Just over half the foreign-born are Hispanic and a little more than a quarter are Asian. They hail from all the corners of the globe, though more from some countries than from others. Mexicans, by far the largest category, account for roughly one in three first-generation immigrants—almost ten times more than any other nationality. The next largest groups are Filipinos and Indians, followed by Chinese, Vietnamese, Koreans, Cubans and Salvadorans—but none of these account for more than 3 or 4 percent of the total.
>
> —TAMAR JACOBY, "THE NEW IMMIGRANTS AND THE ISSUE OF ASSIMILATION"

Jacoby's topic is the new immigrants, the wave of people entering our country now. Their diversity is not easy to grasp. To depict it, she needs to mix some of the many ways new immigrants are classified. First, she contrasts immigrants with all Americans. Then she shifts to two large groups of immigrants in particular, Hispanics and Asian Americans, and compares these to various populations of all Americans. Finally, her third classification is immigrant groups based on national origin.

Any writer can do what Jacoby does *so long as group contrasts are clear.* Notice how Jacoby helps us follow what she has to say by staying with the Hispanic/Asian classification from the fourth sentence on. If she had made the groups she was talking about much more complex, readers would have trouble following her meaning.

Questioning Classifications

Call classifications into question to challenge entrenched or habitual ways of thinking about something. Look at Figure 13.6, an ingenious poster from an organization called the Southampton Anti-Bias Task Force. Its message: "Many skin colors fall into a single category: 'flesh.'" Our humanity is much more important than the shade of our skin.

In the 1950s, boxes of Crayola crayons included a peach-colored one, labeled "Flesh." The company renamed it "Peach" in 1962. So the poster also says: "That crayon is long gone, and with it the assumption that 'white' is normal and all other skin colors deviate from the norm."

FIGURE **13.6**

The Many Colors of "Flesh"

The above image from a poster recalls Crayola boxes that once labeled the center crayon "flesh," now renamed "peach." The bias toward white skin as "normal" is clearly the poster's target.

Unfortunately, classification leads to stereotypes, which in turn lead to discrimination. Here is another potent example of questioning a stereotype that causes many neighborhoods in the United States to remain highly segregated. The author, an African American, had been turned down for a mortgage to buy a house in a white neighborhood.

> The bank was proceeding according to demographic data that show any time black people move into a neighborhood in the States, whites are overwhelmingly likely to move out. In droves. In panic. In concert. Pulling every imaginable resource with them, from school funding to garbage collection, to social workers who don't want to work in black neighborhoods to police whose too frequent relations to black communities is a corrupted one of containment rather than protection. It's called a tipping point, this thing that happens when black people move into white neighborhoods. The imagery is awfully catchy, you must admit: the neighborhood just tipping right on over like a terrible accident, whoops! Like a pitcher I suppose. All that nice fresh wholesome milk spilling out, running away . . . leaving the dark, echoing, upended urn of the inner city.
> —Patricia J. Williams, "The Distribution of Distress"

Afraid of the "tipping point," banks find ways to deny loan requests or impose terms so unfavorable that the applicant cannot afford to accept them. Clearly, our habitual ways of thinking about race as a classification still need to be exposed and challenged.

Comparing-Contrasting

When you write to compare or contrast, you are answering these questions: **How are these things similar? How do they differ?**

Types of comparing-contrasting strategies include

- Comparison
- Contrast
- Analogy

Comparison

To develop a point on any topic, you might compare by drawing parallels between your subject and another to help make your point. For example, the following paragraph compares Iraq and Afghanistan.

> In Iraq, we face a vicious insurgency that will take years to defeat; the same is true in Afghanistan. In Iraq, the insurgency is made more difficult by the overlay of sectarian violence (Sunni versus Shiite); the same is true in Afghanistan (Pashtun versus everyone else). In Iraq, the insurgents are aided by infiltration from neighboring countries (Syria, Iran); the same is true in Afghanistan (Pakistan). In both countries we are trying to rebuild the army and the police—with fitful progress—and fostering a fragile central government whose writ doesn't seem to extend very far across the country.
>
> —Rich Lowry and David B. Rivkin Jr., "It's All the Same Fight"

The strategy is to take two items in the same classification—in this case, a category with only two members, the countries the United States invaded in the years following 9/11—and compare them, show how they are alike.

The similarities are emphasized effectively with a pattern of repetition in the sentences: "In Iraq, . . . the same is true in Afghanistan." "It's all the same fight"—the article's title and central contention—which is why the authors assert parallels.

Look at the graphic in Figure 13.7, a bar graph that compares income inequality among five nations. The Iraq example uses many points of comparison but only two countries. This figure uses five countries but only one point of comparison, the gap between rich and the poor. Why? What looks like a simple five-nation comparison is actually meant to bring out a contrast. It raises this question: As a mature economy, do we in the United States toler-

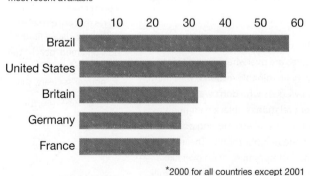

Less equal than others
Gini coefficient—a measure of income equality
most recent available*

Source: OECD: World Bank

*2000 for all countries except 2001 for Germany, and 2003 for Brazil

FIGURE **13.7**

Comparisons of Income Inequality

Use comparisons to make a point—in this case that, where income disparity is concerned, the United States more nearly resembles Brazil than developed countries like Britain or Germany.

ate too great a gap between rich and poor? Are we too close to Brazil and not close enough to other more prosperous countries?

As with other strategies, how comparison and contrast works in any particular case *depends on what a writer is trying to do.* Lowry and Rivkin want to join together something that has been pulled apart. The graphic has much the same motivation: to link the United States with a nation we would not normally compare ourselves to, Brazil.

Contrast

Use contrast to emphasize the differences between things that are similar in some other ways. Contrasting items that most readers would assume are interchangeable can help you make a case for choosing one over the other.

Showing stark contrasts can make a dramatic statement. Consider Figure 13.8, a news photo from *The New York Times*, taken after a snow storm. If you wonder for a moment exactly what the baglike looking objects are in the foreground—uncollected garbage, maybe?—the caption fills you in: They are homeless people, trying to survive the storm under makeshift shelters. And what is that in the background? The White House, the nation's "first home." The picture uses the strategy of contrast to emphasize the gulf between the impressively housed president versus Americans with no homes at all.

In the following example of simple contrast, the writer sets one generation's circumstances against that of current college students:

> Go to college. Work hard. Save money. For the baby boom generation, this mantra was considered the tried and true recipe for getting ahead . . . .
>
> Getting a bachelor's degree is the required ticket for entry into the middle class today, but the security once implied in that status is gone. In addition to the exigencies now felt by middle-class Americans of all ages—rising health care costs, soaring home

FIGURE **13.8**

Homelessness by the White House

Use contrast to make a point—in this case, the irony of the homeless so close to the White House, an American symbol of power, wealth, and prestige.

prices and flat or falling incomes—today's new generation of college grads bear an added vulnerability of massive debt.

—TAMARA DRAUT, "WHAT'S A DIPLOMA WORTH, ANYWAY?"

Analogy

An analogy is an explicit comparison used to bring out similarities in apparently unrelated items or ideas. Writers often use analogies to help readers understand concepts and other complicated points. You can ask, "How is the thing I am talking about, which my audience does not understand, similar to something else that my audience does understand?" In other words, **"What is this like?"** is the key question.

Many common analogies help us to picture information, remember things, solve problems, and make decisions. For example, what analogy describes the structure of the Internet? The World Wide Web, of course. Even if the Internet does not closely resemble a spider's web, the analogy gives us a concept we can understand.

Analogies can also help us make arguments, as in the overworked analogy between alcohol and marijuana that argues if the former is legal, the latter should be also since it is so similar. But analogies can also be fresh and creative, as in the following review of *Harry Potter and the Sorcerer's Stone*:

> This overly familiar movie is like a theme park that's a few years past its prime; the rides clatter and groan with metal fatigue every time they take a curve. The picture's very raggedness makes it spooky, which is not the same thing as saying the movie is intentionally unsettling.
>
> —ELVIS MITCHELL, "THE SORCERER'S APPRENTICE"

Someone who liked the movie might not like Mitchell's analogy, but it makes a strong impression. We do not usually associate movies and theme parks. How did he think of the analogy? Perhaps he thought about the film's primary audience, children, who also love theme parks. Maybe Mitchell happened to recall taking children to a rundown theme park and found enough similarities to the movie to make the link. And so an analogy is born: Likeness suddenly emerges in seemingly unrelated things.

No writer can simply decide to use an original analogy. Rather, analogies come to us or they do not. When something we are writing about reminds us of something else, we can stop and wonder why, and try to uncover the resemblance we sense is there. Being receptive to the working of our own minds is about all we can do.

Overused Analogies

Challenge overused analogies when they block good thinking. Some analogies are so common because people use them too much and without serious thought about what they mean. We can call the value of such analogies into question, as in this example.

> Thirty-five years ago, at the beginning of a twelve-year Senate inquiry into the drug industry, Senator Gaylord Nelson opened the session on psychotropic drugs by

comparing them to the drugs in *Brave New World*. . . . Thirty-five years later, *Brave New World* is still invoked, time and again, as a warning against the dangers that await us if we embark on new enhancement technologies. News stories about psychotropic drugs, stem cells, reproductive technologies, or genetic engineering inevitably appear with headlines reading Brave New Medicine, Brave New Babies, Brave New Minds, or Brave New People. It is as if we have no other metaphors for these technologies, no competing visions of possible futures.

—Carl Elliott, "The Tyranny of Happiness"

Elliott goes on to point out that most of the new technologies are not like the "happy pills" of *Brave New World*, designed to tranquilize a population into accepting totalitarian government. People choose them; they aren't imposed; they choose most of them to gain an apparent competitive advantage, not for escapism.

Writers are often told to avoid overused or trite analogies. That is good advice, but we can also do what Elliott does—challenge them.

Cause and Effect

Cause and effect explains *why something exists or happens*. It answers how and why questions: **How did this happen? Why is this case?** The strategy often arranges information in a chronology to show causation or to suggest an effect: **What happened in what order? What might happen next?**

Types of cause-and-effect strategies include

- Simple causation
- Complex causation

Simple Causation

Writers use simple causation to show why something happened. What happens when you mix blue and yellow paint? Green paint, of course. *The effect must be an inevitable result of the cause* and not just related to it. For example, a study of the dairy industry and federal crime data found that increased ice cream production correlated to an increase in rape cases. The statistics were correct, but the study was created to show how statistics can be used improperly. Increased ice cream production does not cause rape to increase. Both result from seasonal changes in temperature.

Complex Causation

Use complex causation to explain events that have many contributing causes. The typical situation we face in explaining human behavior is **multiple causation,** *many interacting forces and motivations*, as in the following example.

While television has long been suspected as a promoter of consumer desire, there has been little hard evidence to support that view, at least for adult spending. After all, there's not an obvious connection. Many of the products advertised on television are everyday low-cost items such as aspirin, laundry detergent, and deodorant. Those TV ads are hardly a spur to excessive consumerism. Leaving aside other kinds of ads for the moment (for cars, diamonds, perfume), there's another counter to the argument that television causes consumerism: TV is a *substitute* for spending. One of the few remaining free activities, TV is a popular alternative to costly recreational spending such as movies, concerts, and restaurants. If it causes us to spend, that effect must be powerful enough to overcome its propensity to save us money.

Apparently it is. My research shows that the more TV a person watches, the more he or she spends. The likely explanation for the link between television and spending is that what we see on TV inflates our sense of what's normal. The lifestyles depicted on television are far different from the average American's: with a few exceptions, TV characters are upper-middle-class, or even rich.

—Juliet Schor, "When Spending Becomes You"

Note how carefully Schor prepares us for her determination of cause. Instead of creating resistance by claiming "TV causes excessive consumerism," she disarms us by first calling her view into doubt. TV is not *self-evidently* related to excessive spending. It might even work against it, she says. Then, when she asserts the connection between television and spending, she calls it a "link" rather than a cause. In social science terminology, the link would be called *correlation—a relationship in which two things vary in concert, but without evidence of causality*. We do not know and often cannot know for sure. Schor supports the plausibility of her link by attempting to explain why television has the effect she says it has: We watch so many well-off people on television that we come to think of wealthy as normal.

How Can I Develop a Repertoire of Strategies?

This chapter has been just a start for exploring options you have as a writer. The eight strategies covered here do not exhaust the range of possibilities for inventing and developing ideas in your papers and other writing. Like a good vocabulary, strategies for development are part of a writer's toolbox, and the more you use them, the better you become at your craft.

In the long run, what matters most is that you continue to learn from the writers you admire. As you read, note the moves made by good writers, and take time to reflect on why they used a particular strategy and how they put it into sentences, paragraphs, and multiparagraph sections. When working on a project of your own, feel free to imitate the strategies of other authors—in your own way, with your own content, audiences, and purposes. All good writers learn to write this way, by becoming interested in how a better writer handles something. Over time you will internalize the strategies, combine them with others, and transform them in dozens of different ways so that what started as someone else's skill becomes your own.

CHAPTER 14
Editing Fundamentals

IF YOU HAVE EVER GOTTEN A PAPER BACK COVERED WITH CORRECTION marks—for example, with comments in the margins like "What does this mean?" or "Don't follow you here"—and marked with a grade lower than you anticipated, then you know what happens when you do not edit well. Instead of responding to what you have said, your instructor is responding to problems with how you have said it.

Look and listen for problems in the following sentence from a student's paper:

One route that companies have already taken, and been successful, is to have meditation when something like sexual harassment occurs.

If your ear heard how awkward the sentence sounds, you know it needs editing. If your eye saw that the writer meant "mediation" not "meditation"—one little "t" makes a big difference—you can eliminate a significant mistake.

Looking and *listening* are two essential editing skills. A third skill is *rewriting* to solve problems. Consider this edited version of the sentence:

One successful route companies have already taken is to mediate sexual harassment disputes.

No one will be irritated or distracted by this sentence. It says what the writer meant, and the reader will understand its meaning immediately. In short, *nothing interferes with the meaning coming through.* That is what editing is all about.

You can learn to edit. A little knowledge about grammar can help, but you will need practice above all. Editing is a skill, learned as you do it. This chapter provides the fundamentals:

■ Understanding the process of editing and how it fits into the writing process

■ Knowing common problems to look and listen for

■ Applying strategies for solving problems you find

Once you get into the habit of editing, with each paper, you will find it easier to make your writing more clear, concise, and coherent. You will not need instructors' comments to find and correct the rough spots.

What Is Editing?

Editing is an intense effort to find and solve whatever problems remain in a piece of writing after revision. It amounts to paying attention to small details you may have missed earlier in the process. Editing includes

■ Checking for **flow and focus within individual paragraphs**

- Checking for **flow and focus from one paragraph to the next**
- Reworking **awkward, wordy, or unclear sentences**
- Correcting **errors of grammar, spelling, and punctuation**
- Attending to **formalities,** such as parenthetical notation and Works Cited pages

Why Edit?

Perhaps you feel that editing should not matter very much. After all, it is content that counts. Saying something worth reading is the whole point of writing. However, *content cannot be separated from the way it is expressed.* Have you ever been irritated or distracted because background noise or a bad connection interfered with a cell phone conversation? A poorly edited paper is like a bad connection: It irritates and distracts readers. More seriously, if your sentences do not say what you mean, if readers struggle to understand your sentences, if your paragraphs wander, your thoughts and your message get lost.

Edit, then, *to communicate better with your readers.* Edit also because the impression other people have of you matters. An unedited or poorly edited paper says that the writer either lacks the skill or the discipline to attend to details. Judgments like "incompetent" or "careless" or even "illiterate" are common. Such judgments may seem unfair, but the consequences are real: poor grades, lukewarm recommendations, being stuck in low-level jobs.

BEST PRACTICES | Where Does Editing Belong in the Composing Process?

Focus on editing only when you have a draft you consider "final," the best you can do. Why?

First, editing requires undivided attention. Some writers edit as they compose, even while writing first drafts. We do not recommend it. Editing as you write slows down composing and takes attention away from where it ought to be, on saying what you have to say. In subsequent drafts, you can attend to **revision,** which deals with *large-scale changes in a draft* to achieve your purpose or meet the requirements of an assignment, develop your points more adequately, connect with your readers more consistently, improve your organization, and so on. **Revise first, then edit.**

Second, editing too soon is not efficient. If you edit a sentence or a paragraph in the first draft and then delete it during revision, you have wasted time and effort. Still worse, you might resist throwing out a sentence you have edited so carefully when it should be cut. Editing too soon can actually get in the way of something more important—revising and rewriting to solve major problems.

Finally, compulsive editing can easily lead to **writer's paralysis,** *being so critical of everything you write that you can hardly write at all.* When you are composing, let go, let thoughts and words flow. Save editing for later. ■

How Do Writers Edit?

Every semester students come to us with papers covered with correction marks and marginal commentary. They are shocked, puzzled. "But I read it over several times," they say, sometimes adding, "I even had a _____ [tutor, parent, or friend] look it over." To this we say, "But editing is not 'reading' or 'looking over.' You cannot edit a paper by scanning through it."

When we read something, we *look through* the sentences to what is being said. To edit, you have to *look at* the sentences and paragraphs to see *how* things are said.

If you are working on paragraphs, take it one paragraph at a time; if sentences, one sentence at a time. Linger over each one, looking and listening for signs of problems. A good method for slowing down and listening is to read your draft out loud. Your ear will catch things that your eye might miss. Mark anything that bothers you. Then go back and rework the sentence or the paragraph until it does not bother you anymore. In short, **slow down.**

You may be thinking, "Won't this take a long time?" The answer is "Yes, much longer than reading over a paper." If you are working on a five-page, double-spaced paper, expect to spend at least forty-five minutes to an hour editing it. You will get faster with experience, but "fast" and "editing" never go together.

The most important thing to remember when editing your work is to *slow down*. Linger over paragraphs and words, and rework anything that bothers you.

- Budget downtime. Try to get away from a paper for a day or two before editing it. You will be fresher and more detached from your writing.

- Avoid trying to do all the editing at one time. Try fifteen- to twenty-minute sessions, with breaks in between. Otherwise it is hard to maintain the high level of concentration required.

- After editing on your own, find a classmate who is also committed to editing. Exchange papers and help each other find the problems self-editing missed.

What Is the Spiraling Down Method?

We strongly advocate a **spiraling down method** of editing. That is, first address the flow from paragraph to paragraph; then the flow within paragraphs; and finish with attention to individual sentences, word choice, and errors. You will need to make several passes through your paper, once or twice at the paragraph level, once or twice at the sentence level. Spiraling down offers several benefits:

- It keeps you from being overwhelmed by all the details; you can "divide and conquer."

- A key principle of editing is: *The more you look for at one time, the less you find.* If you are examining paragraphs or sequences of paragraphs for coherence and flow, you are not likely to detect individual sentences that need work and vice versa.

- It allows some problems to solve themselves. If you work on paragraphs first, any changes you make may fix or eliminate bad sentences, so you will not have to bother editing them. When you are working at the sentence level, some typos and grammatical errors may simply disappear during rewriting. Why hunt for errors before you give them a chance to go away on their own?

Working on Paragraph Sequences

The first focus of editing is working on paragraph sequences. Paragraphs are the building blocks of any piece of writing. Paragraphs, either singly or in groups, make up the sequence of moves that an author makes while composing. The sequence of paragraphs should create a smooth train of thought and a logical development of points.

Paragraphs may look like independent units, but actually *they mark off a move within a set of connected moves* that make up a section in a paper. A **move** is *an answer to an implied question,* something the reader needs to know. It is common in long essays and book chapters for multiple paragraphs to work together in making any one move. When two or more paragraphs work in unison to make a single move, we refer to them as paragraph groups.

Consider the following passage from "Malnutrition, Poverty, and Intellectual Development," an article from *Scientific American.* We have indicated the implied question each move answers.

Move 1: What was the old theory?

For many years, scientists considered the connection between nutrition and intellectual development to be straightforward. They assumed that poor nutrition was primarily a worry from conception to age two, when the brain grows to roughly 80 percent of its adult size. In this critical period, any degree of malnutrition was thought to halt the normal development of the brain and thereby to inflict severe, lasting damage.

Move 2: What's wrong with the old theory?

Gradually, though, investigators recognized that the main-effect model, as we have termed this view, was too simplistic. For instance, the emphasis on the first two years of life proved somewhat misguided. Brain growth in that period is not always terminated irreversibly in undernourished children. Rather it may be put on hold temporarily; if diet improves by age three or so, growth of the brain may continue at close to a normal pace. Conversely, injury to the brain can occur even when a child suffers malnutrition after the first two years of life—a sign that providing adequate nutrition throughout childhood is important to cognitive development. Focusing exclusively on the first two years of life is thus inadequate.

Move 3: What else is wrong with the old theory?

Furthermore, although severe underfeeding in infancy can certainly lead to irreparable cognitive deficits, as the main-effect model predicts, the model cannot fully account for intellectual impairment stemming from more moderate malnutrition. This flaw became apparent in the 1960s, when researchers showed that mildly undernourished children from middle- or upper-income families (whose nutrient deficits stemmed from medical conditions) did not suffer the same intellectual troubles as did mildly underfed children in impoverished communities. If poor nutrition impaired cognition only by structurally altering the brain, the two groups should have performed alike. Something else had to be at work as well. In other words, factors such as income, education and other aspects of the environment could apparently protect children against the harmful effects of a poor diet or could exacerbate the insult of malnutrition.

Here is the principle at work: *Every paragraph, or paragraph group, implies and answers a key question.* The purpose of each paragraph is to move the line of thought forward, in order, 1, 2, 3. . . . Once you see the logic, it is hard to imagine any other paragraph sequence for presenting the information.

Successful paragraph sequences work this way. Consequently, here is how to edit your own paragraph sequences:

1. Isolate each major section of your paper. If the paper is short, treat the whole paper as one section.

2. Check to see if each paragraph, or paragraph group, makes a *single* move in a sequence of connected moves. Use the implied-question-and-answer test demonstrated above.

3. If this is not happening, ask, **"What are the 1, 2, 3 (and so on) moves you need to say what you want to say?"**

4. Rewrite the section, making paragraphs that correspond to each move.

BEST PRACTICES | Editing Paragraph Sequences

Moving section by section through your paper, concentrate first on the *sequence* of paragraphs. Ask these questions:

1. **Does each paragraph or paragraph group have a definite function or purpose?** If you cannot say what function some paragraph performs, you may need to delete it or reconsider what moves you want to make in your paper.

2. **Do my paragraphs follow a logical sequence in building a train of thought for my reader to follow? Do I need to add more to the sequence or rearrange parts of it?** Add what is needed to existing paragraphs or add a new paragraph.

3. **Are there smooth transitions from one move to the next?** How could you signal the reader where a paragraph or paragraph group makes a new move or takes on a new function in the sequence of your paper? ■

▨▨■■ ACTIVITY 14.1 *Collaborative Activity*

Paragraph Sequencing Practice

The following passage looks like one paragraph but should actually be two. The sentences in both paragraphs have been scrambled and intermixed. Working with one or two other students, sort out the sentences and make them into two separate paragraphs. Be able to say what question each of the two paragraphs answers on the topic of underage drinking.

More multiple-paragraph editing practices appear on pages 349–52.

The laws in Europe do not limit alcohol consumption to people twenty-one or older. People experience alcohol in their earliest years, and therefore Europe does not experience the same problem that the U.S. has. According to Elizabeth Whelan, alcohol-abuse researcher at Harvard, "prohibiting the sale of liquor to reasonable young adults creates an atmosphere where binge drinking and alcohol abuse becomes a problem." Enforcing a younger drinking age is not a way of extending the party to people of all ages, but an attempt to fix our present situation. Those that oppose the age eighteen legal drinking age have two major arguments to support their position. The first is that lowering the drinking age will only increase alcoholism. However, studies indicate that alcoholism is mostly a genetic disease. Furthermore, children imitate their parents. If children grow up in families where alcohol is abused, the chances are high they will misuse it too. The second argument is that drunk driving will increase. Drunk driving is certainly a major problem, but the vast majority of those arrested for it and who get into accidents are not illegal drinkers. The twenty-one drinking age is not the cure; young adults who drink responsibly is. ■

■■■■ ACTIVITY 14.2 *In Your Own Work*

Editing Paragraph Sequences

Select any recent paper you have revised. Next to each paragraph, write down the question it implies and answers. Edit the order of the paragraphs to achieve a 1, 2, 3, and so on sequence. When you are done, print out your edited version and read through it carefully. Does it read better than before? What did you change and why did you make the changes? ■

Working on Individual Paragraphs

Editing paragraphs is the second focus of editing. At the paragraph level, editing focuses on coherence, meaning how well the sentences cohere, or stick together. When sentences cohere, we say the writing flows well, with no gaps in the train of thought.

BEST PRACTICES | Editing Paragraphs

Moving paragraph by paragraph through your paper, ask these questions:

1. **Does the first sentence indicate what the entire paragraph will be about?**
2. **Did you provide explanations, comments, and examples that *develop* the first sentence?**
3. **Is there flow, a smooth movement from sentence to sentence?**
4. **Does the paragraph connect to the previous one and to the following one?** ■

Individual paragraphs function much like paragraph sequences: They are a sequence of connected moves. The difference is that a paragraph is a sequence of connected sentences. Consider the following example, a paragraph from student Lauren Knazze's blog:

> An interesting concept came up in Wellness class today. My instructor used the example of circus elephants to explain the idea. From their youth, circus elephants are trained to be helpless and hopeless. When they are little, they are chained to large boulders so that they cannot escape. Although they try, their efforts prove to be futile. When they grow larger, the elephants believe that they cannot escape, so they don't try. Even though they could pull the rocks and move away, the failures from before are enough to keep them stuck in place, with no resistance. My instructor's point was that people too become so stuck in their ways or so fearful because of past failures that they don't realize that they could change their lives for the better.

Notice how each sentence picks up the idea of the sentence before it and answers the question most likely posed in the reader's mind. In coherent paragraphs, the writer anticipates what the reader is likely to ask—and provides the answer in the very next sentence.

> An interesting concept came up in Wellness class today. (Introduces the topic.)

> My instructor used the example of circus elephants to explain the idea. (Answers the question: **What happened in Wellness class?**)

> From their youth, circus elephants are trained to be helpless and hopeless. (Answers the question: **What was the example?**)

> When they are little, they are chained to large boulders so that they cannot escape. (Answers the question: **What happens to the elephants?**)

> Although they try, their efforts prove to be futile. (Answers the question: **Then what happens?**)

> When they grow larger, the elephants believe that they cannot escape, so they don't try. (Answers the question: **What happens next?**)

> Even though they could pull the rocks and move away, the failures from before are enough to keep them stuck in place, with no resistance. (Answers the question: **What is the point of the example?**)

> My instructor's point was that people too become so stuck in their ways or so fearful because of past failures that they don't realize that they could change their lives for the better. (Answers the question: **Why was this idea important in a Wellness class?**)

Of course, neither writer nor reader is normally aware of the questions that each sentence answers. But when you find a paragraph that is not working, try making the reader's questions explicit and test the next sentence to see if it answers the question. Sometimes the answer comes in a later sentence, and rearranging the sentences solves the problem.

A good paragraph coheres and flows. It **coheres,** *holds together,* because it is about *a single focus or theme*—for example, explaining an idea about personal empowerment. It **flows** because *each sentence answers a question the reader is likely to have asked in response to the previous sentence.*

How Transitions Connect Paragraphs

In addition to the focus of each paragraph, we have to ensure that the beginning and end of each paragraph connect to previous and subsequent ones. These links, called "transitions," function much like turn signals on a car. Imagine that, as a writer, you are taking readers somewhere they have not been, and they are following you. Transitions, like turn signals, tell the reader you are about to turn down another road.

Look back at the first two paragraphs in the *Scientific American* example (pages 338–39). The first paragraph ends by mentioning "the critical period," which was defined as "conception to age two." The first sentence in the second paragraph does two things at once: It refers back to the previous paragraph, by calling the old theory by a name, "the main-effect model," and it announces the new theme or focus, that the model is "too simplistic." The transition helps the reader to anticipate the movement from one focus to another.

Transitions are not all alike. Sometimes the last sentence of the preceding paragraph does the linking, while the first sentence of the next one announces the new focus. How transitions happen matters less than making sure that they do. Look at all endings and beginnings of your paragraphs to make sure the transitions work as smoothly as possible.

■■■■ ACTIVITY 14.3 *Collaborative Activity*

Paragraph Editing Practice

In groups of two or three, edit the following paragraph to make a sequence of sentences with both a single theme or focus and development or movement. Use the implied question-and-answer method we have discussed to help discover a good sentence order. Feel free to cut, add, rearrange, and rewrite sentences. If you think a single paragraph should become two or more, do that as well. Create any needed transitions.

See pages 349–54 for more paragraph editing practices.

My day at the Boys and Girls Club of Greater Houston consisted of running around, playing, and laughing a lot. I graduated from St. Agnes Academy, where one hundred hours of volunteer work were required for graduation. The Boys and Girls Summer Day Camp is a day-care facility where families pay two dollars for an entire summer of supervision of their children while they are at work. From my experiences as a camp counselor I realize that some people you meet leave a strong impression. The children I worked with in the summer of 1997 were underprivileged minorities. I will never forget any of the children, but one little boy was special to me. ■

■■■ ACTIVITY 14.4 *In Your Own Work*

Editing Paragraphs

Select any recent paper you have written and edit the paragraphs for focus and movement. Look at each indentation. Is there a sentence near the opening of each paragraph that contains the main idea and key word or words that unites the paragraph? Look at the flow or connection between each sentence and the next. Does each sentence pick up an idea or key word from the sentence before it? ■

Working on Sentences

Working on sentences is the third focus of editing.

BEST PRACTICES | Editing Sentences

1. Moving sentence-by-sentence through your paper, read each one aloud or subvocalize, "hearing" it in your head. Your ear is the key to detecting sentences that need editing. Mark sentences that sound bad to you.
2. Rework your sentence so the doer of the action comes first, followed by the action itself, the verb.
3. Look for sentence-level errors—for example, fragments, using a comma when you need a semicolon or vice versa, putting a comma after "although," incorrectly punctuating clauses beginning with the word "which." ■

> See the Common Errors section in the Handbook for more on fragments, commas and semicolons, use of "although," and clauses beginning with "which."

Sentences are the basic unit of expression. We speak mostly in sentences. With few exceptions, we write in sentences. Therefore, *reworking sentences is the heart of editing itself.*

What a Sentence Must Do

It is no mystery. A sentence must

- Say precisely what we mean
- Make it easy for our readers to grasp what we mean

A sentence must do these two things; otherwise we have not *communicated*. Anything else takes a back seat. Writing correctly, for example, does not matter if communication has failed.

Why Do Sentences Go Wrong?

Sometimes we are not sure what we mean; we are confused or conflicted. Sometimes we know what we mean but lack confidence in what we want to say. Sometimes we have a general idea of what we want to say but cannot find the words. And sometimes we think we have said what we mean until somebody interprets our sentence in a way we did not intend or points out that our meaning is unclear.

Sentences go wrong because we do not have the point we want to make clearly in mind. Sentences also go wrong because it is difficult to see our own sentences as readers will see them. A sentence that seems perfectly clear to us puzzles or confuses our readers.

Editing is the time to detect uncertainties about what you want to say. You know the sentences you struggled with in writing your drafts and the feeling "this is still not quite right" even after you have revised. Step back and ask, "Why am I confused or conflicted here? What is keeping me from having confidence in what I want to say? What is wrong with that idea that keeps eluding the words to express it?" If you can diagnose the problem, you can get "in here" to line up with "out there." You will not always succeed, but give it your best effort.

Editing is also the right time to seek input from others. When we write a sentence, we get no immediate feedback—nobody is there to look puzzled or ask for clarification as there is in conversation. Instead, we have to *imagine* a reader's response, *anticipate* problems a reader might have, and rework sentences so that he or she will understand. We try, but even the most talented writers cannot always see their sentences "from the outside," as a reader will in responding to them. Therefore, all writers need an actual reader's response, and that is especially true for those sentences that are still bothering us after self-editing.

Edit your own writing first, but then seek out another set of eyes and ears to help you detect more of what you missed.

What Matters Most in Editing Sentences?

In a word: clarity. The first step is to make your writing sound more like something you would say. For example, read this sentence:

> The cessation of the employment of extraordinary means to prolong the life of the body when there is irrefutable evidence that biological death is imminent is the decision of the patient and/or the immediate family.

What does this thirty-five-word sentence mean? It sounds impressive and authoritative, but no one would say it. More likely, you would say something more like this:

> Only the patient or the patient's family can decide to stop life support.

This thirteen-word sentence says what the writer means without making readers struggle to understand it. How did we arrive at this much better sentence? First, *simplify.* The two most important moves you can make in editing are to simplify and find an active verb.

- The "cessation of the employment of extraordinary means to prolong life" equals "stopping life support." What else could it be?
- If we are talking about life support, we must be talking about a patient who would otherwise be dead or likely to die, so why say anything about death at all?
- We found the subject performing the action—"the patient or the patient's family."
- We found the verb, the action the subject was performing, in the noun "decision," so we used the verb "decide."

BEST PRACTICES | Editing for Wordy Phrases

One way to write more plainly, simply, and directly is to look for the following common phrases, each of which has a more concise equivalent.

For these phrases ...	Use ...
at all times	always
biography of the life	biography
close proximity	near
due to the fact that	because
final result	final
first and foremost	first
for the purposes of	to
for the reason that	because
green in color	green
in order to	to
in spite of the fact that	although
in the event that	if
in the not-too-distant future	soon
in this day and age	today
is able to	can
is necessary that	must
mix together	mix
refer back	refer
repeat again	repeat
until such time as	until

We pick up these and many other phrases from conversation and use them without thinking about them. In editing we should weed them out of our sentences. ■

■■■ ACTIVITY 14.5 *Collaborative Activity*

Sentence Editing Practice

Working in groups of two or three, cut the excess verbiage from the following sentences. First, step back and ask: What is the writer trying to say? Find a plain, simple, direct way to say what the writer really means. Delete what you do not need to say it. Find the subject and combine it with an action, a verb.

1. Willy is so frustrated in his futile quest for riches and failure to achieve social approval due to the dreadful reality of his limitations that he consequently turns to a dream world.
2. The lessons I have learned and continue to learn of hard work and entrepreneurship is a great value and truth that shall be passed from me to my kids and to their kids and so on.
3. Americans are starting to worry again, because certain aspects of immigration, such as overpopulation and lack of education, which results in poverty, are beginning to affect America as a whole.
4. On many campuses, gays and lesbians have formed their own fraternities and sororities, not only coming out of the closet, but also benefiting from the social as well as the academic education a school offers.
5. I can only hope by the time my children grow up in this country that affirmative action will no longer be an issue so that they will be looked at as a student for academic ability, character, and personal attributes to do the best they can. ■

For more sentence editing practices, see pages 349–56.

■■■ ACTIVITY 14.6 *In Your Own Work*

Eliminating "Deadwood"

Select any recent paper you have written and revised. Edit the sentences as you did in the previous exercise.

   Tip: Read your sentences aloud to find the ones that need work. They'll sound like something nobody would say. Get rid of "deadwood" and your prose will immediately improve. ■

How Do We Detect Sentence-Level Errors?

Use your ear in editing: Listen to what you have written either in your head or by reading it aloud.

However, certain norms in speech are considered errors in writing, and you cannot rely on your ear to pick them up. In fact, the most common sentence-level errors relate to speech patterns we cannot carry over into writing. For instance:

> As we've moved toward greater equality, a new struggle has emerged in America. New in that it focuses on sexual preference rather than race or gender.

The second sentence is a fragment, common in conversation, but usually considered an error in writing. Fragments are usually easy to fix. Many fragments can be eliminated simply by adding a comma and attaching them to the preceding sentence.

> As we've moved toward greater equality, a new struggle has emerged in America, new in that it focuses on sexual preference rather than race or gender.

Proofreading

Proofreading is the fourth focus of editing. In publications, editors read the final page "proofs" or set type, looking for little errors. In writing a paper, proofreading similarly means looking very closely at the final manuscript to find the small, but nevertheless still important, errors.

BEST PRACTICES | Proofreading

Move sentence by sentence through your paper, *looking* for errors like misspelled words, typos, and word choice problems. *Look because most errors have to be seen, not heard, detected by the eye and not the ear.* Mark the errors. Go back and correct each one. ■

By errors we mean, for example, the following:

- Typing "minorities" (plural) when you mean "minority's" (possessive), or vice versa
- Confusing "there" with "their" and "they're"
- Confusing "to" with "too" and "two"
- Typing "it's" (contraction for "it is") when you mean "its" (possessive form of "it"), or vice versa
- Misspelled words
- Typos
- Omitting a word you meant to include, or typing a word or phrase twice
- Not putting titles in quotation marks or italics

These are the kind of mistakes that proofreading must catch. You will find some of them as you "spiral down," working first with paragraphs, then with sentences. But if you do not proofread, you will miss too many. Furthermore, in reworking paragraphs and sentences, you will probably make a few more errors. Therefore, *proofreading is an essential, last focus of editing.*

It cannot be omitted or done hastily because errors like these are easily and routinely detected by people assessing your writing. Nor can you rely on spell checks and grammar checks to find all such errors for you. Use the programs, but remember that they will miss many mistakes and sometimes tag something as an error that is not wrong.

Our general advice is to approach errors systematically. You will make mistakes. Some of these you will miss even with diligent proofreading. The ones you miss professors marking your papers will usually detect. *It is what you do with the marks on your papers that can make all the difference.*

What matters most are errors that occur regularly. They indicate that you do not recognize the error as an error or do not understand how to correct it in all cases. Talk to your instructor. Or look for the relevant section in our online handbook. Then, having grasped the nature of the error, *make a note about it in an editing checklist you keep for yourself.* Then, write down a description of the error, what you typically do wrong and how to correct it. You might include an example or two, with corrections. Save this list in a notebook or on a computer file. Keep this editing checklist to consult the next time you have to proofread.

■■■■ ACTIVITY 14.7 *Collaborative Activity*

Error Editing Practice

Working with two or three students, correct the errors in the following sentences. If you detect other editing problems, attend to them as well.

1. The administration has done everything they can to improve race relations, now we students must do our part.
2. Looking back at the foundling fathers of our country, they had very similar views about the federal government.
3. Parents install morals in there children; hoping they will make the right decisions as adults.
4. Once she escaped her strict upbringing at college, she lost all restraints, the perfect example of a girl who goes crazy her first year of freedom.
5. The book *The Beauty Myth,* by Naomi Wolf dedicates itself to the fact that women are controlled by their looks.
6. I was perfectly content living in a closed knit community, where everyone felt they were at home.
7. The worst part of the advertisement was their was a girl next to the man, messaging him. ■

■■■■ ACTIVITY 14.8 *In Your Own Work*

Proofreading

Select any recent paper you have revised. Edit the sentences to eliminate errors like the ones discussed and illustrated above. Listening to your sentences can help, especially with some punctuation errors, but concentrate on *looking* for errors. What writing errors have you made in the past? Be sure to check for those in a separate step.

> **Tip:** A good way to proof is by working backward, starting with the last sentence. Reading backward slows the process down and disrupts the flow from sentence to sentence so that you can *look at* the sentences for the errors you need to detect. ∎

Spiraling Down Editing Practice

This concluding section gives you opportunities to practice the editing skills covered in this chapter. In each example:

1. Attend first to paragraph sequencing. Make each paragraph a move in a sequence of moves, as discussed above (pages 338–40).
2. Work with individual paragraphs in the sequence. Be sure to pay attention to the flow from sentence to sentence.
3. Edit sentences. Cut words and phrases you do not need. Find the doer of the action and get it up front, joining it to the action, the verb.
4. Finally, proofread for errors you did not catch in editing the sentences. For now, do not skip or combine steps. As you gain greater experience, working on two levels at the same time becomes easier.

Editing Practice 1: Chunks to Paragraphs to Sentences to Errors

Below are blocks or chunks of writing, with the paragraph indentations removed. Rework them as necessary to achieve a 1, 2, 3 . . . impression of sequence, each paragraph being a distinct "move" in a series of linked moves. (See pages 338–40 for a more detailed explanation.)

After you have edited the chunk for paragraph sequencing, complete the editing by moving through steps 2, 3, and 4 listed above.

1. In "The Substance of Style" Virginia Postrel praises the consumer society. She argues that as humans, we desire beautiful things, because these items "tap deep human instincts." (7) Its human nature to admire beautiful material objects and we have an inate drive to make things special. Aesthetics tap into our deepest emotional drive, therefore pleasing our sensory needs. I can't really argue with these ideas. We are consumers and producers. We have senses of sight, sound, and taste to appreciate the sensory pleasures of the world and many natural resources that we can use to create them. People of all civilizations have decorated the objects used in their daily lives, such as bowls, knives, and clothing. But liking beautiful things does

not mean that we have to judge people by how many things one has. Unfortunately, advertisers exploit humanity's innate desire to consume and indoctrinate society with the beleif that they need to consumer more and more. John Shumaker, in "Dead Zone" describes this as "radical consumerism." A greed in people to consumer everything in sight. In addition to advertising, Shumaker blames the rise or credit cards, inabling people to not have to face the reality of their spending habits (8) and the media in general, where Americans are led to believe that "overindulgence is good for the country" (11). The media fails to cover the destruction that this over consumption is doing to the world's natural resources and to peoples psychological well being.

2. Writing is being "a real person with something to say to a real audience," although as an average student I never considered this. Writing for me was more of a mandatory assignment, written to please my teacher and pass the class. I worried most about my grammar errors and citation mistakes rather than the topic. A way my college writing teacher helped me to break this habit was blogging. Blogging is writing down your ideas, beliefs, and opinions for the world to see. The importance is placed on the topic and the angle of the writer rather than their writing techniques. Motivation for writing a blog, is to reach your audience and stir in them a response. These are the things I needed to work on in finding a voice in my papers. Because of my lack of confidence as a writer I took the anonymous approach as being identified as "someone." This helped me to forget about trying to impress my readers by sounding cool, allowing me to focus on my opinion. With this approach I could hide from snickers of my classmates and really make a statement. The comments directed at my posts were taken less personal this way and I could actually consider my readers' judgment. I decided to interest my readers I would take the approach of talk about the harsher realities of a first year in college. I titled my blog "the world seen through a freshman and spoke about my fears, insecurities and realizations. I decided this angle would work in showing my voice and also intrigue people because of its genuineness. I later found out that I was not only going to reach my audience, but they were going to reach me. Through the number of comments I received, it helped me build my confidence. When I posted "Playing the Game of Life" I was embarassed because I ventured out from the security of purely academic writing and put some of me into it. The next day I received my first comment saying "Wow, you completely explained my four months experiencing college. Thanks for sharing your thoughts." Through this I was able to realize that I do have something to say to the world.

3. From the beginning Park and Preston was cursed with bad luck. Preston Road, initially a trail for immigrants, developed due to frequent usage by both the Comanche people and herding buffalo. Once individuals began to settle in surrounding communities, territory disputes erupted between the immigrants and the Indians. Innocent families were murdered in

there sleep and any attempts to improve the community came to a halt. In 1838 The Texas Congress declared Preston Road an official interstate. The large influx of immigrant travelers turned the road into one of the most important crossings with the old Indian trail while simultaneously creating a permanent traffic jam in western Collin county. Congestion plagued the area as early as 1849. Unbeknowst to the early settlers the negative characteristic would define Preston Road for years to come. The dusty trails and infinite miles of solitude that surrounded Preston in the 1800's have now given way to a bustling quadrant of impatient 5:00 drivers and super sized franchises. The irritating odor of pollution and car exhaust has replaced the calming scent of green grasses and sun riped corn, Since 1890, the population of Plano has increased considerably every year due to a growing business oriented economy. Small independently owned stores crumbled in the late 90's as superstores took over. Wal Mart, Barnes and Nobel, Whole Foods, and Old Navy, amongst others, now dominate Park and Preston. Plano citizens flock to the strip centers for shopping, and sometimes they flock with a bit too much excitement. In 2001, eight accidents occurred in the intersection from red light running alone. Now posted at each of the four crossings are colorful signs warning drivers to not be next in the Plano Police Departments issuance of red light violations. In 1999, State Farm rated Park and Preston the second most dangerous intersection in the country, due to a high number of fatal accidents that year. Oftentimes the speed limit of 45 miles per hour is terribly abused, only worsening the conditions for an accident. Soccer moms rushing their sons and daughters off to practice, along with anxious businessmen drinking coffee while answering cell phone calls, zip through the intersection on a daily basis, unaware of the world outside their SUVs.

4. Americans like to think they have higher moral standards than just about all other places in the world. Los Vegas is an exception to this rule. Vegas is a place that lowers standards and in a way promotes a nontraditional life style. A traditional American life style would be to save rather than spend, think logically over the spur of the moment, and act responsibly rather than erratically. Los Vegas not only goes against the norm, but it intensely encourages foul play, but yet people are infatuated and become addicted to this so-called American lifestyle. Excessive drinking, gambling, and getting married to someone you met no more than a few days ago are common, everyday occurrences in Las Vegas, but are somewhat frowned upon throughout the rest of the country. If Vegas is Sin City then why is it one of the top vacations destinations in the world and also the fastest growing city in America? Is this really a sinful city, or is it a way for Americans to escape the reality of their lives, and live the way they truly want to?

5. If a professor advances viewpoints of their own then they should be completely accepting of other points as well. Once you enter college you are given an academic freedom, meaning the people of the classroom, teachers

and students, can state their ideas and opinions without getting into trouble with any authority. This is given to both students and professors, but professors have more freedom overall. If one is a teacher at elementary through high school they cannot say anything offensive because the school will have to deal with complaining parents, but in college the professors can say whatever they want to say, no one can say anything about it. The students freedom come into play when they sign up for classes because they have the choice of their own environment; choosing the professors and classes. Professors have to hold no self-restraint to what they say. Because at universities there is no restraint. They can bring up and evaluate any controversial opinion they want to. The students on the other hand have to have self-restraint. The teachers are the ones that give the grade, they have a lot more power and therefore more freedom of expression. Legally students have academic freedom, that they cannot use freely. After considering these issues, I believe that professors are doing a good job and keeping the students thinking about issues they probably never thought existed or never really had to think about. I think that this all helps the students out, by broadening their thoughts on everything and making them get out of the bubble of their own thoughts.

Editing Practice 2: Paragraphs to Sentences to Errors

Edit the following paragraphs for focus and flow. Make whatever changes you have to make to create a paragraph with a single theme and movement from sentence to sentence. You can cut sentences, add sentences, rearrange sentences, make two (or more) paragraphs out of one, and so on.

Once you have edited the paragraph, focus on individual sentences. If you locate problems, rework the sentences to solve them while preserving focus and flow. When you are done with the sentences, proofread for any errors you might have missed or introduced when you were editing the paragraph or its sentences.

1. Mandatory drug-testing is an issue that has assumed considerable prominence in the last several years. The drug-testing plan which is currently proposed by the NCAA is an organizational response to a problem which has recently commanded a considerable amount of attention from the atheletes and coaches, as well as from the press and from college administrators. There is a definite agreement that drug abuse is wide-spread throughout collegiate athletics, and may still be growing. The NCAA proposes the selective monitoring of athletes for drug use which is directly related to performance and health.

2. My life had changed. I didn't know Imran and Hanif that well, but I knew them well enough to feel the devastation of their death, the effect it had on our friends, and particularly the effects this traumatic loss experienced by the parents. Imran and Hanif were those parents only children. Four hours I pondered the thought of knowing a parents entire life surrounds the events that take place in their children's lives. I tried to imagine all the feelings rushing through their minds.

3. The guaranteed income principle would give all citizens of a nation a minimum income from which no one can fall. Funiciello provides an example model of guaranteed income in "Ending Poverty as We Know It." The model does prove to be somewhat complicated, but far less than the internal revenue code. Guaranteed income payments may be made in the same form as that of present income tax. Persons whose incomes are less than an agreed minimum should not be taxed at all. From this, it is only a step to the guaranteed income principle. Those who have no income will receive a "refund" check. Those whose incomes are large enough will receive guaranteed income in the form of tax deductions, just as everybody, rich or poor, now receives tax deductions for dependents. The system of guaranteed income can easily fit into the current system and be implemented.

4. Without tolerance for differences in opinion, the abortion debate will never end. If we cannot see past our own stubbornness, the debate will rage as violently as it always has. Without tolerance is when you get protests which end with police riot squads arresting people. Without tolerance is when you get protestors murdering abortion doctors. Without tolerance is when you get desperate women with coathangers performing their own abortions. We cannot continue to fight so violently over any issue and tolerance is the answer. Allow another person the freedom of thought which you take for yourself.

5. The United States has seen many great leaders run the presidency, but John F. Kennedy is one president whose speeches left a mark in history. Kennedy projected a picture of both youth and success as a candidate for the presidency, and would ultimately beat vice president Richard Nixon in the 1960 election. Kennedy's inaugural address of January 1961 would become his most dramatic and moving speeches of all time. In his inaugural address, Kennedy stated many points but his main point involved not just the individual's well being, but the common good of the nation and world as a whole.

6. To begin to solve the problem we must recognize that sexual harassment is common and truly destructive. Sexual harassment creates both mental anguish and monetary losses. In fact, around 60% of working women say they have been harassed. Mental pain exists because 40% of the victims cope by either taking leave time, transferring, or quitting. Change must be made to reduce an estimated annual cost of 6.7 million to Fortune 500 companies, 267 million for the federal government, and 250 million to settle law suits.

7. The ultimate goal of yesteryears was the acceptance of her feminity. This meant living in the "woman's sphere," of domestic life and nurturing her children. Women were looked on as inferior to men and not worthy of the privileges set aside for men. Experts told women how to get a man and keep him happy and how to take care of the family. They were taught to look down upon unmarried, career oriented women because a truly

feminine woman knew her place was in the home. Being truly feminine meant you were satisfied with raising the family and cleaning the home and remaining in the woman's sphere. Today's woman has broken out of the woman's sphere to become more feminist. She is no longer happy with accepting her femininity as the only tool for measuring worth and defining her place in society.

8. Rush Limbaugh recently published his book, *See, I told You So,* in 1993 in order to speak his mind as he questions American values. Limbaugh is known for his outspoken, often outlandish, commentary regarding American politics and society. His chapter entitled, "The Power of You, You Make It Work" focuses on how America looks down on personal achievement and success as not being beneficial to the community. Limbaugh wants this notion to change because he is a big advocate of helping the self. The fact that individuals who succeed are criticized for not being team players has triggered his argument in this chapter.

9. According to Title IX, "no person in the United States shall, on the basis of sex, be excluded from participation in, be denied the benefits of, or be subjected to discrimination under any program or activity receiving Federal financial assistance. With the passage of Title IX, opportunites for women to participate in athletics increased. It has been law for 23 years, and by now you'd think we'd know what it means. It is still being defined today. Title IX regulates many areas, such as admissions, student activities and organizations, counseling, academic advising, financial assistance, and testing. Since there are so many areas, I can see why there is confusion about it. The gender equity problem can be solved by balancing male and female athletic activities.

10. "To the telegraph, intelligence means knowing of lots of things, not knowing *about* them" (Postman 70). All of a sudden we went from a print based society to one that is incredibly fast paced and entirely dependent on catchy phrases and intense short segments of knowledge were thrown at us. Print took time to comprehend, and people had to reflect to evaluate it. With the telegraph people are so overwhelmed that they think they must digest everything. They began to loose sight of what is really relevant. Somehow they picked up the notion that knowing a wealth of information qualifies them as smart. While all the facts that bombard us might make us feel wiser, smarter, and more knowledgeable, they really have no effect or meaning in our lives.

Editing Practice 3: Sentences to Errors

Edit the following sentences. Attend to deadwood, words and phrases not needed, and to having doers of the action in subject position combined with the action, the verb. Then attend to error.

Remember that you must both *listen to* and *look at* the sentences. Your ear does more of the work at the sentence level, your eye at the error level.

Remember also the options to make one sentence into two or more sentences and to combine two or more sentences into one.

1. It is a continuous battle over what each citizens duties should be in terms of his relationship to society.

2. The part of the essay I strongly disagree with is that the author writes about how gays and Jews are both related because they have both experienced violent acts toward them.

3. In the late 1960s with the passage of the Civil Rights Act of 1964 that outlawed job discrimination by race, religion, national origin, or sex, in addition to the Voting Rights Act of 1965 that ensured all people, including blacks, the rite to vote, they accomplished to remove some of the walls that barricaded their lives for so long.

4. Instead of getting upset at them and threatening them with punishment for not complying, I simply told them the importance of being early in the given situation, and even if they did not agree, it would be more beneficial to them in the long run to be early, instead of complaining about it, which would not change anything and also put you on my bad side.

5. I can only hope that by the time my children grow up in this country affirmative action is no longer an issue so that he or she will be looked at as a student for academic ability, character, and personal ambition to do the best they can.

6. Tannen is correct when she says we need to get around dualism, being simply for or against something. It is very important that we get as many views as possible in learning environments, and too many times are arguments dominated by the two sides. There are people with different views and are to afraid to announce them because they will go against the norm.

7. In recent sexual harassment trails, there has bean a failure to convict the perpetrator; lack of evidence, and an uncertainty about the woman's credibility were the main causes of the not convcting.

8. Franklin followed twelve virtues that he set for himself to revise his life and direct him toward success. He devised these virtues from classical and Christian sources. In his autobiography he advocated these virtues.

9. By settling these cases informally, without the interference of the law, the EEOC would rid itself of the task of handling insignificant and potentially embarassing cases of hostile environment sexual harassment cases involving complaints of such things as love notes and dirty jokes so that they could then be able to concentrate on the more serious cases of abusive *quid pro quo* sexual harassment and behavior that unreasonably interferes with the individuals work performance that aren't getting the attention by the courts and public that they deserve.

10. It was the second semester of my junior year, she had moved from the Virgin Islands, and as fate would have it, she ended up in my theater class.

11. He owed some drug dealers a great deal of money which he had not intention of paying.

12. Alcohol plays a major role in todays social scene for most teenagers. Although, most people would like to think differently, this fact is only becoming more evident with each year that passes.

13. After being in school for a few moths I came to the realization of how much I loved the city of Mobile.

14. Feminism is defined as advocating for social, political, and all others rights of equality for women impartial to those of men.

15. In Andrew Cecil's speech, Moral Values in a Free Society, aspects involving individualism and social conscience dominate what comes out to be a provocative look into histories wrongs and rights of the moral system.

16. Sexual harassment always involves an abuse of power. Whether it be a teacher abusing a student, a manager an employee, or simply a stronger person a weaker.

17. The fact is that the past is a very important part in defining the black society because the past created the image of the black society and all the stereotypes it holds.

What Matters Most in Editing? Three Key Points

- **Editing is not just "cleaning up."** Cleaning up is proofreading, and that is important but is only the last step in editing. The purpose of editing is to detect and eliminate *everything* that gets in the way of communicating with your reader—and that means attending to much more than error. You need to work on your paragraphs and sentences even when they have no mistakes.

- **Editing requires time and concentration.** It is not "reading over" your final draft. It is working through your final draft methodically, first focusing on paragraph sequences and paragraphs, then on sentences, and finally on error.

- **Keep an editing checklist** that helps you pay special attention to your particular editing problems. Study the marks and comments on every graded paper. When they relate to editing, add them to your list. If you do not understand an error or problem, ask your instructor to explain or consult our handbook. Add any notes you need to help remember the error or problem and how to fix it. Use the checklist as you edit your next paper.

Do these things, and your editing problems will diminish and you will gain fuller control over the ones that remain. Do them and you will be amazed at how much your writing will improve.

GENRES FOR FURTHER PRACTICE

HOW DO I WRITE A REFLECTION?

"IT MAKES YOU STOP AND THINK," WE SAY, WHEN SOMETHING HAPPENS THAT disturbs our normal expectations, our usually half-awake approach to the world around us. Stopping and thinking is the essence of exploratory writing. The genre that best represents what we can do when we take time to think is reflection.

What Is a Reflection?

In a **reflection,** a writer explores or ponders a subject, examining ideas or feelings about the subject or contemplating connections with related subjects. Rather than making an argument or persuading an audience, reflections offer writer and readers a space to think about experience. Reflections reveal an individual's thought process to others.

ASKING QUESTIONS | Anatomy of a Reflection

Ask and answer the following questions:

1. Topic: **What do I wonder about?** A reflection focuses on one subject that opens further avenues of thought.
2. Personal connection to the topic: **How am I involved with my topic?** Reflection demonstrates the writer's curiosity and ideas; thus, the writer refers to his or her thinking in the writing.
3. Details: **What examples, cases, and details help connect my thoughts with my own and my readers' lived experiences?** Reflection moves back and forth between abstract thoughts and concrete experiences.
4. Conclusion: **Where has my thinking led me?** A reflection is like a journey; your thinking should take you and your readers to a destination, or conclusion. The ending should provide a sense of focus and closure. ■

Why Write a Reflection?

People write reflections in a wide variety of settings: private journals, public blogs, newspaper or magazine columns, and portfolios—basically any place where ideas or subjects can or need to be contemplated. Reflections allow writers to think through any topic that concerns them and to invite readers to comment on what they have written or respond with their own reflections on the same or similar themes.

In your coursework, you might be asked to write reflective essays or journal entries that respond to course readings or class discussions. At the end of a course, you might be asked to reflect on all of the essays that you wrote, on your own writing process, or on what you learned during a class project. You could also be asked in a writing class to write a reflection on whatever interests you. In any of these tasks, the goal is the same: *Explore the subject and demonstrate the thinking that you have done.*

Example of Reflection

The Wonder of Ordinary Places (Blog Post, May 13, 2011)

JULIAN HOFFMAN

Julian Hoffman is a writer living beside the Prespa Lakes in northern Greece. "Notes from Near and Far" is his blog on the nature of place.

When it comes to wonder and the natural world, children are the true specialists. They are particularly open to that state of astonishment that we associate with awe. A child, in the most common of landscapes, is capable, through a combination of intense perception and imagination, of discovering an entire world in the smallest fragment of nature. It might be among wildflowers and weeds at the edge of a scrubby field where an iridescent emerald beetle or the bright flight of a butterfly can hold a child's attention for several minutes. It could be along a river bank

1   Announces topic immediately.

Clarifies the special awareness of children, lost too often in adults.

Photographs and other visuals can help with reflections.

where a child excitedly follows an oak leaf as it travels downstream. It might simply be the prints of an animal, perfectly preserved by snow, that captures a child's imagination.

Photographs are the author's.

What is so remarkable about children's perception, even more so than its intensity, is that it is characterized by an equality of interest. Everything a child encounters in nature, no matter how small, offers possibility and is therefore equally fascinating. Children make little distinction between major and minor motifs. A feather found on the beach is as wondrous as the creature it belonged to.

2

As childhood is left behind, adults tend to shed that capacity for curiosity, that spirit that animates the smallest of things. We yearn for greater and faster excitements; we seek larger vistas, grander views. But in a contemporary Western world increasingly obsessed by speed, style and seduction, there is perhaps all the more need to reclaim the ordinary, to celebrate the everyday. Because the ordinary, when perceived in the spirit of curiosity, is actually extraordinary.

3

Note how the writer moves from an abstract idea to a concrete example that explains the idea.

Skillful use of fragment for emphasis.

The focus is on the value of paying attention to the "ordinary."

The American writer and naturalist, Barry Lopez, once wrote that "with the loss of self-consciousness, the landscape opens." This, I believe, can be understood in two ways. First, when we let go of our constant self-awareness and regain something of a child's immense curiosity and interest in the world 'out there,' the world around us, we become more attuned to its wonders. Leaving something of our self behind, other lives arise in its place. That is when the ordinary transforms into the extraordinary, and a landscape like the shore of Great Prespa Lake becomes something else.

4

Reflection often comments on what others have said.

. . .

Barry Lopez's assertion about landscapes, however, provides a second clue to engaging more deeply with place. To be self-conscious means not only to be aware of one's own mind and actions, but to be conscious of being observed and therefore embarrassed as a result. Self-consciousness prevents us from doing many things, but in the case of a landscape it can stand in the way of knowing it.

5

Great Prespa Lake is near the author's home in Greece. Note that the writer ties his reflection to his own life experiences.

Landscapes are best learned through proximity. Wherever children go, they are tempted to climb trees. They slither through long grasses like snakes, eyeing up insects excitedly from their own height. They make hide-aways in dense shrubs. Children catch frogs in their hands and then slowly open their fingers to reveal them. They collect caterpillars in jars, fascinated by the coming transformation. Children's inquisitive experience of the natural world is hands-on, intimate and utterly without self-consciousness. They are part of a place, not distinct from it.

6

Note how the author uses details to make the actions of children concrete and real.

When we approach similarly, with a sense of freedom unburdened by embarrassment, we open ourselves to the quieter aspects of a landscape. How the light falls through the willow leaves, passing through them like waves. How bear prints and otter tracks lead us first along the beach and then into their lives. The way tiny, resplendent butterflies gather around a flower. There are the curious sounds of water and reptiles in the marsh. How the wind breathes mysteriously through the reeds, their seeds catching the light as they float above the river. The way the bark of a silver birch feels like ancient paper in our hands. Walk into any pocket of the shoreline landscape and there is a world of new moments unfolding.

7

All landscapes contain the seeds of astonishment. Whether we let them take root or not is up to us. But if we become aware of the wonders within easy reach, those close at hand and part of our daily experience, then the everyday places that we live amongst become less easy to dismiss. The greatest threat facing many landscapes is their assumed irrelevance. When a place is perceived to hold little of interest or importance then a whole landscape can turn invisible, and be treated accordingly. Though any child will show you there is no such thing as a place without interest.

> The conclusion arrives at a persuasive point about the consequences of the failure to appreciate the wonders of the ordinary.

■■ ACTIVITY *Thinking as a Writer*

Understanding the Moves in a Reflection

Using Asking Questions: Anatomy of a Reflection (page 358) and the marginal annotations to the reading, discuss "The Wonder of Ordinary Places" in class. How does the author establish his subject? How does he develop it? The photograph is beautiful and eye-catching, but what does it contribute to what the author wants us to think about? How does he connect adult life with the neglect of nature and with indifference to the environment? The blog post is primarily exploratory, but how does it also inform and persuade? ■

Asking Questions: What Can I Write About?

You could write a reflection on anything, from what you ate at breakfast to the best way to avoid nuclear warfare. Whatever topic you choose, remember that a reflection is more than a report or summary of what happened or what you know. It has a goal: To explore an interesting thought, confront a dilemma, prove you read and thought critically about an assigned text, or share an experience. For example, no one really cares what you ate for breakfast, but the process of pondering the statement on your cereal box that no genetically modified organisms (GMOs) are contained in it might lead you on an interesting mental journey. Perhaps thinking about food labeling, GMOs, organic foods, and pesticides makes you wonder whether you need to be trained as a scientist simply to know what to eat for breakfast.

Therefore, whether you have an assigned topic, such as the novel you read for class last week or the essay you just finished revising, or whether you can write on any topic you choose, you can come up with stronger and more interesting ideas by asking yourself the following questions:

- **What interests me? What gets my brain working?** To have something to say in a reflection, you need to be thinking about the topic in a personal and interesting way. So if you are searching for a topic, consider topics you often think about, things that intrigue or bother you, make you angry, or puzzle you. For an assigned topic, such as reflecting on a book or a movie, focus on the moments in the text that you reacted to strongly, that connected with your life and concerns, or that stuck in your head for some other reason or reminded you of something else.

- **What are my own experiences? What is happening around me? What concepts do I know about that will help me evaluate a situation?** Reflective writing comes from you, and so it is crucial to bring your experiences and knowledge to bear. If you try to write about something you have no knowledge of or connection to, your reflection will lack depth. Maybe you are reading Jane Austen's *Emma* and could not care less whether or not she finds a husband. However, you are also taking an economics class and are intrigued by how the whole process of selecting a spouse in this novel seems more like business than love. "Love as Economics" would be a good angle on the novel, a way to reflect on what it shows us about courtship and marriage.

How Do I Prepare to Write a Reflection?

Consider what the task requires, voice and style, development and organization, and visual appeal.

Thinking as a Writer: Task Requirements

Regardless of what your topic is, you need to think about the following intertwined questions in order to help you shape how you write about that topic.

- **What is my purpose in writing? Why am I reflecting on this topic?** The purpose of your writing will influence what aspect of your subject you discuss. If you're writing for an assignment that is designed to measure the thoughtfulness you have put into a required reading, then reflecting only on how it reminds you of what happened to you last week would not achieve your goal. You would instead need to focus on isolating and exploring particular moments from the reading—even if part of how you explore them relates to what happened last week. In contrast, if your goal is to entertain your readers, you would need an angle that opens your subject to humor or a combination of humor and serious insight.

- **Who is my audience?** Your audience will shape not only how you write your reflection but also what direction it takes. If your reflection is just for you, then it might focus on things that only you know. If it is for your instructor or a school magazine, then you will need to think about what others might think about the topic and how you need to connect your ideas and reflection to that broader view.

Thinking as a Writer: Voice and Style

The most crucial aspect of the voice and style for reflection is that it should represent you and the mental exploration in which you are engaged. As long as you are sharing this reflection with an audience, then you are inviting them into your mind, and so you want the writing to reflect your personality. Based on what your purpose is and who your audience is, however, you might need to showcase different aspects of your personality: Are you questioning and speculative about this topic? Are there feelings that need to be evoked when you explore this topic, such as joy, amazement, sorrow, or frustration? Is your attitude on this subject humorous and witty? Your angle will change the voice and style of your reflection, so let it determine your voice and style.

Thinking as a Writer: Development and Organization

Although a reflection may resemble a mental journey through a topic, our minds work in messy and confusing ways we cannot preserve entirely in writing. We free-associate, have random ideas pop into our heads, or have partial images or a vague feeling about events or moments that stand in for more detailed and complete ideas or descriptions. Therefore, when we translate mental contemplation into writing that will be shared with others, we have *to identify the connections that move from one point to the next and develop our ideas and discussions more completely.*

A reflection can be organized rather conventionally: Introduce the topic, explore the several aspects that you want to discuss, and offer a final thought on what this mental journey reveals. Or you may find that you need to move from point to point less predictably, introducing the main idea, following one path of discussion that might lead to a new path, but then coming back to the original idea before beginning again along a new idea. In all cases, the reflection needs to move in directions that will make sense to your audience and offer them something to think about.

Thinking as a Writer: Visual Appeal

Depending upon the goal of your reflection, consider graphics and how your writing will appear on the page. If it is in a blog, you may want the look of the page to be an expression of yourself. If you are writing about an image or a scene, it can help to include a photograph.

What Are the Steps in Writing a Reflection?

The first step is to devote time to thinking, because reflection is thought. The question is: When do you move from thinking about your subject to thinking through your subject as you write about it? Depending upon the topic and goal, you might want to try to preserve the initial thought process as much as possible. In this case, the writing *is* the thinking. In other cases, the reflection might be more of a looking backward—after the fact—in which case you may want to spend a larger chunk of time recalling and thinking before you begin your draft.

1. **Draft your reflection.** Once you begin your draft for a reflection, you should allow your ideas and thoughts to move more freely than you would for an informative or argumentative essay. Even if you are writing your reflection after much thought, the process of writing is a continuation of that thought. Writing without editing your ideas or restricting where they go has the potential to lead you to new ideas or connections. Use the draft as a space for thinking and developing ideas; use the revision as a space for streamlining, reordering, and shaping the ideas.

2. **Revise your reflection.** If you have used your draft as an exploratory space, you might well need to revise to make the logic clearer and the ideas more coherent. However, in a reflection, revision should not eliminate speculation, multiple and even contradictory or overlapping ideas, and, in general, an open-ended quality. Therefore, focus on making the reflection as interesting, as thoughtful, and as coherent as possible. To do that, ask yourself the following questions:

   - **Do I introduce my subject in a way that will interest the reader?** The focus of a reflection should be something that someone would want to join you in contemplating.
   - **Is there logic in the move from one point to another?** Are the connections between the ideas clear? Remember that free association without transitions makes reflection hard for a reader to follow.
   - **Are there any ideas that seem to detract from the reflection or that do not add much to its content or interest?** You do not need to include everything that you think about your subject; even a reflection needs to choose the most relevant and important ideas. Do not be reluctant to cut a line of thought that seemed promising but failed to pay off.
   - **Are there shifts in voice or style?** Have a good reason if your voice and style changes. For example, you could begin a reflection with a humorous scene that leads to a serious point and becomes the focus of what you have to say.
   - **Are there any ideas that need to be more fully developed?** Be attentive to what you have said, for often better ideas will come to you when you let your mind play with what you already have on the page. If you have the sense that "I did not quite arrive at what I wanted to say there," give such places special attention after allowing a day or two to pass. You will be surprised how often what is missing will suddenly occur to you.

3. **Edit your reflection.** Reflections have a more personal or casual style, but when you share them with others you need to edit as you would with any

other piece of writing. Look especially for awkward sentences, wordiness, and transitions between paragraphs. The key question is: Does this sentence say what I mean, not almost, but exactly? Work with it until it does.

4. **Proofread your reflection.** Make sure that your reflection reflects well upon you. Check for misspellings and grammatical errors.

HOW DO I WRITE A VISUAL ANALYSIS?

"IMAGE IS EVERYTHING," A WELL-KNOWN COMMERCIAL TOLD US, AND IF THAT has some truth to it, then images have everything to do with creating an organization, company, university, or individual image. The amount of time and money devoted to creating and managing visual impressions is hard to imagine though we see it everywhere: in the body design of automobiles, clothing, the architecture of buildings, store windows, college catalogs, and so on. Surfing the Internet exposes us to a sea of images, all designed to catch our attention, sell products and services, and form a favorable impression for whoever created each website.

With images everywhere, and image control so important, it is hardly surprising that assessing visuals has also become crucially important. Part of assessment is **visual analysis,** *taking an image apart to see how it works.*

What Is a Visual Analysis?

A visual analysis examines visual "texts," such as print, billboards, online advertisements, photographs, and paintings—anything you can examine that was created by people. It also includes visual aspects that are part of other texts, like the images and graphics on television, in movies, and in printed texts such as books and magazines. A visual analysis examines an image to see how it is constructed, the purpose being to understand its parts and how they work together. Usually an evaluation is at least implied; that is, analysis answers the question, **"How well does the image work?"**

ASKING QUESTIONS | Anatomy of a Visual Analysis

Ask and answer the following questions:
1. The visual text: **How can I represent the visual in my writing?** You cannot analyze visual appeal for a reader without having the image itself in your text. The size and quality of the image matter, especially if you are calling attention to details the reader must be able to see to follow your discussion.
2. Description of the image: **What do I see that matters?** Complex images cannot be fully described, so you have to decide what matters, what you want your reader to notice. In this way, you show the image to your reader through your eyes.

3. Identification of purpose: **What is the image trying to accomplish?** We have already mentioned commercial purposes, the most common motivation for creating an image, but images are also created for critical and artistic purposes, such as the one in the example of visual analysis below.

4. Identification of audience: **Who does the image hope to reach?** Because images are so widely distributed and anyone can view them, it is easy to neglect an important fact: *They always have a target audience in mind.* Becoming aware of the target audience, therefore, is important for analysis.

5. Analysis of key aspects: **What impact do the image's details have? What do they add up to or mean?** You need to say what impact or meaning the image has and how the details relate to impact or meaning. ■

Why Write a Visual Analysis?

Learning to understand how visual texts work helps you observe them critically rather than simply passively receiving the messages. It can also help you understand how to create such images successfully.

Writing a visual analysis amounts to, first, thinking about what comprises the image and how the elements work together to present an idea and, second, writing an explanation of your assessment. Art scholars and critics write visual analyses of paintings and photographs all the time, as do columnists or bloggers who write about contemporary culture and marketing professionals who are working on new advertising campaigns.

You might be asked to write a visual analysis for a variety of different classes, from history and politics to art and business, because visual images are so important in our culture. Writing a visual analysis, like writing any analysis, helps develop skills important to critical thinking generally: the habit of taking things apart to see how they work and the ability to explain their relationships.

An Example of Visual Analysis

Three Girls in a Kentucky Kitchen

ASHLEY JAROL

Background on photographer: part of context for analysis.

William Gedney was a documentary photographer whose best-known photographs are of poor people in India and in the Appalachian coal fields of Kentucky. He received little recognition for his work until after his death

1

of AIDS at age 56 in 1989, even though he had managed to get a one-man show of his work at the Museum of Modern Art in New York in 1968. This picture of three girls in a kitchen was featured in the New York exhibition, and it is now part of its permanent collection (William Gedney Photographs).

He took the picture in July, 1964 during a visit to the mining town of Leatherwood, Kentucky. Gedney lived for eleven days in this family's house. They welcomed him into their home even though the father had been laid off from his job in the mines, and they had twelve children at the time. Gedney kept notebooks and journals about his travels and his pictures, and he recorded the names and ages of everyone in the family. He and the family kept in touch through letters. He sent them Christmas presents, and he visited them again in 1972 and took more pictures of them. In 1977, he sent them $35 with a note that said, "I made myself a promise that if I ever sold any of the pictures I took of your family I would split any money with you. I sold my first picture from those I took. It is of the three girls in the kitchen" (Sartor and Dyer 74).

Gedney's photographs of the Cornett family capture everyday aspects of their lives. In this picture, we see the simple interior of a miner's kitchen and three young girls peeling potatoes. The picture seems to illustrate Gedney's belief that the lives of ordinary people made the best subjects for his pictures. "I prefer the ordinary action, the intimate gesture, an image whose form is an instinctive reaction to the material" ("Short Distances"). Gedney saw something beautiful and intimate in this simple moment and instinctively took his picture. The picture shows that in contrast to the stereotypical view of the never-ending poverty and hopelessness of the Appalachian coalfields, there is grace and beauty in these people's lives.

Even though many details in the kitchen show how poor the family was, there is a cheerful feeling to the room. We see the bare wood floor, the window with no curtain, and the dishes piled up as if there is no cabinet to store them, but the walls are papered with a cheerful floral print that made me think of angels flying upward. Everything is worn, but the floor and table top seem clean and well cared for. The room could be dark and dreary on a different day but at the moment of the picture it is filled with light. The natural sunlight illuminates the room and gives the picture warmth and lightness. Rays of sun fall on the refrigerator and the floor, and there is even a prism of reflected

2

3

4

More context for the analysis: the family of the girls in the photo and artist's relationship with them.

Connects characteristics of photo to artist's interests and intentions.

Main claim: photo counters stereotypes about Appalachian people.

Close attention to details of photo in relation to what the author sees as "lightness and openness." Note organization: first, the scene, then the girls.

368

light on the floor in the right foreground. The sun reflects off of the painted ceiling and makes the single bare light bulb look transparent. Gedney chose to put a lot of ceiling into the picture, maybe because the ceiling was so filled with light. If you took away the ceiling, the picture would lose some of its lightness. Also, through the bright window, the viewer can see out into the sunny backyard. This gives the picture a feeling of lightness and openness.

But it is the girls themselves that give the feeling of summer and lightness. Each of them stands on one foot. They look so animated and graceful. They wear summer dresses, and with their knees pulled up, their skirts look like sails on a boat. But their poses also make me see them as dancers. I have been dancing nearly all my life, and when I first looked at the three girls, I noticed that each one has a natural balance and grace. The tallest and probably the oldest of the sisters stands on the right with a straight back and excellent posture. The sun outlines the curve of her slender arm. The girl in the center balances on the side of her foot. She has positioned her body so that the sunlight falls over her shoulder, making it easier to see what she is doing. I like to imagine that the summer sun is warming her back as she works. The youngest girl is taking a break from peeling her potato and seems to be in the midst of telling a story. She leans against the refrigerator with her back arched, so that only her head and shoulders touch the refrigerator. Although the position might make another person seem clumsy and off balance, she looks perfectly at ease. Her arms are flung outward and behind her, as if she has just reached a point in her story that needed extra body expression.

As Gedney said in the quotation cited above, he wanted to capture the intimate moments in the lives of his subjects. There is an intimacy to the kitchen. Because of the frame of the picture, the viewer seems to be in the room. The girls are surrounded by the ceiling, floor, and walls. We feel like we are looking into their lives, just as Gedney did, but what is interesting is that they don't seem to be even aware that he is there. One critic noted that this is common in Gedney's photographs. "William Gedney's subjects rarely acknowledge the photographer's presence. They appear to ignore the viewer too, frequently showing us their backs . . . . In only a few portraits does the subject lift a wide-eyed gaze to the camera. For the most part, Gedney's people act out the rhythms of unobserved lives" (Gunnell).

Most middle-class people don't see the everyday lives of people as poor as the Cornetts. If we don't see them, we make assumptions about them that may not be true. The Cornett family did live a hard life, but Gedney wanted to show through his photographs that even the poorest families have grace and beauty.

Works Cited

Gunnell, Barbara. "Simple Truth." *New Statesman* 7 Feb. 2000. Print.

Sartor, Margaret, and Geoff Dyer, eds. *What Was True: The Photographs and Notebooks of William Gedney*. New York: W.W. Norton, 2000. Print.

Good connection of analysis to the author's experience as a dancer.

Good use of source to confirm author's analysis.

Short conclusion reminds us of author's main point.

"Short Distances and Definite Places: The Photographs of William Gedney." San Francisco Museum of Modern Art. Web. 8 Oct. 2011.

William Gedney: Photographs and Writings. Digital Collections. Duke University Libraries. Web. 12 Oct. 2009.

Questions for Discussion

Why does Jarol provide the amount and kind of background information she does? How does she understand the point, meaning, or impact of the photograph? What details did she call attention to and why did she select those? How does she connect those details to meaning and impact? How did her analysis help you better understand how the photo works? ■

Asking Questions: What Can I Write About?

You can find an image to analyze simply by looking around you: online resources, magazines, newspapers, advertisements, art galleries, and so on. Choose a visual whose content interests you, either because you know something about the subject or because the subject allows you to talk about other topics that interest you. For example, if you were interested in fashion, you might want to analyze an Abercrombie & Fitch advertisement, but even if you choose your jeans and t-shirts based on comfort over fashion, you might still analyze a Diesel advertisement in relation to something else, such as ideas of masculinity and femininity.

Ask yourself the following questions as you look for an image to analyze:

- **Is this an image (or series of images) that deals with a topic I am interested in, a topic that I have some knowledge about, or a topic that I want to think more about?** If you could not care less about advertising, for instance, analyze an image from a photographic essay, a painting, or the architecture of a building.

- **Is this an image with complexities?** Although any image can be analyzed, some are so simple that a written analysis would not be worthwhile. You want an image complex enough to provide an opportunity for substantial analysis. Bear in mind, however, that an image can *appear* to be simple and become quite interesting and complex as you begin to see more and more in it. The Gedney photograph above is a good example. It is a simple composition that becomes interesting in the student essay above as you contemplate its details.

- **Is this an image with rich cultural connections and implications?** Sometimes the image itself is less interesting than the cultural context in which it functions. For example, for years the "food pyramid" was the standard image for representing good nutrition. However, evidence accumulated to show that many people did not understand the message of the image. Nutritional experts also begin to doubt the accuracy of the information it displayed. And so recently the "food plate" has begun to replace it. In itself, the food plate is not an especially interesting image, but the cultural context of the obesity epidemic makes the image worth analyzing as a way of conveying information effectively.

How Do I Prepare to Write a Visual Analysis?

Consider what the task requires, voice and style, development and organization, and visual appeal.

Thinking as a Writer: Task Requirements

Preparation for writing a visual analysis first requires spending time with the image and thinking about everything you see in it and everything that it brings to mind. Write down what you see and what you are thinking about with each detail. Then analyze the rhetorical situation of the image by asking the following questions:

- **What is the purpose of this image?** Is it an artistic representation, an ad to make you buy something, a photograph of war that argues for peace? You must understand what the goal of the image is before you can assess whether and how it achieves its purpose.

- **Who is the intended audience?** An ad in a magazine, for instance, will often target the magazine's readership. A car company will stress the practicality of a car in a consumer publication, and the fun of driving it in a car magazine.

- **What are the most important elements of the image?** In any image there will be foreground and background. Study both carefully. What you are looking for is pattern, how the elements that make up the foreground and background work together as a whole and how each element contributes to the image's meaning and impact. Remember: You are not just describing the image. You are sharing *your understanding* of it, which means showing readers part-whole relationships.

Thinking as a Writer: Voice and Style

The tone and style of your analysis depend first on why you are writing it. A visual analysis written for a blog will be different in tone from a visual analysis for an art history class. Second, even within those different purposes, how you relate to the image makes a big difference. Are you an objective observer of an artifact from popular culture? Are you a suspicious critic of an advertisement that is trying to push your buttons? Are you interpreting art for an audience unfamiliar with the artwork?

Thinking as a Writer: Development and Organization

The structure of the reading (pages 367–70) offers a good idea of organization:

1. Example visual analysis: Offers your reader information about who created the image and/or the image's function and context.

2. Image description: Calls your reader's attention to features of the image worth close attention.

3. Image explanation: Relates details to a central meaning or intended impact.

4. Conclusion: Leaves the reader with a memorable sense of how the image works.

Of course, this general idea of structure permits many variations, depending on what your image requires for analysis and the particular angle you have on it. For example, analyzing a television ad or a movie scene might require isolating its key moments—perhaps presented as stills—and repeating 2 and 3 above with each key moment.

Development amounts to repeating these four key moves: point to a feature; describe it; comment on the impression you have of it or what you think it means; and connect with related features. Remember that description of an image is not an analysis; you have to explain how the whole image relates to its parts or features. You have to interpret it or show how it works. Having an interpretation without commenting on the details of the image also is not an analysis; you need to show that your understanding of the image can explain what the reader sees.

Thinking as a Writer: Visual Appeal

Whenever possible, include a copy of the image that you are analyzing. You might need to take a photograph of a painting or billboard, scan a print ad, or save a screen image from the web. Remember that your readers need to see an image large enough and clear enough to see what you want them to see. If you are comparing the image to other similar ones, include an example or two to help you make the comparisons.

What Are the Steps in Writing a Visual Analysis?

A good visual analysis requires a very close examination of the image it discusses. Therefore, you need to make sure to keep the image in front of you as you write, thinking about how all of the details of the image work together.

1. **Draft your analysis.** As you write your first draft, you will begin building the argument for the thesis of your analysis, which is the overall point that you want to make about the image. Build your analysis around this point, working your way through the ideas that support your overall analysis with in-depth discussion of specific elements in the composition of the image. Keep an open mind throughout the initial draft process, and you might discover new angles and points to develop. You can adjust your main point in revision as you incorporate new insights.

2. **Revise your analysis.** Read your analysis critically by asking these questions:
   - Does the opening introduce the text and make my main point clear?
   - Am I moving from point to point based on the needs of my argument? Or does the logic of my analysis seem more like a list of points?
   - Does my analysis offer more than a description of the image? Do I need to highlight why these moments are important and identify what they achieve in the text?
   - Have I offered enough detail to support my claims? Are there any comments that I have made but not supported?

3. **Edit your analysis.** A visual analysis needs to smoothly develop its own ideas as it examines and describes the image. Look for lack of transitions between your points and descriptions of the image.

4. **Proofread your analysis.** Any paper should be proofread carefully for errors. Carefully check spelling and punctuation to ensure that your writing is as clear as your point.

HOW DO I WRITE A REVIEW?

REVIEWS ARE EITHER INFORMATIVE OR PERSUASIVE OR SOME MIX OF THESE two purposes or aims for writing. Although many reviews provide little more than information (about a manufactured item, such as a refrigerator), we have chosen to feature what most people have in mind when they use the word *review*: judgments about how good a movie, book, CD, and so on is, judgments that are not facts and thus need explanation and an argument to justify them.

What Is a Review?

A review provides an evaluation of something or someone by establishing a set of standards or criteria, comparing the subject to those criteria, and forming a judgment based on that comparison. Often the goal of a review is to tell you whether the subject is worth your time: Should you eat at Mario Batali's restaurant? Should you see the new movie in the *Fast and Furious* franchise? Should you read Cormac McCarthy's new novel? Sometimes the purpose of a review is to provide justification for taking action in a business or institutional setting: A review of an employee or a teacher, for example, can result in a pay raise, no raise, or even loss of a job. In all cases, however, evaluations should compare like with like: If Mario Batali's restaurant is dine-in Italian, for example, do not compare it to fast-food Chinese establishments. If the criteria for judging something are in doubt, spell them out; if they are in dispute, justify them to your readers. Above all, to be taken seriously, reviews should seem reasonable and fair.

ASKING QUESTIONS | Anatomy of a Review

Ask and answer the following questions:

1. Summary: **How much do I need to tell my readers about what I am reviewing?** A summary offers *necessary* information about the topic. It should be brief and tell readers only what they need to know so that they can understand what you are evaluating.

2. Criteria: **What basis of comparison am I using?** In most reviews, the criteria are not stated explicitly. *They are implicit in the judgment itself*: A movie with a historical setting can be assessed by how faithfully it portrays the time period, for example. But rather than saying, "I am judging this film by how true it is to actual historical facts," the reviewer points instead to anachronisms—depictions not consistent with the time period—which implies the writer's standard of judgment.

3. Evaluation: **What do I think about the value of what I am reviewing?** Evaluations present judgments about the value of the subject under review. How good is the film, book, or CD you are assessing?

4. Argument: **How can I justify or defend my evaluation?** Reviews provide reasons and evidence to support all judgments made. It is not enough to say that a historical drama misrepresents the time period; you need to cite examples of inaccuracies. ■

Why Write a Review?

We write reviews when we want to give our evaluation of something, usually to encourage our audience to take a particular action: read this book, promote this employee, take a class from this professor, do not eat at this restaurant or buy this DVD. Reviews might be formal and professional, like those published in newspapers and magazines. But they can also be informal—written on a blog or on a vendor's website. Professional food and film critics get paid to make such evaluations, and the future success of products and services can sometimes depend upon their reviews.

You might be asked in class to write a review because the process of writing a review requires skills important for other types of thinking and writing, such as

- Thinking critically
- Providing evidence to support your ideas
- Summarizing concisely
- Making fair and balanced judgments

An Example of a Review

Review of *Water for Elephants* (by Sara Gruen)

DANIELLE POIESZ (BLOG POST)

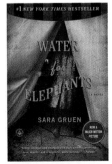

Monday, August 24, 2009
Posted 3:01 p.m.

Spoiler Alert

Water for Elephants by Sara Gruen has spent weeks upon weeks on bestseller lists around the country. With its unique

Indicates that information in the review could lessen the impact of the novel for those who have not read it.

1

Intro identifies book and places it in terms of popularity and favorable print reviews.

premise, readers and reviewers alike have raved about "the tatty glamour of Gruen's meticulously researched world" (*The Washington Post*) and how it "transform[s]a glimpse of Americana into an enchanting escapist fairy tale" (*The New York Times Book Review*).

2   While Gruen fills the pages of this novel with beautiful imagery and richly drawn characters, the hype around this depression-era circus tale is a little overblown. I was, of course, happily ensconced in the depth of feeling toted around by Gruen's main character, Jacob Jankowski, and I found myself reaching for the next page again and again. Gruen's voice is enchanting and thoroughly engaging. So, I won't make any claims to have not enjoyed reading this complexly detailed and excruciatingly emotional story. In fact, I enjoyed it quite a bit. But I do have some qualms about it that I can't seem to shake.

Praise for the book sets up critical comments. Strategy: Negative comments work better after positive ones.

Transitional statement, sets up critical points.

3   First, I did not view *Water for Elephants* in the same light as the reviewers from *Publishers Weekly* do when they say, "With its spotlight on elephants, Gruen's romantic page-turner hinges on the human-animal bonds [. . .]." Jacob, of course, has relationships with the animals in the menagerie, but I don't feel that the book is at all about that bond. He's a vet; of course, he cares about the treatment of the animals. He spends all his working time with them too, so yes, he's going to form some sort of relationship with them. But this book does not hinge on that one bit in my opinion. Instead, Gruen's novel hinges on the personal relationships between the human characters: Jacob, Marlena, August, Walter, Camel, etc. To me, the animal relationships purely influence the reader's feelings toward the humans. The animals liked Jacob and Marlena and they hated August and Uncle Al—their reactions amplified how I already felt about those characters.

Point 1: Disagrees with how the book has been understood by previous reviewers.

4   The only potential horse of a different color here is Rosie, the lovable, hilarious elephant who finally gives August what he deserves when she hits him in the head with a stake, causing him to be stampeded. *Parade* magazine goes so far as to call her the book's "majestic, mute heroine." But I can't wrap my head around that description, even with Rosie's role as the murdering, lemonade-stealing, Polish-speaking pachyderm. She doesn't even enter the book until more than halfway through, and while her presence in the book is supremely entertaining and emotionally quite powerful at times (i.e., when August mistreats her and you watch from Jacob's point of view), I don't feel like she plays that much of a role thematically. She just does the dirty work for the characters, so the reader's opinion of Jacob (who possibly should have sliced August's throat like he intended to) wouldn't be soured and so there can be no legal complications, while providing some comic relief.

Provides reasons and evidence (references to characters and events) in the novel to confirm her understanding.

5   Second, I also am a bit bothered by the structural organization of this novel. I am all for flashbacks and parallel storylines when it's done with purpose, but here I feel it is done for the sake of doing it. The aging Jacob was reminiscing, sure, but he wasn't sharing the tale with another human, as in *Big Fish* where the father tells his son of his life in the circus. Jacob was just remembering on his own, which seems a little bit pointless to me, especially given the fact that nothing really happens in the current day part of the story. All Gruen shows the reader here is a sad, lonely old man who has

Point 2: Takes issue with the structure of the narrative.

Provides argument for contention that story could have been told more effectively.

lost all his family (whether to death or to forgetfulness) and who pines after his youth. Maybe it wouldn't have bothered me so much if he told the story to Charlie at the circus; then at least it would've given the story a purpose. As it is though, it feels to me as if Gruen was trying to use a technique common more in literary than commercial fiction, or that she used it purely to accommodate her prologue so she could tease that pivotal scene. Personally, I think the overall story would have been much more powerful without the older Jacob and had it stuck to being a depression-era novel about a young man who lost everything and then found himself again in the most unlikely of places.

Finally, another thing I'm struggling with after reading *Water for Elephants* is understanding why everyone thinks this is such an original novel. I do agree that Gruen did something special when she exposes the seedy underbelly of the circus in such a gritty and realistic way, but it's not as if it's never been done before. *Big Fish,* which I mentioned previously, is one example. While *Big Fish* is a much more fantastical story than *Water for Elephants,* it still has a lot of the same basic plot points—a life-changing romance and an inside look at the circus. Gruen's voice in telling the story is what's so special here. Additionally, this story is more or less a patchwork of real-life events that took place throughout the history of the circus. While I am a firm believer in writing what you know, in researching a topic before you claim to know it, and in incorporating real life anecdotes and such into a piece of fiction, after reading Gruen's "Author's Note" I was disappointed that she took *so* much from fact and turned it into fiction. Almost all of the unique, humorous (and sometimes not so humorous) scenes in the book are based on actual accounts and were not, as I had thought, a product of Gruen's imagination.

6   Point 3: Novel is not as original as many think.

In sum, then: A brilliantly written (but not-so-brilliantly crafted) and engaging novel with characters who stay with you long after you finish reading—it just could have used a little more editing.

7

Questions for Discussion

In class, discuss "Review of *Water for Elephants*" as an example of the genre. To find points for discussion, use Asking Questions: Anatomy of a Review (page 374) and the marginal annotations to the reading. Are the judgments the author makes clear? Does she provide reasons and evidence for the negative criticisms? If you have read the book, do you think the review is reasonable and fair? If not, do you want to buy the book? That is, what action would you take based on the review, and why would you take it? ■

Asking Questions: What Can I Write About?

When choosing what to review, consider the following:

- **What are your interests?** Do you have good knowledge and experience with any particular field or subject matter?

    Maybe you enjoy a wide variety of video games or listen to a lot of hip-hop music. Perhaps you read a lot of science fiction or you are a film buff. Choosing a subject that you know from experience makes the process of selecting criteria easier.

- **What have you seen, read, or experienced recently that was thought provoking, that stayed with you after the experience was over?**

    Often a book or television show or movie provides entertainment only, enjoyable while it lasts but not memorable. There's nothing wrong with such diversions, but they may not be the best choices for class assignments. Choose a performance or other subject that makes you think about what it means, how it was presented, or how it compares to similar material. A good subject is one that you can analyze, figure out the workings of, and draw some conclusion about its lasting impact. Such subjects result in more interesting reviews.

- **Is this subject something about which I can provide a fair judgment?**

    Part of the validity of a review comes from the reader's sense that it is a fair and thoughtful critique, not a biased snap judgment. If you write a negative review of a country song and you hate country music, it is likely that the only people who would be convinced by your review already had the same opinion or probably would not read the review anyway. Others would find the review worthless in helping them choose whether or not to buy the song. Choosing subject matter that you typically enjoy allows you to create judgments that have a stronger foundation and are more convincing. Of course, this does not mean you should avoid negative comments; rather you should choose a subject on which you can genuinely pass judgments, both good and bad.

How Do I Prepare to Write a Review?

Consider the task requirements, voice and style, and development and organization.

Thinking as a Writer: Task Requirements

In preparation for writing your review, consider your audience, your relationship to the audience and the subject, and your purpose in writing the review. All of these factors will shape the final product.

Perhaps you have decided to review a Korean restaurant for your school newspaper because you just had a wonderful meal there. However, you had never eaten Korean food before. You could compare it to similar food you have eaten in, say, Thai or Chinese restaurants. Perhaps the food seemed spicy to you, but even though you do not usually eat spicy foods, the heat of the peppers did not overwhelm you. Perhaps the meat seemed very tender and full of flavor. Perhaps the entire experience was enjoyable and one that you think others should try.

Thinking as a Writer: Voice and Style

The tone and level of formality in reviews vary widely. They have no single style because the personality of the reviewer (serious literary critic versus beach-reading book lover), the subject being reviewed (the new museum exhibit of Picasso or the latest Final Fantasy video game), and the final evaluation of the subject (rotten tomato or Golden Globe winner) can be so different.

However, voice and style should be a good match for your subject and audience so as not to undermine readers taking your judgments seriously. If a negative review sounds like mudslinging or a positive review like mindless adoration, the reader will discount your opinion. Shape voice and style carefully to support your informative and persuasive purposes.

Thinking as a Writer: Development and Organization

Reviews often follow a pattern of development: Introduce your subject and provide a brief summary; analyze the subject using clear criteria; provide and defend your evaluation. However, reviews can vary from this pattern. Perhaps, for example, you first want to discuss the genre or type of thing your subject belongs to before introducing your subject and describing how it fits into the genre. It depends on your subject and what you want and need to say about it.

Keep in mind that reviewers do not assume the audience has read, seen, or experienced the subject, so your review must share information necessary for the audience to understand your analysis and judgment.

What Are the Steps in Writing a Review?

A review offers a considered judgment, so successful reviews require devoting time to thinking about your subject and everything connected with assessing it. An outline or a list of the features you want to talk about may help, but remember that connecting your points is just as important as making them one by one in a logical sequence. A movie review, for instance, may evaluate the actors' performances and then move on to connect the performances to the director's work.

1. **Draft your review.** Write your review based on the sequence of points you decide to discuss. Provide background information and support for each point and tie them together in the conclusion to an overall assessment.

2. **Revise your review.** Your draft represents your initial effort to analyze and evaluate your subject. When you go back to revise, assess how well the review represents your ideas on the subject, but also assess how well it communicates with your audience, especially in guiding them to take

whatever action you recommend (buy the book, see the movie, purchase the product, and so on). Revise with these questions in mind:

- **Is my evaluation fair and logical?** Have you provided key analysis and examples from the subject to demonstrate how you arrived at your assessment? Make sure that every opinion you present is backed up with analysis or an example. If not, think about how you could support that point.
- **Do my examples and summary convey enough information so that readers who know little about my subject could understand my review?** Do you provide too many unnecessary details or plot descriptions that are not important to your review? A review must carefully measure how much to say. If half of your review is plot summary, then you likely have too much.
- **Does my review cohere?** Is there good flow within paragraphs and are there transitions between paragraphs? Does it move from point to point in a sequence that makes sense? Remember that a review should be organized around what you have to say about your subject, *not around the plot of the movie or the book you are evaluating.*

3. **Edit your review.** Reviews are relatively short, so look for opportunities to cut or shorten material not directly relevant to your evaluation. Use the space you save to explain and support the key points in your evaluation with more specifics. Look for ways to tighten your prose by rewriting wordy sentences.

4. **Proofread your review.** A review depends on the audience's trust in the author's assessment. Eliminate errors, for they will undercut trust in your competence.

BEST PRACTICES | Tact in Reviews

1. Because reviews sometimes deal with plots that have surprise endings, do not spoil the experience for your readers by revealing too much. Do not reveal the murderer in a mystery novel, for instance, or the plot twists in movies that depend on twists for their impact. Think about what you would want to know before you read the book or saw the film. If you feel you must mention a detail that might later ruin the experience for your audience, give them a warning (called a "spoiler alert").

2. Avoid rude attacks on either the subject itself or its creators as you make your evaluation. If you think the writer or director has made a fatal error, do not call her stupid; explain instead how that choice capsized the project. A fair and balanced argument is always more effective than name-calling. ■

HOW DO I WRITE AN EDITORIAL OR OPINION COLUMN?

Rhetorical Analysis

Blog

Reflection

Visual Analysis

Review

Editorial

Proposal

Research Proposal

Annotated Bibliography

Prospectus ⊕

Lab Report ⊕

Instructions ⊕

Abstract ⊕

PERHAPS THE MOST COMMON GENRE FOR CASE-MAKING IS THE EDITORIAL, IN which writers argue for their solutions to problems; for their views on current issues; for the policies they favor at local, state, national, and international levels; and even for which candidate they favor in an upcoming election. Editorials play a significant role in shaping public opinion and therefore matter in the democratic process of our nation. A similar genre is the opinion column, in which regular or guest columnists argue for their position on some current topic or issue.

What Is an Editorial?

An **editorial** is a *short persuasive article in a newspaper, magazine, or news show that expresses the opinion of the editor or editorial board, usually about a current or debatable issue.* Similar in length and style to an editorial, an **op-ed piece** is *an opinion written by someone from outside of the organization.* Called "op-ed" because these pieces were originally published on the page "opposite the editorial page," such writing tries to convince the general reading audience that a particular point of view is valid; it may also try to persuade readers to accept this point of view as the best. Op-eds and editorials are about 250–800 words, and because they are often one article among many that a reader could turn to, the genre attempts to attract and keep reader attention. The point is usually clearly stated within the first few sentences, and the argument needs to be short but adequately supported with logic and evidence.

ASKING QUESTIONS | Anatomy of an Editorial

Ask and answer the following questions:

1. Clear statement of point: **What do I want my readers to believe or do?** The claim (what you are advocating) usually appears within the first few sentences.
2. Background information: **What do my readers need to know?** Any information readers need to understand the argument must be provided. You cannot assume readers know what you know.
3. Logic and evidence: **How can I convince my readers?** Opinions have impact only when readers see them as logical and based on solid evidence. That is, you need to appeal to reason.

4. Appeals to emotions: **How can I move my readers?** In addition to making a good case, editorials appeal to the reader's values, such as love of country or sympathy for people treated unfairly.

5. Consideration of other viewpoints: **How should I handle competing points of view?** Other viewpoints should be treated respectfully even as you show why your opinion is better or best. ■

Why Write an Editorial?

People write editorials and op-eds because they want to make their opinions on current events known as part of their civic life within a community. They write about, for example, green space rezoning in their neighborhood or an issue connected with their business or professional life, such as the impact of taxation on the economy. As a student, you might be asked to write an editorial as an assignment in many courses, such as history, political science, or cultural studies. You could use what you have learned from any course or combination of courses to advocate prison reform, for instance. Writing editorials helps develop important skills, including

- Conveying an opinion persuasively
- Providing evidence and logical analysis
- Expressing ideas concisely and clearly
- Responding to current issues and debates

An Example of an Editorial

Where History Lessons Come Alive

MATT WATSON

Powerful opening that sets the stage for what the author has to say.	*"Nie wieder,"* read the engraving. "Never again." I sat with my head in my hands in the old prison yard, about ready to cry. That's a pretty risky admission coming from a 16-year-old male, but I don't care. I have never been so affected in my entire life as I was last summer when I visited Dachau, the infamous German concentration camp.

1

2

Humbling doesn't even begin to cover it. I was caught completely off-guard by sheer reality. That such a place actually existed, where such terrible events actually occurred, made me temporarily disgusted to be a member of the human race. This

3

revulsion transformed into quiet determination to remember what I had seen that day—and more important, to never let it happen again.

At the risk of sounding contrived, I could never have come close to the deep-seated reality check that I got that afternoon in Germany had I not actually been there. Being confronted by the buildings, standing and smelling and seeing and feeling the claustrophobia of the shower—it gave me a connection to Dachau that enabled me to appreciate the human aspect of the sweep of history. Before Dachau, the Holocaust, as I had learned within the four walls of a classroom, was a part of World War II, one aspect of a brutal regime that could have destroyed democracy, a textbook example of genocide and so on. I learned the facts of the Holocaust without ever examining its soul.

Establishes the importance of being there, of experiencing what you learn about, and how that experience changes perception.

I don't mean to discredit history education or the teachers who taught me about the Holocaust. Not at all. It's quite a valiant undertaking to try to hold the attention of a captive audience who, as a whole, has no initial interest in the political systems of Han China or the causes of the French Revolution. Indeed, to a point, teachers can't be blamed for the apathy of their students. To the average teenager, history is a collection of facts to be memorized, and as anyone can tell you, memorization is never an engaging practice. As a result, kids in class too often utter the phrase dreaded by educators everywhere: What's the point?

Heads off possible reader objection: Are you putting down classroom education? Also insists on his central point: You have to be there.

Traveling showed me the point.

It also made me realize that education should be more than career preparation. It should teach kids how to think in a global context.

Key further point—experience in education helps open the eyes to thinking in real contexts—not just for tests and grades.

On that same trip through Germany, my group and I visited the small portion of the Berlin Wall that's still standing. I experienced the view of so many East Berliners looking hopelessly over that slab of concrete and barbed wire that separated them from the freedom of the West. Again, I was humbled, and again, I felt as if my eyes were pried open to see—to really, truly see—the point. This was education.

To educate in practical matters—to teach to a concrete set of specific standards—is doubtless an important pursuit necessary for the maintenance of society. To educate in human matters—to teach kids how to understand other people, to think in terms of a world no longer confined by geography—is of an entirely different level of importance.

If America is to have any hope of solving the most pressing questions facing society, future leaders will need more than textbook knowledge. They will require a holistic understanding of the fundamental truths that motivate all human action and reaction.

Powerful concluding point about the practical value of education through experience.

Questions for Discussion

After reviewing the Anatomy of an Editorial (pages 381–82) and the marginal annotations to the reading, discuss "Where History Lessons Come Alive" in class. How did the author attempt to catch your attention? How does he make his central point clear, and in what ways does he defend it with logic and evidence? What values does he appeal to? Why are you likely to remember this editorial long after reading it? ∎

Asking Questions: What Can I Write About?

Editorials and op-ed pieces can be written about any subject that people are thinking, talking, and writing about: current events, controversial debates, and cultural events. Because editorials appear in particular publications, people write them for the community the publication serves: an interest group (for example, parents with young children), a neighborhood, a college campus, a city, or a nation.

You need to find a topic that you care about, that you want to express your opinion on, and that you want to convince others in your community to consider. The following questions should help you find an appropriate topic:

- **What current controversial issues are you passionate about?** Controversies and debates taking place in a community appear in the editorials and op-ed pages of newspapers and magazines. Reading them may help you find a topic that interests you.

- **What events are happening around me?** Current events are often the subject of editorials and opinions because people want to weigh in on important decisions that affect them. Perhaps your college is considering restructuring course requirements for graduation or a student group is bringing a controversial speaker to campus. Good editorials can respond to situations that are happening right now and give you a chance to help shape those events.

- **What have you read recently in magazines or newspapers (print or online) that you disagree with?** Sometimes op-ed pieces will respond to something that appeared previously in the publication. The op-ed pages give readers a space to state their own opinions on the subject. When you find yourself talking back to an article, you may have found the topic you should write about.

Regardless of the topic you choose, focus your discussion. Often the best way to get to your point is to think about your relationship to the issue. For example, if your topic is animal rights, think about local problems you have seen that relate to animal rights and experiences you have had, for example, working at an animal shelter.

How Do I Prepare to Write an Editorial?

Consider the task requirements, voice and style, and development and organization.

Thinking as a Writer: Task Requirements

Since editorials and op-ed pieces appear in particular publications, think about who you are writing to by where you would send your piece. A piece defending video games as socially interactive rather than isolating might go to your local newspaper or an online gaming magazine. In either case, writing for the publication's audience would be crucial. The more general reader of the newspaper would not know as much about video games as someone who reads an online gaming magazine. In other words, you could not persuade both audiences with the same article.

The same principle applies to editorials written for a class. Who do you want to reach? Whose opinions do you want to influence most? These questions will help you decide how much background information you should supply, how much and what kind of evidence you need, and what values you can appeal to most effectively.

Thinking as a Writer: Voice and Style

Editorials and opinion pieces necessarily reveal your character and personality. You have choices, however, in how you will sound to your reader. Will emotion or calm rationality be best? Do you need to convey sadness or anger? Is your personal involvement in the issue relevant and therefore does it need to be mentioned and perhaps explained? How you answer these questions matters because readers do respond to how attractive and trustworthy they sense a writer is. In the example of an editorial presented earlier (pages 382–83), Matt Watson presents himself especially well.

Thinking as a Writer: Development and Organization

The editorial is, by convention, short. You must generate a high-impact argument in no more than about 750 words. Unlike a research paper on the same topic, an editorial must focus on persuasion over depth and breadth of coverage, boiling down what you have to say to a central point, a few reasons justifying it, and only the best pieces of evidence you have.

Most editorials follow a simple organizational pattern: Introduce the argument, provide necessary background information, and lay out the evidence and logic to support the claim point by point. Therefore, in preparing to write, the following questions are crucial: Do you have data or information to justify the claims you make? If you are analyzing a problem and proposing a solution, what can you cite that supports your analysis and confirms that your solution can really work? The argument is the heart of the editorial; pay special attention to offering the best reasons you have and selecting the evidence that backs each reason most strongly.

What Are the Steps in Writing an Editorial?

An editorial is not simply your opinion; *it is a demonstration of why this opinion is a good one to hold.* The goal is to find the best way to convince your audience. Therefore, your editorial needs to be shaped thoughtfully.

1. **Draft your editorial.** The draft is the place to get all of your ideas and arguments on the table. You might even find that it is helpful to freewrite the argument section to make sure that you have identified all of your potential points. You might decide later to cut out some of them to develop

better the ones that remain, but give them all free expression in your first draft.

2. **Revise your editorial.** The revision stage is critical to sharpening your argument, especially to making your case using the best strategies. Read over your editorial and ask yourself these questions:
   - Have you clearly stated your argument or point early? You do not have space for a long windup. Get to the point quickly.
   - Have you provided enough information to describe the situation and give crucial background information? Use your sense of your audience to judge which facts you feel certain they already know and which facts need to be introduced or reinforced.
   - Does each point in your argument follow a logical order? Are there some that seem out of place or too weak and need to be cut? Are there some that need more development? Examine your argument for flow: Does it lead from point to point logically and support its points with enough facts?
   - Examine your argument for coherence: Do you have the right tone of voice for your topic? Is the tone consistent throughout? Do you sound trustworthy and believable? Shifting voices, exaggerated or rude tones, and rants will confuse or put off your readers. How you say something is as important as what you say.

3. **Edit your editorial.** When you edit, make sure that you eliminate wordiness, unnecessary points, and excessive discussion. Pay special attention to the implications of the words you select. It makes a difference, for instance, whether you call an immigrant "illegal" or "undocumented."

4. **Proofread your editorial.** Proofread carefully for misspellings and grammatical errors so that mistakes do not detract from your argument.

BEST PRACTICES | Maintaining Editorial Integrity

1. Although any writing will be better when you keep in mind the rhetorical situation, the power of an editorial or op-ed depends especially on your purpose, your audience, and how you portray your relationship to the issue and audience. You need to be aware of what you want to achieve: Are you offering an opinion that has not been aired on the subject but needs to be considered? The best choice among many possibilities? The reasons for taking a particular action? Being clear about your goal matters and makes it easier to reach. Similarly, you need to understand for whom you are writing and how you need to portray yourself to get them to listen. Do you want your audience to see you as one of them? Or is it more important that they see you as a trustworthy observer? Correctly judging what your audience needs and wants is the key to being effective.

2. Often statistics and information are necessary for making an argument. Short quotations from something someone else has said or written are also common. In

academic essays, we cite these sources of information in the text in parentheses or footnotes and include a list of works cited or bibliography at the end. Editorials do not contain such features, but you still need to be careful to attribute any quotations and ideas you use to their sources and say where you got your data.

This reference can be accomplished most easily by introducing the quotations or data with a signal phrase, such as "In a recent report to Congress, the economist George Soros said. . . ." You can also refer your readers to a website, an article, or a book by including a URL for a website or the publication year for a book in parentheses at the end of the sentence. ■

See Chapter 18, pages 433–34 for more discussion of signal phrases.

HOW DO I WRITE A PROPOSAL?

PROPOSALS ARE A MAJOR GENRE IN BUSINESS AND PROFESSIONAL SETTINGS of all kinds, and they take many forms: a request for funding, a project outline, a plan for a dissertation, and so on. Often proposals are elaborate and formal, written by teams of writers, and the results are evaluated by government agencies, corporations, educational institutions, and the like. This treatment deals with the basics of proposal writing at a level appropriate for first-year college writing courses.

What Is a Proposal?

A proposal is an argument that attempts to persuade its audience to see a problem or opportunity in a particular way and convince them to take a particular action proposed. Proposals must be persuasive, so ideas must be presented clearly, with an audience's needs in mind and in a way that draws its support.

ASKING QUESTIONS | Anatomy of a Proposal

Ask and answer the following questions:

1. Identification of the problem: **What problem am I trying to solve?** A proposal must establish a significant problem that needs to be solved or at least addressed in some way.

2. Detailed and clear outline of the solution: **What exactly am I proposing?** Your description of the problem must imply and connect logically to the solution you propose. In other words, the persuasive power of a proposal depends on your readers' seeing the problem as you do and recognizing that the solution follows from your presentation of the problem.

3. Evidence to support the proposed solution: **How can I show that my solution will work?** A proposal must be supported by data and expert opinion in addition to being logically compelling.

4. Consideration of alternative actions or contrary arguments: **How can I establish that only my solution will address the problem adequately?** Especially when other solutions have been or will be proposed, it is important to show why yours has advantages over the competition. Perhaps, for example, you can establish that your solution is cheaper or easier to implement.

5. Conclusion: **How can I motivate my readers to act or support the action I have proposed?** Often the conclusion of a proposal includes a call to action that delineates precisely what you are asking your audience to do and encourages them to do it. ■

Why Write a Proposal?

Proposals are the means for taking effective action on any problem, question, or issue that requires people to cooperate. If you want to enlist the support of others to make life better, proposals are the way to do it.

From a marriage proposal to a business proposal to a grant application to a call by neighbors for greater green space, *people try to persuade others to see a situation the way they do and take the action they propose.* A consulting firm's proposal to evaluate the supply chain efficiency of a retail company and a scientist's proposal asking for research funding for a new DNA sequencing study differ in details, and both differ from a letter to a congressman arguing for public libraries to stay open later. Yet they all have a similar logic and function. Each must identify the problem or need and make a convincing argument for taking the advised action.

Students are often asked to write a research proposal in which they must convince their instructor that what they plan to write about for an upcoming research project is worthwhile. Students in a business course write proposals for solving child labor problems; students in political science propose solutions to problems with campaign funding; students in a writing course write letters to newspaper editors proposing solutions to campus or community problems, large and small. Writing a proposal helps develop important skills:

See How Do I Write a Research Proposal (pages 518–23) for specific information on this kind of proposal.

- Identifying a problem and the best solution
- Clearly articulating how a solution will work
- Making a convincing argument using appropriate evidence
- Considering your audience and shaping your tone and argument for that audience

Example of a Proposal

Stop Marketing Foods to Children

MARION NESTLE

States the problem proposal would solve. Problem too well known to require background, explanation, or evidence.

From a public health perspective, obesity is the most serious nutrition problem among children as well as adults in the United States. The roots of this problem can be traced to farm policies and Wall Street. Farm subsidies, tariffs and trade agreements support a food supply that provides 3,900 calories per day per capita,

1

roughly twice the average need, and 700 calories a day higher than in 1980, at the dawn of the obesity epidemic. In this overabundant food economy, companies must compete fiercely for sales, not least because of Wall Street's expectations for quarterly growth. These pressures induce companies to make highly profitable "junk" foods, market them directly to children, and advertise such foods as appropriate for consumption at all times, in large amounts, by children of all ages. In this business environment, childhood obesity is just collateral damage.

Establishes causes of problem, emphasizing the strong incentives for manipulating children.

Good use of analogy: collateral damage in war, collateral damage in competition for profits.

Adults may be fair game for marketers, but children are not. Children cannot distinguish sales pitches from information unless taught to do so. Food companies spend at least $10 billion annually enticing children to desire food brands and to pester parents to buy them. The result: American children consume more than one-third of their daily calories from soft drinks, sweets, salty snacks and fast food. Worse, food marketing subverts parental authority by making children believe they are supposed to be eating such foods and they—not their parents—know what is best for them to eat.

2

Key point: Children need special attention.

Anticipates possible objection to her proposal: Parents cannot resist $10 billion of advertising directed at their children.

Today's marketing methods extend beyond television to include Internet games, product placements, character licensing and word-of-mouth campaigns—stealth methods likely to be invisible to parents. When restrictions have been called for, the food industry has resisted, invoking parental responsibility and First Amendment rights, and proposing self-regulation instead. But because companies cannot be expected to act against corporate self-interest, government regulations are essential. Industry pressures killed attempts to regulate television advertising to children in the late 1970s, but obesity is a more serious problem now.

3

"Stealth" connects with "collateral damage" as war metaphors, emphasizing the lack of morality in marketing food to children.

Another key point: Companies cannot regulate their own conduct because they are driven by irresistible economic forces.

It is time to try again, this time to stop all forms of marketing foods to kids— both visible and stealth. Countries in Europe and elsewhere are taking such actions, and we could too. Controls on marketing may not be sufficient to prevent childhood obesity, but they would make it easier for parents to help children to eat more healthfully.

4

Simple proposal, clearly stated, not in need of much defense because the logic is so strong.

Defends proposal by pointing to regulation in other countries and by not claiming too much for it.

Questions for Discussion

In class, discuss "Stop Marketing Foods to Children." To find points for discussion, use Asking Questions: Anatomy of a Proposal (page 388) and the marginal annotations to the reading. What is the problem the proposal would address? How does the author lead us to understand why the problem exists? How does she argue that no other solution except government regulation would work? What impact does she claim for her proposal if it were implemented? Do you find her reasoning persuasive? Why or why not? ■

Asking Questions: What Can I Write About?

Good topics for proposals are all around you:

- In campus problems, such as parking, dorm issues, and class scheduling.
- In local community problems, such as zoning, public transportation, and caring for the homeless.
- In state-level problems, such as public school financing, supervision of mental health facilities, and resolution of legalized gambling.
- In national-level problems, such as the war in Afghanistan, the national debt, and financial aid for college students.

Finding problems is relatively easy; finding one that interests you and about which you know something already, either from reading or experience or both, is usually more challenging. The key question is: **Big or small, what problems bother me and seem to have solutions I can advocate with some degree of passion and commitment?**

Here is some good advice: You probably should not take on a very large problem like world poverty. If you are assigned or select a complicated problem, such as child labor in developing countries, a proposal for what a single company could do will probably work better than a sweeping solution for the entire problem. Large-scale problems usually require complex, multifaceted solutions that you will probably not be able to write about in a short paper. Also, focusing on one small aspect of a big problem often proves successful in addressing the big problem because local solutions can be implemented on a larger scale.

If discovering your problem proves to be a problem itself, consider the following:

- **Recent News**   What's happening in your town, your state, the country, or the world and is making the headlines can offer many problems that you might propose solutions to. Glancing through print or online newspapers can call your attention to problems that you did not know existed.
- **Situations around Campus or Town**   What problems are you aware of that people have perhaps not yet taken enough notice of?
- **Your Own Interests**   Perhaps you are interested in animal welfare, environmental causes, child welfare, or other causes. The subjects that you are already involved in are good places to begin.

As you prepare your solution, you need to think about the following:

- **Contributing Factors**   Sometimes the solution to a problem does not focus on the problem itself but on changing the factors contributing to the problem. For example, a proposed solution for childhood obesity might focus not on arguing for more exercise, but on why children are not exercising more. Perhaps recess has been cut from their school, perhaps there are no playgrounds within walking distance. The solution requires understanding the problem in more depth.

- **Previously Proposed or Attempted Solutions**   Investigate what efforts have already been made to solve the problem you are addressing. This research can help you identify what has and has not worked. It will also offer support for your own proposal.

- **Controversies Surrounding Your Topic**   If the solutions for your problem are hotly debated, be sure to consider all sides carefully, including why the topic is so controversial and how your solution might appeal to all sides.

How Do I Prepare to Write a Proposal?

Consider the task requirements, voice and style, development and organization, and visual appeal.

Thinking as a Writer: Task Requirements

Regardless of how passionate you are about your subject, the best proposals come from rational, practical, open-minded investigation. Take time to consider the whole problem carefully, in all of its dimensions, and with a willingness to rethink your preconceptions, biases, or assumptions. Often the key to a good solution is seeing the problem in a fresh "outside the box" way we hear so much about.

Thinking as a Writer: Voice and Style

The voice and style you choose in a proposal depends on your topic, your relation to it, and your readers. Perhaps you are indignant about the use of animals in product safety testing. If you want to propose the use of alternative forms of testing, implying that readers' current choices are cruel and insensitive will not prove persuasive. Instead, give readers better choices and more information for helping to be part of the solution.

Thinking as a Writer: Development and Organization

Each section of the proposal has a function:

1. **Introduction**   In addition to getting the audience's attention, the introduction to a proposal needs to set up the problem and identify the solution that you are attempting to convince your audience to adopt. Readers want information up front, and you want to get your proposal into their heads as soon as possible.

2. **Body**   The organization of the main section of the proposal will vary depending upon the problem and especially the solution. However, in this section you must define the problem, including the scope or urgency of the situation, and identify for your audience why this is a situation in which they need to act. You must describe your proposed solution. In this section, you might consider other options in order to emphasize that yours is the best choice. Finally, if your readers are likely to have objections to your proposal, respond to them after presenting your solution.

3. **Conclusion**   The conclusion should offer more than a recap of the problem and solution. You might have a call to action or examine the consequences of inaction, or make a final appeal for your solution. Make your conclusion memorable and persuasive rather than repetitive and boring.

Thinking as a Writer: Visual Appeal

Visuals such as photographs, maps, tables, or graphs can add to the persuasive impact of your proposal. Remember that to make visuals effective, you must refer to them in writing and comment on them, not just insert them in your paper.

What Are the Steps in Writing a Proposal?

Proposals require extensive thought and, typically, research. A plan or outline helps most writers stay on track with the first draft.

1. **Draft your proposal.** Decide what information you may need to gather in order to describe your problem and its solution in specific terms. See Chapter 16, "Finding Sources," pages 412-24, for more help with this stage of the process. When you sit down to draft your proposal, focus on the logic of how you present the information you have gathered. Logic drives the proposal from point to point and has much to do with its power to persuade.

2. **Revise your proposal.** Read over the proposal with these questions in mind:
   - Is my problem defined early and clearly? Do I provide a sense of why this is a situation that requires action?
   - Is my solution clear and easy to comprehend? Does each piece of the solution have support that makes it convincing? Did I remember to defend the solution against possible objections? As you read, play the role of your readers, imagining what additional information they might need or additional support for your key points.
   - Is the tone of the proposal consistent and appropriate for the audience I envision? If I were a member of that audience, are there any moments that would offend or bore me and make me stop reading?
   - Does my conclusion continue to uphold the proposed solution in a way my readers will likely remember?
   - Have I used transitions to show how the parts of my proposal relate to each other? Where could I do a better job of signaling connections between ideas to the reader?

3. **Edit your proposal.** Work through the prose, eliminating wordiness, making ideas as clear as possible, and fine-tuning the voice and style to match the aim and audience of your proposal.

4. **Proofread your proposal.** For a proposal to be convincing, it must have authority. Errors of grammar and spelling will undermine this authority, so eliminate as many as you can.

Researching Writing

CHAPTER 15
Planning a Research Project

RESEARCH BEGINS WITH QUESTIONS, NOT JUST WITH A TOPIC. WITHOUT questions, research would be a haphazard and aimless task. One question is always relevant: Given what I already know about my topic, what more do I need to know? Asking it exposes the gaps in your existing knowledge and tells you what you need to focus on when doing research.

Research, however, is more interesting and creative than just gathering facts. For example, research can help us ask and answer a more important question: "What do the facts mean?" This question calls for critical thinking, which requires more questions and answers. For example, history textbooks are filled with facts, but they might have different facts or different interpretations of the same facts. A researcher might ask *why* textbooks' explanations of an event might differ. Could the differences have to do with the political climate of the time in which each was published? The writer could attempt to answer this question by finding textbooks published at different times, comparing their depictions of an event, and then relating them to what was going on politically when the books were written.

As a researcher what you are seeking most is *a question that you and your readers will find engaging, worth writing about, and worth reading.* We know, for instance, that wolves thrive in some environments and struggle in others. Why? One question we could ask is, "How does hunting by humans affect the behavior of species that are hunted?" Animal behaviorists are researching how wolf packs behave depending on whether they live in protected areas or in areas where hunting is permitted. What they have learned is worth writing about and sharing with readers—and if we have the opportunity, can even get us out into the field ourselves to do our own firsthand research.

If we think of research as just finding facts and quotations to add to a draft, we have missed what research is all about. *Research is about finding a question worth pursuing. Then, it is about finding information and interpreting it in order to answer the question.* Put simply, research builds the foundation for writing.

When Is Research Necessary?

Research is needed whenever general knowledge and common sense are not enough. Most college writing requires research because instructors want students to go beyond assigned readings to increase the depth of their knowledge, analyze conflicting interpretations, and develop their own understanding of the course subject matter. After college, people conduct research on the job (for example, to analyze markets or prepare proposals for clients) and in community life (for example, to support their claim that a neighborhood should be rezoned or that school funding should be increased).

Research goes on throughout the writing process. In a college writing class, depending on the assignment, you may

- Conduct *preliminary research* to get basic information on a topic and stimulate your curiosity about it.
- Pursue *in-depth research* to satisfy that curiosity, answering your questions and acquiring the solid evidence you need to convince others.
- Continue your research as needed in revision to add support when a point is underdeveloped, your focus shifts, or new questions arise.

What Kinds of Sources Do College Researchers Use?

Most assignments encourage students to consult a variety of sources featuring different opinions on and approaches to a topic. The following discussion offers an overview of the kinds of sources available.

Primary Sources versus Secondary Sources

Primary sources are *data or artifacts, works of art or literature, before they have been interpreted by another researcher.* In the natural sciences and social sciences, primary sources may include data from observational studies, surveys, and laboratory experiments. In the humanities, they may include historical documents (the *Mayflower Compact*, the *Declaration of Independence*), works of art and film, novels and poetry, or letters, diaries, and manuscripts. In all disciplines, researchers may interview experts to learn about their research or their experiences firsthand. Primary sources provide raw materials for your own analysis and

To learn how to conduct observational studies, surveys, and interviews, see Chapter 16, pages 423–25.

Primary sources, such as the Declaration of Independence, are documents or works of art or literature that have not been interpreted by another researcher. They are uninterpreted works in their original form.

Secondary sources, like *National Geographic* magazine, demonstrate other people's ideas and conclusions about a topic, to which you can compare your own thoughts and conclusions.

specific evidence for developing your points and supporting your reasoning.

Secondary sources, in contrast, *result from someone else's research.* For example, in a British literature course, your primary source might be Samuel Taylor Coleridge's poem "The Rime of the Ancient Mariner." Secondary sources would be interpretations of the poem by literary critics. Secondary sources also include general and specialized encyclopedias, most books, and articles in magazines and scholarly journals. They provide useful background or historical information; they communicate other people's ideas and conclusions about a topic, to which you can compare your own thoughts and conclusions. Also, in secondary sources you will find expert opinions that you can use to help formulate your own opinions and to support and develop your opinions. You may also use secondary sources to provide opposing views and opinions you would like to refute. Comparing the perspectives of secondary sources can help you construct a position of your own.

For more on how to compare sources, see Chapter 8, especially pages 173–201.

Popular versus Scholarly Sources

Secondary sources have a wide range of audiences; they may be magazine articles directed to the general public or highly specialized texts written by scholars for other professionals in their field.

Popular works offer accessible introductions to a topic and include the following:

- **Textbooks**   Textbooks offer surveys of a field, such as this guide to writing. They can be a good place to begin research.

- **General Encyclopedias**   Like textbooks, general encyclopedias (such as *Britannica Online* and *Wikipedia*) offer an overview of the basic information on a topic and therefore can serve as starting points for research. However, keep in mind that most assignments will require that you move on to more specialized sources. Footnotes and links in general encyclopedia entries can take you deeper into scholarship on the topic.

- **Magazines and Newspapers**   Magazines and newspapers offer a wide range of information, from celebrity gossip to scientific discoveries. For most college research, instructors prefer that students avoid light reading titles such as *Cosmopolitan* and *USA TODAY* in favor of publications that offer more in-depth articles such as *Women's Health Weekly* and *The New York Times.*

■ **Trade Books**   Trade books are published by commercial presses (like HarperCollins, Knopf, and Simon & Schuster) and aimed at an educated segment of the general public, including students and professors. Trade books are typically more accessible than books published by scholarly presses, but the authors are often experts in their field who also publish more academic works.

Scholarly works include the following:

■ **Specialized Encyclopedias and Dictionaries**   Specialized encyclopedias and dictionaries are works devoted to specific topics and written by experts. You will find many in the reference section of your library; others, like *The New Palgrave Dictionary of Economics* and *The Blackwell Encyclopedia of Sociology*, can be accessed through your library's database offerings. Entries are written by experts and peer reviewed, which means that other scholars have had to approve the credentials of the writer and the accuracy of the material. Entries in specialized encyclopedias and dictionaries provide background information, define terms, and include suggestions for further reading.

■ **Scholarly Journals**   Articles in scholarly journals are written by experts and reviewed by other subject specialists before publication. Scholarly journals are specialized sources, so undergraduates might find reading their articles challenging. Such articles are highly reliable sources of in-depth information, however, so perseverance will pay dividends.

Magazines such as *The Atlantic* are popular sources intended for an intelligent and well-informed readership.

CONCEPT CLOSE-UP | Comparison of a Scholarly Journal Source with a Magazine Source

You can distinguish scholarly journals from popular magazines in several ways. First, scholarly journals do not include glossy advertisements. Second, the titles of scholarly journals, and the articles they publish, usually indicate specifically what they cover. For example, in the *American Journal of Family Therapy,* you will find articles such as "Understanding Online Gaming Addiction and Treatment Issues for Adolescents," whereas an article in a popular magazine such as *Psychology Today* will have a catchier title like "Why Johnny Can't Stop Playing Video Games." Comparing the examples in Figure 15.1 reveals the typical design features, vocabulary, and reading level of academic journal articles and articles in popular magazines. ■

■ **Scholarly Books**   Scholarly books are written by experts in the field and published by university presses. They are rigorously reviewed by other experts in the field (a process known as peer review) before publication, and they are intended for an audience of other scholars in the same field. You can depend on authors of scholarly books to cite their sources and to include a bibliography at the end of the book. The style of the writing can range from accessible at the undergraduate level to highly technical.

FIGURE **15.1**

Understanding How Different Sources Work How does the treatment of the same topic differ in scholarly and popular sources?

The American Journal of Family Therapy, 37:355–372, 2009
Copyright © Taylor & Francis Group, LLC
ISSN: 0192-6187 print / 1521-0383 online
DOI: 10.1080/01926180902942191

Understanding Online Gaming Addiction and Treatment Issues for Adolescents

KIMBERLY YOUNG

The Center for Internet Addiction Recovery, Bradford, Pennsylvania, USA

Massive Muti-user Online Role-Playing Games or MMORPGs as they are often called are one of the fastest growing forms of Internet addiction, especially among children and teenagers. Like an addiction to alcohol or drugs, gamers show several classic signs of addiction (Grusser, Thalemann, and Griffiths, 2007). They become preoccupied with gaming, lie about their gaming use, lose interest in other activities just to game, withdrawal from family and friends to game, and use gaming as a means of psychological

We will talk later about how to find these and other sources (see Chapter 16, pages 414–23) and how to evaluate such sources (Chapter 17, pages 426–32), but this overview should give you an idea of the main kinds of sources available to you.

Print Sources versus Digital Sources

The distinction between online and print sources is not as relevant as it used to be since most print sources are becoming available digitally. Libraries subscribe to databases that provide online the full text of many magazine and journal articles. Increasingly, e-books are available through libraries' book catalogs.

How Do I Plan a Research Project?

Writing a research project can be a big undertaking. To minimize anxiety and keep your progress on track, first break the project down into stages.

Stages of a Research Project

The stages of research include preliminary thinking and research; focused research; informal writing, drafting, and revising; and, finally, editing and proofreading (Figure 15.2).

1. Preliminary Thinking and Research

- If you are writing in response to an assignment prompt, reread it to make sure you understand your instructor's guidelines for the project.
- Brainstorm appropriate topics for questions or problems that interest you personally; confer with your instructor for advice if needed.
- Begin a research log, which is a record of your progress (see Best Practices: Habits of Successful Researchers, page 403).
- Brainstorm possible research questions, and then browse a variety of sources, bibliographies, and indexes to test the availability of resources for answering these questions.
- Decide on a research question, or determine if you need to do more preliminary research before forming a research question.

2. Focused Research and Preliminary Writing

- Identify key words to use as search terms.
- Find and evaluate sources and begin your working bibliography.

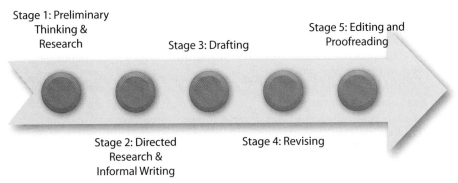

FIGURE **15.2**

Timeline for the Main Stages of a Researched Paper

- Consult a librarian if you need help.
- Write notes about all relevant materials; make printouts and photocopies of the sources you will rely on the most.
- Refine your research question.
- Write a preliminary version of your thesis.

3. Planning and Drafting

See Chapter 24 online, for guidance on using photographs, drawings, tables, and graphs.

- Work out a plan for developing your thesis, such as an outline or flowchart.
- Decide which sources you will draw on to develop each part of the plan.
- Consider what information you could best present visually.
- Begin drafting; *incorporate and cite your sources as you draft.*
- Decide what additional information you need, and do more research.

4. Revising Your Draft

See Chapter 14, pages 335-56, for a systematic approach to editing.

- Refine your thesis if necessary. Rewrite as required to improve your first draft.
- Confer with peers or your instructor to discuss organization and development.
- Do additional research to make underdeveloped sections more specific.

5. Editing and Proofreading Your Draft

For keeping a list of your common errors, see page 356.

- Read your draft aloud for style, flow within and across paragraphs, and conciseness.
- Review suggestions in Chapter 18 for help with smoothly integrating paraphrases and quotations; edit as needed.
- Run spelling and grammar checks.
- Proofread again, paying special attention to your list of common errors.
- Check the correct MLA or APA formats for in-text and end citations.

Scheduling Your Research Project

With your calendar or planner in hand, assign dates for completing each task in the stages described above. You may want to start at your project's due date and work your way backward.

How much time should you allot to each stage? That depends on the length and complexity of the assignment and the amount of time you have. We offer a schedule below for a four-week project. Adjust the schedule accordingly.

- Week 1: Choose a topic, develop a research question, and begin to find and evaluate potential sources.
- Week 2: Continue preliminary research, reading and analyzing sources; finalize your research question, and draft a preliminary thesis.

- Week 3: Outline and write your first draft. Be sure to incorporate and cite your sources as you draft. Decide what further research you will need to develop this draft, and conduct additional research.

- Week 4: Reread and (if possible) get feedback on your draft from a writing tutor, your instructor, or peers; revise your thesis (if necessary), rewrite as needed, edit for style and integration of quotations; proofread and prepare your paper according to your instructor's submission guidelines.

BEST PRACTICES | Habits of Successful Researchers

Following the suggestions below, you can remain in control of any research project.

1. **Plan your work and work your plan.**
   If you stay on schedule and do some work every day, you will greatly reduce the stress of doing a major research assignment. *Consistent work is the key.*

2. **Take initiative.**
   The difference between an outstanding research project and a poor one often comes down to motivation. *Get engaged and stay engaged* from the time you get an assignment until it is ready to turn in.

3. **Keep a research log.**
   Doing research is like making your own path through a forest; if you do not keep track of where you have gone and what you have found, you can waste too much time over the same territory. *Keep a log or daily record of your research* as described later in this chapter on page 407.

   See Chapter 2, pages 13–37, for guidance on critical reading.

4. **Employ a range of reading skills.**
   Researchers change reading styles to suit their purposes. They browse indexes, bibliographies, and the Internet to scout out possible sources. They skim articles and books to get the gist and determine the writer's angle. But when they find a suitable source, they slow down and dive deeper, reading critically and annotating and taking notes.

5. **Avoid premature closure on research and thinking.**
   The best resources are not necessarily the first ones you find. If your instructor suggests a minimum number of sources, you will need to gather more so you can pick the best ones. Keep an open mind. Do not decide you know the answer to your research question and seek out only the information that supports your answer.

6. **Ask for help.**
   Librarians want to help, but you have to initiate contact. If you look for information for more than thirty minutes without success, ask a librarian. ■

How Do I Choose and Narrow a Topic?

An effective research project must focus on a topic that you can do justice to in the allotted space. A typical research project cannot meaningfully examine topics as broad as animal rights, bank regulation, global warming, health care reform, or terrorism. Many complete books have been published on narrower topics than these. To narrow a topic to one that you can usefully explore in a brief assignment, look in some of the places listed below.

- **Course Readings** Many topics for research papers come from course readings. Look at chapter headings and subheadings for ideas about subtopics, and take note of narrower topics while reading. If your text has an index, look at entries and subentries. For example, students reading *The Devil's Highway* by Luis Alberto Urrea, about the deaths of illegal immigrants in the desert Southwest, were interested in writing about the people engaged in human smuggling. To narrow the topic, they looked at the entry for the smugglers, called *coyotes*, and found subentries on coyotes as gangsters, the macho image of coyotes, and the operations of coyotes.

- **Catalogs and Databases** In Chapter 16, Finding Sources, we show how to find resources using library databases and Internet search tools such as Google, Bing, and INFOMINE. (See pages 419–23 for help with searching databases and using Web search engines). Reading the titles of articles and other sources on your general topic is a good brainstorming technique, as the titles alone can suggest interesting ways to focus a research question. For example, some titles that came up in a search about college student debt suggest possible questions for further research:

  - *Article Titles Found in a Database:*

    "A Lifetime of Student Debt? Not Likely"
    "College Students' Knowledge and Use of Credit"
    "Credit Card Debt, Stress and Key Health Risk Behaviors among College Students"
    "When Life Gets in the Way of Paying for College"

  - *Questions for Research Inspired by the Article Titles in a Database:*

    Should colleges offer courses in budget and managing personal finances?
    Is there a relationship between excessive credit card debt and other high-risk behaviors?
    How are high college costs affecting the life choices of young adults?

- **Specialized Reference Sources and Research Guides** You can also find inspiration and background material on your topic in reference works such as specialized dictionaries and encyclopedias (in print and online) and in research guides on college library websites. For more on specialized encyclopedias and reference guides, see pages 415–18 in Chapter 16, Finding Sources.

- **Your Own Interests** Topics for research can be found in your own backyard. For example, a student needing to write a paper on small businesses noticed that a restaurant he frequented had closed recently. He found his topic: the difficulties of running a restaurant. Another student had to write on a class-assigned paper having to do with the environment. Looking around her neighborhood, she noticed many smaller, older homes being torn down, only to be replaced by much larger, new homes that removed existing trees and grass and required more energy to heat and cool. She had found her topic: the teardown epidemic.

How Do I Turn a Topic into a Research Question?

No matter how narrow your topic, you will not write an interesting paper without *a meaningful question that you and your readers will want answered.* Your research question will give you an angle on your topic, something that matters to you.

To turn your topic into a research question, try the following:

- **Use the reporter's questions.** Ask yourself *who, what, where, when, why,* and *how.* On this list, the words most likely to produce a good question are *why* and *how* because these lead to analysis and evaluation. "How did the national debt become so enormous?" is a good example. But do not rule out the other question words because they can also lead to thought-provoking questions like "What personality types are most attracted to social networking sites?"

- **Use critical thinking questions.** Critical thinking is analytical. With x being your topic, you might ask

  - What are the causes of x? (For example, why are rural areas in the United States losing population?)
  - What are the implications or effects of x? (For example, what happens to children's learning when letter grades are abolished?)
  - What larger context or contexts does x belong to? (For example, is graffiti in public places art or vandalism?)
  - What issues are people debating about x? (For example, on the topic of drug wars in Mexico, people are debating the possible entry of United States contract employees to assist the Mexican government. Is this a good idea?)
  - What do most people think about x? How could you question the conventional thinking? (For example, conventional thinking about curing traffic congestion on freeways is to widen them. Is there any evidence that this thinking is wrong?)

- **Look at your topic from different perspectives.** Consider how different groups of people might look at your topic from different angles. On the topic of tearing down houses to build bigger ones: How do developers look at an older neighborhood with small homes, many in dis-

repair, sitting on valuable land? How might a young couple with children who want a large home in a close-in neighborhood? How might members of the neighborhood who want to see their property values go up? Any of these perspectives can furnish an angle on the topic.

Student Example: Turning a Topic into Research Questions

In the case of the student who wanted to write on the topic of teardowns, she could approach research by asking:

- What are the causes of the teardown epidemic?
- Why do people want to replace traditional small homes with giant new ones?
- Why do Americans think they need such large houses?
- How does this change impact the neighborhood?
- Who is hurt by this trend and who gains?
- What is the environmental impact of replacing the smaller houses with bigger ones?

How Do I Manage the Sources I Find?

Once you have your research question, begin gathering sources, assessing their relevance and considering how you might use them. We recommend that you not gather a massive pile of materials to look through later. Instead of one long round of gathering sources, think of this stage as alternating between gathering and reading, note-taking, and reflecting on what you have, and then returning to find more sources as you follow up on leads and questions you encounter. Reading sources as you gather them allows you to develop more interesting research questions and refine your focus. It also helps in developing an understanding of how sources relate to each other and therefore a sense of the big picture you will need to make your own contribution to the topic. Some sources will also direct you to others as you consult the footnotes and bibliographies they provide.

To manage the sources you uncover during this stage, develop a research log, make copies of sources to annotate, and maintain a working bibliography so you can cite sources fully as you draft your project.

Create a Research Log

Keeping track of the sources you consult and the notes you take from them is crucial to avoiding plagiarism and writing a successful research project. Maintaining a research log can help you work more efficiently by making it easier for you to keep track of sources and by helping you to avoid having to retrace your steps.

See Chapter 19, pages 460–62, for help with avoiding accidental plagiarism.

A research log should contain the following:

- Your research question, which you might revise as you move through the research process.
- Ideas and questions that occur to you while browsing and reading.
- Search terms you used, added as you find new terms.
- Notes about catalogs and indexes you searched on any particular day.
- A working bibliography with *complete bibliographical information about each source and notes about what the source contains,* why it is credible and worthy of your and your readers' trust, and how you might use it. See more on working bibliographies on pages 408–11 in this chapter.

Your research log could be a notebook, a computer file, or a series of file folders, or it could be housed online in an electronic source management tool like *Zotero.* You may have folders for different kinds of notes (such as search terms or responses to readings).

Make Copies of Sources

Many sources can be downloaded and stored on your computer. However, we advise that you also print out electronic sources and make photocopies of print sources as well. With paper copies you will be able to read more critically, marking up and annotating the more difficult sources. Making copies also helps you avoid problems when sources are no longer available, as when someone else checks out the book you need or an online source is taken down or moved. Student researchers may also need to submit copies of their sources with their project.

BEST PRACTICES | Storing Copies of Your Sources

1. When photocopying a source, be sure to get all the information you will need later: Avoid cutting off page numbers. Be sure to photocopy not only the chapters or sections of print sources that will help answer your research question but also the title page and copyright pages for books, the front cover or table of contents

for magazines and journals, and the top portion of newspaper pages (where the name of the newspaper, the date of publication, and the edition are located). You will need the information on these portions of your sources in order to cite your source fully and accurately.

2. Clip or staple your printed copies, label them clearly, and keep them in a file folder or binder.

3. For electronic magazine and journal articles, save PDF files, rather than HTML files, whenever possible. PDF files include the source's page numbers and illustrations, which you will need when creating your works cited list (sometimes called a references list or bibliography). HTML files include the text but not the page numbers from the original article. The pages will not match up with the pages of the original.

4. Keep all electronic copies of articles in a file folder; label the files and folders clearly so you know at a glance what it contains. Doing so will save you a good deal of time and trouble later.

5. Bookmark your online sources. Keep a list of websites you want to return to in an Internet browser's Bookmarks or Favorites folders. Make one file for all your bookmarks on a single project. Library databases usually also provide some means for storing links to sources, bibliographic information, and even notes on the source. Check the tools or visit the database vendor's website to learn more. ■

Keep a Working Bibliography

A working bibliography is a list of the publication information for your potential sources, including books, articles, websites, and any other type of source. Keep a separate entry in your working bibliography for each source you might possibly use. The entries in a working bibliography are the same as those in the works cited page or references page that you will eventually include in your final draft. The working bibliography, however, keeps track of all potential sources and all of the sources that you've read regardless of whether you actually use them in the research project itself. It should also include an annotation with notes about the content of the source and your personal responses, such as how you might use the source and how different sources compare or contrast on the same topic or issue.

To save yourself time later on, construct your working bibliography in the appropriate documentation format (see Chapter 20, pages 467–83, for MLA style, and Chapter 21, pages 497–507, for APA style). Doing this will reduce the time and effort required at the end of the project. It will also prevent you from having to track down books and articles you no longer have or search for bibliographic information that you did not know you needed (such as volume numbers or reprint dates).

Citation software like *Zotero* (free on the Web) and *RefWorks* and *EndNote* (sometimes available through your library's webpage or through your school's computer center) can help you format your citations. Be aware, however, that citation software is not perfect. Be sure to check the format against the models in this book or in the style guide you are using in your course before submitting your research project.

Table 15.1 shows the essential information needed for the most common categories of sources.

Annotate Your Working Bibliography

As you skim, evaluate, and read potential sources, annotate your working bibliography by explaining how the source addresses your research question and

Print Sources	Electronic Sources
Book • Author(s), full name • Book title, subtitle • City where published • Publisher • Year published • Medium of publication (Print)	**E-book** • Author(s), full name • Book title, subtitle • City where published • Publisher • Year published • Website title if found online (e.g. *Google Book Search* or *Bartleby.com*) • Date of access • Medium of publication (Web or file format, for example, Kindle e-book file)
Selection from a book or anthology • Author(s), full name • Article or essay title • Book title, subtitle • Editor's name (or editors' names) • City where published • Publisher • Year published • Inclusive page numbers of the article • Medium of publication (Print)	**Selection from an online book or anthology** • Author(s), full name • Article or essay title • Book title, subtitle • Editor's name (or editors' names) • City where published • Publisher • Year published • Inclusive page numbers of the article (if fixed) • Website title if found online (e.g. *Google Book Search* or *Bartleby.com*) • Date of access • Medium of publication (Web or file format, for example, Kindle e-book file)
Magazine article • Author(s), full name • Article title • Title of the periodical • Date of publication (day, month, and year for weekly or biweekly magazines, month and year for monthly magazines) • Page numbers on which article appears • Medium of publication (Print)	**E-zine or online journal article** • Author(s), full name • Article title • Website title (e.g. *TheAtlantic.com, TIME .com*) • Site sponsor (e.g. The Atlantic Monthly Group, Time Inc.; look for this at the bottom of the webpage) • Date of publication (day, month, and year)

TABLE **15.1**

Basic Citation Information for Working Bibliography Entries

TABLE **15.1**
(*continued*)

Print Sources (*continued*)	Electronic Sources (*continued*)
	E-zine or online journal article (*continued*) • Medium of publication (Web) • Name of the database (e.g. Academic OneFile) • Date last accessed • For an article accessed through a database, also include the following: • Name of the database (e.g. Academic OneFile) • Date last accessed
Journal article • Author(s), full name • Article title • Journal title • Volume and issue numbers • Date of publication (year) • Article page numbers (inclusive) • Medium of publication (Print)	**Online journal article** • Author(s), full name • Article title • Journal title • Volume and issue numbers • Date of publication (year) • Article page numbers; use *n.p.* ("no page numbers") if not available or permanent • Medium of publication (Web) • Date last accessed • For an article accessed through a database, add the following: • Name of the database (e.g. Academic OneFile) • Date last accessed
Newspaper article • Author(s), full name, if listed • Article title • Newspaper title (include city name if not included in title) • Date of publication (day, month, and year) • Edition (such as late edition), if specified • Section name or number, if paginated separately • Page numbers on which article appears • Medium of publication (Print)	**Online newspaper article** • Author(s), full name, if listed • Article title • Newspaper website title (e.g. *NYTimes .com, LATimes.com*) • Site sponsor (e.g. The New York Times Company, Los Angeles Times; look for this at the bottom of the webpage) • Date of publication (day, month, and year) • Medium of publication (Web)
	Webpage, website, discussion list, blog • Author(s), full name • Webpage or post title, or subject line (if any) • Title of website, discussion list, or blog • Edition, version (if any) • Site sponsor • Date of publication (day, month, year or whatever is available) • Date last accessed

how you might use the source in your paper. Entries might include the following information:

- ■ **Genre, or Type, of Writing**   Is it, for example, an informational article or an argument, an opinion column or an article in a scholarly journal, a book review or an abstract?

- ■ **Author's Credentials**   Is the author a reporter, a journalist, or a professor? What are the author's areas of expertise, educational background, credentials, and affiliations?

- ■ **Use of Source**   How would you use the source? To answer your research question, provide background information, stimulate thought, represent an alternative viewpoint?

Student Example: Working Bibliography

Below is an example from a student's working bibliography. The research question was: Is there a difference in the experience of reading online versus reading in a printed book?

- · **Author(s):** Not given
- · **Article title:** "Bye Bye Books"
- · **Journal title:** *Wilson Quarterly*
- · **Volume, issue numbers:** 33:2
- · **Publication date (year):** 2009
- · **Article page number(s):** 69
- · **Medium of publication:** Web
- · **Date last accessed:** Aug. 8, 2009
- · **Database:** Academic OneFile

Notes: This unsigned review article in a journal published by Woodrow Wilson International Center for Scholars assesses two essays in other magazines. The essay by Christine Rosen in *The New Atlantis* magazine is relevant to my question. (The other is not—it's about libraries.) The most interesting point is that Rosen thinks that reading printed books and reading online sources are creating two different classes of people, one with book-reading abilities and the other without. The people with only screen-reading abilities have more dopamine, blocking activity in the part of the brain that "controls judgment and measures risk." Both adults and children who read online books wind up becoming more interested in using the technology than in deep reading. I could use this source to argue that the switch is making people less thoughtful. It doesn't have many facts or references about the dopamine studies, but I could go to Rosen's original article for more of her argument. Rosen is a respected writer and editor.

The advice so far should give you an overview of the research process and how it unfolds. In the next chapter, we take you more deeply into the many options for finding good sources.

CHAPTER 16

Finding Sources

ONE OF THE PURPOSES OF A RESEARCHED WRITING PROJECT IS TO INTRODUCE you to the wide array of resources available to anyone who wants to learn more about virtually any topic. An Internet search engine like Google is just one of many resources. Public, college, and government-sponsored libraries and websites offer resources for finding everything from general information to specialized data and scholarly articles. In addition to finding information, you may want to generate your own through interviews, experiments, and observations. This chapter shows you how to stretch your research skills and take advantage of the variety of resources that will help you find not just any sources but the best sources for your project.

How Do I Conduct a Keyword Search?

No matter what kind of index or database you are searching, you will need to think about the words to use. Begin by thinking of *terms that people commonly use to name or describe your topic.* These are known as **keywords** in searching. Keyword searches are good when starting research because databases look for them not only in titles but anywhere in the text of an article.

Develop a List of Keywords as You Find Them

Start generating a list of keywords by examining your research question for words that name and describe your topic. Add words you encounter when reading as well as synonyms or related concepts, and soon you will have a list of words with which to begin. For example, in Chapter 15, we mentioned a student whose topic was the replacement of older homes in her neighborhood by huge new ones. She began her search with the term "teardowns," which she had picked up in neighborhood discussions. She also thought of "neighborhood preservation." As she did preliminary research, she uncovered two more terms she would not have thought of on her own: "McMansions" and "mansionization," which describe the houses built after the tearing down.

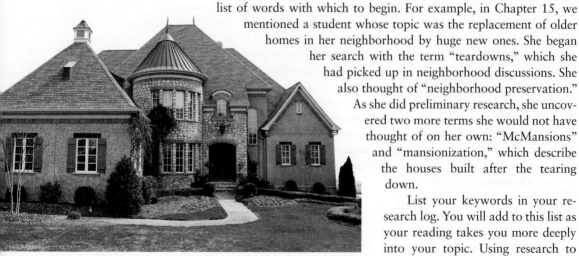

List your keywords in your research log. You will add to this list as your reading takes you more deeply into your topic. Using research to find more keywords is just one example of the ways research is like a branching tree. One good search term leads to more.

See pages 407–11 in Chapter 15 on keeping a research log.

Know How to Narrow or Broaden Your Search

Keywords should be specific to your topic, such as the word "teardowns" in the search described above. If the student had begun her search with a word like "houses" or "neighborhood," she would have found hundreds of irrelevant sources. On the other hand, a term like "McMansion" might be too specific as a starting point and yield few results.

- **Combining Search Terms** Most search engines and library databases use what are called Boolean, or logical, operators to narrow or broaden your search. The operators AND and NOT narrow your search, and the operators OR and the wildcard character—usually an asterisk (*) or a question mark (?)—broaden your search. Table 16.1 shows how these operators work.

- **Advanced Searching** Search engines like Google and online indexes and databases such as those on your library's website offer an advanced search option to help you do more precise searching. In Google, Advanced Search is especially helpful in filtering the vast amounts of material on the Web. By going to the Google Advanced Search screen you can choose webpages by keywords, phrases, and possible alternatives to your keywords. You can also filter out pages with words that you know would be irrelevant to your search, and you can limit the search to certain languages, reading levels,

Search results	Boolean operator	Explanation
	AND	Narrows your search. Use with different concepts. Example: (gas-powered cars) AND (electric-powered cars)
	OR	Broadens your search. Use to search for sources using one or more synonyms. Example: (electric cars) or (fuel cell cars)
	NOT	Narrows your search. Use to eliminate irrelevant material. Example: (gasoline-powered cars) NOT (natural-gas powered cars)
	*	Broadens your search. Use to search multiple versions of a term (photograph, photographs, photographic, photography) simultaneously. Example: Civil War AND photograph*

TABLE **16.1**

Use Boolean Operators to Narrow or Broaden a Search

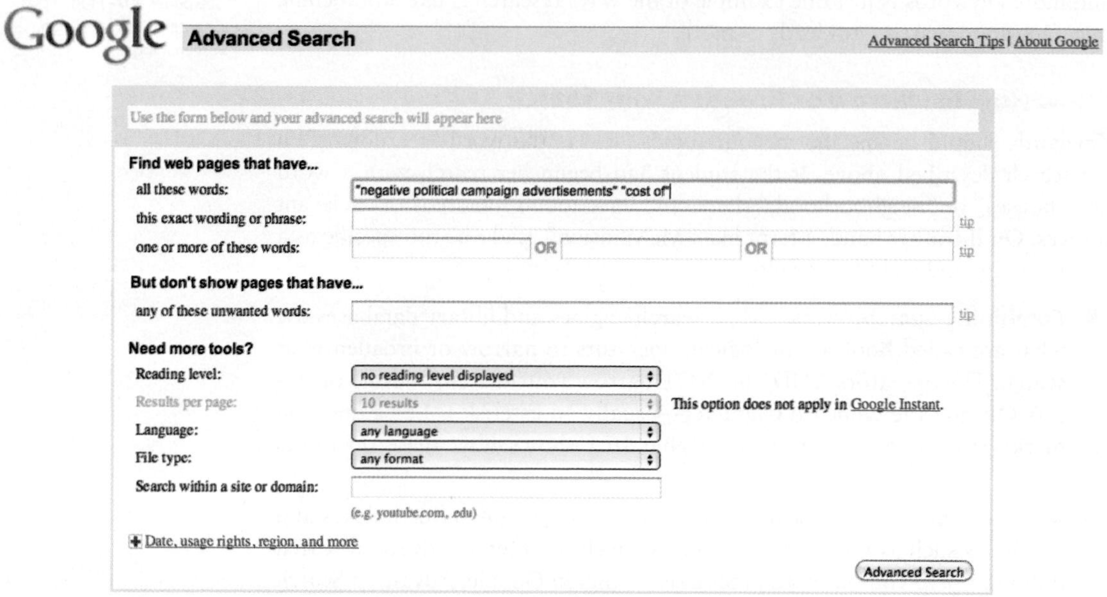

Google **Advanced Search**   Advanced Search Tips | About Google

Use the form below and your advanced search will appear here

Find web pages that have...

all these words: "negative political campaign advertisements" "cost of"

this exact wording or phrase: tip

one or more of these words: OR   OR   tip

But don't show pages that have...

any of these unwanted words: tip

Need more tools?

Reading level: no reading level displayed   ‡

Results per page: 10 results   ‡   This option does not apply in Google Instant.

Language: any language   ‡

File type: any format   ‡

Search within a site or domain:

(e.g. youtube.com, .edu)

➕ Date, usage rights, region, and more

Advanced Search

©2011 Google

FIGURE **16.1**

Advanced Search in Google

> See pages 429–32 in Chapter 17 for more about domains.

websites, or domains. Figure 16.1 shows an example of an advanced search in Google.

The screen above shows a Google Advanced Search narrowed to find sources about the costs of negative political campaign advertisements, eliminating all commercial sites known as "dot com" sites, and written at an intermediate reading level.

Keywords versus Subject Words

Many databases will give you the option of searching by keywords as well as subject words. What is the difference? The subject word option limits the search to the vocabulary preferred by the database; it is less forgiving if you do not know whether the database prefers the word "car" or "automobile," just to give an example. However, most databases provide a thesaurus tool that will direct you to the preferred terms. Once you know the right subject words to search by, the results are going to be good sources, highly relevant to your topic.

What Resources Can I Find through My College Library?

The Internet has not caused libraries and librarians to become extinct. In fact, librarians are more necessary than ever as technology keeps adding to the reserves of information available online.

The library's home page is the gateway to all the resources available to you in print and online, including films, audio recordings, art works, and other me-

FIGURE **16.2**

Example of a College Library Home Page

dia. The example home page in Figure 16.2 gives you an idea of the resources available at one school library; notice the options available under the tab titled "Resources."

How Do I Find Reference Works through My College Library?

To many people, research suggests books, but the library online catalog offers other great resources to inspect before heading across campus to cart home a load of books. For example, consider beginning with **reference works.** Reference works can be books or websites but regardless of the media, *they are compilations of information organized for easy reference.* They are therefore excellent entries into any topic. Too often, students overlook reference works or are unaware of their existence, except for the common encyclopedias.

General Reference Works

Before digging into more detailed books and articles, you can get entry-level knowledge on a topic through general reference works such as encyclopedias, dictionaries, and almanacs. Some examples of general reference works are

> *Oxford English Dictionary*
> *The World Almanac and Book of Facts*
> *Encyclopædia Britannica*
> *Wikipedia*

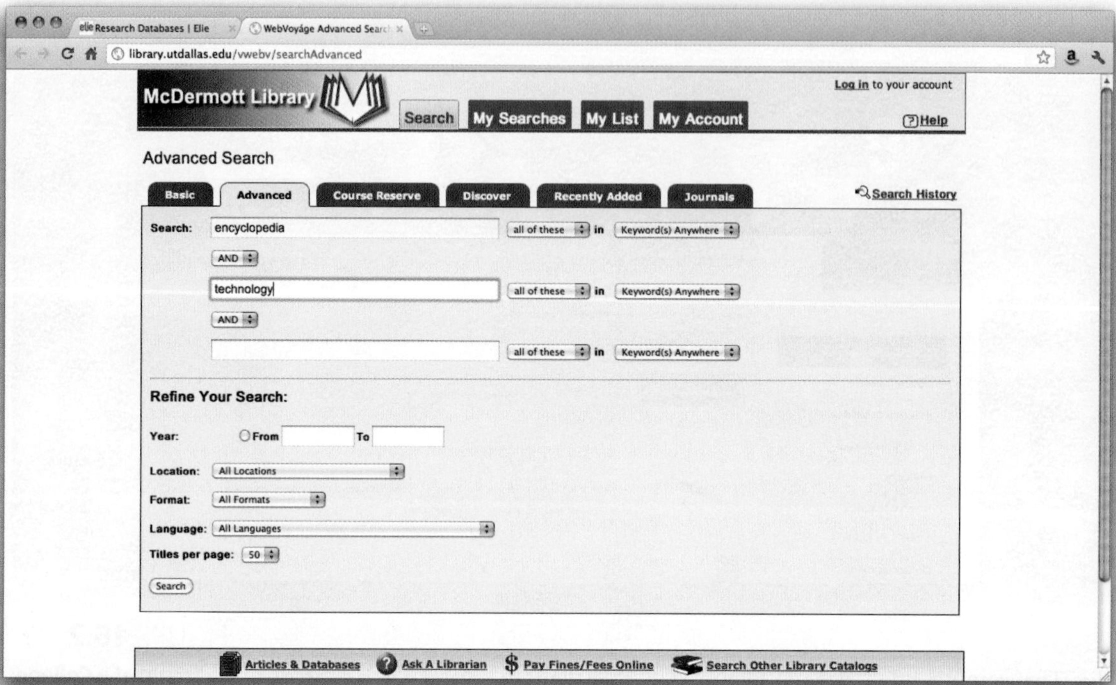

FIGURE **16.3**

Example of a Search for a Specialized Encyclopedia

Many professors prefer that you use general reference works only as starting points for increasing your background knowledge about a topic. General reference works are seldom cited in college writing because the information there is **common knowledge**. That does not mean that everyone knows it; common knowledge is technically defined as *information easily available to anyone from at least three sources*. In the case of *Wikipedia,* many professors advise students to double-check its information because, although it is usually accurate, it is a group-sourced work to which anyone can contribute. For more about *Wikipedia,* see Chapter 17, Evaluating Sources, pages 426–32.

Specialized Reference Works

In contrast to general reference works, libraries also offer more specialized reference works, and these are excellent sources for college papers. You can find them on a wide range of topics, as is evident from these sample titles: *The Almanac of New York City, Encyclopedia of 20th-Century American Humor,* and *Encyclopedia of Multimedia Technology and Networking.* Many are available online through the library, and those that are in print are easy to find. Reference books do not circulate, so you can count on finding them on the shelf.

To find them, do an advanced search in the library's online catalog. As illustrated in Figure 16.3, simply combine your keyword or words with the term "dictionary," "encyclopedia," "atlas," or "almanac" to find these works online or in your library.

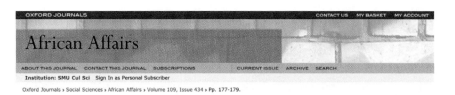

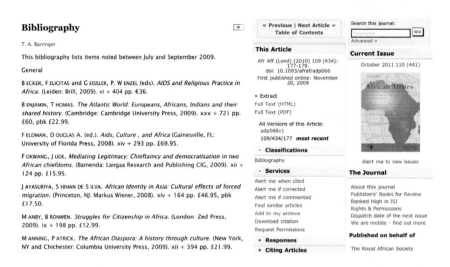

FIGURE **16.4**

Example of an Online Bibliography

Bibliographies

Bibliographies are lists of sources on a topic. You can often find them in the back of books, where authors list works they have consulted or that other readers may wish to consult to get more information. You can also search for bibliographies in your library's catalog using the method described above for specialized encyclopedias, or ask your librarian if there are research guides on the subject of your research. Many will be bound books, but increasingly bibliographies are available online, as in Figure 16.4.

How Do I Use a Library Catalog to Find Books and Other Resources?

Your library's home page will have a link to the library catalog, which is an index of all the library's holdings in all media: print, film, digital, and so on. The home page in Figure 16.5 shows what you can expect to find.

Two main categories of resources are books and audiovisual materials.

- **Books**   You can search for books by subject, author name, title, keyword, and call number, as shown in the advanced search screen in Figure 16.6.

- **Audiovisual Materials**   Audiovisual materials are also found through the catalog and sometimes through a link on the library home page.

FIGURE **16.5**

Example of a Quick Search in a Library Catalog

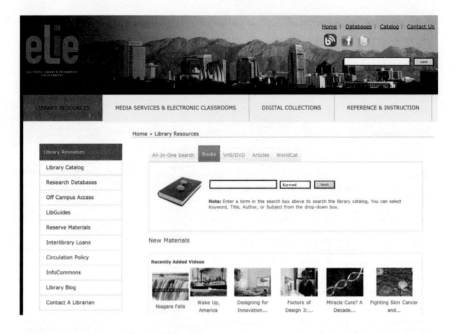

FIGURE **16.6**

Example of an Advanced Library Search

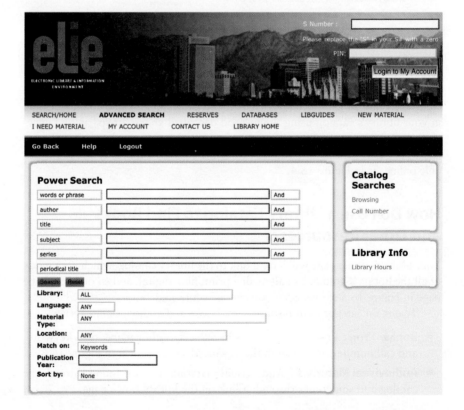

How Do I Use Library Databases to Find Periodicals?

A periodical is any publication that appears on a regular schedule. Newspapers are usually published daily, magazines weekly or monthly, and scholarly journals quarterly. While you can find periodicals through a Web search, the best route to finding reliable articles is through your library's online databases, which are typically accessed through the library's home page. Look for a link under categories like "Find," "Search," or "Research," or look for labels like "articles," "databases," "e-resources," or "online resources."

Thousands of databases are available to researchers, and libraries subscribe to a range, both general and subject-specific. Some of the most popular databases are listed in Table 16.2.

A library's databases will often be listed alphabetically, by title and by subject area, and by popularity. Other search options may also be available, as illustrated below.

Anatomy of a Database Search

Finding articles in subscription databases is a multistep process.

Step 1: Search. Choose one of the databases, and type your keywords in the search field. Advanced search options allow you to narrow or broaden a search. (See Table 16.1 to learn more about Boolean searching.) In a hypothetical search, we wanted to find out if reading literature made people more empathetic. In an advanced search of Academic Search Complete, we

Database	Useful for accessing...
Academic OneFile	Articles in both popular and scholarly periodicals for a broad range of disciplines
Academic Search Complete	Articles in both popular and scholarly periodicals for a broad range of disciplines
LexisNexis Academic	Articles from newspapers around the world
ERIC (Education Resources Information Center)	Resources on education from a wide range of sources
JSTOR	Indexes more than 1,000 academic journals and more than 1 million images, letters, and other primary sources, most of them in the humanities and social sciences
MLA International Bibliography	Indexes articles on topics in literature and languages
ProQuest	Indexes a mix of scholarly journals, trade publications, magazines, and newspapers
PsycARTICLES	Articles on topics in psychology
Web of Science	Articles on topics in the sciences

TABLE **16.2**

Popular Library Databases

FIGURE **16.7**

Example of Results of an Advanced Search

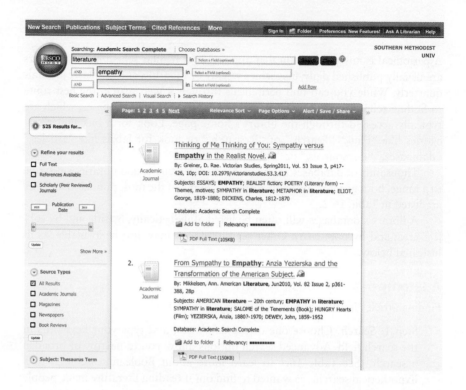

combined the keywords "reading" and "empathy" to get the results shown in Figure 16.7.

Step 2: Survey the results of your search. Figure 16.7 shows some of the titles this search turned up. Some things to note are

Details of the search query appear at the top of the page.

Each entry tells you if the article is available in full text online, and if so, whether in HTML or PDF files.

Results may be filtered further by publication type or by date.

Step 3: Open and examine the entries. Click on a title to find out more about that source. A typical article entry will include useful information such as an abstract of the article and links to related subjects (see Figure 16.8).

How Do I Use the Web to Find Reliable Websites and Online Journals?

The Internet provides access to a vast and ever-changing assortment of files: commercial advertising, personal webpages and blogs, newspapers and magazines, videos and podcasts, images, archives, university projects, government documents, and on and on. In short, the Internet is an unfiltered mass of information.

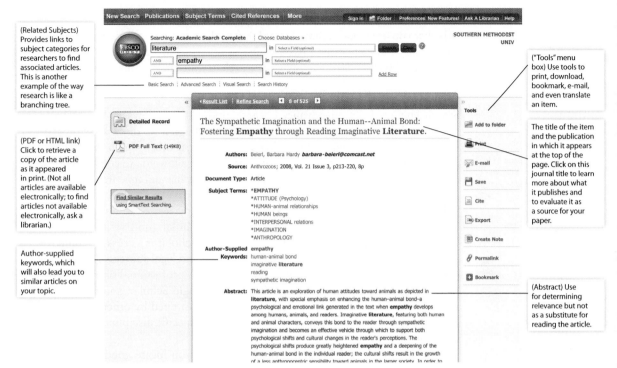

(Related Subjects) Provides links to subject categories for researchers to find associated articles. This is another example of the way research is like a branching tree.

(PDF or HTML link) Click to retrieve a copy of the article as it appeared in print. (Not all articles are available electronically; to find articles not available electronically, ask a librarian.)

Author-supplied keywords, which will also lead you to similar articles on your topic.

("Tools" menu box) Use tools to print, download, bookmark, e-mail, and even translate an item.

The title of the item and the publication in which it appears at the top of the page. Click on this journal title to learn more about what it publishes and to evaluate it as a source for your paper.

(Abstract) Use for determining relevance but not as a substitute for reading the article.

FIGURE **16.8**

Example of an Article Entry

However, it can be an excellent source of free, high-quality information if you know how to use the search engines efficiently and assess the reliability of your results carefully.

CONCEPT CLOSE-UP | Why Care Is Needed in Internet Searching

While the Internet is a great resource, researchers should see it as a complement to the library rather than a substitute, for several reasons:

See the criteria for evaluating websites in Chapter 17, pages 429–32.

- Because anyone can publish online, Web sources must be assessed carefully.

- The quantity of information can be overwhelming. The Internet is so large—estimated to contain more than 11 billion webpages—that one can easily waste valuable time sifting through the mass.[1]

- Many excellent sources are available for free through libraries, but you may have to pay to access them on the Internet. ■

1. de Kunder, Maurice. "The Size of the World Wide Web (The Internet). *WorldWideWebSize.com*. N.p., 25 Oct. 2011. Web. 25 Oct. 2011. <http://www.worldwidewebsize.com/>.

Use Web-Based Databases and Search Engines

Whether you use Google, Bing, Yahoo!, Exalead, or another online search engine, an ordinary Internet search casts a wide net, often yielding an overwhelming list of unfiltered websites. To narrow your search, try the suggestions below.

Advanced Search Options

See Figure 14.1, page 414, for an example of a Google Advanced Search.

Search engines have an advanced search option that allows you to narrow your search by combining terms. Earlier in this chapter, we discussed how Advanced Search in Google helps refine a search. Most other search engines and databases offer similar advanced search options that allow you to combine terms, search by author, and limit your results to specific media and time frames.

Scholarly Searches on the Internet

Some databases on the Internet, such as Google Scholar and INFOMINE, specialize in indexing scholarly publications. Google Scholar is a cross-disciplinary index to journal articles, theses, books, abstracts, and legal sources. The sources are highly credible, coming from academic presses, professional organizations, research centers, and university websites. In Google Scholar, sources are arranged in descending order according to those most cited by other academics. INFOMINE allows you to narrow your search to specific disciplines from a list on its home page.

While Google Scholar and INFOMINE help you locate good sources, be aware that not all the results of your search will be available for free. Many scholarly journals require that you subscribe or pay a onetime fee for single articles. However, if you are enrolled at a school that subscribes to the journal or publishing house, you will have free full-text access through your school library. Many library online resources pages contain a link to Google Scholar so students can use it to search their own library's resources.

Online Periodicals (Newspapers, Journals, and Magazines Not Published in Print)

Articles in some scholarly journals, such as *Kairos: A Journal of Rhetoric, Technology, and Pedagogy,* and magazines, such as *Slate* (www.slate.com), are "born digital" (online only). As such, these sources are not usually listed in library databases. However, you can find a good index to online periodicals at the Internet Public Library at http://www.ipl.org/div/subject/.

Audiovisual and Archived Materials

Resources available online include the following:

■ **Smithsonian Institution** (http://www.si.edu/researchcenters/). This is a searchable website of the Smithsonian's holdings, museums, encyclopedia, and research projects. You can find podcasts at the Smithsonian Institution site at http://www.si.edu/podcasts/.

- **Library of Congress** (http://www.loc.gov). This is also a searchable website. Go to http://www.loc.gov/library/libarch-digital.html to search the digital collections.

Online Reference Works and Bibliographies

You can find some specialized reference works available free online by searching in the same way we advised searching your library's catalog. In a Google Advanced Search, for example, you could type "encyclopedia" and one or more of your keywords.

An excellent source of online bibliographies is available through the Library of Congress website at http://www.loc.gov/rr/program/bib/bibhome.html.

How Do I Find Interactive Online Sources?

Many intelligent discussions take place on blogs, e-mail discussion groups, podcasts, and comment threads in online journals. Online communication can provide you with timely and stimulating debate on a topic. Although the style of this writing is less formal than in published work, these writers often have professional credentials and may be considered experts in their field. Always evaluate interactive sources carefully, however; sources in which anyone can join the conversation or in which participants remain anonymous are unlikely to be reliable. Below is a list of source types that may be useful in a college research project:

- **E-mail Discussion Lists** People subscribe to these lists to participate in conversations on topics of interest. For a good list of groups in the humanities and social sciences, go to H-Net: http://www.h-net.org/lists/.

- **Blogs** For academic blogs in the humanities, social sciences, sciences, and many other disciplines and subject areas, go to: http://www.academicblogs .net/wiki/index.php/Main_Page. Nearly all online versions of newspapers have opinion blogs by their columnists. You can also Google respected authors and scholars to see if they publish a blog by inserting the author's name (in quotation marks) and adding the word "blog."

How Do I Generate My Own Information?

Sometimes a research question will take you out of the library and into the world—into "the field" as researchers call it—to observe some aspect of the world around us: people and other living things, places, nature, buildings, social behavior, institutions, media, and anything that can be observed, measured, drawn, recorded, photographed, or filmed.

The need for field research arises when a researcher simply cannot answer her or his research question with existing sources. Perhaps the research question involves traffic flow in a village center, but the city has collected no traffic data.

Or, the question examines employee responses to changes in health care coverage, but no one has surveyed the workers yet. In such cases, the researcher may need to perform his or her own field research.

The methods for performing field research depend upon the researcher's question and the type of information available to answer that question. Can the information be observed? A researcher could observe and record information about traffic flow in a village center. Can the information be collected? In the case of employee responses to changes in health care coverage, the researcher might conduct surveys or even interview individuals.

Field research is a time-consuming and challenging venture. For example, how many days of traffic would the researcher need to observe—or how many employees would need to be surveyed—before readers would consider the field research complete and accurate? Guidance about research methodology is beyond the scope of this chapter, but it should be required reading for those planning a serious field research project. We offer some brief advice about conducting observations, surveys, and interviews.

Observational Studies

Depending on your topic, firsthand observations can be useful in developing a response to your research question.

Earlier, we described one student's research topic, the tearing down of old homes and their replacement with newer, larger ones. To do research for the project, the student walked the streets of her own neighborhood, noting specifics and taking photographs. More dramatically, a writer can observe undercover, like the anthropologist who posed (with the university's approval) as "Rebekah Nathan," a first-year student living in the dorms and attending classes. Her book, *My Freshman Year* (Cornell UP 2005), aims to give professors an understanding of college from the students' perspective.

Surveys

You may be able to get information on some topics, especially if they are local or campus related, by doing a survey. Be forewarned, however, that it is difficult to conduct a reliable survey questionnaire. First, there is the problem of designing a clear and unbiased survey instrument. If you have ever filled out an evaluation form for an instructor or a course, you know how problems of clarity can arise. An evaluation might ask whether an instructor returns papers "in a reasonable length of time"; what is "reasonable" to some students may be too long for others.

Second, there is the problem of getting a representative response, that is, a response that represents the whole group the survey is intended to represent. A survey of undergraduates taken

This photograph illustrates part of an experiment conducted through Massachusetts Institute of Technology that began when one woman in Seattle asked the question: "Where does my trash go when I toss it out?" Students attached electronic transmitters to trash in order to trace its journey to its ultimate destination.

at the entrance to the library in the evening might have vastly different results from one taken at the gym in the afternoon.

Surveys can be useful, but seek additional advice on how to design and administer them. You might consult a book like T. L. Brink's *Questionnaires: Practical Hints on How to Avoid Mistakes in Design and Interpretation* (Heuristic Books 2004.)

Interviews

Depending on your topic and research question, personal interviews can be a wonderful source of information. Many people in your community, in your workplace, or at your school are experts on specific topics—from city leaders, to environmental activists, to bank presidents. Most will happily share what they know.

Interviews require time from people's often busy schedules, so it is only polite to ask well in advance for their participation, explain what you will be asking them, and give them an estimate of how much of their time you will need. Once you have determined possible sources, begin a courteous round of phone calls and carefully composed e-mails, continuing until you connect with the right person. If necessary, let the person know that you are willing to conduct the interview by e-mail or phone as well as face-to-face.

Prepare for the interview by having questions ready; if you want to record it, be sure to gain permission. Begin the interview by acknowledging the value of the person's time. Tell the person about your research project but withhold your own position on controversial matters. Take careful and complete notes, including the spelling of the person's name as well as the person's title and credentials. Later, follow up with a thank-you note or e-mail. If multiple people in your class are researching the same topic, avoid flooding any one person with requests for interviews. One or two students could conduct the interview and report to the class, or the interview could take place in the class either in person or through live chat or video.

For more about how to do interviews, see Chapter 5, Creating Profiles, pages 88–115.

We suggest that you evaluate sources, covered in Chapter 17, as you do your research rather than making evaluation a separate step. You might spend a day gathering possible sources, and then, before going on to more databases and indexes, look over the ones you have at hand. Evaluating can be as simple as checking a website's home page for information about the credibility of its author or sponsor, or it can be a more time-consuming process of skimming or reading an article or book. Considering the credibility, focus, and angle of the sources you find will help you decide if they are a good fit with your proposed research question and the scope of your project.

CHAPTER 17

Evaluating Sources

OF THE HUNDREDS OF POTENTIAL SOURCES THAT TURN UP IN A SEARCH, how do you select the ones that will be the best for your project? This is an important question because, like a gourmet dish, your paper will be only as good as the ingredients that go into it. Asking two questions will help you make smart choices: (1) How useful will a source be in helping me achieve my purpose for writing? (2) How credible or reliable are the contents of the source? These two questions are equally important. Although we take them up separately here, you should have both of them in mind as you inspect each possible source.

How Do I Decide If a Source Is Useful?

For a source to be useful, it has to fit well with your topic and purpose. The contents need to be relevant to your research question. You cannot always make that determination from the title alone, but there are other ways to predict usefulness. If an article abstract is available, read it; if one is not, skim the article for subheadings or major subdivisions of the content. For a book, read the introduction, preface, or book jacket; skim the index at the back to see what topics are covered. If a book looks promising, you might want to read a couple of reviews to find more about its coverage and the author's angle on your topic.

Below are a few more questions to ask yourself for determining the usefulness of a source.

- **Is the source's angle on your topic a good fit for your purposes?** For example, a search on the topic of bullying in schools might turn up articles on specific kinds, such as bullying of children with autism or bullying of immigrants. You may decide that you want to take your research in that direction, but be aware that doing so may make other sources you already have irrelevant to the new angle. Also, many databases and search engines will turn up articles and websites from foreign countries. Research from and about foreign countries may or may not be relevant to your topic. The point is: Be aware and make an informed decision.

- **Does the source offer the kinds of information you need in order to accomplish your purpose?** Do you need case studies, experts' analyses of a situation, or arguments on an issue? Do you need statistics or other kinds of data? How in-depth is the information? Does the source go beyond the level of what is considered common knowledge—that is, information readily available from multiple other sources? For any source that looks promising, do a preliminary reading and take some notes about how and where it could contribute to your research project.

- **If your topic requires up-to-date information and expert opinions, is the source current enough?** There is no "date of expiration" on a source, and you may want to use a classic or historic work, but if your topic needs recent sources, do enough research to find them before settling on a source that may no longer be relevant.

- **Is the source a good fit with your ability, not just to read but to read critically on your chosen topic?** Sources for college research projects should be challenging, but if a source is so specialized or technical that you have to skip over parts of it, you may not be able to write confidently and clearly about the ideas and information in it. Titles can often clue you to levels of difficulty. For example a database search for articles on school bullying turned up a title that contained the phrase "longitudinal consequences of adolescent bullying perpetration." If a title contains unfamiliar concepts, chances are the article will too.

See Chapter 2, pages 13–16 for an explanation of critical reading.

How Do I Decide If a Source Is Reliable?

The reliability of a source is as important as its usefulness. A source that your readers will not respect and find credible is not a useful one. A reliable source will provide you with credible information, authoritative opinions, and responsible research.

Journals and books that are published by universities can usually be assumed to be reliable. If a book or journal is published by a university press, it has gone through a process known as "peer review," which means it has been critiqued and approved by other scholars working on the topic. You may trust that the books and journals available through your college or university library are credible because they have been selected by librarians and professors.

However, you will also find many sources from publications more broadly available to the public, such as books from popular presses, magazines, and materials on the Internet. Making responsible choices from these more popular sources requires careful scrutiny and critical thinking. For any source, the following questions will help you decide if you should use it.

Who Is the Author?

Information about the author is one of the best clues to a source's credibility. Whether your source is a book, an article, or a website, you should be able to find some information about the author's credentials, such as

- Educational background, advanced degrees
- Professional affiliations, honors, and awards
- Other publications

Information about the author should not be difficult to find. It is usually printed as a headnote or footnote in articles and in the back pages of books and anthologies. For Internet sites, a tab titled "About Me" or "Biography" provides

a link to this important information. Consider whether the person's education and affiliations would indicate that he or she is an authority on the subject. Be suspicious if you cannot find information about an author on the source itself.

If the author is a journalist rather than a scholar or professional in the field of your research, you should consider the credibility of the publication itself, as described below.

Who Published the Source?

Every book, periodical, primary source, and website has a person or organization responsible for its existence. That person or group may be a university press, a government agency, or an organization with an agenda to push or a product to sell. Sometimes a publisher's goals might conflict with the purported topic in a way that may lessen the credibility of the information. To determine credibility of publishers, ask the following questions:

- **Is the publisher well-recognized and respected, such as a major city's newspaper or a newspaper with nationwide circulation?** For books, is the publisher an established house or has the author self-published the book? If so, you need to look further into his or her credentials.

- **Who is the sponsor behind the publication?** Is it an institution, like the Smithsonian? Is it an independent research center or a university?

- **Does the publication list its editorial board, including members' credentials?**

- **What other types of articles or other authors does this publisher publish?**

- **What is the purpose or goal of the publication?** You can often find the mission statement of magazines and newspapers near the masthead inside, and websites also provide descriptions of their purpose through an "About" link on the home page. If you are using a library database like *Academic Search Complete*, the journal or magazine title in the detailed record is a link that takes you to information about the publication, including bias, audience, and topics typically covered.

How Recent Is the Source?

We mentioned this criterion earlier in the chapter, but the date of a source's publication is as important to its credibility as it is to its usefulness. Especially in the social science and science disciplines, information that is more than five years old may well be outdated by more recent research. Although older sources may provide a history of the subject, more recent sources provide more credible information.

How Good Are the Source's Sources?

Just as your instructor expects you to provide documentation for information in your writing, you can expect to find documentation in your sources. When a source includes facts, information, statistics, or quotations, the author should tell you where that information came from. Naming one's sources gives scholarly credibility to work and helps readers in their own research, a professional courtesy. Even if a source does not include footnotes, endnotes, or a list of works cited, you should find specific references to books, articles, and experts woven into the body of the writing.

Will Your Readers Find the Source Authoritative?

Your search may turn up books, articles, and websites aimed at readers of high school age or younger. The information may be perfectly correct, but in making the topic accessible, writers may provide a simplified, less specific treatment than they would give to an older readership.

Clues to audience are the level of vocabulary and specialized terminology as well as visual elements such as graphics. In Figure 17.1, the titles, links, and visuals should clue you to the fact that this government website on bullying is aimed at adolescents and younger readers.

The website on bullying from Hunter College (see Figure 17.2) has a more professional and academic appearance that signals it is a more appropriate choice for college-level research. For more help with evaluating websites, see the following Best Practices.

BEST PRACTICES | Evaluating Websites

No one oversees the reliability or truth of material posted on the Web. Anyone can post almost anything, so users have to take the responsibility for assessing credibility unless the source is a digital version of a reliable print source. All of the questions listed above are relevant to evaluating both print and online sources; however, the questions below are specific to evaluating websites.

What Is the Domain Name Extension?

You can use a website's URL (Uniform Resource Locator) to help you judge reliability. Every URL ends with a period followed by an abbreviation indicating its domain. Some of the more common domain types are:

- **Commercial (.com and .net).** "Dot com" and "dot net" sites include businesses and their publications and other commercial publications. Magazines on the Web usually are "dot com" sites, as are many personal webpages and blogs.

FIGURE **17.1**

Government Website
Dedicated to Prevention of
Bullying

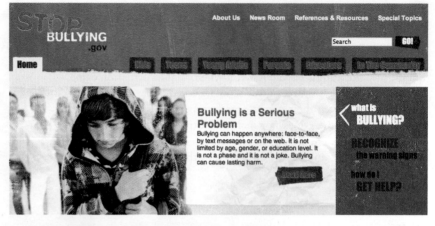

Cyberbullying
Bullying does not just happen face-to-face.
Students and young adults may also struggle
with hurtful or embarrassing messages via text

Webisodes for Kids
Watch the webisodes to find out how KB, Milton,
Josh, and their friends are taking a stand
against bullying. Get ideas for things you can do

LGBT Bullying
If you experience bullying or violence because
you are lesbian, gay, bisexual or transgender
(LGBT) youth, or others think you are, there are

FIGURE **17.2**

College Website with
Resources to Prevent
Bullying

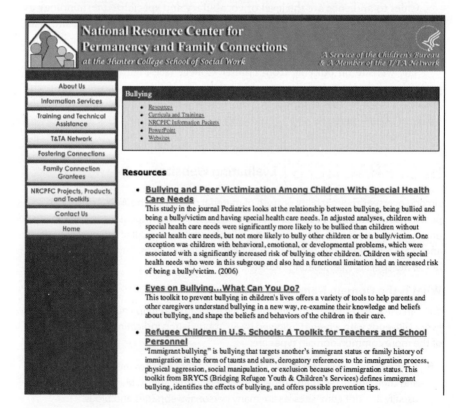

National Resource Center for Permanency and Family Connections
at the Hunter College School of Social Work

A Service of the Children's Bureau & A Member of the T/TA Network

About Us

Information Services

Training and Technical
Assistance

T&TA Network

Fostering Connections

Family Connection
Grantees

NRCPFC Projects, Products,
and Toolkits

Contact Us

Home

Bullying
- Resources
- Curricula and Trainings
- NRCPFC Information Packets
- PowerPoint
- Websites

Resources

- **Bullying and Peer Victimization Among Children With Special Health Care Needs**
  This study in the journal Pediatrics looks at the relationship between bullying, being bullied and being a bully/victim and having special health care needs. In adjusted analyses, children with special health care needs were significantly more likely to be bullied than children without special health care needs, but not more likely to bully other children or be a bully/victim. One exception was children with behavioral, emotional, or developmental problems, which were associated with a significantly increased risk of bullying other children. Children with special health needs who were in this subgroup and also had a functional limitation had an increased risk of being a bully/victim. (2006)

- **Eyes on Bullying...What Can You Do?**
  This toolkit to prevent bullying in children's lives offers a variety of tools to help parents and other caregivers understand bullying in a new way, re-examine their knowledge and beliefs about bullying, and shape the beliefs and behaviors of the children in their care.

- **Refugee Children in U.S. Schools: A Toolkit for Teachers and School Personnel**
  "Immigrant bullying" is bullying that targets another's immigrant status or family history of immigration in the form of taunts and slurs, derogatory references to the immigration process, physical aggression, social manipulation, or exclusion because of immigration status. This toolkit from BRYCS (Bridging Refugee Youth & Children's Services) defines immigrant bullying, identifies the effects of bullying, and offers possible prevention tips.

- **Nonprofit Organizations (.org)** Most nonprofit organizations use the "dot org" extension. These organizations include charities and advocacy groups, such as Autism Speaks (www.autismspeaks.org), which supports research, fundraising, and general awareness of the facts about autism. Be aware, though, that use of the "dot org" extension is open to anyone. On its own, the fact that a website ends in .org does not guarantee that the site is operated by a nonprofit organization or that it is reliable.

- **Educational institutions (.edu).** These are associated with schools, colleges, and universities, including the pages and e-mails of individuals associated with these institutions.

- **Government Agencies (.gov and .mil).** These sites are useful for getting the latest information about any aspect of American government and its agencies, such as the military.

- **Foreign countries (such as .ca or .uk).** These examples are the abbreviations for Canada and United Kingdom sites, but all countries outside the USA have URLs ending in an abbreviation for the name of the country.

In general, sources located on educational (.edu) and government (.gov or .mil) sites are most likely to be reliable. However, an article posted on a website ending in .edu could be the paper of a first-year student or even a student in high school, so you always need to look further into the source. Sources with other domain name extensions, such as .org, .com, .net, or .biz, should be carefully evaluated to determine if they are credible.

Who Is the Publisher of the Website?

A website that serves as the official online presence of a reputable commercial or nonprofit organization is also likely to be reliable. You will need to use critical thinking and reading skills to determine which websites are legitimate. One way to verify that the website is legitimate and reliable is to consider how you arrived at the URL; being directed to a website by a source you already trust indicates that the site is reliable. For example, if *The New York Times* publishes the URL for a company in an article, that's an indication that the website is official and credible. Printed material produced by an organization will also usually include the URL of the organization's website.

The definitive way to determine whether the site is the official arm of the entity it purports to represent is to perform a WHOIS Lookup on the domain and verify that the registration information is real contact information for the organization. Go to http://www.whois.net and enter the domain name in the WHOIS Lookup box. You can verify that the contact information returned by the lookup corresponds to the organization's real contact information by using phone books or other directories. Be wary of any site for which information about the registered owner is not available.

What Is the Purpose or Agenda of the Website?

Websites of reputable institutions and organizations will provide information about the sponsoring person, organization, or body, as well as their mission and funding, on a page with a name like "About Us," "Philosophy," or "Biography." Links to these pages should be available on the home page, which is usually easily accessible by a link on every page on the site.

Do Authors Have Appropriate Credentials?

If articles on a website are signed, check to see if the author has credentials that would ensure he or she has some authority on the topic. If the article is unsigned, the credibility rests on that of the publisher.

Has the Website Been Updated Recently?

Look for the date of the most recent update, commonly located at the bottom of the page. If no one has updated a website in more than a year, it may be abandoned or at least neglected. Avoid websites that offer undated information.

Has the Author Cited Sources for His or Her Information?

Has the author documented his or her sources with links or with footnotes and a works cited or references list? If there are links, do they work? Do the links take you to high-quality sources?

Is the Website Possibly a Hoax?

It is always possible that on the face of things, a website will appear legitimate but actually be satirical or deceitful (See Figure 17.3). You should not be fooled if you have carefully answered the above questions and used some common sense. Having a slightly skeptical attitude is good insurance against fraud. ■

FIGURE **17.3**

This hoax website fooled at least one professional writer who included it as a legitimate source. What clues you that it is satire?

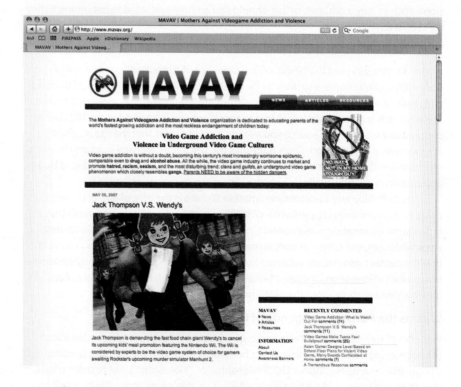

CHAPTER 18

Incorporating Source Materials

SOURCE MATERIALS ARE INTEGRAL TO RESEARCHED WRITING. READING sources generates questions, helps you find an angle, and gives you information and ideas for developing your paper. While some sources will make major contributions and others play lesser roles, all the sources taken together form a foundation for writing with your own voice and purpose. As you read about your topic, a big picture starts to take shape, and your knowledge and confidence grow. Eventually, you are ready to enter the conversation, asserting your own thesis and bringing in sources to develop and support it.

What Does It Mean to Enter the Conversation?

Beginning research is like entering a conversation on your topic. When you write using sources, you join a conversation that includes ideas from the sources you cite, your interpretation of what these other voices are saying, your presentation of your own views, and the responses of people who read your completed paper.

BEST PRACTICES | Read While You Research

Take time to read *while* you research. Reading is a part of research, not something you do after you have gathered up a stack of sources. The following are good reasons to read the sources as you find them:

1. One good source leads to another. Writers will refer to others who have written on your topic. You will find these references in the body of a reading and/or in a bibliography at the end.
2. You will gradually learn the angles and range of opinions on your topic, so when it is time for you to form your own thesis, you will be operating with full knowledge of the conversation already out there.
3. You will be able to compare the sources, deciding which have the best information and arguments to use in your paper. ■

Reading while you research can start lightly with skimming, getting a quick overview of the genre, author, and angle of each potential source. Following are some questions you could ask while skimming, or previewing, sources. Chapter 2 (pages 13–37) gives you more information about how to preview sources and how to read them critically if you decide to use them in your writing.

ASKING QUESTIONS | Previewing a Source

In deciding whether and how to use a source, the most important questions are the following:

1. What is the genre (kind of writing) of this source? For example, is the source an informative and relatively objective entry in a reference book, or is it an argument in an academic or popular journal? Is it an article in a magazine?

2. Who is the author of this source? Is the author an important figure with expertise on your topic?

3. What is the focus, purpose, and angle of this source, and what is its bias? After skimming the source, think about how the author's angle compares with that of other sources you have found or your own angle on the topic, if you have formed one.

4. How might you use this source? Does it contain good facts and data? Does it analyze or explain information? Does it cite experts you could use to support a point? ■

How Does Informal Writing Engage Me in the Conversation?

When you are involved in an oral conversation, you listen to what others have to say, you respond, and you ask questions. In much the same way, while you are reading, you should not simply read to hear what a writer is saying, but think about it, respond to it, and question it. Writing informally helps you engage with sources by preserving your responses and questions before, during, and after you read.

How Do I Annotate to Engage with a Source?

Annotating means taking notes on the source itself—in the margins, between the lines, or on sticky notes if you prefer not to mark up your copy. Annotating supports critical reading, as explained in Chapter 2, pages 21–22. When annotating, you interact with the source, firming up your understanding of what it says as well as what it implies. Students who mark up their sources have better comprehension than those who don't and therefore are able to use sources more competently.

Annotations support research by helping form the big picture of the conversation on your topic, especially if you mark up passages with notes about how author "X" compares with authors "Y" and "Z" on similar points. Annotations can point to places in a text that offer leads to other sources you might want to consult.

The reading that follows is a newspaper article on the topic of fast versus slow reading. Informative newspaper articles are good starting points for research because they present new research in an accessible style and they name people who have written on your topic, thus providing you with leads for further research.

Our annotations show common kinds of notes readers make in the margins to help make good use of a source.

> The full text of Newkirk's argument can be found online at http://www
> .ascd.org/publications/
> educational-leadership/
> mar10/vol67/num06/The
> -Case-for-Slow-Reading.aspx.

READING 18.1

New Hampshire Professor Pushes for Return to Slow Reading

HOLLY RAMER

> Holly Ramer is a writer for Associated Press news service. This article appeared in several major newspapers in June 2010.

Slow readers of the world, uuuuuuuu...niiiiite!   1

At a time when people spend much of their time skimming websites, text   2
messages and e-mails, an English professor at the University of New Hampshire is making the case for slowing down as a way to gain more meaning and pleasure out of the written word.

Thomas Newkirk isn't the first or most prominent proponent of the so-called "slow   3
reading" movement, but he argues it's becoming all the more important in a culture and educational system that often treats reading as fast food to be gobbled up as quickly as possible.

Look for the article by Newkirk.

"You see schools where reading is turned into a race, you see kids on the stopwatch   4
to see how many words they can read in a minute," he said. "That tells students a story about what reading is. It tells students to be fast is to be good."

This is quotable.

Newkirk is encouraging schools from elementary through college to return to   5
old strategies such as reading aloud and memorization as a way to help students truly "taste" the words. He uses those techniques in his own classroom, where students have told him that they've become so accustomed to flitting from page to page online that they have trouble concentrating while reading printed books.

"One student told me even when he was reading a regular book, he'd come to a   6
word and it would almost act like a hyper link. It would just send his mind off to some other thing," Newkirk said. "I think they recognize they're missing out on something."

The idea is not to read everything as slowly as possible, however. As with the slow food movement, the goal is a closer connection between readers and their information, said John Miedema, whose 2009 book "Slow Reading" explores the movement. 7

Look for this book by Miedema.

Important: Clarifies definition of slow reading. Also, the last part is quotable.

"It's not just about students reading as slowly as possible," he said. "To me, slow reading is about bringing more of the person to bear on the book." 8

Miedema, a technology specialist at IBM in Ottawa, Ontario, said little formal research has been done on slow reading, other than studies on physical conditions such as dyslexia. But he said the movement is gaining ground: the 2004 book "In Praise of Slow: How a Worldwide Movement is Changing the Cult of Speed" sprang from author Carl Honore's realization that his "rushaholism" had gotten out of hand when he considered buying a collection of "one-minute bedtime stories" for his children. 9

Another possible source

Another possible source. Author is Lindsay Waters.

In a 2007 article in The Chronicle of Higher Education, the executive humanities editor at Harvard University Press describes a worldwide reading crisis and calls for a "revolution in reading." 10

"Instead of rushing by works so fast that we don't even muss up our hair, we should tarry, attend to the sensuousness of reading, allow ourselves to enter the experience of words," Lindsay Waters wrote. 11

Though slow, or close reading, always has been emphasized at the college-level in literary criticism and other areas, it's also popping up in elementary schools, Miedema said. 12

Here is an example of how to teach slow reading.

Mary Ellen Webb, a third-grade teacher at Mast Way Elementary School in Durham, N.H., has her students memorize poems upward of 40 lines long and then perform them for their peers and parents. She does it more for the sense of pride her students feel but said the technique does transfer to other kinds of reading—the children remember how re-reading and memorizing their poems helped them understand tricky text. 13

This assumption might be shared by my readers.

"Memorization is one of those lost things, it hasn't been the 'in' thing for a while," she said. "There's a big focus on fluency. Some people think because you can read quickly . . . that's a judge of what a great reader they are. I think fluency is important, but I think we can err too much on that side." 14

It's all about balance, said Patti Flynn, an assistant principal in Nashua, N.H., and mother of a 10-year-old girl. 15

This woman has a slightly opposing view.

Her school has offered, and her daughter has participated in, numerous reading challenges that reward students for reaching certain milestones—a pizza party for a class that reads 100 books, for example. Though such contests may appear to emphasize speed rather than reading for pleasure or comprehension, they also are good incentives for children who weren't motivated to read, she said. The challenges have encouraged parents to make reading a priority at home, Flynn said. 16

"The goal shouldn't be to be whipping through a certain number of pages, the goal should be to make sure kids are gaining some conceptual understanding," she said. 17

Her daughter, Lily, said she considers herself a "medium-speed" reader and had to increase her speed to finish about 10 books for her classroom's 100-book challenge. But she said she enjoyed the process and feels like she understood and remembers what she read. 18

"It was fun," she said. 19

How Can a Research Log or a Notebook Help Me Engage with My Source?

Although marginal annotations can include personal responses, it is better to use a notebook or file on your computer to write more expanded informal responses. The more you write to interact with your sources before you use them in your own writing, the more comfortable you will be when it comes time to weave their voices and ideas into your paper. Following are some examples of the kind of background writing that helps you rehearse your use of sources. Performing these actions immediately after reading a source will save you time later because you will have generated raw material for some of your draft.

ASKING QUESTIONS | **What Do I Think about What the Source Is Saying?**

Assert your own voice by freewriting in your Research Log or Writer's Notebook in response to questions such as the following:

- What do I agree with here, and why? What do I know that causes me to agree?

- What do I disagree with here, and why?

- What would I like to know more about, checking for the accuracy of the writer's information?

- What other context or perspective might be possible on the views expressed here?

- What other sources or writers have I found that speak on the same topics, and how do these sources compare?

Below are notebook entries in response to Ramer's article:

> I wonder how college students would respond to being asked to memorize poems and read aloud, as Newkirk has his students do.

Notes can pose a question.

> I agree with the teacher who says there is too much emphasis on speed. If students learn to read everything fast, they read their own writing too fast to critique and catch their errors.

Notes can agree or disagree with a writer or speaker.

> In Newkirk's own article, he disapproves of pizza parties and silly stunts like teachers wearing pajamas to school just to reward kids for reading huge numbers of books. He would disagree with this principal.

Notes can show agreement or disagreement between sources.

> This reading reminds me of how Nicholas Carr ("Is Google Making Us Stupid?") compares digital reading to jet skiing and deep reading to scuba diving. ■

Notes can show your observations of similarities between sources.

How Do I Draw Connections between Sources?

To use your sources well, you must not use each in isolation, taking them up one at a time. You will need to blend them, a critical thinking skill known as **synthesizing,** which means *bringing together.* A good research paper uses multiple sources in any one section, even any one paragraph. (Synthesis is covered in Chapter 8, Comparing Perspectives, pages 173–201.)

As you read a second source, a third, a fourth, and so on, use informal writing to note where authors talk about the same topics. Notice places where they agree or disagree. It is possible that sources will contradict each other; this too, is worth noting and pursuing in further research.

Many kinds of informal writing can help you manage the job of synthesis: We have already suggested annotations and notebook entries. You could also create a chart, like the one shown on page 190 in Chapter 8. All of these methods can help you with the difficult task of organizing ideas across sources.

In a good research paper, the writer weaves material from multiple sources into a coherent whole.

The example notes that follow illustrate how writers can use their notebooks to make connections between points in multiple sources. The student paper in Chapter 20, pages 484–90 shows how these notes helped the writer synthesize his sources.

S T U D E N T   E X A M P L E   **Notes**

Note: Three English professors bring up this idea: Education and books should help us escape the hectic pace of life and slow down and reflect on our lives.

Mark Edmundson, English professor, U. Va.
Says students "skate fast over the surfaces of life." But "To live well, we must sometimes stop and think, and then try to remake the work in progress that we currently are. There's no better place for that than a college classroom where, together, we can slow it down and live deliberately, if only for a while." (no pages)

A good way to draw connections between sources is to paraphrase and directly quote passages from different sources that touch on similar points. The highlighting here shows specific points that run across the three sources.

Thomas Newkirk, English professor, U. of New Hampshire
Schools need to take a stand for an alternative to an increasingly hectic digital environment where so many of us read and write in severely abbreviated messages and through clicks of the mouse. He says "there is real pleasure in downshifting, in slowing down. We can gain some pleasures and meanings no other way." (no pages)

Mark Bauerlein, English professor, Emory U.
Says that reading should be a relief from stress and a way to help us put our lives into better perspective: "Books afford young readers a place to slow down and reflect, to find role models, to observe their own turbulent feelings well expressed, or to discover moral convictions" (58).

Writing informally to note where sources converge in their thinking, or where they diverge, will help you put them together in a plan of your own. The next sections of this chapter address the many ways you can employ sources, working them gracefully into your own writing and documenting them correctly.

What Roles Can Sources Play in My Writing?

As you prepare to start drafting, think of the ways you can use your sources. Remember that sources are integral to the construction of your thinking and the development of your ideas. Bring your sources in as you draft, and cite them correctly so you do not have to find the needed bibliographic information later. Consider the many contributions sources make to academic and workplace writing:

1. Sources provide the background knowledge you need in order to know if your research question is important or already settled.

2. Sources provide awareness of the climate of opinion on an issue, so you can explain opposing views.

3. Sources provide detailed information that makes any kind of writing specific and interesting. Your readers may need background information, concept explanations, and examples that illustrate your topic.

4. In an argument, sources provide evidence and opinions that the writer may use for support.

5. The sources we use not only provide evidence and opinions but also give legitimacy to our writing. Without sources, writing appears untrustworthy.

6. Using a range of sources shows the writer has inquired thoroughly into a topic and considered a wide spectrum of evidence and opinion in order to arrive at a thesis.

What Are My Options for Bringing in Source Material?

To incorporate source information into a paper or project, a writer has three options: direct quotations, paraphrases (also called indirect quotations), and summaries. In the first method, words are taken exactly as they appear in the source, with any alterations noted. In the second, paraphrase, the source material is reworded, and in the third, source material is both reworded and shortened. Each method is appropriate to specific circumstances; making the right choice depends on your purpose as well as the content of the material you plan to include.

Using Direct Quotations

Direct quotations are an efficient way to present material from a source. However, of the three options, direct quotation is the one you should use least. A great deal of source material is not worth quoting directly, and overuse of direct quoting can create a patchwork of voices in your paper, drowning out your own voice. It can also create a choppy, incoherent style if you don't set quotations up with enough context from the source. A good rule of thumb is that no more than 10 percent of a paper should be direct quotations: 100 words in a 1,000-word paper. So when should you use them?

Reserve direct quotations for the words of people whose credentials and opinions will lend weight to your paper or for the words of sources you want to dispute or analyze. You might also use direct quotations for

- Strongly or uniquely worded statements of opinion where capturing the colorful voice of the speaker matters to the point you are making.

- Literary turns of phrase, such as metaphors and analogies, where the style is part of the message.

- Highly technical language, such as professional jargon, where no easy translation is possible.

The example passage below makes good use of a direct quotation.

Appropriate Use of Direct Quotation to Present an Opinion from a Source

Mark Bauerlein, an Emory University professor of English, believes teenagers have stunted their intellects by limiting their use of the Internet and other information technology to peer-to-peer socializing. Although he has called them "the Dumbest

Generation," he says, "These kids have just as much intelligence and ambition as any previous cohort, but they exercise them too much on one another. They are building youth culture into a ubiquitous universe, and as ever youth culture is a drag on maturity" (22).

Bauerlein, Mark. "Generation Text." *America*. 12 October 2009: 20–22. *Academic Source Complete*. Web. 19 June 2011.

Using Paraphrases

Paraphrases are more common in professional researched writing than direct quotations. Unlike quoting, paraphrasing and summarizing let you maintain your role as the paper's dominant voice. Also, readers find direct quotations distracting when there is no good reason for using someone else's exact words instead of your own.

Paraphrase Facts or Background Information

Paraphrase when presenting information such as facts found in reference books, websites, and newspaper articles where the writer is a reporter or journalist, not an expert whose credentials would bolster your paper's credibility. Rewriting an informative passage into your own words may seem like extra work, but it is better to make the effort than to use direct quotations for passages that simply provide information. The following box gives advice on how to write a good paraphrase.

BEST PRACTICES | Writing Paraphrases

Follow these steps to create your own paraphrase:

1. Read the entire source or section. You cannot write a good paraphrase of a passage you have taken out of context. Surrounding sentences will provide information essential for understanding the sentence you are paraphrasing; to make the idea clear to yourself, you may need to add some of that information to your paraphrase. Later, if you use the paraphrase in your paper, you will need to provide enough context, setting it up so that your readers will understand how the passage fit into the source.
2. Read the passage and surrounding sentences several times, including surrounding text, until you understand it and its context. Annotate it. Look up any words that are even slightly unfamiliar to you.
3. Put the text away so you will not be able to look at it while you try to say it in your own way. Recall the main ideas, and try to put each one into your own words and your own wording. A paraphrase must not be an echo of the original's sentence patterns with synonyms plugged in. That is really a form of plagiarism since it involves "stealing" the author's sentence pattern. You may want to break up complex sentences into shorter, simpler ones that make the idea easier to comprehend.

4. If the passage refers to or depends on surrounding material for meaning, put that information into your paraphrase. For example, you may need to replace a pronoun with a noun for clarity.

5. Do not feel that you must find a substitute word for every ordinary word in the passage. For example, if a passage has the word *children,* don't feel you have to say *kids.*

6. Go back and check your paraphrase against the original to see if you have accurately represented the full content of the original passage. Make adjustments as needed. ■

See Chapter 19, pages
460–61, for examples of
plagiarism in poorly written
paraphrases.

A paraphrase should not retain the same syntax, or sentence patterns, as the original, even if the vocabulary is different. A paraphrase that imitates the original sentence is technically plagiarism and does not improve comprehension of the ideas. A good paraphrase is likely to be as long, or even longer, than the original passage, especially if it expresses the same meaning.

Below is an example of a passage from a draft in which the writer uses a long direct quotation. Note that the quoted material is not memorable in style. The wording is not worth reproducing as a direct quotation.

> Food writer Mark Bittman argues that people should take a more sustainable approach to eating: "To reduce our impact on the environment, we should depend on foods that require little or no processing, packaging, or transportation, and those that efficiently convert the energy required to raise them into nutritional calories to sustain human beings" (19).

A revised version uses all of Bittman's point but not any of his exact wording. As you see here, paraphrasing allows you to keep your own voice, vocabulary, and style in the writing. When you paraphrase, you "own" the material, explaining it as you understand it.

> Food writer Mark Bittman believes people need to take a sustainable approach to eating. We should shrink our environmental food footprint by choosing locally grown foods that require minimal processing and packaging. And, in order that energy not be wasted in the production of junk food, he says we should choose nutritious foods that give us a good return in energy for the energy it takes to produce them (19).
>
> Bittman, Mark. *Food Matters: A Guide to Conscious Eating.* New York: Simon & Schuster, 2009. Print.

In the two examples below, the draft passage uses a direct quotation to present purely factual information, while the revised version uses a paraphrase of the basic information in the quoted material. Writers should avoid direct quotations of facts.

Draft Version: Inappropriate Use of a Direct Quotation

Human invention of laws resulted from the need to regulate water use in dry areas such as the Tigris-Euphrates Valley. According to Michael Mares, "our very system of written laws dates back to Hammurabi, king of Babylonia from 1792 to 1750 B.C., whose first laws were written to deal with the use of water for agricultural purposes"(xxix).

In the revision below, the information has been paraphrased.

Revised Version: Appropriate Use of Paraphrase

The human invention of law began under King Hammurabi, who ruled Babylonia from 1792 to 1750 B.C. In the arid region of the Tigris-Euphrates Valley, the Babylonian people needed laws to regulate their use of water, a precious commodity for the development of agriculture (Mares xxix).

Mares, Michael A. *Encyclopedia of Deserts.* Norman: University of Oklahoma Press, 1999. Web. 19 June 2011.

A paraphrase must completely rework the wording and sentence patterns of the original passage. Students can commit plagiarism inadvertently if they do not double-check paraphrases for too much similarity to the wording of the source.

For additional guidance on paraphrasing, see Chapter 19, pages 460–61, and Chapter 2, pages 25–26.

Blend Direct Quotations with Paraphrases

A good way to avoid overly long quotations and to blend your own voice with some key phrases from a source is to embed the quotable bits into paraphrases, as shown in the example below. When you blend paraphrase and direct quotation so that the quoted words are integral to your own sentence, no punctuation is needed to set off the quoted words.

Bauerlein disdainfully describes the world of thirteen- to seventeen-year-olds as a "dynamic 24/7 network" in which "teen activity accrues more and more significance" as the events of the day "are recorded and circulated" (22).

Using a Summary

When you are working with the extended ideas of one of your major sources, you may need to include more than a few quotations and paraphrases in your paper to do the idea justice. In books, it is common to find passages that summarize the entire argument of a source, often with some discussion woven in. Therefore, it is reasonable in some cases to devote one to two paragraphs to a summary, depending upon the length of your paper and the relevance of the source. If you do choose to summarize, make sure that the summary contains only content relevant to your paper and that you comment upon the relevance of the source.

The following Best Practices gives advice on the steps necessary to writing a good summary. Summary writing is also covered in Chapter 2, pages 27–28.

BEST PRACTICES | Summarizing a Source

In your notebook, first write down the author, title, and other source information you'll need for your works cited list (for MLA—Modern Language Association) or list of references (APA—American Psychological Association). Then, follow these suggestions for writing summaries.

1. Read and annotate the entire source, noting the main points and the key supporting points.
2. For long texts, break them into subdivisions. Working with one subdivision at a time, write paraphrases of the main ideas in each. Try working from memory as you write, and check the original later for accuracy. Decide which specific facts would be appropriate to include, depending on the purpose of your summary.
3. Make sure that your sentences restate the points; do not just describe the original passage, as in "The author talks about . . . ." Instead, say what the author's point is.
4. You may include brief direct quotations, but avoid quoting whole sentences. That is not efficient.
5. Do not try to include all of the figurative language and tone of the original. Write the summary in your own voice, not in imitation of the author's voice and style.
6. Keep your summary objective; reserve your commentary for follow-up if you use the summary as part of your paper.
7. Edit your summary to reduce repetition and to combine points into single sentences where possible. ■

A good summary restates the author's points rather than simply describing what the author does. It provides enough detail so that the readers of the summary have something close to the experience of reading the original, but in a more concise version.

Below we offer a passage from a source that is represented in summary form in the student example paper on pages 484–90. If the passage is long and difficult, as is the one below, it helps to annotate it as we demonstrate here, before attempting to draft the summary.

Refresh memory on Socrates: 469–399 B.C. Philosopher who engaged the young men of Athens in debating philosophical questions about virtue and truth. Felt the unexamined life is not worth living. He was sentenced to death for corrupting the youth. Drank the hemlock before he could be executed.

Original Passage with Annotations from "Dwelling in Possibilities" by Mark Edmundson

If Socrates looked out on the current dispensation, what would he see? He'd see the velocity and the hunger for more life, faster, faster—sure. But given his interests,

I think he means the order of things, how things are on campuses.

This section of the reading introduces the question of how well young people know themselves, really, versus how others have defined them.

This paragraph acts as a transition into the role of college in finding identity.

Here, the author is suggesting that reading the great authors helps students see beyond the common views they may have grown up believing.

Should college change you, and make you question prior beliefs?

he'd notice something else, too. He'd see that by the time students get to college, they have been told who they are and what the world is many times over. Parents and friends, teachers, counselors, priests and rabbis, ministers and imams have had their say. They've let each student know how they size him up, and they've let him know what they think he should value. Every student has been submitted to what Socrates liked to call *doxa*, common sense, general belief.

And a student may be all the things the people who raised her say she is; she may want the things they have shown her are worth wanting. She may genuinely be her father and mother's daughter. But then again, she may not.

The primary reason to study Blake and Dickinson and Freud and Dickens is not to become more cultivated, or more articulate, or to be someone who at a cocktail party is never embarrassed (but can embarrass others). The ultimate reason to read them is to see if they may know you better than you know yourself. They may help you to cut through established opinion—*doxa*—about who you are and what the world is. They may give you new ways of seeing and saying things, and those ways may be truer for you than the ones that you grew up with. Genuine education is a process that gives students a second chance. They've been socialized once by their parents and teachers; now it's time for a second, maybe a better, shot. It's time—to be a little idealizing about it—for Socrates to have a turn.

The source of orthodox?

Socrates encouraged questioning common beliefs, for which he was seen as stirring up trouble.

This is clever. He knows that some people read books for superficial reasons, for the status.

This section shows why students should read the great writers for wisdom and new understandings of the world.

After noting the major subdivisions and writing paraphrases of them, the student put the paraphrases together smoothly to make the summary below. (The bibliographic information for this essay by Mark Edmundson appears in the works cited list of the student's paper, pages 484–90.) Note how the following summary also makes use of several direct quotations to convey some of the original language of the source.

Summary

Edmundson imagines that if Socrates were around today, he would worry about the same thing Edmundson worries about—the fast pace of college students' lives and how well they really know themselves and the world. All through their years of school, they've been influenced by adults in their lives—parents, teachers, and clergy—who have told them how to define themselves and interpret the world. Edmundson says these interpretations may be true, but then again, they may not. That is why education and books are important. They challenge "established opinion" and what seems like "common sense" but may not be true. Thus, books give students new perspectives about themselves and the world that may be truer for them than what they had always been told was true.

How Do I Acknowledge, Integrate, and Cite My Source Materials?

When using source information, whether factual data or the opinions and arguments of other people, writers must acknowledge each source and integrate the material smoothly into their own surrounding text. In scholarly and professional writing, they must also document their sources.

BEST PRACTICES | Acknowledging, Integrating, and Citing Sources

Acknowledging sources means *giving credit to a source for paraphrased ideas, direct quotations, and any information that is not common knowledge.* Acknowledging can include citing, as discussed below, but in some genres that do not include documentation, just mentioning a name serves as an acknowledgment. To fail to acknowledge a source is to steal from it, to plagiarize. In magazines, newspapers, trade books, and online writing, authors must acknowledge their sources of information. Authors who do not are considered unethical and irresponsible.

Integrating sources means *blending in source material alongside your own words* so that your paper flows, with no gaps in thought or expression. Smooth integration requires writing in your own voice and signaling readers when you introduce others' words and ideas.

Citing sources (also called documenting) means *providing written information about a source's author, title, date, and place of publication,* in some cases including when and how you found the source. Documentation is not a standard feature in the popular press, but it is usually required in academic articles and scholarly books. While there are many documentation styles, this book covers the two most common ones: those of the Modern Language Association and American Psychological Association.

The following paragraph demonstrates the basic elements of acknowledging, integrating, and citing sources. It uses the MLA documentation form.

Integrates the source material by leading into the history of zombie films.

Documents, or cites, the source by giving the page number.

Integrates the upcoming source by setting up the context of social unrest in the 1960s.

The modern zombie movie has been around for almost forty years and, like other genres, it has gone through periods of feast and famine. According to film scholar Darryl Jones, the genre was born in 1968 with the release of George A. Romero's *Night of the Living Dead* (161), in which a motley group of people, led by an African American antihero named Ben (Duane Jones), must spend the night in a besieged country house, waiting for the authorities to arrive. When the county militia finally does show up, its first response is to shoot and kill Ben, the only survivor of the supernatural abattoir. The violence and graphic images in this low-budget horror film were unprecedented at the time, and the movie

Acknowledges the source by giving the expert's full name on first mention, along with some identification or credentials.

Integrates the source by paraphrasing factual information rather than over-relying on direct quotations.

functions largely as a metaphor for the atrocities of Vietnam and racism. Called "hippie Gothic" by film theorist Joseph Maddrey (51), *Night* protests the war by graphically confronting audiences with the horrors of death and dismemberment and by openly criticizing those who use violence to solve their problems. The politically subversive film gained a cult following and eventually made more than $30 million worldwide ("Business Data for *Night*").

> Unique words taken from a source must be in quotation marks.

> Citations can be placed before the end of a sentence to show precisely what was taken from the source.

> Documents, or cites, the source of this information by title because there is no author.

Works Cited

"Business Data for *Night of the Living Dead*." *Internet Movie Database*. amazon.com, 3 May 2006. Web. 5 July 2009.

Jones, Darryl. *Horror: A Thematic History in Fiction and Film*. London: Arnold, 2002. Print.

Maddrey, Joseph. *Nightmares in Red, White and Blue: The Evolution of the American Horror Film*. Jefferson: McFarland, 2004. Print. ∎

What Are the Options for Acknowledging Sources?

Acknowledging means giving credit. The first time you introduce an important speaker, give the person's first and last name; thereafter, use last names only. Give credentials such as publications or university affiliations.

Acknowledge Sources with Short Phrases or Sentences

You can acknowledge a source in a short phrase, known as a signal phrase because it signals the connection between the material and its source. You can use a complete sentence to acknowledge a source. (The examples below include citations in MLA form.)

The two introductory phrases below, each followed by a comma, provide the name and expertise of the source. (Citations will be explained briefly in this chapter on page 453 and in detail in Chapters 20 and 21.)

Signal Phrase to Identify a Source

According to Maryanne Wolf, a reading expert from Tufts University, "Typically when you read, you have more time to think" than when you look at images or listen to stories (qtd. in Duzbrow).

> In this example, Wolf is not the author of the source. See pages 465–66 and 495 for how to cite sources used by your sources, known as indirect sources. Duzbrow is an online source, so no page number is available.

You should also use signal phrases to acknowledge paraphrased material from a source.

According to Maryanne Wolf, a reading expert from Tufts University, reading is an activity that allows the brain more time for thinking than does listening to a story or watching it in a movie or television show (qtd. in Duzbrow).

> Even if you have paraphrased the words or ideas of a source found in your source, MLA requires that you use "qtd. in" in your parenthetical citation.

You can also acknowledge sources with a complete sentence. In this case, however, you must use a colon rather than a comma between your words and those of the source. The colon is needed here to prevent a comma splice. A comma splice before a quotation is a common punctuation error. (See S-1 in the Common Errors section of the Handbook for more on comma splices.)

Complete Sentence to Identify a Source

Maryanne Wolf, director of the Center for Reading and Language Research at Tufts University, explains why reading is more stimulating to the brain than hearing speech or looking at images: "Typically when you read, you have more time to think" (qtd. in Duzbrow).

In this example, the complete sentence provides more context for the quotation than would a simple signal phrase, making a smooth transition between the quotation and the preceding discussion of the mental benefits of reading.

Vary the Placement of Acknowledgments

To add variety to your writing style, you can place the acknowledgment of a source before the material, after it, or in the middle.

Acknowledgment before a Source

In an *Atlantic* article, Nicholas Carr, an expert on information technology, describes how using the Internet has changed his reading style: "Once I was a scuba diver in the sea of words. Now I zip along on the surface like a guy on a Jet Ski."

Acknowledgment after a Source

"Once I was a scuba diver in the sea of words. Now I zip along on the surface like a guy on a Jet Ski," writes information technology expert Nicholas Carr in an *Atlantic* article about the effects of the Internet on people's reading styles.

Acknowledgment Surrounded by a Source

"Once I was a scuba diver in the sea of words," says information technology expert Nicholas Carr in an *Atlantic* article. "Now I zip along on the surface like a guy on a Jet Ski."

Use a Variety of Verbs to Indicate Acknowledgment

Using the word "says" to lead into quotations becomes repetitive. Think about how you are using the quotation and which verb would best describe the function of the quotation. Here are some options for changing things up:

admits	finds	points out
argues	holds	remarks
claims	insists	shows
comments	maintains	states
contends	observes	suggests

Follow Conventions When Choosing Verb Tenses to Use When Acknowledging Sources

It is customary to use present tense when leading into a quotation or paraphrase from a text you are using as a source. Use past tense only when referring to a past action, as in this example:

> In the 1940s, Edmund Wilson declared that "detective stories [are] simply a kind of vice that, for silliness and minor harmfulness, ranks somewhere between smoking and crossword puzzles."

The author refers to Wilson's action of speaking.

How Can I Integrate Source Material into My Writing?

Integrating sources means blending them smoothly into your own writing. If you've ever received a paper back from your instructor and found the comment "choppy" or "needs to flow" in the margins, then you can understand the difficulties writers face when they bring outside material into their own writing. Making ideas flow can be tricky enough when they are all your own ideas, so adding other voices can make it even trickier.

Researched writing sounds choppy and even incoherent if the writer has not led into quotations, anchored them with a signal phrase, and followed up on quotations with some commentary. Even paraphrases need some setting up, and if your paraphrase is not specific enough, your reader will have trouble getting the point.

BEST PRACTICES | Guidelines for Integrating Sources

Source material should not be dropped into a researched paper like items into a shopping cart. Your paper does not simply contain the sources; it is constructed using the sources.

- Organize around your own points; use sources to develop those points in depth.
- Cite as you write. Do not try to draft without including your source material, correctly worked in and cited.
- Lead up with enough explanation to show your readers how the source fits into your discussion.
- When presenting an authority's viewpoint, introduce the person first, with full name on first mention and any relevant credentials or affiliations. This formality is more common in MLA style than in APA.
- When quoting directly, anchor the words from the source to the surrounding text with a phrase or sentence that introduces the speaker. You should also indicate how the quotation relates to the surrounding text.
- Prefer paraphrase to direct quotation when presenting factual information. Keep direct quotations to approximately 10 percent of your paper.
- Follow up by commenting on the ideas or information to show how the source relates to a point of your own. ■

Avoid Dropped-in Quotations

Direct quotations need to be set up, not dropped into your paper. Provide enough of the original context to fit the quotation coherently into your paragraph. You may need to paraphrase some of the surrounding sentences from which the quotation was taken. If you have not done so already, you may need to introduce the speaker of the words, along with his or her credentials if the speaker is an important writer or authority. If the author is a staff writer, it is sufficient simply to put the last name in a parenthetical citation.

In the following example, the student did not do enough to connect the speaker's words to the idea in the preceding sentence.

> Some people claim that reading on computer screens is the same as reading on paper. "Are you not exercising the same cognitive muscles because these words are made out of pixels and not little splotches of ink?" (Johnson).

The revised version below does a better job of setting up and integrating the quotation.

> Some people claim that reading on computer screens is the same as reading on paper. In an online newspaper column titled "Dawn of the Digital Natives," Steven Johnson, a best-selling nonfiction author, asks his readers, "Odds are that you are reading these words on a computer monitor. Are you not exercising the same cognitive muscles because these words are made out of pixels and not little splotches of ink?"

Set off Long Quotations in Block Style

See pages 465–66 and 495.

The two main documentation styles differ slightly on the rules for block quotes, but they agree that it is necessary to set off longer quotations in order to distinguish them from your own words, as in the example below.

> When the Nielsen researchers used an eye tracker to see how people read on the Internet, they discovered a surprising pattern that creators of websites need to know:
>
>> The pattern looks like the capital letter F. At the top of the page, users read all the way across, but as they proceed their descent quickens and horizontal movement shortens, with a slowdown around the middle of the page. Near the bottom of the page, the eyes move almost vertically, forming the lower stem of the F shape. . . . Whatever content businesses want to communicate to visitors better not be concentrated in the lower-right portions of the screen, Nielsen advised. (Bauerlein 144)

For block style quotes only, the period at the end of a sentence precedes the parenthetical citation.

To Delete Parts of Direct Quotations, Use Ellipses

Sometimes a direct quotation goes into more detail than is necessary for your purpose or contains references or transitional expressions that had a purpose in the original passage but would only be confusing to your readers. When you remove these words from a quotation, you replace them with ellipses. An ellipsis is a series of three spaced periods. When removing words from the end of a sentence, you add a fourth period.

This is the original passage from Steven Johnson's book *Everything Bad Is Good for You:*

> Tools like Google have fulfilled the original dream of digital machines becoming extensions of our memory, but the new social networking applications have done something that the visionaries never imagined: <u>they are augmenting our people skills as well, widening our social networks, and creating new possibilities for strangers to share ideas and experiences.</u>

If you wanted to use only the underlined section of the passage, you should remove the transitional expression "as well" since it no longer serves the purpose of relating the two points in the original passage.

> Some people think that because online communication is not face-to-face, it is causing a decline in our social skills. But Steven Johnson argues that the social networking sites "are augmenting our people skills. . . , widening our social networks, and creating new possibilities for strangers to share ideas and experiences" (124).

In most cases, writers use ellipses to remove passages that are too detailed or irrelevant to the purpose of their own paper.

Use Square Brackets to Change Wording for Clarity and Grammatical Correctness

You can change quotations to make them fit more smoothly into your sentence, provided that you use square brackets around the words you alter. If you take words out and replace them with words in brackets, the brackets will signal to the reader that you have made a substitution, so there is no need for an ellipsis.

Sometimes you need to change the tense of verbs, as in this example from the student paper that appears on pages 484–90. The original passage by University of Virginia professor Mark Edmundson quoted Ralph Waldo Emerson and read

> The idea is to keep moving, never to stop. . . ."In skating over thin ice," Emerson says, "our safety is in our speed." . . . Skate fast over the surfaces of life and cover all the extended space you can, says the new ethos.

To combine his own words smoothly with the quoted passage, the student writer had to change the form of the verb *skate:*

> Too many students are connected to everything and everyone but themselves, as Edmundson says, "[skating] fast over the surfaces of life," depending on energy drinks or someone else's Adderall.

You can also use brackets to alter a word to make a quotation clearer in the context of your sentence, as in the following example. Steven Johnson's book contained this sentence about one drawback of the Internet compared with books:

> But it is harder to transmit a fully fledged worldview.

To fit Johnson's words into his own sentence, the writer had to change the article *a* to *the*:

> Steven Johnson admits in his book *Everything Bad Is Good for You* that the Internet is not so good at "training our minds to follow a sustained textual argument" (187) or to "transmit [the] fully fledged world view" of another person (186).

Avoid Stringing Sources Together with No Commentary

In the following example, the author has not shown how the ideas in the two quotations connect with each other. The result is a paragraph that is purely summary.

> Movies can inspire children to then go out and buy the book of the movie they just watched. Amy Dickinson, writer for *TIME* magazine, says that as "the mother of a typical adolescent, I have to say that *movies* can lead a child to books. . . ." She goes on to say that Stanley Greenspan, the author of *Building Healthy Minds,* believes that "the most important aspect of movie watching is the conversation after the final credits roll, when kids can be encouraged to think critically, be curious, and go looking for answers in a book" (Dickinson).

A revised version takes more of the quotation and makes the connection between the two quotations plain. And the writer wraps up the paragraph neatly with a final comment of her own.

> Movies can inspire children to then go out and buy the book of the movie they just watched, provided that parents or teachers encourage them. Amy Dickinson, writer for *TIME* magazine and parent of an adolescent, says that "*movies* can lead a child to books though sometimes an adult needs to illuminate the way." Parents can help develop children's imaginations by joining with them to write their own scripts for dramas, according to Stanley Greenspan, the author of *Building Healthy Minds*. Dickinson encourages parents not only to watch movies with their children but also to talk about the film afterward: "[T]he most important aspect of movie watching is the conversation after the final credits roll, when kids can be encouraged to think critically, be curious, and go looking for answers in a book" (Dickinson). By interacting with their kids, parents can turn a passive kind of entertainment into an intellectually stimulating one.

Length	Spacing	TABLE **18.1**

Formatting Quotations

Length	Spacing
MLA If a quotation extends to more than four lines in your paper, use the block form. **APA** If a quotation is forty words or longer, use the block form.	**MLA** Begin a new line and indent it one inch (ten spaces) from the left margin. If you are quoting only one paragraph or part of one, do not indent the first line any farther. If the quotation runs more than one paragraph, indent the first line of each new paragraph by three spaces. **APA** Begin a new line and indent it one-half inch (five spaces) from the left margin. If the quotation runs more than one paragraph, indent the first line of each new paragraph by one-half inch (five spaces).

Guidelines for both MLA and APA

How to space it	Double space the quotation. Do not add extra spacing at the top or bottom.
How to cite it	With block quotations, any parenthetical citation follows the final punctuation mark.
How to treat internal quotations	Internal quotations within block form quotes receive the standard double quotation marks.
How to lead into long quotations	Depending on the context, you may need no punctuation between your lead-in or attributive tag and your quotation; however, it is common to lead in with a full sentence and a colon.

How Do I Document My Sources?

Documentation is a two-step process. The first step, which appears in the paper itself and is therefore called an in-text citation, is to identify the author (or title if there is no author) and the page number if one is available. Acknowledgment of an author by name does some of the work of citing but not all of it.

The second step, which appears at the end of the paper, is to provide a full bibliography, an alphabetical list of sources (articles, books, websites, and so on) that are referenced in the paper. This bibliography is called a list of works cited (MLA) or a list of references (APA). In academic writing, every source quoted or paraphrased must appear in the bibliography. These lists appear at the ends of books, articles, and sometimes chapters.

The important point to make here is that when a project calls for documentation, you must have two matching citations: one in the text of your paper and its partner in the list of sources at the back. For every source used in the paper,

Chapter 20, pages 462–90, covers in-text citing and works cited lists in MLA style. Chapter 21, pages 491–516 covers in-text citing and reference lists in APA style.

there must be an item on the list at the back. For every item on the list, there must be a corresponding reference to it in the body of your paper.

How Do I Incorporate Sources without Losing My Own Voice?

To wrap up our advice on incorporating source materials, we want to remind you of the importance of keeping your own voice and perspective in your writing. When a writer brings other people's voices into a paper, one danger is those sources may try to dominate the conversation and determine how the paper develops. The source authors are often, after all, experts on the topic. However, your job as the writer is to politely control the conversation.

Imagine that writing a research paper is like hosting a dinner party. You need to plan the meal and invite the guests. Your sources are like guests who should not monopolize the conversation or take over the dinner. In a paper, you are in charge, organizing around your goals and presenting your perspective. Your thesis drives the paper; your sources are there to help support your points.

Maintain Your Own Angle and Plan

Writers sometimes feel intimidated about asserting their own voices in a conversation of published experts. When you encounter this situation, ask these questions:

- What is my angle and purpose?
- How does this source's information serve my angle and purpose?
- What is the smallest amount of information that I need from this source to make my point?

The following example, illustrating APA documentation style, shows how nutritional scientist Sera L. Young kept her voice in a paper about how attitudes have changed over time on a peculiar type of human behavior. Notice how the writer's tone differs from the tone of her sources' quoted words. Notice also how little of each source's words she needs to convey her point.

> Earth-eating, or geophagia, has always incited strongly negative reactions. Even scientists have done little to conceal their "disgust" for such a "vile habit" (Cragin, 1835) and denounce geophagists: "[W]ith the tenacity of ignorance these people cling to their filthy habits" ("The clay eaters," 1897, p. 150). Positive or even neutral regard for geophagia has only emerged in the last few decades. Yet the grounds for the proclamation of geophagia as "good" or "bad" are limited, even today.
>
> Young, Sera L. (2007). A vile habit? The potential biological consequences of geophagia, with special attention to iron. In J. MacClancy, J. Henry, & H. Macbeth (Eds.), *Consuming the inedible: Neglected dimensions of food choice* (pp. 67–79). New York, NY: Berghahn Books.

By maintaining a neutral tone, Young shows the contrast between her modern perspective and the outdated attitudes of the sources' voices. Also note that Young has successfully acknowledged her sources, integrated their words smoothly into her own sentences, and cited both in-text and in a bibliographic entry at the end.

Chapters 20 and 21 continue our advice about how to cite sources in the text of your papers and in the works cited (MLA) and references (APA) lists at the end of the paper.

CHAPTER 19
Using Sources Responsibly

RESEARCHERS BUILD THEIR WORK ON FOUNDATIONS LAID BY OTHERS. HOW-
ever, the structure falls apart when a researcher steals material. Whether on purpose or not, using another person's work without acknowledging or giving credit to the source is theft.

Word processing software and the Internet have made it easy to copy and paste the words and visual images found in sources. The interactive nature of creative content on the Internet makes borrowing and mashing up seem perfectly acceptable. However, *anytime you put your name on something and claim it as your own work, borrowing without acknowledging is plagiarism.* Universities, the business world, and the law take it very seriously.

Writers who steal not only lose the reader's trust, but they also often face criminal charges. Cases of copyright infringement often make the news, and they damage the careers of popular novelists, song writers, newspaper reporters, and sometimes even professors who have been careless while taking notes or too trusting of assistants' research skills.

By citing your sources, you earn your readers' respect. Readers are more likely to accept your views if you project good character, what the ancient rhetoricians called *ethos.* Honesty is part of good character. Part of writing honestly is distinguishing your ideas from the ideas of others. Therefore, *when in doubt, always cite.*

What Is Plagiarism?

Ethical use of sources requires paying careful attention to the texts of sources, whether written, audio, video, or works of art. Failure to acknowledge sources is plagiarism.

Intentional plagiarism occurs when a student knowingly submits work containing the words, ideas, images, or other intellectual property of another person without acknowledging and citing the source of the material. Note that plagiarism does not have to consist of word-for-word copying of another person's work. Rewording another person's ideas without acknowledging the source of the ideas is every bit as much plagiarism as copying and pasting material from a source into your paper.

Many professors and institutions regard unintentional or accidental plagiarism as seriously as the intentional kind and give it the same penalties. Unintentional plagiarism occurs when a researcher has been sloppy about note-taking and paraphrasing, not realizing that even a single phrase or word group taken verbatim needs quotation marks and a citation. It occurs when a researcher fails to distinguish an opinion found in a source from common knowledge or common facts, which may not need to be cited, as we will explain below. Unintentional plagiarism may not be as unethical as intentional plagiarism, but it is nevertheless serious and can result in an "F" for a paper.

In college, punishment for plagiarism can include failure in the course or even suspension or expulsion from the university. Many universities will indicate on a student's transcript if there has been an honor violation, something that potential employers will see.

When Do I Need to Cite My Sources?

The point of using sources is to combine other people's ideas and knowledge with your own, and the point of citing sources is to distinguish between your sources' knowledge and your own knowledge and ideas. Specifically, acknowledging (giving credit) and citing (with appropriate documentation) are required in the situations described below.

Cite and Quote Exact Words, Phrases, and Sentences

It is easy to understand that you need to put quotation marks around whole sentences that you take from one of your sources. For example, a complete sentence from a book is cited below.

> Yale law Professor Steven L. Carter is concerned about the future of democracy. Noting that many people vote without bothering to inform themselves on the issues, he argues, "Living in a democracy requires hard work that we seem less and less willing to do" (17).

If you wanted to take just a few words from this sentence, the words that express Carter's opinion of Americans' voter apathy, you would still have to enclose the words in quotation marks, as in the example below.

> Yale law Professor Steven L. Carter is concerned about the future of democracy. Noting that many people vote without bothering to inform themselves on the issues, he argues that Americans "seem less and less willing" to carry out the "hard work" of responsible citizenship (17).

Cite Ideas Found in Your Sources

Even if you rework someone else's writing into a paraphrase, *if you use someone else's idea, then you need to cite the source because ideas are intellectual property.* When you paraphrase, you must also acknowledge the source, or you are plagiarizing.

See Chapter 18, pages 441–43, for guidance on paraphrasing.

Cite Paraphrased Ideas from Your Sources

It is a standard practice for writers to draw upon the work of others, including both the information they have gathered and the ideas they have formulated.

Whether you quote them directly or put them into your own words, you need to give credit to the source, so you do not appear to be claiming these ideas as your own.

The following passage comes from a *Wall Street Journal* blog post on the rise of incivility in business settings. The post was written by Sue Shellenbarger. Note that she opens with her own point but develops it with the research of an authority, Christine Pearson. Shellenbarger paraphrases the research in her own words and acknowledges Pearson as the source by naming her.

> Texting has been blamed for a lot of things—harassment among teenagers, driver distraction on the highway, bad grades among students. Now, it is being blamed for bad manners at work.
>
> Based on research on 9,000 U.S. workers and managers, Christine Pearson, a management professor at Thunderbird School of Global Management, says all the texting and emailing interrupting meetings and face-to-face conversations at the office are slowly but surely eroding human civility and making us—well, rude, she writes. All the e-conversations steal our attention away from the people nearby, amounting to what once would have been labeled a snub, writes Ms. Pearson, the author of *The Cost of Bad Behavior.*

Cite Ideas That Coincide with Your Own

You may encounter ideas in sources that coincide with your own. For example, suppose you think that optimistic people do better in life than pessimists. This is a belief you have concluded from observations of family and friends—and perhaps your own attitudes in meeting challenges. Then you read Gregg Easterbrook's book *The Progress Paradox*, and on page 223 you see the following:

> Lisa Aspinwall, a psychologist at the University of Utah, has shown that as a group, the optimistic do better in life than the pessimistic . . . . [O]ptimists . . . are actually better at overcoming negative experiences because they can bounce back rather than be dragged under.

Easterbrook is acknowledging Aspinwall as his source. Easterbrook is your source, but do you need to cite the source of something you could have said on your own? If you do not use Easterbrook's exact words, is it plagiarism to use Aspinwall's opinion without acknowledging Aspinwall's research and citing Easterbrook's book?

A classic book on research, *The Craft of Research*,[1] advises you to take the cautious approach and cite: "In the world of research, priority counts not for everything, but for a lot. If you do not cite that prior source, you risk having people think that you plagiarized it, even though you did not" (203). You do not have to check to see that all of your own ideas are not already out there; however, if you encounter one of your own in a source, you should acknowledge that

---

1. Booth, Wayne C., Gregory G. Colomb, and Joseph M. Williams. *The Craft of Research*. 2nd ed. Chicago: U of Chicago P, 2003. Print.

source. This also strengthens your case: Not only do you believe optimists tend do be more successful in life, but others think so too.

Cite Even a Single Significant Word or Phrase

Verbatim use of some words and phrases cannot be avoided; it would not be necessary to put quotation marks around common words and phrases, such as "fifth-graders" and proper nouns like the White House or Secretary of State Hillary Clinton. However, *when a single word expresses a writer's opinion or judgment, it should go into quotation marks and the source should be acknowledged.*

For example, in this passage from Steven L. Carter's book *Civility*, the word "diabolical" is significant enough to merit a citation:

> As for the automobile itself, it seems an almost diabolical tool, in the traditional sense of the word—a thing of the devil, made to bring out the worst in us.

In your paper, you might put the idea into your own words, acknowledge Carter as the source, and quote the single word.

> Under the cover of anonymity within their cars, drivers become not just uncivil but as Steven Carter puts it, even "diabolical" once behind the wheel (7).

Cite Factual Information That Is Not "Common Knowledge"

Facts that can be easily obtained through multiple sources such as reference books, Google searches, and standard textbooks do not have to be cited. A rule of thumb is that *if the reader could fact-check your information in at least three easily accessed sources, it can count as common knowledge.*

Common knowledge generally includes factual information not in dispute, such as dates or authors of books. For example, a historical date like the bombing of Pearl Harbor on December 7, 1941, is common knowledge. However, the equally important historical date September 6, 1941, when Japanese leaders decided to take the country to war, is not common knowledge, so it is information that must be documented.

If you already knew something that shows up in your research, that is a good indication it is common knowledge, but also consider whether your *readers* would already know it. If your readers know less about your topic than you do, it is good to cite the source, especially if the information might surprise them. Citing sources is a courtesy to readers who may want to pursue their interest in your topic.

It is also not necessary to cite the exact source location for commonly known quotations, such as

Martin Luther King Jr.'s declaration "I have a dream," or commonly available sources, such as the Declaration of Independence. Again, the rule of thumb here is that if readers could easily find a copy of the document, it is not necessary to cite it. However, the motto for research remains important: *When in doubt, cite your source.* You can also consult your professor for advice on when to cite.

Cite Debatable or Unique Information

Some information is disputed or still open to debate. For example, scientists have data supporting the contention that human activity is causing global warming. Others present data that supports another contention: that global temperatures fluctuate independent of human activity.

If information is not generally agreed upon, then the source of the information should always be cited. When in doubt, imagine one of your readers asking, "But how do you know that?" If readers can pose this question, it is best to point them to a source.

Cite Charts, Artwork, and Graphics

Any time you include artwork, photographs, graphics, charts, diagrams, maps, and other audiovisual materials that you got from another source rather than creating the image yourself, you must acknowledge and cite the source.

How Can I Avoid Plagiarizing?

It is easy to avoid blatant forms of plagiarism, such as buying a paper, having someone write your paper for you, or copying and pasting from the Internet into your paper without acknowledging the source. You simply choose not to do it.

However, writers can accidentally plagiarize if, for example, they are careless when taking notes and fail to place quotation marks when they copy something from a source into their notes and then transfer that passage into their paper. Writers are responsible for double-checking paraphrases against the original passage. *Make sure the words and sentence patterns are your own to avoid accidental plagiarism.*

Consider the example of accidental plagiarism below.

Original Passage from *iBrain* by Gary Small and Gigi Vorgan[2]

Our high-tech revolution has plunged us into a state of *continuous partial attention,* which software executive Linda Stone describes as continually staying busy—keeping tabs on everything while never truly focusing on anything. . . . When paying continuous partial attention, people may place their brain in a heightened state of stress. They no longer have time to reflect, contemplate or make thoughtful decisions. Instead they exist in a sense of constant crisis—on alert for a new contact or bit of

2. Small, Gary, and Gigi Vorgan, *iBrain: Surviving the Technological Alteration of the Modern Mind.* New York: HarperCollins, 2008. Print.

exciting news or information at any moment. Once people get used to this state, they tend to thrive on the perpetual connectivity. It feeds their ego and sense of self-worth, and it becomes irresistible.

In the example below, too many words and phrases have been taken directly from the source. *This is plagiarism even though the authors and the page have been cited.*

Irresponsible (Plagiarized) Paraphrase or Short Summary

Our high-tech revolution has put us into a state of continuous partial attention. According to software executive Linda Stone, this is a state of continually staying busy—paying attention to everything while never really focusing on anything. In continuous partial attention, people place their brain in an increased state of stress or constant crisis, without time to reflect or make thoughtful decisions. They are always on alert for exciting tidbits of news. Once they get accustomed to this state, they thrive on being constantly connected because it feeds their ego and gives them a sense of self worth (Small and Vorgan 18).

Responsible Paraphrase or Short Summary

According to Gary Small and Gigi Vorgan, authors of the book *iBrain,* technology has caused some people to experience "continuous partial attention," a state in which people divide their attention among many things at once but never really focus their mind on any one thing at a time. They are always seeking the next exciting piece of information. Small and Vorgan say continuous partial attention is stressful because it leaves people with no time to reflect. But it is also addictive, because once people get used to it, they like the feeling of self-importance they get from being connected at all times (18).

The best way to avoid an inadvertent plagiarism problem is to pay close attention whenever you are using material from sources:

- Take careful notes.
- If you ever cut and paste from an online source into a draft with the intention of reworking the passage into a quotation or summary/paraphrase later, highlight or shadow the entire passage in some bright color so it will stand out as writing that is not your own.
- Summarize fairly and accurately.
- Paraphrase by putting ideas fully into your own words and sentences.
- Choose quotations that accurately depict ideas in the source and carefully use quotation marks to indicate use of exact wording.

Some features of good paraphrasing to note: The paraphrase is set up with the authors' names and credentials; the sentences are new, some longer, some shorter. The words "continuous partial attention" are quoted the first time they appear to show that those are the words of the source. It would be optional to use quotation marks the second time since the term has been established as a technical phrase.

See Chapter 2, pages 25–29, on paraphrasing and summarizing.

See Chapter 18, pages 446–53, on using and documenting sources.

CHAPTER 20

Documenting Your Sources: MLA

THE MODERN LANGUAGE ASSOCIATION (MLA) STYLE OF DOCUMENTATION IS used in the arts and humanities—in particular, by researchers in the fields of language and literature. MLA documentation uses in-text parenthetical citations that are matched to a list of works cited at the end of the paper. This chapter covers the basics of using MLA documentation style. You can find detailed explanations of MLA guidelines for documenting your sources and formatting your papers in the *MLA Handbook for Writers of Research Papers,* 7th edition.

How Do I Make In-Text Citations Using MLA Style?

See Chapter 18, pages 441–46, for guidance on summary and paraphrase.

For an explanation of what is considered common knowledge, see Chapter 19, pages 459–60.

When you quote from, summarize, or paraphrase the work of someone else—and when you provide information that is not common knowledge—cite your sources in the text by providing the author's last name and, if available, the exact page number(s) where the quoted or paraphrased material was found. If the author's name appears in your signal phrase (for example, "As Smith said"), omit it in the parenthetical citation. All in-text citations must match the citations in your works cited list. The examples that follow illustrate the most common ways to cite sources in the text of your papers.

Direct Quotation with Source Named in Signal Phrase

Signal phrase.

As part of his argument that popular culture makes us smarter, Steven Johnson argues, "The rise of the Internet has challenged our minds in three fundamental and related ways: by virtue of being participatory, by forcing users to learn new interfaces, and by creating new channels for social interaction" (118).

Punctuation Alert: Use a comma between a signal phrase and the opening of a quotation that is a complete sentence.

Punctuation Alert: Close direct quotations before parenthetical citations. Place periods after the parenthetical citation unless you have a block quotation (see page 465).

Direct Quotation with Source Named in Parentheses

Popular culture can be mentally stimulating. The Internet, for example, "has challenged our minds in three fundamental and related ways: by virtue of being participatory, by forcing users to learn new interfaces, and by creating new channels for social interaction" (Johnson 118).

Punctuation Alert: In MLA style, there is no comma between the name of the author and the page number. Do not use the word *page* or any abbreviation for it.

Summary or Paraphrase with Source Named in Parentheses

Reading is unlike other natural human functions of seeing, moving, speaking, and thinking. Reading is an invented cognitive function, and understanding how it works illustrates the amazing plasticity of the brain (Wolf and Barzillai).

When you are citing online sources with no page numbers and no numbering of paragraphs, as in the example above, you will not be able to cite a page. You also do not need to cite a page if the source is only one page long or if you are referring to it in its entirety.

Source with Two or More Authors

If your source has two or three authors, give all last names.

In their book *iBrain,* Small and Vorgan claim that Internet use can be addictive, as people get a rush of the brain chemical dopamine when they turn on their computers (48-49).

For four authors or more, you may list all last names or give the first author's name followed by the abbreviation *et al.* (not in italics, but ending with a period).

The nativist opposition to immigration in the 19th century was fueled by the rising numbers of immigrant voters who cast their votes against temperance, antislavery, and other reforms favored by the Protestant native-born majority (Maier et al. 481).

Two or More Works by the Same Author

When you are citing more than one work by an author, you need to specify which one you are referring to; do this by using shortened versions of the titles:

Mark Edmundson believes that people should read good literature with the hope or goal of being influenced by it ("Narcissis Regards"). He argues that this goal is especially important for college students because college reading opens doors to ideas different from the ones students grew up with ("Dwelling" 28).

Two or More Authors with the Same Last Name

If you have sources by two or more authors with the same last name, use initials for first names in parenthetical references (or full names if the initials are also the same). In your discussion, you should use full names the first time you mention an author.

> Although some researchers (C. Smith) have found that this particular gene plays a significant role in promoting cancer cell growth, others (R. Smith) have not been able to discover a link.

Organization or Agency as Author

Treat an organization or government agency the same way you would treat an individual author; the name may be used in a signal phrase or in a parenthetical reference. Try to introduce long names in a signal phrase; if you use the name in a parenthetical citation, you may shorten or abbreviate it, but be certain that it matches the reference list entry. For example, in parentheses you may use Natl. Public Radio instead of National Public Radio.

Work with No Author or Editor

If no author or editor is named, use the title of the work in both in-text citations and works cited entries. If the title is long, abbreviate it. Begin the title or its abbreviation with the first word that is not an article (*the, a, an*) because your works cited list will be organized alphabetically according to the first significant word in the title. The following example is from a page on a website.

> The Law School Aptitude Test (LSAT) measures ability to read and comprehend in-depth texts with insight, to draw "reasonable inferences" from readings, and to analyze and evaluate the reasoning of others' arguments ("About the LSAT").

More than One Source in a Parenthetical Citation

If you have more than one source to cite for a piece of information, list them alphabetically, separated by a semicolon:

> Several researchers believe that reading books puts the brain to work in ways that reading on the Internet does not (Bauerlein; Wolf and Barzillai).

Reference to an Entire Work; Work with No Page Numbers

> Mark Bauerlein's *The Dumbest Generation* argues that people under thirty are not taking full advantage of the Internet's resources for gaining knowledge.

When you do not have page numbers to cite because you are referring to an entire work, try to put the author's name in the text of the sentence rather than in parentheses. The works cited list would contain full bibliographic information for this source. A reference to a source with no page numbers is treated in the same way.

Use of Quotation Marks within a Quotation

In the source from which the following example comes, "truth" appeared in quotation marks. When you quote the entire passage yourself, truth should have single quotation marks:

> According to Wolf and Barzillai, "[Socrates] worried that the seeming permanence of writing would delude young people into thinking that they had learned the 'truth,' when they had just begun the search for it."

> **Punctuation Alert:** In the above example, "he" was used instead of "Socrates" in the source. You need to substitute Socrates because otherwise your reader would not know who "he" was. Use square brackets to substitute proper names for pronouns that have no clear reference in your own sentence.

Long Quotations (Block Quotations)

For direct quotations that will be more than four lines in your paper, omit quotation marks and display the quotation as a block of text set in from the left margin by one inch. Double-space the entire block quotation. In a block quotation, the final period precedes the parenthetical citation. Here is an example of a block quotation:

> In his best-selling book, *The Dumbest Generation,* Mark Bauerlein describes the studies of Jacob Nielsen, who runs a consulting group that designs Web pages for corporations. This group does eye-tracking studies to show how people read on computer screens. The researchers' conclusion was "They *don't*" (qtd. in Bauerlein 143). The eye tracker revealed a surprising pattern that creators of Web sites need to know:
>> The pattern looks like the capital letter F. At the top of the page, users read all the way across, but as they proceed their descent quickens and horizontal movement shortens, with a slowdown around the middle of the page. Near the bottom of the page, the eyes move almost vertically, forming the lower stem of the F shape. . . . Whatever content businesses want to communicate to visitors better not be concentrated in the lower-right portions of the screen, Nielsen advised. (Bauerlein 144)

Indirect Source (a Source Your Source Used)

Sources quote and document their own sources. How do you treat a source within a source? First, do not cite anything that you have not consulted yourself. Second, use "qtd. in" (for "quoted in") and cite the source in which you found the quotation. In the example below, the student's source was an article by William Major.

> Students today are always connected, always in touch. When a professor asked his students to give up cell phones for a few days, they responded as if he had asked them

to take off their clothes (Major). In contrast to Thoreau, who wrote, "I never found the companion that was so companionable as solitude," (qtd. in Major), today's students seem more frightened by than enthusiastic about the possibilities offered by solitude.

Punctuation Alert: As in the example above, use double quotation marks around direct quotes. If your quotation itself contains words or phrases that should be in quotation marks, put these in single quotation marks. *Do not use quotation marks around block quotations* unless they are themselves quotations (dialogue from a novel, for example).

A Work in an Anthology

Cite the author of the individual work, not the editor or compiler of the anthology.

> In "Toadstools," the narrator suspects that the food in supermarket aisles "hold[s] stories of other people's houses" (Nguyen 130).

A Multivolume Work

If your citation requires page numbers, list volume number, followed by a colon and the page numbers. If you are not referring to specific pages, then use the abbreviation for volume: vol. 2.

> In his narrative history of the Civil War, Shelby Foote devotes the chapter "Beleaguered City" to the Battle of Vicksburg (vol. 2: 323-427).

Work of Literature or Classic Work

Because works that are out of copyright (such as nineteenth-century novels) can be found in many editions, citing a page number alone will not help your reader. Along with the page number, provide chapter numbers, section numbers, even paragraph numbers if that is the only way the work is divided. Use abbreviations for parts of books.

> Elizabeth Bennet expresses her recognition of her own pride and prejudice to her sister: "I have courted prepossession and ignorance, and driven reason away. . . . Till this moment I never knew myself" (Austen 136; ch. 36).

Punctuation Alert: Use a semicolon after the page number and before any additional material.

Poetry is cited by line numbers. The first time you cite a poem, use the word *line* or *lines;* after that, give just the numbers.

He did not touch the shroud, or raise the fold
That hid my face, or take my hand in his,
Or ruffle the smooth pillows for my head:
He did not love me living; but once dead
He pitied me; and very sweet it is
To know he still is warm though I am cold. (Rossetti, lines 9-14)

> **Punctuation Alert:** Use a comma after the author's name if what follows is not a number.

Use Arabic numerals to cite act, scene, and lines (if needed) from a play; use periods to separate them.

The warrior Fortinbras has the final words in *Hamlet:* "Take up the bodies; such a sight as this / Becomes the field, but here shows much amiss. / Go, bid the soldiers shoot" (5.2.386-88).

> **Punctuation Alert:** If you are using fewer than four lines of poetry, use a slash (virgule) to separate lines; the slash is preceded and followed by a space.

Religious Texts

Do not italicize the name of sacred texts in your sentences: the Bible, the Koran, the Bhagavad Gita. However, the names of specific editions should be in italics. In parenthetical references, abbreviate the names of biblical books, and separate chapter and verse with periods. The titles of biblical books are not italicized.

The translation in the *New Oxford Annotated Bible* reads: "Now the manna was like coriander seed, and its appearance like that of bdellium. The people went about and gathered it, and ground it in mills or beat it in mortars, and boiled it in pots, and made cakes of it; and the taste of it was like the taste of cakes baked with oil" (Num. 11.7-8).

How Do I Make Entries in the Works Cited List Using MLA Style?

Your works cited list should include complete bibliographic information for all sources you refer to in your paper. The examples in this section indicate how to cite the kinds of sources commonly used in first-year writing assignments.

See Section 1 of the *Engaging Questions Handbook* for more information on works cited lists.

General Guidelines for Your Works Cited List

All the guidelines described below are illustrated in the example research paper at the end of this chapter, pages 484–90.

- The first word of each entry on the works cited list must match the in-text citation. If you refer, for instance, to Edward Hoagland's essay on aging in your paper, there should be an entry in the works cited list that begins with "Hoagland, Edward."

- Put *all* entries in alphabetical order according to the first word in each entry. Usually the first word will be the lead author's or editor's last name or—if no author is named—the first word in the title not including articles (*a, an, the*).

- Do not number the entries.

- Double-space within and between entries.

- Begin each entry at the left margin and indent all subsequent lines by one-half inch. The hanging indent feature of your word processing program will help you.

- Italicize titles of books, periodicals (such as magazines and journals), films, and other major works like websites and blogs.

- Put quotation marks around titles of articles and essays from periodicals or books of collected works (such as anthologies) and around pages or posts found on a website.

See Section II of the *Engaging Questions Handbook* for a list of prepositions.

- Capitalize all words in titles and subtitles except for articles (*a, an, the*), co-ordinating conjunctions (*and, or, but*), and prepositions. Always capitalize the first and last word of a title, regardless of its part of speech.

- Include subtitles of works. Separate them from the title with a colon.

- If some publication information is not given, use the following abbreviations in place of the missing data: n.p. for no place or no publisher, n.d. for no date, and n. pag. for no pagination.

Printed Books

Your entries for printed books should contain the following:

1. Name of author or editor, last name first, followed by a period (unless no author or editor is listed)
2. Title of the work, italicized, followed by a period
3. Place (city) of publication, followed by a colon
4. Publisher, followed by a comma
5. Year of publication, followed by a period
6. Medium, followed by a period

In the works cited list, do not cite page numbers for chapters or portions of books. Do include page numbers, before the medium and followed by a period, for items in an anthology or collected set of works.

Last name, First name. *Title.* City of publication: Publisher, date. Medium of publication.

Book by a Single Author

Urrea, Luis Alberto. *The Devil's Highway: A True Story.* New York: Little, 2004. Print.

Two or More Books by the Same Author

Instead of repeating the author's name in your works cited list, give the name in the first entry only. For subsequent works, use three hyphens in place of the name, followed by a period. Arrange the works in alphabetical order according to the first word in the title of the work, excluding articles (*a, an, the*).

Obama, Barack. *The Audacity of Hope: Thoughts on Reclaiming the American Dream.* New York: Crown, 2006. Print.

———. *Dreams from My Father: A Story of Race and Inheritance.* 1995. New York: Three Rivers, 2004. Print.

Note: For reprinted works, include the original date of publication immediately before current publication information.

Book by Two or Three Authors

Put the name of the lead author first, beginning with his or her last name. Begin with the first name for second and third authors. Use commas between names.

Small, Gary, and Gigi Vorgan. *iBrain: Surviving the Technological Alteration of the Modern Mind.* New York: HarperCollins, 2008. Print.

Suárez-Orozco, Carola, Marcelo M. Suárez-Orozco, and Irina Todorova. *Learning a New Land: Immigrant Students in American Society.* Cambridge: Belknap-Harvard UP, 2008. Print.

In MLA style, use just the city name for place of publication; state names are not used. If the title page shows an imprint (for example, Belknap, an imprint of Harvard University Press, in the second citation above), include both it and the publisher's name, separated by a hyphen.

Book by Four or More Authors

Use only the first author's name and the Latin abbreviation *et al.*, meaning "and others" (not italicized). It is also correct to list all the authors in order, as with two or three authors.

> Chambers, Mortimer, et al. *The Western Experience*. 9th ed. New York: McGraw, 2007.
> Print.

In the Works Cited list, use a comma between the author's first name and *et al*. The parenthetical in-text citation would read (Chambers et al. 2007), with no comma.

Book by a Corporate Author or Government Agency

Treat the corporation or agency as an author.

> Modern Language Association. *MLA Handbook for Writers of Research Papers*. 7th ed.
> New York: MLA, 2009. Print.

If you abbreviate publisher names, use abbreviations that your readers will understand.

Book with No Author or Editor

Begin the citation with the title. In the works cited list, ignore articles *a, an,* and *the* when placing entries in alphabetical order; the following example would be alphabetized under *New*.

> *The New York Times Guide to Essential Knowledge: A Desk Reference for the Curious Mind*.
> 2nd ed. New York: St. Martin's, 2007. Print.

Later Edition of a Book

Directly after the title, add the edition number without italics. Use numerals; abbreviate *edition*.

> Williams, Joseph M. *Style: Ten Lessons in Clarity and Grace*. 9th ed. New York: Pearson,
> 2007. Print.

Reprinted Book

Include the original date of publication before current publication information.

> Adams, Henry. *The Education of Henry Adams: An Autobiography*. 1918. Boston:
> Houghton, 1961. Print.

Translation

> Vargas Llosa, Mario. *The Bad Girl*. Trans. Edith Grossman. New York: Farrar, 2007. Print.

Preface, Introduction, Foreword, or Afterword Not by the Book's Author or Editor

Start the entry with the name of the author of the part of the book; then provide the name of the section, followed by the title of the book. Use the word *by* before the author of the book. If the book is a reprint, include the original date of publication. Indicate the inclusive page numbers for the part of the book you used as your source.

> Bellow, Saul. Foreword. *The Closing of the American Mind.* By Allen Bloom. New York: Simon & Schuster, 1987. 11-18. Print.

If the section has a title of its own, use the following format:

> Mochulsky, Konstantin. "Dostoevsky and *The Brothers Karamazov.*" Introduction. *The Brothers Karamazov.* By Fyodor Dostoevsky. Trans. Andrew R. MacAndrew. 1970. New York: Bantam, 2003. xiii-xxii. Print.

If your source is an e-book file, indicate that as the medium. Use location numbers or other information instead of page numbers.

Scholarly Edition

Important works are often published in scholarly editions, and the scholarship of the editor (on the text, introduction, and footnotes, for example) might be what you cite in your paper. Use the following format if most of your citations are to the work itself:

> Melville, Herman. *Moby Dick.* 1851. Ed. Tony Tanner. New York: Oxford UP, 2008. Print.

Use this format if most of your citations are to the editor's work:

> Tanner, Tony, ed. *Moby Dick.* By Herman Melville. 1851. New York: Oxford UP, 2008. Print.

Anthology or Edited Compilation

Place a comma after the editor's name, and add the abbreviation for editor.

> Shreve, Susan Richards, ed. *Dream Me Home Safely: Writers on Growing Up in America.* Boston: Houghton, 2003. Print.

Work in an Anthology

For works in collections of essays, poetry, and short stories, put the author of the individual work first, followed by its title in quotation marks, then the title of the collection in italics. The editor's name follows. Note that entries for works in anthologies do cite the inclusive page numbers of the selection.

> Nguyen, Bich Minh. "Toadstools." *Dream Me Home Safely: Writers on Growing Up in America.* Ed. Susan Richards Shreve. Boston: Houghton, 2003. 129-132. Print.

The MLA rule for inclusive page numbers is to include all digits for numbers 1–99 but only the last two digits of the second number when the range starts at 100 or higher (unless more are needed for clarity): 23-67, 79-102, 107-23, 1859-75, 1859-917.

Two or More Works from the Same Anthology

If you are using more than one selection from an anthology, you will need at least three entries in your works cited list, one for the entire work, opening with the name of its editor, and one for each of the items, opening with the name of its author. The editor's last name follows the title of the selection and refers your readers to the entire book; it is followed by the inclusive page numbers of the selection. Place each entry in its alphabetically determined spot on the works cited list, as illustrated below.

> Griffith, Patricia. "The Spiral Staircase." Shreve 73-81.
> MacDonald, Michael Patrick. "Spitting Image." Shreve 112-22.
> Shreve, Susan Richards, ed. *Dream Me Home Safely: Writers on Growing Up in America.* Boston: Houghton, 2003. Print.

One Volume of a Multivolume Work

Directly after the title of the work, indicate the volume number you used.

> Foote, Shelby. *The Civil War: A Narrative.* Vol. 2. New York: Random, 1963. Print.

More than One Volume of a Multivolume Work

After the title, indicate the total number of volumes in the work. If the work was published over multiple years, indicate the range of years.

> Foote, Shelby. *The Civil War: A Narrative.* 3 vols. New York: Random, 1958-74. Print.

Book That Is Part of a Series

After the medium (print), put the name of the series and a series number for the work if available. Do not italicize the series title.

> Horning, Alice, and Anne Becker, eds. *Revision: History, Theory, and Practice.* Lafayette: Parlor, 2006. Print. Reference Guides to Rhetoric and Composition.

Signed Article in a Reference Book

Cite the name of the author, the title of the entry, the title of the reference work, name of the editor, publication information. Do not include page numbers if entries are arranged in alphabetical order in the reference book itself.

> Zangwill, O. L. "Hypnotism, History of." *The Oxford Companion to the Mind.* Ed. Richard L. Gregory. New York: Oxford UP, 1987. Print.

Unsigned Article in a Reference Book

Open with the title of the entry. Include page numbers if entries do not appear in alphabetical order.

> "A Technical History of Photography." *The New York Times Guide to Essential Knowledge: A Desk Reference for the Curious Mind.* New York: St. Martin's, 2004. 104-12. Print.

Edition of a Religious Text

Italicize the title and provide names of editors and/or translators and the publication information.

> *The New Oxford Annotated Bible with Apocrypha.* Ed. Michael D. Coogan et al. 4th ed. New York: Oxford UP, 2010. Print. New Revised Standard Version.
> *The Bhagavad Gita: According to Paramhansa Yogananda.* Ed. Swami Kriyananda. Nevada City: Crystal Clarity, 2008. Print.

Art Reproduction

Treat art found in books in the same way you treat selections found in edited collections. Open the entry with the artist's name, followed by the title of the work and the date it was created, if available. Before you list publication information, indicate where the original work of art may be found.

> O'Keeffe, Georgia. *Light /17: Evening Star, No. V.* 1917. McNay Art Museum, San Antonio. *O'Keefe and Texas.* By Sharyn R. Udall. San Antonio: The Marion Koogler McNay Art Museum, 1998. 51. Print.

Articles in Print Periodicals

Your works cited entries for articles in print periodicals should contain the following:

1. Author's name, followed by a period
2. Title of the article, followed by a period, all in quotation marks
3. Title of the periodical, italicized
4. Volume number (if given); issue number (if given)

5. Date (if given), followed by a colon

6. Inclusive page numbers, followed by a period

7. Medium, followed by a period

Article in a Journal with Volume Numbers

Put the volume number (for example, "71" in the example below), a period, and the issue number (if there is one) after the title of the article. Put the year in parentheses.

> Last name, First name. "Article Title." *Journal Title* Vol.issue (date): pages. Medium.

> Bracher, Mark. "How to Teach for Social Justice: Lessons from *Uncle Tom's Cabin* and Cognitive Science." *College English* 71.4 (2009): 363-88. Print.

Some journals are not published by volume. In this case, use issue number only.

Article in a Monthly Magazine

> Last name, First Name. "Article Title." *Magazine Title* date: pages. Medium.

Abbreviate all months except May, June, and July.

> Mooney, Chris. "Climate Repair Made Simple." *Wired* July 2008: 128-133. Print.

Article in a Weekly Magazine

> Levy, Ariel. "Nora Knows What to Do." *New Yorker* 6 July 2009: 60-69. Print.

Although the magazine is titled *The New Yorker*, MLA style calls for dropping *The* before periodical names.

Article in a Newspaper

> Last name, First name. "Article Title." *Newspaper Title* date, edition: pages. Medium.

Give the day, month, year, and edition if specified; use abbreviations. Give section and page number. If pages are not consecutive, put a plus sign after the first page number.

> Keller, Julia. "Sticks and Stones and Presidential Speeches." *Chicago Tribune* 23 Jan. 2011, final ed., sec 4: 4. Print.
> Yoon, Carol Kaesuk. "Reviving the Lost Art of Naming the World." *New York Times* 11 Aug. 2009, natl. ed.: D1+. Print.

If the page number does not include the section number or letter, indicate the section in another way: for example, sec. A, sec. 6, Arts and Entertainment sec. If the city is not named in the newspaper title, add it (not italicized) in brackets after the title, but before the date: *Times Union* [Albany] 13 Jan. 2011.

Editorial in a Newspaper—No Named Author

"Disfigured Democracy: Health Care Extremism Exposes Our Uglier Side." Editorial.
Dallas Morning News 13 Aug. 2009: A14. Print.

Letter to the Editor of a Newspaper or Magazine

Black, Antony. Letter. *Economist* 22 Jan. 2011: 20. Print.
Reed, Glenn. Letter. *Harper's* Aug. 2009: 5. Print.

Review

Open with name of reviewer and title of review, if there is one. Add the abbreviation for *review of*, not italicized, followed by the title of the work being reviewed, and its author or performer.

Hofferth, Sandra. "Buying So Children Belong." Rev. of *Longing and Belonging: Parents,
Children, and Consumer Culture,* by Allison J. Pugh. *Science* 324 (26 June 2009):
1674. Print.

Advertisement in Print Medium

Open with the name of the item or service being advertised.

Daedalus Books. Advertisement. *Harper's* Aug. 2009: 6. Print.

Sources on the Internet

When the information is available, your works cited entries for electronic sources should contain the following:

1. Name of author, editor (ed.), performer (perf.), or translator (trans.), followed by a period
2. Title of work, followed by a period
3. Title of website, followed by a period
4. Publisher or sponsor of the site, followed by a comma
5. Date last updated (or n.d), followed by a period
6. Medium (Web), followed by a period
7. Date you accessed the site, followed by a period

The URL for the website is not needed unless your reader would have difficulty finding the site through a search engine.

Last name, First name. "Title of article or page." *Title of website.* Sponsor/publisher, date
of update. Medium. Access date. <URL (only if needed)>.

Website or Independent Online Work

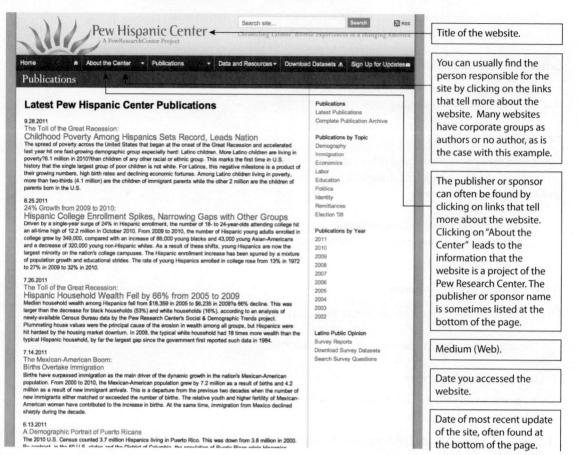

Title of the website.

You can usually find the person responsible for the site by clicking on the links that tell more about the website. Many websites have corporate groups as authors or no author, as is the case with this example.

The publisher or sponsor can often be found by clicking on links that tell more about the website. Clicking on "About the Center" leads to the information that the website is a project of the Pew Research Center. The publisher or sponsor name is sometimes listed at the bottom of the page.

Medium (Web).

Date you accessed the website.

Date of most recent update of the site, often found at the bottom of the page.

Example Entry for Entire Website

Begin with the title of site if there is no author named.

Pew Hispanic Center. Pew Research Center, 22 July 2009. Web. 20 Aug. 2009.

Webpage or Document Found on a Website

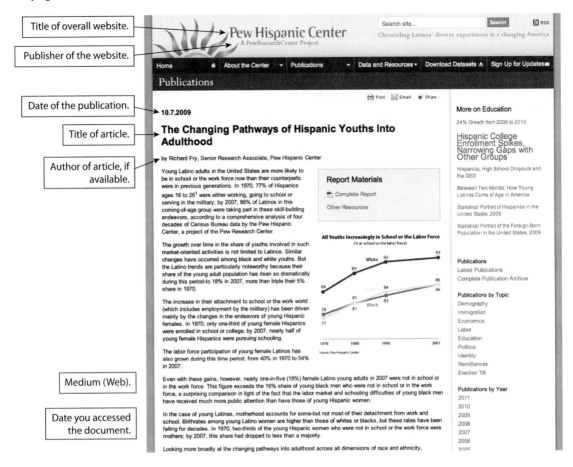

Title of overall website.

Publisher of the website.

Date of the publication.

Title of article.

Author of article, if available.

Medium (Web).

Date you accessed the document.

Example Entry for a Webpage or Document Found on a Website

Author. "Title of Page." *Title of Site*. Sponsor, date of publication. Web. Date accessed.

This format for an individual webpage or document is the basis for many different types of MLA works cited entries, including news stories on television network sites, documents in online archives, online video and audio, and even online performances. Some of the variations on this format follow.

Personal Website

If the site has no title, use "home page" or other descriptive title. If there is no sponsoring organization, use N.p. to indicate no publisher.

> Langer, Ellen. Home page. N.p., 2009. Web. 28 July 2009.

Books Accessed Online

> Austen, Jane. *Pride and Prejudice. Project Gutenberg,* 1998. Web. 7 Jan. 2011.

Use the digital publication date. If the Web source gives print data for the edition used, include it.

> Austen, Jane. *Pride and Prejudice.* Vol. 3. London, 1813. *Google Books,* 2007. Web. 7 Jan. 2011.

For books published before 1900, the publisher's name is not needed.

Article in an Online Journal

Follow the print format, but change the medium to Web and give an access date. The following periodical is published annually, so it has a volume number only.

> O'Dwyer, Kathleen. "Nietzsche's Reflections on Love." *Minerva—An Internet Journal of Philosophy* 12 (2008): 37-77. Web. 12 Oct. 2009.

If no pages are given, use *n. pag.* (not italicized).

Article Accessed through a Library Subscription Database

Give print information and then database information. Italicize the database name.

> Wolf, Maryanne, and Mirit Barzillai. "The Importance of Deep Reading." *Educational Leadership* 66.6 (2009): 32-37. *Academic Search Complete.* Web. 6 Mar. 2009.

Article in an Online Magazine

> Wilson, A. N. "Leo Tolstoy, Russia's Thunderous Prophet. *Slate.*" Washington Post. Newsweek Interactive, 20 Nov. 2010. Web. 23 Jan. 2011.

Article in an Online Newspaper

Put the website in italics; follow with the name of the sponsor or publisher, not italicized.

Hotz, Robert L. "Creative Destruction on a Cosmic Scale: Scientists Say Asteroid
Blasts, Once Thought Apocalyptic, Fostered Life on Earth by Carrying Water and
Protective Greenhouse Gas." *Wall Street Journal.* Dow Jones & Company, 14 Aug.
2009. Web. 15 Aug. 2009.

Editorial in an Online Newspaper or Magazine

"Major Chainsaw." Editorial. *Chicago Tribune.* Tribune Company, 18 Jan. 2011. Web. 19
Jan. 2011.

Online Letter to the Editor

Henderson, Shirley. Letter. *Washington Post.* Washington Post, 16 Jan. 2011. Web. 19
Jan. 2011.

Online Review

Use *Rev. of* (not in italics) to introduce the title of the book being reviewed. If the
review has a title of its own, include it.

Garner, Dwight. "Engagements with History Punctuate a Lifetime in Books." Rev. of
Outside Looking In, by Garry Wills. *New York Times.* New York Times, 2 Nov. 2010.
Web. 19 Jan. 2011.

Article in an Online Reference Work

If unsigned, open with the title of the article. When alphabetizing, ignore opening
article (*a, an, the*).

"The Biological Notion of Individual." *Stanford Encyclopedia of Philosophy.* Metaphysics
Research Lab, Stanford U, 9 Aug. 2007. Web. 26 Mar. 2009.

Blog Entry

Put the title of the post in quotation marks and the blog title in italics.

Jerz, Dennis. "Thoreau's Cellphone Experiment." *Jerz's Literacy Weblog.* 18 Jan. 2011.
Web. 22 Jan. 2011.

Government Document on the Web

United States. Cong. Senate. Special Committee on Aging. *Social Security
Modernization: Options to Address Solvency and Benefits Adequacy.* 111th Cong.,
2nd sess. S. Rept. 111-187. 13 May 2010. Web. 25 Jan. 2011.
United States. Environmental Protection Agency. *Protecting the Stratospheric Ozone
Layer.* 29 Aug. 2008. Web. 24 Jan. 2011.

Broadcast or Published Interview

Open with the names of the interviewee or interviewees, followed by the title of the interview, if there is one; if not, provide the interviewer's name, followed by the correct format for the medium.

> Ganguly, Sumit, and Minxin Pei. "Balancing India and China." *Council on Foreign Relations.* Council on Foreign Relations, 6 Aug. 2009. Web. 13 Aug. 2009.
> Hariri, Saad. Interview by Babak Deghhanpisheh. *Newsweek.* Harman Newsweek, 20 Dec. 2010. Web. 7 Jan. 2011.

Discussion Groups and Online Forums

MLA suggests that postings to online forums and discussion groups are not appropriate sources for research papers and does not provide a format. But there might be a reason for you to cite them in a paper that examined Internet communication, for example. Use the format for e-mail.

> Perlstein, Arnie. "A Novelist's Progress." Message to Austen-L. 26 Jan. 2011. E-mail.

Change the medium to Newsgroup posting or Forum posting as appropriate.

Wiki

> "Herman Melville." *Wikipedia.* Wikimedia Foundation, 18 Jan. 2011. Web. 25 Jan. 2011.

E-mail Message

> Lindahl, Joseph. Message to the Author. 15 May 2010. E-mail.

Other Sources

E-book

Use the format for a print book. The medium of publication should be the type of electronic file used, such as Kindle, Adobe Reader, EPUB, or PDF.

> Hawes, Elizabeth. *Camus: A Romance.* New York: Grove, 2009. Kindle e-book file.

Films

> *The King's Speech.* Dir. Tom Hooper. Perf. Colin Firth, Geoffrey Rush, and Helena Bonham Carter. Weinstein, 2010. Film.

If your paper is about an individual's contribution to the film, then list the director, performer, or other contributor first and cite that person's name in the text. The film's distributor should be listed.

> Fincher, D., dir. *The Social Network.* Perf. Jesse Eisenberg and Rooney Mara. Columbia, 2010. Film.

If you are viewing the film on DVD or via the Web, then change the medium to reflect that. Add the access date at the end for a Web viewing or Internet download.

> *Amazing Grace.* Dir. Michael Apted. Perf. Ioan Gruffudd, Albert Finney, Romola Garai, and Michael Gambon. 20th Century Fox, 2007. DVD.

In this case, you list the DVD distributor.

Television

For an individual episode

> "Cleaning House." *How I Met Your Mother.* By Pamela Fryman. Dir. Steven Lloyd. CBS. WBBM, Chicago, 28 Sept. 2010. Television.

For a series

> *Monk.* Creat. Andy Breckman. Perf. Tony Shalhoub, Jason Gray-Stanford, Ted Levine, and Traylor Howard. USA Network. 2002-2009. Television.

If you watched on DVD or via the Web, change the medium. Add an access date at the end for a Web viewing or Internet download. If you are writing primarily about a contributor to the program, start with the person's name and title.

Performances

> *In the Heights.* By Lin-Manuel Miranda. Dir. Thomas Kail. Chor. Andy Blankenbuehler. Richard Rodgers Theatre, New York. 9 Jan. 2011. Performance.

If you want to emphasize an individual's contribution, use this format:

> Sher, Bartlett, dir. *South Pacific.* By Richard Rodgers and Oscar Hammerstein II. Perf. Kelli O'Hara and Paulo Szot. Vivian Beaumont Theater, Lincoln Center, New York. 3 Apr. 2008. Performance.

Musical Composition and Sound Recording

If your emphasis is on the work, start with the composer. If it is on the performance, start with the conductor or performers. Song names are in quotation marks; longer works are italicized. Add the production company and release date.

> Baez, Joan, perf. "Simple Twist of Fate." By Bob Dylan. *Diamonds and Rust.* A&M, 1988. CD.
> Barenboim, Daniel, cond. *Symphony No. 5.* By Gustav Mahler. Chicago Symphony Orchestra. Rhino, 2006. MP3 file. 19 Jan. 2011.
> Cooder, Ry. *Paradise and Lunch.* Reprise, 1990. CD.

Podcast

> "Rock-Munching Mollusks a Model for Artificial Bones." Narr. Joe Palca. *Morning Edition.* Natl. Public Radio, 13 Jan. 2011. Web. 19 Jan. 2011.

If it is important for your readers to know that your source was a podcast, indicate that in your signal phrase. If the podcast was a digital download, then use MP3 file for the medium.

Cartoon

> Batiuk, Tom. "Funky Winkerbean." Comic strip. *Chicago Tribune* 19 Jan. 2011: 12. Web. 20 Jan. 2011.
> Wilson, Gahan. Cartoon. *New Yorker* 24 Jan. 2011: 24. Print.

Work of Visual Art

For works of visual art, state artist, title (italicized), date of composition (or N.d.), the work's medium, the location (such as the museum, gallery, collection), and city.

> Seurat, Georges. *A Sunday on La Grande Jatte.* 1884. Oil on canvas. Art Inst., Chicago.

If your source comes from the Web, use the following format:

> Seurat, Georges. *A Sunday on La Grande Jatte.* 1884. School of the Art Inst., Chicago. *Art Access.* Web. 19 Jan. 2011.

Map

> "Kingsville, Texas." Map. *Google Maps.* Google, 11 Jan. 2011. Web. 11 Jan. 2011.

A map from a book would be cited this way:

> "The Pusan Perimeter, August 4, 1950." Map. *The Coldest Winter: America and the Korean War.* By David Halberstam. New York: Hyperion, 2007. 165. Print.

Use this form only if the map was your only source from the book; otherwise, list the entire book under Works Cited and indicate in a signal phrase that you are referring to a map.

Oral Presentations

This category includes papers presented at professional conferences as well as readings, speeches, and keynote addresses. Use quotation marks around titles.

> Laurence, David. "The Condition of the Modern Languages in Higher Education: What the Data Tell Us." Paper presented at the Rocky Mountain Modern Language Association Conference. Albuquerque, 15 Oct. 2010. Address.

Pamphlet

Set up works cited entries for pamphlets and brochures as if they were books.

> Divers Alert Network. *Dive and Travel Medical Guide*. N.p.: Divers Alert Network, 2009.
>   Print.

Use N.p. if no place of publication is listed; n.d. for no date.

Legal Sources

> Griswold v. Connecticut. 381 US 479. Supreme Court of the US. 1965. *FindLaw*.
>   Thomson Reuters, 2011. Web. 19 Jan. 2011.
> Patient Protection and Health Care Act. 124 Stat. 119-1025. 2010. Print.

The names of legal cases are italicized in your text: *Griswold v. Connecticut.*

Personal Interview

Give the name of the person interviewed, the kind of interview (personal, telephone), and the date it took place.

> Coman, Carolyn. Telephone interview. 15 Aug. 2009.

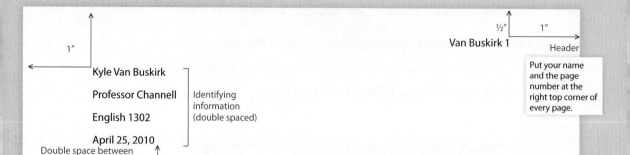

½" 1"

Header

Put your name and the page number at the right top corner of every page.

Kyle Van Buskirk

Professor Channell

English 1302

April 25, 2010

Identifying information (double spaced)

Double space between date and title

The Benefits of Slow Reading Lost in Our Fast-Paced Culture

Double space between title and 1st line

½" For many young adults today, reading anything in depth almost seems like an

ancient pastime. In English class, high school students will search online for the Cliff Notes

rather than actually read the book. When we want news, instead of reading newspapers, we

check the headlines on MSNBC. Doing research, we surf the Internet. A study of computer

activity in the British Library found that researchers skim and "bounce" from site to site. "It

almost seems that they go online to avoid reading in the traditional sense," concluded the

authors of the study (qtd. in Carr). People have lost sight of the many benefits of reading

because we live in such a fast-paced, technology-driven culture. We have become too

impatient to read.

Carr is quoting the authors of the study, but Carr is the source. Use the abbreviation for "quoted in" for indirect sources.

Our pace of life makes everything that takes time seem like a burden. Even sitting

down to drink a cup of coffee takes too long, so we use the drive-through at Starbucks.

What people do not realize is that life is short, and it will be shallow and unsatisfying if we

refuse to slow down to think and reflect. Reading books provides us with that opportunity,

enriching our lives in the long run, but also giving us many immediate, practical benefits.

Some people claim that we read just as much as ever, only we do it on computer

screens. In an on-line newspaper column titled "Dawn of the Digital Natives," Steven

Johnson, a best-selling nonfiction author, asks his readers, "Odds are that you are reading

these words on a computer monitor. Are you not exercising the same cognitive muscles

because these words are made out of pixels and not little splotches of ink?"

Lead into an opinion by first introducing the person who holds that opinion, giving full name on first mention and some identification or credentials.

But there is evidence that on-line reading and on-paper reading are not the same.

In his best-selling book, *The Dumbest Generation,* Mark Bauerlein describes the studies

1"

of Jacob Nielsen, who runs a consulting group that designs Web pages for corporations. This group does eye-tracking studies to show how people read on computer screens. The researchers' conclusion was "They *don't*" (qtd. in Bauerlein 143). The eye tracker revealed a surprising pattern that creators of Web sites need to know:

> The pattern looks like the capital letter F. At the top of the page, users read all the way across, but as they proceed their descent quickens and horizontal movement shortens, with a slowdown around the middle of the page. Near the bottom of the page, the eyes move almost vertically, forming the lower stem of the F shape. . . . Whatever content businesses want to communicate to visitors better not be concentrated in the lower-right portions of the screen, Nielsen advised. (Bauerlein 144)

This study gives scientific evidence that on-line readers could be missing a lot of content. But if people do not read books, they also miss out on important mental exercise.

Even though Steven Johnson defends screen reading as making "Digital Natives" highly informed, he admits in his book *Everything Bad Is Good for You* that the Internet is not so good at "training our minds to follow a sustained textual argument" (187) or to "transmit [the] fully fledged world view" of another person (186). Johnson writes a blog to exchange ideas with readers, but he writes books to present his arguments in full.

Can we get the benefits of book reading from watching the movie version of a novel or listening to an audio book while we drive? According to reading experts, we cannot. Oprah Winfrey, who has promoted book reading on her TV show, published an article in her magazine *O* about the mental benefits of reading. Reading gives your brain more of a neurobiological workout than hearing speech or looking at images (Duzbow). Maryanne Wolf, director of the Center for Reading and Language Research at Tufts University, explains why: "Typically, when you read, you have more time to think. Reading gives you a unique pause button for comprehension and insight. By and large, with oral language— when you watch a film or listen to a tape—you don't press pause" (qtd. in Duzbow). In a more technical article, Wolf explains that experienced readers' brains have developed

---

Marginal notes:

Use block form for quotations of more than four lines of type. Double-space as normal before, after, and within block quotations.

Period ending a block quotation goes before the parenthetical citation.

Work quotations into a paraphrase to present key ideas concisely. Use square brackets where you have had to alter a quotation to fit it into your sentence.

Use a colon before a direct quotation if you lead into it with a complete sentence instead of a phrase.

Use ellipses to show where parts of quotations have been deleted. An ellipsis is a series of three spaced periods. The first period here is not spaced because it ends the sentence before the deleted portion.

Cite the source of paraphrased information that is not common knowledge.

"streamlined" circuits that allow them to go far beyond just decoding the words. As they read, experienced readers can also "question, analyze, and probe" and "go beyond the wisdom of the author to think their own thoughts," a process that involves "all four lobes and both hemispheres of the brain" (Wolf and Barzillai). Reading gives our brains a workout, but because on-line readers click on links and allow their eyes to jump around in the F-shaped pattern described earlier, they are not developing these critical reading skills.

However, even when a person sits down with a book, he or she may not take the time to hit the pause button and read deeply. In an article for *Atlantic Monthly* titled "Is Google Making Us Stupid?" Nicholas Carr, who writes about information technology, describes how switching to the Internet as his main source of information has changed his style of reading. He went from loving to read long books to having to struggle to pay attention to them: "I get fidgety, lose the thread, begin looking for something else to do. I feel that I am always dragging my wayward brain back to the text." Carr has lost the ability to immerse himself in a book. As he describes it, "Once I was a scuba diver in the sea of words. Now I zip along the surface like a guy on a Jet Ski."

One would think that schools would encourage reading for pleasure, but too often they encourage reading for speed. This bothers Thomas Newkirk, Professor of English at University of New Hampshire. He criticizes the Accelerated Reading Program, which awards points for numbers of books read, and standardized testing "in which reading is always 'on the clock.'" A slow reader himself, Newkirk says fast readers miss out on a lot, just as riders on high-speed European trains miss out on the details of the scenery and see the distant landscape as a blur. Newkirk says that "there is real pleasure in downshifting, in slowing down. We can gain some pleasures and meanings no other way." The pleasure is not just a result of going slow, explains John Miedema, who wrote a book on slow reading. "To me," he says, "slow reading is about bringing more of the person to bear on the book" (qtd. in Ramer). This is what people mean when they say they "got into" a book. Getting lost in a book is fun.

Grade 12 in 2005

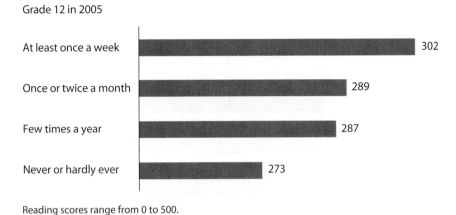

Reading scores range from 0 to 500.

Fig. 1. Average Reading Scores by Frequency of Reading Fiction Books or Stories Outside School

Source: United States, Department of Education, National Center for Education Statistics, reported in United States, National Endowment for the Arts, *To Read or Not to Read: A Question of National Consequence;* Nov. 2007; Web; 22 Apr. 2009: 71.

Setting aside time to read for pleasure also pays off in practical ways. Students who read for pleasure have distinctly higher reading comprehension scores and better writing scores. Fig. 1 shows the correlation between twelfth graders' reading scores and the amount of time they spend reading fiction for fun.

Fig. 2 shows the results of a slightly older study on writing ability. Students who read every day scored almost thirty points higher than those who did almost no reading for fun.

Reading for pleasure is also a way of improving mental wellness. Most students live at too fast a pace. We are distracted and stressed, constantly worrying about the next quiz, test, project, or research paper. Bauerlein believes leisure reading provides relief from stress and helps us put our lives into perspective. He explains, "Books afford young readers a place to slow down and reflect, to find role models, to observe their own turbulent feelings well expressed, or to discover moral convictions" (58). Slowing down to think is necessary in college, when students are making important decisions about their morals, goals, and identity.

Grade 12 in 2002

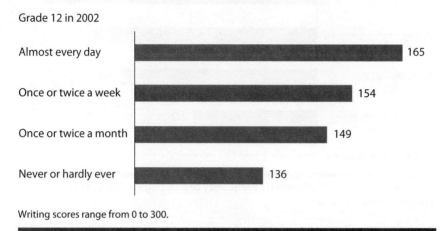

Writing scores range from 0 to 300.

Fig. 2. Average Writing Scores by Frequency of Reading for Fun

Source: United States, Department of Education, National Center for Education Statistics, reported in United States, National Endowment for the Arts, *To Read or Not to Read: A Question of National Consequence;* Nov. 2007; Web; 22 Apr. 2009: 72.

Likewise, Newkirk argues that schools should encourage slow reading to show students "an alternative to an increasingly hectic digital environment where so many of us read and write in severely abbreviated messages. . . ." Encouraging slow rather than fast reading would be one way to help students keep their lives in balance. Even before the Internet, media critic Neil Postman argued that a "major role" for schools "is to help conserve that which is necessary to a humane survival is threatened by a furious and exhausting culture" (qtd. in Newkirk). In other words, reading quality literature at a leisurely pace helps to keep us human.

Another English professor, Mark Edmundson, at the University of Virginia, is also concerned that the lifestyle of college students is too hectic. He sees that his students are always connected through their cell phones and laptops, working too hard, playing too hard, and taking ADD drugs to keep going (25). Edmundson worries that the fast pace of his students' lives keeps them from really knowing themselves and reflecting on the world. He imagines that Socrates would worry that today's students do not slow down enough to question what they have been told is true, what Socrates referred to as "*doxa*, common sense, general belief"(27). All through their years of growing up, adults in their lives—parents, teachers, and clergy—have told them how to define themselves and interpret the world. Edmundson says these interpretations may be true, but then again, they may not. That is why education and books are important. Edmundson wants professors to slow their classes down: "to live well, we must sometimes stop and think, and then try to remake the work in progress that we currently are" (28).

We do a disservice to ourselves when we do not take time to read slowly. In addition to preparing us for success in our careers, deep reading helps us put our lives into perspective. Too many students are connected to everything and everyone but themselves, as Edmundson says, "[skating] fast over the surfaces of life," but not thinking about where we are going and why" (25). Reading books for leisure helps to connect us with our own lives because books contain wisdom, not just more information, which we are already drowning in. To read for wisdom, we have to slow down the pace.

Use summary to present a large section of a source, citing pages for paraphrases as well as where brief quotations help to preserve the voice of the source's author.

Use brackets when changing verb tenses to make them fit grammatically into your sentence.

Works Cited

Bauerlein, Mark. *The Dumbest Generation: How the Digital Age Stupefies Young Americans and Jeopardizes Our Future.* New York: Tarcher-Penguin, 2008. Print.

Carr, Nicholas. "Is Google Making Us Stupid?" *TheAtlantic.com.* Atlantic Monthly Group, July-Aug. 2008. Web. 10 Apr. 2010.

Duzbow, Lauren. "Watch This. No. Read It!" *Oprah.com.* Harpo Productions, June 2008. Web. 16 Apr. 2010.

Edmundson, Mark. "Dwelling in Possibilities: Our Students' Spectacular Hunger for Life Makes Them Radically Vulnerable." *Arts Education Policy Review* 110.2 (2008): 22-28. Web. 2 Apr. 2010.

Johnson, Steven. "Dawn of the Digital Natives." *guardian.co.uk.* Guardian News and Media Ltd., 7 Feb. 2008. Web. 19 Apr. 2010.

——. *Everything Bad Is Good for You: How Today's Popular Culture Is Actually Making Us Smarter.* New York: Riverhead, 2005. Print.

Newkirk, Thomas. "The Case for Slow Reading." *Educational Leadership* 67.6 (2010): 6-11. Web. 15 Apr. 2010.

Ramer, Holly. "NH Professor Pushes for Return to Slow Reading." *Seattle Times.* Seattle Times, 17 June 2010. Web. 20 June 2010.

United States. Natl. Endowment for the Arts. *To Read or Not to Read: A Question of National Consequence.* Nov. 2007. Web. 14 Apr. 2010.

Wolf, Maryanne, and Mirit Barzillai. "The Importance of Deep Reading." *Educational Leadership* 66.6 (2009): 32-37. *Academic Search Complete.* Web. 19 Apr. 2010.

CHAPTER 21

Documenting Your Sources: APA

THE AMERICAN PSYCHOLOGICAL ASSOCIATION (APA) STYLE OF DOCUMENTA-
tion is used not only in the field of psychology, but also in education, anthropology, social
work, business, and other behavioral and social sciences. In APA documents, it is common
to find authors referred to by their last name only rather than their full names, as in Modern
Language Association (MLA) documents.

Like MLA style, APA documentation requires that a writer acknowledge the source of all
direct quotations, paraphrased and summarized ideas from sources, and information that is
not common knowledge. Citing is a two-step process that includes a brief in-text reference to
the author and date of publication and a longer entry with complete bibliographical information in the reference list at the end of the article or book.

How Do I Make In-Text Citations Using APA Style?

For direct quotations and paraphrases of information that is not common knowledge, the basic in-text citation provides the last name of the author of the source,
directly followed by the year the source was published. Citing page numbers is
required for direct quotations and highly specific data but not for summarizing
or paraphrasing ideas found throughout a text. The following examples show
options for citing in text.

Summary or Paraphrase with One Author Named in Your Sentence

The playground is a space where gender identities are constructed. Paechter (2007)
argues that boys who are physically passive on the playground move into the marginal
spaces occupied by girls and younger children and thus become stigmatized by other
boys as effeminate.

Summary or Paraphrase with One Author Named in Parentheses

The playground is a space where gender identities are constructed. Boys who are
physically passive on the playground move into the marginal spaces occupied by
girls and younger children and thus become stigmatized by other boys as effeminate
(Paechter, 2007).

> **Punctuation Alert:** Place a comma between the author's name and the date of
> publication.

The parenthetical citation does not include page numbers because the information is a summary.

Direct Quotation with Author Named in the Sentence

> According to Yoon (2009) anthropologists have found that people around the world create remarkably similar categories when labeling plants and animals, a phenomenon known as folk taxonomy. Yoon finds consensus about such categories as trees, vines, and bushes especially interesting "since there is no way to define a tree versus a bush" (p. D4). In naming the world around them, people appear "unconsciously to follow a set of unwritten rules" (p. D1).

Use the abbreviations *p.* or *pp.* for page references. Also cite figure numbers, table numbers, or other parts of a book if they are the source of specific information.

Punctuation Alert: Close direct quotations before parenthetical citations. Place periods after the parenthetical citation unless you have a block quotation (see page 495).

Direct Quotation with Author Named in Parentheses

Unless the author is named in a sentence, all references in parentheses must include the last name and the year.

> Anthropologists have found that people around the world create remarkably similar categories when labeling plants and animals, a phenomenon known as folk taxonomy (Yoon, 2009). Consensus about such categories as trees, vines, and bushes is especially interesting "since there is no way to define a tree versus a bush" (Yoon, 2009, p. D4). In naming the world around them, people appear "unconsciously to follow a set of unwritten rules" (Yoon, 2009, p. D1).

Source with Two Authors

Give both authors' last names each time you refer to the source. If you name them as part of your sentence, use *and* to join them.

> Wolf and Barzillai (2009) describe the cognitive work of the reading brain.

If you name them in parentheses, use an ampersand (&).

> Reading is very much unlike our other natural human functions of seeing, moving, speaking, and thinking. Reading is an invented cognitive function, and understanding how it works illustrates the amazing plasticity of the brain (Wolf & Barzillai, 2009).

Source with Three or More Authors

For three, four, or five authors, give all authors' last names in your first reference to the work. Write out "and" when the list is part of your sentence. Subsequent references should give only the first author's last name followed by the abbreviation *et al.* (not in italics).

First Reference

> Radeloff, Hammer, and Stewart (2005) studied the impact of housing density on forests in the midwestern United States.

Later References

> Radeloff et al. (2005) argue that rural sprawl has more impact on forests than urban sprawl because even though rural sprawl is less dense, its effects are spread over larger areas that once were forests.

For six or more authors, give only the first author's last name, followed by et al.

> Mottron et al. (2007) studied locally oriented perception in children with autism.

More than One Publication by an Author in the Same Year

When you are citing more than one publication by an author, with the same year of publication, label the years a, b, c, and so on; the letter *a* would be assigned to the publication that comes first alphabetically. See the reference list example on page 501.

> Developmental psychologists often focus on the stresses of adolescence rather than on the positive aspects of that stage of life (Steinberg, 2005a, 2005b).

Punctuation Alert: Works by the same author are separated by commas.

Two or More Authors with the Same Last Name

Include identifying initials before each last name.

> S. Young (2007) complains that scientists study earth-eating, or geophagia, only from the standpoint of their own disciplinary interests. Thus, there is no "global perspective of all the possible benefits and all the possible negative consequences of geopaghia" (p. 67).

Organization or Agency as Author

Spell out the name the first time you use it.

> According to the National Collegiate Athletic Association (2010), the Academic
> Progress Rate is a way to measure academic performance for college and university
> sports teams.

If the name is long and has a familiar abbreviation, you may use that in subsequent citations.

> (NCAA, 2010)

Always spell out brief names or names that do not have familiar abbreviations.

Work with No Author or Editor

If no author or editor is named, use the title of the work in both in-text citations and reference list entries. If the title is long, abbreviate it in the text but not on the reference list. Use double quotation marks around the title of an article, a chapter, or a webpage in your discussion, but not in the reference list. Italicize the title of a periodical, book, or report. The example below shows a webpage.

> The Law School Aptitude Test (LSAT) measures ability to read and comprehend in-
> depth texts with insight, to draw "reasonable inferences" from readings, and to analyze
> and evaluate the reasoning of others' arguments ("About the LSAT," 2009).

More than One Source in a Parenthetical Citation

If you have more than one source for the same information, include all sources in the parenthetical citation, in alphabetical order, as they would appear in the reference list. Use a semicolon to separate sources by different authors.

> (Steinberg, 2005a, 2005b; Stewart, 1987)

Work with No Page Numbers (Including Web Pages and E-books)

If online material, e-books, or even print material is unpaged and you need to cite a specific passage, use chapters, paragraphs, headings, or whatever other indicators will help readers find the passage.

> According to Friend (2009), "Extraordinary oddities of conduct are tolerated among
> Wasps so long as you show up for Christmas" (Chapter 4, para. 78).

If the chapters have further numbered subdivisions, include them.

> (Section 5, para. 4, for example)

Reprinted Works

When you cite a work that has been republished, give both the original date and the date of the version you are using. The in-text citation for the example on page 499 would be (Obama 1995/2004). The date of original publication comes first, although on the reference list the date following the author's name will reflect the edition you used (2004, in this case).

Citations within Quotations

You will often find that your source cites other sources. Do not put these sources on your References list unless you also read them and used them in your paper. When quoting, include the citations as they appear in the passage you are quoting.

> Hunters seldom wear protection for their hearing, resulting in hearing loss among practitioners of the sport, as Flamme et al. (2010) explain:
>> Firearm impulse sound exposure contributes to the poorer hearing ability and hearing handicap evident in sports hunters when compared to nonhunters (Taylor & Williams, 1966; Stewart et al., 2002). Nondahl et al. (2000) calculated a 7% increase in the likelihood of having a marked high-frequency hearing loss for every 5 years of hunting.

Long Quotations

For direct quotations of forty or more words, omit quotation marks and display the quotation as a block of text set in from the left margin by one-half inch (in the same place as a new paragraph's opening). Double-space the entire quotation. See the example above on citations within quotations.

> **Punctuation Alert:** With block quotations, place final period before the parenthetical citation.

Indirect Sources

A good researcher relies on primary sources. But if your only source for information was cited in another source, use this format.

> . . . as noted by Conley (as cited in McMaster, 2009).

Include McMaster on your reference list, not Conley.

Work in an Anthology

If you are citing a selection from an anthology, list the author of the selection. If you are citing the collection as a whole, list the editor or compiler of the book.

Classics and Religious Works

When you are citing a work whose original publication date is not known or is not relevant, show the date of the version you are using—(Defoe, 2005 version), for example—for a modern version of *Robinson Crusoe,* first published in 1719. For a translation of a classical work, show the date of translation (Sophocles, trans. 1911). Religious works are cited only in the text, not in the reference list. Instead of page numbers, cite books, chapters, verses, lines, and so forth. Use standard abbreviations for biblical books: Num. 11.7–8, for instance.

A Multivolume Work

Cite all the years of publication if you are referring to the entire work.

> (Foote, 1958–1974)

If you have used all the volumes but are citing from just one, include the volume number.

> (Foote, 1958–1974, Vol. 2, p. 165)

An Entire Website

When your source is an entire website, cite it in the text by providing the uniform resource locator (URL), but do not provide a reference list entry.

> The PsychCentral website, sponsored by mental health professionals, offers news, information, and support group hosting for people interested in or affected by mental health disorders (http://psychcentral.com).

Personal Communications

Personal communications such as letters and interviews are not listed in the reference list; they are cited in text as in the following example.

> Carolyn Coman described her use of storyboarding to focus on the emotional impact of significant scenes in her fiction (C. Coman, personal communication, August 15, 2009).

Note that the names of months are not abbreviated in APA style and that month precedes day.

How Do I Make Entries in a Reference List Using APA Style?

This section includes examples of how to cite the most common kinds of sources in papers using the APA style of documentation.

General Guidelines for Your Reference List

- Begin the list on a new page and center the word *References* at the top. (Do not italicize.)
- The first word of each entry must match the in-text citation.
- Put all entries, regardless of genre and medium, in alphabetical order according to the author's (or editor's) last name, followed by the initials of the author's first name or names. Use an ampersand before the last author's name.
- If no author is named, use the first word in the title that is not an article (*a, an, the*). See page 498 for an example.
- Do not number the entries.
- Double-space within and between entries.
- Begin each entry at the left margin and indent all subsequent lines by one-half inch. The hanging indent feature of your word processing program will help you do this.
- Italicize titles of books and periodicals.
- Do not enclose titles of articles in quotation marks, although you do use quotation marks for titles when you refer to them in text.
- Capitalize only the first words of titles and subtitles of books and articles; however, capitalize all proper nouns in any title or subtitle (for example, a person's name).
- Capitalize the full names of periodicals, journals, and newspapers.
- Use city and state, unless the state is included in the publisher's name (Albuquerque: University of New Mexico Press). Use postal abbreviations for state names (New Haven, CT).
- In general, when the entry ends with something other than a publisher's name or page number, such as the DOI (digital objective identifier), URL, accession number, or original publication date, there is no end punctuation.

See the list of examples for more help with citing specific kinds of sources.

Printed Books

Your entries for printed books should contain the following:

1. Name of author (or editor) in inverted order, followed by a period (unless no author or editor is listed)
2. Date of publication in parentheses, followed by a period
3. Title of the work, in italics, followed by a period
4. City and state of publication, followed by a colon
5. Publisher, followed by a period

Last name, Initial(s). (Date). *Title*. City, State: Publisher.

Book by a Single Author

> Paechter, C. F. (2007). *Being boys, being girls: Learning masculinities and femininities.* New York, NY: McGraw-Hill.

Use a brief form of the publisher's name. Do not include words like *Company, Corporation, Inc.* Words like *Books* and *Press* should be retained. Do not use abbreviations.

Two or More Books by the Same Author

List the works in order of publication, with the earliest first. Repeat the author's name for each entry.

> Obama, B. (2004). *Dreams from my father: A story of race and inheritance.* New York, NY: Three Rivers. (Original work published 1995)
> Obama, B. (2006). *The audacity of hope: Thoughts on reclaiming the American dream.* New York, NY: Crown.

Book by Two or More Authors

List all authors by last name and initials, separated by commas. Use an ampersand (&) before the final name. If a work has up to seven authors, list them all. If there are more than seven, list the first six, then an ellipsis (three spaced dots), then the last author. (See the example for a journal article on page 503.)

> Booth, W., Colomb, G., & Williams, J. (2003). *The craft of research* (2nd ed.). Chicago, IL: University of Chicago Press.
> Small, G., & Vorgan, G. (2008). *iBrain: Surviving the technological alteration of the modern mind.* New York, NY: HarperCollins.

Book by a Corporate Author or Government Agency

Treat the corporation or agency as an author. If the author and publisher are the same, put "Author" after the place of publication.

> American Psychological Association. (2010). *Publication manual of the American Psychological Association* (6th ed.). Washington, DC: Author.

Book with No Author or Editor

Start with the title of the work. Use "Anonymous" only if that is what the title page says.

> *The Chicago Manual of Style.* (2010). Chicago, IL: University of Chicago Press.

Later Edition of a Book

Put the edition number in parentheses after the title.

> Williams, J. M. (2007). *Style: Ten lessons in clarity and grace* (9th ed.). New York, NY: Pearson Longman.

Reprinted Book

Indicate the original date of publication in parentheses.

> Obama, B. (2004). *Dreams from my father: A story of race and inheritance.* New York, NY: Three Rivers. (Original work published 1995)

Note: The in-text citation should include both dates, with the original publication date first (1995/2004).

Anthology or Compilation

Between the editor's name and the date, put the abbreviation for editor(s), followed by a period.

> MacClancy, J., Henry, J., & Macbeth, H. (Eds.). (2007). *Consuming the inedible: Neglected dimensions of food choice.* New York, NY: Berghahn Books.

Selection in an Anthology or Compilation

For articles in edited works, put the author of the individual work first, followed by the year of publication, and then the title of the article, followed by the word *In* and the editor or editors' names (not in inverse order) and the title of the collected work. The inclusive pages of the selection follow the title of the book, in parentheses. End the citation with place and name of publisher.

> Young, S. (2007). A vile habit? The potential biological consequences of geophagia, with special attention to iron. In J. MacClancy, J. Henry, & H. Macbeth (Eds.), *Consuming the inedible: Neglected dimensions of food choice* (pp. 67–79). New York, NY: Berghahn Books.

Note that APA style for inclusive numbers uses all digits.

Translation

Put the translator's initials and last name, followed by the abbreviation for translator in parentheses after the book's title.

> Ariès, P. (1965). *Centuries of childhood* (R. Baldick, Trans.). New York, NY: Vintage Books. (Original work published 1962)
> Sophocles. (1911). *Oedipus Rex* (J. E. Thomas, Trans.). Clayton, DE: Prestwick House. Retrieved from http://www.gutenberg.org/wiki/Main_Page

For classical works, such as *Oedipus Rex*, cite the date of translation in your text: (Sophocles, trans. 1911). This example also illustrates the format for a book retrieved online.

Preface, Introduction, Foreword, or Afterword Not by the Book's Author or Editor

Open the entry with the name of the author of the part of the book; then put the date in parentheses and write out the name of the section written by this author. Follow with author or editor, title, and publication information for the entire book.

> Gore, A. (2008). Foreword. In B. McKibben (Ed.). *American earth: Environmental writing since Thoreau.* New York, NY: Library of America.

Multivolume Work

Directly after the author, indicate the inclusive dates of the volumes. After the title of the work, indicate in parentheses the number of volumes.

> Churchill, W. (1956–1958). *A history of the English-speaking peoples* (Vols. 1-4). London, England: Cassell.

One Volume of a Multivolume Work

If the individual volumes in a multivolume work have their own titles, use the following format when only one of them should be included in your reference list.

> Churchill, W. (1957). *A history of the English-speaking peoples: Vol. 3. The age of revolution.* London, England: Cassell.

If the volume does not have its own title, then put the volume number in parentheses after the title, as when citing all volumes.

Signed Article in a Reference Book

Include inclusive page numbers for the entry in parentheses after the title of the book.

> Zangwill, O. L. (1987). Hypnotism, history of. In R. L. Gregory (Ed.), *The Oxford companion to the mind* (pp. 330–334). New York, NY: Oxford University Press.

Unsigned Article in a Reference Book

Open with the title of the entry.

> A technical history of photography. (2004). In *The New York Times guide to essential knowledge: A desk reference for the curious mind* (pp. 104–112). New York, NY: St. Martin's.

Articles in Print Periodicals

Your reference list entries for print periodicals should contain the following:

1. Name of author (or editor) in inverted order, followed by a period (unless no author or editor is listed

2. Date of publication in parentheses, followed by a period

3. Title of the article, not in italics, followed by a period

4. Title of the periodical, in italics, followed by a comma (and, for a journal, further publication information)

5. Inclusive page numbers, followed by a period

Article in a Journal with Volume and/or Issue Numbers

Last name, Initial(s). (Date). Title of article. *Title of Periodical, Vol. no*(issue), pages.

Put a comma after the journal title, followed by the volume number in italics; then (with no space) put the issue number, if one is needed, in parentheses, followed by a comma and inclusive page numbers. For journals, use the issue number *only* if the journal is paged by issue, not by volume.

Bracher, M. (2009). How to teach for social justice: Lessons from *Uncle Tom's Cabin* and cognitive science. *College English, 71,* 363–388.

Wolf, M., & Barzillai M. (2009). The importance of deep reading. *Educational Leadership, 66*(6), 32–37.

Multiple Publications by the Same Author in the Same Year

Use letters to distinguish works by the same author in the same year; assign the letters according to the alphabetical order of the reference list.

Steinberg, L. (2005a). Cognitive and affective development in adolescence. *Trends in Cognitive Sciences, 9,* 69–74.

Steinberg, L. (2005b). *The ten basic principles of good parenting.* New York, NY: Simon & Schuster.

Article in a Monthly Magazine

For magazine articles, do not use *p.* or *pp.* Instead, put the volume number in italics followed by the issue number in parentheses, a comma, and page numbers. Because magazines are paged by issue, the issue number is required.

Mooney, C. (2008, July). Climate repair made simple. *Wired, 16*(7), 128–133.

Article in a Weekly Magazine

Include the day as well as the month and year.

Gladwell, M. (2009, October 19). Offensive play: How different are dogfighting and football? *The New Yorker,* 50–59.

Article in a Newspaper

Give the day, month, year, and edition if specified. For newspaper articles, use the abbreviations *p.* and *pp.* before page number (not italicized). List all page numbers if the article appeared on discontinuous pages.

> Yoon, C. K. (2009, August 11). Reviving the lost art of naming the world. *The New York Times,* pp. D1, D4.

Do not abbreviate the names of months. Include articles at the beginning of periodical titles.

Newspaper Article with an Anonymous Author

Start with the title of the article. When alphabetizing, ignore opening articles (*a, an, the*).

> Moon travel uncertain. (2009, August 14). *Dallas Morning News,* p. 12A.

Editorial in a Newspaper—No Author Given

Put the genre (editorial) in square brackets.

> Disfigured democracy: Health care extremism exposes our uglier side [Editorial]. (2009, August 13). *Dallas Morning News,* p. A14.

Letter to the Editor of a Newspaper or Magazine

Put the genre (letter to the editor) in square brackets.

> Meibers, R. (2009, July). Thou shall kill [Letter to the editor]. *Harper's,* 4.

Review

Open with the name of the reviewer, the date, and the title of the review, if there is one. Put "Review of," followed by the item being reviewed, in square brackets.

> Denby, D. (2011, January 24). Man up. [Review of the films *The Green Hornet,* dir. M. Gondry, and *The Dilemma,* dir. R. Howard]. *The New Yorker,* 82–83.
> Hofferth, S. (2009, June 26). Buying so children belong [Review of the book *Longing and belonging: Parents, children, and consumer culture* by A. J. Pugh]. *Science, 324,* 1674.

Although *Science* is a scholarly journal, it is published weekly; APA style treats it and similar journals like a magazine.

Advertisement in Print Medium

> Daedalus Books. (2009, August). [Advertisement]. *Harper's,* 6.

Sources on the Internet

Your reference list entries for Internet sources will vary according to the kind of source: online periodical, database, reference work, public service site, government site, and so on. Each entry should contain the following:

1. Name of author (or editors) in inverted order, followed by a period (unless no author or editor is listed

2. Date of publication in parentheses, followed by a period

3. Title (including a format description in square brackets for unusual sources), followed by a period

4. Retrieval path, often a DOI or URL, or a database name and accession number (if available)

Other information may be included, such as periodical titles and page numbers, where available.

> Last name, Initial(s). (Date). Title [label if needed]. Retrieval path.

Website

Do not list entire websites in the reference list. Give the URL in your discussion. See page 496.

Webpage

> Tartakovsky, M. (2011). Asperger's syndrome. Retrieved from http://psychcentral.com
> /lib/2010/aspergers-syndrome/

If the source is something unusual, such as a lecture, a data file, or a video, put that in square brackets after the title.

Journal Article Retrieved Online—with DOI

Because URLs often change, a new method of locating online materials has been developed. Increasingly, you will find that articles have an alphanumeric identification string, usually located near the copyright date in the article. You can also find it in the bibliographic information in the library's full-record display. Always use the DOI, if available, instead of the URL from which you retrieved the online article. Use the format for a print journal. Conclude the entry with the DOI. There is no space between the colon and the number when giving a DOI.

> Mottron, L., Mineau, S., Martel, G., St.-Charles Bernier, C., Berthiaume, C., Dawson,
> M., . . . (2007). Lateral glances toward moving stimuli among young children
> with autism: Early regulation of locally oriented perception. *Development and
> Psychopathology, 19,* 23–26. doi:10.1017/S0954579407070022

Note the treatment of more than seven authors. The first six are listed; an ellipsis follows, and then the last author is named. This article has ten authors.

Journal Article Retrieved Online—without DOI

Follow the format for a print article. Follow with "Retrieved from" and the URL for the journal home page.

> O'Dwyer, K. (2008). Nietzsche's reflections on love. *Minerva—An Internet Journal of Philosophy, 12,* 37–77. Retrieved from http://www.ul.ie/~philos/

Source Accessed through a Database

Cite books and periodicals according to the guidelines already given. Include the name of the database only if you think it would be difficult to find the source in any other way. In that case, at the end of the citation, add "Retrieved from" and the database name. Give the accession number, if there is one, in parentheses. Put information identifying the genre in square brackets after the title.

> Van der Woude, G. (2002). *Harriet Tubman integrated unit* [Classroom guide]. Retrieved from ERIC database. (Accession No. ED476397).

Article in an Online Magazine

Conclude the entry with "Retrieved from" and the URL for the home page of the magazine. Use the DOI if there is one.

> Vanderbilt, T. (2011, January 13). Streetcars vs. monorails. *Slate.* Retrieved from http://slate.com

Article in an Online Newspaper

Use the URL for the home page of the newspaper if the article can be found by searching the site, as is usually the case.

> Hotz, R. L. (2009, August 14). Creative destruction on a cosmic scale: Scientists say asteroid blasts, once thought apocalyptic, fostered life on earth by carrying water and protective greenhouse gas. *The Wall Street Journal.* Retrieved from http://online.wsj.com/home-page

Article in an Online Encyclopedia or Reference Work

If the entry is unsigned, open with its title, as in the first example below.

> The biological notion of individual. (2007, August 9). In E. N. Zalta (Ed.), *Stanford Encyclopedia of Philosophy.* Retrieved from http://plato.stanford.edu/entries/biology-individual/

Botstein, L. (2005). Robert Maynard Hutchins and the University of Chicago. In J. Reiff, A. D. Keating, & J. R. Grossman (Eds.), *Encyclopedia of Chicago*. Retrieved from http://www.encyclopedia.chicagohistory.org/pages/2190.html

Use the URL that will get you to the specific article.

Abstract

Sweeten, G., Bushway, S. D., & Paternoster, R. (2009). Does dropping out of school mean dropping out into delinquency? *Criminology, 47,* 47–92. Abstract retrieved from http://www.ncjrs.gov

Blog Post

Give the title of the post and the URL for the post but not the title of the blog.

Agapakis, C. (2010, December 8). Making blind mice see [Web log post]. Retrieved from http://scienceblogs.com/oscillator/2010/12/making_blind_mice_see.php

Published or Broadcast Interview

Include the format in which the interview was published and follow style for that format.

Emanuel, R. (2010, July 8). Interview by J. Lehrer [Web]. Retrieved from http://www.pbs.org/newshour/bb/politics/july-dec10/rahmemanuel_07-08.html

Discussion Groups and Online Forums

Simmons, J. (2010, June 27). Hiroshima and Nagasaki: Justified? [Online forum comment]. Retrieved from http://www.armchairgeneral.com/forums/showthread.php?t=94802

Bracketed labels could also include:

[Discussion list message]
[Newsgroup posting]

Video on the Internet

Hirsh, M. (2010, December 16). Richard Holbrooke: A friend to journalists [Video file]. Retrieved from http://www.youtube.com/watch?v=IeGGGEUsCl0

Other Kinds of Sources

E-book

Friend, T. (2009). *Cheerful money: Me, my family, and the last days of Wasp splendor* [Kindle version]. Retrieved from Amazon.com

Indicate the type of e-book file. If there is a DOI for the e-book file, include it at the end.

Films

Fincher, D. (Producer & Director). (2010). *The social network* [Motion picture]. United
States: Columbia.

List the producer and the director, the studio, and the country of origin.

Television Program (Episode from a Series)

Fryman, P. (Writer), & Lloyd, S. (Director). (2010). Cleaning house [Television series
episode]. In C. Bays, P. Fryman, R. Greenberg, & C. Thomas (Executive Producers),
How I met your mother. New York, NY: CBS.

If you want to cite the entire series, list the creators and producers first, along
with inclusive dates.

Live Performance

Sher, B. (Director). (2008, April 3). *South Pacific* [Live performance]. Vivian Beaumont
Theater, Lincoln Center, New York, NY.

Musical Compositions and Sound Recordings

Cooder, R. (1990). *Paradise and lunch* [CD]. New York, NY: Reprise.
Mahler, G. (Composer), & Barenboim, D. (Conductor). (2006). *Symphony no. 5* [Recorded
by Chicago Symphony Orchestra]. [MP3]. New York, NY: Rhino. Retrieved January
21, 2011 from Amazon.com

Podcast

Palca, J. (Narrator). (2011, January 13). *Rock-munching mollusks a model for artificial
bones* [Audio podcast]. Retrieved from http://www.npr.org

Map

Google Maps. (2011, January 21). Kingsville, Texas [Road map]. Retrieved from http://
maps.google.com/

For a map in a book or article, cite the map number or page number in text and
indicate in your signal phrase that you are referring to a map.

Visual Art

Seurat, G. (1884). *A Sunday on La Grande Jatte* [Painting]. Art Institute, Chicago, IL.

Give the medium and the location. If you cite a work of art in a book, indicate what you are referring to (painting, sculpture, etc.) in your text and list the entire book in the reference list.

Dissertation or Thesis Retrieved from Database

Neland, L. S. (1989). *Correlates of marital satisfaction in chemically dependent women* [Doctoral dissertation]. Retrieved from ProQuest. (AAT 9007511)

Unpublished Dissertation or Thesis

Pendleton, R. (2005). *Teaching biography: History as lives, lives as history* (Unpublished master's thesis). University of Rochester, Rochester, NY.

Paper Presented at a Professional Conference

Jones, S. L., and Yarhouse, M. A. (2009, August 9). *Ex-gays? An extended longitudinal study of attempted religiously mediated change in sexual orientation.* Paper presented at the meeting of the American Psychological Association, Toronto, Canada.

Legal Sources

Griswold v. Connecticut, 381 U.S. 479 (1965).
Patient Protection and Affordable Care Act, Public Law 111-148, 124 Stat. 119-1025 (2010).

Your in-text citations should italicize the names of court cases.

Wikipedia Entry

Sigmund Freud. (n.d.). In *Wikipedia*. Retrieved January 28, 2011, from http://en.wikipedia.org/wiki/Sigmund_Freud

Because APA requires publication dates (not dates of update), n.d. is usually used for Wikipedia entries. The retrieval date is given because the material you cite is likely to change over time on Wikipedia.

Personal Communications

Personal communications such as interviews and letters are not included in the list of references in APA style. However, you need to cite them in the text as described on page 496.

Running head: POPULARITY'S DOWNSIDE

½"   1"
1

Use your title, but not your subtitle, as a running head on every page. Number all pages, starting with title page.

Popularity's Downside:

Valuing Quantity over Quality in Friendship

Audra Ames

Southern Methodist University

Center the title, name, course, instructor, and date in upper half of page. Do not set title off in any other way. This should appear on own page centered.

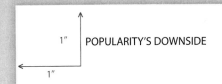

½″   1″

1″

1″

1″

Do not indent first
line of abstract.

Abstract   Heading (centered), new page

Abstract is
an objective
summary of the
main points in the
essay or article.

Adolescents commonly value popularity over having a few high-quality friends, as they see popularity as a mark of status. However, making popularity one's main goal causes young people to miss out on the benefits of real friendship because the values and behavior required for popularity conflict with those that would allow true friendships to form. True friendship encourages personal growth and deep intimacy while an obsession with popularity encourages aggression, mean competition, and conformity to peer group preferences. It also causes young people to keep personal problems to themselves and to become self-absorbed to the point of narcissism. Young people with poor self-image and values may seek the security of groups whose friendship can be destructive, but most settle for superficial friendships that are not harmful, but do not promote personal growth or offer the deep rewards of true friendship. Popularity itself is good but should be seen as a means for finding potential friends with whom to form deep relationships.

Keywords: popularity, competition, peers, friendship

Abstract should
be between 150
and 250 words.

509

Popularity's Downside:

Valuing Quantity over Quality in Friendship

⟵⟶ In middle school, junior high, and high school, social hierarchies are very important, with the top rungs of the ladder usually occupied by cheerleaders, athletes, and the physically attractive people. There is a high correlation between these sources of status and being popular. Popularity itself is a source of status. Even after high school, some people want to continue to play the popularity game; they seek quantity of friends, not quality in friendships. Studies show that this is a mistake. Having large quantities of friends is not as worthwhile as having a few high quality friendships. Real friendships are based not on status and hierarchies but on shared interests and equality. Making popularity one's main goal causes young people to miss out on the benefits of real friendship because the values and behavior required for popularity conflict with those that would allow true friendships to form.

The Value of Friendship

High-quality friendships have been described as relationships in which people are willing to put aside some of their own self-interests to invest attention in each other's goals and personal growth. Friendships support mutual growth. Relationships with friends are not static and unchanging because friends keep each other moving forward, as described by Csikszentmihalyi (1997): "We try new things, activities, and adventures; we develop new attitudes, ideas, and values; we get to know friends . . . deeply and intimately" (pp. 81–82). Similarly, Berndt (2004) found that "friendships are higher in quality when friends feel free to disclose their most intimate thoughts and feelings to each other" (p.1). With true friends, no one feels the need to hide who they are, or what they really think and feel, or fear being seen as weak if they confide about insecurities and doubts.

The rewards of friendship are great; studies have shown that people's most positive experiences occur with friends, and this is "especially true for adolescents" (Csikszentmihalyi, 1997, p. 81). Growing up is just easier with a good friend. Studies have found that having

1"

1"

a close friend and being in a reciprocated friendship helps children of middle-school age adjust to their changing environment with less stress and depression (Dittmann, 2004).

How Popularity Conflicts with Friendship

However, a problem for many adolescents is the importance of popularity over having a few quality relationships. A study of middle school girls found that although they highly valued friendship as a source of trust and intimacy, "friendship was seldom a serious contender with popularity when girls had to choose" (Merten, 2004, p. 362). Similarly, Closson (2009) found that clique members were willing to give up their personal preferences in friends to comply with the leaders' preferences. He concluded that "the desire for popularity may be stronger than the desire for a stable, high-quality friendship in early adolescence" (p. 429).

It seems that young people are torn between their desire for friendship and their desire for status. Studies confirm what most people know from personal experience: Social status is "a central aspect of daily life" for young adolescents (Closson, 2009, p. 407). The desire for status conflicts with the desire for friendship because young people choose to associate with those who can help boost their status rather than those who share their interests and goals. Csiksentzmihalyi (1997) argued that "friendships are expected to provide mutual benefits, with no external constraints that might lead to exploitation" (p. 82). The desire for status puts constraints on the choice of friends, and young people might act friendly to someone simply for the social benefits that person brings.

Too much concern for popularity can keep young people from discussing personal problems, and thus getting the benefit of a peer's sympathy and support. In his study of junior high girls, Merten (2004) noted that true friendships encouraged sharing of all experiences (inclusion), while the desire for popularity caused girls to exclude from conversations any experiences that might cause them to be judged as weak. In friendships, Merten saw girls "respecting and valuing each other's experiences, rather than having the demands of popularity select which experiences were worthy of inclusion in a relationship" (p. 364). Basically, the girls seeking popularity had to filter what they said around their popular friends in order to not have a vulnerability exploited. Popularity is accompanied by a fear of vulnerability. If you show weakness, you are picked apart or criticized for it.

The Downside of Popularity

The fact is that popularity is associated with some bad traits, such as aggression and gossip. Even within cliques, Closson (2009) found that members act aggressively to gain and keep status, and this happened most frequently in cliques that were recognized as having high status within the school:

> Compared to members of lower status cliques, those in perceived popular cliques used more instrumental relational aggression. Some researchers have suggested that peer-directed relational aggression may be used intentionally to damage another peer's social reputation, thereby . . . maintaining or increasing one's status within the clique by decreasing the social position of others. (p. 428)

Closson (2009) also found that popular people were described by their peers as "cool, nice, and funny yet also conceited, exclusionary, and mean" (p. 408). But conceited people are not usually happy because they are too self-absorbed.

A desire for popularity inspires narcissism, which can be described as overly high self-esteem and self-absorption. Narcissistic people are "looking for happiness by way of what they can draw toward themselves, rather than what they can share with others" (Schumaker, 2007, p. 175). People who are obsessed with being popular are buying into a system that almost rules out the possibility of real friendship because as Merten (2004) found, "Popularity was based on hierarchy, public recognition, and self-interest [while] friendship was based on equality . . ." (p. 363). The main focus of popularity seems to be popularity in itself, and especially the attributes that go along with being popular, like physical attractiveness (p. 363). It is not surprising that narcissism has been connected with aggressive behavior, including bullying. Schumaker (2007) described narcissists as aggressive, with a tendency to bully (p. 168). When their self-esteem is threatened, narcissists put others down in order to build up their egos again.

Sometimes people can be popular in another way that creates malignant growth. They can be popular with the wrong crowd, and this can inspire aggressive, antisocial behavior. Interactions with a certain group of people may change a person or encourage violence and aggression, so that the person is more willing to commit unlawful, harmful acts in order to impress his peers. Berndt (2004) summarized studies related to "the three A's of friendship: adjustment, attachment, and aggression." In one study done on aggression in children, surprising data was collected. "Students higher in relational aggression actually had higher quality friendships, perhaps because these students needed friends to join them in attacking or excluding their victims" (Berndt, 2004, p. 2). These relationships are of high quality, but only because peers bond over acts of violence, which does not create a stable, high quality life. An extreme example of destructive friendship would be gangs, in which individuals support each other in a kind of "malignant growth" (Csikszentmihalyi, 1997, p. 82).

Putting Popularity in Its Place

More commonly, people of all ages settle for superficial "friendships" that are more like high school cliques. Csikszentmihalyi (1997) describes these groups as "safe cocoon[s]" for people not seeking to change: "The superficial sociability of teenage peer groups, suburban clubs and coffee klatches, professional associations, drinking buddies, gives a soothing sense of being part of a like-minded set of people without demanding much effort or growth" (p. 82). Having a large circle of acquaintances is not a bad thing if people do not see it as sufficient for the real happiness of true friendship.

One argument in favor of popularity is that it enables people to find friends and to be friends: Nangle, Erdley, Newman, Mason, and Carpenter (2003) found that popularity laid the groundwork for children with good social skills to find potential friends from a large "pool" of others with similarly good social skills (p. 551). Most important, these researchers found that young people with good social skills were able to form deep and long-lasting close friendships. Popularity is not a substitute for real friendship, just a stepping stone to it.

Conclusion

When you have a few good quality friendships versus a lot of acquaintances, you are able to explore, challenge and push yourself into becoming a better person. Equally important is the social support of a good friend. Studies have shown that the most frequent complaint of people dealing with an emotional crisis is that they do not have any true friends to turn to (Csikszentmihalyi, 1997, p. 83). People that do not have social support when they experience a rough patch are more likely to become depressed. Young people need to make it through adolescence with an appreciation for real friendship, and not give in to an immature obsession with popularity as a status symbol. Overall, quality over quantity in friendship is a much more successful route through all of one's life.

References

Berndt, T. J. (2004). Friendship and three A's (aggression, adjustment, and attachment). *Journal of Experimental Child Psychology 88*(1), 1-4. doi:10.1016/j.jecp.2004.03.004

Closson, L. M. (2009). Aggressive and prosocial behaviors within early adolescent friendship cliques: What's status got to do with it? *Merrill-Palmer Quarterly: Journal of Developmental Psychology, 55,* 406–435. doi:10.1353/mpq.0.0035

Csikszentmihalyi, M. (1997). *Finding flow: The psychology of engagement with everyday life.* New York, NY: Basic Books.

Dittmann, M. (2004, July). Friendships ease middle school adjustment. *American Psychological Association.* Retrieved from http://www.apa.org/monitor/julaug04 /friendships.aspx

Merten, D. E. (2004). Securing her experience: Friendship versus popularity. *Feminism & Psychology, 14,* 361–365. doi:10.1177/0959-353504044635

Nangle, D. W., Erdley, C. A., Newman, J. E., Mason, C. A., & Carpenter, E. M. (2003). Popularity, friendship quantity, and friendship quality: Interactive influences on children's loneliness and depression. *Journal of Clinical Child and Adolescent Psychology, 32,* 546–555. doi:10.1207/S15374424JCCP3204_7

Schumaker, J. F. (2007). *In search of happiness: Understanding an endangered state of mind.* Westport, CT: Praeger Publishers.

Include the issue number if a journal is paginated by issue.

Begin references on a separate page.

If your source has a Digital Object Identifier, it is not necessary to give the URL or the date of access.

Include information about databases for on-line articles only if the article is rare and not easily found in several databases.

If a source has multiple authors, list all in the order given. Use an ampersand (&) before the final name.

For a journal paginated by volume, it is not necessary to give the issue number.

GENRES FOR FURTHER PRACTICE

HOW DO I WRITE A RESEARCH PROPOSAL?

AS PART OF PLANNING A RESEARCH PROJECT, WRITERS ARE OFTEN REQUIRED to present a proposal. For professors, graduate students, and other researchers, the research proposal can be part of a request for funding or for approval so a project can go forward. For undergraduates, the research proposal demonstrates that the project poses a worthwhile question and that sources are available for pursuing the answer.

What Is a Research Proposal?

See "How Do I Write a Prospectus?" online, for further discussion.

Similar to a prospectus, a research proposal demonstrates to your instructor or manager that you have done the preliminary work for a research project. Research proposals adhere to the following arrangement of parts.

ASKING QUESTIONS | Anatomy of a Research Proposal

Ask and answer the following questions:

1. Overview of the project: **What question will my research answer?** You need to explain the focus and purpose of the research and tell why the question needs answering. Who will care about the answer to your question? Will the finished project be primarily informative, exploratory, or argumentative?

2. Review of the literature: **What research has already been done on this question?** Show that you have acquainted yourself with what has already been written on your topic. You need to describe the major contributors—who thinks what and why—and indicate how your sources agree and disagree. The literature review section ends by showing how your research relates to previous research or to a question not yet adequately answered.

See Chapter 8, pages 173–201, for help with comparing sources' viewpoints.

3. Methods: **How will I conduct my research?** In the sciences, research involves actual experiments or surveys, so the methods section is a detailed plan for conducting the research and measuring the results. In the humanities, this section describes the primary and secondary sources containing information and opinions about your topic. It also explains your research strategy, such as databases you will search and what search terms you will use.

See Chapter 15, pages 396–411, for guidance on kinds of sources.

See Chapter 16, pages 412–25, for guidance on databases and search terms.

4. Working Bibliography: **What sources have I already found on my topic?** To show that you have a foundation for your project, list the potentially relevant sources that you have found so far, using whatever documentation style your instructor requires. ■

See Chapter 20, pages 462–90, for help with MLA documentation and Chapter 21, pages 491–516, for APA. If your instructor wants an annotated bibliography, see pages 524–28 for guidance.

Why Write a Research Proposal?

Research proposals are part of a longer class assignment. One goal is to ensure projects have gotten off to a timely start. Beyond keeping up with your work, a research proposal helps you move beyond selecting a topic to formulating the question your research will answer. Writing a research proposal encourages you to take stock of where you are after preliminary research and to map out the next steps.

Asking Questions: What Can I Write About?

Writing the research proposal will direct your attention to the following questions:

Significance: **Is my research question worthwhile?** Is the question genuinely open to debate? Does the answer matter to me and my readers? How could having an answer matter in changing how people think or behave?

Knowledge of the conversation: **Who are the major people writing on this topic?** Do these authors refer to each other? About what do they agree and disagree? How do their angles (points of view) differ and which angles are most relevant to my question and point of view?

Feasibility of my research plan: **Can I find the answer to my question?** That is, does information exist that can help answer my question or are there ways to do field research to generate my own information? Can I gather the materials I need in time to complete the assignment?

See Chapter 16, pages 412–25, for guidance in conducting field research.

Student Sample Research Proposal

The following proposal was written in a first-year course for an informative paper. The finished paper appears on pages 140–46.

Amie Hazama

English 1302

May 4, 2010

Research Proposal for a Paper, "Civility in the Workplace"

Overview of the Project: Within the large topic of incivility in American society, I will look

at the question "What are the actual costs of incivility in the workplace?" Incivility makes

for a stressful workplace, and this is becoming common knowledge. However, people do

not know enough about the costs in terms of lost productivity and time. My preliminary

research shows that rudeness, insensitivity, and hostility cost money. I want to make bosses

and managers aware of the size of the problem and the benefits of improving the level of

civility in the workplace. Students in the workforce or about to enter it should also know

how important civility is.

Review of the Literature: I have discovered that incivility has gotten a lot of attention

in the last ten years. P. M. Forni of Johns Hopkins (2002) wrote a best-selling book called

Choosing Civility: The Twenty-five Rules of Considerate Conduct. This book does not focus on

the workplace, but many of the "rules" are relevant, such as the importance of listening and

of giving praise when it is deserved.

In that same year, another book was published that focused just on incivility at work,

Rude Awakenings: Overcoming the Civility Crisis in the Workplace, by a civility consultant,

Giovinella Gonthier. Unlike Forni, Gonthier puts incivility into a historical context, showing

what developments since the 1960's have contributed to people's increasing lack of polite

behavior. Like Forni, Gonthier devotes most of her book to "rules" or advice about behavior.

Most important to my research, however, is her chapter on "The Business Imperatives of

Civility." Here, she reports on research into how incivility affects workers' performance.

Two other academic researchers, Christine M. Pearson and Christine L. Porath (2009),

published *The Cost of Bad Behavior: How Incivility Is Damaging Your Business and What to

Do About It*. The authors previewed their research in an article published in *Academy of

Management Executives* in 2005. They based the book on interviews with over 9,000 workers

who were victims, witnesses, or perpetrators of "bad behavior" at work. They argue that

---

Marginal annotations:

Clearly states the research question.

Why this question is worth asking and answering.

Who would be an audience for my project?

The student has surveyed major works on the topic of civility published in the last ten years.

Shows how this work takes a different angle from Forni's.

Shows how the angle of this book differs from those already mentioned.

Students were to narrow the assigned topic of incivility in daily life.

What is the aim or genre that the project will take?

Shows how this book is relevant to the research question.

Shows another difference.

How this source is similar to Forni.

Shows the breadth of this research.

workplaces can be transformed into more civil places if managers realize the costs and take steps to change the climate, not just the behavior of a few really bad offenders. Their view is similar to Forni's, because they believe that people need to pay attention to the little ways people are discourteous without even realizing it.

Shows how this source differs in angle from Forni.

In my research, I intend to use some of the older sources to lay out some definitions and examples but then move to Pearson and Porath and others in order to document the cost to business and how training can help solve the problem.

Explains the direction of the research for this project. Shows the need for current data and where it might be found.

Methods: I will rely on secondary sources, that is, the work of experts like Pearson and Porath, who have done interviews and surveys. I will look at their book and their 2005 article. They are the most prominent writers right now on this topic, so I will search the library databases to find other articles written by them.

Identifies a starting point and how those sources will lead to further sources with the same angle.

Page break

References

Forni, P.M. (2002), *Choosing civility: The twenty-five rules of considerate conduct.* New York, NY: St. Martin's Press.

Gallup study: Feeling good matters in the workplace. (2006, January 12). *Gallup Management Journal.* Retrieved from http://gmj.gallup.com/content/20770/Gallup -Study-Feeling-Good-Matters-in-the.aspx

Gonthier, G. (2002), *Rude awakenings: Overcoming the civility crisis in the workplace.* Chicago, IL: Dearborn Trade Publishing.

Hauser, S. (2011). The degeneration of decorum: Stress caused by rude behavior in the workplace might be costing the U. S. economy billions of dollars a year. *Workforce Management,* 90.1, 16. Retrieved from http://find.galegroup.com.proxy.libraries.smu .edu/gtx/start.do?prodId=AONE&userGroupName=txshracd2548

Pearson, C., & Porath, C. (2009). *The cost of bad behavior: How incivility is damaging your business and what to do about it.* New York, NY: Penguin Portfolio.

Pearson, C., & Porath, C. (2005). On the nature, consequences and remedies of workplace incivility: No time for "nice"? Think again. *Academy of Management Executive,* 19.1, 7–18. Retrieved from http://www.realmarcom.com/documents/conflict/pearson_ incivility.pdf

Ramsey, R. (2008). The case for civility in the workplace. *Supervision,* 69.12, 3–6. Retrieved from http://find.galegroup.com.proxy.libraries.smu.edu/gtx/start.do?prodId= AONE&userGroupName=txshracd2548

How Do I Prepare to Write a Research Proposal?

Thinking as a Writer: Task Requirements

In preparation for writing your research proposal, be aware of the specific requirements of the kind of proposal you will be writing. Different fields of study and programs have formats you should follow. Check your instructor's guidelines.

Gather together all of the results of preliminary research: copies of sources, notes on sources, your research journal or notes, and a working bibliography if you have one.

Thinking as a Writer: Voice and Style

The tone of your research proposal should be consistent with the purpose of the project itself, but a relatively formal tone is appropriate. You want to sound knowledgeable and confident, in control of the research and the project it supports; the formal tone helps to communicate the right impression.

Thinking as a Writer: Development and Organization

A basic outline might include Overview, Literature Review, Methods, and Bibliography, but be sure to discuss *the significance of the project or the purpose of the study* in the Overview or a separate section. Your reader must understand the contribution your project is making. Of course, add whatever sections you need to satisfy special requirements in a particular field or for an individual instructor's assignment.

What Are the Steps in Writing a Research Proposal?

You will be moving back and forth between your notes and your proposal as you work your way through each section. Focus on the information that needs to be included in each section while you write your draft; you can then go back during your revision and work on style and language.

1. **Draft your research proposal.** Before drafting, make an outline that includes the major sections your proposal needs to contain. Then, for each section, jot down the major points you want to include. For example, in your Overview, you might describe the topic, tell what you hope to accomplish with your research, and explain what question you hope to answer. In your Review of the Literature section, jot down the authors and texts you will discuss in the order you think they should be presented. This may not be the order in which you read them. Present them instead to show how they relate to one another and how you see their relevance and significance to the question you want to pursue.

2. **Revise your research proposal.** After drafting, consider all of the following questions:

- Have I introduced my research proposal in a way that would engage a reader's attention by, for example, giving some context that would show why the topic and question are interesting and relevant to my readers? If your readers are classmates, have you shown how your research question relates to ideas the class has been studying?
- Do I develop and connect all of the points within each section? Is it clear that I have not only collected the relevant sources, but that I also understand how the ideas all fit together? Remember: *Communicating your understanding of the sources is more important than summarizing what they say.* See the Hazama example (pages 520–21) for a good model.
- Is my research plan made clear in the Methods section? Were you specific about search terms and databases that you plan to use? Have you identified good sources that will serve as leads to other possible good sources? Be sure to consult Chapter 15, Planning a Research Project, pages 396–411, and Chapter 16, Finding Sources, pages 412–25 to get further ideas if you are having trouble with Methods.

3. **Edit your research proposal.** Read through the proposal trying to identify places where the ideas are overly complicated or where you have said too much about a source. You do not need to summarize entire sources to compare how they relate to key issues and points, so look for unnecessary details that might be getting in the way.

4. **Proofread your research proposal.** A research proposal full of errors and awkward sentences does not inspire confidence in the instructor or manager reviewing your proposal. Edit to eliminate grammatical and spelling errors. Make sure your bibliography entries conform exactly to the documentation style required for the assignment.

HOW DO I WRITE AN ANNOTATED BIBLIOGRAPHY?

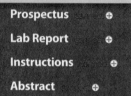

ANNOTATED BIBLIOGRAPHIES SERVE MANY PURPOSES, AND THEIR CONTENTS can vary from a one-sentence description of a source to a fully developed paragraph with an evaluation of the source and its possible uses.

What Is an Annotated Bibliography?

A **bibliography** is *an organized list of sources (books, articles, websites, maps, and so on) on a particular topic.* The citations in a bibliography conform to standard documentation formats, such as a works cited list in Modern Language Association style or a Reference list in American Psychological Association style. Whatever style is used, it is important that all the citations conform to the same style of documentation.

To **annotate** a bibliography means to *add a note to each of the citations,* just as annotating a reading means to add notes to the margins. In the case of an annotated bibliography, the note follows the bibliographic information. It is customary to start a new line and indent annotations to set them off from the citation. The content of the annotations will depend on the writer's purpose in creating the bibliography.

Why Do Writers Create Annotated Bibliographies?

There are many reasons for creating an annotated bibliography.

- Scholars create them as research tools for other scholars. These published annotated bibliographies are good places to start a research project since they provide a list of possible sources and a description of the contents of each. An annotated bibliography can be a complete stand-alone book, an article in a scholarly journal, or a list of suggestions for further reading at the end of a book or article. For advice on finding these resources for research, see Chapter 16, Finding Sources, pages 412–25.

- Writers create them as annotated works cited or annotated reference lists so that readers of their papers can see what research went into it and use the list to pursue their own interest in the topic. Instructors may require such lists as part of a research project to ensure that students have read sources well enough to give a brief summary of each.

- Students in a class working on the same project create annotated bibliographies collaboratively in a wiki or discussion board to share the results of their research as they gather and evaluate sources.

- Researchers create annotated bibliographies as they find their sources. Known as working bibliographies, they are informal writing that the writer does just for himself or herself to keep track of the bibliographic information and record notes about the content and usefulness of a source as well as about how sources compare. This kind of annotated bibliography would be useful as a step before planning a paper or before writing a **literature review,** *an overview of previous research,* often required for science papers.

What Should an Annotation Include?

Depending on your purpose and audience, an annotation might include one or more of the following items:

- Description of what the source contains or covers, possibly including how it is organized.
- Summary of the contents of the source—its angle or argument.
- Information about the author of the source and his or her credentials.
- Genre or type of writing of the source, such as news article, editorial, scholarly book, and so on.
- Description of the audience the author was addressing.
- Description of the bias or agenda of the source.
- Suggestions about how the source, or portions of the source, is relevant to research on a particular topic.
- An evaluation of the quality of the source, possibly comparing it to other similar sources.
- A mention of any special features contained in the source such as illustrations, indexes, and bibliographies.
- Comments about the author's voice or style of writing and how it contributes to the quality and overall purpose of the source.

What Do Annotated Bibliography Entries Look Like?

Annotations can be single sentences or much longer, as the following examples from a professional scholar's bibliography illustrate.

Scholarly Annotated Bibliography

Note the range of works on just one novel, *The Awakening* by Kate Chopin, compiled by Neal Wyatt, a former graduate student at Virginia Commonwealth University. The entries are succinct summaries.

> Tells more about the genre, what kind of book it is.

> Shows the angle and context in which *The Awakening* will be discussed.

Abel, Elizabeth, Marianne Hirsch, and Elizabeth Langland, eds. *The Voyage In: Fictions of Female Development*. Hanover: UP of New England, 1983. Print.

> A collection of essays on novels dealing with female development.

Anastasopoulou, Maria. "Rites of Passage in Kate Chopin's *The Awakening*." *Southern Literary Journal* 23.2 (1991): 19-30. Print.

> Describes the argument of the source, an article in a scholarly journal.

Maintains that *The Awakening* follows the structure of a rite of passage but that Edna fails in that passage due to two flaws.

Batten, Wayne. "Illusion and Archetype: The Curious Story of Edna Pontellier." *The Southern Literary Journal* 28.1 (1985): 73-88. Print.

> Again, this describes the argument of the article in a single sentence.

Interprets *The Awakening* as a series of illusions that Edna fails to incorporate into a workable and realistic life.

Culley, Margaret, ed. *The Awakening. Kate Chopin. Norton Critical Edition*. New York: Norton, 1976. Print.

> Assesses the quality of the source.

> Describes the genre and content.

An authoritative text and collection of both contemporary and modern critical views of *The Awakening*.

Class Annotated Bibliographies

Class annotated bibliographies have the purpose of helping other students decide whether and how to use a source for a project assigned to the class. The three examples below, all part of a shared or "common" bibliography for a class project, show detailed annotations.

Booth, Wayne C. "For the Love of It: Spending, Wasting, and Redeeming Time." *The Essential Wayne Booth*. Ed. Walter Jost. Chicago: U of Chicago, 2006. 301-312. Print.

> Tells what genre the source is.

> Tells the audience for the source.

> Tells when the source was first published.

> Tells who the author is.

> Summarizes the content and angle of the source.

> Tells how the source might be useful for others writing with this angle.

> Gives additional helpful information about accessing the source.

This essay is actually a speech given to high school and college students. It was originally published in 1999 and is reprinted here in a collection of essays, all by Wayne C. Booth (1921–2005), who was the George M. Pullman Distinguished Professor Emeritus at the University of Chicago. Booth was a professor of English and Rhetoric with many publications in that field, but his interests were widespread, and the topic of this essay is the value of pursuing hobbies—or as he puts it "amateuring." Being an amateur means doing something just for the love of it. In his case, it was taking up the cello at age forty, an experience he describes here. If you can get past the somewhat preachy tone of the essay, it has some inspiring ideas and examples in it. This would be a good source for people writing on the rewards of investing mental effort in leisure activities. The book containing this essay is on reserve in Fondren Library.

Glier, Ray. "Putting Civility and Sportsmanship Back in Game, if Not in the Stands." *New York Times* 22 Feb. 2008: pD4(L). *Academic OneFile*. Web. 25 Feb. 2011.

This news article is about how civility among sports fans has gone down and describes several events, in the NBA and college basketball, where incidents have occurred that highlight this ugly trend. It also talks about what has been done to curb the bad behavior. Ray Glier is a freelance writer who has written for *The New York Times, MSNBC, The Miami Herald,* and other papers.

Gives the genre.

Summarizes the contents of the article.

Tells credentials of the writer.

Twenge, Jean. *Generation Me: Why Today's Young Americans Are More Confident, Assertive, Entitled—and More Miserable Than Ever Before.* New York: Free Press, 2006. Print.

This book is by a San Diego State U. psychology professor who has made a name for herself by arguing that people are becoming increasingly narcissistic. The chapter most relevant to our topic is the first one, titled "You Don't Need Their Approval: The Decline of Social Rules." Another relevant chapter is "Sex: Generation Prude Meets Generation Crude." As you can tell from these titles, Twenge writes with a reader-friendly style.

Gives the genre.

Gives author's credentials.

Gives the author's angle or agenda.

Directs readers to the chapters most relevant to the assigned projectt.

Comments on the style and accessibility of the writing.

How Can I Support Academic Honesty When Writing Annotations?

You will find many sources that contain abstracts. The abstract may be in the database along with the citation, and it may also be at the opening of the text itself. While it might seem efficient to copy and paste the abstract into your annotated bibliography, doing so constitutes plagiarism. An annotated bibliography *must be your own writing and must reflect your own understanding of the source.* (For more on plagiarism, see Chapter 19, Using Sources Responsibly, pages 456–61.)

CREDITS

Photo Credits

Text/Figure Credits

INDEX

A

"A Dark, Skinny Stranger in Cleveland Park" (Carter), 69–70
"About Me" (Lopez), 88
abstracts, 527–28
academic honesty, 527
accidental plagiarism, 139, 456, 460–61
accurate information, 6–7, 128
acknowledgments, 448–49
advanced search options, 413–14, 422
advertising, 258–59
analogy, 216, 332–33
and (coordinating conjunction), 304–05
anecdotes, 119, 317
angle. *See* writer's angle
annotated bibliography
    academic honesty, 527
    class, 526
    defined, 524
    entries, 525–27
    library database abstract, 528
    reasons to write, 524–25
    scholarly, 526
annotations, 21, 411, 434–35, 524
APA style. *See also* in-text citations, APA style; works cited list, APA style
    in-text citations, 491–96
    parenthetical citations, 462–63
    sample research paper, 508–16
    works cited list, 496–508
appealing for action. *See* persuasion
appeals, strategies for, 270
archived materials, 422–23
argument
    critiquing, 203–04
    defined, 231
    exploration of, 218
    good and bad, 203
    questions for critique of, 216
    and reality, 219
    structure of, 278–79
    vs. critique, 203
    vs. exploration, 193
argument writing. *See* case making; critique; evaluations; perspectives, comparison of; persuasion
Aristotle, 258
Armario, Christine
    "Study: Students Need More Paths to Career Success," 10–12
artwork, citation of, 460
audience-based reasons, 272
audiovisual materials, 422–23
author's voice, source materials and, 453–55
autobiographical narratives, 76

B

background information, 250
background writing, 437
bibliographies, 417
bibliography, 524
block style quotations, 450
blog
    anatomy of, 57
    best practices, 61
    comments, 61–62
    crediting sources, 61
    defined, 56
    development and organization, 59
    good character in, 62
    reasons to write, 56
    sources in, 61
    as sources of information, 212–13
    special considerations, 61–62
    suggested topics, 58–59
    task requirements, 59
    topic selection, 58–59
    uses for, 56–58
    visual appeal, 60
    voice and style, 59
    writing process, 60
Boolean search operators, 413
brief, 272
brief examples, 314–16
"Building a Better Life through Greenways and Trails" (Trails and Greenways Clearinghouse), 235–37

C

Carey, Kevin, 175
Carr, Nicholas
    "Is Google Making Us Stupid?," 14
Carter, Stephen L.
    "A Dark, Skinny Stranger in Cleveland Park," 69–70
case, parts of a, 232–33
case making
    audience, 241
    best practices, 250–51
    common ground, 249, 250
    concessions, 249
    considered opinion, 244
    counterargument, 249
    defined, 231, 232
    development and organization, 250
    evidence, 247–48
    example, 231–32
    purpose, 241
    questioning, 247–48, 251
    readings, 235–37, 238–40
    reasons for, 233–34
    refutations, 249
    revision checklist, 251–52
    rhetorical situation, 237–38, 240, 241–42
    sensationalism, 249
    sources, 244–45
    stance, 249
    strategy, 234
    structure, 232, 234
    student examples, 248, 251–54, 254–57
    topic exploration, 242–43
    topic selection, 241–42, 268
    understanding other positions, 249
    voice, 249
    writing process, 242–53
case structure, 232–33
causation, 333
cause and effect, 333–34
cause-and-effect reasoning, 240
central question, 177
"Changes in Narcissism" (Twenge), 181–82
charts, citation of, 460
Chavez, Linda
    "Right to Bear Arms," 229–30
"Chevrolet Volt, Car of the Year" (MacKenzie), 289–92
citation software, 409
claims, 203, 232, 245–46, 271–72
classification, 327–29
classifications, questioning, 329
closure, postponement of, 158
Codrescu, Andrei
    "Notes of an Alien Son: Immigration Paradoxes," 19–20
Coman, Carolyn, 80–81
common ground, 249, 250
common knowledge, 416
common knowledge, citation of, 459–60
communication, key variables in, 158
comparative grid, 190
comparison, 330–31
complex causation, 333–34
complex definition, 325–26
composing process, editing fundamentals in, 336
concept exploration. *See* exploratory writing
concepts, 148–50
conceptual description, 321–22
concessions, 249
conclusions, 177, 250
concrete details, 67, 68
conflict, 67, 68
considered opinion, 244
context, 119, 202–03, 250
contrast, 331–32
conventional expectations, 120